The New Chess Player
Le Nouveau Joueur d'Échecs
Der neue Schachspieler
De Nieuwe Schaakspeler
Den nye Schackspelare
Il Nuovo Giocatoré di Scacchi
El Nuevo Ajedrecista
Новый Шахматист

1

1978

A

PITMAN

PITMAN PUBLISHING LIMITED
39 Parker Street, London WC2B 5PB

Associated Companies
Copp Clark Limited, Toronto
Fearon-Pitman Publishers Inc., Belmont, California
Pitman Publishing New Zealand Ltd., Wellington
Pitman Publishing Pty Ltd., Melbourne

Distributed in Italy by
Edizioni Scholastiche APE SpA
Via Tanaro 14, 20128 Milano

First published in Great Britain 1978

Printed and bound in England by
Billing & Son Ltd., Guildford

ISBN 0 273 01263 0

Contents

+ = white stands slightly better les blancs ont jeu un peu meilleur Weiss steht etwas besser wit staat er iets beter voor vit står något bättre il bianco sta un po' meglio el blanco está algo mejor белые стоят немного лучше

= + black stands slightly better les noirs ont jeu un peu meilleur Schwarz steht etwas besser zwart staat er iets beter voor svart står något bättre il nero sta un po' meglio el negro está algo mejor черные стояат немного лучше

± white has the upper hand les blancs ont le meilleur jeu Weiss steht besser wit staat beter vit står bättre il bianco sta meglio el blanco está mejor белые стоят лучше

∓ black has the upper hand les noirs ont le meilleur jeu Schwarz steht besser zwart staat beter svart står bättre il nero sta meglio el negro está mejor черные стоят лучше

+ – white has a decisive advantage les blancs ont un avantage décisif Weiss hat entscheidenden vorteil wit heeft een beslissend voordeel vit har avgörande fördel il bianco è in vantaggio decisivo el blanco tiene una ventaja decisiva белые имеют решающее преимущество

– + black has a decisive advantage les noirs ont un avantage décisif Schwarz hat entscheidenden vorteil zwart heeft een beslissend voordeel svart har avgörande fördel il nero è in vantaggio decisivo el negro tiene una ventaja decisiva черные имеют решающее преимущество

= the game is even le jeu est égal das Spiel ist ausgeglichen de stellingen zÿn gelÿkwaardig spelet är jamnt giuoco pari el juego está equilibrado игра равна

≂ approximately equal plus où moins égal ungefähr gleich ongeveer gelÿkwaardig narmelsevis jämnt piu o meno eguale más o menos igual приблизительно равно

∝ the position is unclear le jeu est incertain das Spiel ist unklar de posities zÿn onduidelÿk ställningen är oklar il giuoco è poco chiaro la posición no es clara неясная позиция

! a very good move un tres bon coup ein sehr guter Zug een zeer goede zet ett bra drag una buona mossa una jugada muy buena очень хороший ход

!! an excellent move un excellent coup ein ausgezeichneter Zug een uitstekende zet ett utmärkt drag una mossa ottima una jugada excelente отличный ход

? a mistake un coup faible ein schwacher Zug een fout ett dåligt drag una mossa debole una mala jugada плохой ход

?? a blunder une grave erreur ein grober Fehler een ernstige fout ett grovt fel un grave errore un gran error грубая ошибка

!? a move deserving attention un coup qui mérite l'attention ein beachtenswerter Zug een zet die de aandacht verdient ett drag som fortjäner uppmärksamhet una mossa degna di considerazione una jugada que merece atención ход, заслуживающий внимания

?! a dubious move un coup d'une valeur douteuse ein Zug von zweifelhaftem wert een dubieuze zet ett tvivelaktigt drag una mossa dubbia una jugada de dudoso valor ход, имеющий сомнительную ценность

Δ with the idea . . . avec l'idée . . . mit der Idee . . . met het idee om . . . med idén . . . con l'idea . . . con idea . . . с идеей…

N a novelty une innovation eine Neuerung een nieuwtje en nyhet un'innovazione una novedad новинка

Contributors

B. Balogh	
G. Botterill	
W. S. Browne	GM
V. Ciocaltea	IM
J. Dorfman	IM
A. Filipowicz	IM
G. Forintos	GM
T. Georgadze	GM
F. Gheorghiu	GM
A. Gipslis	GM
E. Gufeld	GM
E. Haag	IM
P. Hardicsay	
T. D. Harding	
K. Honfi	IM
M. H. Horton	
S. Joksic	
A. Z. Kapengut	
A. Kochiev	IM
L. Kovacs	IM
A. Kuligowski	
B. Kurajica	GM
R. Maric	IM
E. Mednis	IM
A. Miles	GM
L. Ochoa	
E. Paoli	IM
M. Pavlov	IM
T. Petrosian	GM
J. Pribyl	IM
K. Pytel	IM
V. Raicevic	GM
D. Rajkovic	GM
L. Shamkovich	GM
G. Sigurjonsson	GM
A. Suetin	GM
E. Sveshnikov	GM
J. Tompa	
L. Vadasz	GM
L. Vogt	GM
M. Vukic	GM
S. Webb	IM

Journals

Ajedrez, British Chess Magazine, Butlleti D'Escacs, Ceskoslovensky Sach, Chess, Chess Bulletin (Canada), Chess in Australia, Chess Life and Review, Deutsche Schachblatter, Deutsche Schachzeitung, Europe Echecs, Fernschach, Jaque, Jaque Mate, Le Courrier Des Echecs, L'Italia Scacchistica, Magyar Sakkelet, Modern Chess Theory, Revista Romana de Sah, Rochade, Sahovski Glasnik, Scacco, Schaakbulletin, Schach, Schach-Echo, Schack nytt, Schakend Nederland, Shahmat, Shakhmatna Mis'l, Skakbladet, South African Chessplayer, Suomen Shakki, Szachy, Tidskrift for Schack, 64 **Шахматы** **Шахматный Бюллетень** **Шахматы в СССР**

Bulletins

1977: Amsterdam, Auckland, Baku, Bar, Biel, Brighton, Buenos Aires, Budapest, Decin, Erevan, Frankfurt, Glucksburg,Katowice, Kragujevac, Las Palmas, Ljubljana, London (2), Montreux, Moscow, Nis, Pernik, Rim. Sobota, Sochi, Tilburg, Vrn. Banja, Vrsac, Zalaegerzeg;
1978: Hastings, Stockholm, Wijk aan Zee.

Novelties

10	Diesen	– Andersson	234	Tal	– Spassov
17	Stefanov	– Neamtu	237	Gipslis	– Tukmakov
51	Balashov	– Miles	245	Spassky	– Miles
110	Ogaard	– Miles	295	Kapengut	– Vorotnikov
117	Gheorghiu	– Kouatly	300	Shamkovich	– Tarjan
175	Chiburdanidze	– Alexandria	301	Loktev	– Grebenskikov
181	Chiburdanidze	– Alexandria	313	Shamkovich	– Stopa
211	Matulovic	– Bohmfeld	319	Zaitsev	– Zuravlev
217	Biriescu	– Georgescu	345	Tatai	– Korchnoi
223	H.Olafsson	– Mednis	367	Bangiev	– Hait

Combinations

6	Raicevic	– Mestrovic	211	Matulovic	– Bohmfeld
18	Kasparov	– Kapengut	215	Timman	– Mecking
37	Smejkal	– Bueno	218	Lanka	– Bangiev
66	Shamkovich	– Anguiano	220	Tratatovici	– Stefanov
90	Sosonko	– Smyslov	243	Bukic	– Romanishin
97	Gligoric	– Timman	268	Formanek	– Wagman
120	Ivkov	– Timman	270	Furman	– Beljavsky
148	Petran	– F.Portisch	310	Timoshenko	– Klovan
150	Smejkal	– Vogt	320	Mititelu	– Ene
175	Chiburdanidze	– Alexandria	348	Planinc	– Kovacevic
184	Lanka	– Efimov	354	Knezevic	– Planinc
204	Honfi	– Cserna	359	Sveshnikov	– Botterill
208	Kagan	– Shamkovich	362	Pribyl	– Seifert

Theory

English/Englisch

1 c4 ♘f6 2 ♘f3 c5 3 ♘c3 d5 4 cxd5 ♘xd5 5 e4 ♘b4 6 ♗b5+ 6 ♗c4 ♗e6! 7 ♗xe6 ♘d3+ 8 ♔f1 fxe6 9 ♘g5 ♕d7 10 ♕f3!? TN ♘e5 11 ♕h3 ♕d3+ 12 ♕xd3 ♘xd3 13 ♔e2 ♘f4+ 14 ♔f3 e5∞ Vadasz-Lukacs, Budapest 1977 **6...♘8c6** 6...♗d7 7 a3 ♘4c6 8 d4! cxd4 9 ♘xd4 ♘xd4 10 ♕xd4 ♘c6 11 ♕d3 a6 12 ♗a4 ♘e5 13 ♗xd7+ ♕xd7 14 ♕g3± Bukic-Smejkal, Banja-Luka 1976 **7 0-0** TN 7 a3 ♘d3+ 8 ♔e2 ♘f4+ 9 ♔f1 ♘e6 10 b4 ♘ed4 =+ Bukic-Smejkal, Belgrade 1977; 10... g6! 11 bxc5 ♗g7 12 e5 ♘d4 13 ♘xd4 ♕xd4 14 ♗b2 0-0∓ Poutiainen-Tal, Tallinn 1977 **7...a6 8 ♗a4 b5 9 a3 ♘d3 10 ♘xb5 axb5 11 ♗xb5 ♕d6 12 ♕b3 ♗a6! 13 ♕a4 ♗xb5 14 ♕xa8+ ♘d8**∓ Tukmakov-Tal, USSR Final 1977

1 c4 c5 2 ♘f3 ♘f6 3 ♘c3 ♘c6 4 d4 cxd4 5 ♘xd4 e6 6 g3 ♕b6 6...♗c5 7 ♘b3 ♗b4 (7...♗e7 8 ♗g2 d6 9 0-0 0-0 10 ♘d4 ♗d7 11 ♘db5 ♕b8 12 ♗f4 ♘e5 13 b3 += Vukic-Minic, Vinkovci 1977) 8 ♗g2 d5 9 cxd5 ♘xd5 10 a3 ♗xc3+ 11 bxc3 0-0 N 12 ♕c2 ♕c7 13 c4 ♘e5 14 ♘d2 b5∞ Korchnoi-Spassky (1) 1977 **7 ♘b3 ♘e5** 7...♗b4 8 ♗g2 ♕a6 (8...♘e5 9 ♗e3 ♕a6 10 c5 ♘c4 11 ♗c1 d5 12 cxd6 0-0 13 0-0 ♗xd6 14 ♕d3 ♖b8 15 a4!± Romanishin-Hulak, USSR v Jugoslavia 1976) 9 ♘d2 ♗xc3 10 bxc3 0-0 11 0-0 d5 12 ♕b3 Korchnoi-Spassky (5) 1977, 12...♘a5! **8 e4 ♗b4**

Diagram

9 ♕e2 a5 9...0-0 10 f4 ♘c6 11 ♗e3 N (11 e5 ♘e8 12 ♗d2 f6 13 exf6 ♘xf6 14 ♗g2 d5!∓ Beljavsky-Geller, Moscow 1975) 11...♕c7 12 ♗g2 d5 13 e5 ♘e4 14 0-0 ♗xc3 15 cxd5! += Korchnoi-Spassky (3) 1977 **10 ♗e3** 10 f4 ♘c6 11 e5 a4 Zaitsev **10...♕c6 11 f3 0-0 12 ♘d4 ♕a6** 12...♗xc3+ 13 bxc3 ♕a4 **13 ♘b5 d5?** 13...a4 **14 ♘c7** 14 cxd5 exd5 15 ♗d4 dxe4 16 ♗xe5 exf3 17 ♕c4 f2+∓ Miles-Stean, BBC 1977 **14...♕d6** 14...♕c6 15 ♘xa8 ♘xc4 16 ♖c1 b5 17 ♘b6 +− **15 ♘xa8** +− Karpov-Miles, Tilburg 1977

1 c4 ♘f6 2 ♘c3 c5 3 ♘f3 e6 4 d4 cxd4 5 ♘xd4 ♗b4 6 ♘b5 6 ♗g5 ♕a5 7 ♗d2 ♘c6 8 e3 ♕b6 9 a3 ♗e7 10 b4 d5= Gulko-Alburt, USSR Final 1977; 6 g3 ♕c7?! (6...♘e4 7 ♕d3 ♕a5 8 ♘c2 [8 ♘b3 ♘xc3 9 ♘xa5 ♘e4+ 10 ♗d2 ♗xd2+ 11 ♕xd2 ♘xd2 12 ♔xd2 ♘c6 13 ♘xc6 dxc6= Alburt-Razuvaev, Baku 1977] 8...♗xc3+! 9 bxc3 ♘c5 10 ♕d2 b6∓ Lombard-Rogoff, Biel 1976) 7 ♕b3 ♗c5 8 ♗e3 a6 9 ♘c2 b6 10 ♗g2 ♘c6 11 ♘a4 ♗xe3 12 ♘xe3 ♖b8= Popov-Tseshkovsky, Erevan 1977 **6...d5** 6...0-0 7 a3 ♗xc3+ 8 ♘xc3 d5 9 cxd5 exd5 10 ♗e3 ♘c6 11 ♗d4 ♖e8 12 e3 ♘g4 13 ♗e2 ♘h6 14 0-0 ♘f5 =+ Debarnot-Miles, Las Palmas 1977 **7 cxd5** 7 ♗f4 0-0 8 a3 ♗xc3+ 9 bxc3 ♘c6 10 ♗d6 ♖e8 11 ♗c7 ♕d7

12 ♗g3 e5∓ Galasov-Mikhalchishin, USSR 1977 **7...exd5 8 ♗g5 0-0 9 a3 ♗xc3+ 10 ♘xc3 ♘c6 11 e3** 11 ♗xf6 ♕xf6 12 ♕xd5 ♘d4 **11...♗e6 12 ♗d3 h6 13 ♗xf6 ♕xf6**= Miles-Furman, Bad Lauterberg 1977

1 c4 ♘f6 2 ♘c3 e6 3 e4

3...c5 3...d5 4 e5 (4 cxd5 exd5 5 e5 d4 6 exf6 dxc3 7 ♕e2+ ♗e6 8 dxc3 ♘d7 9 fxg7 ♗xg7 10 ♘f3 0-0 11 ♕c2 ♖e8 12 ♗e2 += Korchnoi-Partos, Montreux 1977) 4...d4 (4...♘fd7 [4...♘e4 5 ♘xe4 dxe4 6 ♕g4 ♘c6!∞] 5 cxd5 exd5 6 d4 c5 7 ♘f3 ♘c6 8 ♗b5! cxd4 [8...a6 9 ♗xc6 bxc6 10 0-0 ♗e7 11 dxc5 ♘xc5 12 ♘d4± Smyslov-Farago, Hastings 1976/77] 9 ♘xd4 ♘dxe5 10 ♕e2! ♕e7 11 ♘xd5 ♘d3+ 12 ♗xd3 ♘xd4 13 ♕xe7+ ♗xe7 14 ♘c7+ +− Quinteros-Nunn, London 1977) 5 exf6 dxc3 6 bxc3 ♕xf6 7 d4 c5 (7...b6 8 ♘f3 ♗b7 9 ♗d3 ♗d6?? [9...h6] 10 ♗g5 ♗xf3 11 ♕d2 ♗f4 12 ♗xf4 ♗xg2 13 ♖g1 ♗b7 14 ♗e5± Miles-Sosonko, Amsterdam 1977) 8 ♘f3 cxd4 9 ♗g5 ♕f5 10 cxd4 ♗b4+ 11 ♗d2 ♘c6 (11...♕a5 12 ♖b1 N ♗xd2+ 13 ♕xd2 ♕xd2+ 14 ♔xd2 0-0 15 ♗d3 += Adamski-Kostro, Katowice 1977) 12 ♗xb4 ♘xb4 13 ♖b1 ♕a5 N (13...♘c6 14 ♗d3 ♕f6 15 ♗e4 0-0 16 0-0 ♖d8 17 ♗xc6 bxc6 18 ♕a4± Tal-Sosonko, Wijk aan Zee 1976) 14 ♕d2 ♘c6 15 ♗d3 ♕xd2+ 16 ♔xd2 b6 17 ♖hc1± Miles-Sosonko, Tilburg 1977 **4 e5 ♘g8 5 ♘f3** 5 d4 cxd4 6 ♕xd4 ♘c6 7 ♕e4 ♗b4 N 8 ♗d2 d6 9 ♕g4 dxe5 10 ♕xg7 ♕f6 11 ♕g3 ♘h6 12 0-0-0 ♘f5 13 ♘e4 ♗xd2+ 14 ♖xd2 ♕e7 15 ♕c3± Hort-Jelen, Ljubljana 1977 **5...♘c6 6 d4 cxd4 7 ♘xd4 ♘xe5 8 ♘db5** 8 ♗f4; 8 ♕a4

8...a6 8...f6 9 ♗e3 (9 ♗f4 a6 10 ♗xe5 axb5 11 ♗g3 ♘h6 12 ♕h5+ g6 13 ♕xb5 ♘f5 14 ♖d1 ♖a5∞ Keene-Furman, Bad Lauterberg 1977; 9 f4 ♘f7 10 f5∞ Keene) 9...b6 10 f4 ♘c6 11 f5 g6 12 fxe6 dxe6 13 ♕xd8+ ♔xd8 14 0-0-0+ ♔e7 15 g4 ♖b8 16 ♗g2± Miles-Flesch, Biel 1977 **9 ♘d6+ ♗xd6 10 ♕xd6 f6 11 ♗e3** 11 ♗f4 ♘f7 12 ♕a3 ♘e7 13 ♗e2 0-0 14 ♖d1 d5 15 cxd5 ♘xd5 =+ Timman-Karpov, Las Palmas 1977 **11...♘e7** 11...♘f7 12 ♕g3 ♘e7 13 ♕xg7 ♘f5 14 ♕g4 ♘xe3 15 fxe3 ♕b6 16 ♕d4 += Keene-Partos, Montreux 1977 **12 ♗b6 ♘f5 13 ♗xd8 ♘xd6 14 ♗c7 ♔e7 15 c5 ♘e8 16 ♗b6 d5 17 cxd6+ ♘xd6** 17...♔xd6? 18 f4 ♘d7 19 ♗d8 ♘c7 20 ♘e4+ ♔d5 21 ♘xf6+ gxf6 22 ♗xe7 +− Gulko-Diesen, Polanica 1977 **18 0-0-0** 18 ♗c5 Miles-

L.Bronstein, Sao Paulo 1977; 18... b6!∞ **18...Nec4!** 18...Bd7 19 Bc5 Nf7 20 Ne4 Rac8 21 Kb1 Rc6 22 Be2 e5 23 Ba3 Bf5= Miles-Karpov, BBC 1977 **19 Bxc4 Nxc4 20 Bc5+ Kf7 21 Rd4 b5 22 b3 e5**∓ Miles-Huebner, Tilburg 1977

1 c4 e5 2 Nc3 Nf6 3 Nf3 Nc6 4 e3 Bb4 5 Qc2 0-0 6 Nd5 Re8 7 Qf5 d6 8 Nxf6+ gxf6 9 Qh5 9 Qc2? e4 10 Nh4 f5 11 g3 d5 12 cxd5 Ne5 13 Qb3 Be7 14 d4 exd3 15 Bxd3 Bxh4∓ Keene-Timman, Bad Lauterberg 1977 **9...d5 10 a3!** 10 cxd5? Qxd5 11 Be2 Be6 12 0-0 e4 13 Qxd5 Bxd5 14 Ne1 Rad8∓ Keene-Korchnoi, Montreux 1977 **10...Bf8 11 d4 Be6** TN 11...exd4 12 Bd3 h6 13 0-0± **12 Bd3 h6 13 cxd5 Qxd5 14 e4 Qb3 15 Bb1 Nxd4 16 Nxd4 exd4 17 0-0** += Fedorowicz-Tarjan, Hastings 1977/78

1 c4 e5 2 Nf3 Nc6 3 Nc3 f5 4 d4 e4 5 Ng5 Nf6 6 e3 6 h4 d6 7 g3 g6 8 Nh3 Bg7 9 Bg5 h6 10 Bc1 Qe7 11 Nf4 Qf7 12 e3 Bd7 13 Bd2 0-0-0∓ Georgadze-Hort, Decin 1977 **6...Bb4 7 Bd2** 7 Nh3 Bxc3+ 8 bxc3 b6 9 Ba3 Ba6 10 Qa4 += Uhlmann-Karner, Tallinn 1977 **7...Qe7 8 Nh3 Nd8 9 a3 Bxc3 10 Bxc3 d6 11 Nf4 0-0 12 Be2 c6 13 d5 c5 14 h4 Nf7 15 b4**± Polugaevsky-Balashov, USSR Final 1977

1 c4 Nf6 2 Nf3 g6 3 Nc3 d5 4 cxd5 Nxd5 5 e4 Nxc3 6 dxc3 Qxd1+ 7 Kxd1 f6 TN 7...Nd7 8 Bc4 Bg7 9 Re1 c6 10 Kc2 0-0 11 Be3 h6 12 a4 a5 13 e5 e6 14 Rad1± Romanishin-Grigorian, USSR Final 1976 **8 Bc4 e5 9 Be3 Nd7 10 Ke2 Bc5 11 Rhd1 Bxe3 12 Kxe3 Nb6 13 Nd2 Ke7 14 Bb3 Be6 15 Bxe6 Kxe6**= Najdorf-Mecking, Wijk aan Zee 1978

QGA/Ang.Damengambit

1 d4 d5 2 c4 dxc4 3 e4 3 Nf3 Nf6 4 e3 Bg4 5 Bxc4 e6 6 Qb3 (6 Nc3 Nbd7 7 h3 Bh5 8 Be2 Bd6 9 0-0 0-0 10 e4 e5 11 dxe5 Nxe5 12 Nxe5 Bxe2 13 Qxe2 Bxe5 14 Bg5 Qe8= Balashov-Miles, Tilburg 1977) 6... Bxf3 7 gxf3 Nbd7 8 Qxb7 c5 9 dxc5 Bxc5 10 Nc3 0-0 11 f4 (11... Rb8 12 Qf3 Qc7 13 Bb3 Bb4 14 Bd2 Nc5∓ Tal-Shianovsky, USSR Final 1962) 11...Nb6!? N 12 Be2 Nfd5 13 0-0 Qh4 14 Bf3 Rab8∞ Quinteros-Miles, Amsterdam 1977 **3...e5 4 Nf3 exd4 5 Bxc4 Bb4+** 5...Nc6 6 0-0 Bg4? 7 Qb3 Qd7 8 Bxf7+! Qxf7 9 Qxb7 +− Pytel-Castro, Dortmund 1977 **6 Bd2 Bxd2+ 7 Nbxd2 Nh6!?** N 7...Nc6 8 0-0 Nf6 9 e5 Nd5 10 Qb3 Nce7 11 Nxd4 0-0 12 Rad1± Bagirov-Petrushin, Baku 1977 **8 0-0 c5 9 Nb3 Qe7 10 Re1 b6 11 Bd5 Bb7 12 Nxc5!?** ∞/± Partos-Miles, Biel 1977

Benko Gambit

1 d4 Nf6 2 c4 c5 3 d5 b5 4 cxb5 a6 5 bxa6 5 e3 g6 (5...e6 6 Nc3 exd5 7 Nxd5 axb5 8 Bxb5 Bb7 9 Bc4 Be7 10 Ne2 Nxd5 11 Bxd5 Bxd5 12 Qxd5± Tukmakov-Bednarski, Decin 1977) 6 Nc3 Bg7 (6...d6 7 a4 Bg7 8 Qb3 Nbd7 9 Nf3 0-0 10 Ra3 axb5 11 Bxb5 Ne8 12 0-0 Nc7 13 Bc6 Rb8 14 Nb5± Donner-Miles, Amsterdam 1977) 7 e4 (7 Nf3 0-0 8 a4 e6 9 bxa6 Nxa6 10 Bc4 Nb4 11 0-0 exd5 12 Nxd5 Nfxd5 13 Bxd5 Rb8∓

Reinhardt-Szmetan, Argentina 1977) 7...d6 8 ♘f3 0-0 9 a4 e6 10 dxe6 fxe6 11 e5!?∞ Farago-Filipowicz, Polanica-Zdroj 1977 **5...♗xa6 6 ♘c3 g6 7 ♘f3 d6**

8 g3 8 e4 ♗xf1 9 ♔xf1 ♗g7 10 g3 ♘bd7 (10...0-0 11 ♔g2 ♕a5 12 ♖e1 ♘fd7 13 ♖e2 ♘a6 14 ♗e3 ♖fb8 15 ♖c1 ♖a7 16 ♕d2 ♘c7 17 e5± Tarjan-Webb, Hastings 1977/78) 11 ♔g2 ♘g4 12 ♘d2 ♘ge5 13 ♕e2 += Hort-Rajkovic, Stip 1977 **8...♗g7 9 ♗g2** 9 ♗h3 0-0 10 0-0 ♘bd7 11 ♖e1 ♕c7 12 ♗f4 ♖fb8 13 ♕d2 ♖b4 14 ♖ac1 h5= Beljavsky-Vaganian, Baku 1977 **9...♘bd7 10 0-0 ♘b6 11 ♖e1 0-0 12 ♘d2 ♕c7 13 ♖b1 ♕b7 14 b3 ♘fxd5 15 ♘xd5 ♘xd5 16 ♘f1 ♘c3!! 17 ♗xb7 ♗xb7 18 ♕d3 ♗e4∓** Hort-Alburt, Decin 1977

Benoni

1 d4 ♘f6 2 c4 e6 3 ♘c3 c5 4 d5 exd5 5 cxd5 d6 6 ♘f3 g6 7 e4 ♗g7 8 ♗g5 h6 8...0-0 9 ♘d2! ♖e8 (9...♕e7 10 ♗e2 ♘bd7 11 0-0 h6 12 ♗h4 g5?! 13 ♗g3 ♘e5 14 f4! += Botterill-Century, Brighton 1977) 10 ♗e2 a6 11 a4 ♘bd7 12 0-0 ♖b8 13 ♗h4 ♕c7 14 h3 c4?! 15 ♗xc4 ♘c5 16 ♖e1 ♗d7 17 ♕f3 ♘h5 18 ♗f1± Kavalek-Ljugojevic, Manila 1976 **9 ♗h4 g5** 9...a6 Londz (10 a4) 10...b5 11 ♗e2 0-0 12 0-0 ♖e8 13 f4?! ♘bd7 14 ♕c2 ♕c7 15 ♖ae1 ♘b6 16 ♔h1 ♗d7 17 ♗f3 b4∓ Spassov-Hulak, Athens 1976; 9...0-0 10 ♘d2 b6 11 ♗e2 ♗a6 12 0-0 ♕d7 (12...♗xe2 N 13 ♕xe2 a6 14 a4 ♖e8 15 f4 ♕c7 16 ♖ae1 ♘bd7 17 ♔h1 += Miles-Robatsch, Biel 1977) 13 a4 ♖e8 14 h3 ♕b7 15 ♗b5!± Matera-Feuerstein, New York 1977 **10 ♗g3 ♘h5 11 ♗b5+! ♔f8** 11...♗d7 12 ♗xd7+ ♕xd7 13 ♘e5!± **12 e5!**

12...g4 N 12...♘xg3 13 fxg3 a6?! 14 ♗d3 ♕b6? (14...c4!? N 15 ♗xc4 b5 16 ♗b3 ♕b6 17 ♕e2 dxe5 [17...♖a7∞] 18 0-0-0 b4 19 ♘a4 ♕d6 20 ♘d2± Gulko-Savon, USSR Final 1977) 15 ♘d2 ♗xe5 16 ♘c4 ♗xc3+ 17 bxc3 ♕c7 18 0-0 ♔g7 19 ♕h5 ♖f8 20 ♖f6! +− Miles-Wedberg, Stockholm 1976; 13...dxe5 14 0-0 a6 15 ♗e2 (15 ♗d3 N ♔g8 Matera-Rohde, New York 1977, 16 ♘d2±; 15...b5 16 ♘d2 c4 17 ♕h5 f6 18 ♗c2 ♗d7 19 a4!± Miles-Hernandez, Biel 1977) 15...♖a7 16 a4 b6 17 ♕b3∞ f5 Stean-Nunn, Birmingham 1976 18 ♖ad1 +−; 12...a6!? N 13 ♗e2 (13 ♗d3 dxe5 14 ♗xe5 g4 15 ♗xg7+ ♔xg7 16 ♘d2 ♖e8+∓) 13...♘xg3 14 fxg3 g4 15 ♘h4 ♗xe5∞

13 0-0 13 ♗h4! ♕b6 14 0-0 gxf3 15 e6! +– **13...dxe5** 13 gxf3 14 ♕xf3 ♕g5 15 ♗e2 ♘xg3 (15...♗g4 16 ♕xg4 ♕xg4 17 ♗xg4 ♘xg3 18 fxg3 ♗xe5∞) 16 fxg3 ♗f5 17 ♘e4! +– **14 ♗h4 ♗f6 15 ♗xf6 ♕xf6 16 ♘d2 ♕g6** 15...a6; 16...b6;

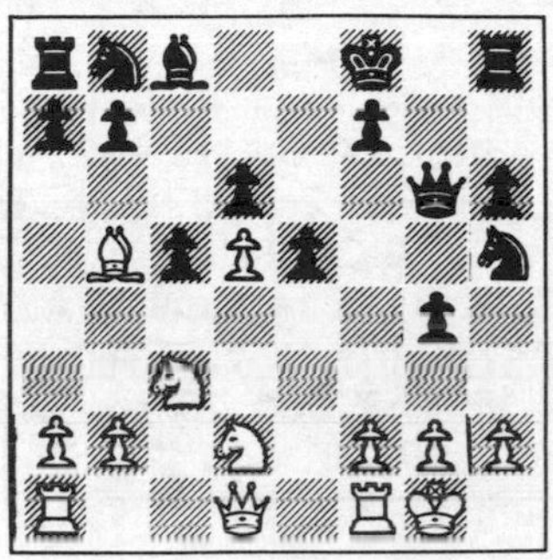

17 ♕e2 f6 18 ♘de4 b6 19 ♘d6 ♘f4 20 ♕e3 ♗d7 21 ♗c4! ♖h7 22 g3 ♘h3+ 23 ♔h1 ♖e7 24 f3∞ Hartston-Wahlbom, Copenhagen 1977

1 d4 ♘f6 2 c4 c5 3 d5 e6 4 ♘c3 exd5 5 cxd5 d6 6 e4 g6 7 f4 ♗g7 8 ♗b5+ 8 e5!? (Mikenas) 8...♘fd7 9 ♘e4 dxe5 10 ♘d6+ ♔e7 11 ♘xc8+ ♕xd8 12 ♘f3 ♖e8 (12...e4!) 13 fxe5 N (13 ♗c4 ♔f8 14 0-0 ♘b6 15 ♗b5 ♖d8 16 fxe5 ♖xd5= Mikenas-Suetin) 13...♘xe5 (13...♔f8 14 e6 fxe6 15 ♗e2 exd5 16 0-0∞) 14 ♗b5! ♘bd7 15 0-0± Littlewood-Povah, British Final 1975

Diagram

8...♘fd7 8...♘bd7 9 e5 dxe5 10 fxe5 ♘h5 11 e6 fxe6 12 dxe6 0-0 13 ♘f3! ♖xf3 14 ♕xf3!± **9 a4** 9 ♗e2!? N 0-0 10 ♘f3 ♘a6 11 0-0 ♘c7 12 a4 ♖b8 13 ♔h1 (13 ♘d2 ♘f6 14 ♘c4 b6 Δ ♗a6∞) 13...a6 14 a5 b5 15 axb5 ♖xb6 16 ♘d2 ♘f6 17 ♘c4 ♖b4 18

♘xd6 ♖d4 19 ♕e1 ♕xd6 20 e5 ♕b6 21 exf6 ♕xf6∞ Hollis-Nunn, Oxford 1978 **9...0-0 10 ♘f3 ♘a6 11 0-0 ♘b4?! 12 ♗e3** 12 ♔h1 ♘f6 13 f5!? a6 14 ♗c4 ♘g4 15 ♗g5 ♗f6 16 ♗xf6 ♕xf6 17 ♕d2 += Butnorus-Bangiev, USSR 1977 **12...♘f6 13 h3!** N **a6 14 ♗c4 ♘xe4?! 15 ♘xe4 ♖e8 16 ♘e5!**± Soos-Povah, Birmingham 1977

1 d4 ♘f6 2 c4 c5 3 d5 e6 4 ♘c3 exd5 5 cxd5 d6 6 ♘f3 g6 7 ♘d2 ♘bd7 7...♗g7 8 ♘c4 0-0 9 ♗g5 (9 ♗f4 b6 10 ♗xd6 ♖e8 11 ♗g3 ♘e4 12 ♘xe4 ♖xe4 13 e3 b5 14 ♘d6 ♖b4 Donner-Planinc, Wijk aan Zee 1973 15 b3!±) 9...h6 10 ♗f4!? N b6 11 ♗xd6 ♖e8 12 ♗g3 ♘e4 13 ♘xe4 ♖xe4 14 e3 b5 15 ♘d2 ♖b4 16 b3! ♗xa1 17 ♕xa1 ♕xd5 18 a3 ♖g4 19 ♗e2 ♘c6 20 ♗f3!± Petrosian-Nunn, Hastings 1977/78 **8 e4** 8 ♘c4 ♘b6! 9 e4 ♘xc4 10 ♗xc4 ♗g7 11 0-0 0-0 12 ♗f4 a6 13 a4 ♘h5 14 ♗e3 ♖e8= Gligoric-Trifunovic, Jugoslav Final 1957 **8... ♗g7 9 ♗e2 0-0 10 0-0 ♖e8**

Diagram

11 a4 11 ♕c2 ♘h5 12 ♗xh5 gxh5 13 a4 ♘e5 14 ♘d1 b6 15 ♖a3 ♗a6 16 ♘e3! ♗xf1 17 ♘dxf1 ♔h8 18 ♘f5±

Plachetka-Sikora, CSSR Final 1974; 15...f5 16 exf5 ♗a6 17 ♘e4! ♗xf1 18 ♔xf1± Gligoric-Taimanov, Leningrad 1973; 11...♘b6! N 12 ♗b5 ♗d7 13 a4 ♗xb5 14 ♘xb5 a6 15 ♘c3 ♘fd7 16 a5 ♘c8 17 b3 ♘a7 18 ♗b2 ♘b5= Polugaevsky-Mecking (3) 1977 **11...g5!?** N 11...♘e5 12 ♖a3 ♗d7 13 ♕c2 Petrosian-Ljubojevic, Milan 1975, 13...c4 14 ♘xc4 ♘xc4 15 ♗xc4 ♖c8; 13...♕e7; 11...a6 12 ♖a3 ♖b8 13 a5 ♕c7 14 h3 Petrosian-Quinteros, Lone Pine 1976, 14...g5! Byrne; 11...♘e5 12 ♖a3 b6 13 ♕c2 ♘h5 14 ♗xh5 gxh5 15 ♘d1 ♗a6 16 ♖h3 ♗xf1 17 ♘xf1 b5 18 ♘de3 bxa4 19 ♘f5± Petrosian-Rashkovsky, USSR Final 1976

12 ♘c4 12 f3 ♘e5 13 ♘c4 ♘xc4 14 ♗xc4 h6 15 ♘e2 a6 16 ♘g3 ♘h7= Popov-Spassov, Varna 1971; 12 ♕c2 ♘e5 13 ♘f3 ♘xf3+ 14 ♗xf3 Gligoric-Fischer, Palma 1970, 14...♘d7 15 ♗g4 ♘e5 16 ♗xc8=; 13 ♘d1 g4 14 ♘e3 ♘h5 15 g3 ♕f6 16 f4? gxf3 17 ♘xf3 ♗h3∓ Farago-Szilagyi, Hungary Final 1974; 13 b3 g4 14 ♗b2 ♘h5 15 ♘c4 ♘xc4 16 ♗xc4 ♘f4 17 ♘d1 ♗e5= Gligoric-Tatai, Venice 1971; 13 ♘c3 ♘xc4 14 ♗xc4 ♘g4 15 ♘e2 Najdorf-Ree, Wijk aan Zee 1971, 15...♘e5 Δ g4 =; 12 ♖a3!? Petrosian **12...♘xe4 13 ♘xe4 ♖xe4 14 ♘xd6** 14 ♗d3 ♖d4 15 ♗e3 ♖xc4! 16 ♗xc4 ♗xb2∞ **14...♖d4 15 ♕b3 ♘b6 16 a5 ♘xd5 17 ♘xc8 ♖xc8 18 ♕xb7 ♖c7** Bonchev-Tseitlin, Bulgaria 1977 **19 ♕b5∞**

1 d4 ♘f6 2 c4 e6 3 g3 c5 4 d5 exd5 5 cxd5 d6 6 ♘c3 g6 7 ♗g2 ♗g7 8 ♘f3 0-0 9 0-0 ♖e8 9...a6 10 a4 ♘bd7 11 e4?! (11 ♘d2 [11 ♗f4 ♕e7 12 ♖e1 ♖b8 13 e4 ♘g4 14 ♗f1 ♘ge5 15 ♘d2 ♖e8 16 ♗e3 f5 17 h3 ♕f8 18 f4± Inkiov-Ermenkov, Bulgaria Final 1977] 11...♖e8 12 h3 ♖b8 13 ♘c4 ♘b6 14 ♘e3 ♘bd7 15 ♘c4 ♘b6 16 ♘e3 ♘fd7 N 17 a5 ♘a8 18 ♘c4 ♘e5= Pachman-Mecking, Manila 1976) 11...♖e8 12 ♖e1 c4! 13 ♕e2 Sosonko-Ligterink, Wijk aan Zee 1977, 13...♘c5!∓; 9...b6 10 ♖e1 ♖e8 11 ♗f4 a6 12 e4 ♘g4 13 a4 ♖a7 14 h3 ♘e5 15 ♗xe5± Zaitsev-Rashkovsky, Sochi 1976; 9...♕e7!? 10 ♘d2 ♘bd7 (10...b6 11 ♘c4 ♗a6 12 ♕b3±) 11 a4 (11 ♖e1 ♘e8 12 e3 ♘c7 13 a4 ♘a6 14 f4 ♘b4 15 ♘c4 ♘b6 16 ♘a3 a5∞ Korchnoi-Kaplan, Hastings 1975/76) 11...♘h5 12 e4 ♘e5 13 ♕e2 f5 Hort-Nunn, Hastings 1975/76, 14 exf5 ♗xf5 15 ♘de4∞

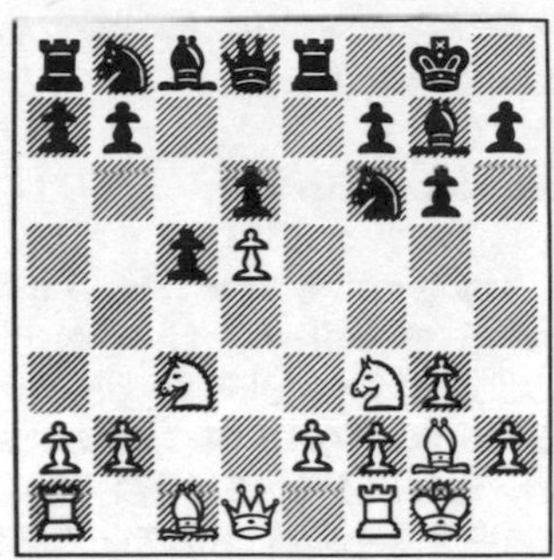

10 Bf4 Nh5 10...a6 11 a4 Bg4 12 Qd2 Bxf3 13 Bxf3 Qc7 14 Rfc1 Nbd7 15 b4 Ne5 16 Bxe5 Rxe5 17 bxc5 Qxc5 18 Rab1 Qc7 19 Qb2 Rb8 20 Ne4± Sosonko-Smejkal, Biel 1976 **11 Bg5 Qd7** N 11...Qb6 12 Qd2 Na6 13 h3 f6 14 Be3 f5 15 Rab1 Bd7 16 Bh6 Bh8= Ivanov-Kapengut, USSR 1977 **12 e4?!** 12 a4 **12...b5 13 Rc1 b4 14 Na4 Na6 15 h3 Bb7 16 a3 Nf6 17 Nd2** 17 Qc2 Nxe4 18 Rxe4 Rxe4 19 Qxe4 Qxa4∓; 17 Bxf6!? **17...Nxd5 18 exd5 Rxe1+ 19 Qxe1 Qxa4 20 Qe7∝** Sosonko-Smyslov, Tilburg 1977

Nimzo-Indian/Nimzo-Indisch

1 d4 Nf6 2 c4 e6 3 Nc3 Bb4 4 f3 d5 5 a3 Bxc3+ 6 bxc3 c5 7 cxd5 Nxd5 7...exd5 8 e3 0-0 9 Bd3 b6 10 Ne2 Ba6 11 0-0 Bxd3 12 Qxd3 Re8 13 g4 Nc6 14 Ng3 Rc8 15 Ra2 += Partos-Andersson, Biel 1977

Diagram

8 dxc5 f5 8...Qa5 9 e4 Ne7 10 Be3 Qxc3+ 11 Kf2 0-0 12 Ne2 Qa5 13 Qb3? f5!∓ Kozlovskaya-Fatalibekova, (1) 1977; 13 Qd2 Qxd2 14 Bxd2 **9 Qc2 0-0** 9...f4 10 g3∝ **10 e4 fxe4** 10...Nf6 11 Bf4 b6 12 Rd1 Qe8 13 Bd6 Rf7 14 Nh3 h6 15 exf5! exf5+ 16 Kf2 Ba6 17 Bxa6 Nxa6 18 Rfe1 +− Hollis-Sokolsky, corres 1976/77 **11 fxe4 Qh4+ 12 g3 Qf6 13 Bd3 Qxc3+ 14 Qxc3 Nxc3 15 Bf4 Bd7** 15...Rd8 16 Bc2 Bd7 **16 Rc1 Na4 17 Bd6 Rc8 18 Nf3 b6 19 Ne5 Nxc5 20 Bxc5!** TN **Rxc5 21 Rxc5 bxc5 22 0-0 +−** Hollis-Kauranen, corres 1977/78

1 d4 Nf6 2 c4 e6 3 Nc3 Bb4 4 Qc2 c5 4...d6 5 g3 e5!? 6 Nf3 (6 Qa4+ Nc6 7 d5 Bd7 8 Bd2 Bxc3 9 Bxc3 Ne4) 6...e4 7 Nd2 Nc6 8 Ndxe4 Nxd4 9 Qd3 Bf5 10 Bg2 Qe7 11 0-0 += Grigorian-Savon, Baku 1977 **5 dxc5 Bxc5** 5...0-0 6 Bf4 (6 Nf3 Na6 7 a3 Bxc3+ 8 Qxc3 Nxc5 9 b4 Nce4 10 Qd4 a5 11 Bb2 axb4 12 axb4 Rxa1+ 13 Bxa1 d6 =+ Farago-Orso, Hungary 1977) 6...Na6! 7 Bd6 Re8 8 a3 Bxc3+ 9 Qxc3 Ne4 10 Qd4 Qa5+ 11 b4 Nxb4 12 axb4 Qxb4+ 13 Kd1 Nxf2+ = Bagirov-Gaprindashvili,

Tibilisi 1974 **6 Nf3 Nc6 7 Bg5 h6** N **8 Bh4 g5 9 Bg3 Bb4 10 e3 Qa5 11 Bd3 Nh5 12 0-0-0**

1 d4 Nf6 2 c4 e6 3 Nc3 Bb4 4 e3 c5 5 Bd3 Nc6 6 Nf3 Bxc3+ 7 bxc3 d6 8 0-0 8 e4 e5 9 d5 Ne7 10 Nh4 (10 Nd2 Qa5 11 Qc2 Bd7 12 0-0 h6 13 f4 exf4 14 Nb3 Qc7 15 Bxf4 Ng6 16 e5∞ Gligoric-Barle, Ljubljana 1977) 10...h6 11 f4 Ng6 12 Nxg6 fxg6 13 0-0 0-0 14 f5 gxf5 15 exf5 Bd7 16 Rb1 Rb8 = Lombard-Panno, Biel 1977 **8...e5 9 Nd2 cxd4 10 cxd4 exd4 11 exd4 Nxd4 12 Re1+ Ne6 13 Ba3 0-0 14 Nb3 Qd7 15 Re3 Qc6 16 Bxd6±** Portisch-Timman, Wijk aan Zee 1978

1 d4 Nf6 2 c4 e6 3 Nc3 Bb4 4 e3 0-0 5 Bd3 d5 6 Nf3 c5 7 0-0 dxc4 8 Bxc4 Nbd7 8...Bd7 9 Qe2 Bc6 10 Rd1 Qe7 11 a3 Bxc3!? 12 bxc3 Nbd7 13 a4! N ± Gligoric-Taimanov, Montilla 1977 **9 Qe2** 9 Bd3 b6 10 a3 cxd4 11 exd4 Bxc3 12 bxc3 Bb7 13 c4 Rc8 14 Bb2 Qc7 15 Re1 Qf4 16 Qd2! Qd6!∞ Gligoric-Balashov, Tilburg 1977

9...b6! 9...cxd4 10 exd4 b6 11 Bg5 Bxc3 12 bxc3 Qc7 13 Bd3 Bb7 14 c4 += Gligoric-Parma, Jugoslavia 1977 **10 d5 Bxc3 11 dxe6 Ne5 12 exf7+ Kh8 13 bxc3 Bg4 14 e4 Qe7! 15 Re1 b5! 16 Bxb5 Nh5!=** Knaak-Holmov, Balashikha 1977

QID/Damen-Indisch

1 d4 Nf6 2 c4 e6 3 Nf3 b6 4 g3 Bb7 4...Ba6 5 Qa4 (5 b3 Bb4+ N 6 Bd2 Be7 7 Bg2 Bb7 8 Nc3 d5 9 cxd5 exd5 10 0-0 0-0 11 Bf4 Na6= Miles-Panno, Biel 1977) 5...Be7 (5...c6 6 Nc3 b5!? 7 cxb5 cxb5 8 Nxb5 Qb6 9 Nc3 [9 e3 Bb7 10 Be2 Bc6 11 Qc4 Qb7∞ Kluger-Portisch, Hungary Final 1959] 9...Bb4 10 Bg2 0-0 11 Qc2 Nc6 12 0-0 Rfc8 13 a3 Bxc3 14 bxc3 Nd5!∞ Tukmakov-Gulko, USSR Final 1977; 5...Be7 6 Bg2 0-0 7 0-0 c6 8 Nc3 d5 9 cxd5 b5 10 Qb3 exd5 11 a3 Nbd7 12 Bf4 Nb6= Bagirov-Smyslov, USSR Final 1977; 5...Bb7 6 Bg2 Be7 7 0-0 0-0 8 Nc3 c5 9 Rd1 cxd4 10 Nxd4 Bxg2 11 Kxg2 Qc7 12 Bf4 Qb7+ 13 f3 a6 14 Rd3 += Webb-Barcza, Decin 1977 **5 Bg2 Be7 6 0-0 0-0 7 Nc3 Ne4** 7...d5 8 Ne5 Na6 9 Be3 (9 cxd5 exd5 10 Qa4 N [10 Nd3 Ne4 11 Nf4 Nxc3 12 bxc3 c6 13 e4 dxe4 14 Bxe4± Bukic-Lengyel, Stip 1977] 10...Qe8 11 Qxe8 Rfxe8 12 Bg5 Ne4= Andersson-Balashov, Tilburg 1977; 9 Qa4 Qe8 10 Qxe8 Rfxe8 11 Rd1 Ne4 12 Be3 Nxc3 13 bxc3 c6 14 cxd5 cxd5= Kochiev-Karpov, Leningrad 1977) 9...c5 10 Rc1 Ne4 11 cxd5 exd5 12 Nxe4 dxe4 13 dxc5 Bxc5 14 Bxc5 Nxc5 15 b4 Ne6 16 Nc6 Bxc6 N (16...Qe8 17 Bxe4 Nd8 18 Qc2 Nxc6= Browne-Tal, Las Palmas 1977) 17 Rxc6 Qe7= Bagirov-Balashov, USSR Final 1977

Diagram

8 Qc2 8 Bd2 d5 (8...Bf6 9 Qc2 Nxd2

10 Qxd2 d6 11 e4 [11 Rad1 Nd7 12 d5 Bxc3 13 Qxc3 e5 14 e4 Qe7= Damjanovic-Smyslov, Hastings 1976/77] 11...Nd7 12 d5 Ne5! N 13 b3 Nxf3+ 14 Bxf3 g6 15 Bg2 Bg7= Mecking-Polugaevsky (10) 1977) 9 cxd5 exd5 10 Rc1 Nd7 11 Qb3 Ndf6 12 Rfd1 c5 13 dxc5 Bxc5= Smyslov-Tal, Leningrad 1977 **8...Nxc3 9 Qxc3 f5 10 b3 Bf6 11 Bb2 Nc6 12 Rad1** 12 Ne5 Nxd4 13 Qxd4 Bxg2 14 Kxg2 d6 15 Qe3 Bxe5 16 Bxe5 dxe5 17 Qxe5 Qd7 18 Rad1 Qc6+= Dorfman-Gulko, USSR Final 1977 **12...Qe7** N 12...Ne7 13 Ne1 Bxg2 14 Nxg2 g5!? 15 Qc2 Ng6 16 e4 += Polugaevsky-Korchnoi (2) 1977 **13 Qd2 Nd8 14 d5 Bxb2 15 Qxb2 d6 16 dxe6 Nxe6 17 b4 f4 18 Rd2 Rf6 19 Qc3 Raf8∓** Miles-Korchnoi, Wijk aan Zee 1978

Gruenfeld

1 d4 Nf6 2 c4 g6 3 Nc3 d5 4 Bf4 Bg7 5 e3 0-0 6 Qb3 c5 7 cxd5 cxd4 8 exd4 Nbd7 9 Be2 Nb6 10 Bf3 e6 10...Bg4 11 Bxg4 Nxg4 12 Nf3 Nf6 13 d6 exd6= **11 d6! Nfd5** N 11...Nfd7 12 Nge2 e5 13 dxe5 Nxe5 14 Bxe5 Bxe5 15 Rd1± Kluger-Benko, Budapest 1954 **12 Bxd5 exd5 13 Nge2 Re8 14 0-0** += Petrosian-Grigorian, USSR Final 1977

1 d4 Nf6 2 c4 g6 3 Nc3 d5 4 Nf3 Bg7 5 Bg5 Ne4 5...dxc4 6 e4 0-0!? 7 Bxc4 Bg4 8 Be2 Nfd7 9 0-0 Nb6 10 d5 += Pytel-Ghinda, Zabrze 1977 **6 Bh4** 6 cxd5 Nxg5 7 Nxg5 e6 (7...c6 8 dxc6 Nxc6 9 d5 Ne5 10 e4 0-0 11 Be2 e6 12 Nf3 Nxf3+ 13 Bxf3 exd5 14 Qxd5 Be6 15 Qxd8 Rfxd8α) 8 Nf3 (8 Qd2 h6! 9 Nh3 exd5 10 Nf4 0-0 11 e3 c5!∓) 8...exd5 9 e3 a5!? 10 Be2 0-0 11 0-0 c6 12 a3 Re8 13 Ne1 (13 b4 axb4 14 axb4 Rxa1 15 Qxa1 b5!∓ Uhlmann-Simagin, Budapest 1961) 13...Bf5 14 Qb3? Ra7 15 Bd3 Be6 16 Rd1 Nd7 =+ Ivanov-Tseshkovsky, Erevan 1977

6...Nxc3 6...c5 7 cxd5 Nxc3 8 bxc3 Qxd5 9 e3 Nc6 10 Be2 cxd4 11 cxd4 Qa5+ 12 Qd2 Qxd2+ 13 Kxd2 e5 14 dxe5 Nxe5 15 Nd4!± Gheorghiu-Jansa, Sochi 1976 **7 bxc3 dxc4!** 7...c5 8 cxd5 Qxd5 9 e3 Nc6 10 Be2 cxd4 11 cxd4 0-0 12 0-0 b6 13 Rc1 N Bb7 14 Bc4 Qd6 15 Bg3 Qb4= Beljavsky-Grigorian, Baku 1977 **8 e3** 8 Qa4+ Nd7 9 Qxc4 0-0 10 e3 c5! 11 Be2 cxd4 12 Nxd4 Nf6 13 0-0 e5∓ Mikenas-Tukmakov, 1970 **8...b5 9 a4 c6 10 axb5** 10 Be2 a6 11 Nd2 0-0 12 Bf3 Ra7 13 0-0 h6 14 Ne4 Re8∓

Lengyel-Gulko, Sombor 1974 **10... cxb5 11 ♘e5 ♗b7 12 ♕b1** N 12 ♖b1 ♕a5! 13 ♘xc4 (13 ♗xc4 ♗xe5 14 ♗xb5+ ♘c6 15 ♗xc6+ ♗xc6 16 dxe5 ♕xc3+ 17 ♔e2 ♕c4+ Δ 18...♘xe5∓) 13...♕xc3+ 14 ♘d2 a6∓ **12...♕b6 13 ♕b4 f6 14 ♖a5 ♘c6 15 ♘xc6 ♗xc6 16 d5 ♗xd5!**∓ Pytel-Smejkal, Dortmund 1977

1 d4 ♘f6 2 c4 g6 3 ♘c3 d5 4 ♘f3 ♗g7 5 ♕b3 dxc4 6 ♕xc4 0-0 7 e4 a6 7...c6 8 ♕b3 ♗g4!? N (8...e5!=) 9 ♕xb7 ♘fd7 10 ♕xa8 ♕c7 11 ♘d5 cxd5 12 ♕xd5 ♘c6 13 ♕c4 ♗xf3 14 gxf3 ♗xd4∞ Blackstock-Castro, Budapest 1977; 7...♗g4 8 ♗e3 ♘fd7 9 0-0-0 (9 ♕b3 ♘b6 10 ♖d1 ♗xf3?! N [10...e6!? 11 ♗b5 ♗xf3! N 12 gxf3 ♕h4 13 ♘e2 a6 14 ♗d3 ♘c6 15 ♗b1 ♖fd8 =+ Forintos-Smejkal, Bar 1977] 11 gxf3 e6 12 h4 ♘c6 13 e5 ♘e7 14 h5± Sosonko-Timman, Amsterdam 1977) 9...c6 10 h3 ♗xf3 11 gxf3 b5 12 ♕b3 a5 13 d5 a4∞ Sosonko-Castro, Biel 1976

8 ♗e2 8 ♕b3 b5 9 e5 ♗e6!? (9...♘fd7 10 ♗e3 ♘b6 11 a4 ♗e6 12 ♕d1 b4=) 10 exf6 ♗xb3 11 fxg7 ♔xg7 12 axb3 ♘c6 13 ♗e3 ♘b4 14 ♖c1 N (14 ♖d1 ♕d7 15 ♗e2 ♕e6 16 d5!∞ Filep-Barcza, Hungary 1969) 14...♕d7 15 ♗e2 c6 16 ♘e4 ♕f5 17 ♘fd2± Bronstein-Poutianen, Tallinn 1977; 8 ♗f4 b5 9 ♕xc7 ♕xc7 10 ♗xc7 ♗b7 11 e5 ♘d5 12 ♘xd5 ♗xd5 13 ♗e2 ♖c8 14 ♗a5 ♘c6 15 ♗c3 ♖ab8 16 0-0 b4∓ Plaskett-S.Webb, Brighton 1977 **8...b5 9 ♕b3 c5** 9...♗b7 10 e5 ♘d5 11 0-0 ♘xc3 12 ♕xc3 ♗d5 13 a4 ♘c6 14 ♗e3± Sosonko-Sax, Ljubljana 1977 **10 dxc5 ♘bd7** 10...♕c7? 11 ♗e3 ♗b7 12 ♘d5 ♕a5+ 13 ♘d2 ♘xe4 14 ♗f3!± Moisseev-Florian, corresp 1976/77; 10...♗e6 11 ♕c2 ♕c7 12 ♘d4 ♗c4 13 ♗e3 e5 14 ♘b3 ♘c6 15 0-0 ♖ad8≈ Gulko-Kirov, Polanica 1977; 10...♗b7! Moisseev **11 e5 ♘xc5 12 ♕b4 ♘fd7 13 0-0 a5 14 ♕h4 ♗b7**≈ Sosonko-Mecking, Wijk aan Zee 1978

1 d4 ♘f6 2 c4 g6 3 ♘c3 d5 4 ♘f3 ♗g7 5 e3 0-0 6 cxd5 ♘xd5 7 ♗c4 ♘xc3 7...♘b6 8 ♗b3 c5 9 0-0 cxd4 10 ♘xd4 ♘c6 11 ♕e2 (11 ♘xc6 bxc6 12 ♕f3 a5 13 ♘a4 ♕c7 14 ♖d1 ♘xa4 15 ♗xa4 ♗b7 16 e4 ♗e5= Panno-Gheorghiu, Las Palmas 1973) 11...a5 12 ♖d1 ♘xd4 13 exd4± Gligoric-Portisch, Skopje 1972 **8 bxc3 c5 9 0-0 ♕c7 10 ♗e2** 10 ♕e2 b6 11 ♗b2 ♘c6 12 ♖ac1 ♗b7 13 ♖fd1 e6 14 ♗b5 ♖fd8 15 ♗a3 ♘a5= Kuzmin-Kochiev, Minsk 1976 **10...b6 11 a4 ♘c6 12 ♘d2 ♖d8 13 ♘c4 ♗a6! 14 ♘a3 ♗b7 15 ♗b2 ♘a5 16 ♗f3 e5 17 d5 e4!**∓ Plachetka-Tukmakov, Decin 1977

1 d4 ♘f6 2 c4 g6 3 ♘c3 d5 4 cxd5 ♘xd5 5 e4 ♘xc3 6 bxc3 ♗g7 7 ♗c4 c5 7...0-0 8 ♘e2 (8 ♗e3!? b6 9 h4 ♘c6 10 ♗d5 ♕d7 11 h5 e6 12 ♗b3 ♘a5 13 hxg6 fxg6∓ Knaak-Sax, Budapest 1977) 8...♘c6 9 0-0 b6 10 f4 (10 ♗g5 ♗b7 11 f4? ♘a5 N 12 ♗d3 c5!∓ Gligoric-Hartston, Moscow 1977) 10...♘a5 11 ♗d3 c5 12 e5!? N cxd4 13 cxd4 f5∞ Munder-Hartston, Hamburg 1977

8 ♘e2 0-0 9 0-0 ♘c6 10 ♗e3 ♕c7 10... cxd4 11 cxd4 ♗g4 12 f3 ♘a5 13 ♗d3 ♗e6 14 d5 ♗xa1 15 ♕xa1 f6 16 ♗h6 (16 ♖b1 ♗d7 17 ♗h6 ♖f7 18 e5 fxe5 19 ♕xe5 b5 20 ♗e3 ♕b8 21 ♕c3 ♕d8 22 ♕e5 ♕b8 23 ♕c3 ♕d8 ½-½ Kavalek-Timman, Wijk aan Zee 1978) 16... ♖e8 17 ♔h1 ♖c8! 18 ♕d4 ♗d7 19 ♖b1 N b6 20 e5 ♖c5 21 ♘f4 ♕c7∓ Deze-Pribyl, Zalaegerszeg 1977 **11 ♖c1 ♖d8 12 ♕d2 ♘e5!? 13 ♗d5 e6 14 dxe5** 14 ♗b3 **14...exd5 15 ♗g5 ♖e8 16 exd5 ♗xe5 17 f4** 17 ♘g3?! f5 18 f4 ♗d6 =+ Gligoric-Savon, Ljubljana 1977 **17...♗g7 18 d6 ♕c6 19 ♗e7 b5!? 20 f5±** Gligoric-Tseshkovsky, Ljubljana 1977

King's Indian/Koenigs-Indisch

1 d4 ♘f6 2 c4 g6 3 ♘c3 ♗g7 4 g3 d6 5 ♗g2 0-0 6 ♘f3 ♘c6 6...c6 7 0-0 ♕a5 (7...♗f5 8 ♘h4 ♗d7 9 e4 e5 10 ♘f3 ♖e8 11 h3 ♘a6 12 ♖e1 exd4 13 ♘xd4 ♕b6 14 ♘b3 += Portisch-Larsen (10) 1977) 8 h3 e5 9 e4 exd4 10 ♘xd4 ♕c5 11 ♘b3 ♕b4 12 ♗e3 a5 13 ♘d2 += Ribli-Vaganian, Leningrad 1977 **7 0-0 a6 8 h3** 8 ♗d2!? ♗d7 9 e3 e5 10 d5 ♘e7 11 e4 h6 12 ♘e1 ♘e8 13 ♘d3 f5 14 ♖b1 b5= Smejkal-Sax, Belgrade 1977

8...e5 8...♖b8 9 ♗g5 b5 10 cxb5 axb5 11 ♖c1 b4 12 ♗xf6 exf6 13 ♘d5 ♘e7 14 ♘xe7+ ♕xe7 15 d5 += Larsen-Timman, Las Palmas 1977 **9 d5 ♘e7 10 c5 b5** N **11 cxb6 cxb6 12 e4 b5=** Marovic-Smejkal, Vrsac 1977

1 d4 ♘f6 2 c4 g6 3 ♘c3 ♗g7 4 e4 d6 5 h3 0-0 6 ♗g5 c5 6...c6 7 ♘f3 a6 8 a4 a5 9 ♗e2 ♘bd7 10 0-0 e5 11 d5 ♘c5 12 ♘d2 ♕b6 13 ♕c2 h6 14 ♗e3 ♘fd7 15 ♔h1 ♕d8 16 ♖ad1 f5 17 exf5 gxf5 18 f4± Partos-Planinc, Nice 1974 **7 d5 b5!** 7...♘a6 8 ♘f3 ♘c7 9 ♗d3 a6 10 a4 ♗d7 11 a5 ♖b8 12 0-0± Larsen-Westerinen, Helsinki 1969 **8 cxb5 a6** 8...♕a5 9 ♗d2 a6 10 a4 axb5 (10...♕b4!) 11 ♗xb5 ♗a6 12 ♖a3! ♘bd7 13 ♘f3 ♗xb5 14 ♘xb5± Suba-Plachetka, Moscow 1977 **9 bxa6** 9 a4 ♕a5 10 ♗d2 ♕b4! 11 ♕c2 axb5 12 ♗xb5 ♗a6∞ Partos-Haik, Bagneux 1974 **9...♕a5 10 ♗d2 ♕b4! 11 ♕c2 ♗xa6 12 ♗xa6 ♘xa6 13 a3 ♕c4 14 ♖b1 ♘b4∓** Rashkovsky-Geller, Sochi 1977

1 d4 ♘f6 2 c4 g6 3 ♘c3 ♗g7 4 e4 d6 5 ♘f3 0-0 6 ♗e2 e5 7 ♗e3 ♘g4 7...exd4 (7...♕e7 8 dxe5 [8 ♗g5 ♘bd7 9 ♕d2 ♖e8 10 ♘d5 ♕d8 11 dxe5 dxe5 12 ♖d1 c6 13 ♘xf6+ ♗xf6 14 c5 ♕e7= Miles-Kavalek, Wijk aan Zee 1977] 8...dxe5 9 ♘d5 ♘xd5 10 cxd5 c6 11 d6 ♕d8 12 0-0 ♖e8 13 ♕d2 f6 14 ♖fd1 ♗e6 15 ♕c3 ♕d7 16 b4± Miles-Torre, Bad Lauterberg 1977) 8 ♘xd4 ♖e8 9 f3 c6 10 ♗f2 d5 11 exd5 cxd5 12 c5 ♘c6 13 0-0 ♘h5 14 ♕d2 ♗e5 15 g3 ♘g7 N 16 ♖fe1 ♘e6= Gligoric-Hort, Tilburg 1977

8 ♗g5 f6 9 ♗c1 ♘a6 9...♘c6 10 h3 ♘h6 11 0-0 ♘f7 12 ♗e3 ♔h8 13 c5 += Miles-Hort, Tilburg 1977 **10 0-0 f5 11 exf5 exd4 12 ♗g5 ♕e8 13 ♘d5 ♗xf5 14 ♘e7+ ♔h8 15 ♘xd4** += Hort-Nicevski, Stip 1977

1 d4 ♘f6 2 c4 g6 3 ♘c3 ♗g7 4 e4 d6 5 ♘f3 0-0 6 ♗e2 e5 7 0-0 ♘bd7 8 ♖e1 8 ♕c2 c6 9 ♖d1 ♕e7 10 d5 c5 11 ♖b1 ♘h5 12 g3 ♘b6 13 b4 cxb4 14 ♖xb4 f5 15 c5 dxc5 16 d6 ♕d7 17 ♖xb6! +- Dorfman-Grigorian, USSR Final 1977 **8...c6 9 ♗f1 a5** 9...h6 10 ♖b1 ♘h7 11 dxe5 ♘xe5 12 ♘xe5 dxe5 13 ♗e3 ♕xd1 14 ♖exd1 ♖e8= Taimanov-Rashkovsky, Baku 1977

10 ♖b1 10 ♗e3 exd4 11 ♘xd4 ♖e8 12 f3 d5 13 cxd5 cxd5 14 ♘db5 dxe4 15 ♘d6 ♖f8 Dorfman-Kochiev, USSR 1977, 16 f4!?; 10 h3 exd4 11 ♘xd4 ♖e8 12 ♗f4 ♘c5 13 ♕c2 ♘fd7 14 ♖ad1 ♗xd4 15 ♖xd4 ♘e6 =+ Rashkovsky-Kochiev, Baku 1977 **10...exd4** 10...♖e8 11 d5 ♘c5 (11...♕c7 12 a3 a4! 13 ♘xa4 ♘xe4 14 ♖xe4 ♖xa4 =+ Nesis-Skuja, corresp 1977) 12 b3 ♗d7 13 ♘d2 ♗h6 14 a3 cxd5 15 cxd5 ♖f8 16 ♘c4 ♗xc1 17 ♕xc1 ♕c7 N 18 b4± Ftacnik-Tal, Sochi 1977

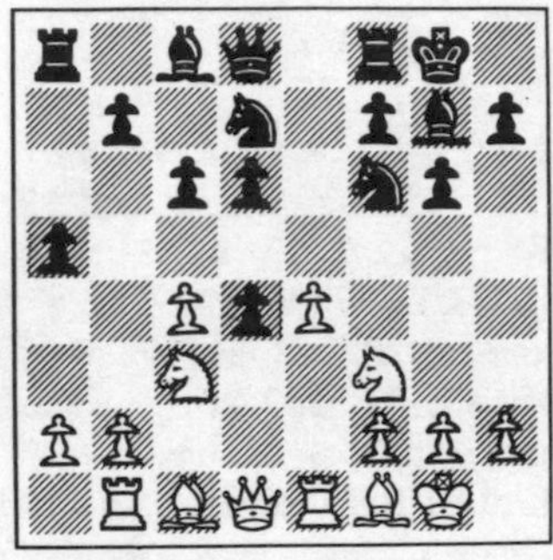

11 ♘xd4 ♖e8 11...♘c5 12 f3 ♖e8 13 ♗e3 a4 14 ♕d2 ♘fd7 15 b4 axb3 16 axb3 += Ogaard-Larsen, Copenhagen 1977 **12 ♘c2** 12 f3 d5 13 cxd5 cxd5 14 ♘db5 dxe4 15 ♘d6 exf3 16 ♘xe8 ♘g4∞ Polugaevsky-Kochiev, USSR Final 1977; 12 ♗f4 ♘c5 13 f3 (13 ♕c2 ♘g4 14 ♖bd1 ♗e5 15 ♗xe5 dxe5 16 ♘b3 ♕h4= Smejkal-Kochiev, Dortmund 1977) 13...d5 14 exd5 ♖xe1 15 ♕xe1 ♘xd5 16 cxd5 ♗xd4+ 17 ♗e3 ♗xe3+ 18 ♕xe3 += Tal-Grigorian, USSR Final 1977 **12...♕e7 13 ♗f4 ♘e5 14 ♕d2 ♘h5 15 ♗g5 f6 16 ♗e3** += Baumbach-Syre, West Germany 1977

Sicilian/Sizilianisch

1 e4 c5 2 ♘f3 e6 3 d4 cxd4 4 ♘xd4 ♘f6 5 ♘c3 d6 6 ♗e2 6 ♗e3 a6 7 f4 (7 ♗e2 ♕c7 8 f4 b5 9 ♗f3 ♗b7 10 a3 ♘bd7 11 ♕e2 += Suetin-Platanov, USSR 1977) 7...b5 8 a3 ♗b7 9 ♗d3 ♘bd7 10 ♕f3 ♖c8 11 0-0 ♗e7 12 ♖ae1 ♘c5 13 ♗f2 0-0 =+ Ligterink-Kavalek, Wijk aan Zee 1977

6...♗e7

(1) 6...a6 7 0-0 ♘bd7 (7...♕c7 8 f4 ♘bd7 9 a4 b6 10 ♗f3 ♗b7 11 ♕e2 e5? 12 ♘d5! ♘xd5 13 exd5 g6 14 ♘c6± Smyslov-Grigorian, USSR Final 1976) 8 a4 (8 f4 b5 9 ♗f3 ♗b7 10 e5 ♗xf3 11 ♘xf3 ♘g4 12 ♕e2 b4 13 ♘e4 d5 14 ♘eg5 ♗c5+ 15 ♔h1 Ligterink-Ghizdavu, Amsterdam 1974, 15...h6 16 ♘h3 g6 Δ ♕b6) 8...b6 9 f4 ♗b7 10 ♗f3 ♖c8 11 ♕e1 ♕c7 12 ♔h1 += Geller-Barczay, Wijk aan Zee 1977;

(2) 6...a6 7 f4 ♘c6 8 ♗f3 ♕c7 9 ♗e3 ♗e7 10 0-0 0-0 11 ♔h1 ♗d7 12 a4 ♘a5 13 g4 += Vasyukov-Tukmakov, Erevan 1976;

(3) 6...a6 7 f4 ♗e7 8 0-0 0-0 (8...♕c7 9 ♕e1 0-0 10 ♕g3 ♕b6 11 ♗e3 ♕xb2 12 ♗f2 ♕b4 13 e5 dxe5 14 fxe5 ♘e8 15 ♘e4 ♘d7 16 ♗d3 ♕a5 17 ♗f3 f5∓ Sigurjonsson-Sax, Amsterdam 1976) 9 ♔h1 (9 ♗e3 ♕c7 10 ♕e1 ♖e8 11 ♕g3 ♘bd7 12 ♘f3 e5 = Tal-Andersson (1) 1976) 9...♕c7 (9...♘c6 10 ♗e3 ♕c7 11 a4 ♖d8 12 ♕e1 ♘xd4 13 ♗xd4 e5 14 ♗e3 exf4 15 ♗xf4 ♗e6 16 ♕g3 ♘d7= Karpov-Ribli, Leningrad 1977) 10 ♕e1 b5 (10...♖e8 11 ♕g3 ♘bd7 12 ♗f3 ♖b8 13 a4 ♗f8 14 ♗d2 ♔h8 15 ♖ae1 e5 16 ♘f5 b5= Vogt-Andersson, Cienfuegos 1976; 10...♘bd7 11 ♗f3 ♖e8 12 g4 ♘b6 13 a4 ♗f8 14 ♕g3 ♘c4 15 g5 ♘d7 16 ♘de2 ♖b8 17 b3 ♘a5 18 ♗b2 ♘c5 = Tal-Andersson, Wijk aan Zee 1976) 11 ♗f3 ♗b7 12 e5 dxe5 13 fxe5 ♘fd7 14 ♕g3 ♔h8 15 ♗f4 ♘b6 (15...♘c6 16 ♘f5!? g5!∝ Sibarevic-Antunac, Jugoslavia 1977) 16 ♘e4 ♘8d7 17 ♗g5 ♗xg5 18 ♘xg5 ♗xf3 19 ♖xf3 ♔g8 20 ♕h3 h6 21 ♘xf7 ♕c4 22 ♕h5± Beljavsky-Ribli, Leningrad 1977 **7 0-0 0-0** 7...♘c6 8 ♗e3 ♗d7 9 ♘db5 ♕b8 10 a4 0-0 11 g4 ♖d8 12 g5 ♘e8 13 f4 a6 14 ♘a3 ♘b4 15 ♗b6 ♖c8 16 ♘c4± Grefe-Szmetan, Quito 1976; 9 f4 a6 (9...♘xd4 10 ♗xd4 ♗c6 11 ♕e1 0-0 12 ♕g3 g6 13 ♕e3 ♕a5 14 e5 dxe5 15 fxe5 ♘d7 16 ♗f3 ♗xf3 17 ♖xf3 ♗c5 18 ♖e1 ♗xd4 19 ♕xd4 ♕b6 20 ♕xb6 ♘xb6 21 ♘e4± Browne-Timman, Amsterdam 1976) 10 ♔h1 ♕c7 11 ♕e1 b5 12 a3 (12 ♗f3 b4 13 ♘d1 ♘xd4 14 ♗xd4 e5 =+ Planinc-Kurajica, Banja Luka 1976) 12...0-0 13 ♕g3 ♘xd4 14 ♗xd4 ♗c6 15 ♖ae1! ♕b7 16 ♗d3 g6 17 f5 ♘h5 18 ♕h3 exf5 19 ♖xf5∝ Honfi-Janosevic, Majdanpek 1976

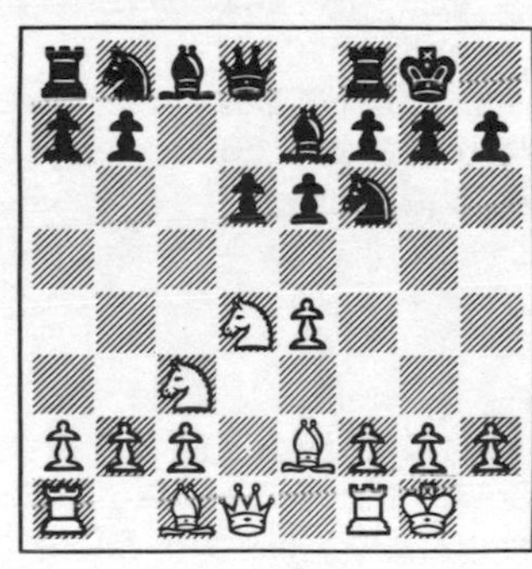

8 f4 ♘c6
8...a6 9 ♗f3 ♕c7 10 ♔h1 ♘c6 11 g4 ♘xd4 12 ♕xd4 ♘d7 13 g5 ♖e8 14 a4 b6 15 ♕f2 ♗b7 16 ♗e3 ♗f8 17 ♖g1 g6 18 ♖g3 ♗g7= Padevsky-Andersson (2) 1976;
(2) 9 ♔h1 ♕c7 10 ♗e3 ♘bd7 11 a4 b6 12 ♗f3 ♗b7 13 ♕e2 ♘c5 14 ♗f2 += Timoshenko-Boensch, Varna 1977;
(3) 9 ♔h1 ♘c6 10 ♗e3 ♗d7 11 a4 ♕c7 12 ♘b3 b6 13 ♗f3 ♖ab8 14 ♕e2 [14 g4 ♗c8 15 g5 ♘d7 16 ♗g2 += Jansa-Ree, Sochi 1976] 14...♘a5 15 ♘xa5 bxa5 16 ♖ab1 ♗c8 17 g4 ♖e8 18 g5 ♘d7 19 ♕f2 ♗b7 20 ♗g2 ♗c6 21 ♗d4 ♗f8 22 f5 ♘e5 =+ Vogt-Schmidt, L'Aja 1976;
(4) 9 ♗e3 ♕c7 10 a4 (10 g4 ♘c6 11 g5 ♘d7 12 f5 ♘de5 13 f6 ♗d8∝ Sax-Stean, Moscow 1977) 10...♘c6 11 ♔h1 (11 ♕e1 ♗d7 12 ♕g3 ♘xd4 13 ♗xd4 ♗c6 14 ♔h1 g6 15 f5 e5 16 ♗e3 ♔h8 17 ♗g5 gxf5 18 ♕h4 ♘g8 19 ♖xf5 ♗xg5 20 ♖xg5 f6 21 ♖f5 ♖ad8= Christiansen-van der Vliet, Wijk aan Zee 1977) 11...♖d8! 12 ♘b3 b6 13 ♕e1 ♖b8 14 ♕f2 ♘b4 15 ♗f3 e5 16 a5 bxa5 17 ♘xa5 ♘c6 18 ♘c4 Reshevsky-Ree, Amsterdam 1977, 18...♘b4 = **9 ♗e3** 9 ♔h1
(1) 9...♗d7 10 ♘b3 a6 11 a4 b6 12 ♗f3 ♕c7 13 ♕e2 ♖fd8 14 g4 ♗e8 15 g5 ♘d7 16 ♗e3 += Ermenkov-Vogt, Albena 1976;
(2) 9...a6 10 ♗f3 ♕c7 11 a4 ♖d8 12 ♗e3 ♘e5! 13 ♗e2 b6 =+ Haag-Jansa, Budapest 1976

Diagram

9...a6
(1) 9...♗d7 10 ♘b3 a5 (10...a6 11 a4 e5 12 ♘d5!± Sax-Hulak, Vinkovci 1976; 10...♕c7 11 ♗f3 ♖fd8= Tal-Beljavsky, Moscow 1975) 11 a4 ♘b4 12 ♗f3 e5 13 ♖f2 ♗c6 14 ♖d2 ♕c7 15 ♔h1± Tukmakov-Plachetka, Odessa 1976; 9...e5 10 ♘b3 a5 (10...exf4 11 ♖xf4 ♗e6 12 ♘d4 ♘xd4 13 ♗xd4 ♘d7 14 ♔h1 ♗g5 15 ♖f1 ♘e5 16 ♗g1∝ Matanovic-Vogt, Vratsa 1975) 11 a4 ♘b4 12 ♔h1 ♗d7 (12...♕c7 13 ♖c1 ♗e6 14 ♘d2 exf4 15 ♘b5 ♕d8 16 ♗xf4 d5 17 ♘c7 ♖c8 18 ♘xe6 += Kavalek-Spassky, Manila 1976) 13 ♗b5 (13 ♗f3 ♕c7 14 ♖f2 ♖fe8 15 ♖d2 b6 16 ♘c1 ♗c6 17 ♘1e2 ♕b7 18 ♘g3 ♗f8 =+ Mecking-Spassky, Manila 1976) 13...♗g4 14 ♕d2 ♖c8 15 ♖ac1 ♗e6 16 fxe5± Suetin-Sax, Budapest 1976;
(2) 9...♕c7 10 ♕e1 (10 ♔h1 ♘xd4 11 ♕xd4 e5 12 ♕d3 ♗d7?! 13 fxe5 dxe5 14 ♖xf6!± Ivanovic-Sofrevsky, Jugoslavia 1976) 10...♗d7 11 ♕g3 ♘xd4 12 ♗xd4 ♗c6 13 ♗d3 b6 14 ♖ae1 ♖ad8 15 ♔h1 ♕b7 16 ♖f3 ♖fe8 17 ♕h3 += Akvist-Kuzmin, Reggio-Emilia 1976/77 **10 ♕e1**
(1) 10 ♔h1 ♗d7 11 ♕e1 b5 12 a3 ♕b8! 13 ♕g3 (13 ♗f3 ♘xd4 14 ♗xd4 e5 15 ♘d5 ♘xd5 16 exd5 exd4 17 ♕xe7 ♗f5∓ Szabo-Larsen, Costa Brava 1976) 13...b4 14 axb4 ♕xb4 15 ♘xc6 ♗xc6 16 e5 dxe5 17 fxe5 ♘e4 18 ♘xe4

♗xe4 19 ♗d3 ♗xd3 20 cxd3 ♔h8∞ Jansa-Sakharov, Sochi 1976;
(2) 10 ♔h1 ♕c7 11 ♕e1 ♘xd4 12 ♗xd4 b5 13 e5 dxe5 14 ♗xe5 ♕b6 15 ♗d3 ♗b7 16 ♕h4 h6 17 ♕g3 ♘e8 18 f5 exf5 19 ♖xf5 ♗d6 20 ♖af1 ♖d8 21 a4 ♗xe5 22 ♖xe5 b4 23 ♘e4± Barczay-Westerinen, Budapest 1976; 13 ♕g3 ♗b7 14 a3 ♗c6 15 ♖ae1 ♕b7 (15...♖ac8 16 ♗d3 e5 17 fxe5 ♘h5 18 ♕h3 dxe5 19 ♘d5 ♗xd5 20 ♗xe5 ♕xe5 21 exd5 ♕d6 22 ♕xh5 g6= Balashov-Karpov, Leningrad 1977; 15...♖ab8 16 e5 ♘e8 17 ♗d3 g6 18 ♕h3 ♘g7 19 ♕h6 f6! 20 ♖e3 ♖f7 – Tal-Andersson, Las Palmas 1975) 16 ♗d3 b4 17 axb4 (17 ♘d1 g6 18 ♘f2 bxa3 19 bxa3 d5 20 e5 ♘e4∞ Sznapik-Smejkal, Sandomierz 1976) 17...♕xb4 18 ♘e2 ♕b7 19 e5 ♘h5 20 ♕h3 g6 21 ♘g3 dxe5 22 ♗xe5 ♘g7 22 ♘e4 f6 23 ♗c3 Ermenkov-Estevez, Kecskemet 1977, 23...♗b4=;
(3) 10 a4 ♗d7 11 ♔h1 ♘xd4 12 ♕xd4 ♗c6 13 ♗f3 ♖c8 14 a5 d5! =+ Pritchett-Andersson, Haifa 1976
(4) 10 a4 ♕c7 11 ♔h1 ♖e8 (11...♗d7 12 ♕e1 ♘xd4 13 ♗xd4 ♗c6 14 ♕g3 g6 15 f5 e5 16 ♗e3 ♔h8 [16...b5? 17 ♗h6 ♖fc8 18 ♗d3 ♔h8 19 ♕h3 b4 20 fxg6 fxg6 21 ♕e6± Shamkovich-Sherwin, Lone Pine 1976] 17 ♗g5 (17 fxg6 fxg6 18 ♗h6) 17...♕d8 18 ♕h4 gxf5 19 ♖xf5 ♘g8 =+ Barle-Janosevic, Jugoslavia 1977) 12 ♗f3 ♖b8! 13 ♕e2 ♘xd4 14 ♗xd4 e5 15 ♗e3 ♗e6 16 ♖fd1 ♗c4 17 ♕f2 b5 18 axb5 axb5 19 ♖a7 ♖b7 20 ♖xb7 ♕xb7= Balashov-Kavalek, Manila 1976

10...♞xd4

(1) 10...♘d7?! 11 ♖d1 ♖e8 12 ♗c4 ♘f8 13 a3 ♗d7 14 ♕f2 b5 15 ♗a2 ♖b8 16 f5± Beljavsky-Andersson, Cienfuegos 1976;
(2) 10...♕c7 11 ♖d1 ♘xd4 12 ♗xd4 b5 13 a3 (13 e5 dxe5 14 fxe5 ♘d7 15 ♘e4 ♗b7 16 ♘f6+! ♔h8 17 ♕h4 h6 18 ♕h5 ♗c5!= Geller-Tal, USSR Final 1976) 13...♗b7 14 ♕g3 g6 15 f5! e5 16 ♗e3 ♖fe8 17 ♖f3 += Polugaevsky-Suetin, USSR 1976;
(3) 10...♕c7 11 ♕g3 ♗d7 12 ♔h1 (12 ♖ae1 ♘xd4 13 ♗xd4 ♗c6 14 ♗d3 ♖ad8 15 ♔h1 += Byrne-Fraguela, Las Palmas 1976) 12...b5 13 e5 dxe5 14 fxe5 ♘x e5 15 ♗h6 ♘e8 16 ♗f4 f6 17 ♗g4 ♕c4 18 ♗xe5 fxe5 19 ♖xf8+ ♖xf8 20 ♕f3+ +– Klovan-Sher, USSR 1976;
(4) 10...♗d7 11 ♖d1 (11 ♕g3 ♘xd4 12 ♗xd4 ♗c6 13 ♗d3 b5 14 a3 ♕d7 15 e5 [15 ♖ae1 a5 16 ♕h3 e5! 17 fxe5 dxe5 18 ♗xe5 ♕xh3 19 gxh3 b4= Vukcevic-Sigurjonsson, Reykjavik 1976] 15... dxe5 16 ♗xe5 g6 17 f5 ♘h5 18 ♕g4 exf5 19 ♗xf5 ♕a7+ 20 ♗d4 ♗c5 21 ♗xc5 ♕xc5+ 22 ♔h1 ♖ad8= Byrne-Najdorf, Haifa 1976) 11...♘xd4 12 ♗xd4 ♗c6 13 ♗f3 ♕c7 14 e5 ♘e8 15 ♔h1 ♖d8 16 ♖d3 dxe5 (16...b5) 17 fxe5 g6 18 ♕f2 += Geller-Sigurjonsson, Wijk aan Zee 1977 **11 ♗xd4 b5 12 a3** 12 ♖d1 b4 13 e5 bxc3 14 exf6 ♗xf6 15 ♕xc3 ♗xd4 16 ♕xd4±; 12...♕c7 13 e5 dxe5 14 fxe5 ♘d7 15 ♘e4 ♗b7 16 ♘f6+ ♔h8 17 ♕h4 h6 18 ♕h5± Kasparov-Mageramov, USSR 1977; 12...♗b7 13 ♗f3 b4 (13...♕c7 14 e5 dxe5 15 fxe5 ♘d7 16 ♗xb7 ♕xb7 17 ♘e4 ♕c7!= Kaplan-Weinstein, New York 1976) 14 e5 ♗xf3 15 ♖xf3 dxe5 16 fxe5 ♘d5 17 ♘e4 ♕c7 18 ♕f2 ♖ac8 19 c3 ♕c6 20 ♘f6+! ± Geller-Grigorian, USSR Final 1976 **12...♝b7 13 ♛g3 ♜c8** 13...♗c6 14 ♖ae1 ♕d7 15 ♗d3 ♖ae8 16 ♔h1 ♗d8 17 e5 dxe5 18

♗xe5 g6 19 ♕h3± Ostojic-Kaplan, Cleveland 1975; 13... g6 (Geller) 14 ♗d3 ♖c8 15 f5 e5 16 ♗e3 ♖xc3! 17 bxc3 ♘xe4 18 ♕g4 ♘f6 19 ♕h3 ♕c8 20 ♗h6 ♖e8=+ Jansa-Hartston, Reykjavik 1975 **14 ♔h1 g6 15 ♗d3 ♘h5 16 ♕e3 ♕d7 17 ♗e2 ♘xf4! 18 ♕xf4 e5 19 ♕g3 exd4 20 ♗g4 ♕c7 21 ♗xc8 dxc3 22 ♗xb7 cxb2 23 ♖ab1 ♕xb7 24 ♕d3 ♕c6 25 ♖xb2±** Karpov-Andersson, Tilburg 1977

1 e4 c5 2 f4 ♘c6 2...♘f6 3 ♘c3 d5 4 e5 d4 5 exf6 dxc3 6 fxg7 cxd2+ 7 ♕xd2 ♕xd2+ 8 ♗xd2 ♗xg7 9 0-0-0 ♗f5 (9...♘c6 10 ♗b5 ♗d7 17 ♗e3 b6 12 ♘f3 ♘e5 13 ♗xd7+ ♘xd7 14 ♖he1 h5 15 ♗f2 ♗h6 16 g3± Bisguier-Hartston, Hastings 1975/76) 10 ♘e2 ♘c6 11 ♗e3 ♖c8 (11...b6 12 ♘g3 ♗d7) 12 ♘g3 ♗g4 13 ♖d5 ♗d4 14 ♗xd4 cxd4 15 ♗b5± Miles-Plachetka, Dubna 1976; 2...g6 3 ♘f3 ♗g7 4 ♘c3 ♘c6 5 b3?! d6 6 ♗b2 ♘f6 7 ♘d5 0-0 8 ♘xf6+ exf6!∓ Bohm-Timman, Wijk aan Zee 1977 **3 ♘f3 ♘f6** 3...e6 4 ♗b5 ♘ge7 5 0-0 a6 6 ♗e2 g6 7 d3 ♗g7 8 c3 0-0 9 ♗e3 b6 10 d4 f5 11 e5 += Miles-Reshevsky, Amsterdam 1977 **4 ♘c3 d5 5 e5 d4 6 exf6 dxc3 7 fxg7 cxd2+ 8 ♕xd2 ♗xg7 9 ♕xd8+ ♘xd8 10 ♗b5+ ♗d7 11 ♗xd7+ ♔xd7 12 c3 f5 13 ♗e3** += Miles-Gligoric, Tilburg 1977

1 e4 c5 2 ♘f3 ♘c6 3 ♗b5 g6 3...e6 4 0-0 (4 ♗xc6 bxc6 5 0-0 ♘e7 6 b3 ♘g6 7 ♗b2 f6 8 e5 [8 d4 cxd4 9 ♘xd4 ♗c5 10 c4 0-0 11 ♘c3 ♕c7 12 ♔h1 ♗e7 13 ♖c1± Timman-Visier, Las Palmas 1977] 8...♗e7 9 exf6 ♗xf6 10 ♗xf6 ♕xf6 11 ♘c3 0-0 12 ♘e4 ♕e7 13 ♘fg5 h6= Uusi-Gulko, USSR 1977) 4...♘ge7 5 b3 (5 c3 a6 6 ♗a4 d5 7 exd5 ♕xd5 8 d4 ♗d7 9 ♖e1 ♖d8 10 c4! ♕xc4 11 ♘bd2 ♕d5 12 ♗b3 ♕h5 13 ♘e4! ♘f5 14 dxc5± Spassky-Timman (1) 1977) 5...♘d4 6 ♘xd4 cxd4 7 c3 a6 8 ♗e2 ♘c6 9 ♗b2 ♗c5 10 b4 ♗b6 11 a4 d5 =+ Barczay-Adorjan, Budapest 1977 **4 0-0 ♗g7 5 c3** 5 ♖e1 e5 (5...♘f6 6 ♘c3 0-0 7 e5 ♘e8 8 ♗xc6 dxc6 9 h3 ♘c7 10 b3 ♘e6 11 ♗b2 += Panno-Szmetan, Bogota 1977) 6 c3 ♘ge7 7 d4 cxd4 8 cxd4 exd4 9 ♗f4 a6 10 ♗f1 d6 11 ♘bd2 0-0 12 h3 ♗e6 N (12...h6 13 ♘c4 d5∓ Castro-Geller, Biel 1976) 13 ♘b3 ♕b6 14 ♗xd6 ♖fd8∓ Dankert-Radulov, Hamburg 1977 **5...♘f6 6 d4 cxd4 7 cxd4 ♘xe4 8 d5 ♘b8** 8...♘d6 9 ♘a3 ♘e5 10 ♘xe5 ♗xe5 11 ♖e1 ♘xb5 12 ♖xe5! f6 13 ♘xb5 fxe5 14 d6 +− Lutikov-Ermenkov, Albena 1976 **9 ♖e1 ♘d6 10 a4 0-0 11 ♗g5 ♖e8 12 ♘c3±** Lalev-Asparuhov, Pernik 1977

1 e4 c5 2 ♘f3 d6 3 d4 cxd4 4 ♘xd4 ♘f6 5 ♘c3 ♘c6 6 ♗g5 e6 7 ♕d2 a6 8 0-0-0 ♗d7 8...h6 9 ♗e3 (9 ♗f4 ♗d7 10 ♘xc6 ♗xc6 11 ♕e1 [11 f3 d5 12 ♕e1 ♗e7 13 exd5 ♘xd5 14 ♘xd5 ♗xd5 15 ♗c4 ♗g5 16 g3 ♗xf4 17 gxf4 0-0= Beljavsky-Radulov, Leningrad 1977] 11...b5 12 e5 ♘d5 13 ♘xd5 ♗xd5 14 ♖xd5! exd5 15 ♗d3± Torre-Ivanovic, Vrsac 1977) 9...♗d7 10 f4 (10 f3 ♕c7 11 g4 b5 12 ♖g1 ♘e5 N 13 a3 ♖b8 14 h4 g6 15 g5 hxg5 16 hxg5 ♘h5 17 f4 ♘c4 18 ♗xc4 bxc4 19 ♕f2± Tal-Csom, Moscow 1977) 10...♗e7 11 ♔b1 ♕c7 12 ♕e1 b5 13 ♗d3 0-0∞ Torre-Hort, London 1977 **9 f4 b5** 9...♗e7 10 ♘f3 b5 11 ♗xf6 gxf6 12 f5 ♕b6 13 ♔b1 0-0-0 14 g3 ♔b8 15 fxe6 fxe6 16 ♗h3 ♗c8 17 ♕e1! N (17 ♕h6 ♕c5 18 ♖hf1 a5 =+ Beljavsky-Tal, Leningrad 1977) 17...

♖he8 18 ♘e2± Karpov-Liberzon, Bad Lauterberg 1977 **10 ♗xf6 gxf6**

11 f5 11 ♔b1 (11 ♘xc6 ♗xc6 12 ♕e1 – 12 ♕e3 ♕e7 13 ♗d3 ♕a7 14 ♕e1! N [14 ♕h3 ♕c5 15 f5 b4 16 ♘c2 e5 17 ♘g3 a5= Torre-Kinlay, London 1977] 14...0-0-0 15 ♔b1 ♕c5 16 ♖hf1 ♔b7 17 ♖c1 += Zaid-Lanka, USSR 1977) 11...♕b6 12 ♘f3 0-0-0 13 f5 (13 ♗d3 ♔b8 14 ♖hf1 ♗c8 15 f5 h5 16 ♕e1 ♘c5= Klovan-Beljavsky, USSR 1977) 13...h5 14 fxe6 fxe6 15 ♘e2 ♔b7 16 ♕e1 += Matulovic-Ciocaltea, Nis 1977 **11...♘xd4 12 ♕xd4 ♗h6+ 13 ♔b1 ♗f4 14 fxe6** N 14 ♕f2 ♗e5 15 ♘e2 ♕c7 16 ♘f4 ♕c5 17 ♕xc5 dxc5 =+ Speelman-Dorfman, Mexico 1977 **14...fxe6 15 ♘e2 ♗e5 16 ♕d2 0-0=** Mecking-Panno, Wijk aan Zee 1978

1 e4 c5 2 ♘f3 d6 3 d4 cxd4 4 ♘xd4 ♘f6 5 ♘c3 a6 6 ♗g5 e6 6...♘c6 7 ♗xf6 gxf6 8 ♗e2 ♕b6 (8...♖g8!) 9 ♘b3 e6 10 0-0 ♗d7 11 ♗h5 (11 ♔h1) ♘e5 ∞/= Nunn-Quinteros, London 1977 **7 f4 ♗e7** 7...♕c7 8 ♗xf6!? gxf6 9 ♗e2 ♘c6 10 ♘b3 ♕b6 N 11 ♕d2 h5= Tal-Balashov, USSR Final 1977; 7...b5 8 e5 dxe5 9 fxe5 ♕c7 10 ♕e2 ♘fd7 11 0-0-0 ♗b7 12 ♕g4 ♕xe5 13 ♗e2 ♗c5 N (13...♘f6 14 ♗xf6 gxf6 15 ♖he1± Balinas-Tarjan, Odessa 1976) 14 ♖hf1! N (14 ♗f3? ♗xd4 15 ♗xb7 ♗xc3!∓ Stean-Sigurjonsson, England v Iceland 1977) 14...♗xd4 15 ♖xd4 0-0 16 ♖d3 f5 17 ♕h4 b4 18 ♕xb4± Westerinan-Sigurjonsson, New York 1977; 7...♕b6 8 ♕d2 (8 ♘b3 ♘bd7 9 ♕f3 ♕c7 10 a4 b6!? 11 ♗d2 ♗b7 12 0-0 ♗e7= Sax-Nunn, Hastings 1977/78) 8...♕xb2 9 ♖b1 (9 ♘b3 ♘c6 10 ♗xf6 gxf6 11 ♘a4 ♕a3 12 ♘b6 ♖b8 13 ♘c4 ♕a4 14 ♔f2! N f5? [14...e5 15 ♗d3 ♗e6 16 ♘b6 ♕b4= Ligterink-Barczay, Wijk aan Zee 1977] 15 a3!± Timman-H.Olafsson, Reykjavik 1976) 9...♕a3 10 f5 ♘c6 11 fxe6 fxe6 12 ♘xc6 bxc6 13 e5 dxe5 14 ♗xf6 gxf6 15 ♘e4 ♗e7 16 ♗e2 h5 17 ♖b3 ♕a4 18 c4 (18 ♘xf6+! N ♗xf6 19 c4 ♗h4+ 20 g3 ♗e7 21 0-0 ♖a7 22 ♖b8 ♖c7 Vitolins-Gavrikov, USSR 1977, 23 ♗d3!?±) 18...f5 19 ♘h3 (Bronstein) 19...h4 20 ♘h5 ♖a7≈ Fedorowicz-Nunn, Hastings 1977/78; 7...♘bd7 8 ♕f3 ♕c7 9 0-0-0 b5 10 ♗d3 (10 ♗x b5!?) 10...♗b7 11 ♖he1 ♕b6 12 ♘b3 b4 13 ♘a4 ♕c7 14 ♘d4 ♗e7 15 ♕h3 0-0-0 16 f5± Timman-Mecking, Wijk aan Zee 1978

8 ♕f3 ♕c7 9 0-0-0 ♘bd7 10 ♗d3 b5 10...h6 11 ♗h4 (11 ♕h3 ♘b6 12 f5 e5 13 ♘b3 ♗d7 14 ♗e3 ♘a4 15 ♘d5

♘xd5 16 exd5 Jovicic-Bukic, Belgrade 1977, 16...♘b6! Quinteros-Szmetan, Fortaleza 1975) 11...g5 12 e5 gxh4 13 exf6 ♘xf6 14 f5 e5 15 ♘de2 ♗d7 16 ♘e4! N d5! (16...♗c6 17 ♘xf6+ ♗xf6 18 ♗e4 0-0-0 19 ♘c3± Parma-Bukic, Ljubljana 1977) 17 ♘xf6+ ♗xf6 18 ♕xd5 ♗c6 Biriescu-Georgescu, Rumania Final 1977, 19 ♕c4= **11 ♜he1 ♝b7 12 ♛g3 b4! 13 ♞d5 exd5 14 e5 dxe5 15 fxe5 ♞h5 16 ♛h4** 16 e6 ♘xg3 17 exf7+ ♔xf7 18 ♖xe7+ ♔g8 19 hxg3 ♕xg3 20 ♘e6 ♕e5 21 ♖f1 Baliev-Vidican, corresp 1976, 21...♘f8!= **16...♝xg5+ 17 ♛xg5 g6 18 g4** N **♞g7** 18...h6 19 ♕d2 ♘g7 20 e6± **19 e6 ♞c5! 20 exf7+ ♚xf7 21 ♜f1+ ♚g8 22 ♚b1** ∞/± Weigel-Hauernherm, corresp 1974/77

1 e4 c5 2 ♞f3 d6 3 d4 cxd4 4 ♞xd4 ♞f6 5 ♞c3 a6 6 ♝g5 e6 7 ♛d3 h6 7... b5 8 f4 ♘bd7 9 0-0-0 ♗b7 10 e5 dxe5 11 fxe5 (11 ♘dxb5 axb5 12 fxe5 h6 13 ♗h4 g5 14 exf6 gxh4 15 ♕xb5 ♕c7 16 ♖xd7? ♕xd7 −+ Castro-Galarza, Quito 1977) 11...♘xe5 12 ♕g3 ♘ed7 13 ♘cxb5 (13 ♗xf6 gxf6 14 ♗e2∞) 13...axb5 14 ♗xb5 ♖xa2!∓ Katalimov-Gofstein, USSR 1977 **8 ♝h4 ♞bd7 9 f4 ♝e7 10 0-0-0 g5** 10... ♕c7 11 ♗e2 b5 12 ♗f3 ♗b7 13 ♘xe6!! fxe6 14 e5 dxe5 15 ♕g6+ +− Mukhin-Platanov, USSR Final 1969 **11 fxg5 ♞g4 12 ♞f3 hxg5 13 ♝g3 ♛b6 14 ♜d2 ♛e3 15 ♛c4**∞ Katalimov-Doroshkevich, Erevan 1977

1 e4 c5 2 ♞f3 d6 3 d4 cxd4 4 ♞xd4 ♞f6 5 ♞c3 a6 6 ♝c4 e6 7 ♝b3 b5 8 0-0 ♝e7 9 f4 9 ♕f3 ♕b6 10 ♗e3 ♕b7 11 ♕g3 ♗d7 (11...g6 12 ♗h6! N ± Ermenkov-Ostojic, Kecskemet 1977) 12 ♖fe1 ♘c6 13 f4 b4 14 ♘d5 exd5 Nicevski-Rodriguez, Tbilisi-Suhumi 1977 15 e5∞ **9...0-0** 9...♗b7 10 e5 dxe5 11 fxe5 ♗c5 12 ♗e3 ♘c6 13 exf6 ♘xd4 14 ♕h5 ♕c7! Janosevic-Marjanovic, Vrsac 1977 15 fxg7∞ **10 e5 dxe5 11 fxe5 ♞fd7** 11...♗c5 12 ♗e3 ♘c6 13 exf6 ♗xd4 14 ♕e1± Perecz-Kovacs, Hungary 1977 **12 ♛h5 ♞c6 13 ♞xc6 ♛b6+ 14 ♚h1** 14 ♗e3 ♕xc6 15 ♖f3 ♗b7 16 ♖af1 N ♗c5 17 ♖1f2 ♗xe3 18 ♖xe3± Hartston-Georgieva, Belgrade 1977 **14...♛xc6 15 ♜f3 ♝b7 16 ♝f4 ♞c5** =+ Adorjan-Hulak, Amsterdam 1977

1 e4 c5 2 ♞f3 e6 3 d4 cxd4 4 ♞xd4 ♞f6 5 ♞c3 ♞c6 6 ♞db5 6 ♘xc6 bxc6 7 e5 ♘d5 8 ♘e4 f5 9 exf6 ♘xf6 10 ♘d6+ ♗xd6 11 ♕xd6 ♗a6 N 12 c4? (12 ♗xa6 ♕a5+ 13 ♗d2 ♕xa6 14 b3 ♘e4 15 ♕d4 ♘xd2 16 ♕xd2) 12...♕b6 13 ♗d3 (13 f3) 13...♗xc4! −+ Adorjan-Quinteros, Amsterdam 1977 **6...d6** 6...♗b4 7 a3 ♗xc3+ 8 ♘xc3 d5 9 exd5 exd5 10 ♗d3 d4 11 ♘e2 ♗f5 12 0-0 ♗xd3 13 ♕xd3 += Karpov-Kuzmin, Leningrad 1977 **7 ♝g5** N **a6 8 ♝xf6 gxf6 9 ♞d4 ♛a5 10 ♞b3 ♛g5 11 g3 f5 12 ♝g2**± Radulov-Semkov, Bulgaria Final 1977

1 e4 c5 2 ♞f3 ♞c6 3 d4 cxd4 4 ♞xd4 ♞f6 5 ♞c3 e5 6 ♞db5 d6 7 ♝g5 7 ♘d5 ♘xd5 8 exd5 ♘e7 9 c4 ♘f5 (9... ♘g6 10 ♕a4 N ♗d7 11 ♕b4 ♕b8 12 ♗e3 b6 13 h4 h5 14 g3 ♗e7 Westerinen-Barle, Esbjerg 1977, 15 ♗e2±) 10 ♗d3 ♗e7 (10...a6? 11 ♕a4! ♔e7 12 ♘c3 +− Mestel-Fedorowicz, Hastings 1977/78) 11 0-0 a6 12 ♘c3 0-0 13 f4 exf4 14 ♗xf4 ♘h4 15 ♔h1 N (15 ♕c2 ♘g6 16 ♗e3 += Holmov-Gurgenidze, Tbilisi-Suhumi 1977) 15...♘g6 16 ♕h5 f5 17 ♗g3 ♘e5 18 ♗xe5 dxe5 19 ♖xf5∞

Shamkovich-Tisdall, Hastings 1977/78

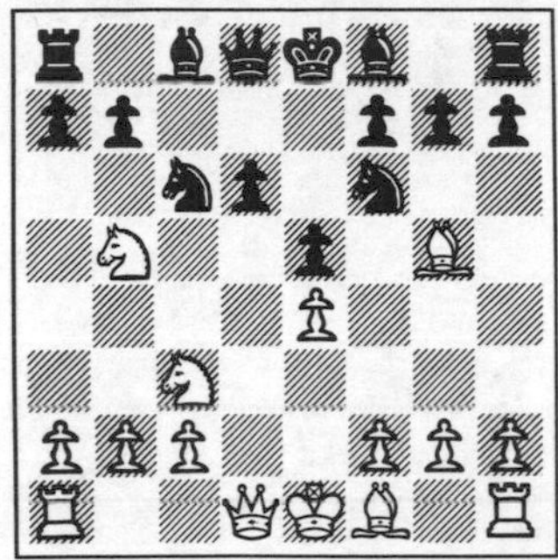

7...a6 8 Na3 b5 9 Bxf6 9 Nd5 Be7 (9...Qa5! 10 Bd2 Qd8 11 Nxf6+ Qxf6 12 Bd3 d5 13 exd5 Nb4 14 Be4 Qh4∞ Smyslov-Kuzmin, USSR Final 1977) 10 Bxf6 (10 Nxe7 Nxe7 11 Bd3 Bb7 12 Qe2 Nd7! =+ Petrushkin-Timoshenko, Baku 1977) 10...Bxf6 11 c3 0-0 12 Nc2 Bg5 13 a4 bxa4 14 Rxa4 += Smyslov-Sveshnikov, USSR Final 1977 **9...gxf6 10 Nd5 f5 11 c3** 11 exf5 Bxf5 12 c3 Bg7 13 Nc2 0-0 14 Nce3 Be6 15 g4 Ne7=; 15...Qh4 16 Bg2 e4 N ∞ Dementiev-Majorov, USSR 1977; 11 Bxb5!? axb5 12 Nxb5 Ra7 (12...Ra4 13 Nbc7+ Kd7 14 exf5 Ne7 15 0-0 Ra4∓ Levchenkov-Gorelov, USSR 1977) 13 Nxa7 Nxa7 14 exf5 N Bxf5 15 Qf3± Vitolins-Katisonok, USSR 1977; 11 Bd3 Be6 12 Qh5 Bg7 13 0-0 f4 14 c3 (14 Rfd1! N 0-0 15 c3 Ra7 16 Nc2 += Geller-Lombard, Biel 1976) 14...0-0 15 Nc2 f5 16 Ncb4 Nxb4 17 Nxb4 d5? 18 exd5± Damjanovic-Ligterink, Karlovac 1977; 11 g3 fxe4 12 Bg2 Be6 (12...Ra7 13 Bxe4 Bg7 14 Qd3 0-0 15 Ne3 Nd4∞ Lonka-Vasyukov, Leningrad 1977) 13 Bxe4 Bg7 14 Qh5 Rc8 15 0-0 (15 Rd1 Ne7 16 c3 Rc5 17 Nb4 Qb6 18 Nd3± Browne-Ghizdavu, USA Final 1977) 15...Ne7 16 Rad1 Rc5! 17 Nb4 N (17 Ne3 d5 18 b4 Rc7 19 c4± Gaprindashvili-Peters, Lone Pine 1977) 17...Qb6 18 Qg5 Kf8∞ Lanka-Efimov, USSR 1977

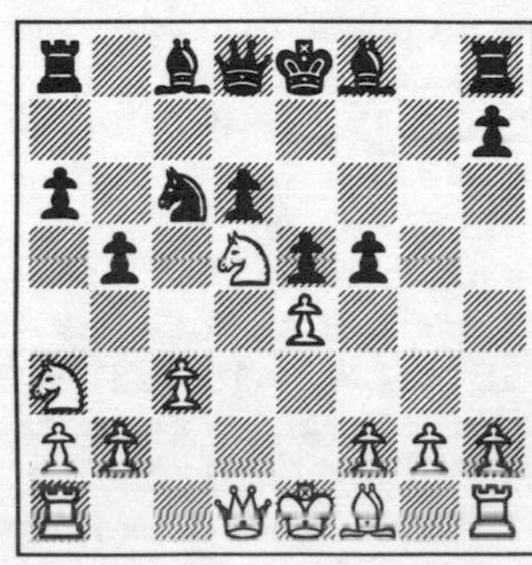

11...Bg7 12 Bd3 Be6 13 Qh5 0-0 14 exf5 Bxd5 15 f6 e4 16 fxg7 Re8 17 Be2 Re5 18 Qh6 Rg5 18...Qg5 19 Qxg5 Rxg5 20 Nc2 Bc4 Nunn-Birnboim, London 1977, 21 a4 +=; 18...b4 19 Nc2 bxc3 20 bxc3 Qa5 21 Qd2 Rc8 22 0-0± Nunn-Tisdall, Hastings 1977/78 **19 Nc2 Ne5 20 Ne3 Bc4 21 Bxc4 bxc4 22 0-0 Rb8** Nunn-Piasetski, London 1978 **23 Rad1**±

1 e4 c5 2 Nf3 d6 3 d4 cxd4 4 Nxd4 Nf6 5 Nc3 g6 6 Be2 Bg7 7 0-0 Nc6 8 Nb3 0-0 9 Bg5 Be6 9...Ne5 10 f4 Neg4 11 Bxg4 Bxg4 12 Qd3 Be6 13 f5 Bd7 14 Rae1 b5 15 Rae1± Tarjan-Castro, Quito 1977

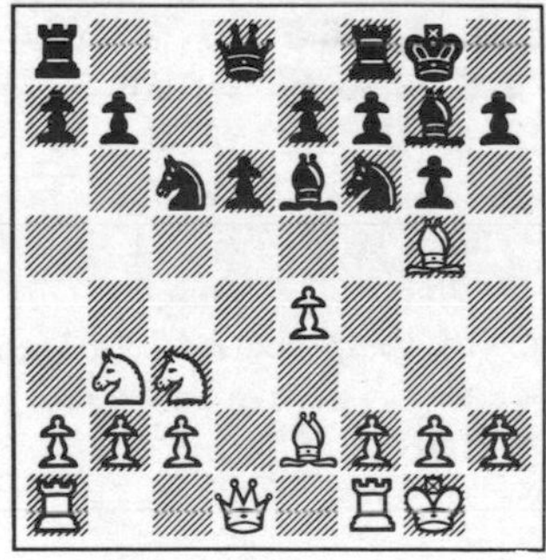

10 Kh1 10 f4 Na5 11 f5 Bc4 12 Kh1 Rc8 13 Bd3 b5 14 Qd2 b4 15 Ne2 d5 16 Nxa5 Qxa5 17 e5 Ne4 18 Bxe4 dxe4 19 f6 exf6 20 Bxf6 Qd5= Sigurjonsson-Sosonko, Wijk aan Zee 1977 **10...a5** 10...Qc8 11 f4 Rd8 12 Bf3 Bc4 13 Rf2 e6 14 Rd2 Qc7 15 Qe1 h6 16 Bh4 Rd7 17 Rad1 e5 18 Bxf6 Bxf6 19 Bg4± Karpov-Miles, Bad Lauterberg 1977; 10...a6 11 f4 b5 12 Bf3 Rc8 13 Nd5 Nd7 14 c3 Nb6 15 Qe2 Nc4 16 Rad1 Qc7 17 Rfe1 Qa7 18 Bh4± Karpov-Martin, Las Palmas 1977; 10...Na5 11 Nd5 Bxd5 12 exd5 Ne4 13 Bc1 Rc8 14 Bf3 Nf6 15 Be3 Nc4 16 Bd4± Veroci-Milivojevic, Gosa 1977 **11 a4 Nd7** 11...Rc8 12 f4 Nb4 13 Nd4 Bc4 14 Ndb5 Qb6 15 Bh4 Bxe2 (15...Qc5 16 Bd3 Rfd8 17 Bf3 Qh5 18 Bb6 Qxd1 19 Rfxd1 Rf8 20 Na7± Karpov-Hernandez, Las Palmas 1977) 16 Qxe2 Qc5 17 Rad1 Qc4 18 Rfe1 += Gaprindashvili-Beljavsky, USSR 1977 **12 f4 Nb6 13 f5 Bc4 14 Bxc4 Nxc4 15 Qe2 Nb6 16 Qb5 Nd4 17 Nxd4 Bxd4 18 Rad1 Bg7 19 Be3 Nd7 20 Nd5±** Karpov-Sosonko, Bad Lauterberg 1977

1 e4 c5 2 Nf3 d6 3 d4 cxd4 4 Nxd4 Nf6 5 Nc3 g6 6 Be3 Bg7 7 f3 Nc6 8 Qd2 0-0 9 0-0-0 d5 9...Nxd4 10 Bxd4 Be6 11 Nd5! N Bxd5 12 exd5 Rc8 13 g4 Qc7 14 c3 Qa5 N (14... e5 15 dxe6 fxe6 16 Bd3 e5 17 Be3 d5 18 Kb1 Kh8 19 h4± Timman-Miles, Holland v England 1977) 15 g5 Nh5 16 Bxg7 Nxg7 17 Kb1 e5 18 dxe6 fxe6≈ Timman-Sosonko, Wijk aan Zee 1978

Diagram

10 exd5 Nxd5 11 Nxc6 bxc6 12 Bd4 e5 13 Bc5 Be6 14 Ne4 Re8 15 h4 Rb8 15...h6 16 c4 (16 g4 Nf4 17 Qc3 Bd5 18 h5 g5 19 Qa3 Qc7 20 Ba6 Re6 21 Rh2± Lidtke-Nikanter 1975) 16...Qc7 17 Bd6 Qb6 18 Nc5 Nc7 19 h5 g5 20 Bd3± Tringov-Despotovic, S. Palanka 1977 **16 g4 f5 17 gxf5 gxf5 18 Nd6 Bf8** 18...Rf8 19 Nc4 Kh8 20 Rg1 Bf6 21 Qh6 Rf7 Timman-Miles, Bad Lauterberg 1977, 22 Rg6! Δ Bd6, Rxf6± **19 Bc4** 19 c4! **19...Re7 20 Rhg1 Kh8 21 Bxd5 cxd5 22 Qe3 Bg8** Sigurjonsson-Miles, Wijk aan Zee 1977 **23 Nc4!**

Ruy Lopez/Spanisch

1 e4 e5 2 Nf3 Nc6 3 Bb5 f5 4 d3 fxe4 4...d6? 5 c3 (5 0-0 Δ d4) 5...fxe4 6 dxe4 Nf6 7 Nbd2 Bg4 8 h3 Be6 9 Qa4 Bd7 10 Qb3 += Steczkowski-Widera, Katowice 1977; 4...Nf6!? 5 0-0 fxe4 (5...Bc5!?) 6 dxe4 d6 7 Nc3 Be7 8 Nd5!; 7 Qd3 a6 (7...Bg4!) 8 Bxc6+ bxc6 9 Qc4 += Grabczewski-Antowicz, Katowice 1977 **5 dxe4 Nf6 6 Qd3** N **d6 7 Nc3 a6 8 Bc4 Na5 9 Be3 b5 10 Bb3 Nxb3 11 axb3 c6 12 0-0-0 +=** Jasnikowski-Antowicz, Katowice 1977

1 e4 e5 2 ♘f3 ♘c6 3 ♗b5 f5 4 ♘c3 fxe4 5 ♘xe4 d5 5...♘f6 6 ♕e2 (6 ♘xf6+ ♕xf6 7 0-0 ♘d4 8 ♘xd4 exd4 9 ♖e1+ ♗e7 10 ♕e2 c6 11 ♗d3 d5 12 b3 0-0!= Adorjan-Parma, Moscow 1977) 6...d5 7 ♘xf6+ gxf6 8 d4 e4 9 ♘h4 ♕e7 10 ♗f4! N f5 (10...♗e6) 11 g3 ♗g7 12 ♕h5+ += Savon-Parma, Ljubljana 1977 **6 ♘xe5 dxe4 7 ♘xc6 ♕g5 8 ♕e2 ♘f6 9 f4 ♕h4+ 10 g3 ♕h3 11 ♘e5+ c6 12 ♗c4 ♗c5 13 d3** 13 d4! ♗xd4 14 ♗e3 ♗xe5 15 fxe5 ♘g4 16 ♗c5 ♘xe5 17 ♕xe4 ♕f5 18 ♕e3! ♗d7 19 ♖f1 1-0 Golze-Dohl, corresp 1977/78 **13...♘g4 14 ♘f7 ♗f2+ 15 ♔d1 e3 16 ♕f3 ♘f6?** 16...♘xh2 17 ♕e4+ ♔f8 18 ♗xe3 +− Kavalek-Ljubojevic, Amsterdam 1975; 16...♘h6!= **17 f5 ♖f8 18 ♘d6+?** 18 ♗xe3! **18...♔d7≈** Nunn-Rumens, London 1977

1 e4 e5 2 ♘f3 ♘c6 3 ♗b5 f5 4 d4 fxe4 5 ♘xe5 5 ♗xc6 dxc6 6 ♘xe5 ♘f6 7 ♗g5 ♗d6 N (7...c5 8 ♘c3 ♗f5 9 f4 cxd4 10 ♗xf6± Schonmann-Ljublinsky, corresp 1959) 8 ♘d2 0-0 9 ♕e2 ♕e8 10 0-0-0 ♗f5 11 g4 ♗e6 12 ♗xf6 gxf6 13 ♘ec4= Ciocaltea-Maric, Bar 1977; 6...♕h4 7 ♕e2! ♗e6 8 h3 0-0-0 9 g3 ♕e7 10 ♗e3 ♘f6 11 ♘c3 ♕b4 12 0-0-0 c5 13 a3 ♕a5 14 d5! +− Grabowski-Wittmann, corresp 1977/78 **5...♘xe5 6 dxe5 c6 7 ♘c3 cxb5** 7...d5 8 exd6 ♘f6 9 ♗c4 ♗xd6 10 ♗g5 ♗f5 11 ♕d4 ♕e7 12 0-0-0± Lind-Briem, Stockholm 1977/78 **8 ♘xe4 d5 9 exd6 ♘f6**

Diagram

10 ♕d4 10 ♗g5 ♕a5+ 11 ♗d2 b4∞; 10...♗f5 11 ♗xf6 gxf6 12 ♕h5+ ♗g6 13 ♕xb5+ ♔f7 14 ♕xb7+ ♔g8 15 0-0 ♗xe4; 11 ♕h5+ g6 12 ♕e5+ ♔f7 13 ♕xh8 ♘f6! 14 ♗g5 ♗c6 15 ♖ad1 ♗g7 16 ♕xd8 ♖xd8∓ Mallee-Parma, Mannheim 1975 **10...♗e7!?** 10...♘xe4 11 ♕xe4+ ♔f7 12 ♗f4 ♕e8 13 ♗e5 ♗xd6!? 14 ♕d5+ ♕e6 15 ♕xd6 ♕xd6 16 ♗xd6 ♖e8+ 17 ♔f1 ♗f5 =; 14 ♕f3+!?∞ **11 ♗g5 ♗f5 12 0-0-0!?∞**

1 e4 e5 2 ♘f3 ♘c6 3 ♗b5 ♘ge7 4 d4 4 0-0 a6? (4...♘g6 Larsen) 5 ♗c4 ♘g6 6 d4 exd4 (6...♗e7! 7 dxe5 ♘cxe5 8 ♘xe5 ♘xe5 9 ♗b3 += Westerinen-Larsen, Siegen 1970) 7 ♘xd4 ♗c5 8 ♘f5 0-0 9 ♕h5 d6 10 ♗g5 ♕e8 11 ♘d2!± Ornstein-Larsen, Ribe 1973; 4 ♘c3 ♘g6 5 d4 exd4 6 ♘xd4 ♗c5 7 ♗e3 ♗xd4 8 ♗xd4 0-0 Metchkarov **4...exd4 5 ♘xd4 g6** 5...♘xd4 6 ♕xd4 ♘c6 7 ♕d5 ♘b4 8 ♕b3 ♗c5= Larsen **6 ♘xc6** 6 0-0 ♗g7 7 ♗e3 0-0 8 ♘c3 d6 9 ♗e2 f5= Kolbak-Larsen, Grenaa 1973 **6...♘xc6 7 ♗xc6 bxc6 8 ♕d4 f6 9 ♗e3** N **♗d6 10 ♘c3 ♕e7 11 0-0-0 +=** Zaitsev-de Greiff, Quito 1977

1 e4 e5 2 ♘f3 ♘c6 3 ♗b5 ♘f6 4 0-0 ♗c5 5 ♘xe5 ♘xe4 6 ♕e2 ♘xe5 7 ♕xe4 ♕e7 8 d4 8 ♘c3 N ♘g6 (8...c6) 9 ♕xe7+ ♗xe7 10 ♘d5 ♗d6 11 ♖e1+ ♔d8 12 ♗f1 += Petryk-Lokasto, Katowice 1977 **8...♘c6** 8...♘g6? 9 ♗xd7+! **9 ♕g4 h5!?** 9...f5!? 10 ♕h5+

g6 11 ♕d1 ♘xd4 12 b4 ♗b6 13 c4 0-0 (13...♕e2 14 c5 ♕xd1 15 ♖xd1 ♘xb5 16 a4± Dorfman-Gulko, USSR Final 1976) 14 c5 ♘xb5 15 cxb6 c6 16 a4± Timoshenko-Donchenko, USSR 1976; 9...♘xd4 N 10 ♕xg7 ♕f8 11 ♕e5+ ♘e6 12 ♗e3 ♗e7= Jansa-Knezevic, Vranjacka-Banja 1977

10 ♕xg7 10 ♕d1 ♘xd4 11 b4 ♗b6 12 c4 0-0! 13 c5 ♘xb5 14 a4 ♕f6∓ Timoshenko-Gulko, Baku 1977 **10... ♗xd4 11 ♕g3 a6 12 ♗xc6 dxc6 13 c3 h4 14 ♕f3 ♗e5 15 ♕e3 ♗f5 16 ♘d2 0-0-0 17 ♘f3 ♗d6 18 ♕xe7 ♗xe7 ½-½** Vogt-Kirov, Polanica 1977

1 e4 e5 2 ♘f3 ♘c6 3 ♗b5 ♘f6 4 0-0 4 ♕e2 d6 (4...a6 5 ♗a4 d6 6 c3 ♗d7 7 d4 ♕e7 8 d5 ♘b8 9 ♗c2 g6 10 c4 a5 11 ♘c3± Torre-Reshevsky, Amsterdam 1977) 5 d4 exd4 6 e5!? dxe5 7 ♘xe5 ♗b4+ 8 c3 0-0! 9 ♗xc6 ♘xc6 10 cxb4 ♖e8 11 0-0 ♗g4 12 f3 ♗h5 13 ♕e1 ♘d7∓ Quinteros-Kavalek, Amsterdam 1977 **4...♘xe4**

Diagram

5 d4 ♘d6 5...♗e7 6 ♕e2 (6 dxe5 0-0 7 ♕d5 ♘c5 8 ♗e3 a6 Gulko-Sanguinetti, Biel 1976, 9 ♗c4 d6 10 exd6+=; 6...d5 7 ♘d4 [7 exd6 ♘xd6 8 ♗xc6+ bxc6 9 ♘e5 ♗b7 10 ♘c3 0-0 11 ♕f3 ♗h4 12 ♗f4± Kagan-Kestler, Biel 1977; 7 c4 a6! 8 ♗a4 dxc4 9 ♘d4 ♘c5! 10 ♗xc6+ bxc6 11 ♘xc6 (11 ♗e3 ♗b7 12 ♘f5! ♕xd1 13 ♖xd1 ♗f8 14 ♘d2 g6 15 ♘d4± Nunn-Formaniek, London 1977) ♕xd1 12 ♖xd1 ♘d3!= Formanek-Pachman, Reggio Emilia 1975/76] 7...♗d7 8 ♗xc6 bxc6 9 f3 ♘c5 10 ♘c3 0-0 11 ♗e3 ♘e6 N 12 ♘b3 f6! 13 exf6 ♖xf6 =+ Tringov-Knezevic, Vrnjacka Banja 1975) 6...♘db7 7 ♗xc6 bxc6 8 dxe5 ♘b7 9 c4 (9 ♖e1 0-0 10 ♘c3 ♘c5 – 10...d5!? TN 11 exd6 ♗xd6 12 ♗g5 ♕d7 13 ♘e4 c5! 14 ♖ad1 ♕c6 15 ♕d2 f6 16 ♗f4 ♗g4∞ Balashov-Smyslov, Leningrad 1977; 11 ♗e3 ♘e6 12 ♖ad1 d5 13 exd6 cxd6 14 ♘d4 ♘xd4 15 ♗xd4 ♖e8 [15...♗e6 16 ♕f3 ♕d7 17 ♕g3 f6 18 ♕e3 ♔f7 19 ♘e4 += Torre-Knezevic, Vrsac 1977] 16 ♕f3 d5 17 ♘a4 ♗f8 18 ± Balashov-Knezevic, Leningrad 1977) 9...0-0 10 ♘c3 f6 11 ♖d1 (11 ♖e1 fxe5 12 ♘xe5 ♗f6 13 ♗f4 ♗xe5 14 ♗xd5 d6= Tal-Dorfman, USSR Final 1976) 11...♕e8 12 exf6 ♗xf6 13 ♘e4 ♗e7 14 b3 d6 15 h3 ♕g6 =+ Milicevic-Knezevic, Vrnjaca Banja 1977 **6 ♗xc6** 6 dxe5 ♘xb5 7 a4 d6 8 e6 fxe6 9 axb5 ♘e7 10 ♘c3 ♘f5 11 ♘d4 ♕f6 Nunn-Romanishin, Mexico 1977; 12

b6! ∝/± cxb6 13 ♘db5 ♕d8 14 ♘e4±

6...dxc6 7 dxe5 ♘f5 8 ♕xd8+ 8 ♕e2 ♘d4 9 ♘xd4 ♕xd4 10 ♖d1 ♗g4– (Keres) 11 ♖xd4 ♗xe2 12 ♘c3 ♗h5 13 ♗g5 += Janosevic-Smejkal, Vrsac 1977 **8...♔xd8 9 ♘c3** 9 b3 h6 10 ♘c3 ♗e6 11 ♘e2 ♗d5 12 ♘d5 c5 13 ♗b2 ♔c8 14 ♘f4 += Tseshkovsky-Romanishin, USSR Final 1976; 11... c5!? Romanishin **9...h6 10 h3** 10 b3 ♗e6 11 ♗b2 [11 ♗xe6 ♘xe6 12 ♘b3 dxc3 13 ♕c2 Kuzmin] 11...♔c8 12 h3 c5 13 ♖ad1 b6= Gulko-Romanishin, USSR Final 1976 **10...♗e6 11 g4 ♘e7 12 ♘d4 ♗d7 13 ♗f4 c5 14 ♘de2 ♔c8 15 ♖ad1 g5 16 ♗g3 ♘g6=** Geller-Romanishin, USSR Final 1977

1 e4 e5 2 ♘f3 ♘c6 3 ♗b5 a6 4 ♗a4 ♘f6 5 0-0 ♘xe4 6 d4 b5 7 ♗b3 d5 7...♗e7 8 ♘xe5 (8 dxe5) 8...♘xe5 9 dxe5 ♗b7 10 ♕g4 0-0 11 f3 ♘g5 Tal-Smyslov, USSR Final 1977, 12 ♘c3

Diagram

8 dxe5 ♗e6 9 c3
9 ♘bd2 ♘c5 (9...♗e7? 10 ♘xe4 N dxe4 11 ♗xe6 fxe6 12 ♘g5 ♕xd1 13 ♖xd1 ♗xg5 14 ♗xg5 ♖f8 15 ♗h4 e3 16 fxe3 += Sax-Tarjan, Hastings 1977/78) 10 c3 ♘xb3? (10...d4! 11

cxd4 [11 ♘e2 ♗d5 12 ♘d2 a5! N 13 c4 ♗e6 14 ♘f4 a4 = Tal-Romanishin, Leningrad 1977] 11...♘xd4 12 ♘xd4 ♕xd4 13 ♗xe6 ♘xe6 14 ♕f3 ♖d8= Nenarokov) 11 ♘xb3 ♗e7 12 ♘fd4± ♘xe5? 13 ♖e1 ♘g6 14 ♘xe6 fxe6 15 ♘d4 ♘f8 16 ♕g4 +– Kuzmin-Beljavsky, Baku 1977; 9 ♕e2 ♗c5 (9...♗e7 10 ♖d1 ♘c5 11 c4 d4 12 cxb5 ♘xb3 13 axb3 axb5 14 ♖xa8 ♕xa8 15 ♘xd4 ♘xd4 16 ♖xd4 0-0 17 ♕xb5 ♕a1! TN [17...c5 18 ♖d1 ♕e4 19 ♘c3 ♕xe5 20 ♕b7= Korchnoi] 18 ♕d3 ♖a8 19 ♕c2 ♕a5 20 ♕c3 ♕xe5∓ Nunn-Tarjan, Hastings 1977/78) 10 ♗e3 0-0 11 ♖d1 ♗xe3 12 ♕xe3 ♘e7 13 ♘bd2 [13 ♘d4] 13...♘f5 14 ♕e2 ♘xd2 TN (14...♘c5 15 c3 += Sokolov-Karaklaic, Jugoslavia Final 1958) 15 ♕xd2 c6 16 a4 ♕b6 17 axb5 axb5 18 c3± Balashov-Smyslov, Tilburg 1977

9...♗c5 10 ♘bd2 0-0 11 ♗c2 ♗f5 11... ♘xf2 12 ♖xf2 f6 13 exf6 ♗xf2+ 14 ♔xf2 ♕xf6 15 ♘f1?! (15 ♔g1) 15... ♘e5 16 ♗e3 ♖ae8 17 ♗d4 Balashov-Tukmakov, USSR Final 1977, 17... ♕h4+ 18 ♔g1 ♘xf3+ 19 ♘xf3 ♕h5 =+ **12 ♘b3 ♗g4 13 ♘xc5 ♘xc5 14 ♖e1** 14 ♗e3 ♘e4 15 a4 N ♕d7 16 ♗b3 ♖ad8= Baljavsky-Tukmakov, USSR 1977 **14...♖e8 15 ♗f4 ♗h5** 15...d4 16 h3 ♗h5 17 cxd4 ♗xf3 18 ♕xf3 ♘xd4 19 ♕c3± Karpov-Beljavsky, Leningrad 1977; 16...d3! 17 hxg4 dxc2 18 ♕xc2 ♕d3= Pereira-Weiner, corresp 1976/77 **16 ♗g3** TN **♘e6 17 ♕d2 ♘e7 18 ♘h4 d4 19 ♗e4 c6 20 ♕c2 ♗g6 21 ♖ad1 ♕b6 22 f4**± Karpov-Smyslov, Tilburg 1977

1 e4 e5 2 ♘f3 ♘c6 3 ♗b5 a6 4 ♗a4 ♘f6 5 0-0 ♗e7 6 ♖e1 b5 7 ♗b3 d6 8 c3 0-0 9 h3 ♗b7 10 d4 10 d3 h6 N 11 ♘bd2 d5 12 exd5 ♘xd5 13 ♘e4 ♖e8 14 ♕e2 ♗f8? 15 ♗xh6 +− Castro-Hidalgo, Quito 1977 **10...♖e8 11 ♘g5** 11 ♘bd2 ♗f8 12 ♗c2 g6 13 b3 (13 d5 ♘e7 14 b3 ♗g7 15 c4 c6 16 ♘f1 += Suetin-Zaitsev, Sochi 1977) 13...♗g7 14 d5 ♘b8 15 ♘f1 c6 16 c4± Karpov-Balashov, USSR Final 1976; 11 dxe5 ♘xe5 12 ♘xe5 dxe5 13 ♘d2 c5 14 a4 c4 15 ♗c2 ♘d7∓ Galarza-Zaitsev, Quito 1977 **11...♖f8 12 f4 exf4 13 ♘f3** TN 13 ♗xf4 ♘a5 14 ♗c2 ♘d5! =+ **13...♘h5 14 ♘bd2 g6 15 a4 ♖e8**∓ A.Rodriguez-Milicevic, Vrnjacka Banja 1977

1 e4 e5 2 ♘f3 ♘c6 3 ♗b5 a6 4 ♗a4 ♘f6 5 0-0 ♗e7 6 ♖e1 b5 7 ♗b3 d6 8 c3 0-0 9 h3 h6 10 d4 ♖e8 11 ♘bd2 ♗f8 12 ♘f1 ♗d7 13 ♘g3 13 ♗c2 g6 14 ♗d2 ♗g7 15 ♕c1 ♔h7 16 ♘g3 ♘a5 17 b3 c5= Tal-Geller, USSR Final 1969 **13...♘a5 14 ♗c2 ♘c4 15 ♘h2** 15 b3 ♘b6 16 ♗e3 c5 17 d5 a5 18 ♘d2 g6 19 ♕e2 ♗g7 20 ♗d3 b4 21 c4 a4= Sigurjonsson-Geller, Las Palmas 1976; 16 ♗b2 c5 17 dxc5 dxc5 18 c4 ♕c7 19 ♘d2= Tal-Geller, Moscow 1967 **15...c5 16 b3 ♘b6 17 f4 cxd4 18 cxd4 ♕c8!=** Tal-Geller, USSR Final 1977

1 e4 e5 2 ♘f3 ♘c6 3 ♗b5 a6 4 ♗a4 ♘f6 5 0-0 ♗e7 6 ♖e1 b5 7 ♗b3 d6 8 c3 0-0 9 h3 ♘b8 10 d4 10 a4 ♗b7 11 d3 ♘bd7 12 axb5 axb5 13 ♖xa8 ♗xa8 14 ♘a3 ♗c6= Matulovic-Smejkal, Vrbas 1977 **10...♘bd7 11 ♘bd2 ♗b7 12 ♗c2 ♖e8 13 ♘f1 ♗f8 14 ♘g3 g6 15 a4** 15 ♗d2 ♗g7 16 ♕c1 d5! 17 ♗g5! ♕b8 18 ♘xe5 ♘xe5 19 dxe5 ♘xe4 20 ♗xe4 dxe4 21 ♗f6 ♗xf6 22 exf6 ♖e6 23 ♕g5 ♕d8 Liberzon-Gligoric, Bad Lauterberg 1977, 24 ♖ad1 +=

15...c5 16 d5 ♘b6 17 ♕e2 17 b3 bxa4 18 bxa4 a5!=; 17 a5 ♘bd7 18 b3 ♗g7 19 c4 b4 20 ♖a2 ♕e7= Damjanovic-Gligoric, Krk 1977; 17 ♗g5 h6 18 ♗e3 ♘c4 19 ♗c1 ♘b6 20 b3 bxa4 21 bxa4 a5 22 ♗d3 += Kuzmin-Vogt, Polanica 1977 **17... ♘xa4 18 ♗xa4 bxa4 19 ♖xa4 ♗c8** 19...♘d7 20 ♖a3 ♘b6 21 ♘h2 ♗g7 22

Ng4 Bc8 23 c4 Bxg4 24 hxg4 a5!= Torre-Gligoric, Bad Lauterberg 1977 **20 b3** 20 Bd2 a5? (20...Rb8) 21 b4!± Tal-Vogt, Leningrad 1977 **20...Rb8 21 Ra3 Re7 22 c4 Reb7 23 Qc2 Ne8 24 Bd2 Ng7 25 Nh2 f5=** Karpov-Smejkal, Moscow 1977

1 e4 e5 2 Nf3 Nc6 3 Bb5 a6 4 Ba4 Nf6 5 0-0 Be7 6 Re1 b5 7 Bb3 d6 8 c3 0-0 9 d4 Bg4 10 d5 10 Bd3 cxd4 (10...Bh5 N [Δ Ng4] [10...d5!? 11 exd5 exd4 12 Bg5 Nxd5!! N ∓ Toth-Perenyi, Hungary 1977] 11 h3 Bg6 12 Nbd2 exd4 13 Nxd4 Na5 14 Bc2 c5 15 N4f3 += Panchenko-Zaitsev, Sochi 1977) 11 cxd4 Na5 12 Bc2 c5 (12...Nc4 13 Bc1 c5 14 b3 Na5 15 dxc5 N [15 d5 Nd7 16 Nbd2 Bf6 17 Rb1 Bc3 18 h3 Bh5 N 19 g4 Bg6 20 Re3± Gulko-Unzicker, Tallinn 1977] 15...dxc5 16 Nbd2 Nc6 17 Bb2 Nd4∓ Rumens-Hindle, Brighton 1977) 13 dxc5 dxc5 14 Nbd2 Nd7 N (14...Nc6 15 Rc1 Nd7 16 h3 Be6 17 Nb3 a5∞ Gulko-Podgaets, Vilnius 1971) 15 h3 Bh5 16 g4 Bg6 17 Nh2 Nc6 18 f4 f6 19 Ndf3 Qc7 20 Nh4 Bf7 21 Nf5 += Kurajica-Jelen, Ljubljana 1977

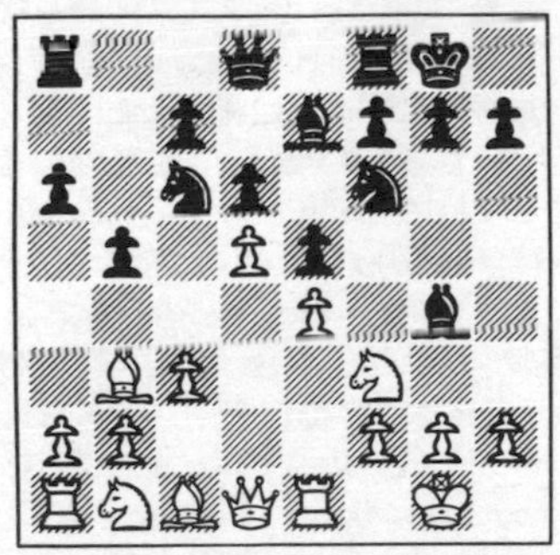

10...Na5 11 Bc2 c6 11...c5 12 Nbd2 Ne8 13 h3 Bd7 14 Nf1 g6 15 Bh6 Ng7 16 g4 += Vogt-Balashov, Leningrad 1977 **12 h3 Bxf3** (12...Bc8 – 12...Bd7 13 Nxe5 dxe5 14 d6 Be6 15 dxe7 Qxe7 16 Qf3 N [16 f4 exf4= Sigurjonsson-Tseshkovsky, Las Palmas 1976] 16...Rfd8 17 Qg3 Nd7 18 Nd2 f6= Adorjan-Lengyel, Budapest 1977; 13 dxc6 Qc7 14 Nbd2 [14 a4! += Stein-Gerschberg, Ukraine 1966] 14...Qxc6 15 Re3!? g6 16 b4 Nc4= Soltis-Reshevsky, USA Final 1977; 12...Bh5 N 13 dxc6 Nxc6 14 Nbd2 d5 15 exd5 Qxd5 16 Qe2± Tseshkovsky-Malevinsky, Erevan 1977 **13 Qxf3 cxd5 14 exd5 Nc4** 14...Rc8 15 Nd2 (15 b3 g6 16 Bh6 Re8 17 Nd2 Qc7 18 Re3 += Vasyukov-Vogt, Cienfuegos 1975) 15...Qc7? (15...g6 16 Bd3 Nh5 17 a4 f5 =+ Stein-Geller, Kislovodsk 1966) 16 Nf1 Ne8 17 Ng3 g6 18 Nf5!± Adorjan-Lukacs, Budapest 1977 **15 Nd2 Nb6 16 Nf1 Ne8 17 a4 Nxa4** 17...bxa4 18 Ne3 N Bg5 19 Bxa4 Nxa4 20 Rxa4 f5 21 Nc4 e4 22 Bxg5 Qxg5 23 Qe3± Sax-Jelen, Ljubljana 1977 **18 Bxa4 bxa4 19 Ne3 g6 20 Nc4 f5 21 Rxa4 Nf6** TN 21...Nc7 (Romanishin-Karpov, USSR Final 1976, 22 Na5 Δ Nc6, Be3 += **22 Na5 Ne4 23 Nc6 Qd7=** Diesen-Kuzmin, Polanica 1977

Vienna/Wiener

1 e4 e5 2 Nc3 Nf6 3 f4 3 g3 d5 4 exd5 Nxd5 5 Bg2 Nxc3 6 bxc3 Bd6 7 Nf3 0-0 8 0-0 c5 N (8...Nc6 9 d4 Bg4= Gufeld-Nei, USSR Final 1961) 9 d3 Nc6 10 Nd2 Qd7? 11 Qf3! Qc7 12 Ne4 Be7 13 Be3 c4 14 d4± Spassky-Korchnoi (14) 1977 **3...d5 4 fxe5 Nxe4 5 Nf3 Bc5 6 Qe2 Bf2+ 7 Kd1 Nxc3+ 8 dxc3 Bh4!?** TN 8...Bb6 9 Bg5 Qd7 10 Kd2 (10 Qd2

Keres) 10...0-0 11 ♖d1 += Larsen, 11...♖e8 12 ♔c1 f6= Euwe **9 ♗f4 ♗e7 10 ♔d2 0-0 11 ♖d1 c5 12 ♔c1 ♕a5 13 a3 ♖d8** Luksic-Vukovic, Jugoslavia 1977 14 c4!±

Kings Gambit/Koenigsgambit

1 e4 e5 2 f4 exf4 3 ♘f3 ♗e7 4 ♗c4 ♘f6 5 e5 ♘g4 6 0-0 ♘c6 7 ♕e2 TN 7 d4 d5 8 exd6 ♗xd6 9 ♖e1+ ♘e7 10 h3 ♘h6! Euwe **7...♗c5+ 8 ♔h1 0-0 9 h3 ♘h6 10 ♕e4 d5! 11 ♕xd5** 11 exd6 ♘f5 **11...♕xd5 12 ♗xd5 ♘f5 13 ♔h2 ♘b4 14 ♗b3 ♗e6 15 a3 ♘g3∓** Luksic-Marojevic, Jugoslavia 1977

Ponziani

1 e4 e5 2 ♘f3 ♘c6 3 c3 d5 4 ♕a4 f6 4...♗d7 5 exd5 ♘d4 6 ♕d1 ♘xf3+ 7 ♕xf3 ♘f6 8 ♗c4 ♗d6 9 d3 ♗g4 10 ♕e3 N (10 ♕g3 h5 11 ♗g5 ♕d7 12 h3 ± Dueckstein-Fuderer, Zagreb 1955) 10...0-0 11 0-0 ♕e8 12 h3 ♗d7 13 ♕f3 e4 ∝/+= Novak-Schinzel, R.Sobota 1977; 8 c4 Karpov; 4...dxe4 5 ♘xe5 ♕d5 6 ♘xc6 bxc6 7 ♗c4 ♕d7 (7...♕d6 += – Karpov) 8 d3 exd3 9 0-0 ♗d6 N (9...♘f6 10 ♖d1 ♗d6 11 ♗g5 Karpov) 10 ♘d2 ♘e7 11 ♘e4 0-0 12 ♖d1 ♖e8 Ljubojevic-Karpov, Ljubljana 1975; 13 ♗xd3±

5 exd5 TN 5 ♗b5 ♘e7 6 exd5 ♕xd5 7 d4 ♗g4 8 ♗c4!? += Eales-Beljavsky, Groningen 1969/70 **5...♕xd5 6 ♗b5 ♗d7 7 d4 a6 8 c4 ♕e4+ 9 ♗e3 ♗b4+ 10 ♘bd2 ♗xd2+ 11 ♘xd2 ♕xg2 12 0-0-0 0-0-0∝** Petronic-Veroci, Gosa 1977

French/Franzoesisch

1 e4 e6 2 d4 d5 3 ♘d2 3 e5 c5 (3...b6!? 4 c3 ♕d7 5 a4 [5 ♘f3 ♘e7 6 ♗d3 ♗a6 7 ♗xa6 ♘xa6 8 ♕d3 ♘b8 9 ♘bd2 ♘bc6= Hedman-Romanishin, Cienfuegos 1977] 5...a5 6 ♗b5 c6 7 ♗d3 ♗a6 8 ♘e2 ♘e7 9 0-0 ♘f5= Menvielle-Romanishin, Cienfuegos 1977) 4 c3 ♘c6 5 ♘f3 ♗d7 6 ♗e2 ♘ge7 7 ♘a3 cxd4 8 cxd4 ♘f5 9 ♘c2 ♘b4 N 10 ♘e3 ♘xe3 11 fxe3!?∝ Spassky-Korchnoi (18) 1977/78 **3...c5** 3...dxe4 4 ♘xe4 ♗d7!? 5 ♘f3 ♗c6 6 ♗d3 ♘d7 7 0-0 ♘gf6 8 ♘g3 ♗e7 9 ♖e1 0-0 10 ♕e2 ♖e8 11 ♗d2 ♗xf3 12 ♕xf3 c5∝ Balashov-Suba, Moscow 1977; 3...♗e7 4 ♗d3 (4 c3 dxe4 5 ♘xe4 ♘f6 6 ♘xf6+ ♗xf6 7 ♘f3 b6 8 ♗b5+ c6 9 ♗d3 ♗a6= Adorjan-Romanishin, Hastings 1976/77) 4...♘c6 5 ♘gf3 ♘b4 6 ♗e2 dxe4 7 ♘xe4 ♘f6 8 ♘xf6+ ♗xf6 9 0-0 0-0 10 c3 ♘d5 11 ♗d3 += Radulov-Romanishin, Leningrad 1977; 3...♘f6 4 e5 ♘fd7 5 c3 c5 6 ♗d3 ♘c6 7 ♘e2 (7 ♘df3 cxd4 8 cxd4 f6 9 exf6 ♘xf6 10 ♘e2 ♗d6 11 0-0 0-0 12 ♗f4 ♗xf4 13 ♘xf4 ♕b6 N 14 ♕d2 Parma-Planinc, Maribor 1977, 14...♔h8∝) 7...cxd4 8 cxd4 f6 9 exf6 ♘xf6 10 0-0 ♗d6 11 ♘f3 ♕c7 12 ♗g5 0-0 13 ♗h4 e5= Smyslov-Vaganian, Leningrad 1977 **4 exd5** 4 ♘gf3 ♘c6 5 ♗b5 dxe4 6 ♘xe4 ♗d7 7 0-0 N (7 ♗g5 ♕a5+ 8 ♘c3 a6! N 9 ♗xc6 ♗xc6 10 d5 ♗xd5

11 0-0 ♗c6 12 ♘e5 ♕c7∓ Nicevski-Uhlmann, Skopje 1976) 7...♘xd4 8 ♗g5 f6 9 ♘xd4 cxd4 10 ♗h4 ♗e7 11 c3 (11 ♕h5+ ♔f8 12 ♗c4 ♖c8 13 ♗b3 ♘h6 14 ♖ad1 ♘f5 15 ♘g3±) 11... ♗xb5 12 ♕h5+ ♔f8 13 ♕xb5 ♕d5= Tal-Uhlmann, Tallinn 1977

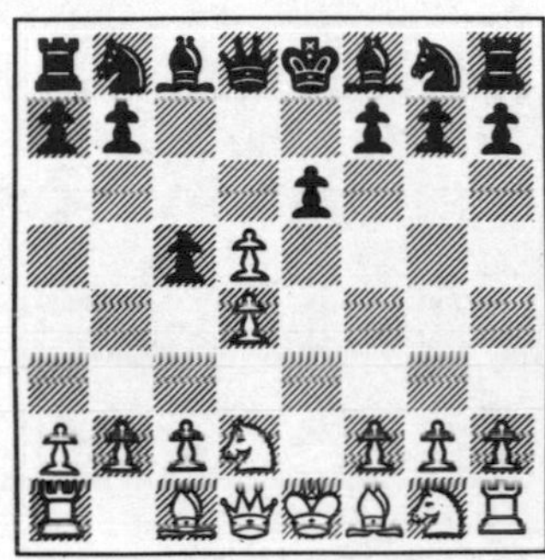

4...exd5 4...♕xd5 5 ♗c4 ♕d6 6 ♘gf3 cxd4 7 0-0 ♘f6 (7...♘c6 8 ♖e1 ♘h6 N 9 ♘e4 ♕b4 Radulov-Gulbrandsen, Oslo 1977, 10 ♗h6!±) 8 ♘b3 ♘c6 9 ♘bxd4 ♘xd4 10 ♘xd4 a6 11 ♗b3 ♘e7 12 c3 0-0 13 ♕f3 += Jansa-Petrosian, Moscow 1977 **5 ♘gf3 ♘c6** 5...a6 6 dxc5 ♗xc5 7 ♘c3 ♗d6 8 ♗d3 ♘e7 9 0-0 h6 10 h3 ♘bc6 11 ♘bd4 0-0 12 c3 ♗c7 13 ♗e3 ♕d6 14 ♖e1 += Timoshenko-Vaganian, Baku 1977 **6 ♗b5 ♗d6 7 dxc5 ♗xc5 8 0-0 ♘e7 9 ♘b3 ♗d6 10 ♖e1 0-0 11 ♗g5 ♗g4 12 ♗e2** 12 c3 f6 13 ♗h4 ♗h5 14 ♗e2 ♗f7 15 ♗g3 ♗e5= Gipslis-Bronstein, Tallinn 1977 **12...♕c7** 12...h6 13 ♗xe7 ♗xe7 14 h3 ♗h5 15 c3 ♕d6= Gipslis-Uhlmann, Tallinn 1977 **13 h3 ♗d7 14 ♘fd4 ♘xd4 15 ♘xd4** += Karpov-Debarnot, Las Palmas 1977

1 e4 e6 2 d4 d5 3 ♘c3 ♗b4 4 e5 c5 4...b6 5 ♗d2 ♕d7 6 ♘f3 ♗a6 7 ♗xa6 ♘xa6 8 ♘e2 ♗f8 9 ♘f4 c5 10 ♕e2 ♘b4 11 ♗e3 ♘h6 12 dxc5 bxc5 13 c3 ♘c6 14 c4 += Liberzon-Hubner, Bad Lauterberg 1977 **5 a3** 5 ♕g4 ♔f8 6 ♘f3 ♘c6 7 ♗d2 cxd4 8 ♘xd4 ♕b6 9 ♘xc6 bxc6 10 ♗d3 += Zuckerman-Hook, New York 1976; 5 ♗d2 ♘e7 6 ♘b5 ♗xd2+ 7 ♕xd2 0-0 8 f4 a6 9 ♘d6 cxd4 10 ♘f3 ♘bc6 11 ♗d3 f6 12 0-0 fxe5 13 fxe5 ♖xf3! 14 ♖xf3 ♘xe5 =+ Janosevic-Marovic, Vrsac 1977 **5...♗xc3+ 6 bxc3 ♘e7 7 ♕g4** 7 a4 ♗d7 8 ♘f3 ♕a5 9 ♗d2 ♘bc6 10 ♗e2 f6! (10...c4 11 ♘g5 h6 12 ♘h3 0-0-0 13 ♘f4 ♔b8 N 14 0-0 ♘c8 15 ♘h5 ♖hg8 16 ♗g4± Kavalek-Uhlmann, Manilla 1970, 7 ♘f3 ♗d7 8 dxc5!? N ♕c7 9 ♗d3 ♗a4 10 ♖b1 (10 ♗e3 ♘d7 11 ♕b1 ♘c6 12 ♘d4 ♘dxe5 =+ Spassky-Korchnoi (6) 1977; 10 0-0 ♘d7 11 ♘d4!? ♘xc5 12 ♗b5 ♗xb5 13 ♘xb5 ♕xe5 14 ♖e1 ♘e4! 15 f3 a6 16 ♘d4 ♘xc3 17 ♕d2 ♕c7 18 a4!∝ Spassky-Korchnoi (8) 1977) 10...♘d7 11 ♖b4 ♗c6 12 0-0 ♘xc5 13 ♖g4! ♘g6 14 ♘d4 0-0-0 15 f4± Spassky-Korchnoi (10) 1977

7...cxd4 7...♕c7 8 ♕xg7 ♖g8 9 ♕xh7 cxd4 10 ♘e2 ♘bc6 11 f4 ♗d7 12 ♕d3 dxc3 13 ♗e3 (13 ♖b1 0-0-0 14 ♕xc3! N ♘f5 15 ♖g1± Mecking-Uhlmann, Manilla 1976; 13 h4 0-0-0 14 h5 ♘f5 15 h6 ♖g6 16 h7 ♖h8 17 ♖h3 d4!! N 18 ♖b1 ♗e8 19 ♕f3 ♕d8∓

Bronstein-Uhlmann, Tallinn 1977; 13 ♘xc3 a6 14 ♖b1 ♘a5 15 h4 ♘f5 16 ♖h3 0-0-0 17 h5 ♖g4 18 ♕f3! ♖dg8 19 h6! ♖4g6 20 h7! Hasin) 13...d4 N 14 ♗f2 0-0-0 15 ♘xd4 ♘xd4 16 ♕xd4 b6 17 ♗h4 ♗b5 18 ♕e4 ♗xf1 Spassky-Korchnoi (2) 1977, 19 ♕a8+ = **8 cxd4!? ♕c7 9 ♔d1 0-0 10 ♘f3 f6 11 ♗d3 ♘f5 12 ♕h3 ♘c6** 12... fxe5 13 ♘xe5 g6 **13 g4 fxe5 14 dxe5 ♘xe5 15 ♘xe5 ♕xe5 16 ♖b1 ♘h6 17 ♖e1≈!?** Spassky-Korchnoi (12) 1977

Alekhine/Aljechin

1 e4 ♘f6 2 e5 2 ♘c3 d5 3 e5 ♘e4 4 ♘ce2 f6 5 ♘f3 dxe5 N 6 d3 ♘d6 7 ♘xe5 ♘d7 8 ♘xd7 ♗xd7 9 ♘f4 c6 10 ♕e2 ♘f7 11 d4 g6 12 ♘e6 ♗xe6 13 ♕xe6 += Smyslov-Alburt, USSR Final 1977 **2...♘d5 3 d4** 3 c4 ♘b6 4 c5 ♘d5 5 d4 (5 ♘c3 e6 6 ♗c4 ♘xc3 7 dxc3 ♘c6 8 ♗f4 ♗xc5?! 9 ♕g4 g5 10 ♗xg5 ♖g8 11 ♘h3 ♗e7 12 ♗xe7 N ♖xg4 13 ♗xd8 Oszvath-Orev, Bulgaria 1977, 13...♖xc4 14 ♗xc7 ♘xe5=) 5...d6 (5...b6 6 cxb6 axb6 7 ♗c4 e6 8 ♘e2 Δ ♘g3 +=) 6 cxd6 exd6 (6... cxd6 7 ♘f3 ♘c6 8 ♗c4 ♘b6 9 ♗b5 dxe5 10 ♘xe5 ♗d7= Sveshnikov-Petrosian, USSR Final 1977) 7 ♘f3 ♗e7 N (7...♘c6 8 ♗b5! a6 9 ♗xc6+ bxc6 10 ♗g5 ♗e7 11 ♗xe7 ♘xe7 12 0-0 += Sveshnikov-L.Popov 1973) 8 ♘c3 c6 (8...dxe5 9 ♘xe5 ♗e6 10 ♗d3 ♘d7=) 9 ♗e2 0-0 10 0-0 ♘xc3 (10... ♗e6 11 ♘e4∝) 11 bxc3 += Sveshnikov-Shamkovich, Hastings 1977/78; 3 ♗c4 ♘b6 4 ♗b3 c5 5 d3 ♘c6 6 ♘f3 e6 7 ♘c3 d5 8 exd6 ♗xd6 9 ♘e4 ♗e7 10 ♗e3 ♘d5 11 ♗d2 0-0= Ivanovic-Matovic, Vrsac 1977 **3...d6 4 ♘f3 ♗g4** 4...dxe5 5 ♘xe5 g6 6 ♗c4 ♗e6 7 0-0 ♗g7 8 ♕e2 ♘d7 9 ♘f3 ♘7f6 10 ♗b3 c6 11 c4 ♘c7 12 ♘c3 0-0 13 ♗e3 += Matanovic-Knezevic, Vrsac 1977; 4... ♘b6 5 a4 c6 N 6 a5 ♘d5 7 ♗e2 g6 8 0-0 ♗g7 9 c4 ♘c7 10 exd6 ♕xd6 11 ♘c3 += Sigurjonsson-Larsen, Ljubljana 1977

5 ♗e2 5 h3 ♗xf3 6 ♕xf3 dxe5 7 dxe5 e6 8 ♕e4 ♘d7 9 ♗c4 c6 10 0-0 ♗c5 11 ♘d2 ♘e7 12 ♘f3 ♘f5 13 ♗f4 += Prandstetter-Alburt, Decin 1978 **5...e6 6 0-0 ♗e7 7 h3** 7 c4 ♘b6 8 exd6 cxd6 9 b3 0-0 10 ♗b2 ♘c6 11 a3 N a5 12 ♘bd2 ♗f5 13 ♖e1 d5 14 c5 ♘d7= Kagan-Vukic, Biel 1977 **7...♗h5 8 c4 ♘b6 9 ♘c3** 9 exd6 cxd6 10 ♘bd2 ♘c6 11 b3 0-0 12 ♗b2 ♗g6 (12...d5 13 c5 ♘d7 14 ♖c1 N – 14 a3 f6 15 b4 a6 16 ♖e1 += Medina-Hecht, Malaga 1972 – 14...a5 15 a3 b6 16 ♗b5!± Anikaev-Gurgenidze, USSR 1976) 13 a3 (13 ♗c3 a5 14 a3 ♗f6 15 ♖e1 ♕b8 16 ♘f1 ♗e4 17 ♘3h2 d5 18 c5 += Kuzmin-Alburt, USSR Minsk 1976; 13 ♘e1?! d5 14 c5 ♘d7 15 ♘df3 b6= Blumenfeld-Vukic, New York 1976) 13...a5 14 ♗c3 ♗f6 15 ♖e1 e5 N 16 ♘f1 e4 17 ♘3h2 d5= Tal-Bagirov, USSR Final 1977 **0-0 10 ♗e3 d5**

Diagram

11 cxd5 11 c5 ♗xf3 12 ♗xf3 ♘c4 13 ♗f4 ♘c6 14 b3 ♘4a5 15 ♕d2 += Geller-Timman, Teesside 1975 **11... ♞xd5** 11...exd5 N 12 ♗d3 ♘c6 13 g4 ♗g6 14 ♗f5 ♕e8 15 ♘e2 f6= Gulko-Bagirov, Baku 1977 **12 ♛b3 ♞xe3** 12...♘b6 13 ♖fd1! N ♕c8 14 d5 ♘xd5 15 ♘xd5 exd5 16 ♖xd5 += Sznapik-Schmidt, Poland Final 1977 **13 fxe3 b6 14 d5** 14 ♗d3 ♘c6 15 ♗e4 ♘a5 16 ♕c2 ♗g6 17 ♗xg6 hxg6 18 ♖ad1± Pytel-Bohm, Le Havre 1977 **14...♝c5 15 dxe6 ♝xe3+ 16 ♚h1 fxe6 17 ♛xe6+ ♚h8 18 ♜ad1** +− Georgadze-Alburt, Tbilisi-Suhumi 1977

Pirc

1 e4 d6 2 d4 g6 3 ♞f3 ♝g7 4 ♞c3 ♞f6 5 ♝c4 0-0 6 ♛e2 c6 7 ♝b3 7 ♗g5 **7...d5** 7...♗g4 8 h3 ♗xf3 9 ♕xf3 e6!= Medina-Botvinnik, Palma 1967 **8 exd5** 8 e5 ♘e8 9 ♗g5 **8...cxd5 9 ♝g5 ♞c6** =+ Kestler-Torre, Biel 1977

1 e4 d6 2 d4 ♞f6 3 ♞c3 g6 4 ♞f3 ♝g7 5 ♝e2 0-0 6 0-0 ♞c6 7 d5

Diagram

7 h3 e5 8 dxe5 ♘xe5 9 ♘xe5 dxe5 10 ♕xd8 ♖xd8= Hort-Bronstein, Krems 1967; 7 ♗g5!? h6 8 ♗f4 ♘g4!? N (8...e5! 9 dxe5 ♘h5) 9 h3 e5 10 dxe5 ♘gxe5 11 ♘xe5 dxe5 12 ♗e3 ♘d4 13 ♗c4 ♕h4 14 ♘d5 c6 15 ♘c7 ♗xh3! −+ Zaharov-Adorjan, Sochi 1976 **7...♞b4!?** 7...♘b8 8 a4 c6 9 ♖e1 ♗g4 10 h3 ♗xf3 11 ♗xf3 ♘bd7 12 g3!± Hardiczay-Kubicek, Olomouc 1976

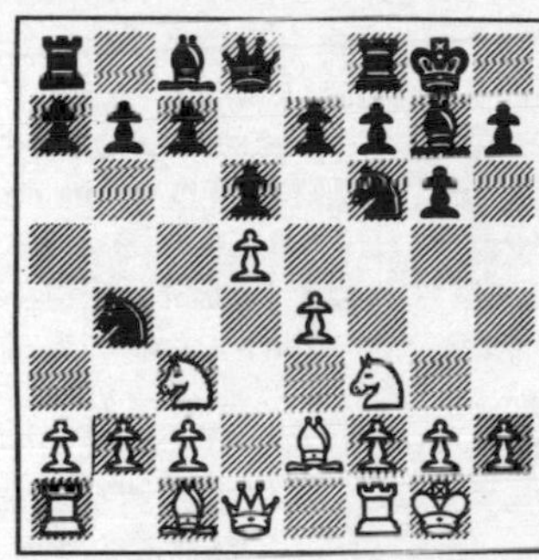

8 a3 8 ♗e3 ♗d7 (8...e6 9 a3 ♘a6 10 ♗xa6 bxa6 11 ♘d4 exd5 12 ♘c6 ♕e8 13 exd5 ♗d7= Stean-Jansa, Cirella 1976/77) 9 h3 c6 10 ♖e1 cxd5 11 exd5 ♕a5 12 ♗c4 ♖ac8 13 ♗b3 ♖xc3!? ∝ Blackstock-Vadasz, Budapest 1977; 8 h3 a5 (8...e6 9 ♗g5 h6 10 ♗e3 exd5 11 exd5 ♔h7 12 a3 ♘a6 13 b4 ♘b8 14 ♖b1± Gipslis-Vadasz, Budapest 1977) 9 ♖e1 e6 10 a3 ♘a6 11 dxe6 ♗xe6 12 ♘d4 (12 ♗f4 ♘c5 13 ♗f1 ♖e8 14 ♕d2 d5∝ Weinstein-Sax, Budapest 1976) 12...♗d7 13 ♗f4 ♖e8 14 ♗f3 ♘c5= Jansa-Mednis,

Nis 1977; 8 Bg5 h6 9 Be3 e6 10 a3 Na6 11 dxe6 Bxe6 12 b4?!∞ Timman-Adorjan, Amsterdam 1977 **8...Na6 9 Re1** 9 Bxa6 bxa6 10 Nd4 Bb7 Δ Qd7 **9...Nc5 10 Bf1 e6 11 dxe6 Nxe6 12 h3 b6 13 Bc4 Bb7=** Gaprindashvili-Vadasz, Budapest 1977

1 e4 d6 2 d4 Nf6 3 Nc3 g6 4 Nf3 Bg7 5 Be2 0-0 6 0-0 c6 6...Bg4 7 Be3 Nc6 8 Qd2 e5 9 d5 Ne7 10 Rad1 Kh8 (10...Bd7 11 Ne1 Ng4 12 Bxg4 Bxg4 13 f3 Bd7 14 f4 Bg4 15 Rb1 c6 16 h3 Bd7 TN 17 fxe5 dxe5 18 d6± Karpov-Timman, Tilburg 1977) 11 h3 Bxf3 12 Bxf3 Nd7 13 Be2 f5 14 f4 Karpov-Keene, Moscow 1977, 14...a6= **7 a4 a5 8 h3** 8 Be3 Qc7 N (8...Na6; 8...Ng4) 9 Ne1!? Na6 10 f3 Bd7 11 Qd2 Rfd8= Barcza-Alster, Decin 1977; 8 Re1 Na6 9 Bf1 Nb4 10 Nb1 Bg4 11 Nbd2 e5 12 c3 Na6 13 dxe5 dxe5 14 h3 Bxf3 15 Qxf3± Miles-Panno, Amsterdam 1977 **8...Na6 9 Re1 Nb4** 9...Qc7 N 10 Bf4 Nh5 11 Bh2 e5 12 Qd2 Nb4 13 Rac1 Re8 14 Bc4± Barlov-Dimitrievic, Kraguevac 1977 **10 Bf1** N 10 Bf4 Nd7 11 Nb1 e5 12 Bg5 f6 13 Be3 d5 14 Nbd2 dxe4 15 Nxe4 Nd5= Kossikov-Vitolins, Cheliabinsk 1975 **10...Ne8 11 Bg5 Nc7 12 Qd2 Ne6 13 Bh4 d5 14 exd5 cxd5 15 Nb5±** Zakharov-Sejkora, Decin 1977

1 d4 g6 2 e4 d6 3 Nc3 Nf6 4 Bg5 Bg7 5 Qd2 5 e5 Nfd7 6 exd6 (6 f4) 6... cxd6 7 Qd2 N 0-0 8 0-0-0 Nc6 9 h4!?∞ Ivanovic-Borkowski, Pristina 1976 **5...h6 6 Bh4 c6 7 f4 0-0** 7...Be6 8 Nf3 d5 9 Bd3 dxe4 10 Nxe4 Nxe4 11 Bxe4 Bd5 12 Qe2± Fuderer-Pirc, Opatija 1953 **8 Nf3 Bg4 9 Be2 d5 10 e5 Ne4 11 Qe3 Qd7 12 0-0-0 +=** Romanishin-Balashov, USSR Final 1977

1 e4 d6 2 d4 Nf6 3 Nc3 g6 4 f4 Bg7 5 Nf3 5 e5 dxe5 6 dxe5 Qxd1+ 7 Kxd1 Nfd7 8 Nd5 Kd8 9 Nf3 c6 10 Ne3 f6 11 b3 (11 exf6 exf6 12 Nc4 Nc5 13 Nd6 Be6 14 f5! += Adorjan-Vadasz, Budapest 1970) 11...Nb6 12 c4 fxe5 13 fxe5 Na6 14 Bd3 Nd7= Rogulj-Vadasz, S.Palanka 1977 **5...c5 6 Bb5+** 6 dxc5 Qa5 7 Bd3 Qxc5 8 Qe2 Bg4 (8...0-0 9 Be3 Qc7 10 0-0 Bg4 [10...Nbd7 11 h3 a6 12 a4 b6 13 Qf2 Bb7 14 f5 N ∞ Timman-Sigurjonsson, Wijk aan Zee 1977] 11 Nb5!? TN (11 h3 Bxf3 12 Qxf3 Nbd7 13 Qf2 a6 14 a4 e6 15 Qh4 Rae8= Kupreichik-Razuvaev, Batumi 1969) 11...Qa5! 12 b4 Qd8 13 c4 Nc6 14 Rab1 a5! 15 a3 axb4 16 axb4 Ra4∓ Ljubojevic-Marangunic, Jugoslavia Final 1977) 9 Be3 Qa5 10 0-0 Nc6 11 h3 Bxf3 12 Qxf3 0-0 13 a3 Nd7 14 Bd2 Qb6+ 15 Kh1 Nc5 16 Rab1 Nxd3 17 cxd3 Qb3? (17...f5! TN – Nunn) 18 f5 Qc2 (18...Rfe8 19 Bg5 Rac8 20 Nd5 Ne5 21 Qg3± Adorjan-Suttles, Hastings 1973/74) 19 Bg5 Ne5 20 Qg3 f6 21 Bf4± Nunn-Torre, London 1977) **6...Bd7**

7 e5 7 Bxd7+ N Nfxd7 8 d5 Na6 9

♕e2 0-0 10 0-0 ♘c7 11 a4 a6 12 ♖d1 ♖b8 13 a5 += Hort-Torre, Polanica 1977 **7...♘g4 8 h3** 8 e6 ♗xb5 9 exf7+ ♔d7 10 ♘xb5 ♕a5+ 11 ♘c3 cxd4 12 ♘xd4 ♗xd4 13 ♕xd4 ♘c6 14 ♕c4 ♕b6 (14...♕a6 15 ♘b5 ♖hf8 16 ♗d2 ♖ac8 17 0-0-0 ♘f2 −+ Skrobek-Maciejewski, Katowice 1977; 14...♕f5 15 h3 ♘f6 16 0-0 ♕e6 17 ♕b5 ♖ab8 18 f5± Bednarski-Rukavina, Decin 1978) 15 ♕e2 h5 16 ♗d2 ♘d4 17 ♕d3 ♘f5≈ Van Wijgerden-Timman, Amsterdam 1977 **8...cxd4 9 ♕xd4 ♘h6** 9...♗xb5 10 ♘xb5 ♘c6 11 ♕e4 ♕a5+ 12 ♘c3 ♘h6 13 g4 0-0-0 14 0-0 += Timman-Sigurjonsson, Geneva 1977 **10 ♗d2 ♗xb5 11 ♘xb5 ♘c6 12 ♕f2 dxe5 13 fxe5** Sigurjonsson-Westerinen, Geneva 1977 **13...0-0≈**

1 e4 d6 2 d4 ♘f6 3 ♘c3 g6 4 f4 ♗g7 5 ♘f3 0-0 6 ♗d3 6 ♗e3 b6 N e5 (7 ♗d3 ♗b7 8 f5) 7...♘g4 8 ♗g1 c5 9 h3 ♘h6 10 d5 ♘f5 11 ♗f2 dxe5 12 fxe5 ♘d7 13 ♕e2 ♗b7 14 0-0-0± Balashov-Timman, Tilburg 1977; 6 e5 dxe5 7 dxe5 ♕xd1+ 8 ♔xd1 ♘h5!? N 9 ♗c4 (9 ♗e3? ♘c6 10 ♗c4 ♗g4 11 ♖f1 ♘a5 12 ♗d3 f6 13 exf6 ♗xf6! 14 h3 ♗e6 15 ♘d2 ♘g3 16 ♖e1 ♗f5∓ Panchenko-Adorjan, Sochi 1977) 9...♘c6 (9...♗g4 10 ♔e2 ♘c6 11 ♗e3 g5! 12 fxg5 ♗xe5 13 ♔f2 ♗xf3 14 gxf3 ♖ad8 =+ Martin-Djindjihashvili, Haifa 1976) 10 ♖f1! ♗h6?! (10...♗g4 11 ♔e1 ♘a5 12 ♗d3 f6 13 exf6 ♗xf6 14 h3∞) 11 ♘e2 ♖d8+ 12 ♔e1 ♘b4 13 ♗b3 ♗e6≈ Zhuravlev-Adorjan, Sochi 1977 **6...♘c6** 6...♗g4 7 h3 ♗xf3 8 ♕xf3 ♘c6 9 ♗e3 e5 (9...♘d7 10 e5! ♘b4 11 0-0-0± R.Byrne-Korchnoi, Moscow 1975) 10 dxe5 dxe5 11 f5 ♘d4 12 ♕f2 b5 13 0-0 c5 14 ♘xb5 ♘xb5 15 ♗xb5 ♘xe4 16 ♕f3 += Parma-Planinc, Ljubljana 1977; 6...♘a6 7 0-0 (7 e5) 7...c5 8 d5 ♘c7 (8...♘b4) 9 a4 a6 10 ♕e1 ♗d7 11 a5 ♗b5 12 f5 (12 ♕h4 e6 13 f5 exf5 14 exf5 ♗xd3 15 cxd3 ♘d7 16 ♗g5± Gligoric-Larsen, Beverwijk 1967) 12...gxf5 13 ♕h4 e5 14 ♗g5 f4 15 g3 c4 16 ♗e2 ♘ce8 17 gxf4± Adorjan-Bohm, Amsterdam 1977

7 0-0 e5 7...♗g4 8 e5 ♘d7 N 9 ♗e3 ♘b4 10 ♗e4 c5 (10...f5!? 11 exf6 ♘xf6 12 ♗xb7 ♖b8 13 ♗e4 ♘xe4 14 ♘xe4 ♘d5∞) 11 dxc5 ♘xc5 12 ♗xc5 dxc5 13 ♗xb7 ♖b8 14 ♗e4 f5 15 ♗d5+ ±/+− van Wijgerden-Adorjan, Amsterdam 1977 **8 fxe5** 8 dxe5 dxe5 9 f5 gxf5 10 exf5 e4! N 11 ♘xe4 ♗xf5 12 ♘xf6+ ♕xf6 13 ♗g5 ♕e6 14 c3 ♗g6 15 ♕e2 ♕xe2= Sax-Haxai, Budapest 1977 **8...dxe5 9 d5 ♘e7** 9...♘d4 N 10 ♘xe5 ♘xe4 11 ♗xe4 ♗xe5 12 ♗f4 ♗xf4 13 ♖xf4 ♘f5= van Wijgerden-Donner, Amsterdam 1977 **10 ♘xe5 c6!** TN 10...♘fxd5 11 ♘xf7 ♘xc3 12 bxc3 ♖xf7 13 ♖xf7 ♔xf7 14 ♗c4+ +− **11 ♗c4** 11 dxc6? ♕d4+; 11 ♗g5!? **11...♕d6 12 ♘d3 cxd5 13 exd5 ♘exd5 14 ♘xd5 ♘xd5 15 ♔h1 ♘b6 16 ♗b3 ♗f5∓** Bellin-Botterill, Brighton 1977

Hradec Kralove 25.xii.77-5.i.78

				1	2	3	4	5	6	7	8	9	0	1	2	
1	Gurgenidze	GM	2510	x	½	½	½	½	½	½	1	½	1	1	1	7½
2	Gipslis	GM	2535	½	x	0	½	½	½	1	1	1	1	1	½	7½
3	Moehring	IM	2405	½	1	x	1	½	½	0	½	1	½	½	1	7
4	Knezevic	GM	2500	½	½	0	x	½	½	½	1	1	1	½	1	7
5	Pribyl	IM	2485	½	½	½	½	x	1	1	½	1	0	½	½	6½
6	Sapi		2420	½	½	½	½	0	x	½	½	½	½	½	½	5
7	Mojzis		2300	½	0	1	½	0	½	x	0	½	½	½	1	5
8	Gonsior		2385	0	0	½	0	½	½	1	x	1	½	1	0	5
9	Jasnikowski		2340	½	0	0	0	0	½	½	0	x	1	1	1	4½
10	Seifert		2320	0	0	½	0	1	½	½	½	0	x	½	½	4
11	G.Szilagyi	IM	2370	0	0	½	½	½	½	½	0	0	½	x	½	3½
12	Nun		2340	0	½	0	0	½	½	0	1	0	½	½	x	3½

Category 7 (2402) GM = 8 IM = 6½

Reggio Emilia 27.xii.77-6.i.78

				1	2	3	4	5	6	7	8	9	0	1	2	
1	L.Kovacs	IM	2395	x	½	1	½	1	1	0	1	1	1	1	½	8½
2	Averbakh	GM	2520	½	x	½	1	½	½	1	½	½	1	½	1	7½
3	Formanek	IM	2410	0	½	x	1	1	1	½	1	1	½	0	½	7
4	Niklasson		2380	½	0	0	x	½	0	1	1	1	1	½	1	6½
5	Coppini		2215	0	½	0	½	x	½	½	1	½	½	1	1	6
6	Wirthensohn	IM	2390	0	½	0	1	½	x	½	1	1	0	½	½	5½
7	Passerotti		2380	1	0	½	0	½	½	x	0	½	½	1	1	5½
8	Haik	IM	2400	0	½	0	0	0	0	1	x	1	1	1	1	5½
9	Valenti		2240	0	½	0	0	½	0	½	0	x	1	1	1	4½
10	Wagman		2325	0	0	½	0	½	1	½	0	0	x	1	½	4
11	Martorelli			0	½	1	½	0	½	0	0	0	0	x	½	3
12	Magrin			½	0	½	0	0	½	0	0	0	½	½	x	2½

Category 4 (2339) IM = 7½

Alicante 1978			1	2	3	4	5	6	7	8	9	0	1	2	3	4	
1	Beljavsky	GM 2545	x	1	1	1	1	1	1	1	1	1	1	1	1	1	13
2	Ermenkov	GM 2520	0	x	½	½	1	½	½	½	½	1	½	1	1	½	8
3	Diesen	IM 2440	0	½	x	½	1	½	1	½	½	½	½	½	1	1	8
4	Damjanovic	GM 2455	0	½	½	x	½	½	½	½	½	½	1	1	½	1	7½
5	Medina	2425	0	0	0	½	x	1	½	1	1	½	½	1	0	1	7
6	Vilela	2435	0	½	½	½	0	x	1	½	½	1	0	½	½	1	6½
7	O.Rodriguez	IM 2485	0	½	0	½	½	0	x	1	½	½	1	½	½	1	6½
8	Rohde	IM 2425	0	½	½	½	0	½	0	x	1	0	1	1	½	1	6½
9	Sanz	2330	0	½	½	½	0	½	½	0	x	½	½	1	1	1	6½
10	Ochoa	2345	0	0	½	½	½	0	½	1	½	x	½	0	1	1	6
11	A.Fernandez	2310	0	½	½	0	½	1	0	0	½	½	x	0	1	1	5½
12	Hernando	2340	0	0	½	0	0	½	½	0	0	1	1	x	½	½	4½
13	Ang.Martin	2390	0	0	0	½	1	½	½	½	0	0	0	½	x	1	4½
14	Verdu		0	½	0	0	0	0	0	0	0	0	0	½	0	x	1

Category 6 (2390) GM = 9½ IM = 8

Montpelier 26.xii.77-3.i.78			1	2	3	4	5	6	7	8	9	0	
1	O.Castro	IM 2410	x	1	1	½	½	½	1	1	½	1	7
2	Preissmann	2315	0	x	1	½	1	½	1	½	1	1	6½
3	Medina	IM 2345	0	0	x	½	1	½	1	1	1	1	6
4	Pytel	IM 2435	½	½	½	x	1	½	1	½	1	½	6
5	Seret	2350	½	0	0	0	x	½	0	1	1	1	4
6	Weill		½	½	½	½	½	x	0	½	½	½	4
7	Giffard	2270	0	0	0	0	1	1	x	½	0	1	3½
8	J.Gonzalez	2450	0	½	0	½	0	½	½	x	½	½	3
9	Villeneuve	2270	½	0	0	0	0	½	1	½	x	½	3
10	Dussol		0	0	0	½	0	½	0	½	½	x	2

Category 3 (2325) IM = 6½

Reykjavik 4-22.ii.78

				1	2	3	4	5	6	7	8	9	0	1	2	3	4	
1	Browne	GM	2550	x	½	1	0	0	½	1	½	1	1	1	½	1	1	9
2	Miles	GM	2565	½	x	½	½	0	½	½	1	1	½	1	½	1	1	8½
3	Hort	GM	2620	0	½	x	0	1	½	½	½	½	1	1	½	1	1	8
4	Larsen	GM	2620	1	½	1	x	1	0	0	1	0	1	½	1	0	1	8
5	Lombardy	GM	2540	1	1	0	0	x	½	1	½	½	0	½	1	1	1	8
6	F.Olafsson	GM	2530	½	½	½	1	½	x	½	½	1	½	1	½	½	½	8
7	Polugaevsky	GM	2620	0	½	½	1	0	½	x	½	0	1	½	1	1	1	7½
8	Kuzmin	GM	2535	½	0	½	0	½	½	½	x	½	1	1	1	1	0	7
9	Smejkal	GM	2555	0	0	½	1	½	0	1	½	x	½	0	1	1	½	6½
10	Sigurjonsson	GM	2500	0	½	0	0	1	½	0	0	½	x	1	½	½	½	5
11	Ogaard	IM	2435	0	0	0	½	½	0	½	0	1	0	x	½	½	½	4
12	H.Olafsson		2420	½	½	½	0	0	½	0	0	0	½	½	x	½	½	4
13	Petursson		2350	0	0	0	1	0	½	0	0	0	½	½	½	x	1	4
14	Arnason		2470	0	0	0	0	0	½	0	1	½	½	½	½	0	x	3½

Category 11 (2522) GM = 7½ IM = 6

45 USSR Final i.78

			1	2	3	4	5	6	
Dorfman	IM	2550	½	0	½	1	½	½	3
Gulko	GM	2575	½	1	½	0	½	½	3

Poland Final Warsaw 11-15.iii.78

			1	2	3	4	
Kuligowski		2325	0	1	1	0	2
Sznapik	IM	2430	1	0	0	1	2

Bulgaria Final 9-15.i.78

			1	2	3	
Radulov	GM	2490	1	0	1	2
Inkiov	IM	2450	0	1	0	1

Itoh

				1	2	3	4	5	6	7	8	9	0	
1	Torre	GM	2490	x	0	1	1	1	1	1	½	1	1	7½
2	R.Rodriguez		2415	1	x	½	0	½	0	1	1	1	1	6
3	Kileng			0	½	x	1	½	0	1	1	½	1	5½
4	Rogers		2400	0	1	0	x	½	1	½	½	1	½	5
5	Maninang		2305	0	½	½	½	x	½	½	½	1	1	5
6	K.Jhunjhnuwala			0	1	1	0	½	x	0	1	1	½	5
7	Shaw		2385	0	0	0	½	½	1	x	1	½	1	4½
8	Laird			½	0	0	½	½	0	0	x	½	1	3
9	Chen Te			0	0	½	0	0	0	½	½	x	½	2
10	Shiomi			0	0	0	½	0	½	0	0	½	x	1½

Itoh

				1	2	3	4	5	6	7	8	9	0	
1	Balinas	GM	2440	x	1	½	1	0	1	1	0	1	1	6½
2	Bachtiar	IM	2335	0	x	1	1	½	1	½	1	0	1	6
3	Green			½	0	x	1	0	½	1	1	1	1	6
4	Fuller		2390	0	0	0	x	1	½	1	1	1	1	5½
5	C.H.Chi			1	½	1	0	x	0	0	1	½	1	5
6	Chiong			0	0	½	½	1	x	0	1	1	1	5
7	Sinuraya			0	½	0	0	1	1	x	0	½	½	3½
8	Gonda			1	0	0	0	0	0	1	x	1	½	3½
9	M.K.Wong			0	1	0	0	½	0	½	0	x	½	2½
10	Sinprayoon			0	0	0	0	0	0	½	½	½	x	1½

Itoh (Final)

				1	2	3	4	5	6	7	8	
1	Torre	GM	2490	x	0	1	1	1	1	0	1	5
2	R.Rodriguez		2415	1	x	½	1	0	1	½	1	5
3	Kileng			0	½	x	1	1	½	½	½	4
4	Balinas	GM	2440	0	0	0	x	1	1	1	½	3½
5	Rogers		2400	0	1	0	0	x	1	½	1	3½
6	Bachtiar	IM	2335	0	0	½	0	0	x	1	1	2½
7	Fuller		2390	1	½	½	0	½	0	x	0	2½
8	Green			0	0	½	½	0	0	1	x	2

Wijk aan Zee 19.i.-2.ii.78

				1	2	3	4	5	6	7	8	9	0	1	2	
1	Portisch	GM	2630	x	½	½	½	1	1	½	½	1	1	½	1	8
2	Korchnoi	GM	2665	½	x	½	½	½	1	1	1	1	½	1	0	7½
3	Andersson	GM	2545	½	½	x	½	½	½	1	½	0	½	1	1	6½
4	Ree	IM	2500	½	½	½	x	½	½	½	½	½	½	½	1	6
5	Timman	GM	2585	0	½	½	½	x	½	1	1	½	½	½	½	6
6	Panno	GM	2580	0	0	½	½	½	x	½	½	½	1	½	1	5½
7	Mecking	GM	2630	½	0	0	½	0	½	x	1	½	½	½	1	5
8	Miles	GM	2565	½	0	½	½	0	½	0	x	1	½	1	½	5
9	Najdorf	GM	2525	0	0	1	½	½	½	½	0	x	½	½	1	5
10	Sosonko	GM	2575	0	½	½	½	½	0	½	½	½	x	½	½	4½
11	Kavalek	GM	2570	½	0	0	½	½	½	½	0	½	½	x	½	4
12	v.d. Sterren		2400	0	1	0	0	½	0	0	½	0	½	½	x	3

Category 13 (2564) GM = 5½ IM = 4

Santos Lugares ii.78

				1	2	3	4	5	6	7	8	9	0	1	2	
1	Sanguinetti	IM	2485	x	½	½	½	½	1	½	1	½	1	1	1	8
2	J.Szmetan	IM	2420	½	x	½	0	1	1	0	1	½	1	1	1	7½
3	Schweber	IM	2450	½	½	x	½	0	½	1	1	1	½	1	1	7½
4	R.Garcia	IM	2430	½	1	½	x	½	½	1	0	1	½	½	1	7
5	Panno	GM	2580	½	0	1	½	x	½	1	0	1	1	½	1	7
6	Guimard	GM		0	0	½	½	½	x	½	½	1	1	1	1	6½
7	Balduzzi			½	1	0	0	0	½	x	1	1	½	½	1	6
8	Rubinetti	IM	2430	0	0	0	1	1	½	0	x	0	½	1	1	5
9	Rossetto	GM	2405	½	½	0	0	0	0	0	1	x	1	1	0	4
10	Castelli		2225	0	0	½	½	0	0	½	½	0	x	½	½	3
11	Agdamus			0	0	0	½	½	0	½	0	0	½	x	1	3
12	Rios			0	0	0	0	0	0	0	0	1	½	0	x	1½

Torremolinos 15-26.ii.78

				1	2	3	4	5	6	7	8	9	0	1	2	
1	Bellon	IM	2350	x	1	1	½	0	1	1	½	1	1	1	½	8½
2	Sanz		2330	0	x	½	1	½	½	1	½	½	1	1	1	7½
3	Andersson	GM	2545	0	½	x	½	½	½	½	1	1	1	1	1	7½
4	Tarjan	GM	2510	½	0	½	x	½	1	½	1	½	1	1	½	7
5	Rivas			1	½	½	½	x	½	0	½	1	1	½	½	6½
6	Pavlov	IM	2405	0	½	½	0	½	x	½	½	½	1	1	1	6
7	Piasetski	IM	2410	0	0	½	½	1	½	x	½	½	0	1	1	5½
8	Diesen	IM	2440	½	½	0	0	½	½	½	x	½	½	½	1	5
9	Damjanovic	GM	2455	0	½	0	½	0	½	½	½	x	1	0	½	4
10	Durao	IM	2315	0	0	0	0	0	0	1	½	0	x	1	1	3½
11	Duran			0	0	0	0	½	0	0	½	1	0	x	1	3
12	Ruiz		2250	½	0	0	½	½	0	0	0	½	0	0	x	2

Category 5 (2368) GM = 8½ IM = 7½

Roskilde 1-12.ii.78

				1	2	3	4	5	6	7	8	9	0	1	2	
1	Schneider	IM	2430	x	½	1	½	½	½	½	1	1	½	1	1	8
2	Westerinen	GM	2450	½	x	½	½	1	½	1	½	½	1	1	1	8
3	O.Jakobsen	IM	2400	0	½	x	1	½	0	½	1	1	½	½	1	6½
4	Kristiansen		2395	½	½	0	x	½	½	½	½	½	1	½	1	6
5	Webb	IM	2445	½	0	½	½	x	½	½	½	½	1	½	1	6
6	Helmers		2345	½	½	1	½	½	x	1	½	0	0	½	½	5½
7	Fedder		2400	½	0	½	½	½	0	x	0	1	1	1	½	5½
8	Filipowicz	IM	2360	0	½	0	½	½	½	1	x	½	½	½	1	5½
9	Ghitescu	IM	2450	0	½	0	½	½	1	0	½	x	½	½	½	4½
10	Rajna	IM	2410	½	0	½	0	0	1	0	½	½	x	½	1	4½
11	Rosenlund		2340	0	0	½	½	½	½	0	½	½	½	x	0	3½
12	Danielsen			0	0	0	0	0	½	½	0	½	0	1	x	2½

Category 6 (2385) IM = 7

Hamar 3-10.i.78

				1	2	3	4	5	6	7	8	9	0	
1	Wibe	IM	2420	x	1	0	½	½	½	1	1	1	1	6½
2	Ogaard	IM	2435	0	x	1	½	1	½	0	1	1	1	6
3	Westerinen	GM	2450	1	0	x	½	½	½	½	1	1	1	6
4	Johannessen	IM	2400	½	½	½	x	1	½	½	½	1	½	5½
5	Farago	GM	2510	½	0	½	0	x	½	1	1	1	1	5½
6	L.Lengyel	GM	2430	½	½	½	½	½	x	½	½	½	1	5
7	de Lange		2290	0	1	½	½	0	½	x	½	½	1	4½
8	Johnsen		2280	0	0	0	½	0	½	½	x	½	½	2½
9	Goichberg			0	0	0	0	0	½	½	½	x	1	2½
10	T.A.Nilsen			0	0	0	½	0	0	0	½	0	x	1

Beersheva 18.ii.-4.iii.78

				1	2	3	4	5	6	7	8	9	0	1	2	3	4	
1	Korchnoi	GM	2665	x	1	1	½	½	1	1	1	1	1	1	1	1	1	12
2	Bleiman	IM	2440	0	x	1	½	1	1	1	0	½	½	0	½	1	1	8
3	Stean	GM	2510	0	0	x	½	1	1	½	½	½	½	½	1	½	1	7½
4	Keene	GM	2480	½	½	½	x	0	1	0	½	½	1	½	½	½	1	7
5	Murei		2420	½	0	0	1	x	0	1	1	½	1	1	0	1	0	7
6	Birnboim		2465	0	0	0	0	1	x	1	½	0	1	1	1	½	½	6½
7	Lederman	IM	2405	0	0	½	1	0	0	x	1	0	1	0	1	1	1	6½
8	Liberzon	GM	2555	0	1	½	½	0	½	0	x	½	½	½	½	1	1	6½
9	Tatai	IM	2455	0	½	½	½	½	1	1	½	x	0	½	½	½	½	6½
10	Kraidman	GM	2455	0	½	½	0	0	0	0	½	1	x	1	1	½	1	6
11	Vanger		2470	0	1	½	½	0	0	1	½	½	0	x	1	0	1	6
12	Kagan	IM	2465	0	½	0	½	1	0	0	½	½	0	0	x	1	1	5
13	Formanek	IM	2410	0	0	½	½	0	½	0	0	½	½	1	0	x	1	4½
14	Pasman			0	0	0	0	1	½	0	0	½	0	0	0	0	x	2

Category 9 (2457) GM = 8½ IM = 6½

Hastings 28.xii.77-14.i.78				1	2	3	4	5	6	7	8	9	0	1	2	3	4	5	
1	Djindjihashvili	GM	2535	x	½	½	½	½	1	½	1	½	½	1	1	1	1	1	10½
2	Petrosian	GM	2645	½	x	½	½	½	1	½	½	1	½	½	1	1	1	½	9½
3	Sax	GM	2565	½	½	x	½	½	½	1	½	0	1	½	1	1	1	1	9½
4	Hort	GM	2620	½	½	½	x	½	½	½	½	½	½	1	½	1	1	1	9
5	Mestel	IM	2420	½	½	½	½	x	0	½	½	1	1	1	½	1	1	0	8½
6	Tarjan	GM	2495	0	0	½	½	1	x	½	½	1	0	½	1	½	1	1	8
7	Sveshnikov	GM	2520	½	½	0	½	½	½	x	½	1	1	½	0	1	1	0	7½
8	Speelman		2395	0	½	½	½	½	½	½	x	½	½	½	½	1	½	½	7
9	Nunn	IM	2410	½	0	1	½	0	0	0	½	x	1	1	1	0	0	1	6½
10	Shamkovich	GM	2485	½	½	0	½	0	1	0	½	0	x	0	1	½	1	1	6½
11	Fedorowicz		2480	0	½	½	0	0	½	½	½	0	1	x	½	½	0	1	5½
12	Webb	IM	2430	0	0	0	½	½	0	1	½	0	0	½	x	1	1	½	5½
13	Tisdall		2375	0	0	0	0	0	½	0	0	1	½	½	0	x	1	1	4½
14	Botterill		2350	0	0	0	0	0	0	0	½	1	0	1	0	0	x	1	3½
15	Kagan	IM	2440	0	½	0	0	1	0	1	½	0	0	0	½	0	0	x	3½

Category 10 GM = 8½ IM – 7

Sarajevo 26.ii.-15.iii.78				1	2	3	4	5	6	7	8	9	0	1	2	3	4	5	6	
1	Raicevic	GM	2450	x	½	½	½	½	½	½	½	½	½	1	1	½	1	1	1	10
2	Forintos	GM	2435	½	x	½	½	1	½	½	½	½	1	½	½	1	1	1	0	9½
3	Matulovic	GM	2525	½	½	x	½	1	0	½	½	0	1	1	½	½	1	½	1	9
4	Radulov	GM	2490	½	½	½	x	½	½	0	½	½	½	½	1	½	1	1	1	9
5	Arapovic		2415	½	0	0	½	x	½	1	½	1	½	½	½	½	1	1	1	9
6	Kelecevic		2410	½	½	1	½	½	x	½	1	½	½	½	½	½	1	0	1	9
7	Osmanovic		2255	½	½	½	1	0	½	x	0	1	½	½	1	½	1	1	½	9
8	Knezevic	GM	2505	½	½	½	½	½	0	1	x	½	½	0	½	½	½	1	1	8
9	Plachetka	IM	2460	½	½	1	½	0	½	0	½	x	½	0	½	½	1	1	1	8
10	Kirov	GM	2465	½	0	0	½	½	½	½	½	½	x	½	½	½	½	1	1	7½
11	Maslesa		2305	0	½	½	½	½	½	½	1	1	½	x	0	½	½	½	½	7½
12	G.Szilagyi	IM	2365	0	½	½	0	½	½	0	½	½	½	1	x	0	½	1	1	7
13	L.Popov	IM	2435	½	0	0	½	½	½	½	½	½	½	½	1	x	0	1	0	6½
14	Covic			0	0	0	0	0	0	0	½	0	½	½	½	1	x	0	1	4
15	Dizdarevic			0	0	½	0	0	1	0	0	0	0	½	0	0	1	x	1	4
16	Ikonic			0	1	0	0	0	0	½	0	0	0	½	0	1	0	0	x	3

Category 6 (2382) GM = 11 IM = 9

Santa Fe de Bogota 11-30.iii.78				1	2	3	4	5	6	7	8	9	0	1	2	3	4	5	6	
1	Geller	GM	2590	x	1	1	½	0	1	1	1	1	1	½	1	0	1	1	1	12
2	L.Garcia		2325	0	x	½	0	½	½	½	1	1	1	1	½	1	1	1	1	10½
3	R.Hernandez	IM	2465	0	½	x	0	1	½	0	1	1	½	1	1	1	1	1	1	10½
4	G.Sigurjonsson	GM	2500	½	1	1	x	½	½	½	0	1	0	1	1	1	½	0	1	9½
5	Guild.Garcia		2365	1	½	0	½	x	0	½	1	0	1	½	1	½	1	1	1	9½
6	Panno	GM	2580	0	½	½	½	1	x	1	0	0	1	1	0	1	½	1	1	9
7	C.Cuartas	IM	2415	0	½	1	½	½	0	x	½	0	½	1	1	1	1	0	1	8½
8	Cuellar	IM	2365	0	0	0	1	0	1	½	x	½	½	½	1	0	½	1	1	7½
9	J.A.Gutierrez	IM	2380	0	0	0	0	1	1	1	½	x	0	½	1	1	0	0	1	7
10	Guil.Garcia	GM	2535	0	0	½	1	0	0	½	½	1	x	½	0	½	½	1	½	6½
11	Minaya		2355	½	0	0	0	½	0	0	½	½	½	x	½	½	1	½	1	6
12	Zapata		2355	0	½	0	0	0	1	0	0	0	1	½	x	1	½	½	½	5½
13	J.Gonzalez	IM	2370	1	0	0	0	½	0	0	1	0	½	½	0	x	½	1	0	5
14	Szmetan	IM	2420	0	0	0	½	0	½	0	½	1	½	0	½	½	x	½	½	5
15	Velandia		2220	0	0	0	1	0	0	1	0	1	0	½	½	0	½	x	0	4½
16	Acosta			0	0	0	0	0	0	0	0	0	½	0	½	1	½	1	x	3½

Category 7 (2403) GM = 10½ IM = 9

Bugojno 26.ii.-16.iii.78				1	2	3	4	5	6	7	8	9	0	1	2	3	4	5	6	
1	Karpov	GM	2725	x	½	0	1	½	1	1	½	½	1	½	1	½	½	1	½	10
2	Spassky	GM	2630	½	x	½	0	½	1	1	½	½	1	½	½	1	½	1	1	10
3	Timman	GM	2585	1	½	x	½	½	½	0	1	1	½	0	1	½	½	1	½	9
4	Ljubojevic	GM	2605	0	1	½	x	½	½	1	½	0	0	½	½	1	½	1	1	8½
5	Tal	GM	2625	½	½	½	½	x	½	½	½	½	½	½	½	1	½	½	1	8½
6	Hort	GM	2620	0	0	½	½	½	x	0	½	1	1	½	½	1	1	½	½	8
7	Larsen	GM	2620	0	0	1	0	½	1	x	1	½	½	1	1	½	½	½	0	8
8	Balashov	GM	2590	½	½	0	½	½	½	0	x	½	1	½	½	½	1	½	½	7½
9	Huebner	GM	2595	½	½	0	1	½	0	½	½	x	½	½	1	½	0	½	1	7½
10	Miles	GM	2565	0	0	½	1	½	0	½	0	½	x	½	½	½	1	½	1	7
11	Ivkov	GM	2515	½	½	1	½	½	½	0	½	½	½	x	½	½	½	0	0	6½
12	Portisch	GM	2630	0	½	0	½	½	½	0	½	0	½	½	x	½	1	½	1	6½
13	Byrne	GM	2550	½	0	½	0	0	0	½	½	½	½	½	½	x	½	1	½	6
14	Vukic	GM	2480	½	½	½	½	½	0	½	0	1	0	½	0	½	x	½	½	6
15	Bukic	GM	2500	0	0	0	0	½	½	½	½	½	½	1	½	0	½	x	½	5½
16	Gligoric	GM	2565	½	0	½	0	0	½	1	½	0	0	1	0	½	½	½	x	5½

Poland Final 5-25.ii.78	1	2	3	4	5	6	7	8	9	0	1	2	3	4	5	6	7	8	
1 Kuligowski	x	1	½	1	½	½	½	1	0	1	0	½	½	½	1	1	½	1	11
2 Sznapik	0	x	½	½	1	0	1	1	1	1	½	½	½	0	1	1	1	½	11
3 W.Schmidt	½	½	x	½	½	1	½	½	½	0	½	½	1	½	1	1	½	½	10
4 J.Adamski	0	½	½	x	½	½	½	1	½	1	½	½	½	1	½	½	½	1	10
5 Swic	½	0	½	½	x	½	½	½	1	½	½	½	½	½	½	1	1	1	10
6 Pytel	½	1	0	½	½	x	½	½	½	1	1	½	½	1	0	½	½	½	9½
7 Sydor	½	0	½	½	½	½	x	½	½	½	½	½	½	½	½	½	1	1	9
8 Bielczyk	0	0	½	0	½	½	½	x	1	½	½	1	1	1	½	½	½	½	9
9 A.Adamski	1	0	½	½	0	½	½	0	x	½	1	1	½	½	0	1	½	1	9
10 Skrobek	0	0	1	0	½	0	½	½	½	x	1	1	½	1	1	0	0	1	8½
11 Gralka	1	½	½	½	½	0	½	½	0	0	x	½	½	½	½	½	1	½	8
12 Doda	½	½	½	½	½	½	½	0	0	0	½	x	1	1	1	0	1	0	8
13 Witkowski	½	½	0	½	½	½	½	0	½	½	½	0	x	½	½	½	1	½	7½
14 Kruszynski	½	1	½	0	½	0	½	0	½	0	½	0	½	x	½	0	1	½	6½
15 Dobrzynski	0	0	0	½	½	1	½	½	1	0	½	0	½	½	x	1	0	0	6½
16 Lipski	0	0	0	½	0	½	½	½	0	1	½	1	½	1	0	x	½	0	6½
17 Pinkas	½	0	½	½	0	½	0	½	½	1	0	0	0	0	1	½	x	1	6½
18 Pokojowczyk	0	½	½	0	0	½	0	½	0	0	½	1	½	½	1	1	0	x	6½

DDR Final Eggesin 78	1	2	3	4	5	6	7	8	9	0	1	2	3	4	5	
1 Knaak	x	½	1	½	1	1	1	1	1	1	1	1	1	1	1	13
2 L.Espig	½	x	½	½	½	½	1	½	½	1	1	1	1	½	1	10
3 Bruggemann	0	½	x	½	1	½	1	1	½	0	½	½	½	1	½	8
4 Vogt	½	½	½	x	½	½	½	0	½	0	1	1	½	1	1	8
5 Hesse	0	½	0	½	x	½	½	1	½	1	½	½	½	1	1	8
6 Heinig	0	½	½	½	½	x	0	½	½	½	½	½	1	1	1	7½
7 Uhlmann	0	0	0	½	½	1	x	1	½	1	½	0	0	1	1	7
8 Liebert	0	½	0	1	0	½	0	x	½	1	1	½	½	½	1	7
9 T.Espig	0	½	½	½	½	½	½	½	x	0	½	½	½	1	½	6½
10 Enders	0	0	1	1	0	½	0	0	1	x	0	1	½	0	1	6
11 Raitza	0	0	½	0	½	½	½	0	½	1	x	½	½	½	1	6
12 Mohring	0	0	½	0	½	½	1	½	½	0	½	x	1	0	½	5½
13 Starck	0	0	½	½	½	0	1	½	½	½	½	0	x	½	½	5½
14 Okrajek	0	½	0	0	0	0	0	½	0	1	½	1	½	x	½	4½
15 Bodach	0	0	½	0	0	0	0	0	½	0	0	½	½	½	x	2½

Trstenik 4-18.iii.78

				1	2	3	4	5	6	7	8	9	0	1	2	3	4	
1	Todorcevic	IM	2435	x	½	½	1	1	½	½	1	½	1	1	0	1	1	9½
2	Sahovic	IM	2490	½	x	½	0	½	1	½	1	1	½	1	1	1	1	9½
3	Ciric	GM	2430	½	½	x	½	½	½	½	½	1	½	½	1	1	1	8½
4	Augustin	IM	2430	0	1	½	x	1	½	½	½	1	1	0	½	½	1	8
5	Rajkovic	GM	2490	0	½	½	0	x	0	1	½	1	½	½	1	1	1	7½
6	Spasov	GM	2450	½	0	½	½	1	x	½	½	½	½	½	1	0	1	7
7	Lechtynsky	IM	2420	½	½	½	½	0	½	x	½	½	½	1	½	½	1	7
8	Tringov	GM	2480	0	0	½	½	½	½	½	x	½	1	0	1	1	1	7
9	Janosevic	GM	2455	½	0	0	0	0	½	½	½	x	1	1	1	½	1	6½
10	Martinovic	IM	2460	0	½	½	0	½	½	½	0	0	x	1	½	1	1	6
11	Haik	IM	2425	0	0	½	1	½	½	0	1	0	0	x	½	1	½	5½
12	Giffard		2365	1	0	0	½	0	0	½	0	0	½	½	x	½	1	4½
13	Nedeljkovic			0	0	0	½	0	1	½	0	½	0	0	½	x	0	3
14	Jankovic			0	0	0	0	0	0	0	0	0	0	½	0	1	x	1½

Category 7 (2409) GM = 9½ IM = 7½

Havana 24.ii-8.iii.78

			1	2	3	4	5	6	7	8	9	0	1	2	
1	S.Garcia	GM	x	½	1	½	½	1	1	½	½	½	1	1	8
2	R.Hernandez	IM	½	x	½	½	½	½	½	½	1	1	1	1	7½
3	Guil.Garcia	GM	0	½	x	1	1	½	0	1	1	1	1	0	7
4	J.Diaz	IM	½	½	0	x	½	1	1	½	½	1	1	½	7
5	Nogueira	IM	½	½	0	½	x	½	0	1	1	1	1	1	7
6	Estevez	IM	0	½	½	0	½	x	½	½	1	1	1	1	6½
7	Vera		0	½	1	0	1	½	x	½	½	0	0	1	5
8	Jimenez	IM	½	½	0	½	0	½	½	x	½	½	½	½	4½
9	F.J.Perez	IM	½	0	0	½	0	0	½	½	x	0	1	1	4
10	Veliz		½	0	0	0	0	0	1	½	1	x	0	1	4
11	Gilb.Garcia		0	0	0	0	0	0	1	½	0	1	x	1	3½
12	Ortega		0	0	1	½	0	0	0	½	0	0	0	x	2

Bucharest 7-23.iii.78			1	2	3	4	5	6	7	8	9	0	1	2	3	4	5	6	
1	Alburt	GM 2510	x	1	½	½	0	1	1	½	1	1	½	½	½	½	1	1	10½
2	Ciocaltea	IM 2455	0	x	½	1	½	½	½	½	1	½	½	1	1	½	1	1	10
3	Uhlmann	GM 2575	½	½	x	0	0	½	½	1	1	½	½	½	1	1	1	1	9½
4	Ftacnik	IM 2380	½	0	1	x	0	½	½	0	1	½	1	1	1	½	½	1	9
5	Stoica	IM 2420	1	½	1	1	x	0	½	½	½	½	½	½	½	½	½	½	8½
6	Marjanovic	IM 2450	0	½	½	½	1	x	½	1	½	0	½	½	½	½	1	1	8½
7	Ghinda	2445	0	½	½	½	½	½	x	1	½	½	½	½	½	1	½	½	8
8	Ungureanu	2410	½	½	0	1	½	0	0	x	½	½	½	½	1	½	1	1	8
9	Biriescu	2390	0	0	½	0	½	½	½	½	x	1	½	½	½	1	1	1	8
10	Padevsky	GM 2450	0	½	½	½	½	1	½	½	0	x	½	½	½	½	½	1	7½
11	Minev	IM 2390	½	½	½	0	½	½	½	½	½	½	x	½	½	0	½	1	7
12	Adamski	IM 2470	½	0	0	0	½	½	½	½	½	½	½	x	1	½	½	0	6
13	Suba	IM 2430	½	0	0	0	½	½	½	0	½	½	½	0	x	1	½	1	6
14	Lukacs	IM 2460	½	½	0	½	½	½	0	½	0	½	1	½	0	x	½	0	5½
15	Vaisman	IM 2400	0	0	0	½	½	0	½	0	0	½	½	½	½	½	x	½	4½
16	Bellon	IM 2350	0	0	0	0	0	½	½	0	0	0	0	1	0	1	½	x	3½

Category 8 (2437) GM = 10 IM = 8

33 Jugoslavia Final 78		1	2	3	4	5	6	7	8	9	0	1	2	3	4	5	6	7	8	
1	Ivkov	x	½	½	½	½	1	½	½	½	½	½	½	½	½	½	1	1	½	10
2	Matanovic	½	x	0	½	½	½	½	½	½	½	½	1	1	1	½	½	1	½	10
3	Velimrovic	½	1	x	1	1	0	1	0	½	½	0	0	1	0	½	1	½	1	9½
4	Matulovic	½	½	0	x	½	1	½	½	½	½	1	0	½	1	½	½	1	½	9½
5	Kovacevic	½	½	0	½	x	½	½	½	½	½	1	1	½	0	1	1	0	1	9½
6	Nikolac	0	½	1	0	½	x	½	½	½	1	½	0	1	½	1	½	½	1	9½
7	Knezevic	½	½	0	½	½	½	x	½	½	½	½	½	½	1	½	½	1	1	9½
8	Parma	½	½	1	½	½	½	½	x	½	½	½	½	0	½	½	½	1	½	9
9	Bukic	½	½	½	½	½	½	½	½	x	½	½	½	½	½	1	½	1	0	9
10	Kurajica	½	½	½	½	½	0	½	½	½	x	½	1	½	½	½	½	1	½	9
11	Rajkovic	½	½	1	0	0	½	½	½	½	½	x	1	0	½	½	½	1	1	9
12	Ivanovic	½	0	1	1	0	1	½	½	½	0	0	x	1	½	½	½	0	½	8
13	Vukic	½	0	0	½	½	0	½	1	½	½	1	0	x	1	0	1	0	½	7½
14	Hulak	½	0	1	0	1	½	0	½	½	½	½	½	0	x	½	0	0	1	7
15	Raicevic	½	½	½	½	0	0	½	½	0	½	½	½	1	½	x	0	0	1	7
16	Mestrovic	0	½	0	½	0	½	½	½	½	½	½	½	0	1	1	x	0	½	7
17	Planinc	0	0	½	0	1	½	0	0	0	0	0	1	1	1	1	1	x	0	7
18	Ostojic	½	½	0	½	0	0	0	½	1	½	0	½	½	0	0	½	1	x	6

Baguio City 3-19.iii.78

				1	2	3	4	5	6	7	8	9	0	1	2	3	4	
1	Quinteros	GM	2480	x	½	1	1	½	½	1	1	0	½	0	1	1	1	9
2	Torre	GM	2490	½	x	1	½	½	0	1	1	1	1	1	0	½	1	9
3	Ardijansjah	IM	2330	0	0	x	1	1	1	0	1	0	1	1	1	1	1	9
4	Harandi	IM	2390	0	½	0	x	½	1	1	½	1	½	½	½	1	1	8
5	Balinas	GM	2440	½	½	0	½	x	½	0	1	1	1	1	½	1	½	8
6	Sharif	IM	2380	½	1	0	0	½	x	½	½	1	1	1	½	½	½	7½
7	Sampouw		2315	0	0	1	0	1	½	x	½	1	½	1	1	0	1	7½
8	Mascarinas		2355	0	0	0	½	0	½	½	x	1	1	1	1	1	1	7½
9	Shirazi		2285	1	0	1	0	0	0	0	0	x	0	1	1	½	1	5½
10	Bachtiar		2335	½	0	0	½	0	0	½	0	1	x	0	1	½	1	5
11	Cardoso	IM	2320	1	0	0	½	0	0	0	0	0	1	x	1	½	1	5
12	R.Rodriguez		2415	0	1	0	½	½	½	0	0	0	0	0	x	1	1	4½
13	Laird			0	½	0	0	0	½	1	0	½	½	½	0	x	½	4
14	Hon			0	0	0	0	½	½	0	0	0	0	0	0	½	x	1½

Category 5 (2353) GM = 10 IM = 8½

Washington iii.78

			1	2	3	4	5	6	7	8	9	0	
Kavalek	GM	2570	½	½	½	½	½	½	1	½	1	1	6½
Andersson	GM	2545	½	½	½	½	½	½	0	½	0	0	3½

Bialystok 5-19.iii.78

1	Butnorius		2350	8
2	Holm		2380	8
3	Pahtz		2385	7½
4	Meduna		2425	7
5	Bielczyk		2380	6
6	Pokojowczyk		2385	5½
7	Lehmann	IM	2405	5½
8	Szymczak	IM	2390	5½
9	Gorski			4½
10	Liangov		2325	3½
11	Klimaszewski			3½
12	Cywlik			1½

Stockholm 27.xii.77-4.i.78

1	Jansson		2395	7
2	L.Karlsson		2360	7
3	L.Schneider	IM	2430	7
4	Schussler		2365	6½
5	Kaiszauri		2420	6½
6	Rantanen	IM	2420	6½
7	Salonen			6½
8	Ekstrom		2360	6½
9	Hansson		2345	6½
10	O.Jakobsen	IM	2400	6
11	Renman		2400	6
12	Wedberg		2360	6
13	Rorvall		2350	6
14	Ivarsson		2355	6
15	Rooze		2355	6
16	Hammar		2385	6
17	Ornstein	IM	2425	5½
18	W.Ott		2215	5½
19	Cramling		2355	5½
20	Poutiainen	IM	2425	5½
21	Marszalek		2340	5½
22	Sznapik	IM	2430	5½
23	Brinck-Claussen		2385	5½
24	Jonsson		2230	5½
25	Helmertz		2305	5½
26	Petursson		2350	5½

... (91)

Bergen 14-19.i.78 9rd

1	Farago	GM	2510	6½
2	Westerinen	GM	2450	6
3	Rantanen	IM	2420	6
4	Kaiszauri	IM	2420	5½
5	Niklasson		2340	5½
6	Helmers		2345	5½
7	L.Lengyel	GM	2430	5
8	Iskov		2395	5
9	Ogaard	IM	2435	5

... (18)

Zurich 26-29.xii.77

1	Govedarica	IM	2405	6½
2	B.Toth	IM	2480	6
3	Nemet	IM	2425	6
4	Zichichi	IM	2360	6
5	Hartmann		2240	6
6	Ostojic	GM	2420	5½
7	Mariotti	GM	2475	5½
8	Karl			5½
9	Rukavina	IM	2435	5½
10	Miltner			5½
11	Engel			5½

... ( )

Groningen 20.xii.77-5.i.78 13 rds

1	Taulbut	2405	9
2	Dolmatov	2495	9
3	Georgiev	2415	9
4	Foisor	2310	8½
5	Groszpeter	2230	8
6	Goodman	2320	8
7	Mokry	2310	8
8	Upton		8
9	Pasman		7½
10	Arnason	2350	7½
11	Pederson	2380	7½

... (32)

Trinec 25.xii.77-5.i.78

1	Bukal	IM	2410	7½
2	Sikora		2415	7½
3	Adamski	IM	2470	6½
4	Jankovec		2370	6½
5	Estrin	IM	2430	6
6	Mrdja			6
7	Gliksman	IM	2340	5½
8	Kornasiewicz		2275	5½
9	Kupka		2355	5½
10	Schrancz		2300	4½
11	Mesiarik		2345	3½
12	Marosczyk			1½

Category 4 IM = 7½

Sandanski 14-25.ii.78

1	Inkiov	IM	2450	8
2	Velikov	IM	2430	8
3	Spassov	GM	2450	6½
4	V.Antonov		2345	6½
5	S.Kostadinov			6½
6	A.Kostadinov			6½
7	Grigorov		2340	5½
8	Vagalinski			4½
9	Mitov			4½
10	Gochev			4½
11	Grancharov			4
12	Gelemerov			1

Brno 25.xii.77-6.i.78

1	Hausner		2365	9½
2	Petrienko		2340	9
3	Kizlov			8½
4	Mozny			8
5	Blatny		2325	7½
6	Mista	IM	2360	7½
7	Lukovnikov			7
8	Beil		2350	6
9	Danek			6
10	Petrusiak		2310	6
11	Pise			6
12	Vechet			5½
13	Spevak			3
14	Jaros			1½

Kringsja Oslo 6-12.i.78 9rd

1	Ornstein	IM	2425	7
2	P.Littlewood		2345	6
3	Petursson		2350	6
4	B.Toth	IM	2480	5½
5	Rantanen	IM	2420	5
6	Niklasson		2340	5
7	Gereben	IM	2270	5
8	Whiteley		2385	5
9	Petterson			5
10	Helmers		2345	5
11	Iskov		2395	4½
12	Orseth			4½
13	Lekander		2280	4½
14	T.Kristiansen		2320	4½

... (22)

1 b3

1 Petrosian-Sveshnikov Hastings 77/8

1 c4 e6 2 Nf3 d5 3 b3 Nf6 4 Bb2 Bd6 5 g3 b6 6 Bg2 6 cxd5 exd5 7 Bg2 0-0 8 0-0 Re8 9 Nc3 Bb7 10 Rc1 a6 11 Nh4 Nbd7 12 d3 Rae8? Grigorian-Sveshnikov, USSR Final 77; 12...Nc5! **Bb7 7 0-0 0-0 8 Nc3 a6 9 Rc1 Nbd7 10 Qc2 Qe7** 10...Rfe8! **11 cxd5 exd5 12 e3** 12 Nh4 g6∞ **Rfe8 13 Rfe1 Ne5?!** 13...c5 14 d4 Rac8= **14 Nxe5 Bxe5 15 Ne2! Bxb2 16 Qxb2 a5 17 a3 c5 18 d4 Ne4 19 Nf4 Qf6** 19...Rac8 **20 Rc2 cxd4 21 Qxd4 Qxd4 22 exd4 Nf6 += 23 Rec1 g5! 24 Nd3** 24 Rc7 gxf4 25 Rxb7 Rac8 26 Rd1 f3 =+ **Rac8 25 Rc7 Ba6 26 Ne5 Rxc7 27 Rxc7 Rc8 28 Rxc8+ Bxc8 29 Kf1 Be6 30 Ke2 Ne8 31 Nf3 f6 32 Nd2 Kf7 33 Nb1 Ke7 34 Nc3 Kd6 35 Kd2 Ng7 36 Nd1 ½-½ Sveshnikov**

2 Begun-Kapengut Minsk 78

1 Nf3 Nf6 2 b3 g6 3 Bb2 Bg7 4 g3 d6! 4...0-0 5 Bg2 d6 6 d4 e5 7 dxe5 Ng4 8 h3 Nxe5 9 Nxe5 dxe5 Smyslov-Polugaevsky, Palma 70 **5 d4 c5 6 c4?!** 6 dxc5! Qa5+ 7 Nbd2 Qxc5 8 Bd4 Qh5 9 c4 Keene **Ne4! =+** 6...cxd4 7 Nxd4 d5! 8 Bg2 dxc4 Keene **7 Bg2 Qa5+ 8 Kf1** 8 Nbd2 Nc3 **Nc6 9 e3 0-0 10 Ne1?** 10 Qe2 =+ **f5 11 f3 cxd4! 12 exd4 e5! 13 fxe4?** −+ 13 dxe5 Be6∓; 13 d5 Qb6 14 Qe2 Nd4 **fxe4+ 14 Kg1 Bg4 15 Qd2** 15 Bc3 Bxd1 16 Bxa5 exd4 −+ **Bh6! 0-1 Kapengut**

1 c4 c5

3 Tal-Zuravlev Sochi 77

1 c4 c5 2 Nf3 Nf6 3 Nc3 d5 4 cxd5 Nxd5 5 d4 cxd4 5...Nxc3 6 bxc3 g6∞ **6 Qxd4 Nxc3 7 Qxc3 Nc6 8 e4 Qa5??** 8...e6 9 Bb5 += **9 Qxa5 Nxa5 10 Bb5+ Bd7 11 Bxd7+ Kxd7 12 0-0 Nc6 13 Bf4 e6** 13...h6!? (Δ g5, Bg7) 14 Rfd1+ Ke6 15 h4 g6 Δ Bg7 **14 Rac1 Rd8 15 Rfd1+ Ke8 16 Rxd8+ Kxd8 17 Ne5 Nxe5 18 Bxe5 h5** 18...f6 19 Bb8+− **19 Bb8 a6 20 e5! Be7 21 Rc7 Re8 22 Kf1!** 22 Rxb7? Kc8 23 Rb6 Bc5 24 Rc6+ Kxb8 25 Rxc5 Rd8=; 23 Rb3 Rd8= **b6 23 Ke2 Bc5 24 Rxf7 Re7 25 Rxe7 Kxe7 26 f4 +− Kd7 27 Kd3 b5 28 Ke4 g6 29 h3 Ke8 30 g4 hxg4 31 hxg4 Bb6 32 Bd6 Bf2 33 Bb4 Bb6 34 Bc3 Bf2 35 f5 gxf5+ 36 gxf5 Kf7 37 f6 Bb6 38 Bd4 Ba5 39 Bc5 Be1 40 Kd3 Bg3 41 Bd4 Be1 42 Kc2 Bb4 43 Kb3 Bf8 44 Be3 Ke8 45 Kc3** Δ b4, a3, Kh5 **a5 46 Kb3 a4+ 47 Kc3 Kf7 48 Kd4 Ke8 49 Bd2 Kf7 50 a3** Δ Bb4, Kc5 **1-0 Petrosian**

4 Tukmakov-Tal 45 USSR Final 77

1 Nf3 Nf6 2 c4 c5 3 Nc3 d5 4 cxd5 Nxd5 5 e4 Nb4! 5...Nxc3 6 bxc3 g6=; 6 dxc3 Qxd1+ 7 Nxd1 += **6 Bb5+** 6 Bc4 Be6! **N8c6** 6...Bd7 7 a3!+= **7 0-0?** TN 7 a3 Nd3+ 8 Ke2 Nf4+ 9 Kf1 Ne6 =+ **a6 8 Ba4 b5 9 a3 Nd3 10 Nxb5 axb5 11 Bxb5 Qd6 12 Qb3** 12 b4!? **Ba6!** 12...Nxc1 13 Raxc1 Δ d4, Qc3; 12...Nf4? 13 d4!

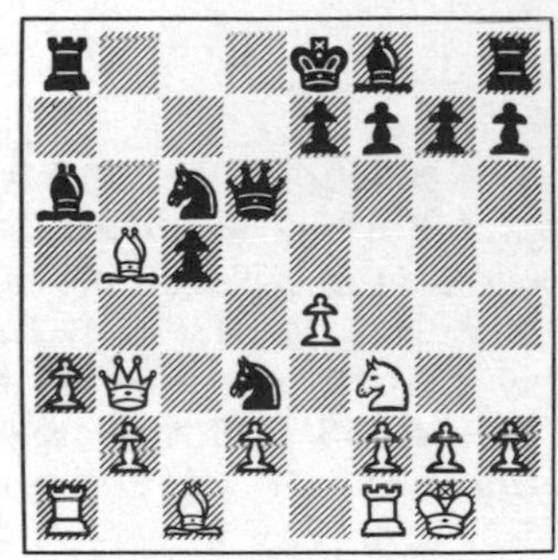

13 ♕a4 ♗xb5! 13...♗b7 14 ♕b3∞ **14 ♕xa8+ ♘d8 15 b4 ♗c6 16 bxc5 ♕g6 17 ♕b8 ♕xe4** −+ 17...♗xe4 −+ **18 a4 e5 19 ♖a3 ♗xc5 20 ♖xd3 ♕xd3 21 ♘xe5 ♕e4 22 ♘xc6 ♕xc6 23 ♖e1+** 23 ♕e5+ ♔f8 Δ f6, ♔f7 −+ **♔d7 24 d4 ♗xd4 25 ♖d1 ♕xa4 0-1 Petrosian**

5 Rukavina-L.Lengyel
Virovitica 77

1 ♘f3 ♘f6 2 c4 c5 3 ♘c3 d5 4 cxd5 ♘xd5 5 g3 ♘c6 6 ♗g2 ♘c7 7 d3 7 ♕a4 ♗d7 8 ♕e4! ♘e6 9 e3 g6 10 d4 cxd4 11 exd4 ♗g7 12 ♗e3 f5 13 ♕d5 Romanishin-Tal, USSR Final 76 **e5 8 ♗e3?!** 8 ♘d2 **♗e7 9 ♘d2 ♗d7 10 0-0 0-0 11 ♘c4 f6 12 f4 exf4 13 gxf4 ♖b8! 14 ♖c1?!** 14 ♗f2 **♘d4 15 ♗f2 ♗g4 16 ♘e3 ♗h5 17 ♕d2 f5 18 ♖ce1?** 18 ♖fe1 **♖e8 19 ♗g3** 19 ♘ed5 ♘xd5 20 ♗xd5+ ♔h8 21 ♗g3 ♗f6! 22 e3 ♘e2+ 23 ♘xe2 ♕xd5 24 ♘c3 ♕d7 **b5! 20 ♘cd5 ♗d6 21 ♖f2 ♔h8 22 a3 c4! 23 dxc4 ♗c5 24 b4** 24 ♘xc7 ♖xe3! 25 ♘d5 ♘xe2+ **♘xd5 25 cxd5 ♗b6** 25...♘b3 Δ ♗xe3 **26 ♕d3 ♖xe3 27 ♕xe3 ♘c2 28 ♕d2 ♘xe1 29 ♕xe1 ♕e7 30 ♔h1 ♗xf2 31 ♗xf2 ♖e8 32 h3 ♕c7** 32...♕xe2 33 ♕xe2 ♖xe2 34 ♗xa7 **33 e3 ♕c2 34 ♔g1 ♗f7 35 ♕a1 ♕d2 36 ♕b1 ♖c8 37 ♕xf5 ♖c2 38 ♕xc2 ♕xc2 39 e4 ♕c1+ 40 ♔h2 ♕xf4+ 41 ♗g3 ♕d2 42 d6 ♗g6 0-1**

6 Raicevic-Mestrovic
Jugoslavia Final 78

1 c4 c5 2 ♘f3 ♘c6 3 ♘c3 e5!? 4 d3 f5 5 g3 ♘f6 6 ♗g2 ♗e7 7 0-0 0-0 8 ♘e1 ♕e8 9 f4 9 ♘d5 ♗d8 **d6 10 a3 ♗d8!** Δ ♗a5xc3 **11 e3 ♗e6 12 b3** Δ ♘c2, d4 **♗a5! 13 ♗d2 ♖d8= 14 ♖c1 exf4 15 gxf4 d5!? 16 cxd5 ♗xd5!? 17 ♘xd5 ♘xd5 18 b4?** 18 ♗xd5+ ♖xd5 19 b4 cxb4 20 ♕b3+ ♕f7 21 d4∞

18...♘xe3!!∓ 19 ♕b3+ ♔h8 20 ♗xc6 bxc6 21 bxa5 21 ♖f3 c4! 22 ♕b2 (22 ♖xe3 ♗b6 −+) ♗b6∓ **♕g6+! 22 ♔f2 ♘g4+ 23 ♔e2 ♕h5! −+ 24 d4 ♘xh2+ 25 ♔f2 ♖fe8! 26 ♘f3 ♘xf3 27 ♕xf3 ♕h2+ 28 ♕g2 ♖e2+ 29 ♔xe2 ♕xg2+ 30 ♖f2 ♖e8+ 31 ♗e3 ♕e4 0-1 Maric**

7 Quinteros-Tringov Bar 77

1 c4 ♘f6 2 ♘c3 c5 3 ♘f3 e6 4 g3 ♘c6 5 ♗g2 d5 6 cxd5 ♘xd5 7 0-0 ♗e7 8 d4 0-0 9 e4 ♘xc3 9...♘b6 10 d5 exd5 11 exd5 ♘b4 12 ♘e5! Quinteros-Diesen, Polanica 77 **10 bxc3 cxd4 11 cxd4 b6 12 ♗e3** 12 d5 exd5 13 exd5 ♘b4 14 ♘d4 ♗a6 Pachman-Hutchings, Barcelona 75 **♗b7 13 ♖c1 ♘a5 14 ♕d3 ♖c8 15 ♖xc8 ♕xc8 16 ♖c1 ♕a8 17 d5!**

17...exd5 17...♖d8 18 ♗g5 f6 19 ♗h3! fxg5 20 ♗xe6+ ♔h8 21 ♘e5 ♖f8 22

♘g6+! hxg6 23 g4; 20...♔f8 21 ♘e5 ♗c8 22 ♕f3+ ♗f6 23 ♖c7 ♗xe6 24 dxe6 ♖e8 25 ♘d7+ ♔g8 26 ♕xf6 +−; 24...♖c8 25 ♘d7+ ♔g8 26 e5! ♕xf3 27 ♖xc8+ +−; 19...exd5 20 ♗e6+ ♔h8 21 ♘h4! g6 22 ♘xg6+! hxg6 23 g4 fxg5 24 ♕d4+ ♔h7 25 ♖c3 +− **18 exd5 ♝xd5 19 ♞g5 ♝xg5 20 ♝xd5 ♛d8 21 ♝xg5 ♛xg5 22 ♜c7! h5** 22... ♕f6 23 ♕e4 a6 24 ♖xf7 +− **23 ♛f3 ♛g6 24 ♜xa7 h4 25 ♚g2 hxg3 26 hxg3 ♛f6 27 g4! ♛xf3+ 28 ♚xf3 ♜d8 29 ♝xf7+ ♚f8 30 ♜c7! ♜d6 31 g5 ♞c6 32 ♚e4 g6 33 ♝b3 ♞e7 34 f4 ♜d2 35 ♜b7 ♜d6 36 ♚e5 ♜c6 37 ♝e6! ♞f5! 38 ♜f7+ ♚e8 39 ♝d7+ 1-0**

8 Gheorghiu-Ilijin Rumania Final 77

1 c4 c5 2 ♞f3 ♞f6 3 ♞c3 e6 4 g3 ♝e7!? 5 ♝g2 0-0 6 0-0 ♞c6 7 d4 cxd4 8 ♞xd4 ♞e5 9 b3 a6 10 ♝b2 ♞g6 11 e4 ♛c7 12 f4! d6 13 f5! exf5 13...♘e5 14 fxe6 fxe6 15 ♗h3!± **14 ♞xf5 ♝xf5 15 exf5 ♞e5 16 ♚h1 ♜fe8 17 h3 ♜ab8 18 ♜c1** 18 a4 Δ ♗c1± **♛a5 19 g4 h6 20 a4 ♛b6!** Δ ♕e3-g5-h4∝ **21 ♞e2! ♝f8 22 ♞f4 ♛d8 23 ♛d2 ♞fd7 24 ♝d4 ♝e7 25 ♜cd1 b5??** 25...♘c5 **26 cxb5 axb5 27 a5! +− b4 28 a6 ♛a5 29 a7 ♜a8 30 ♝xa8 ♜xa8 31 ♛g2! ♛d8** 31...♖xa7 32 ♖a1 **32 ♞d5** 32 ♕b7 Δ ♘d5 +− **♝f8 33 ♞c7 ♜xa7 34 ♞e6! +− ♛b8** 34...fxe6 35 ♗xa7 exf5 36 ♖xf5 +− **35 ♝xa7 ♛xa7 36 ♞xf8 ♞xf8 37 ♜xd6 ♛e3 38 ♜d8! ♛xb3 39 f6??** Zeitnot; 39 ♖fa1! +− **gxf6 40 ♜xf6 ♚g7 41 ♜f5 ♞fg6! 42 ♜d2! ♞h4?! 43 ♛d5!! +− ♛xd5** 43...♕xh3+ 44 ♖h2 **44 ♜xd5 ♞xf5 45 ♜xe5 ♞d6 46 ♜d5 ♞e4 47 ♜b5 ♞g5 48 ♚g2 ♞e6 49 ♚g3 ♚g6 50 h4! b3 51 ♜xb3 ♚g7** 51...f5 52 ♖b6 ♔f6 53 g5+! +− **52 ♜b6 ♞c7 53 ♚f3 ♞e6 54 ♚e4 ♞f8 55 ♚d5 ♞g6 56 h5! ♞f8 57 ♚d6 ♚f6 58 ♜b5! ♞h7 59 ♜f5+ ♚g7 60 ♚e7 1-0** 60...♘g5 61 ♖f6! **Gheorghiu**

9 Vukic-Parma
Jugoslavia Final 78

1 ♞f3 c5 2 c4 ♞c6 3 ♞c3 ♞f6 4 g3 e6 5 ♝g2 d5 6 cxd5 ♞xd5 7 0-0 ♝e7 8 d4 0-0 9 ♞xd5 exd5 10 dxc5 ♝xc5 11 a3 ♝e7! 11...a5?! 12 ♘e1 d4 13 ♘d3! += **12 ♞e1?!** 12 b4! ♗f6 13 ♖a2 Δ ♖d2 **♝f6!** 12...♗e6?! 13 ♘d3 Δ 14 ♘f4 **13 ♞d3** 13 ♗xd5? ♗e6 14 e4 ♘e7!; 13 ♕xd5? ♘d4 14 ♕c4 b5!∓ **♝f5 14 ♞f4 d4 15 ♝d2 ♜e8 16 ♜e1 ♝e4 17 ♝xe4?!** 17 ♕b3! **♜xe4 18 ♛b3 ♛d7 19 ♛d5?** 19 ♖ad1! **♛e7= 20 ♜ad1 ♜ad8 21 ♛b3 ♛d7 22 ♞d3 ♛c7 23 ♞f4 ♛d7?** 23...♗g5! =+ **24 ♛f3 ♜de8 25 ♞d3 ♜4e7 26 ♝f4 ♛f5 27 ♜c1 h6 28 h4 ♛g6 29 ♚f1 ♝e5 30 h5! ♛d6 31 ♝d2 ♝f6 32 ♝b4! += ♞xb4 33 axb4 ♝g5 34 ♜c2 ♛e6 35 ♜a1 ♛b3 36 ♞e1 ♛xb4 37 ♜xa7 ♛b5 38 ♜a3 ♛d7 39 ♚g2** 39 ♖b3? ♕h3+ 40 ♔g1 ♖e3! −+ 41 fxe3 ♖xe3 42 ♖xe3 ♗xe3+ **♜e5 40 ♜a7 ♜b5 41 ♞d3 ♝f6 42 b4** 42 ♘c5? ♕c8! **♝e7 43 ♜c4 ♝f8 44 ♜c2 ♜c8 45 ♜xc8 ♛xc8 46 ♜a5 ♛e8=** 46...♖xa5?! 47 bxa5 ♕d7 48 ♕e4 Δ ♘e5 += **47 ♜a7 ♝xb4?!** 47...♕c8= **48 ♜xb7 ♜xb7 49 ♛xb7 ♝d2 50 ♛f3 ♝g5 51 g4! ♛e7 52 ♚f1 ♝f6 53 ♛d5 ♛c7 54 ♚g2 ♛e7 55 ♚f3 ♛c7 56 ♛a8+ ♚h7 57 ♛e4+ ♚g8 58 ♚g2 ♛c8 59 ♞b4?!** 59 ♔h3! Δ f4, ♘e1-f3, g5± **♛d7 60 ♞d5 ♛d8 61 f3 ♛d7 62 ♚h3 ♛d8 63 f4 ♛d7 64 ♞b4 ♛a4 65 ♞d3 ♛c2 66 ♚g2 ♚h8 67 ♚f3 ♛d2 68 ♚g2 g6? 69 ♛e8+ ♚g7 70 hxg6 fxg6** 70...♔xg6? 71 ♕g8+ ♗g7 72 ♘e5+ ♔f6 73 ♕d8+ ♔e6 74 ♕d7+ +− **71 ♞c5! ♝h4??** 71...♔h7!? 72 ♕f7+ ♗g7 73 ♕e7 += **72 ♞e6+ ♚f6 73 ♞xd4 +− ♛e1?**

73...♕xf4? 74 ♕f8+ ♔e5 75 ♘f3+ ♔e4 76 ♕b4+ ♔e3 77 ♕d2+ ♔e4 78 ♕d4 mate **74 ♛f8 mate 1-0 Vukic**

10 Diesen-Andersson
Torremolinos 78
1 d4 ♞f6 2 c4 e6 3 g3 c5 4 ♞f3 4 d5 exd5 5 cxd5 g6 6 ♗g2 d6 7 ♘f3 ♗g7 8 0-0 0-0 9 ♘c3 a6 10 a4 ♘bd7 **cxd4 5 ♞xd4 ♝b4+! 6 ♝d2** 6 ♘c3 ♘e4 7 ♕d3 ♕a5 8 ♘c2 ♘xc3 9 ♘xb4 ♘xa2 10 ♖xa2 ♕xb4+ 11 ♗d2 ♕e7 12 ♗c3 0-0! 13 ♗g2 d5! 14 cxd5 exd5 15 ♗xd5 ♗xe6= **♛b6! 7 ♝xb4 ♛xb4+ 8 ♞c3! ♞c6!** TN 8...♕xb2? 9 ♘db5! ♕b4 10 ♕b3!; 8...♕xc4 9 e4! ♕c5 10 ♖c1 += **9 ♞b5 0-0 10 e3 d5! 11 a3 ♛a5** 11...♕e7 **12 c5 ♛d8 13 ♜c1** 13 ♗g2 b6 **♜b8! 14 b4 a5! 15 ♛a4 ♝d7 16 ♛b3 axb4 17 axb4 e5!± 18 ♝g2** 18 ♘xd5 ♘xd5 19 ♕xd5 ♘xb4 Δ ♕a5! **♝e6! 19 ♜d1 d4! 20 ♛b1 ♛e7! 21 ♞e4 dxe3! 22 ♞xf6+ ♛xf6 23 fxe3 ♜a8! 24 ♜d6 ♛g5 −+ 25 ♛c1 ♜a1!!**

26 ♛xa1 ♛xe3+ 0-1 27 ♔f1 ♗c4+ 28 ♖d3 ♗xd3 mate; 27 ♔d1 ♗b3 mate **Pavlov**

11 Sosonko-Timman Tilburg 77
1 d4 ♞f6 2 c4 e6 3 g3 c5 4 ♞f3 cxd4 5 ♞xd4 d5 6 ♝g2 e5 7 ♞b3 d4 8 e3 8 ♗g5 ♘c6 9 0-0 ♗e7 Hort-Smejkal, Novi Sad 76 10 e3= **♝g4! 9 f3** 9 ♕d3?! ♘c6 10 exd4 ♘b4! 11 ♕d2 exd4 12 0-0 d3∓; 10 ♗xc6+ bxc6 11 exd4 e4! Δ ♗h3∓ **♝e6 10 exd4 ♝xc4!? 11 dxe5 ♞d5≈ 12 ♞c3 ♝b4 13 ♝d2 ♝xc3 14 ♝xc3 ♞c6 15 ♛d2 ♛b6 16 ♞a5! ♞e3** 16...♘xa5? 17 ♗xa5 ♕e3+ 18 ♕xe3 ♘xe3 19 ♔f2±; 17...♕b5? 18 b3 +−; 17...♕e6 18 f4 Δ b3± **17 ♞xc4 ♞xc4 18 ♛f2 ♞e3 19 ♚e2! ♞xg2 20 ♛xb6 axb6 21 ♚f2 ♞h4 22 gxh4 ♚e7 23 ♜hg1 ♜hg8 24 ♜g4** 24 h5!? **h5= 25 ♜e4 ♚e6 26 a3 ♜ad8 27 ♜g1 ♞e7 28 ♜b4 ♞d5 29 ♜b5 ♜c8 30 ♜d1 ♜c5 31 ♜b3 ♜gc8 32 ♚g3 ½-½ Webb**

12 Karpov-Miles Tilburg 77
1 c4 c5 2 ♞f3 ♞f6 3 ♞c3 ♞c6 4 d4 cxd4 5 ♞xd4 e6 6 g3 ♛b6 7 ♞b3 ♞e5 8 e4 ♝b4 9 ♛e2 a5? 9...a6!? 10 ♗e3 ♕c6 11 f3 b5 12 cxb5 **10 ♝e3 ♛c6 11 f3 0-0** 11...b5 12 cxb5 ♗xc3+ 13 ♔f2 ♘g4+ 14 ♔g1 **12 ♞d4 ♛a6 13 ♞b5 d5** 13...♘e8 14 f4 ♘c6 15 a3 ♗e7 16 0-0 **14 ♞c7 ♛d6 15 ♞xa8 dxe4 16 fxe4 ♞xe4 17 ♜d1 ♛c6 18 ♝g2 ♞xc4 19 ♝d4 ♝xc3+ 20 bxc3 f5 21 0-0 ♞cd6** 21...b5 22 ♗xe4 fxe4 23 ♖xf8+ ♔xf8 24 ♖f1+ ♔e7 25 ♕f2 **22 ♞b6 e5 23 ♞xc8** Δ ♘e7+ **♜xc8 24 ♝xe5 ♛c5+ 25 ♝d4 1-0**

13 Vukic-Nemet Vinkovci 77
1 ♞f3 g6 2 c4 ♝g7 3 d4 ♞f6 4 g3 0-0 5 ♝g2 c5 6 ♞c3 cxd4 7 ♞xd4 ♞c6 8 0-0 d6?! 8...♘xd4!? 9 ♕xd4 d6 10 ♕d3 a6 **9 ♞xc6 bxc6 10 ♝xc6 ♝h3** 10...♖b8!? **11 ♝xa8 ♛xa8 12 f3 ♝xf1 13 ♚xf1 ♜c8 14 ♛d3 += ♛b7** 14...♕c6 15 ♗e3± **15 ♜b1 ♞d7** 15...♕a6? 16 b3 d5 17 ♘xd5 ♘xd5 18 ♕xd5 ♕xa2 19 ♕d3± **16 b3!** 16 ♗f4? ♗xc3! 17 ♕xc3 d5! **♞e5** 16...♗xc3!? 17

♕xc3 d5 18 ♗b2 f6∝ **17 ♛d5 ♛d7 18 ♞e4± ♜c6 19 ♝e3 h6 20 ♚g2 ♚h7 21 ♜d1 ♛c7** 21...f5? 22 ♘c5! **22 ♛b5 f5 23 ♞f2 a6 24 ♛d5 ♛c8 25 ♞d3 e6 26 ♛a5 ♜xc4 27 ♞xe5** 27 bxc4? ♘xc4 −+ **♜c2 28 ♞c4 ♜xe2+ 29 ♚f1 ♜xh2 30 ♝g1 ♛c6 31 ♜d3 ♜c2 32 ♛b6?!** 32 ♘xd6! ♖c1+ 33 ♔g2 ♕c2+ 34 ♖d2 ♕b1 35 ♕b6 +− **♛xb6 33 ♞xb6 d5 34 a4 g5 35 ♞d7 ♜c6 36 ♞c5?!** 36 f4! **d4 37 b4 a5?** 37...e5!?∝ **38 ♝xd4 e5?? 39 b5 +− ♜c8 40 ♝f2 e4 41 fxe4 fxe4 42 ♜d7 ♚g6 43 b6 ♝e5 44 b7 ♜e8 45 ♞xe4 ♚f5 46 ♞c5 ♚g4 47 ♚g2 h5 48 ♜d5 ♝b8 49 ♞d7 1-0 Vukic**

14 Korchnoi-Portisch
Wijk aan Zee 78
1 c4 c5 2 ♞f3 ♞f6 3 g3 d5 4 cxd5 ♞xd5 5 ♝g2 ♞c6 6 ♞c3 e6 7 0-0 ♝e7 8 d4 0-0 8...cxd4?! 9 ♘xd5 ♕xd5? 10 ♘xd4!± **9 c4** 9 ♘xd5 exd5 10 dxc5 ♗xc5 11 b3 ♕f6 12 ♗g5 ♕e6 13 ♖c1 ♗b6 14 ♖c2 += Uhlmann-Velimirovic, Tallinn 77 **♞db4! 10 a3** 10 d5?! exd5 11 exd5 ♘d4 12 a3 ♘bc2 =+ **cxd4 11 axb4 dxc3 12 bxc3 ♛c7 13 ♝e3 b6** 13...e5? 14 b5 ♘a5 15 ♘xe5± **14 ♛e2 e5 15 ♞d2 ♝e6 16 f4 f6** 16...exf4? 17 gxf4 f6 18 e5! Δ b5± **17 f5 ♝f7 18 ♜fc1 ♜ad8** 18...♖fd8!? **19 ♝f2 a5! 20 ♞c4 ♜b8 21 ♞e3 axb4 22 ♞d5** 22 cxb4 ♕d6 =+ **♛d6**

Diagram

23 ♛b5! Δ ♕xc6; 23 ♘xb6? bxc3 Δ ♘d4∓ **♜fc8 24 cxb4** 24 ♘xb6? ♖d8∓ **♝xd5 25 exd5 ♞d4 26 ♝xd4 exd4 =+ 27 ♛e2 ♜c3** 27...♖xc1+ 28 ♖xc1 ♕xb4!? 29 ♖c7 ♗f8 =+; 29 ♕e6+ ♔h8 30 ♖c8+ ♖xc8 31 ♕xc8+ ♗f8 32 ♗f1 =+; 32 d6!? ♕xd6 33 ♗d5 =+ **28 ♜ab1 ♜e3 29 ♛c4 d3 30 ♜d1 b5 31 ♛d4** 31 ♕c3 ♕e5 =+ **♝d8! 32 ♚h1 ♝b6 33 ♛c3 ♛e5 34 ♛c6 ♛d4** 34...d2!? 35 ♕e6+ ♕xe6 36 fxe6 ♖d3 =+; 36 dxe6 ♖d8 =+ **35 d6 ♜e5 36 ♛f3 ♜be8** 36...d2! 37 ♕f4 ♖be8? 38 ♕xd4 ♗xd4 39 d7 =; 37...♕xf4 38 gxf4 ♖e2 =+ **37 d7!= ♜8e7** 37...♕xd7 38 ♖xd3= **38 d8♛+ ♛xd8 39 ♜xd3 ♛c8 40 ♜f1 h6 ½-½ Webb**

15 Najdorf-Miles Wijk aan Zee 78
1 c4 c5 2 ♞f3 ♞f6 3 ♞c3 d5 4 cxd5 ♞xd5 5 e3 ♞xc3 6 bxc3 g6 7 d4 ♝g7 8 ♝e2 0-0 9 0-0 b6 10 a4 ♞d7 11 ♛b3 11 a5 ♖b8 **♛c7 12 e4!? cxd4 13 cxd4 ♝b7 14 e5** 14 ♗d3 ♘c5 15 ♕c2 ♖fc8 **e6 15 ♞g5 ♜fc8 16 ♝f3 h6! 17 ♝xb7** 17 ♘e4? ♘xe5! 18 dxe5 ♕xe5 **♛xb7 18 ♞f3 =+/∓ ♜c7 19 ♝d2 ♜ac8 20 h3 ♜c4 21 ♜fb1 a6** 21...♕d5 22 ♕b5 **22 ♜c1** 22 ♗a5 ♕d5 Δ ♖c1+ **♛d5 23 ♜xc4 ♜xc4 24 ♛b1 ♛c6 25 ♛d1 ♝f8 26 ♝e3 b5 27 axb5 axb5 28 ♞d2 ♜c2?** 28...♖c3 **29 ♚h2 b4 30 ♜a7 ♜c3 31 ♛b1?** 31 ♕g4!? ♖a3! 32 ♖xd7 ♕xd7 33 ♘e4 ♗e7! 34 ♗xh6 ♖d3! 35 ♗g5 ♗xg5 36 ♕xg5 ♕xd4 −+; 35 ♗e3 b3; 31 ♕f3! ♕xf3 32 gxf3 ♘b6 33 ♘e4 ♖c8 34 ♘f6+ ♔g7 35 ♖b7!≈; 33...♖c6 34 ♘f6+ ♔g7 35 ♘e8+ ♔g8 36 ♘f6+ = **♜a3 32 ♜xa3**

bxa3 −+ 33 ♕a2 ♘b6 34 ♘b1 ♕c4 35 ♕xc4 ♘xc4 36 ♘c3 ♘xe3 37 fxe3 ♗b4 38 ♘a2 ♗d2 39 e4 ♗e3 40 d5 exd5 41 exd5 ♗f4+ 42 ♔g1 ♗xe5 43 ♔f2 ♔f8 44 ♔e3 ♔e7 45 ♔d3 ♔d6 46 ♔c4 ♗b2 47 ♘b4 f5 48 ♔b3 g5 0-1 Miles

16 Miles-Andersson
Wijk aan Zee 1978

1 c4 c5 2 ♘f3 ♘f6 3 ♘c3 e6 4 e3 d5 5 cxd5 ♘xd5 6 d4 cxd4 7 exd4 ♗e7 8 ♗d3 0-0 9 0-0 ♘c6 10 ♖e1 ♗f6 11 ♗e4 ♕d6!? 11...♘ce7 **12 ♕d3** 12 ♘b5!? **h6** 12...♘db4 13 ♕b1 ♘xd4 14 ♘xd4 += **13 ♗xd5** 13 ♘b5 **exd5 14 ♘b5 ♕b8 15 g3 ♗g4 16 ♗f4 ♕d8 17 ♘e5 ♗xe5 18 dxe5** 18 ♗xe5 =/=+ **♕d7?** 18...d4!=+ **19 ♘d4= ♖ac8 20 ♖ac1 ♘xd4 21 ♕xd4 b6 22 ♗d2 ♗f3? 23 ♕f4 ♗e4 24 f3 ♗g6 25 ♕d4 += ♖fe8 26 ♔g2 ♖xc1 27 ♖xc1 h5 28 ♗c3 ♕e6 29 ♖d1 ♖d8 30 h3 ♖d7 31 ♖d2 ♗f5 32 g4 ♕g6 33 a3 ♗e6 34 ♕d3 ♕xd3 35 ♖xd3 ♔h7 36 ♔g3** △ f4-f5 **g5! 37 gxh5 ♔h6 38 h4 ♔xh5 39 ♖d4 ♖c7 40 hxg5 ♔xg5** 40...♖c4!? **41 ♗d2+ ♔g6** 41...♔f5? 42 ♖g4 **42 ♖f4 += ♖c8! 43 ♖f6+ ♔h7 44 ♗g5 ♖g8 45 ♖h6+** 45 f4 ♖g6= **♔g7** △ ♖h8 **46 ♖h2 ♔f8 47 f4 ♔e8 48 ♔f3 a5 49 ♔e3 ♔d7 50 ♖h6 ♔c6 51 ♔d4 ♔b5 52 ♖f6 ♖g6= 53 ♖xg6 fxg6 54 ♗d8 a4 ½-½ Miles**

17 Stefanov-Neamtu
Rumania Final 77

1 ♘f3 c5 2 c4 ♘f6 3 ♘c3 d5 4 cxd5 ♘xd5 5 e4 5 d4!?; 5 g3 **♘b4** 5...♘xc3 6 dxc3! += **6 ♗c4 ♗e6!? 7 ♗xe6 ♘d3+ 8 ♔f1 fxe6 9 ♘g5 ♕d7 10 ♕f3!** TN 10 ♕g4∞

10...♘e5 11 ♕h3!± ♕d3+ 12 ♕xd3 ♘xd3 13 ♔e2! ♘xc1+ 14 ♖axc1 ♔d7 15 d4! cxd4 16 ♖hd1 ♘c6 17 ♘b5 e5 18 ♘f7!! e6 18...♖g8 19 ♘xe5+ ♘xe5 20 ♖xd4+ ♔e6 21 ♘c7+ **19 ♘xh8 a6 20 ♘c3 ♔e7 21 ♘a4 ♔f6 22 ♖d3! +−** △ ♖f3+ **1-0 Gheorghiu**

18 Kasparov-Kapengut Minsk 78

1 ♘f3 ♘f6 2 c4 c5 3 ♘c3 d5 4 cxd5 ♘xd5 5 g3 ♘c6 6 ♗g2 ♘c7 7 ♕a4 ♗d7 8 ♕e4 g6 9 ♘e5 ♗g7 10 ♘xd7 ♕xd7 11 0-0 11 ♕a4?! 0-0 12 ♗xc6 bxc6 13 d3 ♘b5 14 ♗d2 ♖fb8 Vaganian-Tseshkovsky, Baku 77; 11...♘d4! 12 ♕d1 (12 ♕xd7+ ♔xd7 13 ♗xb7 ♘c2+∓) 12...♖b8 13 d3 0-0 14 0-0 b6 15 ♖b1 ♖fd8 16 ♗d2 ♘f5 17 ♘e4 ♘d5 18 ♗h3 e6 19 ♗xf5 exf5∓ Malisov-Kapengut, Minsk 77; 11 h4?! 0-0 12 h5 ♕d4! 13 h6 ♗h8 14 d3 ♕xe4 15 ♘xe4 ♘d4 =+ Guzevic-Andreev, USSR 75 **♖c8!** 11...0-0 12 d3 ♘e6 13 ♕d5?! ♕c7 14 ♕c4 ♖ab8 15 ♗e3 ♘cd4 16 a4 ♖fd8 17 ♖fc1 ♕e5 18 ♖a2 b6 19 b3 ♖d7 20 ♗h3 ♕h5 =+ Vaganian-Polugaevsky, Leningrad 71; 13 ♗d2 ♖ac8 14 ♖ab1 b6 15 ♖fc1 c4? (15...♘ed4=) 16 ♘d5 cxd3 17 ♕xd3 ♘e5 18 ♕a3 ♘c4 19 ♕xe7 +− Piasetsky-Krpanec, Karlovec 77; 12 a3!? ♖c8 13 b4 ♘e6 14 b5 ♘a5

15 ♖b1 e6 16 ♘d5 ♖fe8 17 e3 c4!∞ **12 a3** 12 ♕a4 ♘e6 13 d3 0-0 14 ♗e3 b6 15 ♖fc1 ♖fd8 16 ♖ab1 ♘ed4 17 a3 ♘a5 =+ W.Schmidt-Alburt, Decin 76 **♞e6 13 b4 b6 14 ♜b1 0-0 15 ♞d5!** 15 ♗h3 f5 16 ♕d5 ♕xd5 17 ♘xd5 ♘ed4 18 e3?! ♘f3+ 19 ♔h1 g5!=+ Iljinsky-Kapengut, 13/35 **♞cd4** 15...f5 16 ♕c4 ♘e5 17 ♕a2 c4 18 ♗b2 f4 19 ♗xe5 ♗xe5 20 d3 c3 21 gxf4 ♗xf4 22 ♗h3 ♖c6 23 ♘xc3 ♔g7 24 ♘e4 1-0 Romanishin-Pinter, Costa Brava 77 **16 ♝b2 f5!?** 16...♖fe8 17 ♖fc1 ♘g5 18 ♕c3 ♕g4 **17 ♛e3 c4 18 d3?!** 18 ♖fc1

18...f4!∓ 19 gxf4 c3! 20 ♝xc3 ♞f5 21 ♛d2 ♝xc3 22 ♞xc3 ♞h4? 22...♘fd4! 23 e3 ♖xc3 24 exd4 ♘xd4∓; 23 ♘d5 ♖c2 24 ♕e3 ♖xe2 25 ♕g3 ♖f5∓ **23 ♝h3±** 23 e3? ♘xf4 −+ **♛c6 24 b5! ♛xc3 25 ♛xc3 ♜xc3 26 ♝xe6+ ♚g7 27 ♝b3 ♜c5 28 ♜fc1 ♜xb5 29 a4 ♜b4 30 ♜c7 ♜fxf4 31 ♜xe7+ ♚h6 32 ♜xa7 ♜g4+ 33 ♚h1 ♜gf4 34 f3 ♞f5 35 ♚g2 ♜h4 36 e4 ♞d4 37 ♝a2 ♜xb1 38 ♝xb1 ♜f4 39 ♜b7 ♞xf3 40 ♜xb6 ♚h5 41 ♚g3 g5 42 ♝c2 ♞xh2 43 ♝d1+ ♞g4 44 ♚h3 1-0 Kapengut**

19 Georgadze-Alburt Decin 77

1 c4 c5 2 ♞f3 ♞f6 3 ♞c3 d5 4 cxd5 ♞xd5 5 g3 ♞c6 6 ♝g2 e6 7 0-0 ♝e7 8 d4 0-0 9 ♞xd5 exd5 10 dxc5 ♝xc5 11 a3 11 b3!? ♕f6!? 12 ♖b1 ♗f5 13 ♗b2 ♕e7 14 ♖c1 ♗e4 =/+= Uhlmann-Alburt, Decin 77; 12 ♗g5 ♕f5∞ Meduna-Tukmakov, Decin 77 **a5 12 ♞e1! d4 13 ♞d3 ♝b6** 13...♗a7 Dorfman-Alburt, USSR 73 **14 ♞f4 ♜e8 15 ♞d5 ♝e6 16 e4! dxe3 17 ♝xe3 ♝xd5 18 ♝xd5 ♝xe3** 18...♖e7?? 19 ♗g5 +−; 18...♘e7?? 19 ♗xf7+ ♔xf7 20 ♕b3+ +− **19 fxe3 ±/+= ♜f8 20 ♛b3 ♛e7 21 e4 a4 22 ♛c3 ♜ac8 23 ♜ac1 h6! += ½-½** 24 ♕c5 ♖c7? 25 ♕xe7, 24...♕d7 +=/∞

20 Hubner-Karpov Tilburg 77

1 c4 ♞f6 2 ♞c3 c5 3 ♞f3 d5 4 cxd5 ♞xd5 5 g3 g6 6 d3 6 ♗g2 ♗g7!? 7 ♕a4+ ♘c6 8 ♘g5 e6 9 ♘ge4 ♘b6! 10 ♕b5 c4 11 ♘a4≈ Tatai-Karpov, Las Palmas 77; 6...♘c7 **♝g7 7 ♝d2 b6!** 7...0-0 8 ♗g2 b6? 9 ♘xd5 +− **8 ♛a4+ ♝d7 9 ♛h4** 8 ♕e4? ♗c6 9 ♘e5 ♗xe5 10 ♕xe5 f6 −+ **♝c6 10 ♝g2 e6!** 10...0-0= **11 ♛xd8+ ♚xd8 12 ♜c1 ♞a6! =+ 13 ♞xd5 ♝xd5 14 ♝c3 f6** 14...♗xc3+? 15 bxc3= **15 a3 ♚e7 16 0-0 ♜hc8 17 ♞d2** 17 b4?! cxb4 18 axb4 ♘c7 Δ ♘b5, a5∓ **♞c7 18 b4** 18 e4 ♗b7 19 e5 ♗xg2 20 exf6+ ♗xf6 21 ♗xf6+ ♔xf6 22 ♔xg2 ♘b5 =+; 19 d4 ♘b5 20 dxc5 ♘xc3 21 ♖xc3 ♖xc5 =+ **♝xg2 19 ♚xg2 cxb4 20 ♝xb4+ ♚d7 21 ♝c3?!** 21 ♘c4!? ♘d5 22 ♗d2 =+ **♞d5 22 ♝b2 ♝h6! 23 e3** 23 ♖fd1 ♖xc1 24 ♗xc1 ♖c8∓ **♞xe3! 24 fxe3 ♞xe3+ 25 ♚f3 ♞xf1 26 ♞xf1 ♜xc1 27 ♝xc1 ♜c8∓ 28 ♝b2** 28 ♗d2 ♖c2 Δ a5, ♖a2 **♜c2** 28...e5? 29 ♘e3 **29 ♝xf6 ♜a2 30 ♚e3 ♜xa3 31 ♞d2 b5 32 ♞e4 b4 33 ♚d4 a5 34 ♚c4 ♜a2 35 h4 ♚c6 36 ♝d4 ♜e2 37 ♝e5 ♜e1 38 ♝f6** 38 ♔b3 ♔d5 39 ♗c7 ♖e3 −+

♖b1 39 ♗e7 e5! –+ 40 g4 ♖c1+ 41 ♔b3 ♔d5 42 ♗g5 ♖b1+ 43 ♔c2 ♖h1 44 ♔b3 ♖h3 45 ♘f6+ ♔d4 46 ♘xh7 ♖xd3+ 47 ♔c2 a4 48 ♗e7 48 h5 a3 Δ b3+ **♖c3+ 49 ♔b1 ♖c7 0-1 Webb**

21 Korchnoi-Andersson
Wijk aan Zee 78

1 c4 e6 2 ♘c3 ♘f6 3 ♘f3 c5 4 g3 b6 5 ♗g2 ♗b7 6 0-0 ♗e7 7 d4 cxd4 8 ♕xd4 0-0 9 e4 d6 10 ♖d1 10 ♕e3 a6 11 ♘d4 ♕c7 12 b3 ♘bd7 13 ♗b2 ♖fe8 14 ♔h1 ♗f8 15 f4 += Uhlmann-A.Rodriguez, Halle 76 **a6 11 ♕e3 ♕c7 12 b3 ♘c6!?** 12...♘bd7 13 ♘d4 **13 ♗b2 ♘d7 14 ♖ac1** Δ ♘d5 **♕b8 15 ♖d2 ♖c8 16 ♖cd1 ♖a7 17 ♗f1 ♘c5 18 ♗a3** Δ 19 e5 dxe5 20 b4 **♘d8 19 ♗e2** 19 e5?! ♗xf3 **♗c6 20 e5 dxe5 21 ♘xe5 ♗e8 22 b4** 22 ♗f3!? **♘a4 23 ♘d7 ♗xd7 24 ♖xd7 ♘xc3 25 ♕xc3 ♘c6!= 26 ♖xa7 ♕xa7 27 b5?!** 27 ♗b2 ♗f6 28 ♕b3= **♗f6** 27...axb5 28 ♗xe7 ♘xe7 29 cxb5! **28 ♕e3 axb5 29 cxb5 ♘d4! 30 ♗d3** 30 ♗b2? ♘xe2+ 31 ♕xe2 ♕xa2 **g6 31 ♗b2 ♘f3+** 31...♕a4!? 32 ♖d2 ♕b4 =+ **32 ♕xf3 ♗xb2 33 ♗f1 ♗a3=** 33...♕xa2 34 ♕b7 **34 ♖d3 ♗c5 35 ♕e2 ♕e7 36 ♗g2 ♖d8 37 ♖xd8+ ♕xd8 38 ♗e4 ♕d4 39 ♔g2 ♔g7 40 ♗c2 h5 41 h4 e5 42 ♕f3 f5 43 ♗b3 e4 44 ♕f4 ½-½ Webb**

22 Kochiev-Gulko USSR Final 77

1 ♘f3 ♘f6 2 c4 c5 3 g3 d5 4 ♗g2 ♘c6 5 d4?! 5 0-0 e5= **dxc4 6 ♕a4 cxd4 7 0-0** 7 ♘xd4 ♕xd4 8 ♗xc6+ ♗d7 9 ♗e3∝ **♗d7 8 ♕xc4 ♕b6!** 8...♖c8 9 ♘d4 +=; 8...e5?! 9 ♘g5! ♕e7 10 b3 Δ ♗a3± **9 e3!? ♖c8!** 9...dxe3 10 ♗xe3 ♕xb2 11 ♘d2≈ **10 ♘xd4 ♘a5!? 11 ♕d3! e5 12 ♘b3 ♘c6?** 12...♗b5?! 13 ♕f5!; 12...e4!? **13 ♘c3 ♗e7 14 e4 ♘b4 15 ♕e2 ♗g4 16 ♗f3 ♗xf3 17 ♕xf3 ♘c2 18 ♖b1 ♘d4 19 ♘xd4 exd4 20 e5!? dxc3 21 exf6 c2 22 fxg7 ♖g8 23 ♖a1 ♖xg7 24 ♖e1?** 24 ♗d2 ♕xb2 25 ♖ae1!∝ **♖g6=+ 25 ♗f4 ♕xb2 26 ♖ac1 ♖e6 27 ♖xe6 fxe6 28 ♕h5+ ♔d8 29 ♕xh7 ♕d4 30 h4 ♖c4 31 ♕h5 ♕d3 =+ ½-½ Kochiev**

23 Bukic-Raicevic
Jugoslavia Final 78

1 ♘f3 e6 2 c4 c5 3 g3 ♘f6 4 ♗g2 ♗e7 5 0-0 0-0 6 ♘c3 ♘c6 7 d4 d5 8 cxd5 ♘xd5 9 e4 ♘xc3?! 9...♘db4!= **10 bxc3 b6 11 ♗e3 ♘a5 12 ♕e2 ♗b7 13 ♘d2 ♖c8 14 ♖fd1 cxd4 15 cxd4 ♕d7 16 ♘b3 ♕a4?** 16...♘xb3 17 axb3 a5 18 d5 ♗c5 19 ♗h3 +=; 16...♘c4 17 ♗f4 +=

17 d5± exd5 18 exd5 ♗f6 19 ♗d4 ♖fe8 20 ♕d3 ♗xd4 21 ♕xd4 ♖c4 21...♕xd4 22 ♖xd4 ♘c4? 23 d6 +–; 22...♖c4? 23 ♘xa5 +– **22 ♕d2 ♖b4 23 ♘xa5 ♕xa5 24 ♖ac1 +– ♕b5 25 d6 ♖b2 26 ♕f4 ♗a6** 26...♖b4 27 d7 **27 ♗c6 1-0 Webb**

24 Raicevic-Velimirovic
Jugoslavia Final 78

1 c4 c5 2 ♘f3 g6 3 ♘c3 ♗g7 4 e3 ♘f6 5 ♗e2 0-0 6 0-0 ♘c6 7 d4 cxd4 8 exd4?! 8 ♘xd4 **d5! 9 ♗f4?! dxc4 10 d5?! ♘a5 11 ♗e5 ♗g4 12 ♕d4**

♗xf3 13 ♗xf3 ♘e8 14 ♖fe1 f6 15 ♗g3 e5!∓ 16 ♕d2 ♘d6 17 ♗d1 ♘f5? 17...b5 **18 ♗g4! ♘xg3 19 ♗e6+ ♔h8 20 hxg3 ♘c6 21 ♖e4!∝ ♘d4**

22 ♖xd4! exd4 23 ♕xd4 f5 24 ♕xc4 ♕b6 25 ♕e2 ♖ad8 26 ♖d1 ♖fc8 27 ♕c2 ♕c5 =+ 28 ♕b3 b5 29 ♖c1 a6 30 ♘e2 ♕d6 31 ♘f4 ♖e7 32 ♖c6 ♕e5 33 d6!∝ ♖xd6 34 ♖c8+ ♗f8 35 ♖xf8+ ♔g7 36 ♖g8+ ♔h6 37 ♗d5± ♖cd7! 38 ♗f3 ♕c1+ 39 ♔h2 ♕xf2 40 ♕c3 ♕d4 41 ♕c1 ♕d2 42 ♕h1!? ♕e3!= 43 b3! ♖d2 44 ♕a1! ♕xf3 45 ♕f6! 45 ♖xg6+? hxg6 46 ♕h8+ ♖h7 47 ♕f8+ ♔g5+ −+ **♖xg2+!! 46 ♘xg2 ♕h5+ 47 ♔g1** 47 ♔h4 ♖d2 Δ ♖xa2= **½-½ Maric**

25 Larsen-Miles Reykjavik 78

1 g3 g6 2 ♗g2 ♗g7 3 c4 c5 4 ♘c3 ♘c6 5 ♘f3 a6 6 0-0 d6 7 ♖b1 ♖b8 8 a4 ♘f6 9 d3 0-0 10 ♗d2 ♗d7 11 ♘e1 ♘e8 12 ♘c2 ♘c7 13 b4 cxb4 14 ♘xb4 ♘xb4 15 ♖xb4 b5 16 ♕c2!? 16 axb5 axb5 17 cxb5 ♘xb5= **bxc4 17 ♖xb8 ♕xb8 18 dxc4 ♗f5! 19 e4 ♗d7≈ 20 ♖b1 ♕a7 21 ♕b3 ♗d4 22 ♗e1 ♖c8 23 a5 ♘e6 24 ♘d5 ♗c6 25 ♕d1 ♗c5 26 h4 ♔f8 27 ♕d2 ♘d4 28 h5 ♗xd5 29 cxd5 ♖b8 30 ♖xb8+?** 30 ♕d3 ∝/+= **♕xb8 31 ♕d3 ♕b2 32 ♗d2!** 32 ♕xa6? ♕c1! 33 ♕f1 ♘c2 34 ♗c3 ♗xf2+! **f6 33 ♔h2 ♘b5!? 34 ♗e3 ♕a2 35 ♗h3?!** 35 e5! fxe5 36 hxg6 hxg6 37 ♗xc5 dxc5 38 ♕xg6 ♘d6 39 ♕h6+ ♔f7 ∝/= **♕xa5 36 ♗xc5 dxc5 37 ♕e3 ♔g7 38 h6+ ♔f8 39 ♕xc5 ♕c7∝ 40 ♕e3!?** 40 ♕b4 ∝/=+ **a5 41 ♗e6 a4 42 ♕d3 ♕c5**

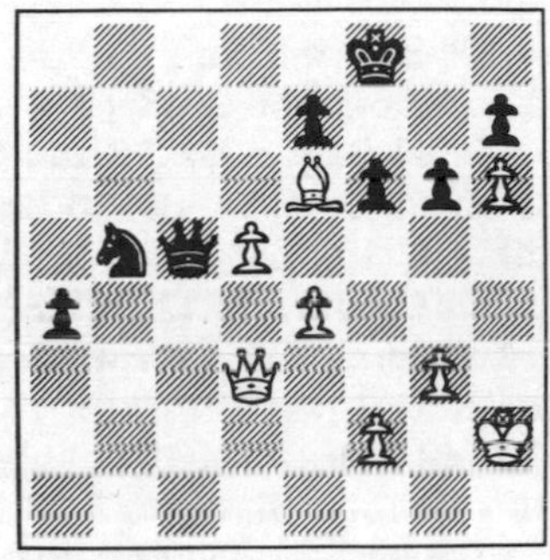

43 e5! 43 ♔g2 a3∓ **a3** 43...♕xf2+!? 44 ♔h1 ♘d4 45 ♕a6 ♕e1+ 46 ♔g2 ♕e2+ −+; 45 ♕c3 ♕g1+! −+; 45 ♕b1 ♕f3+ 46 ♔h2 ♕c2+ 47 ♔h3 ♕xe5 −+; 44 ♔h3 ♕g1!? 45 ♕xb5? ♕h1+ 46 ♔g4 f5+! 47 ♔g5 ♕c1+! 48 ♔h4 ♕xh6 mate; 47 ♔f4 ♕e4 mate; 47 ♗xf5 ♕h5+ 48 ♔f4 ♕xf5+ 49 ♔e3 ♕xe5+ −+; 45 exf6! exf6 46 ♕xb5 ♕h1+ 47 ♔g4 =; 44...♕c5!? **44 exf6 exf6 45 ♕f3** Zeitnot **♔e7** 45...♕c3 46 ♕e2∝ **46 ♗g8! ♘d4!?** Zeitnot 46...a2 47 d6+ = **47 ♕e4+ ♔f8?** 47...♔d7! 48 ♗xh7! a2 49 ♗xg6 a1♕ 50 h7! ♘f3+! 51 ♕xf3! ♕f8!?= **48 ♗xh7 a2 49 ♗xg6 ♘f3+ 50 ♔g2?** 50 ♕xf3! a1♕ 51 h7 ♔g7? 52 h8♕+ ♔xh8 53 ♕h5+ ♔g7 54 ♕h7+ ♔f8 55 ♕f7 mate; 51...f5 52 ♕xf5+ ♔e7 53 ♕f7+ ♔d8 54 d6! +− **♘e5 51 h7 ♔g7 52 h8♕+ ♔xh8 53 ♕h4+ ♔g7 54 ♕h7+ ♔f8 55 ♕h8+ ♔e7 56 ♕e8+** 56 ♕g7+ ♔d8 57 ♕xf6+ ♕e7= **♔d6 57 ♕f8+ ♔xd5 58 ♗f7+ ♔d4!** 58...♘xf7 59 ♕xf7+ ♔e5 60 ♕xa2 ♕f8! += **59 ♕xc5+**

59 ♕d8+ ♔c3! 60 ♗xa2 ♘g4!= **♚xc5 60 ♝xa2 ♚d6= 61 ♚h3 ♚e7 62 ♝b1 ♚f7 63 ♝f5 ♞c6 64 ♚g4 ♞e5+ 65 ♚f4 ♞c4 66 ♝c2 ♞d6 67 ♚e3 ♚e6 68 ♚d4 ♞b5+ 69 ♚c5 ♞d6 70 ♝b3+ ♚e7 71 ♚d5 ♞e8 72 ♝c2 ♞d6 73 ♝g6 ♚d7 ½-½ Miles**

26 Raicevic-Zivkovic Bar 77

1 ♞f3 c5 2 c4 ♞f6 3 g3 g6 4 ♝g2 ♝g7 5 0-0 0-0 6 d4 cxd4 7 ♞xd4 ♞c6 8 ♞c3 ♞xd4 9 ♛xd4 d6 10 ♝d2?! 10 ♕d3 **♝e6** 10...♘g4!? 11 ♕d5 ♗e6 12 ♕b5∞ **11 ♛d3 ♞d7 12 b3 ♜b8 13 ♜ac1 a6 14 a4?!** 14 ♖fd1 **♛b6 15 ♛b1 ♜fc8∞ 16 ♛a2 a5!** 16...♘c5 17 b4 ♘d7 18 a5! ♕d8 19 ♘d5± **17 ♞b5 ♞c5 18 e4?** 18 ♗c3! += **♝d7 19 ♝g5 ♝xb5 20 axb5** 20...cxb5!? **♛c7 21 ♜cd1?!** 21 ♖fd1!? **♜a8 22 ♜fe1 a4! 23 b4 ♞e6** 23...♘b3 24 b6 ♕xb6 25 ♗xe7 ♗e5!∓ **24 b6 ♛xc4?** 24...♕xb6 25 ♗xe7 ♗e5!∓ **25 ♛xc4 ♜xc4 26 ♝xe7 ♝d4 27 e5! dxe5 28 ♝xb7 ♜e8 29 ♝d5!± ♜c2 30 ♜xd4! exd4 31 b7 d3 32 ♜d1 d2 33 ♚g2** 33 ♔f1? ♘d4 **a3 34 ♝f6 a2 35 ♝e4 ♜c1 36 ♜xd2 a1♛ 37 ♝xa1 ♜xa1 38 ♜c2 ♜d1! 39 ♜c8 ♜dd8 40 b8♛ ♜xc8 41 ♛d6 ♜cd8 42 ♛b6 ♜b8 43 ♛a5 ♞d4 44 ♝d5 ♞b5 45 h4 h5 46 ♛a6 ♚g7 47 ♛a1+ f6 48 ♛a6 ♜e7 49 ♝c4 ♜a7 50 ♛e6 ♜ab7 51 f3? ♞d4! 52 ♛e4 ♞f5 53 ♝d5 ♜xb4= 54 ♛e6 ♜d4 55 ♛f7+ ♚h6 56 ♚h3 ♜d2 57 ♝e6 ♞g7 58 ♛xf6 ♞xe6 59 ♛xe6 ♜bb2 60 ♛e3+ ♚g7 61 g4 ♜h2+ 62 ♚g3 ♜hg2+ 63 ♚f4 ♜b4+ 64 ♚e5 ♜bb2 65 ♛c3 hxg4 66 ♚e6+ ½-½ Raicevic**

1 c4 e5

27 Mohring-Gipslis
Hradec Kralove 77-78

1 c4 e5 2 ♞c3 ♞f6 3 ♞f3 ♞c6 4 d3 ♝b4 5 ♝d2 5 ♗g5 h6 6 ♗xf6 ♗xc3+ 7 bxc3 ♕xf6= Petrosian-Keene, Nice 74 **0-0 6 e3 ♜e8** 6...d5 7 cxd5 ♘xd5 8 ♗e2 ♖e8!= **7 ♝e2** 7 ♕c2 a5 8 ♗e2 d6 9 a3 ♗c5 10 0-0 ♗f5 11 b3 e4! 12 dxe4 ♘xe4 13 ♘xe4 ♗xe4 14 ♕b2! += Csom-Jansson, Nice 74 **♝f8** 7...♗xc3 8 ♗xc3 d5 9 0-0 d4 10 exd4 exd4 11 ♗d2 a5= Lombardy-Gipslis, Tallinn 75 **8 0-0** 8 ♘e4 d6 9 0-0 h6 10 ♗c3 ♘h7 11 b4 f5 12 ♘g3 ♘e7 13 ♘d2 f4∞ Kjarner-Gipslis, Tallinn 77 **d6 9 ♞g5** 9 a3 ♘e7 10 b4 ♘g6 11 ♕c2 ♗f5 12 ♘e4 c6 13 ♗c3 d5= Larsen-Lombardy, Orense 75 **♞d7 10 f4 exf4 11 exf4 ♞d4! 12 ♝h5 g6 13 f5 ♞f6! 14 fxg6** 14 ♘xf7?! ♔xf7 15 fxg6+ hxg6∓ **fxg6 15 ♞e2 ♞f5** 15...♘xh5!? **16 ♝f3 c6!= 17 ♞c3 d5??** 17...♘e3 18 ♗xe3 ♖xe3 =+ **18 cxd5! +−** 18 ♕b3?! ♘d4!∓ **cxd5 19 ♛b3! ♚g7** 19...♘d4 20 ♗xd5+ Δ ♕c4 +− **20 ♞xd5 ♝c5+ 21 ♚h1 ♝d4 22 ♞f4** Δ ♘e6+ +− **♛b6 23 ♛f7+ ♚h8 24 ♞d5 1-0 Gipslis**

28 Ubilava-Bobovich USSR 77

1 c4 e5 2 ♞c3 ♞f6 3 ♞f3 ♞c6 4 d3 ♝c5 4...♗b4 5 ♗d2 0-0 6 e3 ♖e8 7 ♗e2 ♗xc3 8 ♗xc3 d5=; 5 g3!? **5 e3** 5 ♗g5 h6 6 ♗h4 g5 7 ♗g3 d6=; 5 g3 **0-0 6 ♝e2 d6 7 0-0 h6 8 a3 a5 9 d4 ♝b6** 9...exd4 10 exd4 ♗b6 11 ♗e3 ♘g4 12 ♗f4 +=; 9...♗a7?! 10 b4! axb4 11 axb4 ♘xb4 12 ♘b5 ♘c6 13 d5 **10 c5?! dxc5 11 d5 ♞e7 12 e4 ♞g6?** 12...c6! 13 d6 ♘g6 14 ♗e3 ♘e8 15 ♘a4 ♗d7 16 ♘xc5 ♘xd6 =+ **13 ♞d2! += ♞e8 14 ♞c4 ♞d6 15 a4 f5 16 f3 ♝d7** 16...fxe4 17 fxe4 ♗g4! 18 b3 ♗xe2 19 ♕xe2 ∞/+=; 17 ♘xe4!? Δ ♗d3 **17 ♝e3 f4?! 18 ♝f2 ♚h7 19 ♚h1 ♞xc4 20 ♝xc4 ♜f6 21 ♞b1?**

21 ♕e2 Δ ♖ad1, g3 += **♞e7! 22 ♞c3** 22 ♘d2 c6! **♞c8 23 b3 ♞d6 24 g3 fxg3 25 ♝xg3 ♛e7 26 ♛c2** Δ f4 **♚h8 27 ♚g2** 27 f4 exf4 28 ♖xf4 ♖xf4 29 ♗xf4 ♖f8 30 ♗g3 ♖f3!∓ **g5 28 ♛b2 ♜e8 29 ♞d1 h5 30 ♞e3 h4 31 ♝e1 h3+ 32 ♚h1! ♛f7** 32...♖ef8!? **33 ♝g3 ♜xf3 34 ♝e2 ♜f4** 34...♖xf1+ 35 ♖xf1 ♕g7 36 ♘c4 += **35 ♝xf4 gxf4 36 ♞c4 ♛f6** 36...♘xe4 37 ♘xe5 ♕xd5 38 ♘xd7+ ♔h7 39 ♗f3 **37 ♝f3 ♞f7 38 ♝h5! ♚g7 39 ♜g1+ ♚f8 40 ♜af1 +− ♛h8 41 ♝xf7 ♚xf7 42 ♜g5 ♛h6 43 ♞xe5+ ♚e7 44 ♞g6+ 1-0 Gufeld**

29 Miles-Portisch
Wijk aan Zee 78

1 c4 e5 2 ♞c3 ♞f6 3 ♞f3 ♞c6 4 e3 ♝b4 5 ♛c2 0-0 6 ♞d5 a5?! N 6...♖e8 **7 a3 ♝e7 8 d4 exd4** 8...d6 += **9 exd4 ♜e8 10 ♝e3 ♝f8 11 ♝d3± h6?! 12 h4!?** 12 0-0-0! d6 13 h4! ±/+−; 12...♗d6 13 g4!?± **♝d6!** 12...♘xd5? 13 cxd5 ♘e7? 14 ♗h7+ ♔h8 15 ♘e5 −+; 12...d6 13 ♘g5! +− **13 0-0-0 ♞xd5 14 cxd5** ∝/+=/± **♞e7 15 ♝h7+ ♚f8 16 ♝e4 c6 17 ♛d2 ♞xd5 18 ♝xd5 cxd5 19 ♝xh6 ♛f6** 19...♕c7+ 20 ♔b1 gxh6 21 ♕xh6+ ♔g8 22 ♘g5 +− **20 ♝e3 ♛f5 21 h5! ♜a6 22 ♛d3 ♛xd3 23 ♜xd3 ♜c6+?** 23...♗b8 += **24 ♚b1 f6 25 ♞h4 ♚f7 26 ♞g6** 26 ♘f5!? ♗f8 27 h6 d6! 28 h7 ♗xf5 29 h8♕ ♗xd3+∝ **b6 27 ♝f4? ♝a6 28 ♜d2 ♝c4 29 ♝xd6 ♜xd6 30 ♞f4 b5 31 ♚c2** Zeitnot **a4 32 ♚c3 ♜c6 33 ♚b4 ♝b3 34 h6** 34 ♖h3 ♖c4+ −+ **g5?** 34...♖a8! 35 h7 ♖c4+ 36 ♔xb5 ♖b8+ 37 ♔a6 ♖c7 38 ♖c2! ♖xc2 39 h8♕ ♖xh8 40 ♖xh8 ♖xf2 −+ **35 h7 ♜h8** 35...♔g7? 36 ♘g6 **36 ♞e2 ♚g7 37 ♜c1 ♝c4 38 ♜h1 ♜xh7 39 ♜xh7+ ♚xh7 40 ♞c3 ♜c8 41 ♜d1 ½-½ Miles**

30 Shamkovich-Lebredo Mexico 78

1 c4 e5 2 ♞c3 ♞c6 3 ♞f3 ♞f6 4 e3 d5?! 4...♗b4; 4...♗e7 **5 cxd5 ♞xd5 6 ♝b5!** Δ ♘xe5 **♞xc3 7 bxc3 ♝d6 8 d4 += ♝d7 9 0-0** 9 ♗xc6?! ♗xc6 10 dxe5 ♗xf3 11 ♕xf3 ♗xe5 12 ♕xb7 ♗xc3+ 13 ♔e2 0-0!=; 13...♗xa1? 14 ♗a3! **0-0 10 ♝e2 ♜e8 11 c4!?** 11 ♕c2! ♕e7 12 ♗b2 += **exd4!** 11... e4?! 12 ♘d2 ♗xh2+? 13 ♔xh2 ♕h4+ 14 ♔g1 ♖e6 15 f4! ♖h6 16 ♘xe4 +− **12 exd4 ♝g4 13 ♝e3 ♛f6 17 ♛d2 ♜e4!∝**

15 h3 15 ♗g5? ♖xe2!; 15 ♘g5? ♖xe3! 16 ♕xe3 ♗f4 17 ♕c4 ♗xc2! 18 ♕xh7+ ♔f8 19 ♕h8+ ♔e7 20 ♕xa8 ♕xg5 21 ♖fe1 ♘xd4∓; 15 d5? ♘e5 16 ♘g5 ♖xe3 17 ♕xe3 ♗xe2 18 ♘e4 ♘f3+!∓ **♝h5 16 ♜ab1! ♜ae8!?** 16...b6 17 ♖b5!± **17 ♜xb7** 17 ♖b5? ♗xf3 18 ♗xf3 ♖xd4! 19 ♗xd4 ♘xd4= **♝f4?** 17...♗xf3! 18 ♗xf3 ♘xd4 19 ♗xe4 ♕e5 20 ♗xh7+! ♔xh7 21 ♕d3+ ♔g8 22 g3±; 18...♖xd4!? 19 ♗xd4 ♘xd4 20 ♗d1 ♕e5 21 g3 h5∝ **18 ♜b3 ♝xf3** 18...h6 19 d5! ♘e5 20 ♗xf4! ♖xe2 21 ♗xe5!± **19 ♝xf3 ♜xd4 20 ♛c2! ♜d6** 20...♗xe3 21 fxe3 ♖d6 22 ♗d5 +− **21 ♝xc6 ♜xc6 22 ♛e4!! ♝e5** 22...♖xe4 23 ♖b8+ **23 f4 1-0 Shamkovich**

31 Gheorghiu-Radovici
Rumania Final 77
1 c4 e5 2 ♞c3 ♞c6 3 ♞f3 g6!? 3...♘f6 **4 d4! exd4 5 ♞xd4 ♝g7 6 ♞xc6 bxc6 7 g3 ♞e7 8 ♝g2 0-0 9 0-0 ♜b8 10 ♛a4!** 10 ♕c2 += **a6?** 10...d6! 11 ♕xa7 ♗e6 12 ♕a4 c5!∝ **11 c5! ♞f5 12 ♜d1! ♛e8** 12...♕f6!± **13 e4 ♞h6 14 ♛c2 ♛e7 15 ♝f4! ♜b7** 15...♕xc5 16 ♗xc7 ♖b7 17 ♗d6 **16 ♞a4 ♞g4 17 ♛d2! ♞e5 18 ♜ac1 ♛e6 19 b3 f5 20 ♜e1!** 20 ♗xe5 ♗xe5 21 f4 Δ e5± **♛f7 21 ♜e2!!** +− Δ ♖ce1 **♞g4 22 exf5 ♛xf5 23 ♜ce1** 23 h3 ♘f6? 24 ♖e5 +−; 23...♘e5! **d5 24 cxd6 ♜b5 25 dxc7 ♞xh2?! 26 ♚xh2 ♜d5 27 ♝xd5+ cxd5 28 ♜e8 ♛h5+ 29 ♚g1 ♝g4 30 ♜1e5! 1-0** 30...♗xe5 31 ♕xd5+ **Gheorghiu**

32 Wolf-Liberzon Israel 77
1 c4 ♞f6 2 ♞c3 g6 3 g3 ♝g7 4 ♝g2 0-0 5 d3 d6 6 ♝d2 e5 7 ♛c1 ♞c6 8 ♞d5 ♞d4 9 e3 ♞e6 10 ♞e2 ♞h5 11 0-0 c6 12 ♞c3 f5 13 f4 g5 14 ♚h1 gxf4 15 gxf4 ♛f6 16 fxe5 dxe5 17 ♞e4 ♛g6 18 ♞d6 ♞c5 19 ♞xc8 ♜axc8 20 ♛c2 f4 21 exf4 ♞xd3 22 ♛b3 exf4 23 ♝f3!= ♜ce8 24 ♛xb7 ♜f7 25 ♛b3 ♜fe7 26 ♝xh5 ♛xh5 27 ♛xd3 ♛xe2 27...♖xe2 28 ♗xf4= **28 ♛xe2 ♜xe2 29 ♝xf4 ♜xb2 30 ♜ad1 ♜xa2 31 ♜d7 ♜f8! 32 ♜g1 ♜xf4** 32...♖f7 33 ♖d8+ ♖f8 34 ♖d7= **33 ♜dxg7+ ♚f8 34 ♜xh7 ♜xc4 35 ♜b1 ♚g8 ½-½** 36 ♖c7=

33 Kuligowski-W.Schmidt
Poland Final 78
1 c4 g6 2 e4 e5 3 d4 ♞f6 4 ♞f3! ♝b4+ 5 ♝d2 ♛e7 6 dxe5 6 ♗d3= Malich-W.Schmidt, Poland Final 78 **♞xe4 7 ♝xb4 ♛xb4+ 8 ♞bd2 ♞xd2 9 ♛xd2 ♛xd2+** 9...♕e7?! **10 ♞xd2!** Δ ♘b1-c3 **♞c6 11 f4 0-0 12 g3!** 12 0-0-0?! f6 13 exf6 ♖xf6 14 g3±; 12...d6! 13 exd6 ♗f5!!= **d6 13 exd6 cxd6 14 ♞b1??** 14 ♔f2! ♗f5 15 ♘b1!± **d5!= 15 ♞c3 dxc4 16 ♝xc4 ♜e8+ 17 ♚f2 ♝e6 18 ♝xe6 ♜xe6 19 ♜ad1 ♜ae8 ½-½ Kuligowski**

34 Gulko-Smyslov
45 USSR Final 77
1 c4 e5 2 g3 ♞c6 3 ♝g2 g6 4 ♞c3 ♝g7 5 e3 d6 6 ♞ge2 ♞ge7 7 ♜b1 a5?! 8 d3 ♝e6 9 ♞d5 ♛d7 10 a3 0-0 11 0-0 ♚h8?! 11...♘c8 Δ ♘d8/♘6e7, c6∝ **12 ♝d2 f5 13 f4! ♝g8 14 ♛a4 ♞xd5 15 cxd5 ♞b8 16 ♛c2 c6 17 ♞c3 ♜c8 18 dxc6 ♞xc6±** 18...bxc6 19 e4!± **19 ♛a4 ♜e8?!** 19...exf4 Δ d5 **20 ♛b5 ♝e6 21 ♞d5 ♛f7 22 ♜bc1 ♜ad8 23 ♞b6 exf4 24 ♜xf4 g5?** +− 24...d5!?± **25 ♜ff1 ♛g6 26 ♞c4 ♝xc4 27 ♜xc4 f4 28 ♝e4 ♛h5 29 exf4 ♛e2 30 ♜f2 ♛d1+ 31 ♚g2 gxf4 32 ♝xf4 ♞d4 33 ♛g5 ♞e2 34 ♜c7 ♜g8 35 1-0 Petrosian**

1 c4 ♞f6

35 Webb-Petrosian Hastings 77/8
1 c4 ♞f6 2 g3 c6 3 ♝g2 d5 4 cxd5 4 b3 dxc4 5 bxc4 ♕d4∓; 4 ♕c2 e5=+; 4 ♘f3 dxc4 5 ♘a3 b5 =+ **cxd5 5 ♞f3 ♞c6 6 0-0?!** 6 d4+= **e5 7 d4 e4 8 ♞e5 ♝d6 9 ♝f4 0-0 10 ♞c3 ♜e8 11 ♞xc6 bxc6 12 ♝xd6?!** 12 ♗g5 h6 13 ♗xf6 ♕xf6= **♛xd6 13 ♜c1?!** 13 ♕d2 h5 14 ♕g5∝ **h5 14 ♛d2 h4 15 ♛g5?** 15 ♘d1 Δ ♘e3=

Diagram

15...h3! 15...♘h7!? 16 ♕xh4 g5 17 ♕h5 ♖e6! 18 e3 ♖h6 19 ♕d1 g4 Δ ♘g5, ♔g7, ♗d7, ♖ah8 **16 ♝h1 ♛b4! 17 ♛d2 ♜ab8 18 b3 ♞g4!** Δ ♘xf2, e3

19 ♕f4 ♖b7 20 ♘xe4!? 20 ♖fd1 ♕e7 21 f3 exf3 22 ♗xf3 ♘e3 23 ♖d3 g5 24 ♕e5 ♕d8! −+ **dxe4 21 ♗xe4 ♗d7 22 ♖c5** 22 ♗xc6 ♗xc6 23 ♖xc6 ♘f6∓; 22 ♖xc6 ♘f6∓ **♖b5 23 ♗xc6? ♖xc5 24 ♗xd7 ♕b7! 25 f3 ♕xd7 26 dxc5 ♘e3 0-1 Petrosian**

36 Miles-Panno
Wijk ann Zee 78

1 c4 ♘f6 2 ♘c3 d5 3 cxd5 ♘xd5 4 g3 g6 5 ♗g2 ♘b6 6 d3 ♗g7 7 ♗e3 0-0 8 ♕d2 e5 9 h4 h5 10 ♗h6 ♖e8 11 ♗xg7 ♔xg7 12 ♖c1 c6 12...♘c6? 13 ♗xc6! **13 ♘f3 ♘a6 14 0-0 ♘c7 15 ♖fd1 f6 16 e3 a5 17 ♕c2 ♕e7 18 ♘e4 ♗g4 19 ♖d2 ♖ed8?** 19...♗f5 **20 ♕c5! ♕xc5 21 ♘xc5 ♖a7 22 d4!± ♗xf3 23 ♗xf3 f5** Δ e4 **24 e4! fxe4 25 ♗xe4 a4** 25...♖xd4 26 ♖xd4 exd4 27 ♖d1± **26 ♘xb7! ♖xb7 27 ♖xc6** ±/+− **♖xd4 28 ♖xg6+ ♔f7 29 ♖xd4 exd4 30 ♖h6 ♔g7 31 ♖xh5 ♖a7 32 ♖h7+?** 32 ♖c5 +− **♔g8 33 h5 ♘b5 34 ♖h6** 34 ♖xa7 ∞/± **♘c8 35 ♖g6+? ♖g7! 36 ♖a6 ♖a7 37 ♖xa7 ♘cxa7 38 f4 ♘d6 39 ♗d3 ♘c6 40 a3? ♘a5!= 41 ♔f2 ½-½** 41...♘ac4 42 ♗xc4+ ♘xc4 43 ♔e2 ♘xb2 44 g4 **Miles**

37 Smejkal-Bueno Leipzig 77

1 c4 e5 2 ♘c3 ♘f6 3 ♘f3 e4 4 ♘g5 b5 5 d3 exd3 6 cxb5 h6 7 ♘f3 dxe2 8 ♗xe2± ♗b7 8...a6 9 0-0 ♗c5 10 ♘d4 0-0 11 ♗f3 ♖a7 12 ♗e3± Stean-Regan, New York 77; 8...♗c5 9 0-0 ♗b7 10 ♘d4 0-0 11 ♗e3 ♗b6 12 ♗f3 d5 13 ♘f5± Ghitescu-Ermenkov, Moscow 77; 9...0-0 10 ♘e5 ♗b7 11 ♗f3± Alburt-Pribyl, Decin 76 **9 0-0 ♗e7 10 ♘d4 0-0 11 ♗f3 d5 12 ♘f5 ♗b4** 12...♗c5 13 ♗e3± **13 ♕d4! c5 14 ♕h4** Δ ♗xh6/♘xg7 **♗xc3 15 bxc3 ♘e4 16 ♕g4 ♘g5 17 ♗xg5 hxg5 18 ♖fe1 g6 19 ♘e7+ ♔h7 20 ♕xg5 a6**

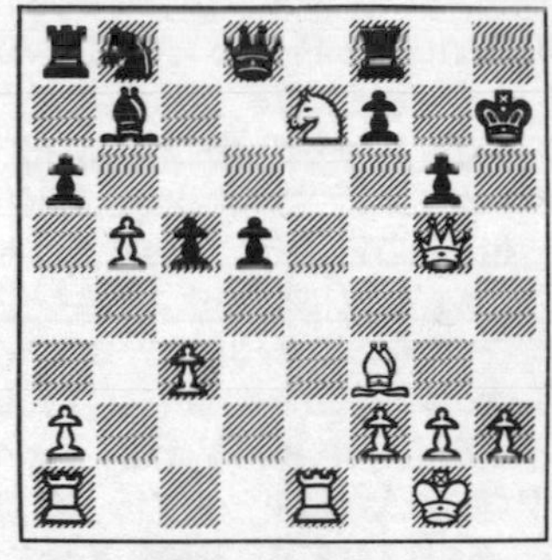

21 ♖e6! ♖g8 22 ♕h4+ 1-0 22...♔g7 23 ♘f5+ **Webb**

38 Olafsson-Hubner Tilburg 77

1 c4 ♘f6 2 ♘c3 e6 3 ♘f3 b6 4 e4 ♗b7 5 ♕c2 c5 6 ♗e2 6 d4 cxd4 7 ♘xd4 ♗b4 8 f3 0-0 **♘c6 7 0-0 d6 8 ♖d1 ♘d4! 9 ♘xd4 cxd4 10 ♘b5 ♗xe4 11 d3 ♗b7 12 ♘xd4 ♗e7 13 ♕a4+ ♕d7 14 ♕xd7+ ♔xd7 15 ♗e3 d5 16 ♖ab1 ♖hc8 17 b4** 17 ♗f3 e5 18 ♘f5 ♗f8 19 cxd5 g6 20 ♘g3 ♗xd5 21 ♗xd5 ♘xd5 22 ♖bc1 ♖xc1 Δ ♘b4 **♔e8 18 a4 ♘d7 19 a5?** 19 f4 **dxc4 20 dxc4 bxa5 21 bxa5 ♗e4** 21...♗a6 22 ♘b5 ♘e5 23 ♖bc1 **22 ♖b2** 22 ♖a1 ♘e5 23 ♖dc1 a6 **a6 23 f3 ♗g6 24 ♔f2?!** 24 f4 **♘e5 25 ♖c1?? 0-1** 25... ♗a3 −+

39 Smejkal-Miles Reykjavik 78

1 c4 b6 2 ♘c3 ♗b7 3 e4 e6 4 ♘f3 ♗b4 5 ♕b3 ♗xc3!? N 5...c5? Csom-Keene, Dortmund 76 **6 ♕xc3 ♗xe4 7 ♕xg7 ♕f6 8 ♕xf6 ♘xf6≈ 9 ♗e2 ♖g8 10 d3 ♗b7 11 ♖g1!** 11 0-0? ♘c6 **♘c6 12 ♗d2 d6** 12...0-0-0 13 ♗c3 ♖g6? 14 ♘h4 ♖h6 15 g3 +− **13 ♗c3 ♘g4!?** 13...♘d7 **14 h3 ♘ge5 15 0-0-0 0-0-0 16 ♘h2! ♘e7 17 ♘g4?** 17 f4 += **♘d7!= 18 g3 ♖g6! 19 ♘e3 ♘e5** Δ ♗/♘f3 **20 g4?** 20 f4 ♘f3 21 ♗xf3= **♖f6! =+ 21 ♖df1 ♘7g6 22 g5 ♖f4 23 ♘g2 ♖f5** 23...♗xg2!? 24 ♖xg2 ♖h4 =+ **24 ♘e3** Zeitnot **♘f4! 25 ♔d2** 25 ♘xf5 ♘xe2+ −+ **♘xe2 26 ♔xe2 ♖f4 27 ♖g3 ♖g8 28 ♗xe5 dxe5 29 f3 h6 30 ♘g2 ♖d4** 30...♖f5 31 h4 hxg5 32 ♘e3! **31 h4 b5!∓ 32 ♖h3 ♖gd8 33 ♘e1** 33 ♖d1? e4 **♔d7 34 ♘c2** 34 ♖f2!? Δ ♔f1, ♖e2 **♖f4 35 ♘e3 ♔e7 36 ♘d1? e4! 37 fxe4** 37 dxe4 ♗xe4 38 ♔e3 ♗d3! −+ **♖xf1 38 ♔xf1 ♗xe4 39 ♘f2** 39 ♔e2 ♗f5 Δ ♖d4 −+ **♗f5 40 ♖e3 ♖d4 41 ♘e4 ♗xe4 42 dxe4 ♖xc4 −+ 43 ♖e2 ♖d4 44 ♔g2 ♖d3 45 ♖c2 c5 46 ♖e2 c4 0-1 Miles**

40 Neamtu-Ilijin
Rumania Final 77

1 ♘f3 ♘f6 2 c4 b6 3 ♘c3 e6 4 e4 c5 4...♗b7 **5 e5 ♘g8 6 d4 cxd4 7 ♘xd4 ♕c7 8 ♗f4 a6 9 ♗e2 ♗b7 10 0-0 ♗b4 11 ♘a4! ♘e7 12 a3 ♘g6 13 ♗e3 ♗e7** 13...♗c5 14 ♘xc5 bxc5 15 ♘b3±; 14 f4± **14 f4 0-0 15 ♘b3 ♘h4 16 ♖f2 ♗xg2!? 17 ♖xg2 ♕c6 18 ♖f2 ♕xa4 19 ♘d4!± ♕xd1+ 20 ♖xd1 ♖a7 21 b4 ♖b7** 21...g6! **22 f5 ♗d8 23 ♗g4** 23 fxe6 dxe6 24 ♘xe6!± **exf5 24 ♘xf5 ♘xf5 25 ♗xf5 ♘c6 26 ♗f4! ♘b8 27 ♗e4 ♖c7 28 e6! ♖xc4 29 exf7+ ♔h8 30 ♗d6 ♖xe4 31 ♗xf8 ♖g4+ 32 ♔f1 1-0 Gheorghiu**

41 Miles-Hubner Tilburg 77

1 c4 ♘f6 2 ♘c3 e6 3 e4 c5 4 e5 ♘g8 5 ♘f3 ♘c6 6 d4 cxd4 7 ♘xd4 ♘xe5 8 ♘db5 a6 8...d6? 9 c5!±; 8...f6 9 ♗f4 a6 10 ♘d6+ ♗xd6 11 ♕xd6 ♘f7 12 ♕a3 ♘e7 13 ♗e2 0-0≈ Timman-Karpov, Las Palmas 77; 9 f4!? ♘g6 10 f5≈ **9 ♘d6+ ♗xd6 10 ♕xd6 f6 11 ♗e3** 11 b3 ♘e7 12 ♗b2 0-0 13 0-0-0 ♘f7 14 ♕g3 ♘f5 ½-½ Spassky-Hort (11), 77 **♘e7!** 11...♘f7?! 12 ♕g3 ♘e7 13 ♕xg7 ♘f5 14 ♕g4 ♘xe3 15 fxe3 ♕b6 16 ♕d4 += Keene-Partos, Montreux 77 **12 ♗b6 ♘f5 13 ♗xd8 ♘xd6 14 ♗c7 ♔e7 15 c5** 15 0-0-0? ♘exc4 16 b3 ♘e8! **♘e8 16 ♗b6 d5 17 cxd6+ ♘xd6 18 0-0-0 ♘ec4** 18...♘d7?! 19 ♗a5 b6 20 ♗b4 ♘c5 21 ♘a4! ♘xa4 22 ♖xd6± **19 ♗xc4** 19 ♗c5? b6 20 ♗b4 a5∓ **♘xc4 20 ♗c5+ ♔f7 21 ♖d4** 21 b3 b6! 22 bxc4 bxc5 23 ♘e4 ♖b8 **b5 22 b3 e5 23 ♖d5 ♘a5 24 ♗b6 ♘b7 25 ♖hd1 ½-½** 25...♖e8 =+ **Webb**

42 Miles-Sosonko IBM 77

1 c4 ♘f6 2 ♘c3 e6 3 e4 d5 4 e5 d4 5 exf6 dxc3 6 bxc3 ♕xf6 7 d4 b6 7...c5 **8 ♘f3 ♗b7 9 ♗d3!? ♗d6?** 9...♗xf3?! 10 gxf3 Δ ♕e2-e4 **10 ♗g5! ♗xf3 11 ♕d2! ♗f4! 12 ♗xf4 ♗xg2 13 ♖g1 ♗b7 14 ♗e5± ♕f3 15 ♗xg7 ♖g8 16 ♗xh7!! ♖xg7 17 ♖xg7 ♕h1+ 18 ♔e2 ♕f3+** 18...♕xa1 19 ♕f4! +− ♕b2+ (19...f5 20 ♗xf5) 20 ♔d3!? (20 ♔d1!) f5 21 ♗g6+ ♔f8 22 ♖f7+ ♔g8 23 ♖f8+!! ♔xf8 24 ♕h6+ ♔e7 25 ♕g7+ ♔d6 26 ♕f8+ ♔c6 27 ♗e8+ ♘d7 28 d5+ exd5 29 ♕f6+ ♔c5 30 ♕e7+ ♔c6 31 ♗xd7 mate! **19 ♔f1 ♘d7 20 ♕e3 ♕h1+ 21 ♖g1 ♕xh2 22 ♗e4 ±/+− ♗xe4 23 ♕xe4 ♕h3+ 24 ♔e2 0-0-0 25 ♖g3 ♕h5+ 26 ♕f3 ♕h7 27 ♕d3 ♕h5+ 28 ♕f3 ♕h7 29 ♖c1** 29 ♔d2 ♘e5 30 ♕e2 ♕f5 **♔b8 30 a4?**

e5 31 a5 e4 32 ♕h1 ♕f5 33 ♕h4 ♘f6 34 axb6 axb6 35 ♖a1 ♕e6 36 ♖a4 ♖e8 37 ♕g5 e3!∝ 38 ♖xe3 ♘e4 39 ♕f4 39 ♕g2?? ♕c6! −+ **f5 40 ♔e1?=** 40 ♖b4! △ f3 +=/± **♕g6 41 ♖b4 ♕g1+ 42 ♔e2 ♔b7!?** 42...♕c1= **43 c5!? ♘xc3+ 44 ♔d3?! ♘d5 45 ♕f3 ♖e4! 46 c6+! ♔xc6** 46...♔b8 47 ♖xe4 △ ♕f8+; 46...♔a6!? 47 ♖xe4? fxe4+ 48 ♔xe4 ♘xb4 49 ♕a3+ ♔b5 −+; 47 ♕e2!? ♘f4+? 48 ♔d2 ♘xe2? 49 ♖a3 mate; 47...♘xb4+ 48 ♔c3+ ♔a5 −+; 47 ♔d2!! ♘xe3? 48 ♕e2+ ♔a7 49 ♖a4+ ♔b8 50 ♖a8!! +−; 47...♘xb4 48 ♖a3+ △ ♕xf5+; 47...♖xe3 48 ♖a4+ △ ♕xd5+ **47 ♖c4+ ♔b5 48 ♖xe4 fxe4+ 49 ♔xe4 ♕g6+ 50 ♔xd5 ♕d6+ 51 ♔e4 ♕e6+ 52 ♔d3 ♕xc4+ 53 ♔e3 ♔b4= 54 ♕f8+ ♔c3 55 ♕a3+ ♔c2 56 f4 ♕e6+ 57 ♔f2 ♕d5 58 ♔e3 ½-½ Miles**

43 Larsen-Balashov Bugojno 78

1 c4 ♘f6 2 ♘c3 e6 3 ♘f3 b6 4 b3 ♗b7 5 ♗b2 ♗e7 6 e3 0-0 7 ♗e2 ♖e8?! 7...c5= **8 0-0** 8 d4 d5; 8 d3 d6 **a6 9 d4 d5 10 cxd5 exd5 11 ♘e5 ♗d6 12 f4 c5 13 ♘a4! += ♘bd7 14 ♖c1 ♖c8 15 ♗f3 ♘f8 16 dxc5 ♗xc5!** 16...bxc5?! 17 ♕d2 △ ♖fd1/♗c3/♘c4/♘d3 **17 ♘xc5 bxc5 18 ♕d2 ♕b6 19 ♕c3 ♖c7** 17...♘e6!? △ d4 **20 ♘g4 ♘8d7 21 b4 ♖ec8 22 ♘xf6+ ♘xf6 23 bxc5 ♖xc5 24 ♕d2 ♖xc1 25 ♖xc1 ♖xc1+ 26 ♕xc1 ♘e4 27 ♗d4 ♕b5** 27...♕c6 28 ♕b2 += **28 h3 ♗c6 29 ♔h2 f6 30 ♗e2! ♕b7** 30...♕xe2 31 ♕xc6 ♕b5 32 ♕e6+ ♔f8 33 ♗b6± **31 ♕a3 ♗b5 32 ♗g4 ♔f7 33 ♕a5 ♔e7 34 ♗f5! g6 35 ♕b4+ +− ♔f7** 35...♘d6? 36 ♗xf6+ **36 ♗xe4 dxe4 37 a4 ♗c6 38 ♕d6 ♗xa4** 38...f5 39 ♕f6+ ♔e8 40 ♕h8+ +− **39 ♕xf6+ ♔e8 40 ♕h8+ ♔d7 41 ♕xh7+ 1-0 Webb**

44 Suba-Stefanov
Rumania Final 77

1 c4 ♘f6 2 ♘c3 e6 3 ♘f3 b6 4 g3 ♗b7 5 ♗g2 ♗e7 6 0-0 0-0 7 ♖e1 d5 8 cxd5 exd5 9 d4 ♘a6 10 ♗g5 ♘e4 11 ♗xe7 ♕xe7 12 ♕b3 ♖fd8 13 ♖ad1 c5 17 dxc5 ♘axc5 18 ♕b4?? ♘xf2! 16 ♖d2 d4!! 17 ♖xd4 ♕e3 18 ♔f1 ♗xf3 19 ♘d5 ♖xd5 20 ♖xd5 ♘g4! 0-1 Pavlov

45 Portisch-Najdorf
Wijk aan Zee 78

1 c4 ♘f6 2 ♘c3 e6 3 ♘f3 ♗b4 4 ♕c2 0-0 5 a3 ♗xc3 6 ♕xc3 b6 7 b4! += ♗b7 8 ♗b2 d6 9 e3 ♘bd7 10 ♗e2 c5 11 0-0 ♖c8 12 d3 d5 13 b5 ♖e8 14 a4 e5 15 cxd5 ♘xd5 16 ♕b3 ♕f6 17 ♘d2 △ ♗f3 **♘b4?!** 17...♘c7!?

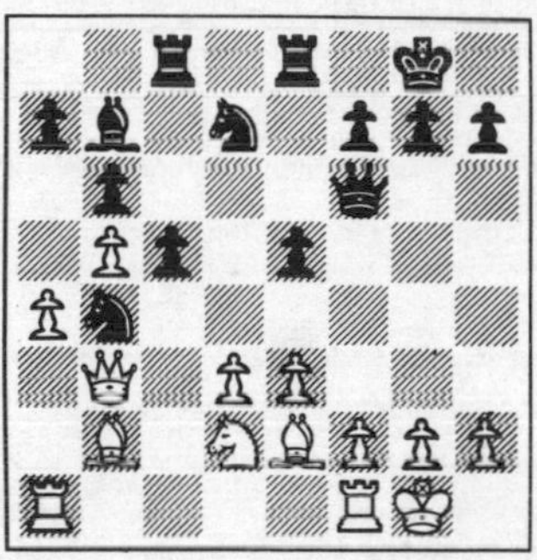

18 e4!± ♕e6 19 ♘c4 ♖cd8 20 f4 exf4 21 ♖xf4 ♔h8 22 ♗g4 ♕e7 23 ♗xd7! ♕xd7 24 ♘e5 ♖xe5 25 ♗xe5 ♖f8 25...f6? 26 ♖xf6! **26 ♖af1 ♔g8** 26...f6? 27 ♖xf6! gxf6 28 ♖xf6 +− **27 ♗d6?** 27 d4! +− **♗d5! 28 exd5 ♕xd6± 29 ♖f5 g6 30 ♖f6 ♕e5 31 d6 ♘d5 32 ♖6f3 ♕xd6 33 ♕c4** △ d4 **♕e5 34 ♕e4 ♕d6 35 h3 ♘c3 36 ♕e1 ♕d4+ 37 ♔h1 f5 38 ♕e6+ ♔g7 39 ♖e1 ♖f7 40 ♕e8 ♘d5 41 ♕d8 ♘c3 42 ♕b8 ♘d5 43 ♕d6 ♘c3 44 ♕b8 ♘d5 45 ♖e8! ♘f6 46 ♖e6 ♕xa4 47 ♖fe3 +−**

♛xb5 48 ♜e7 ♛b1+ 49 ♚h2 ♛a2 50 ♜1e6 Δ ♕d6 **♛d5 51 ♜d6 ♛a2 52 ♛d8** Δ ♖xf6 **♜xe7 53 ♛xe7+ ♚f7 54 ♛e5** Δ ♖e6, ♖e7 **g5 55 ♛xf5 h6 56 ♛e5 1-0** time/zeit 56...♔g6 57 g4 Δ ♖e6, ♖e7 **Webb**

46 Panno-Sosonko
Wijk aan Zee 78

1 c4 ♞f6 2 ♞c3 e6 3 ♞f3 ♝b4 4 ♛c2 0-0 5 a3 ♝xc3 6 ♛xc3 b6 7 g3 7 b4! += **♝b7 8 ♝g2 d5!** 8...d6 9 0-0 ♘bd7 10 b4 += Szmetan-Christiansen, Wijk aan Zee 2 77 **9 cxd5** 9 d4?! dxc4 10 ♕xc4 ♗d5 11 ♕c3 ♘bd7 12 b4 a5! =+ Ree-Korchnoi, Amsterdam 76 **♞xd5 10 ♛c2 c5 11 0-0 ♞c6= 12 b3 e5** Δ ♘d4 **13 e3 ♜e8 14 d3 ♜c8 15 ♝b2 f6 16 ♜fd1 ♚h8 17 ♞d2 ♜c7 18 ♞c4 ♝c8?! 19 d4! cxd4 20 exd4 e4!** 20...exd4 21 ♗xd4 += **21 ♝xe4 b5**

22 ♝xd5 22 ♗xh7? ♘ce7 −+; 22 ♘e3?! ♘cb4 23 ♕b1 ♘xe3 24 fxe3 f5!≈ 22 ♘d2?! ♘xd4 23 ♕d3 ♘c3!?≈ **♛xd5 23 ♜e1** 23 ♘e3 += **♝e6** 23...♘e7?! 24 ♘e3 ♖xc2 25 ♘xd5± **24 ♞e3** 24 ♘d2 ♖cc8≈ **♛xb3 25 d5! ♛xc2** 25...♗xd5? 26 ♘xd5 +− **26 ♞xc2 ♞d8 27 ♞d4 ♝d7 28 ♜xe8+ ♝xe8 29 ♜e1 ♝g6 30 d6 ♜d7 31 ♞xb5 ♚g8** 31...a6 32 ♖e7 ♖xe7 33 dxe7 ♘c6 34 ♘c7 ♘xe7 35 ♘xa6 += **32 ♝c3 ♞b7 33 ♜d1 ♚f7 34 f4 ♞d8 35 ♝a5 a6 36 ♞c7** 36 ♗xd8!? ♖xd8 37 ♘c7±; 36...axb5 37 ♗c7∓ **♞b7 37 ♝b6 ♜xd6 38 ♜xd6 ♞xd6 39 ♞xa6 += ♚e6 40 ♝c5 ♞c4 41 ♝f8 ♝e8 42 ♞c7+ ♚f7 43 ♝b4 ♝c6 44 ♚f2 g5 45 f5 h5 46 ♞e6 ♝d7 47 ♞d4 ♞e5 48 h3 ♝a4?** 48...♘c6! 49 ♘xc6 ♗xc6 50 ♔e3 ♗g2 51 h4 ♗h3 52 ♔e4 ♗g2+ = **49 ♚e3 ♞c6 50 ♞f3 ♞e5?!** 50...♗c2!?; 50...g4!? **51 ♞d2! ♝d7 52 ♞e4 ♞c4+ 53 ♚d4 ♝xf5 54 a4 ♝g6 55 a5 +− ♞e5 56 ♚d5 ♞d7 57 ♞d6+ ♚e7 58 a6 1-0 Webb**

47 Hort-Sosonko Tilburg 77

1 c4 ♞f6 2 ♞f3 e6 3 ♞c3 ♝b4 4 ♛c2 0-0 5 e4!? e5! 6 a3 6 ♘xe5?! ♖e8 7 ♘f3 ♗xc3 8 dxc3 ♘xe4=; 7...♘xe4!? 8 ♘xe4 d5≈ **♝xc3 7 dxc3 b6** 7...h6!? **8 ♝g5 d6 9 ♝e2 ♝b7 10 ♞d2 ♞bd7 11 f3 ♞c5 12 ♞f1 ♞e6 13 ♝h4 ♞f4 14 ♞e3 ♞g6 15 ♝f2 ♞f4 16 ♝f1 a5 17 a4 ♝c8** 17...c6 18 0-0-0 ♕c7 19 g3 ♘e6 20 ♕b3 ♘c5 21 ♕a2 += **18 h4 += ♛e8 19 0-0-0 ♞d7 20 g3 ♞e6 21 h5 ♞dc5 22 b3 ♜b8 23 ♝e2 ♞g5 24 h6 g6 25 ♞d5 ♛d8 26 b4 axb4 27 cxb4 ♞ce6 28 b5±** 28 f4? c6 29 fxg5 cxd5≈; 29 ♘xb6 ♖xb6 30 ♗xb6 ♕xb6 31 fxg5 ♕xb4≈ **f5?!** 28...f6!?

29 ♝e3! 29 exf5? ♖xf5≈ **♝b7** 29...f4

30 gxf4 exf4 31 ♗d2 Δ ♗c3±; 29... fxe4 30 f4!± **30 exf5 ♜xf5 31 f4! exf4 32 gxf4 ♝xd5 33 cxd5 ♞xf4 34 ♝g4 ♜f6?** 34...♕e7! 35 ♖he1 ♖e5 36 ♕f2 ♘xd5!?; 36 ♕d2 ♘e4!? **35 ♝d4 ♜f7 36 ♝a1! +− ♜e7 37 ♝f6 ♜e2 38 ♝xd8 ♜xc2+ 39 ♚xc2 ♜xd8 40 ♜he1 ♞f7 41 ♜e7 ♞xh6 42 ♝e6+ ♞xe6 43 dxe6! ♞f5 44 ♜xc7 ♞e3+ 45 ♚d2 ♞xd1 46 ♚xd1 h5** 46...♖e8 47 e7 ♔f7 48 a5! +− **47 a5 h4 48 ♚e1 ♜f8 49 axb6 h3 50 e7 ♜b8 51 ♚f2 h2 52 ♚g2 ♚f7 53 b7 1-0 Webb**

48 Portisch-Andersson
Wijk aan Zee 78

1 c4 ♞f6 2 ♞c3 e6 3 ♞f3 b6 4 e4 ♝b7 5 d3 5 ♗d3 **c5 6 g3 ♝e7 7 ♝g2 0-0 8 0-0 a6 9 ♜e1 ♞c6 10 b3 d6 11 d4 cxd4 12 ♞xd4 ♞xd4 13 ♛xd4 ♛c7 14 ♝b2 ♜ab8 15 ♜ac1 ♜fd8 16 ♜ed1 ♝f8 17 ♝a3 ♝a8 18 h3 h6 19 ♝b4 ♝e7 20 ♚h2 ♞e8 21 ♛e3 ♞f6 22 e5!? dxe5 23 ♝xe7 ♛xe7 24 ♝xa8 ♜xa8 25 ♛xb6 += h5!? 26 ♛e3 ♛c7 27 ♜e1?!** 27 ♘e4 ♘xe4 28 ♕xe4 f5 29 ♕h4 += **♞d7 28 ♛g5** 28 ♘e4 h4!≈ **f5!≈ 29 ♛xh5 e4 30 ♜ed1 ♞e5 31 ♛e2 ♚f7** 31...♖d3!? **32 ♛h5+ ♚g8 33 ♚g2? ♛c6 34 ♛e2 ♜d3 35 h4 ♜f3!** Δ e3 **36 ♚h3 ♞d3** 36...♘g4! 37 ♖f1 ♖d8 Δ ♖dd3 −+ **37 ♛xf3! exf3 38 ♜xd3 g5∓ 39 ♜e1 ♚f7 40 ♜de3 ♜e8** 40...♖d8!? 41 ♖xe6 ♕xe6 42 ♖xe6 ♔xe6 43 ♘d5 g4+ 44 ♔h2 ♔e5∓ **41 g4!? ♜h8 42 h5 ♛d6 43 ♜xf3 ♜xh5+ 44 ♚g2** 44 gxh5 g4+ 45 ♔g2 gxf3+ 46 ♔xf3 ♕d4 −+ **♛h2+ 45 ♚f1 ♜h3 46 ♜ee3 ♜xf3 47 ♜xf3 ♚g6** 47...f4!? 48 ♘e4 ♕h4∓; 48 c5 ♕h4 49 c6 ♔e7∓ **48 ♜e3 ♚f7** 48...f4!? **49 ♜f3 ♚g6 50 gxf5+ exf5 51 ♞d5 ♛e5** 51...f4?! 52 c5! **52 ♜e3 ♛d4** 52...♕a1+ 53 ♔g2 ♕xa2 54 c5≈ **53 ♞e7+ ♚f6 54 ♞xf5!= ♚xf5 55 a4 ♛d2 56 ♚g2 ♛c1 ½-½ Webb**

49 Petrosian-Tarjan
Hastings 77/8

1 ♞f3 ♞f6 2 c4 g6 3 ♞c3 d5 4 ♛a4+ ♝d7! 4...c6 5 cxd5 ♘xd5 6 d4 +=; 4...♘c6?! 5 ♘d4! ♗d7 6 cxd5±; 5...♕d7 6 cxd5 ♘xd5 7 ♘xd5 ♕xd5 8 ♘xc6± ♗d7 9 ♕d4 +− **5 ♛b3 dxc4! 6 ♛xc4** 6 ♕xb7 ♘c6 7 ♘b5 ♘d5!∓ **♝g7 7 g3 0-0 8 ♝g2 ♞c6 9 0-0?!** 9 d3! **♝g4!** Δ ♗xf3, ♘e5xf3+∓ **10 ♛a4 ♛d7** Δ ♗h3 **11 ♞g5 ♜ab8!?** 11...h6 12 ♘ge4 ♘xe4 13 ♗xe4= **12 d3** 12 h3!? h6 13 hxg4 hxg5 14 d3 +=; 12...♗f5 13 g4 ♗e6 14 d3 +=; 12...b5! 13 ♕d1 h6 14 hxg4 hxg5 15 d3 b4 16 ♘e4 ♘xe4 17 ♗xe4 ♘d4 18 ♗xg5 ♕xg4 19 ♗xe7 ♘xe2+ =+; 18 e3 ♘e6= **♞d4 13 ♛xd7 ♝xd7= 14 ♝f4 ♜fc8 15 ♞f3** 15 ♖fc1!? ♗g4 16 ♔f1 h6=; 16 e3! += **♞h5!** 15...♘xf3+ 16 ♗xf3+ = **16 ♝g5 e5 17 ♜fc1** 17 ♘xd4 exd4 18 ♘d5 ♔h8 19 ♗f3 c6 20 ♗xh5 cxd5 21 ♗f3= **♚f8 18 ♞d2 ♞f6 19 h3 ♝c8 20 ♞b3 c5! 21 ♞xd4 cxd4 22 ♞d5 f6 23 ♝d2 ♚f7 24 e3 ♝f8?** 24...dxe3 25 ♗xe3 b6= **25 exd4 exd4 26 ♞f4 +=** Δ ♗d5+, ♘e2± **f5??** 26...♘c7 27 ♘e2 ♘e6= **27 ♞e2 +− ♝b5 28 ♜xc8 ♜xc8 29 ♞xd4 ♝xd3 30 ♝xb7 ♜d8 31 ♞c6 ♜d5 32 ♞b4! ♜b5 33 ♝d5+ ♚g7 34 ♝c6 ♜b6** 34...♗xb4 35 ♗xb5 +−; 34...♖xb4 35 ♗xb4 ♗xb4 36 ♗xe8 +− **35 ♝c3+ ♚h6 36 ♞xd3 ♜xc6 37 ♜e1 ♞f6 38 ♜c1 ♜a6 39 ♝d2+ g5 40 h4 ♞e4 41 hxg5+ ♚h5** 41...♘xg5 42 ♘e5 ♔h5 43 ♔g2 +− **42 ♝e3 ♜xa2 43 ♚g2 ♚g6 44 ♜c7 ♝d6 45 ♜c6** Δ f3/♗f4 **1-0 Petrosian**

1 d4 d5 2 c4 dxc4

50 Kuzmin-Miles Reykjavik 78

1 d4 d5 2 c4 dxc4 3 Nf3 Nf6 4 Nc3 a6 5 e3 5 e4!? **b5 6 a4 b4 7 Nb1 e6 8 Bxc4 Bb7 9 0-0 Nbd7 10 Nbd2 c5= 11 Ne5!? cxd4 12 exd4 Nb6!? 13 a5** 13 N2f3 Nxc4 =+ **Qxd4!** 13...Nxc4? 14 N2xc4 Δ Qa4+, Nb6±; 13...Nbd7 **14 Nef3 Bxf3 15 Qxf3 Nbd5 16 Bb3** ∝/=+ **Be7** 16...Bd6 17 Nc4 **17 Ba4+ Kf8 18 Bc6 Rd8 19 Qe2 Qa7 20 Nf3 Rc8 21 Ba4 h6 22 Bd2 g6 23 Ne5 Kg7 24 Nc6 Qb7 25 Rac1** 25 Nxe7 Qxe7 26 Qxa6 Ra8∓ **Bd6 26 Rc4 Rc7 27 Rfc1 Rhc8 28 Qd3 Ng8! 29 b3 Nge7 30 Qc2 Nxc6 31 Bxc6 Qb8 32 Qb2+?** 32 g3∝ **f6!∓ 33 Bd7 Bxh2+ 34 Kf1 Be5 35 Qb1 Rd8 36 Bxe6** 36 Rxc7? Nxc7 **Nc3 37 Qc2** 37 Bxc3∓ **Rxc4 38 Bxc4 Bf4! −+ 39 Bxc3** 39 Bxf4 Qxf4 (Δ Rd2, Qh2) 40 Re1 Rd2 41 Re7+ Kf8 42 Rf7+ Ke8 −+; 39 Re1 Rxd2 40 Re7+ Kf8 41 Rf7+ Ke8 −+ **Bxc1 40 Qe4 Qd6** 40...Re8 41 Qd5 **41 Be1 h5 42 Qb7+ Rd7 43 Qxb4 Qxb4** 43...Qh2!? **44 Bxb4 Bd2 45 Bc5** 45 Bxd2 Rxd2 46 Bxa6 Ra2 47 b4 Ra4 −+ **Bxa5 46 Bxa6 Bb6! 47 Bb4** 47 Bxb6 Rd6 −+ **Ra7 48 Bc4 Ra2** 48...Ra1+ **49 Be1 Rc2 50 g3 Bd4 51 Bd3 Rc1 52 Ke2 Bc3 53 Bd2 Bxd2 54 Kxd2 Rc7 55 b4 g5 56 b5 Kf8 57 Be4 Rc4 58 Kd3 Rb4 59 Bc6 Ke7 0-1 Miles**

51 Balashov-Miles Bugojno 78

1 d4 d5 2 Nf3 Nf6 3 c4 dxc4 4 Nc3 a6 4...Nc6!? **5 e4 b5 6 e5 Nd5 7 a4 Nxc3 8 bxc3 Qd5 9 g3 Be6** 9...Bb7 10 Bg2 Qd7 11 Ba3 e6 12 Bxf8 Kxf8 13 0-0 g6 14 Nh4 += Bronstein-Korchnoi, Moscow 64 **10 Bg2 Qb7 11 0-0 Bd5 12 e6!** N; 12 Ba3 e6 13 Bxf8 Kxf8 14 Nh4 Bxg2 15 Nxg2 Nd7= Ivkov-Filip, Zagreb 65 **Bxe6 13 Ng5 Bd5 14 Bxd5 Qxd5 15 axb5 axb5 16 Rxa8 Qxa8 17 Qg4 Nc6** 17...Qb7 18 Qf5 f6 19 Ne6 +−; 17...e6 18 Nxe6 +−; 17...Nd7 18 Nxf7 +−

18 Qf3 f6 19 Ne6 +− Qb7 20 Qd5 g5 21 Bf4! Bh6 22 Re1 Qb6 23 Nxc7+ Kf8 24 Re6 gxf4 25 Rxc6 Qb8 26 Ne6+ Ke8 27 Rc7 Kf7 28 Nxf4+ Kf8 29 Qc5 1-0 Webb

52 Kavalek-Miles
Wijk aan Zee 78

1 d4 d5 2 c4 dxc4 3 Nf3 Nf6 4 Nc3 a6 5 e4!? b5 6 e5 Nd5 7 a4 Nxc3 7...c6!?; 7...Bb7 8 e6∝ **8 bxc3 Qd5 9 g3 Bb7 10 Bg2 Qd7 11 Nh4! c6** 11...Bxg2 12 Nxg2 e6 13 Qf3 Ra7 14 axb5 Qxb5 15 Nf4 Δ d5 ∝/±; 12...Qd5 13 0-0 Δ Nf4, d5± **12 f4!?** 12 Ba3!?≈ Bronstein-Korchnoi, USSR 64 **e6 13 f5! exf5 14 0-0 g6 15 Bg5 ∝/± Be7** 15...Bg7 16 Bf6 0-0 17 Nxf5 gxf5 18 Qh5 h6 19 Rxf5 Δ Rg5 +−; 16... Kf8!? **16 Bf6 Rg8** 16...Bxf6 17 exf6 Qd6 18 Re1+ Kf8 19 Re7 Nd7 20 axb5±; 18...Kd8 19 axb5 ∝/±; 19 Re7!? **17 Qd2 Qe6** 17...Bf8?! **18 axb5 Bxf6** 18...axb5 19 Rxa8 Bxa8 20 Ra1 Bb7 21 Ra7 Qc8 22 Bxe7 Kxe7 23 d5 +− Rd8 24 Qg5+ Ke8

25 d6 ♖d7 26 ♘xf5 **19 exf6 ♕xf6 20 ♖ae1+ ♔d8** ∞/± **21 bxc6?!** 21 ♕h6 Δ ♘xf5± **♗xc6 22 d5 ♗d7** 22...♗b5 23 d6± **23 ♘f3** 23 d6 ♘c6 **♖e8 24 ♖b1 ♗b5 25 ♘d4 ♘d7 26 g4** 26 ♘xb5? axb5 27 ♖xb5 ♕e5 ∞/=+ **♕d6 27 gxf5 f6** Zeitnot 27...♘e5 28 fxg6 Δ ♕g5+, ♖f6± **28 ♕h6 ♘e5 29 fxg6?** Zeitnot 29 ♕xh7 ∞/± **hxg6 30 ♕f4?** 30 ♘e6+ ♔c8 31 ♕f4 **f5 31 ♖fe1 ♔d7! 32 ♘c6? ♘d3!** −+ **33 ♖xe8** 33 ♕xd6+ ♔xd6 −+ **♕xf4 34 ♖xa8 ♕e3+ 0-1 Miles**

53 Gligoric-Portisch Bugojno 78
1 d4 d5 2 c4 dxc4 3 ♘f3 ♘f6 4 e3 e6 5 ♗xc4 c5 6 0-0 a6 7 a4 ♘c6 8 ♕e2 cxd4 9 ♖d1 ♗e7 10 exd4 0-0 11 ♘c3 ♘d5 12 ♗d3 12 h4!?; 12 ♕e4 ♘f6 13 ♕h4 ♘d5 14 ♕g4 ♘f6 15 ♕g3 ♘h5 16 ♕h3 Polugaevsky-Hort, Manila 76; 16...g6!?= **♘cb4 13 ♗b1 b6!** 13... ♗d7 14 ♘e5 ♗c6 15 ♖a3 ♘f6 16 ♗g5 g6 17 a5 += Gligoric-Ivkov, Novi Sad 76 **14 a5?!** 14 ♘e5!? ♗b7 15 ♖a3=; 15 a5!? **bxa5 15 ♘e4** 15 ♘e5!? **♗d7 16 ♘e5 ♗b5 17 ♕h5 f5!** 17...g6 18 ♕h6 Δ ♖a3/♘g5≈; 17...f6? 18 ♘g5! **18 ♘c3** 18 ♘g5!? **♗f6∓ 19 ♘xb5 axb5 20 ♖a3 ♕e8 21 ♕e2 a4 22 ♖h3 ♖c8** Δ ♖xc1 **23 ♗d2 ♘c2 24 ♕d3 ♘xd4!** −+ **25 ♖e1** 25 ♕xd4 ♖c4 **♘b3 26 g4 ♗xe5! 27 ♖xe5 ♘f6 28 ♗c3 ♘xg4 29 ♖xb5 ♕c6 30 ♖b4 ♘f6 31 ♖g3 ♖c7 32 ♕e2 ♘c5 33 ♕e5 ♘cd7 34 ♕e2 ♔h8 35 ♗a2 ♖e8 36 ♗c4 e5 37 ♗b5 ♕e6 38 ♖xa4 f4 39 ♖g5 h6 40 ♖g6 ♕f5 41 ♖xf6 gxf6 0-1 Webb**

1 d4 d5 2 c4 c6

54 Knaak-I.Fischer Leipzig 77
1 d4 d5 2 c4 c6 3 ♘f3 ♘f6 4 ♘c3 dxc4 5 a4 ♗f5 6 e3 e6 7 ♗xc4 ♗b4 8 0-0 ♘bd7?! 8...0-0! **9 ♘h4** 9 ♕b3 += **♗g4 10 f3 ♗h5** 10...♘d5?! 11 fxg4 ♕xh4 12 e4 ♘xc3 13 bxc3 ♗xc3 14 ♖a3± **11 g4 ♘d5?! 12 ♕e1 ♗g6 13 e4! ♘5b6** 13...♘xc3?! 14 bxc3 ♗xc3 15 ♕xc3 ♕xh4 16 ♗a3 0-0-0? 17 ♗a6! +−; 13...♕b6!? **14 ♗b3 a5 15 ♗e3± ♗e7 16 ♘g2 h5 17 ♖d1!?** 17 ♘f4 ♘f8 18 ♖d1± **hxg4 18 fxg4 ♘f6**

19 d5! cxd5 20 exd5 ♘fxd5 20...exd5 21 g5 ♘g4 22 ♗f4± **21 ♘f4 ♕c7 22 ♗xd5 ♘xd5** 22...exd5 23 ♘b5 +− **23 ♖xd5! exd5 24 ♘cxd5 ♕d6 25 ♗d4 ♖h7 26 ♖f2 ♕d7** 26...♔d7 27 ♘b6+ ♔e8 28 ♘fd5 +− **27 ♘xe7 1-0 Webb**

55 Petrosian-Klaric Sochi 77
1 c4 ♘f6 2 ♘c3 c6 3 d4 d5 4 cxd5 cxd5 5 ♗f4 e6 6 e3 a6?! 6...♗e7 7 ♗d3 ♘c6 8 h3 0-0 9 ♘f3 ♗d7 10 0-0 ♕b6 11 a3 += Portisch-Petrosian (12) 74 **7 ♗d3 ♘bd7 8 ♘f3 ♗e7 9 h3 b5 10 0-0 ♗b7 11 a4! b4 12 ♘a2** Δ ♘c1-b3± **♖c8 13 ♘c1 ♘b6 14 ♕e2 ♘c4!? 15 ♘b3!?** 15 b3 ♘a3 16 ♗xa6 ♖c2 17 ♗xb7 ♖xe2 18 ♗c6+ Δ ♘xe2±; 15... ♘a5 16 ♗xa6 ♗xa6 17 ♕xa6 0-0 += **♘a5 16 ♘fd2! 0-0?** 16...♕b6 17 ♘xa5 ♕xa5 18 ♘b3 ♕b6 19 a5± **17 ♗xa6 ♗xa6 18 ♕xa6 ♘c4 19 ♖a2! ♘d7 20 ♘f3 +− g5 21 ♗g3 h6 22 a5 ♖a8 23 ♕b5 f5 24 ♕c6 ♖f6 25 ♘e5**

♘dxe5 26 ♗xe5 ♖g6 27 a6 ♖a7 28 ♘a5! ♘xa5 29 ♖xa5 ♔f7 30 ♖b5 ♖g8 31 ♖b7 ♕a8 32 ♕d7 ♖xb7 33 axb7 ♕a7 34 ♕c8 1-0 Petrosian

56 Bukic-Portisch Bugojno 78

1 d4 d5 2 c4 c6 3 ♘f3 ♘f6 4 cxd5 cxd5 5 ♘c3 ♘c6 6 ♗f4 ♕b6?! 7 ♘a4 7 a3!? **♕a5+ 8 ♗d2 ♕d8 7 e3 e6 10 ♖c1 ♘e4 11 ♗b5** 11 ♗d3 ♗d6 12 0-0 0-0 13 a3 ♕e7 14 b4 e5 15 dxe5 ♘xe5 16 ♘xe5 ♕xe5 17 f4 ♕e7 18 ♘c3 ♘xc3 19 ♖xc3 ♖d8 20 ♕c2 h6 21 e4 d4! 22 ♖c4 ♗e6 23 ♖xd4 ♖ac8 24 ♕b2 ♗c7 ½-½! Ivkov-Portisch, Bugojno 78 **♗d7 12 0-0 ♖c8 13 ♘c5 ♗xc5 14 dxc5 0-0 15 b4 += a6 16 ♗e2 ♘a7 17 ♗e1!?** 17 a4 b5 18 ♖a1 +=; 17...a5 18 bxa5!? **♗b5 18 ♘d4 ♗xe2 19 ♕xe2 ♕d7 20 ♖c2** 20 f3 ♘d6!? **e5 21 ♘b3 ♘c6 22 a3 ♕e6 23 ♖b2 ♖fe8 24 f3 ♘f6 25 ♗h4 ♘d7 26 ♖d1 ♘f8 27 ♗e1 ♘g6 ½-½** 28 a4 ♘a7?! 29 ♘a5!± ♕d7? 30 ♘c4; 28...♕d7!? 29 ♘d2 ♕e6= **Webb**

1 d4 d5 2 c4 e6

57 Timman-Gligoric Bugojno 78

1 d4 d5 2 c4 e6 3 ♘c3 c5 4 cxd5 exd5 5 ♘f3 ♘c6 6 g3 ♘f6 7 ♗g2 ♗e7 8 0-0 0-0 9 dxc5 ♗xc5 9...d4?! 10 ♘a4 ♗f5 11 ♗f4 ♗e4 12 ♖c1 ♕d5 13 ♕b3 += **10 ♗g5 d4 11 ♗xf6 ♕xf6 12 ♘d5!?** 12 ♘e4= **♕d8 13 ♘d2 ♖e8 14 ♖c1 ♗f8 15 ♘b3 ♗g4** 15...♗e6 16 ♘f4 ♗xb3 17 ♕xb3± **16 ♖e1 ♖e5 17 ♘f4 ♗b4 18 ♘d2 d3! 19 ♘xd3 ♗xe2 20 ♖xe2 ♕xd3 21 ♗e4 ♕d4** 21...♕d6?! 22 a3 ♗a5 23 ♘c4 +=; 22...♗e5 23 b4± **22 ♖c4 ♕d6** 22...♕xb2? 23 ♘f3 **23 ♗xc6 ♖xe2 24 ♕xe2 ♗xd2 25 ♗xb7 ♖d8 += 26 ♖e4 g6 27 ♗a6 ♗g5 28 ♗c4** 28 h4!? ♗f6 29 b3 ♕d1+ 30 ♔g2 +=; 28...♗h6 29 ♗c4 ♕d1+ 30 ♔g2 Δ ♖e7 += **♕d1+ 29 ♔g2 ♕xe2 30 ♖xe2 ♖d2= 31 ♖xd2 ♗xd2 32 ♔f3 ♗c1 33 b3 ♗a3 34 ♔e4 ♔f8 35 ♔d5 ♔e7 36 ♔c6 g5 37 g4 h6 38 f3 a5 39 ♔b5 ♗b4 40 a3 ♗xa3 41 ♔xa5 f6 42 b4 ♔d6 43 b5 ♗c5 ½-½ Webb**

58 Ljubojevic-Gligoric Bugojno 78

1 d4 d5 2 c4 e6 3 ♘c3 c5 4 cxd5 exd5 5 ♘f3 ♘c6 6 g3 ♘f6 7 ♗g2 ♗e7 8 0-0 0-0 9 ♗g5 cxd4 10 ♘xd4 h6 11 ♗e3 ♖e8 12 ♖c1 ♗f8 13 ♘xc6! 13 ♘b3 ♗e6 14 ♘b5 ♗g4 15 h3 ♗f5 16 ♘5d4 ♘xd4 17 ♘xd4 ♗d7= Petrosian-Spassky (18), 69 **bxc6 16 ♘a4 ♗d7 15 ♗c5 ♗xc5 16 ♘xc5 ♗g4 17 ♖e1 ♕b6 18 ♕c2 ♖ad8 19 h3 ♗c8** 19...♗h5!? **20 b3 ♕b8 21 e3±**

♖e7 22 ♖ed1 ♖de8 23 ♖d4 ♘h7 24 ♕d2 ♘g5 25 h4 ♘e6 26 ♘xe6 ♖xe6 27 ♕b4 ♕b6 28 ♕c5 Δ ♗h3 **♖f6 29 ♖a4 ♕xc5 30 ♖xc5 a6 31 ♗f1 ♔f8 32 ♗xa6! +− d4!? 33 exd4** 33 ♗xc8? dxe3! **♖e1+ 34 ♔g2 ♗e6** 34...♗xa6 35 ♖xa6 ♖e2 36 ♖a8+ ♔e7 37 ♖e5+ **35 ♗c4 ♗xc4 36 ♖a8+ ♔e7 37 bxc4 ♖d1 38 ♖e5+ ♖e6 39 ♖a7+ ♔f6 40 ♖e3! ♖xd4 41 ♖f3+ ♔e5 42 ♖axf7 g6 43 ♖e3+ ♖e4 44 ♔f3 ♖xe3+ 45 ♔xe3 ♖e8 46 a4 h5 47 a5 ♖a8 48 ♖e7+ ♔f5 49 ♖c7 ♖xa5 50 ♖xc6**

Ra3+ 51 Kd4 Rf3 52 Rc8 Ke6 53 Re8+ Kd6 54 c5+ Kd7 55 Rg8 1-0 Webb

59 Sveshnikov-Nunn Hastings 77/8

1 Nf3 d5 2 c4 e6 3 d4 c5 4 cxd5 exd5 5 Nc3 Nc6 6 Bg5?! 6 g3; e3; 6 Bf4 **Be7** 6...f6!? 7 Be3 c4 Δ Bb4, Ne7∞ **7 Bxe7 Ngxe7 8 e3 c4?!** 8...Qb6! 9 Qd2 cxd4 10 Nxd4 Nxd4 11 exd4 0-0= **9 Be2 0-0 10 0-0 b5!? 11 Ne5** 11 Nxb5 Rb8 12 Qa4 Qb6 =+ **Nxe5** 11...b4 12 Nxc6 Nxc6 13 Na4 += **12 dxe5 Rb8!?** 12...a6 13 Bf3 Be6 14 Qd2= **13 a4! b4 14 Nb5 Nc6?** 14...a6 15 Nd4 Qc7 16 f4 f6 17 exf6 Rxf6∞ **15 f4! Qb6 16 Qxd5!** 16 Nd4 Nxd4 17 exd4 f5!= **Qxe3+ 17 Rf2** 17 Kh1?? Qxe2 18 Qxc6 Bb7 −+ **Na5** 17...Rxb5 18 axb5 Nd4 19 Qxc4± **18 Nd6 Qb6** 18...Nb3 19 Nxc4! Qd4 20 Qxd4 Nxd4 21 Bf1± **19 Qf3!** 19 Bxc4 Be6 20 Qd3 Nxc4 21 Nxc4 Bxc4 22 Qxc4 Rfc8 23 Qf1 b3≈ **Bd7 20 f5 Qd4 21 Qg3 f6** 21...Qxb2 22 Rd1 Qc2 23 Bf3 Δ f6 +− **22 Rd1 Qxe5 23 Qxe5 fxe5 24 Nxc4 Bxa4 25 Ra1 +− Bb5 26 Rxa5 e4 27 Ne3 Bxe2 28 Rxe2 1-0 Sveshnikov**

60 Diesen-Kovacs Stip 77

1 c4 c5 2 Nf3 Nf6 3 Nc3 Nc6 4 e3 e6 5 d4 d5 6 cxd5 Nxd5 7 Bd3 cxd4 8 exd4 Be7 9 0-0 0-0 10 Re1 Ncb4 11 Bb1 b6 12 Ne5 Bb7 13 a3 Nxc3 14 bxc3 Nd5 15 Qd3 15 Qf3! Rb8 16 Qh3 += Muratov-Jurkov, USSR 67 **g6 16 Bh6 Re8 17 Qf3 Bf6!** 17...f6? 18 Bxg6! hxg6 (18...Nf4 19 Qxf4 hxg6 20 Qg4 +−) 19 Qg4 Nf4 20 Bxf4 Bf8 21 Qxg6+ Bg7 22 Qf7+ Kh7 23 Re3 +− **18 Ng4** 18 c4!? Bxe5 19 dxe5 (19 Rxe5 Qh4 20 Be4 Qxh6 21 cxd5 f5∞) 19...Qh4 20 Be4 Qxh6 21 cxd5 exd5 22 Bxd5 Bxd5 23 Qxd5 Qf8= **Bg7 19 Bxg7** 19 c4 Nf6 20 Nxf6+ Qxf6 21 Qxb7 Bxh6= **Kxg7 20 Ba2 h5** 20...Nf6? 21 Qxb7 Nxg4 22 Bxe6 += **21 Ne5 ½-½** 21...Qf6 22 Qxf6+ Nxf6 = **L.Kovacs**

61 Deze-Adamski Zalaegerrzeg 77

1 c4 Nf6 2 Nc3 e6 3 Nf3 c5 4 e3 Be7 5 d4 cxd4 6 exd4 d5 7 cxd5 Nxd5 8 Bd3 Nc6 9 0-0 0-0 10 Re1 Nf6 11 a3 b6 11...a6 12 Bc2 b5!? **12 Bg5 Bb7 13 Bb1!?** 13 Bc2 Rc8 14 Rc1 Re8 15 Qd3 g6 16 Bh6 Qd6 17 h3 Bf8 18 Bg5 Bg7 **Rc8 14 Qd3 g6 15 Ba2 Re8?!** 15...Ng4!? Neamtu-Korchnoi, Bucharest 66 **16 Rad1 Nd5 17 h4!? Nxc3 18 bxc3 Na5?!** 18...Bxg5 19 Nxg5 h6 20 Nf3 Qf6 Δ Na5 **19 Bxe7! Qxe7?** 19...Rxe7!? 20 h5!± **20 d5!± Qxa3**

21 dxe6!! Qxa2 22 Ng5! +− f6 22...fxe6 23 Qd7 +− **23 Qd7 fxg5 24 Qf7+ Kh8 25 Rd7 1-0 Maric**

62 Gulko-Grigorian USSR Final 77

1 c4 Nf6 2 Nc3 e6 3 Nf3 d5 4 d4 c5 5 cxd5 Nxd5 6 g3 Nc6 6...cxd4 7 Nxd5 Qxd5 8 Qxd4 Qb5! 9 e4 Qb4+ 10 Bd2 Nc6!= **7 Bg2 Be7 8 0-0 0-0 9 e4** 9 Nxd5 exd5= **Nxc3!?** 9...Nb6 10 d5 exd5 11 exd5 Nb4 12 Ne1 += **10**

bxc3 cxd4 11 cxd4 b6 12 Bb2 TN 12 d5!? exd5 13 exd5 Nb4∞; 12 Bf4?! Ba6 13 Re1 Nb4 14 Bf1 Bxf1 15 Kxf1 Rc8 16 Re2 f5 =+ **Bf6 13 Qe2 Bb7 14 Rfd1** += **Na5 15 Ne5 Rc8 16 d5 exd5 17 exd5 Qd6 18 Nc6 Rfe8 19 Qc2 Bxb2 20 Qxb2 Bxc6!= 21 dxc6 Qe6 22 Rd7 Nxc6 23 Rad1 Qg4 24 Qd2 h5 25 Rc1 Ne5 26 Rxc8 Rxc8 27 Rxa7 h4! 28 h3 Nf3+ 29 Bxf3 Qxf3 30 Rc7 Rxc7 31 Qd8+ Kh7 32 Qxc7 Qd1+ 33 Kh2 hxg3+ 34 Kxg3 Qg1+ 35 Kf3 Qg6 36 Qc4 Qf5+ 37 Kg3 Qe5+ ½-½ Petrosian**

63 Knaak-A.Petrosian Leipzig 77
1 d4 d5 2 c4 e6 3 Nc3 Be7 4 cxd5 exd5 5 Bf4 c6 6 e3 Bd6?! 6...Bf5 7 g4 Be6 8 h4!? **7 Bxd6 Qxd6 8 Bd3 Ne7 9 Qc2 Nd7 10 Nf3 Nf6 11 Ne5± Ng4 12 Nxg4 Bxg4 13 0-0 Bh5?!** 13...h6± **14 e4! dxe4 15 Nxe4 Qxd4** 15...Qc7 16 Qc5! **16 Ng3 Bg4 17 Rfe1 Be6 18 Bf5 0-0-0!?** 18...0-0 19 Rad1 Qf6 20 Bxe6 fxe6 21 Rd7± **19 Bxe6+ fxe6 20 Rxe6 Nd5 21 Nf5 Qf4 22 g3 Qc7 23 Rae1± g6** 23...Kb8!? **24 Nd4! Kb8 25 R6e5 Qb6 26 Ne6 Nb4 27 Qe2 Nd3**

28 Ra1!! 28 Rd1 Nxe5 29 Qxe5+ Kc8 30 Nxd8 Rxd8 31 Rxd8+ Qxd8 = **Nxe5** 28...Rd7/Rd6 29 Rd1! +− **29 Qxe5+ Kc8 30 a4 c5** 30...a5 31 b4! **31 Rc1 Qd6 32 Rxc5+ Kb8 33 Nxd8 Rxd8 34 Qc3!** 34 Qxd6+?!± **Qe6 35 Qf3 Qb6 36 Rb5 Qc7 37 Kg2 a6 38 Rb3 Qe7 39 Rc3 Qd7 40 Qf4+ Ka8 41 Rc7** +− **Qd3 42 Qf3 Qxf3+ 43 Kxf3 Rd3+ 44 Kg2 h5 45 Rg7 Rd6 46 a5 Rd5 47 Rxg6 Rxa5 48 Re6 Ra2 49 Re2 a5 50 f4 a4 51 Rf2 1-0 Webb**

64 Georgadze-Bednarski Decin 77
1 c4 e6 2 Nc3 d5 3 d4 Nf6 4 Nf3 Be7 5 Bf4!? 0-0 5...dxc4 **6 e3 c5 7 dxc5 Bxc5 8 a3!?** 8 Qc2 Nc6 9 a3 Qa5 10 Nd2 Be7 11 Bg3 Qd8 Petrosian-Liberzon, Biel 76 **dxc4 9 Bxc4 Qxd1+ 10 Rxd1 Nc6 11 Ke2!?** 11 Ne5 Nxe5 12 Bxe5 b6= **Bd7?!** 11...b6 **12 Ne4 Nxe4 13 Rxd7+= Rfd8 14 Rhd1** 14 Rxd8+ Rxd8 15 Bd3? Nxf2 16 Bxh7+ Kxh7 =+ **Rxd7 15 Rxd7 Rd8 16 Rxd8+** 16 Rxb7 Na5 **Nxd8 17 Bd3 Nf6 18 h3 Kf8 19 Nd2 Nc6** 19...Ke7 20 Nc4± Δ b4 **20 Nc4 Be7 21 Bh2?!** Δ Nd6; 21 g4! **Bd8 22 g4** 22 Nd6 Bc7 **g6 23 Bd6+ Be7 24 Bg3! h5** 24...Bd8 25 Nd6 Bc7 26 Nxb7 +− **25 g5 Nd7 26 h4 Nc5 27 Bc2 Nd8 28 Ne5?** 28 b4! Nd7 29 Nd6 Δ Nc6± **b5 29 f3 Ke8 30 Bf4 Bd6?** 30...Ncb7+= **31 Nxg6 1-0 Georgadze**

65 Ogaard-Sigurjonsson Reykjavik 78
1 d4 Nf6 2 c4 e6 3 Nf3 d5 4 Nc3 Be7 5 Bg5 Nbd7 6 e3 0-0 7 Rc1 a6 8 c5 8 cxd5 **c6 9 Bd3 e5!?** 9...b6 **10 dxe5 Ne8! 11 Bf4 Nxc5 12 Bb1 f5!?** 12...Bg4 **13 exf6 Nxf6 14 Ng5!? Ne6 15 Qd3?!** 15 Nxe6 Bxe6 16 0-0= **Nxf4 16 exf4 h6 17 0-0??** 17 Nh7 Rf7 18 Nxf6+ Rxf6 19 Qh7+ Kf7 =+ **hxg5 18 fxg5 Ne4 19 Nxe4 dxe4 20 Qxe4 Bf5 21 Qc4+ Qd5** −+ **22 Qxd5+ cxd5 23 Bxf5 Rxf5 24 f4 Bd6 25 g3 Re8**

25...d4! **26 ♔f2 ♔f7 27 ♔f3 ♖e4 28 ♖fd1 ♖a4 29 a3 d4 30 ♖c2 ♔e6 31 ♖d3 ♖c5 32 ♖e2+ ♔d5 33 ♖e4? ♖c2! 34 f5 ♖f2+ 35 ♔xf2 ♔xe4 36 f6 gxf6 37 g6 ♖c4 38 ♖b3 ♖c2+ 39 ♔e1 b5 40 h4 ♗f8 41 h5 d3 42 ♔d1 ♔e3 0-1 Sigurjonsson**

66 Shamkovich-Anguiano Mexico 78
1 c4 ♘f6 2 ♘c3 e6 3 ♘f3 d5 4 d4 ♗e7 5 ♗g5 ♘bd7 6 e3 0-0 7 ♖c1 c6 8 ♕c2 ♖e8 8...b6 **9 a3 h6** 9...b6 **10 ♗f4! dxc4?! 11 ♗xc4 b5 12 ♗a2 ♗b7 13 0-0 ♕b6** Δ c5 **14 ♘e5! ♖ed8** 14...c5? 15 ♘xd7 ♘xd7 16 d5!±; 14...♘xe5 15 dxe5 ♘d7 16 ♗b1 ♘f8 17 ♘e4±; 14...♘f8!?

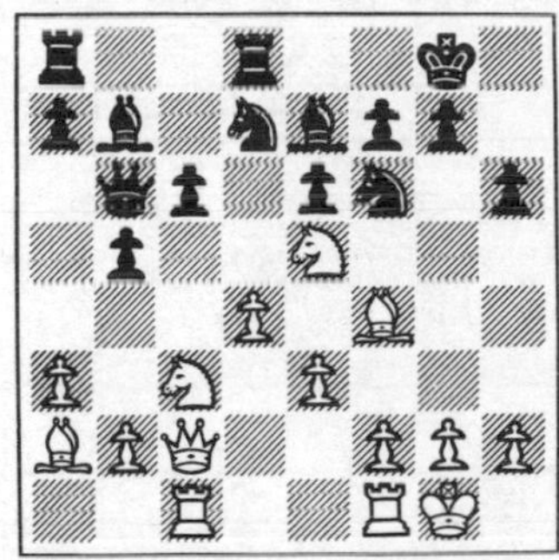

15 ♗xh6!! gxh6 15...♘xe5 16 dxe5 gxh6 16 exf6 ♗xf6 17 ♘e4± **16 ♗xe6!** Δ ♕g6+ **♘xe5** 16...♔g7!? 17 f4! ♘xe5 18 fxe5 fxe6 19 exf6+ ♗xf6 20 ♖xf6! ♔xf6 21 ♕h7! (Δ ♖f1+) +− **17 dxe5 ♘d5?** 17...fxe6 18 ♕g6+ ♔h8 19 exf6 ♗f8 20 f7 ♗g7 21 ♘e4! +− Δ ♘f6/♘g5 **18 ♕g6+ ♔h8 19 ♕xh6+ 1-0 Shamkovich**

67 Petrosian-Suba Sochi 77
1 d4 ♘f6 2 c4 e6 3 ♘f3 d5 4 ♗g5 ♗e7 5 ♘c3 0-0 6 ♕c2 ♘bd7 7 e3 c6 7...h6 8 ♗h4 c5 9 ♖d1 cxd4 10 ♘xd4 ♘b6!? 11 ♗e2 ♗d7 12 cxd5 ♘fxd5 13 ♗xe7 ♕xe7 14 ♘xd5 ♘xd5 15 0-0 ♖ac8 16 ♕b3 ♖c7= Korchnoi-Petrosian (7) 77 **8 a3 a6 9 ♖d1 ♖e8 10 h3 ♘h5?!** 10...b6 11 cxd5 cxd5= **11 ♗xe7 ♕xe7 12 b4** 12 g4 ♘hf6 13 g5 ♘h5 14 ♖g1 Δ ♘e5!? **♘hf6 13 ♕b3 b5 14 cxd5 exd5!∝** 14...cxd5± **15 ♗d3 a5 16 0-0 axb4 17 axb4 ♗b7?** 17...♘b6 18 ♘e5 ♗b7 Δ ♘c4=; 18 ♖fe1 ♗e6!= **18 ♖fe1 ♘e4?** 18...♕d6 19 e4 dxe4 20 ♘xe4 ♘xe4 21 ♗xe4 ♘f6 +=; 20 ♘g5!? **19 ♗xe4 dxe4 20 ♘d2± ♘f6 21 ♖a1 g6?** 21...h5 Δ h4 **22 ♖ec1 h5 23 ♖xa8 ♖xa8 24 ♕b1! ♖e8 25 ♘e2 ♕d6?** 25...h4! **26 ♘g3 ♕e6 27 ♖c5! +− h4** 27...♘d7 28 ♖g5 ♘f6 29 ♖e5 +−; 28...f6 29 ♖xg6+ ♔h7 30 ♕d1 +−; 30 ♘xh5 +− **28 ♖e5 hxg3 29 ♖xe6 gxf2+ 30 ♔xf2 ♖xe6 31 ♕a2 ♔g7 32 ♕a7 ♗c8 33 ♕c7 ♗d7 34 ♘b3 ♖e8 35 ♘c5 ♗e6 36 ♕xc6 ♗c4 37 g4 ♖e7 38 g5 ♘d5 39 ♕d6 ♖e8 40 ♘d7 ♔g8 1-0 Petrosian**

68 Grigorian-Geller USSR Final 77
1 d4 d5 2 c4 e6 3 ♘c3 ♗e7 4 ♘f3 ♘f6 5 ♗g5 0-0 6 e3 h6 7 ♗h4 b6 8 ♕b3 ♗b7 9 ♗xf6 ♗xf6 10 cxd5 exd5 11 ♖d1 ♖e8 12 ♗d3 ♘c6! 13 0-0 13 ♘xd5 ♘a5 14 ♘xf6+ ♕xf6 Δ ♗xf3∝; 13 ♕xd5 ♗xd4 14 ♘xd4 ♕xd5 15 ♘xd5 ♘xd4 16 ♘xc7 ♗xg2= **♘a5 14 ♕c2 c5 15 dxc5 bxc5∝ 16 ♘a4 c4 17 ♗e2 ♖b8! 18 ♘d4?!** 18 ♘c3!? **♘c6! 19 ♘xc6 ♗xc6=**

Diagram

20 ♗xc4?? 20 ♘c3= **♕a5 21 ♗b3 ♗xa4 22 ♗xa4 ♖ec8 23 ♗c6 ♕a6!** 23...♖b6? 24 ♕a4 **24 ♖c1 ♗xb2 0-1 Petrosian**

69 Ftacnik-Krogius Sochi 77
1 c4 ♘f6 2 ♘c3 e6 3 ♘f3 d5 4 d4 ♗e7

5 ♗g5 h6 6 ♗h4 0-0 7 e3 b6 8 ♗e2 ♗b7 8...dxc4!? 9 ♗xc4 ♗b7 Δ ♘bd7, c5= **9 ♗xf6 ♗xf6 10 cxd5 exd5 11 ♕b3 c6?!** 11...a6 12 0-0 ♕d6 Δ ♘d7 **12 0-0 ♘d7 13 ♖fe1 ♗e7 14 ♖ad1 ♕c7?!** 14...♘f6 15 ♘e5 ♗d6∞ **15 ♖c1 ♘f6 16 ♘e5** 16 ♘xd5 ♘xd5 17 ♕xd5 ♕xh2+ 18 ♘xh2 cxd5 19 ♖c7 ♗b4 20 ♖ec1 ♖ab8 Δ ♗d6, ♖fd8 **♕d6 17 f4± ♘d7?** 17...♖ac8 Δ c5 **18 ♗d3 ♘xe5 19 fxe5 ♕d7 20 ♘e2!** Δ ♘f4, ♗b1, ♕d3 +− **f6 21 exf6 ♖xf6** 21...♗xf6 22 ♗b1 ♔h8 23 ♕d3 g5 **22 ♗b1 ♕g4 23 ♕d3 g6 24 ♘f4 +− ♔g7 25 ♘xd5! cxd5 26 ♖c7 ♖f7 27 ♖xb7 ♖af8 28 ♖xa7 h5 29 ♖c7! h4 30 a3? h3 31 ♖c2??** −+ 31 g3 ♖f2 (Δ ♖g2+, ♖xh2+, ♖f2+) 32 ♖xe7+ ♔h8 33 ♕xg6 ♕xg6 34 ♗xg6 ♖g2+ 35 ♔h1 ♖ff2 36 ♖h7+ +−; 32...♔h6 33 ♕xg6+ ♕xg6 34 ♗xg6 ♔xg6 35 ♖c1≈ **♗d6??** 31...♗h4! −+ **32 ♕e2** 32 e4 hxg2 33 ♖xg2 ♗xh2+ **♕h4 33 gxh3 ♗xh2+ 34 ♔h1 ♗g3 35 ♖c6 ♕xh3+ 36 ♔g1 ♗h2+ 37 ♔h1 ♗f4+ 38 ♔g1 ♗xe3+ 0-1 Petrosian**

70 Gulko-Dorfman (1) 78

1 d4 ♘f6 2 c4 e6 3 ♘f3 d5 4 ♗g5 c6 5 ♘bd2 h6 6 ♗xf6 ♕xf6 7 g3?! 7 e3, 8 ♗d3 **dxc4 8 ♘xc4 ♗b4+ 9 ♘cd2 0-0 10 a3 ♗a5 11 b4 ♗b6 12 ♘c4 ♖d8 13 e3 ♗c7 14 ♗g2 ♘d7 15 0-0 ♕e7** 15...e5 16 ♘cxe5 ♘xe5 17 ♘xe5 ♗xe5 18 dxe5 ♕g5 **16 ♕c2** 16 ♗h3!? **e5 17 ♖ac1 a6 18 ♘cd2 ♗b6 19 ♖fe1 ♖e8 20 ♘xe5 ♘xe5 21 dxe5 ♕xe5 22 ♘c4 ♕c7 23 ♘xb6 ♕xb6 24 ♖ed1 ♗e6 ½-½**

71 Gulko-Dorfman (3) 78

1 d4 ♘f6 2 c4 e6 3 ♘f3 d5 4 ♗g5 h6 5 ♗xf6 ♕xf6 6 ♘c3 c6 7 e3 ♘d7 8 a3 8 ♕b3 ♗d6 9 ♗e2 ♕e7 10 ♘d2 0-0= Vidmar-Capablanca, Nottingham 36; 8 ♗d3 dxc4 9 ♗xc4 ♗d6 10 0-0 ♕e7 11 ♖c1 0-0 12 ♘e4 ♗c7 13 ♗b3 ♖d8 14 ♕c2 ♘f8 = Petrosian-Dorfman, USSR Final 76 **♕d8 9 ♗d3 ♗d6 10 0-0 0-0 11 ♖c1 a6** 11...dxc4!? 12 ♗xc4 e5 **12 ♖e1 f5 13 cxd5 cxd5** 13...exd5!? 14 ♕b3 ♘f6 15 e4 fxe4 16 ♘xe4 ♘xe4 17 ♗xe4 ♔h8 18 ♗b1 ♕f6 **14 ♕b3 ♘f6 15 ♘e2 g5 16 ♘e5 ♖b8 17 f3 ♕a5 18 ♖c3** 18 ♘c3!? Δ e4 **♘d7 19 f4 ♘xe5 20 fxe5 ♗e7 21 ♖ec1 b5**

22 ♘g3 22 ♗xf5! exf5 (22...♖xf5 23 ♖xc8+) 23 ♕xd5+ ♔h8 24 ♖c6! ♕d2 25 ♖xh6+ ♔g7 26 ♕c6 **♗b7 23 ♕d1 g4 24 ♗xf5** 24 ♘h5 ♗g5 25 ♘f4 **exf5 25 ♘xf5 ♖xf5 26 ♕xg4+ ♖g5 27 ♕e6+ ♔h7 28 ♖c7 ♖bg8 29 ♖xe7+** 29 ♖xb7? ♖xg2+ 30 ♔h1 ♖xh2+ 31 ♔xh2 ♕d2+ **♖8g7 30 ♖xg7+ ♖xg7 31**

♕f5+ ♔g8 32 ♕e6+ ♔h7 33 ♕f5+ ♔g8 34 ♕e6+ ½-½

QP

72 Gulko-Dorfman (5) 78

1 d4 d5 2 ♘f3 ♗f5 3 c4 e6 4 ♕b3 ♘c6 5 c5 5 ♕xb7? ♘b4 **♕c8** 5...♖b8 6 ♘c3 e5 7 e4 exd4 8 exf5 dxc3 9 ♗b5 ♗xc5 10 0-0 ♘f6 11 ♕xc3 ♕d6 12 ♗f4! += Portisch-Keres, Wijk aan Zee 69 **6 e3** 6 ♗f4 ♘f6 7 ♘c3 ♗e7 8 e3 += Euwe-Kmoch, Amsterdam 33 **♘f6 7 ♗b5 ♘d7 8 ♕a4** 8 0-0 ♗e7 9 ♕a4 ♘cb8 10 b4 c6 11 ♗e2 += van den Bosch-Euwe, Amsterdam 35 **♗e7 9 ♗xc6 bxc6 10 ♕xc6 0-0 11 0-0 ♖b8 12 ♕a4** 12 ♘c3 ♖b4 13 ♘b5 ♘b8 (13...♗d3? 14 ♘xa7 ♕d8 15 ♖e1 ♘b8 16 ♕a8) 14 ♕xc7 ♕xc7 15 ♘xc7 ♖b7 =+; 13 a3 ♘b8 14 ♕a8 ♖b7 Δ c6, ♕c7, ♘d7 **♗d3 13 ♖e1 e5 14 ♘c3 c6 15 e4 dxe4 16 ♘xe4 exd4 17 ♕xd4** 17 ♗f4 ♗xe4 18 ♗xb8 ♕xb8 19 ♕xd4 ♘xc5=; 19 ♖xe4 ♘xc5= **♗xe4 18 ♕xe4 ♗xc5 19 b3** 19 ♕c2!; 19 ♘g5 ♘f6 20 ♕c2 += **♖e8 20 ♕xe8+** 20 ♕f5? ♖b5; 20 ♕c4 ♖b4 21 ♕f1 **♕xe8 21 ♖xe8+ ♖xe8 22 ♔f1 ♘e5 23 ♘xe5 ♗d4 24 ♖b1 ♖xe5 25 ♗d2 ♔f8 26 ♖c1 ♖e6 27 ♗b4+ ♔e8 28 ♗c5 ♗xc5 29 ♖xc5 ♔d8 30 ♖h5 h6 31 ♖a5 ♖e7 32 ♖a6 ♖c7 33 ♔e2 ♔c8 34 h4 ♖e7+ 35 ♔d3 ♖d7+ 36 ♔c3 ♔b7 37 ♖a5 ♖e7 38 ♖f5 ♔c7 39 b4 f6 40 ♔d3 ♖e1 41 a3 ♔b6 ½-½**

73 Klaric-Geller Sochi 77

1 d4 ♘f6 2 ♘f3 c5 3 c3 e6 4 ♗g5 d5 5 e3 ♘bd7 6 ♘bd2 ♗e7 7 ♗d3 b6 8 ♘e5? 8 0-0 ♗b7 9 ♘e5? ♘xe5 10 dxe5 ♘d7 11 ♗f4 ♕c7 12 ♘f3 h6 13 ♗g3 g5∓ Spassky-Petrosian 66; 9 ♕b1!? Δ e4= **♘xe5 9 dxe5 ♘d7 10 ♗f4?** 10 ♗xe7 ♕xe7 11 f4= **♗b7 11 0-0 g5! 12 ♗g3 h5 13 f4 h4 14 ♗e1 gxf4 15 exf4 ♕c7 16 ♕g4 0-0-0 −+ 17 ♕h3 ♖dg8 18 ♘f3 ♔b8 19 ♗f2?** 19 ♖f2 **f5 20 exf6 ♗xf6 21 ♕xe6 d4 22 ♗e1 ♕xf4 23 ♕f5 ♕xf5 24 ♗xf5 ♘e5 25 ♔f2 h3 26 ♖g1 ♘xf3 27 gxf3 ♗h4+ 0-1 Petrosian**

1 d4 f5

74 Aberbakh-Wagman
Reggio Emilia 77/78

1 c4 f5 2 ♘c3 g6 3 e4 d6 4 h4!? ♘f6 5 h5 ♗g7 5...♘xh5 6 ♖xh5!; 5...gxh5 6 ♗e2 **6 d3 c6 7 ♗g5 ♘a6 8 h6! ♗f8 9 ♕d2 fxe4 10 dxe4 ♘c5 11 f3 ♗e6 12 ♖b1 a5 13 ♗e3** Δ e5 **♘fd7 14 b3 ♗f7 15 f4 e5 16 ♘f3 ♕c7 17 g3 ♗e7 18 ♗h3 ♖d8** 18...0-0-0? 19 ♗xc5 dxc5 20 ♘xe5± **19 0-0 ♖f8?!** 19...0-0! **20 ♕h2! ♗f6 21 f5 ♖g8 22 ♘g5 ♗xg5 23 ♗xg5 ♖a8 24 ♕d2 gxf5 25 ♗xf5 ♗g6 26 ♔h2 ♘f8 27 ♗h4 ♘ce6** 27...♘fe6 28 ♗h3 ♘d4 29 ♕e3 += **28 ♗h3 b6 29 ♖f6 ♘d4 30 ♖bf1 ♖a7 31 ♕f2 ♗f7 32 ♘e2 ♘de6 33 ♕e3 ♘d8 34 ♖6f2 ♗e6?** Zeitnot; 34...♘g6 += **35 ♗xd8 ♕xd8 36 ♖xf8+ ♖xf8 37 ♖xf8+ ♔xf8 38 ♗xe6 ♕f6 39 ♗f5 a4 40 b4 d5 41 ♕xb6 ♕xh6+ 42 ♔g2 ♖f7 43 ♕b8+ ♔g7 44 ♕xc5+ ♔f8 45 ♘f4 dxc4 46 ♘e6+ 1-0 Paoli**

75 Browne-Byrne USA Final 77

1 d4 f5 2 ♘c3!? ♘f6 3 ♗g5 d5 4 ♗xf6 exf6 4...gxf6!? **5 e3 ♗e6 6 ♗d3 g6** 6...♕d7 **7 ♕f3! c6 8 ♘ge2 ♘d7** 8...♕b6 **9 h3!** 9 h4?! h5!= **♕b6** 9...h5 10 g4! fxg4 11 ♗xg6+ ♔e7 12 hxg4 hxg4 13 ♕g2; 9...♘e5? 10 dxe5 fxe5 11 ♕g3 e4 12 ♘d4 +− **10 g4! ♕xb2?** 10...fxg4 11 hxg4 ♗f7 12 0-0-0 0-0-0 13 ♖h3!± **11 ♖b1 ♕a3 12 gxf5 ♗f7**

12...gxf5 13 ♖xb7 0-0-0 14 ♖b3 ♕a5 15 0-0± **13 ♖xb7 ♗b4 14 0-0!** 14 ♔d2?! **0-0-0?** 14...♗xc3 15 ♖b3 ♕xa2 16 ♖xc3± **15 ♖xb4! +− ♕xb4 16 ♗a6+ ♔c7 17 ♖b1 ♕d6 18 ♖b7+ ♔c8 19 ♖b3+ ♔c7 20 ♖b7+ ♔c8 21 e4!!**

21...♘b8 21...dxe4 22 ♘xe4 ♕e7 23 ♕f4 +−; 21...♖df8 22 exd5 ♘b8 23 dxc6 ♘xa6 24 ♘b5 ♕d5 (24...♕d8 25 ♘xa7 mate) 25 ♕xd5 ♗xd5 26 ♘d6+ ♔d8 27 ♖d7 mate **22 ♘b5! cxb5 23 ♕c3+ ♘c6** 23...♕c6 24 ♖xf7+ +− **24 e5! ♕c7 25 e6! 1-0** 25...♗e8 26 ♖xb5+ **Browne**

76 Kraidman-Murei Netanya 77

1 d4 f5 2 g3 ♘f6 3 ♗g2 e6 4 c4 ♗b4+ 5 ♗d2 a5 6 ♘f3 0-0 7 0-0 d5 8 ♗g5! += Δ c5! **♗e7 9 ♘bd2 ♘c6 10 cxd5 exd5 11 ♘b3 ♘e4 12 ♗xe7 ♕xe7 13 ♖c1 ♖a6 14 ♘c5 ♖b6 15 ♘d3!±** Δ ♘fe5 **g5! 16 e3 f4 17 exf4 ♗g4∞**

Diagram

18 ♘de5 ♘xe5 19 dxe5 c6! 20 h3 ♗xf3 21 ♗xf3 gxf4 22 ♗xe4 dxe4 23 gxf4 ♖xf4 24 ♖c3! ♖b5! 25 ♔h1 ♖xe5 26 ♖g3+ ♔h8 27 ♖fg1 ♖f8 28 ♕b3 ♖d5 29 ♖g7 ♕f6 30 ♕g3 ♖dd8 31 ♖g2 b5 32 ♕g4 ♕h6 33 ♖g3 ♖de8 34 ♕d7! 1-0 Gheorghiu

77 Kochiev-Tal USSR Final 77

1 ♘f3 g6 2 c4 ♗g7 3 d4 d6 4 g3 f5 5 ♗g2 ♘f6 6 b3 0-0 7 ♗b2 e6 8 0-0 ♕e7 9 ♘c3! += ♘bd7 9...♘c6 10 d5± **10 ♖c1?** 10 ♕c2! Δ e4± **e5! 11 dxe5 dxe5 12 ♘d5 ♘xd5 13 cxd5** 13 ♕xd5+ = **♘b6! =+ 14 ♘d2! ♖d8 15 ♘c4 e4** 15...♗e6 16 dxe6!? **16 ♗xg7 ♕xg7 17 ♘xb6 axb6 18 ♕c2!= ♖xd5 19 ♕xc7 ♕xc7 20 ♖xc7 ♖c5 21 ♖e7 ♔f8 ½-½** 22 ♔xh7 ♔g8 23 ♖e7 ♔f8= **Kochiev**

78 Dorfman-Bellin Moscow 77

1 ♘f3 e6 1...g6 2 d4 f5? 3 h4! ♘f6 4 h5! ♘xh5 5 ♖xh5 gxh5 6 e4 d6 7 ♘g5 c6 8 ♕xh5+ ♔d7 9 ♘e6!! +− Vadasz-Holzl, Hungary-Austria 74 **2 d4 f5 3 ♗g5 ♘f6** 3...♗e7 4 ♗xe7 ♕xe7 5 ♘bd2 ♘f6 6 e3 0-0 7 ♗d3 d6 8 0-0 e5 9 dxe5 dxe5 10 e4 +=; 5 ♘c3!? (Δ ♕d3, 0-0-0 +=) **4 ♘bd2 ♗e7 5 ♗xf6 ♗xf6 6 e4 d5! 7 exd5 exd5 8 ♕e2+ ♕e7 9 0-0-0 ♕xe2 10 ♗xe2 ♗e6?!** 10...0-0 **11 ♖he1** 11 ♖de1! ♔f7 12 h4 h6 13 h5!± **♔f7 12 ♘e5+ ♗xe5 13 dxe5 ♘c6!** 13...♘d7 14 ♘f3 h6 15 ♘d4± **14 ♘f3?!** 14 f4! Δ ♘f3, h4± **h6 15 h4 g6 16 a3 ♖hd8 17 ♗d3 a6 18 ♘g1 d4** 18...♘d4 19 ♗xa6 ♘xc2∞; 19 ♗f1 c5 20

♖xd4 cxd4 21 ♘f3 d3 22 c3! ∞/± **19 ♞h3 ♞e7 20 ♞f4 b5 21 ♝e2! c5** 21...♘d5 22 ♘xd5 ♗xd5 23 g4± **22 g4! ♞d5 23 ♞xd5 ♝xd5 24 f4** 24 h5 f4! **♝e4?** 24...fxg4 25 ♗xg4 h5 26 ♗h3 ♗e6 += **25 h5 g5** 25...gxh5 26 gxf5 ♗xf5 27 ♖h1!± **26 fxg5 hxg5 27 gxf5 ♝xf5 28 ♝f3!** 28 ♖g1 ♖g8 29 ♗f3 ♖ad8 **♜a7 29 ♜g1 ♜e7 30 ♜de1** 30 ♖df1 ♖xe5 31 ♗g4 ♖dd5! **d3! 32 cxd3 ♜xd3 32 ♝e4 ♝xe4 33 ♜xe4 ♚e6 34 ♜xg5 ♜h3 35 ♜e2! ♜eh7 36 ♜g6+ ♚e7 37 ♜xa6 ♜7xh5 38 ♜b6?!** 38 ♖c6 c4 (38...b4 39 a4 +−) 39 ♖c5 +− **b4?** +− Zeitnot **39 axb4 cxb4 40 ♜xb4 ♜d3 41 ♜b7+ 1-0 Dorfman**

2...c5

79 Gligoric-Vukic Bugojno 78

1 d4 ♞f6 2 c4 c5 3 d5 b5 4 cxb5 a6 5 bxa6 ♝xa6 6 ♞c3 d6 7 ♞f3 g6 8 e4 ♝xf1 9 ♚xf1 ♝g7 10 g3 0-0 11 ♚g2 ♛b6!? N 11...♘bd7 (+= Webb) 12 h3 ♕a5 13 ♖e1 ♖fb8 14 ♕c2! ♘b6 15 ♘d1 ♕a6 16 ♗d2 ♕c4 17 ♘c3! +=; 11...♕a5 12 ♖e1 ♘a6 13 ♖e2 ♘d7?! 14 ♗f4! += Tarjan-Webb, Hastings 77/8 **12 ♜e1 ♞a6!** Webb **13 ♜e2** 13 e5 dxe5 14 ♘xe5 ♘b4! Δ ♕b7= **♞b4!** Δ ♕a6, ♘d3/♕d3 Webb **14 ♝g5** 14 ♗f4 ♕a6 15 e5? dxe5 16 ♘xe5 ♘fxd5! Webb **♛a6** 14...h6!? 15 ♗f4 ♕a6∓ Webb **15 ♛d2** 15 ♖d2!? ♖fb8 16 a3 ♕a5 17 ♖c1 ♘a6 18 e5! **♜fb8** =+ Webb **16 ♜d1!?** Webb **♞xa2 17 e5** 17 ♖a1 ♕c4= **♞xc3!= 18 bxc3 ♞xd5** 18...dxe5 19 ♖xe5! Webb **19 ♜e4!** 19 ♖de1? e6 −+ **♞b6** 19...e6? 20 c4 ♘b6 21 exd6 +− **20 exd6 exd6 21 ♛xd6 ♞a4 22 ♛f4!** Webb **♞xc3 23 ♜e7 ♜f8 24 ♜dd7 ♛a2 25 ♛d6 ♜ac8** 25...♕c4 26 ♘d2= Webb; 25... c4? 26 ♕e6 +− **26 ♝e3** Δ ♘g5 Webb **♛a8 27 ♜b7! ♜cd8** 27...c4 28 ♕d7 ♖cd8 29 ♕c7 ♖c8 30 ♕d7= **28 ♛xc5 ♞d5 ½-½ Vukic**

80 Petrosian-Alburt USSR Final 77

1 d4 ♞f6 2 c4 c5 3 d5 b5 4 ♞f3 g6 5 cxb5 a6 6 e3!? ♝g7 7 ♞c3 0-0 8 a4 axb5 9 ♝xb5 d6 10 0-0 ♞a6 11 ♜a3 ♞c7 12 ♞d2 ♞d7 12...♘fxd5 13 ♘xd5 ♘xd5 14 ♗c6 ♗e6 15 ♗xa8 ♕xa8 Δ ♘b4∞ **13 ♝xd7!? ♝xd7 14 ♞c4 ♜a6** 14...♕b8 15 ♖b3 ♕a7 16 ♘b6± **15 e4 ♛b8! 16 ♛c2 ♛b4 17 ♞a2 ♛b7 18 ♝d2 ♜fa8?** 18...e6 19 dxe6 fxe6∞; 19...♘xe6 =+ **19 a5 ♞b5 20 ♜b3 ♛c7 21 ♝c3 ♞d4 22 ♝xd4 ♝xd4 23 ♞c3! +− ♜b8 24 ♜b6 ♜aa8 25 ♛b3 ♛d8 26 ♞b5 ♝g7 27 ♞a7! +− ♛e8 28 ♜a1 ♝f8 29 ♞c6 ♜c8** 29...♖xb6 30 ♘xb6 ♗xc6 31 dxc6 +− **30 a6 ♜c7** 30...♗xc6 31 dxc6 ♖xc6 32 a7 +− **31 ♜b7 ♜xc6 32 dxc6 ♝xc6 33 a7 ♝xe4 34 ♜b8 ♛d7 35 ♜xa8 ♝xa8 36 ♞b6 ♛b7 37 ♛f3 1-0 Petrosian**

81 Tukmakov-Georgadze Decin 77

1 d4 c5 2 d5 ♞f6 3 ♞c3 3 c4 b5! **g6 4 e4 d6 5 ♝e2 ♝g7 6 ♞f3 0-0 7 0-0 ♝g4 8 ♞d2! ♝xe2 9 ♛xe2 ♞a6 10 ♞c4 ♞c7 11 a4 += a6 12 a5 ♞d7** 12...♘b5! 13 ♘xb5 axb5 14 ♘b6 ♖a7 15 f3 ♘d7= **13 ♞a4 ♞b5 14 c3 ♛c7 15 ♝f4 ♜ae8** 15...f5!? 16 exf5 ♖xf5 17 ♗g3 += **16 ♜ad1 e5!? 17 dxe6 ♜xe6 18 ♛d3 ♛c6 19 f3** 19 ♘xd6?? ♘xd6 20 ♗xd6 ♕xa4 21 ♗xf8 ♘xf8 −+ **♝e5** 19...f5? 20 ♕d5 ♕xd5 21 exd5 +− **20 ♝xe5 ♞xe5 21 ♞xe5 ♜xe5 22 ♞b6 += ♚g7?!** 22...♖fe8! **23 ♞c4 ♜e6 24 ♛d5 ♛c7 25 f4! ♜fe8 26 e5 dxe5 27 fxe5 f6** 27...♖8e7 28 ♘d6 ♕c6 29 ♖xf7+ ♖xf7 30 ♕xe6 +−; 27...♕c6 28 ♕xc6 ♖xc6 29 ♖d7 +− **28 exf6+ ♜xf6 29 ♜xf6**

♚xf6= 30 ♞b6 ♚g7 31 ♞d7 c4? Zeitnot 31...♖d8 32 ♕e6 ♘d4 33 ♕f6+ ♔g8 34 ♖xd4 cxd4 35 ♕e6+ ♔g7 36 ♕e7+ ♔h8= **32 ♞c5 ♛e5 33 ♛xc4** 33 ♕xe5 ♖xe5 34 ♘xb7 ♖e2 35 ♖b1 **♛e3+ 34 ♚h1 ♞d6! 35 ♛d4+ ♛xd4 36 cxd4 ♜e2 37 b3 ♚f6** 37...♖a2 =+ **38 h3?! ♞e4 39 ♞xe4+ ♜xe4 40 d5 ♚e7 41 d6+ ♚d7 42 ♚h2 ♜e3 43 ♜f1 ♜xb3 ½-½ Georgadze**

82 Niklasson-Averbakh
Reggio Emilia 77/78

1 d4 ♞f6 2 c4 c5 3 d5 e5 4 ♞c3 d6 5 e4 ♞bd7 5...♗e7 **6 ♞f3 ♝e7 7 ♝e2** 7 ♗d3 **0-0 8 0-0 ♞e8 9 a3 b6 10 b4 g6 11 ♝h6 ♞g7** Δ ♗g5 **12 ♛d2 ♞f6 13 ♞e1?! ♞g4!** 13...♔h8 14 bxc5 bxc5 15 f4 ♘g8 16 ♗xg7+ ♔xg7 17 fxe5 dxe5 18 ♘f3 ♗d6 19 ♘b5 +=; Malich-Polugaevsky, Havana 66 **14 ♝xg4** 14 h3? ♘xh6 15 ♕xh6 ♗g5; 14 ♗xg7 ♔xg7 15 ♘d3 ♗g5 16 f4 exf4 17 ♘xf4 ♘e5 =+ **♝xg4 15 bxc5 bxc5 16 f4?!** 16 ♖ac1 **exf4 17 ♛xf4**

17...f5!!∓ 18 ♞f3 18 h3 ♗f6! 19 hxg4 fxe4! (Δ ♗d4+) 20 ♔h1 ♗xc3 21 ♕xf8+ ♖xf8 22 ♖xf8+ ♖xf8 −+ **♝f6 19 ♜ac1 ♝xf3 20 ♛xf3 fxe4 21 ♛e2** 21 ♕xe4? ♗d4+! 22 ♔h1 ♗xc3 −+ **♝d4+ 22 ♚h1 ♜xf1+ 23 ♛xf1 ♞f5 24 ♝f4 ♝xc3 25 ♜xc3 ♛f6 26 ♜c2 ♞e3 0-1 Paoli**

83 Didishko-Kapengut Minsk 78

1 d4 ♞f6 2 c4 c5 3 d5 e6 4 ♞c3 exd5 5 cxd5 d6 6 ♞f3 g6 7 e4 ♝g7 8 ♝e2 0-0 9 0-0 ♝g4 10 ♝f4 10 ♗g5 h6 11 ♗h4 ♕b6! Mochalov-Kapengut, Minsk 72; 10 h3 ♗xf3 11 ♗xf3 ♘bd7 12 ♗f4 ♘e8 13 a4 a6 14 ♗h2 Smyslov-Filip, Baden-Baden 57; 14...♖b8 15 ♗e2 ♗d4! 16 ♔h1 ♕e7 17 f4 f5 18 exf5 gxf5 19 ♗d3 ♘g7; 10 ♘d2 ♗xe2 11 ♕xe2 ♘bd7! 12 ♘c4 ♘b6 13 ♘xb6 ♕xb6 14 a4 a6 15 ♗e3 W.Garcia-A.Rodriguez, Cuba 74; 15...♖ac8! 16 f3 ♘d7 **♜e8 11 ♞d2** 11 h3 ♗xf3 12 ♗xf3 a6 13 ♖e1 ♘fd7!? 14 ♗xd6 ♕b6 15 ♗xb8 ♕xb2∞ **♝xe2 12 ♛xe2 ♞h5 13 ♝e3 ♞d7 14 g4 ♞f6 15 h3 ♞b6!? 16 ♜ae1?!** 16 a4 a6 17 ♖ac1 ♖c8 18 b3 ♘xe4!?∞ **♛d7 17 ♛f3 h5! 18 g5 ♞h7 19 ♛g3 ♜ad8 20 ♝f4 ♞a4! =+ 21 ♞c4** 21 ♘xa4 ♕xa4 22 ♗xd6 h4! 23 ♕f4 ♘xg5 24 ♕xg5 ♖xd6 =+ **h4 22 ♛d3** 22 ♕f3 ♘xc3 23 bxc3 b5 24 ♘xd6 ♖e5!∓ **b5 23 ♞xd6 ♞xb2 24 ♛f3** 24 ♕xb5 ♕xh3 25 ♘xe8 ♕g4+ 26 ♗g3 ♗xc3 −+ **♜e5!∓ 25 ♞dxb5 ♞xg5 26 ♝xg5 ♜xg5+ 27 ♚h1 ♞c4 28 d6 a6! −+ 29 ♞c7 ♞d2 0-1** 30 ♕d3 ♖g3! 31 fxg3 ♕xh3+ 32 ♔g1 ♗d4+ 33 ♖f2 hxg3 −+ **Kapengut**

84 Botterill-Fedorowicz
Hastings 77/78

1 d4 ♞f6 2 c4 c5 3 d5 e6 4 ♞c3 exd5 5 cxd5 d6 6 e4 g6 7 ♞f3 ♝g7 8 ♝g5 h6 9 ♝h4 a6! 9...g5 10 ♗g3 ♘h5 11 ♗b5+ ♔f8 12 e5! **10 ♞d2 b5 11 a4?!** 11 ♗e2 **b4 12 ♞cb1 ♛e7! 13 ♝d3 g5 14 ♝g3 ♞xd5 15 ♞c4! ♞f4! 16 ♝xf4 gxf4 17 ♞b6 ♝b7 18 ♞xa8 ♝xa8 19 0-0 ♝xb2 =+ 20 ♜a2 ♝d4 21 ♞d2 ♜g8 22 ♛f3 ♛f6 23 ♚h1 ♚f8**

24 Bc4 Bc6? 24...a5! =+ **25 a5! Bd7 26 Qe2 Qg5 27 Rg1 Bc3 28 Nf3 Qg6 29 Bxa6± b3 30 Ra3 d5 31 Bb7 b2 32 Nh4 Qf6 33 a6 Be5** Zeitnot **34 Nf3** 34 a7 Qxh4 35 f3 Rg5! **Qg7 35 Rb3! +− Nxa6 36 Bxa6 c4 37 Nxe5 cxb3 38 Nxd7+ Ke7 39 exd5+ Kxd7 40 Qb5+ Ke7 41 Qb4+ 1-0 Botterill**

85 Petrosian-Nunn Hastings 77/8

1 d4 Nf6 2 c4 c5 3 d5 e6 4 Nc3 exd5 5 cxd5 d6 6 Nf3 g6 7 Nd2 Bg7 7... Nbd7 8 Nc4 Nb6= **8 Nc4 0-0 9 Bg5!? h6?! 10 Bf4 b6!?** 10...Ne8 11 e3 +=; 10...Re8 11 Nxd6 Nh5 12 Nxe8 Bxc3+ 13 bxc3 Nxf4 14 e3? Nh5?? 15 g4 +−; 14...Qxe8∓; 14 g3!? Nh5 15 Bg2 Δ e4, f4 **11 Bxd6 Re8 12 Bg3 Ne4 13 Nxe4 Rxe4 14 e3 b5 15 Nd2 Rb4 16 b3!?** TN **Bxa1 17 Qxa1 Qxd5 18 a3 Rg4?** +− 18...Rxb3! 19 Be2 Rd3! 20 Bf3 Qd8 21 Qc1 Rd5!∞; 19 Nxb3 Qxb3 20 Be2 Bb7 21 0-0≈

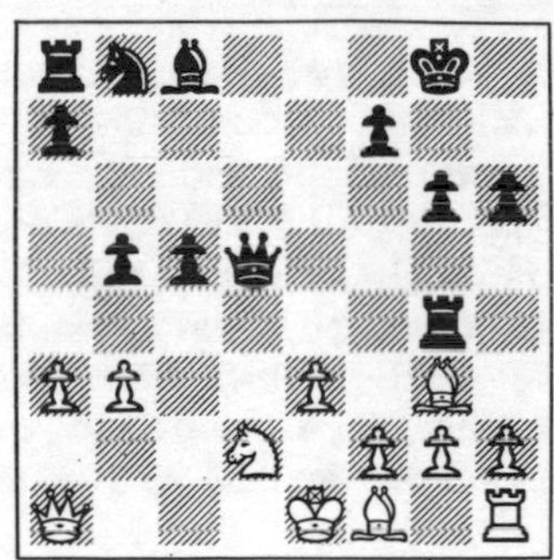

19 Be2! Nc6 19...Rxg3 20 hxg3 +− Δ Bf3/Rxh6 **20 Bf3! Qe6 21 Bxg4 Qxg4 22 0-0 Bb7 23 f3 Qe6 24 Ne4 Rd8 25 Nxc5 Qxe3+ 26 Bf2 Qe7 27 Re1 Qc7 28 h4** 28 Ne4!? f5± **h5 29 Ne4! +− Ne7** 29...f5 30 Nf6+ Kf7 31 b4 +−; 30 Ng5 +− **30 Nf6+ Kf8 31 b4** Δ Bc5 **Bc8 32 Nxh5 gxh5 33 Qh8+ Ng8 34 Bc5+ Rd6 35 Qe5 1-0 Petrosian**

86 Bukic-Velimirovic
Jugoslavia Final 78

1 d4 Nf6 2 c4 c5 3 d5 e6 4 Nc3 exd5 5 cxd5 d6 6 Nf3 g6 7 Bf4 a6 7... Bg7 8 Qa4+!? Bd7 9 Qb3≈ **8 a4 Bg7 9 e4 0-0 10 Nd2 Nh5 11 Be3 Nd7** 11... Bd4 12 Nc4 Bxe3 13 Nxe3 Nd7 14 g3 Rb8 15 a5 Ng7 16 Bg2 f5 17 0-0 Nf6= Bukic-Velimirovic, Jugoslavia Final 77 **12 Be2 Ne5 13 0-0** 13 Bxh5 gxh5 14 0-0 Qh4≈ **Qh4 14 f4! Ng4 15 Bxg4 Bxg4 16 Qe1 Qe7** 16...Qxe1? 17 Raxe1 Bd7 18 Nc4± **17 Qf2 += Rfe8 18 Rae1** Δ f5/e5 **b5! 19 h3** 19 f5 Be5!; 19 e5?! dxe5 20 Bxc5 Qd7≈ **b4!** 19...Bd7?! 20 g4? b4 21 Nd1 Nf6∓; 20 e5!? **20 hxg4 bxc3 21 gxh5 cxd2 22 Bxd2 Bxb2** 22...Bd4 23 Be3 Qxe4 24 Bxd4 Qxd4 25 Qxd4 cxd4 26 h6!± **23 e5! dxe5 24 fxe5 Bd4** 24...Bxe5?! 25 Rxe5! Qxe5 26 Qxf7+ Kh8 27 h6! Qd4+ 28 Rf2 Qa1+ 29 Kh2 Qe5+ 30 g3 Δ Bg5 +− **25 Be3 Qxe5!?** 25...Bxe5 26 Bxc5 Qd7 27 Qf3 += **26 Qxf7+ Kh8 27 Bf2 Bxf2+ 28 Qxf2 Qxd5 29 Qf6+ Kf8 30 hxg6 Qd4+ = 31 Qxd4 cxd4 32 gxh7+ Kxh7 33 Rxe8 Rxe8 34 Rf4 Rd8 35 Kf1 d3 36 Ke1 d2+ 37 Kd1 Kg6 38 Rb4 Kf5 39 Rb6 Rg8 40 Kxd2 Rxg2+ 41 Kc3 a5 42 Kc4 Ke5 43 Kb5 Kd5 44 Rh6 Rg8 45 Kxa5 Kc5 ½-½ Webb**

87 Kerchev-Rogulj Varna 77

1 d4 Nf6 2 Nf3 c5 3 d5 g6 4 Nc3 Bg7 5 e4 d6 6 Be2 0-0 7 0-0 Bg4 8 Nd2 Bxe2 9 Qxe2 e6 10 Nc4 exd5 11 exd5 Qd7 12 a4 Re8 13 Qf3 Ng4 14 Bf4 Ne5 15 Bxe5 dxe5 16 d6 Nc6 17 Nd5 Nd4 18 Qd1 Rad8 19 Ne7+ Kf8 20 Nd5 Qe6 21 Nde3 a6 22 c3 b5 23

axb5 axb5 24 ♞a5 ♜xd6 25 cxd4 exd4 26 ♞c2 ♛d5 27 ♛d3 c4 28 ♛a3 ♚g8 29 ♜fd1 ♜de6 30 ♞e3 ♛e4 31 ♞f1 ♝f8 32 ♛f3 ♛xf3 33 gxf3 ♝g7 34 ♞d2 c3 35 ♞e4 f5 36 ♞c5 ♜e2 37 ♞d3 c2 38 ♜f1 ♜d2 39 ♞c1 d3 40 ♞cb3 ♜d1 41 ♞d1 ♜xa1 0-1

88 Sosonko-Balashov Tilburg 77
1 d4 ♞f6 2 c4 c5 3 d5 g6 4 ♞c3 ♝g7 5 e4 d6 6 ♞f3 0-0 7 ♝e2 e6 8 0-0 ♜e8 9 ♝f4 exd5 10 exd5 ♞a6 11 ♛d2 ♞c7 12 ♜fe1 ♝f5 13 h3 ♞e4 14 ♞xe4 ♝xe4 15 ♞g5! += h6 15...♗f5 16 g4 ♗c8 17 ♗d3± **16 ♞xe4 ♜xe4 17 ♝d3** 17 ♗xh6?! ♖d4 18 ♕e3 ♗xh6 19 ♕xh6 b5 += **♜xe1+ 18 ♜xe1 g5 19 ♝g3 ♛f6 20 b4! ♞a6!** 20...b6 21 bxc5 bxc5 22 ♕a5± **21 b5 ♞c7 22 ♜e4 b6 23 ♛e2 ♚f8 24 ♛g4 ♜d8 25 ♚h2± ♞e8 26 ♜e3 ♛d4 27 ♛f5 ♝e5** 27...♕f6 28 ♕h7 Δ ♖f3±; 27...♘f6? 28 ♗xd6+ **28 ♜xe5!** 28 ♗xe5 dxe5 29 ♕xe5 ♕xe5 30 ♖xe5 ♘d6 +=; 29 ♖xe5 ♖d6 30 ♖e4 ♕f6± **dxe5 29 ♝xe5 ♛h4 30 g3?** 30 g4! +− **♛h5 31 g4 ♛g6 32 ♛f3 ♛g8 33 d6?!** 33 ♕f5!? **♜xd6!** 33... ♘xd6 34 ♕f6 ♘b7 35 ♗e4 +− **34 ♝xd6+ ♞xd6 35 ♛f6 ♞e8 36 ♛xh6+ ♚e7 37 h4** 37 ♕c6!? **gxh4 38 ♛xh4+ f6 39 ♛g3 ♞d6 40 ♛e3+ ♚d7 41 ♛f4 ♚e7 42 ♚g3 ♛e6 43 g5 fxg5 44 ♛xg5+ ♛f6 45 ♛xf6+ ♚xf6= 46 ♚f4 ♚e6 47 ♝e2 ♚f6 48 ♝f1 ♚e6 49 ♝e2 ♚f6 50 ♝d3 ♚e6 51 f3 ♚f6 52 ♚e3 ♚g5 53 f4+ ♚f6 54 ♚f3 ♚e6 55 ♚g4 ♚f6 56 ♝f1 ♞e4 57 ♝g2 ♞d6 58 ♝d5 ♞f5 59 ♚f3 ♞d6 60 ♝g8 ♚g7 61 ♝e6 ♚f6 62 ♝d5 ♚f5 63 ♝g8 ♚f6 64 ♚g4 ♞f5 65 ♚f3 ♞d6 66 ♚e3 ♚g7 67 ♝d5 ♚f6 68 ♚f3 ♚f5 69 a3 ♚f6 ½-½ Webb**

89 Tal-Velimirovic Moscow 77
1 c4 c5 2 ♞f3 g6 3 d4 ♝g7 4 d5 4 e4?! **♞f6 5 ♞c3 d6 6 e4 0-0 7 ♝f4 ♞h5 8 ♝g5 h6 9 ♝d2?! e5 10 dxe6 ♝xe6 11 ♝e2 ♞c6 12 0-0 ♜e8 13 ♝e3 ♛b6! 14 ♛d2 ♞d4! 15 ♝xd4** 15 ♗xh6 ♘xe2+ 16 ♘xe2 ♕xb2 17 ♖ab1 ♕xd2 18 ♗xd2 b6∓ **cxd4 16 ♞d5** 16 ♘b5 ♗g4 =+ **♝xd5 17 exd5 ♞f6= 18 ♜ad1?!** 18 ♗d3 **♞e4 19 ♛c2 a5! 20 ♞e1** 20 ♗d3 **a4 21 ♞d3 ♛c7** Δ b5 **22 ♜c1 a3∓ 23 b3 ♞c3 24 ♜fe1 h5** Δ ♗h6, ♘xd5 −+ **25 ♝f3 b5! 26 cxb5 ♛a5 27 g3 ♛xb5 28 ♚g2 h4 29 ♞f4 ♜e5! 30 gxh4? ♜ae8 31 ♞d3**

♞xa2! −+ 32 ♛xa2 ♛xd3 33 ♜ed1 ♛a6 34 ♜xd4 ♜e1 35 ♜dc4 ♝b2 36 ♜xe1 ♜xe1 37 b4 ♝e5? 37...♖a1 38 ♕b3 a2 −+ **38 h5 ♜a1?! 39 ♛c2 a2 40 hxg6 ♜g1+ 41 ♚xg1 a1♛+ 42 ♚g2 ♝f6 43 ♝h5! fxg6** 43...♕xc4 44 gxf7+ +− **44 ♛xg6+ ♚h8 45 ♛h6+ ♚g8 46 ♜g4+ ♝g7 47 ♛e6+ ♚h8 48 ♛e8+ ♚h7 49 ♝g6+ ♚h6 50 ♛e3 mate 1-0 Maric**

90 Sosonko-Smyslov Tilburg 77
1 d4 ♞f6 2 c4 e6 3 g3 c5 4 d5 exd5 5 cxd5 d6 6 ♞c3 g6 7 ♝g2 ♝g7 8 ♞f3 0-0 9 0-0 ♜e8 9...a6; 9...♗g4 **10 ♝f4 ♞h5!** 10...a6 11 a4 ♗g4 12 ♕d2 ♗xf3 13 ♗xf3 ♕c7 14 ♖fc1 ♘bd7 15 b4! += Sosonko-Smejkal, Biel 76 **11 ♝g5 ♛d7** 11...♕b6 12 ♕d2 ♘a6

13 h3 f6 14 ♗e3 f5≈ Ivanov-Kapengut, USSR 77 **12 e4! b5** 12...♗xc3? 13 bxc3 ♖xe4 14 ♕d2 Δ ♖fe1± **13 ♖e1** 13 ♕c2?! b4 14 ♘d1 a5∓; 14...c4!? **b4 14 ♘a4 ♘a6 15 h3 ♗b7** 15...♘f6 16 ♘d2 ♘xd5?! 17 exd5 ♖xe1+ 18 ♕xe1 ♕xa4 19 ♘c4±; 19 ♘e4!? **16 a3!? ♘f6 17 ♘d2 ♘xd5!? 18 exd5 ♖xe1+ 19 ♕xe1 ♕xa4 20 ♕e7** 20 ♘c4?! bxa3 21 ♘xd6 ♕d7≈ **♗xb2 21 ♖a2** 21 ♖b1? bxa3 22 ♕xb7 ♖b8∓ **♗d4 22 ♕xb7 ♖b8 23 ♕c6**

23...b3!! 23...♕xc6 24 dxc6 b3 25 ♘xb3 ♖xb3 26 ♗f1 ♘c7 27 ♗d8 +−; 23...♕d1+ 24 ♗f1 b3 25 ♘xb3 ♕xb3 26 ♖e2 ♕b6 27 ♖e7!± **24 ♕xa4** 24 ♘xb3 ♕xb3 25 ♖e2 ♕d1+? 26 ♗f1 ♖b1 27 ♖e8+ ♔g7 28 ♕xa6 ♕f3! 29 ♗e3 ♗e5±; 25...♕b6! 26 ♖e7≈ **bxa2 25 ♕xa6 a1♕+ 26 ♗f1 ♕e1 27 ♕e2 ♕xe2 28 ♗xe2± f6 29 ♗h6 ♔f7 30 ♘c4 ♔e7 31 ♔g2 ♖b3 32 ♗d2** 32 ♗f4 ♗e5 33 ♘xe5? dxe5 34 ♗e3 ♔d6∓ **♖b1 33 ♗a5 ♖c1 34 ♗d2** 34 ♗c7 ♔d7 35 ♗b8 ♖c2= **♖a1 35 ♗d3 ♔d7 36 h4 ♖a2 37 ♗b1 ♖a1 38 ♗d3 ♖d1 39 h5?** 39 ♗c2± **♗c3! 40 hxg6 hxg6 ½-½** 41 ♗xc3 ♖xd3 42 ♗xf6 ♖xd5= **Webb**

3...♗b4

91 Knezevic-Bukic
Jugoslavia Final 78

1 d4 ♘f6 2 c4 e6 3 ♘c3 ♗b4 4 ♕c2 c5 5 dxc5 ♘a6 6 a3 ♗xc3+ 7 ♕xc3 ♘xc5 8 f3! += a5 9 e4 0-0 9...d6 10 ♗e3 ♕c7 11 ♘e2 ♗d7 12 ♖c1 a4 13 ♘d4 0-0 14 ♗e2 ♖fc8 15 0-0 += Idovcic-Damjanovic, Zagreb 64 **10 ♗e3** 10 ♗f4 ♕b6 11 ♖d1 ♘e8 12 ♘e2± Bogoljubov-Alekhine, 29 **♕c7 11 ♖d1** Δ b4 **a4 12 e5!?** 12 ♘e2 Δ ♘d4 += **♘e8 13 ♘h3 b6 14 ♗e2 ♗b7 15 0-0 ♖d8 16 ♘f2 f6** 16...d6 17 ♗f4± **17 ♘d3! fxe5 18 ♕xe5 ♕xe5 19 ♘xe5 d6 20 ♘d3± ♖c8 21 ♘f4 ♔f7 22 ♖fe1 ♖d8 23 ♗xc5** 23 ♗f1!? ♘c7 24 ♘e2± **bxc5 24 ♗d3 e5 25 ♘e2 ♗c6 26 ♘c3 ♖b8 27 ♖d2 h6 28 ♗c2 ♖a8 29 ♘b5 ♔e6 30 ♖ed1 ♗xb5 31 cxb5 ♖a5**

32 f4!? 32 b6 ♖b5 33 ♗xa4 ♖xb6= **exf4?!** 32...♖xf4 33 b6 ♔d7 34 ♗g6= **33 ♖e1+ ♔f7** 33...♔d7 34 ♖de2 ♘f6 35 ♖e7+± **34 ♖de2 ♖a7 35 ♗e4** 35 b6!? ♖b7 36 ♗e4 ♖xb6 37 ♗d5+ ♔f6 38 ♖xe8± **♘f6 36 b6 ♖a6 37 b7 ♖b6 38 ♗f3 d5 39 ♖e7+ ♔g6 40 ♖c7 ♖b8 41 ♖ee7 ½-½** 41...♖g8 42 ♖e2 ♖b8=; 41...♖xb2!? **Webb**

92 Forintos-Haag Hungary 78

1 d4 ♘f6 2 c4 e6 3 ♘c3 ♗b4 4 ♕c2 d5

5 a3 Bxc3+ 6 Qxc3 Ne4 7 Qc2 c5 8 dxc5 Nc6 9 Nf3 9 cxd5∝ **Qa5+ 10 Bd2** 10 Nd2∝ **Qxc5 11 e3 Nxd2 12 Nxd2 0-0?!** 12...d4 13 b4 Qe7 14 e4!? TN; 14 Nf3 += TN **13 b4 Qe7 14 Bd3 g6** 14...h6 15 0-0 dxc4±; 14...f5 15 f4±; 15 0-0 **15 0-0 Rd8?!** 15...d4! += **16 f4! a6 17 Rae1 dxc4 18 Nxc4 Qc7?** 18...Bd7 19 Nb6 Rab8 20 Be4± **19 Ne5 Bd7 20 Qc3! f5 21 Bc4 Rac8 22 Nxg6!! hxg6 23 Qf6 Ne5** 23...Ne7 24 Rf3; 24 Rc1; 23...Be8 +−; 23... Qd6 24 Qxg6+ Kf8 25 Rf3 Qe7 26 Rg3 +− **24 fxe5 Qxc4 25 Rf3! Qg4 26 Rh3** 26 Rg3?? Rf8−+ **Qxh3 27 gxh3 Be8 28 Kf2 Rd2+ 29 Kf3** 29 Re2 +− **Rc4 30 Rg1 Bc6+ 31 Kg3 Bd5 32 e4! Rd3+ 33 Kf4 Rxe4+ 34 Kg5 Rxh3 35 Kxg6 1-0 Haag**

93 Ivkov-Karpov Bogojno 78

1 d4 Nf6 2 c4 e6 3 Nc3 Bb4 4 Qc2 0-0 5 Nf3 c5 6 dxc5 Na6 7 e3 Nxc5 8 Bd2 b6 9 Be2 Bb7 9...Ba6 **10 0-0 Qe7** 10...Nce4 11 Nxe4 Bxe4 12 Bd3 Bxd3 13 Qxd3 Bxd2 14 Qxd2 Flohr-Najdorf, Budapest 50 **11 a3 Bxc3 12 Bxc3 Rac8 13 Rac1 Rfd8 14 b4 Nce4 15 Bd4 d6 16 Bd3 e5 17 Bb2 Qe6 18 Qe2 Qg4 19 h3 Qe6 20 Rfd1 Rd7 21 Nh2 Rdc7 22 f3 Ng3 23 Qe1 Nf5 24 Bxf5 Qxf5 25 Rxd6 Ne8 26 e4 Qg5 27 Qd2 Qxd2 28 Rxd2 f6 29 Rdc2 Ba6 30 c5 bxc5 31 Rxc5 Rxc5 32 bxc5 Rc6 33 Ng4 Bc8 34 Ne3 Nc7 35 a4 Ne6 36 Nf5 Kf8 37 Rd1 g6 38 Nd6 Bd7 39 Ba3 Ra6 40 a5 Nd4** 40...Rxa5?? 41 Nc4 **41 Bb4 Ke7 42 Nc4 Ba4 ½-½**

94 Gligoric-Hubner Bugojno 78

1 d4 Nf6 2 c4 e6 3 Nc3 Bb4 4 e3 b6 5 Bd3 Bb7 6 Nf3 0-0 7 0-0 d5 8 a3 Bxc3 9 bxc3 dxc4 10 Bxc4 c5 10...Nc6 11 Re1 Na5 11 Bd3 Be4= **11 Bd3 Qc7** 11...Nbd7 12 Re1 Ne4 13 Bb2 Rc8 14 c4 Rc7= **12 Bb2 Be4 13 c4 Nbd7 14 Bxe4 Nxe4 15 Qe2 Rfe8 16 Rfd1 Rac8 17 Rac1 Nd6 18 Qd3 Nb7 19 d5 e5 20 Ng5 Nf6 21 e4 h6 22 Nf3** Δ d6 **Nd7 23 Nd2 Nd6 24 Re1** Δ f4 **f6 25 Qh3** 25 g3!? Δ f4 **Nf8 26 Qg3 Qd7 27 Rf1** 27 f4 exf4 28 Qxf4 Ng6 29 Qg3 Ne5= **Kh7 28 Qd3 a6 29 f4 Ng6 30 f5 Nf8 31 a4 Rc7 32 Ra1 Rb8 33 Bc3 Qc8 34 h3** 34 Rfc1 Nd7 35 Nb3 b5 36 axb5 axb5 37 Na5 b4∓ **Nd7 35 Kh2** 35 Rfc1 b5 36 Ba5 Ra7 37 axb5 axb5 38 cxb5 Rba8∓ **b5!∓ 36 axb5 axb5 37 Ra5 b4 38 Bb2 Ra8 39 Rfa1 Rxa5 40 Rxa5 Qb8 41 Nb3 Ra7 42 Rxa7** 42 Rxc5?! Nxc5 43 Nxc5 Qb6 44 Ne6 Qf2 −+ **Qxa7 43 Bc1 Qa6 44 Be3 Qxc4 45 Qxc4 Nxc4 −+ 46 Bf2** 46 Bxc5 Na5! 47 Nxa5 Nxc5 48 Nc4 Nxe4 49 d6 Nc5 50 Nb6 b3 −+ **Kg8 47 g4 Kf7 48 Kg2 Ke7 49 Bxc5+** 49 Nxc5 Nd2 50 Be3 b3! −+ **Nxc5 50 Nxc5 Nd2 51 Kf2 b3 52 Na4 Nxe4+ 53 Ke3 Nc5 0-1 Webb**

95 Portisch-Hubner Bugojno 78

1 d4 Nf6 2 c4 e6 3 Nc3 Bb4 4 e3 b6 5 Ne2 Ba6 6 a3 Bxc3+ 7 Nxc3 d5 8 b4!? 8 b3; 8 Qf3; 8 cxd5 **0-0?!** 8... bxc4 9 Bxc4 dxc4 10 Qe2 a5! 11 b5 Nd5= **9 b5 Bb7 10 cxd5** 10 Be2 dxc4 11 0-0 += **Nxd5 11 Nxd5 Qxd5 12 f3 a6 13 Bd3 f5! 14 a4! axb5 15 Ba3 b4** 15...c5 16 Bxb5 +=; 15...Rf7 16 axb5 += **16 Bxb4 += Rf7 17 Rc1?!** 17 0-0 += **Ba6 18 Bc2≈ Nc6 19 Bb3 Qd7 20 Bc3 Ne7 21 Kf2 Nd5 22 Bd2** 22 Re1 f4!? **Qd6 23 Qc2** Δ Qc6 **Bb7 24 Qc4 Rf6 25 g3 h5!∓ 26 Rhd1 h4 27 Rg1 Raf8 28 a5 Rh6 29 axb6 cxb6 30 Ra1 Kh7 31 Ra7**

♛b8 32 ♜aa1 ♞f6 33 ♝d1 ♛d6!?

34 ♛c2 34 ♗b4!? hxg3+ 35 hxg3 ♖h2+ 36 ♖g2? ♘g4+ 37 fxg4 ♖xg2+; 36 ♔d1 ♖c8 37 ♗xd6 ♖xc4 38 g4≈ **hxg3+ 35 hxg3 ♜h3 36 ♜c1 ♜f7 37 ♝e2?** 37 ♖g2 ♘g4+; 37 ♕a4!?∓ **♞e4+! 38 fxe4 fxe4+ 39 ♚e1 ♛xg3+! 0-1 Webb**

96 Gligoric-Sosonko Tilburg 77
1 d4 ♞f6 2 c4 e6 3 ♞c3 ♝b4 4 e3 c5 5 ♝d3 ♞c6 6 ♞f3 ♝xc3+ 7 bxc3 d6 8 e4 e5 9 d5 ♞e7 10 ♞d2 10 ♘h4 **♛a5 11 ♛b3 0-0 12 ♞f1** 12 0-0!? **♞h5 13 ♞e3 ♞f4 14 ♝c2 f5 =+ 15 ♝d2 ♛c7 16 ♛b1 g6 17 ♛d1 fxe4 18 ♝xe4 ♝f5! 19 ♞xf5 gxf5 20 ♝c2!** 20 ♗xf4 exf4 21 ♗c2 ♘g6∓ **♞xg2+ 21 ♚f1 ♞f4** 21...♘h4?! 22 ♗g5 ♘hg6 23 h4≈ **22 ♝xf4 exf4 23 ♛h5 ♚h8 24 ♜e1 ♞g6** 24...♖ae8? 25 ♗xf5 **25 ♝xf5 ♞e5** Δ ♕f7 **26 ♝e6! ♛g7 27 ♜g1 ♛f6 28 ♜e4 ♞d3?** 28...a6 29 ♖g5 b5 30 ♖f5 ♕g6 =+; 29...♘f3!?; 28...b5!? 29 cxb5 a6 **29 ♜g4! ♞e5** 29...♕xc3 30 ♗f5 ♕c1+ 31 ♔g2 f3+ 32 ♔xf3! **30 ♜h4 ♛g7 31 ♜exf4 ♜xf4 32 ♜xf4 ♜f8 33 ♜xf8+ ♛xf8 34 ♝f5 ♛f7?** 34...♕e7 35 h4 ♘xc4 36 ♕g5 ♕xg5 37 hxg5 ♘b6≈; 35 f4 ♘xc4 36 ♗e6≈ **35 ♛xf7 ♞xf7 36 f4 +− ♚g7 37 ♚e2 h6 38 ♚f3 ♚f6 39 ♝c8 b6 40 ♚g4 ♚g6 41 ♝f5+ ♚f6 42 ♝d7 ♞d8 43 ♚h5 ♚g7 44 h4 ♞f7 45 ♝e8 ♞d8 46 f5 a6** 46...♔f8 47 ♔xh6! **47 f6+ ♚xf6 48 ♚xh6 ♞b7 49 ♝g6 b5** 49...♘a5 50 ♗d3 ♘b7 51 h5 ♘d8 52 ♗g6 ♘b7 53 ♔h7 Δ ♔g8 +− **50 cxb5 axb5 51 h5 c4** 51...b4 52 cxb4 cxb4 53 ♔h7 ♘c5 54 ♔g8 ♘d7 55 ♗e8 +− **52 ♝e8 1-0 Webb**

97 Gligoric-Timman Tilburg 77
1 d4 ♞f6 2 c4 e6 3 ♞c3 ♝b4 4 e3 c5 5 ♝d3 ♞c6 6 ♞f3 ♝xc3+ 7 bxc3 d6 8 e4 e5 9 d5 ♞e7 10 ♞d2 ♛a5 11 ♛b3 0-0 12 0-0 += ♞h5 13 g3 ♝h3 14 ♜e1 ♛c7 15 ♛d1 g6 16 ♞f1 ♛d7 17 ♝h6 ♞g7 18 f4 18 ♘e3 f5= **♝xf1** 18...f6 19 ♘e3 Δ ♕f3, g4± **19 ♜xf1!?** 19 ♗xf1 += **♛h3**

20 ♝g5! 20 fxe5?! ♕xh6 21 exd6 ♕g5! = **f6** 20...♕d7 21 ♗f6 ♕c7 22 g4± **21 fxe5! fxg5 22 exd6 ♛d7 23 dxe7** 23 e5!? ♘ef5 24 ♕d2± **♛xe7 24 ♛d2± ♛e5 25 ♝c2 ♞h5** 25...♘e8? 26 ♖xf8+ ♔xf8 27 ♕f2+ **26 ♜xf8+ ♜xf8 27 ♜f1 ♞f6** 27...♖xf1+? 28 ♔xf1 ♘f6 29 d6 +− **28 d6 ♚g7** 28...♖d8 29 ♖xf6! **29 d7 ♜d8 30 ♝a4 a6** 30...♘xe4? 31 ♕e3 **31 ♛f2 h5 32 ♛f3 h4 33 ♜d1** 33 ♖b1!? ♕c7 34 e5 ♕xe5 35 ♖xb7 ♕e1+ 36 ♕f1≈ **♛e6** 33...♕xe4? 34 ♕xe4 ♘xe4 35 ♖e1 Δ ♖e8! +− **34**

gxh4 gxh4 35 ♕f4 ♕xc4 35...♘xd7!? 36 ♕g5 ♘e5! 37 ♕xd8 ♕g4+ =; 36 ♕d6 ♕g4+ =; 36 ♖d6 ♕e7 37 ♕d2 ♘e5!∓ **36 ♖f1 ♕e6 37 e5!** 37 ♗b3 ♕e7; 37 ♕xh4 b5 **♘xd7 38 ♕xh4 ♖f8 39 ♗xd7 ♖xf1+ 40 ♔xf1 ♕xd7 41 ♕f6+ ♔h7 42 e6 ♕g7! 43 ♕d8 ♕xc3 44 ♕d7+ ♔h6 45 e7 ♕f3+ 46 ♔e1 ♕e3+ 47 ♔d1 ♕f3+ 48 ♔c2 ♕e4+ 49 ♔d2 ♕f4+ 50 ♔d3 ♕f3+ 51 ♔c4 ♕e4+ 52 ♔xc5 ♕e3+ 53 ♔c4** 53 ♔d6 ♕f4+ **♕e4+ 54 ♔c3 ♕e3+ 55 ♔b2 ♕e2+ 56 ♔b3 ♕e3+ 57 ♔a4 ♕c3! 58 ♕xb7 ♕c4+ 59 ♔a5** 59 ♔a3 ♕c1+ 60 ♕b2 ♕e3+ **♕xa2+ 60 ♔b6 ♕e6+ 61 ♔c5** 61 ♔a7 ♕g5! Δ ♔f6 **♕e5+ 62 ♔c4 ♕f4+ 63 ♔d3 ♕f1+ 64 ♔d4 ♕a1+ 65 ♔e3 ♕g1+ 66 ♔d3 ♕d1+ ½-½ Webb**

98 Portisch-Timman
Wijk aan Zee 78

1 d4 ♘f6 2 c4 e6 3 ♘c3 ♗b4 4 e3 c5 5 ♗d3 ♘c6 6 ♘f3 ♗xc3+ 7 bxc3 d6 8 0-0 8 e4 e5 9 d5 ♘e7 10 ♘h4 h6 11 f4 ♘g6! 12 ♘xg6 fxg6 13 0-0 Larsen-Ivkov **e5 9 ♘d2 cxd4 10 cxd4 exd4 11 exd4 ♘xd4 12 ♖e1+ ♘e6?!** 12... ♗e6 **13 ♗a3 0-0 14 ♘b3 ♕d7?!** 14...b6 15 ♗xd6 ♖e8; 14...♘f4 15 ♗c2 **15 ♖e3!** 15 ♗xd6? ♖d8 16 c5 ♘xc5 **♕c6?** 15...♖d8 **16 ♗xd6 ♖d8 17 ♗e5 ♘d7 18 ♕h5 h6** 18...g6? 19 ♕xh7+ +− **19 ♗b2 ♕xg2+** 19...♘f4 20 ♕g4 **20 ♔xg2 ♘f4+ 21 ♔g1 ♘xh5 22 ♖d1! ♖f8 23 ♗a3 ♖d8 24 ♗b2 ♖f8 25 ♗a3 ♖d8 26 ♗f5** Δ ♗xd7 +− **♘hf6 27 ♗e7 ♖e8 28 ♗xf6 ♘xf6 29 ♖xe8+ ♘xe8 30 ♖d8 ♔f8 31 ♗xc8 1-0**

99 Gligoric-Spassky Bugojno 78

1 d4 ♘f6 2 c4 e6 3 ♘c3 ♗b4 4 e3 c5 5 ♗d3 d5 6 ♘f3 0-0 7 0-0 b6 8 cxd5 exd5 9 ♘e5 ♗b7 9...♗xc3; 9...♗a6? 10 ♘c6! **10 ♗d2 ♘c6 11 a3** 11 ♘xc6 ♗xc6 12 dxc5 bxc5 13 ♘e2 +=; 12... ♗xc5 += **♗xc3** 11...♗a5 **12 ♗xc3 ♖e8 13 ♘xc6 ♗xc6 14 ♖c1?!** 14 dxc5 bxc5 15 b4 d4! 16 exd4 ♕d5 =+; 15 ♗xf6 ♕xf6 16 ♕c2 c4!≈; 14 b3!? **c4 15 ♗b1 b5 =+ 16 ♖e1** 16 b4 ♘e4 17 ♗e1 ♕g5 =+ **♘e4 17 f3 ♘xc3 18 ♖xc3** 18 bxc3 ♕d6 19 ♕c2 g6 20 ♕b2 f5∓ **♕b6 19 ♕c2 g6 20 ♕f2** Δ e4 **♖ad8∓ 21 f4?!** 21 g4!? **f5 22 ♕h4** Δ g4/♗xf5 **♗d7 23 ♔h1 ♔g7 24 ♖f1 ♕f6 25 ♕f2 a5 26 ♖cc1 b4 27 axb4 axb4 28 ♕d2 ♕e7 29 ♖f3 ♖a8 30 h3 ♖a6 31 ♕f2 ♖e6 32 ♖e1 ♖a6 33 ♖g1 ♖a1 34 ♔h2** 34 g4 fxg4 35 hxg4 ♗xg4 36 ♖fg3 ♖xb1! **♖ea8 35 ♖g3** 35 g4!? **♕f6 36 ♖f3 ♕b6 37 ♕h4 ♕f6 38 ♕f2 ♖8a7 39 h4 h5! −+ 40 ♔h3 ♖c7 41 ♖c1 ♗a4 42 ♖g3 c3 43 ♖g5 ♕a6 44 ♔h2 ♗b5 45 bxc3 bxc3 46 ♕c2 ♗d3 47 ♕b3 ♖xb1 48 ♕xd5 ♔h7! 49 ♖xc3 ♖g7 50 ♔g3 ♗e4 51 ♕c4 ♕a1 0-1 Webb**

100 Portisch-Panno
Wijk aan Zee 78

1 d4 ♘f6 2 c4 e6 3 ♘c3 ♗b4 4 e3 c5 5 ♗d3 0-0 6 ♘f3 d5 7 0-0 b6?! 8 cxd5 exd5 9 ♘e5 9 dxc5 bxc5 10 ♘e2 Δ b3, ♗b2 += **♗xc3** 9...♗a6 10 ♘c6! **10 bxc3 ♗a6 11 f3!** +=; 11 ♗xa6 ♘xa6 12 dxc5? ♖e8∓; 12 a4 ♖e8 13 ♕f3 ♕c8 14 ♗b2 ♕e6= Farago-Forintos, 68 **♖e8 12 ♖e1 ♘fd7** 12...♗xd3 13 ♘xd3 Δ ♘f2 +=; 13 ♕xd3 ♘bd7 14 ♘xd7 ♕xd7 15 e4 dxe4 16 fxe4 cxd4 17 cxd4 ♕c6= **13 ♗xa6 ♘xa6 14 ♘d3 ♘f6 15 ♘f2!± ♘c7 16 e4 ♘e6 17 e5 ♘d7 18 ♕d3 ♕h4 19 ♗e3 ♖ac8** 19... f6 20 g3 ♕h5 21 f4 c4 22 ♕b1 Δ ♕b5/f5± **20 g3 ♕h5 21 f4 f5** 21... cxd4 22 cxd4 Δ ♕b5/f5; 21...c4 22 ♕b1± **22 dxc5 ♘dxc5 23 ♕xd5 ♖ed8**

24 Qc4 Kf7 25 Bxc5 Rxc5 26 Qa4 Rc7 27 Rad1 +– Rxd1 28 Rxd1 Ke7 29 Rd6 Qf3 30 Qb3 Nd8 31 Qg8 Nf7 32 Rd3 Qe2 33 Qxg7 Qxa2 34 Qf6+ 1-0 Webb

101 Portisch-Karpov Bugojno 78

1 d4 Nf6 2 c4 e6 3 Nc3 Bb4 4 e3 0-0 5 Bd3 c5 6 Nf3 d5 7 0-0 dxc4 8 Bxc4 cxd4 9 exd4 b6 10 Bg5 Bb7 11 Re1 11 Ne5 Nc6 12 Bxf6!?; 11...Be7; 11 Qe2 Bxc3 12 bxc3 Nbd7 13 Bh4 Rc8 14 Rac1 Bxf3= Kuzmin-Polugaevsky, Sochi 76; 11 Bd3 Nc6 12 Be4 Be7 13 Bxf6 Bxf6 14 Qa4 a6!≈ Portisch-Gheorghiu, Montana 76 **Nbd7 12 Rc1 Rc8 13 Bd3 Bxc3 14 bxc3 Qc7 15 c4 Rfe8 16 Qe2 h6 17 Bd2 Bxf3!? 18 Qxf3 e5 19 Qg3?** 19 d5 e4!? 20 Bxe4 Ne5 21 Qg3 Nxc4≈; 19...Nc5 20 Bb1 +=; 19 dxe5= **exd4 20 Rxe8+ Nxe8 21 Bf4 Qc6 22 Bf5 Rd8 23 h3 Nc5 24 Rd1 Qf6 25 Bb1 Qe6 26 Kh2 Kf8! –+**

27 Be5 Qxc4 28 Qf4 Ne6 29 Qe4 Qd5 30 Qe2 Nd6 31 a4 Nc4 32 Bg3 Nc5 33 Ba2 d3 34 Qe1 Qd4 35 f3 Ne3 36 Rd2 Re8 37 Qc1 Nxa4 38 Kh1 Nc5 39 Bf2 Qe5 40 Bb1 Kg8 0-1 Webb

102 Szmetan-Suba Rumania 78

1 d4 Nf6 2 c4 e6 3 Nc3 Bb4 4 e3 0-0 5 Bd3 d5 6 Nf3 c5 7 0-0 dxc4 7... b6?! –14/355 **8 Bxc4 Nbd7** 8...cxd4 –14/356; 8...Qe7 –14/357 **9 a3** 9 Qe2!?; 9 Bd3 **cxd4 10 axb4** 10 Nb5= **dxc3 11 bxc3 Qc7 12 Qb3!** 12 Qe2?! Nb6 13 Bd3 e5! =+ **Nb6 13 Be2 e5 14 Ra5** N 14 c4 Be6 15 Ra5= Timman-Keene, Reykjavik 76 **Be6 15 Qa3** 15 c4!? **Nfd7 16 Nd2 a6 17 Bb2 Nc4 18 Nxc4 Bxc4 19 Bxc4 Qxc4 20 b5= Nc5 21 bxa6 b6 22 Qa2 Qd3** 22... Qxa2 **23 Ra3 Rxa6 24 Rxa6 Nxa6?** 24...Qxa6= **25 c4! Nb4?! 26 Qb1?** 26 Qa4! Qxc4 27 Rc1 Qe4 28 Ba3 +–; 26...Nc2 27 Rc1 Nxe3 28 fxe3 Qxe3+ 29 Kh1 +– **f6 27 Bxe5 Qxb1 28 Rxb1 Nd3 29 Bd4 Rc8 ½-½ Ciocaltea**

103 Botterill-Petrosian Hastings 77/8

1 d4 e6 2 c4 Nf6 3 Nc3 Bb4 4 e3 0-0 5 Ne2 d5 6 a3 Be7 7 Nf4 a5 TN? 7...c6 8 b4 Nd7 9 c4 e5 10 dxe5 Nxee5= **8 b3 c6 9 Be2 Nbd7 10 cxd5?!** 10 0-0 dxc4?! 11 bxc4 e5 12 Nd3± **Nxd5 11 Ncxd5 exd5 =+ 12 0-0 Bd6 13 Nd3 Qh4! 14 g3 Qe7 15 Bb2 Re8 16 Re1 Nf6 17 Bf1 Bf5 18 Bg2 Qc7 19 Rc1 Re7 20 f3** Δ e4 **Rae8 21 Qd2 h5! 22 Ne5 Qb6! 23 Kh1?** 23 Qd1 Nd7 24 Nxd7 Rxd7 **Qxb3 24 e4 Bh7! –+** 24...dxe4 25 fxe4 Be6 26 Nd3!? (Δ Nc5, d5, e5) Bxa3 27 Rc3 Bb4 28 Nxb4 Qxb4 29 Ba3±; 26...Bc4!; 26 Nxc6 bxc6 27 e5 Bd5! –+ **25 Bc3** 25 Nxc6 bxc6 26 e5 Bxa3 27 Bxa3 Qxa3 28 exf6 Rxe1+ 29 Rxe1 Rxe1+ 30 Qxe1 gxf6 –+ **dxe4 26 fxe4 Bxe5 27 dxe5 Ng4 28 Bxa5 Nxe5 29 Bb4 Rd7 30 Qg5 Bg6 31 Rc3 Qa2 32 Rce3 Nd3 33 Rxd3 Rxd3 34 e5 Qb3 35 Qc1 0-1 Petrosian**

3...Bb4+ Bogolyubov

104 Diesen-Tarjan Torremolinos 78

1 d4 Nf6 2 c4 e6 3 Nf3 Bb4+ 3...b6 4. g3 Bb7 5 Bg2 Be7 6 0-0 0-0 7 Nc3 Ne4 8 Qc2 Nxc3 9 Qxc3 f5 10 b3 Bf6 11 Bb2 Nc6! 12 Rad1 Ne7 Δ g5, Ng6 Polugaevsky-Korchnoi (2) 77 **4 Bd2 Qe7** 4...a5!? Bronstein **5 g3 Nc6 6 Bg2** 6 Nc3! Bxc3 7 Bxc3 Ne4 8 Rc1 +=; 6...d6 7 Bg2 **Bxd2+! 7 Nbxd2?!** 7 Qxd2 Ne4 8 Qc2 Qb4+ 9 Nd2 Nxd2! −+ **d6 8 0-0 e5 9 d5 Nb8 10 e4 a5! 11 b3 0-0 12 a3 Nc6 13 b4** 13 Ne1 Δ Nd3 **Bg4! 14 Qb3 Rfb8 15 Qc3 Bxf3! 16 Bxf3 axb4 17 axb4 c5!! =+**

18 b5 Nb4 19 Be2 b6 20 f4 Ne8! 21 Bg4 g6 22 fxe5 Qxe5 23 Qxe5 dxe5 24 Rxa8?! Rxa8 25 Bd7 Kf8! 26 Bxe8 Kxe8 27 Rf6 Ra1+! 28 Nf1 28 Kf2 **Nc2! 29 Kg2 Ra2 30 Kh3 Ra1** Zeitnot **32 Nd2?** 31 Kg2 Δ g4 **Rd1 32 Nf3 Rf1! −+ 33 d6 Ne1! 34 d7+ Kd8 35 Rxf7 Rxf3 0-1 Pavlov**

Queen's Indian

105 Kraidman-Gheorghiu
Netanya 77

1 d4 Nf6 2 c4 e6 3 Nf3 b6 4 g3 Ba6!? 4...Bb7 **5 Nbd2** 5 Qa4; 5 b3 **Bb7 6 Bg2 c5 7 0-0 cxd4 8 b3** 8 Nxd4 Bxg2 9 Kxg2 Nc6=; 9...Qc8= **Be7** 8...Bb4 9 Bb2 Bc3 10 Qc1 += **9 Bb2 0-0 10 Qc2 d6** 10...Nc6! =+ **11 Bxd4 Nbd7 12 Rfd1 a6 13 Ng5 Bxg2 14 Kxg2 Rc8 15 Qd3 Qc7 16 Nde4 Nxe4 17 Nxe4 Rfd8** 18 Bb2 Qc6 19 Qf3 f5 20 Nd2 Bf6! =+ **½-½ Gheorghiu**

106 Kuligowski-J.Adamski
Poland Final 78

1 d4 Nf6 2 c4 e6 3 Nf3 b6 4 g3 Bb7 5 Bg2 c5 6 d5! exd5 7 Ng5!? 7 Nh4 Rubinstein **Nc6! 8 cxd5 Na5 9 Nc3!? Be7** 9...d6? 10 Qa4!± **10 0-0 d6 11 b3?! 0-0** 11...a6!? **12 Nh3** 12 Qc2 **a6! 13 Qc2 b5 14 e4 Rc8?** 14...b4! 15 Nd1 c4 16 bxc4 Rc8 17 Ne3 Nxc4!≈ **15 Nd1! +=/± Re8** 15...b4 16 Bd2! **16 Ne3 Nd7?** 16...Bf8 **17 Bb2 Bf6 18 Nf5± Ne5 19 f4 Ng4 20 Bf3 Bxb2 21 Qxb2 Nf6 22 g4** 22 Nf2± Rf8 23 Ng4 Ne8; 22 e5 dxe5 23 fxe5 Nxd5 24 Nd6± **c4?** 22...Rf8 Δ Ne8± **23 g5 +−** 23 b4 c3!± **c3 24 Qf2! Nxe4 25 Qd4 Nf6 26 gxf6 gxf6 27 Kh1 c2 28 Qg1+ 1-0 Kuligowski**

107 Tukmakov-Kuzmin
USSR Final 77

1 d4 Nf6 2 c4 e6 3 Nf3 b6 4 g3 Bb7 5 Bg2 Be7 6 0-0 0-0 7 Nc3 Ne4 8 Qc2 Nxc3 9 Qxc3 c5 10 Rd1 d6 11 b3 Nd7 12 Bb2 Nf6 13 d5 exd5?! 13...e5 14 Nxe5 dxe5 15 d6 Bxg2 16 Qxe5 Re8 17 dxe7 Qxe7 18 Qxe7 Rxe7 19 Kxg2 Rxe2 20 Bxf6 gxf6 21 Rd7 += Petrosian-Karpov 76 **14 cxd5 Re8 15 e4 Bf8 16 Nd2± b5 17 a4 Ba6 18 axb5 Bxb5 19 Re1! a5 20 Qc2 Qd7 21 Nc4! Ra6** 21...Bxc4 22 Qxc4 Reb8 23 e5±; 23 Bc3± **22 e5?!** 22 Bxf6 gxf6 23 Ne3 +− **dxe5 23 Nxe5 Qc7 24 Bc3± Rd8 25 Red1**

♜e8 26 ♞c4 a4 27 ♞e3 ♛d7 28 bxa4 ♝xa4 29 ♛d3 ♝b5 30 ♛c2 ♝a4 31 ♛f5 ♛xf5 32 ♞xf5 ♜ea8 33 ♜e1 ♜8a7 34 ♝f1 ♜b6 35 d6! +− ♜bb7 35... ♗xd6 36 ♗xf6 gxf6 37 ♖e4 +− **36 ♝g2 ♜b6 37 ♝xf6 gxf6 38 ♜xa4 ♜xa4 39 d7 ♜b8 40 ♜e8 ♜a1+ 41 ♝f1 ♜aa8 42 ♞e7+ 1-0 Petrosian**

108 Miles-Korchnoi
Wijk aan Zee 78

1 d4 ♞f6 2 ♞f3 e6 3 g3 b6 4 ♝g2 ♝b7 5 c4 ♝e7 6 0-0 0-0 7 ♞c3 ♞e4 8 ♛c2 ♞xc3 9 ♛xc3 f5 10 b3 10 d5! += **♝f6 11 ♝b2 ♞c6 12 ♜ad1 ♛e7!** 12... ♘c7 13 ♘e1 ♗xg2 14 ♘xg2 g5 15 ♕c2! ♘g6 16 e4± Polugaevsky-Korchnoi (2) 77 **13 ♛d2** 13 ♘e1? ♘xd4! 14 ♖xd4 ♗xg2 15 ♘xg2 c5 −+; 13 ♕c2!? d6 14 ♗a3 +=; 13...g5!? **♞d8 14 d5** 14 ♘e1 **♝xb2 15 ♛xb2 d6 16 dxe6 ♞xe6 17 b4** 17 e3!? **f4!∓**

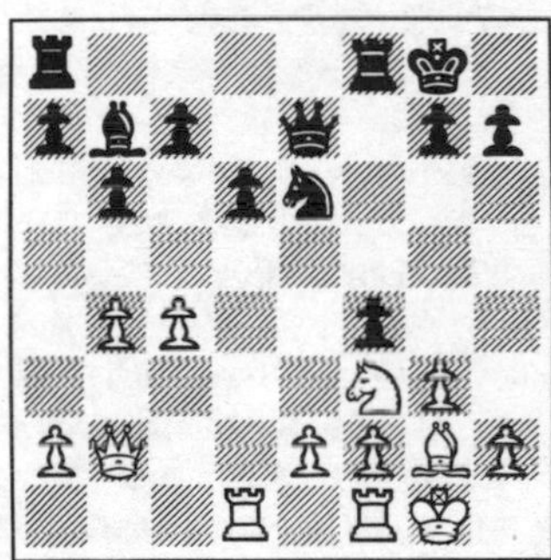

18 ♜d2 18 ♘e1 ♗xg2 19 ♘xg2 ♖f6∓; 19...g5!? **♜f6 19 ♛c3 ♜af8 20 a3 ♛e8 21 ♛d3 ♛h5 22 ♜dd1 ♚h8 23 ♞h4 ♝xg2 24 ♚xg2 g5 −+ 25 ♞f3 ♜h6 26 h4** 26 ♖h1 ♕h3+ 27 ♔g1 fxg3 28 fxg3 ♖hf6 −+ **gxh4 27 ♛c3+ ♚g8 28 gxh4** 28 ♘xh4 f3+ 29 exf3 ♘f4+ 30 ♔h2 ♕f5 −+ **♛g4+ 29 ♚h2 ♞g5! 30 ♞xg5 f3! 31 ♛xf3 ♜xh4+ 32 ♛h3 ♛xg5 0-1 Webb**

109 Vukic-Larsen Bugojno 78

1 ♞f3 e6 2 c4 b6 3 g3 ♝b7 4 ♝g2 ♞f6 5 0-0 g6?! 5...c5 **6 ♞c3 ♝g7 7 ♜e1!** 7 d4 ♘e4= **d5 8 d4 0-0 9 cxd5 exd5 10 ♝g5 ♞bd7 11 ♛b3 ♜e8 12 e3 a6 13 ♜ac1! += h6 14 ♝xf6 ♞xf6 15 ♞e5! ♜e6** 15...♘e4? 16 ♗xe4 ♗xe5 17 ♗xd5 +− **16 ♞d3 h5 17 ♜c2 ♝h6 18 ♜ec1 ♜a7 19 ♞e2 ♝a8 20 ♞e5! ♞g4** 20...c5? 21 dxc5 ♖xe5 22 cxb6 +− **21 ♞f4 ♝xf4 22 exf4 ♞f6 23 f5 gxf5 24 ♛f3 ♞g4! 25 ♞d3** 25 ♕xf5? ♘xe5 26 dxe5 c5! Δ d4∓ **♛g5** 25... ♖e4?! 26 h3 ♘f6 27 ♕xf5 ♖xd4 28 ♘f4 c5 29 ♕g5+ Δ ♘xh5 +− **26 h3 ♞f6 27 ♜xc7 ♜xc7 28 ♜xc7 ♝c6 29 ♛f4** 29 ♘e5? ♕c1+ 30 ♔h2 ♘g4+! 31 hxg4 hxg4 Δ ♖h6+ −+ **♛xf4 30 gxf4 ♝e8 31 ♞e5 ♚f8 32 ♝f1 a5 33 ♝a6 ♜e7 34 ♜c8 ♚g7 35 h4! ♞e4 36 f3 ♞d6 37 ♜d8 ♜e6 38 ♚f2 ♚f8 39 ♜b8 b5 40 ♝c8 ♜e7 41 ♝d7! +− a4** 41...f6? 42 ♘g6+ +− **42 b3 axb3 43 axb3 ♚g7 44 ♝xe8 ♜xe8 45 ♜b6 ♜e6 46 ♜c6 f6 47 ♜c7+ ♚h6 48 ♞d3 ♜e8 49 ♞b4 ♜a8 50 ♜c6 ♞e8 51 ♞xd5 ♜a2+ 52 ♚g3 ♚g7 53 ♜b6 ♜d2 54 ♞e7 ♚f7 55 ♞xf5 ♚g6 56 ♜xb5 ♞c7 57 ♜a5 ♜d3 58 b4 ♞e6 59 ♜d5?** 59 d5! ♔xf5 60 dxe6+ ♔xe6 61 ♖xh5 +− **♞c7 60 ♞e7+ ♚f7 61 ♜d7 ♞b5 62 ♞c6+ ♚e6 63 ♜d8 ♞d6! 64 ♜h8 ♞f5+ 65 ♚f2 ♞xd4?** 65...♘xh4! 66 ♖xh5 ♖xf3+ 67 ♔e2 ♖xf4 68 b5 ♔d6 69 d5 ♔c5!= **66 ♞xd4 ♜xd4 67 ♜e8+ ♚f5 68 ♜e4 ♜e1?!** 68...♖d2+ **69 ♜e1 ♜d4 70 ♜e4?** 70 ♖b1!! ♔xf4 71 b5 ♖d2+ 72 ♔e1 ♖d8 73 ♖b3! ♔g3 74 b6 ♔xh4 75 b7 ♖b8 76 ♔f2 +− **♜d2+ 71 ♚e3 ♜b2 72 ♜d4 ♜b3+ 73 ♚e2 ♚e6 74 ♚d2?** 74 ♔f2! Δ ♔g3 **♜xf3 75 ♚c2 ♜g3!= 76 b5 ♚f5 77 b6 ♜g8 78 ♚d3 ♚g4 79 ♚e3**

♔xh4 80 ♔f2 ♔g4 81 b7 ♖b8 82 ♖b4 h4 83 ♔g1 83 ♔g2 h3+ 84 ♔h2 f5=; 84 ♔f2 f5= **h3 84 ♔f1 ♔g3 ½-½ Vukic**

110 Ogaard-Miles Reykjavik 78

1 d4 e6 2 c4 b6 3 d5?! ♕h4! TN 3...♗b7 4 a3 ♕h4?! 5 ♘c3! ♕xc4 6 e4±; 3...♗b4+ **4 e3** 4 ♘c3 ♗b4! **♘f6 5 a3** 5 ♘f3 ♕h5=+; 5 ♘c3 ♗b4 **♗b7 6 ♘f3?!** 6 ♘c3 exd5 7 cxd5 ♘e4 8 ♕c2 ♘xc3 9 ♕xc3 ♗xd5 10 ♕xc7 ♘c6 ∞/=+ **♕h5 7 dxe6 fxe6** =+/∓ **8 ♗e2 ♕g6 9 ♘h4** 9 0-0 ♘c6/♗d6∓ **♕h6 10 ♗f3?!** 10 ♘f3 **♘c6 11 g3 g5! 12 e4** 12 ♘g2 g4 13 ♗xg4 ♘xg4 14 ♕xg4 ♘e5 −+; 13 ♗e2 ♘e5 −+ **♘e5 13 ♗g2 ♕g7 14 f4** 14 ♘f3 ♘xf3+ 15 ♗xf3 g4 −+; 14 ♗xg5 ♕xg5 15 f4 ♕g7 16 fxe5 ♘g4 −+ **gxh4 15 fxe5 ♘g4! −+ 16 ♗f4 0-0-0 17 ♘c3 ♗c5 18 ♕d2 ♘xe5 19 b4 h3! 0-1 Miles**

111 Petrosian-Tal Sochi 77

1 d4 ♘f6 2 c4 e6 3 ♘f3 b6 4 g3 ♗b7 5 ♗g2 ♗e7 6 0-0 0-0 7 ♘c3 d5 8 ♘e5 ♘a6 9 ♗g5 9 ♗e3 c5 10 ♖c1 ♘e4 11 cxd5 exd5 12 ♘xe4 dxe4 13 dxc5 ♗xc5 14 ♗xc5 ♘xc5 15 b4 ♘e6 16 ♘c6 ♗xc6 17 ♖xc6 ♕e7!= 18 ♗xe4 ♖ad8 19 ♗d3 ♕xb4 20 ♕b1 ♕xb1 21 ♖xb1= Bagirov-Balashov 77 **c5 10 ♖c1 ♘e4 11 ♗xe7 ♕xe7 12 dxc5 ♘axc5 13 ♘xe4 dxe4** 13...♘xe4± **14 b4 ♖ad8** 14...♘a6 15 a3± **15 ♕c2 ♕g5!** 15...♘a6 16 a3±; 15...♘d7 16 ♘xd7 ♖xd7 17 a3 += **16 bxc5 ♕xe5 17 cxb6 axb6 18 ♖b1 ♕a5!** 18...♖d6 19 ♖b5 Δ ♖fb1± **19 ♖b5=** 19 ♗xe4 ♖d2 20 ♗xh7+ ♔h8 21 ♖b5! ♖xc2 22 ♗xc2 Δ ♖h5+, ♗h7+ = **♖d2 20 ♕b1 ♕xa2 21 ♖xb6 ♗a8 22 e3 ♕xc4 ½-½ Petrosian**

112 Petrosian-Krogius Sochi 77

1 c4 ♘f6 2 ♘c3 e6 3 ♘f3 d5 4 d4 ♗e7 5 g3 0-0 6 ♗g2 ♘bd7 7 0-0 c6 8 ♕d3 b6 9 e4 ♗a6 10 b3 ♖c8 11 ♖d1 11 ♗f4 ♖e8 12 ♖fd1 ♘f8 13 a4 ♗b4 14 e5 ♘6d7 15 ♗d2± Korchnoi-Petrosian 75 **b5?! 12 cxd5 cxd5 13 e5 ♘e8 14 ♘xb5 ♘c7 15 a4 ♖b8 16 ♕e3!**± **♗xb5 17 axb5 ♘xb5 18 ♗f1 a5**

19 ♖a4? 19 ♗d2! ♘a3 20 ♖a2 ♗b4 21 ♖da1 ♕e7 22 ♗c1 ♘b5 23 ♖xa5 ♗xa5 24 ♖xa5 ♕b4 25 ♗d2 +−; 19...♗b4 20 ♗xb4 axb4 21 ♗xb5 ♖xb5 22 ♖dc1± **♘a7!= 20 ♗d2 ♘c6 21 ♖da1 ♕b6 22 ♗xa5 ♕xb3** 22...♘xa5?! 23 ♖xa5 ♕xb3 24 ♖a7 Δ ♖c1-c7± **23 ♗d2 ♕xe3 24 ♗xe3 ♘b6 25 ♖a6 ♘b4 26 ♖a7 ♘c6 27 ♖c7 ♖fc8 28 ♖xc8 ♖xc8 29 ♗b5 ♘c4 30 ♗xc6 ♖xc6 31 ♖a8+ ♗f8 32 ♗g5 ♖c7 33 ♔g2 h6 34 ♗d8 ♖b7 35 g4 ♔h7 ½-½ Petrosian**

113 Sosonko-Karpov Tilburg 77

1 d4 ♘f6 2 c4 e6 3 g3 d5 4 ♗g2 dxc4 5 ♘f3 a6 6 0-0 ♘c6 6...b5 7 ♘e5 ♘d5 8 e4 ♘f6 9 a4 c6≈ **7 e3!** 7 ♘c3?! ♖b8 8 e4 ♗e7 9 d5 ♘b4 10 ♘e5 exd5 11 exd5 ♗f5∓ **♘b4!?** 7...♖b8 8 ♘fd2 += ♘a5? 9 ♕a4+ c6 10 b4!± **8 ♘e5 c5 9 a3 ♘bd5?!** 9...♘d3

10 ♘xd3 cxd3 11 ♕xd3 ♗e7= **10 dxc5 ♕c7** 10...♗xc5? 11 e4 **11 ♘xc4 ♕xc5** 11...♗xc5?! 12 e4 ♘b6 13 ♗f4 ♗xf2+ 14 ♖xf2 ♕xc4 15 ♖c2± **12 b3 b5** 12...♗e7? 13 e4± **13 ♘a5 ♕c7 14 b4 ♗b7?!** 14...♗e7 15 e4 ♘b6 16 ♗e3± **15 e4 ♘b6 16 ♗f4! e5 17 ♘xb7 ♖c8!** 17...exf4 18 e5! +− **18 ♕e2 ♘fd7 19 ♘c5 exf4 20 ♘xa6 ♕e5 21 ♘d2 fxg3 22 hxg3± ♗e7 23 ♘f3 ♕h5 24 e5 ♘c4 25 e6 fxe6 26 ♕xe6 ♕f7 27 ♘g5?!** 27 ♕e2! 0-0 28 ♗h3 ♕xf3 29 ♕xe7! **♕xe6 28 ♘xe6 ♔f7 29 ♖fe1 += ♗f6 30 ♖ad1 ♘db6 31 ♘ac7 ♘xa3 32 ♘d5 ♘ac4 33 ♘xb6** 33 ♘xf6!? **♘xb6 34 ♖d6 ♖b8 35 ♘c7 ♖hd8 36 ♘xb5 ♗e7 37 ♖xd8 ♖xd8 38 ♘a7. ♗xb4 39 ♘c8 ½-½ Webb**

114 Romanishin-Grigorian
USSR Final 77
1 ♘f3 ♘f6 2 c4 e6 3 g3 d5 4 ♗g2 ♗e7 5 0-0 0-0 6 d4 dxc4 7 ♕c2 a6 8 a4 ♘c6 9 ♕xc4 ♕d5 10 ♕xd5 TN **exd5?** 10...♘xd5 11 e4 += **11 ♗f4 ♗g4 12 ♖d1 ♖ac8?±** 12...♗xf3 13 ♗xf3 ♖ac8+= **13 ♘e5!±**

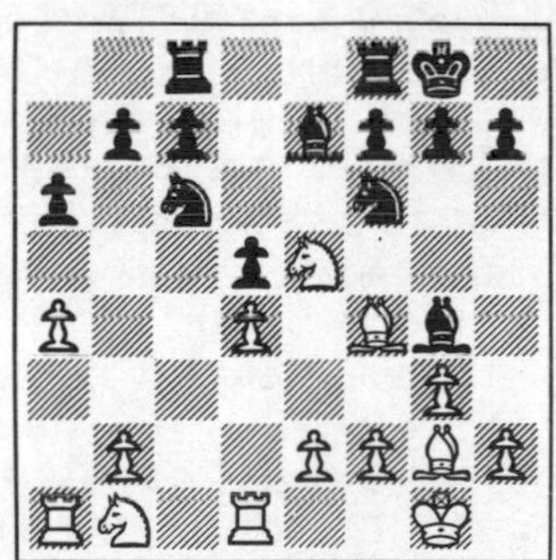

13...♘xe5 +− 13...♗xe2 14 ♖e1 +−; 13...♗e6 14 ♘c3 ♖fd8 15 a5± **14 dxe5 ♘h5 15 ♗e3 g6 16 ♗xd5 ♗xe2 17 ♖d2 c6 18 ♗xf7+ ♔xf7 19 ♖xe2 ♘g7 20 ♘c3 ♘f5 21 e6+ ♔g8 22 ♗b6 ♗f6 23 ♖d1 ♗d8 24 e7! ♗xb6 25 exf8+ ♖xf8 26 ♖d7 ♗c5 27 ♘e4 ♗d4 28 ♖e3 1-0 Petrosian**

115 Quinteros-L.Kovacs Stip 77
1 ♘f3 ♘f6 2 c4 e6 3 g3 d5 4 ♗g2 ♗e7 5 0-0 0-0 6 d4 ♘bd7 7 ♕c2 c5 8 cxd5 ♘xd5 9 ♘c3 ♘b4 10 ♕b1 ♘f6!? 10...♘c6 11 dxc5 ♘xc5 (11...♗xc5 12 ♘g5! g6 13 ♖d1 += Keres) 12 ♖d1 ♕a5 13 ♗d2 ♘d7 14 ♘e4 ♕f5 15 ♗c3 += Keres-Levenfish, USSR Final 47 **11 ♖d1 ♘bd5 12 e4!? ♘xc3 13 bxc3 ♗d7! 14 ♗f4** 14 ♕xb7 ♖b8 15 ♕xa7 ♖a8 16 ♕b7 ♖b8= 17 ♕a6 ♗b5 18 ♕a3? cxd4 −+ **♗a4 15 ♖d2 ♕a5! 16 ♕xb7!? ♖fe8 17 ♖c1 ♖ac8** △ ♗c6, ♘xe4 **18 ♕b1 cxd4 19 ♖xd4** 19 cxd4? ♖xc1+ 20 ♕xc1 ♘xe4 =+; 19 ♘xd4? e5 −+ **♗c5 20 ♖d2 ♗a3 21 ♖e1 e5! =+ 22 ♗g5 ♕xc3 23 ♗xf6 ½-½** 23...gxf6 =+ **L.Kovacs**

Grunfeld

116 Tarjan-Pavlov Torremolinos 78
1 d4 ♘f6 2 c4 g6 3 ♘c3 d5 4 cxd5 ♘xd5 5 e4 ♘xc3 6 bxc3 ♗g7 7 ♗c4 c5 8 ♘e2 0-0 9 0-0 ♘c6 10 ♗e3 ♘a5 11 ♗d3 b6!? 12 e5?! ♗b7 13 ♘f4 cxd4 14 cxd4 ♖c8 15 ♕g4 ♘c6 16 ♖ad1 ♘b4 17 ♗b1 ♗d5!? TN 17...♘d5! 18 ♖e1 ♘xf4 19 ♗xf4 ♗d5 =+ Sax **18 ♖d2 ♖c3 19 h4 ♗c4 20 ♖fe1 ♘d5 += 21 h5 ♘xf4 22 ♗xf4 ♗d5 23 f3 ♕c8 24 ♕h4 ♖c1 25 ♖dd1 ♖xd1 26 ♖xd1 ♕e6 27 ♖c1 ♗c4 28 a3 a5?** 28...b5! **29 ♔f2!** △ ♖h1 **♖c8 30 ♖h1 f5 31 g4! ♗a2?! 32 hxg6 ♗xb1** Zeitnot **33 ♕xh7+ ♔f8 34 ♗h6 ♗xh6 35 ♕h8+ ♕g8 36 ♕xh6+ ♔e8 37 ♕h8 ♔f8?** 37...♗a2! **38 ♕xg8+ ♔xg8 39 ♖xb1 f4 40 ♖xb6 ♖c2+ 1-0** 41 ♔f1 ♖c3 42 ♔g2 ♖c2+ 43 ♔h3 △ g5 **Pavlov**

117 Gheorghiu-Kouatly
Val Thorens 77

1 c4 Nf6 2 Nc3 d5 3 cxd5 Nxd5 4 g3 4 Nf3 g6 5 Qa4+ += **g6 5 Bg2 Nb6 6 d3 Bg7 7 Nf3** 7 Be3± **c6!** TN 7...0-0 8 0-0 Nc6 9 Be3 e5 10 Qc1± **8 0-0 0-0 9 Bd2** 9 Be3 Nd5!∞ **h6 10 Qc1 Kh7 11 Ne4** 11 b4 += **Na6 12 Bc3! f6!** 12...Bxc3± **13 Rd1 Nd5 14 Be1 e5 15 Nc3 Be6 16 e4! Nb6** 16...Nxc3 17 bxc3 Δ d4± **17 d4 Qc8! 18 b3 Bg4 19 Qe3 f5!?** 19...Qe6∞ **20 dxe5 fxe4 21 Nh4!!±**

21...Bxd1 22 Rxd1 22 Bxe4? Bh5!∓ **g5 23 Bxe4+ Kg8 24 Ng6 Re8 25 f4 Qg4! 26 f5! Nd5** 26...Bxe5 27 Nxe5 Rxe5 28 Qd4! Δ Bd5+ **27 Qd4! Nxc3 28 Bxc3! +-** 28 Bd5+ Nxd5 29 Qxg4± **Qe2 29 Re1** 29 f6! +- **Qb5 30 f6 Qc5 31 Rf1 Bxf6 32 exf6! Kf7** 32...Rxe4 33 f7+ Kh7 34 Qxc5 Nxc5 35 f8Q +- **32 Ne7! 1-0 Gheorghiu**

118 Diesen-Pavlov Torremolinos 78

1 d4 Nf6 2 c4 g6 3 Nc3 d5 4 Nf3 Bg7 5 Qb3 dxc4 6 Qxc4 0-0 7 e4 a6 7... Bg4 8 Be3 Nfd7; 7...Na6 **8 Be2** 8 Bf4 b5! 9 Qxc7 Qxc7 10 Bxc7 Bb7 =+ **b5 9 Qb3 Bb7?!** 9...c5! **10 e5 Nd5** 10...Ne4 **11 0-0 Nb6 12 a4 bxa4 13 Nxa4 Bd5 14 Qc3! += Nxa4 15 Rxa4 Qd7!? 16 b3! Nc6 17 Be3!** 17 Rxa6 Rxa6 18 Bxa6 Bxf3 19 gxf3 Nxd4= **Rab8 18 Nd2 a5 19 Rfc1 Rb6 20 Nc4 Rb7 21 Nxa5 Nxa5 22 Rxa5 Rxb3 23 Qxc7 Qxc7 24 Rxc7 Rb1+ 25 Rc1 Rxc1+ 26 Bxc1 e6 27 Bf3! Rc8 28 Be3 Bxf3 29 gxf3 h6?** 29...Rd8 **30 Kg2 Bf8 31 d5! exd5 32 Rxd5 Re8 33 f4 h5 34 Kf3 Bh6??** Zeitnot **35 f5! Bxe3 36 Kxe3 gxf5 37 Kf4 Ra8 38 Kxf5 Ra2 39 f4 Rf2 40 h4??** Zeitnot 40 Rd3! +- Rxh2 41 Kf6; 40...Kf8 41 Rh3 +- **Rg2! 41 Kf6 Rg6+ 42 Ke7 Re6+ 43 Kd7 Kf8 44 f5 Ra6 45 f6 Ra4! 46 Kc6 Kg8 47 Rd8+ Kh7 48 Kd6 Ra6+ 49 Kd5** 49 Ke7 Re6+ 50 Kxf7 Rxe5= **Kg6 50 Rg8+ Kh6!** 50...Kf5? 51 Rg5+ **51 Rg7 Ra5+! 52 Kd6 Rxe5!! 53 Rxf7** 53 Rg6+ Kxg6 54 Kxe5 Kh6 55 Kd6 Kh7 56 Ke7 Kg8 57 Ke8 +-; 53...Kh7! 54 Rh6+? Kxh6 55 Kxe5 Kg6 56 Kf4 Kxf6 -+ **½-½ Pavlov**

119 Sosonko-Mecking
Wijk aan Zee 78

1 d4 Nf6 2 c4 g6 3 Nc3 d5 4 Nf3 Bg7 5 Qb3 dxc4 6 Qxc4 0-0 7 e4 a6 8 Be2 b5 9 Qb3 c5!? 9...Bb7 10 e5 Nd5 11 0-0 Nxc3 12 Qxc3 Bd5 13 a4 Nc6 14 Be3 bxa4 15 Rxa4 a5 16 Nd2 Qd7 17 Rfa1± Sosonko-Sax, Ljubljana 77 **10 dxc5 Nbd7 11 e5!?** 11 Be3? Ng4; 11 c6 Nc5 12 Qc2 b4 13 Nd5 Ncxe4 14 Nxf6+ Nxf6≈; 12...Bg4!? **Nxc5** 11...Ng4!? 12 e6 Nxc5 13 Qb4 Nd3+ 14 Bxd3 Qxd3∓ **12 Qb4 Nfd7 13 0-0 a5?!** 13...Bb7 14 Rd1 a5 15 Qh4 e6 16 Bg5 Qb8 17 Be7 b4! 18 Bd6 Qd8 19 Be7 Qb8 20 Bd6 Qd8 21 Be7 ½-½ Ree-Mecking, Wijk aan Zee 78 **14 Qh4 Bb7** 14...Nxe5 15 Rd1 += **15 Bg5 Qb6?!** 15...f6!? **16 Bxe7 Rfe8 17 Bxb5 Bxf3 18 Bxc5**

18 gxf3? ♘xe5 **♕xc5 19 ♗xd7 ♖e7 20 gxf3 ♖xd7 21 f4 += ♕b4! 22 ♖ad1 ♖ad8 23 ♕xd8+** 23 ♕g4 h5 24 ♕f3 ♕xb2≈; 23 ♖xd7 ♖xd7 24 ♕g4 ♖d2≈ **♖xd8 24 ♖xd8+ ♗f8 25 ♘d5 ♕xb2 26 ♖e1 ♔g7 27 ♖e3 ♗c5 28 ♖f3 ♕e2 29 ♔g2 ♗xf2!** ½-½ 30 ♘c3 ♕e1 31 ♖xf2 ♕xc3= **Webb**

120 Ivkov-Timman Bugojno 78

1 d4 ♘f6 2 c4 g6 3 ♘c3 d5 4 ♘f3 ♗g7 5 ♕b3 dxc4 6 ♕xc4 0-0 7 e4 ♗g4 8 ♗e3 ♘fd7 9 ♕b3 ♘b6 10 ♖d1 ♘c6 11 d5 ♘e5 12 ♗e2 ♘xf3+ 13 gxf3 ♗h5 14 ♖g1! += 14 h4; 14 f4 **♕b8?!** 14... ♕c8 15 ♖g3 c6 16 ♖c1 ♕d7 += **15 f4 ♗xe2 16 ♘xe2 c6 17 dxc6 bxc6 18 h4± ♖d8 19 ♖xd8+ ♕xd8 20 h5 ♖b8** 20...♕d6 21 hxg6 hxg6 22 f5 gxf5 23 ♘g3!

21 hxg6 hxg6 22 ♖xg6!! ♘d5 23 ♖xg7+ ♔xg7 24 ♗d4+ ♘f6 25 ♕c3!± ♕h8 25...♔f8 26 ♘g3 Δ ♘f5 **26 ♘g3 ♔f8 27 ♗xa7! ♖b7 28 ♗d4 ♖d7 29 ♗e5 ♕h4** Δ ♕g4; 29...♕h2 30 ♕xc6 ♕g1+ 31 ♘f1 ♕g4 32 ♘e3!; 31...♖d1+ 32 ♔xd1 ♕xf1+ 33 ♔c2 +− **30 ♕xc6 ♖d8?!** 30...♕g4!? 31 ♘e2 ♕h3; 31 ♕c8+ ♘e8 32 ♗d4!? ♕e6≈; 31 ♕a4!? **31 ♕c7 ♔e8** 31...♖d3? 32 ♗xf6 Δ ♕c8+ **32 ♕c6+ ♔f8 33 ♕b6! ♔e8** 33...♖d7? 34 ♗xf6 Δ ♕b8+; 33...♖c8!? **34 ♗c7 +− ♘d7** 34...♖c8 35 ♕b7 ♕g4 36 f5 +− **35 ♕b7 e6 36 ♗xd8 ♔xd8 37 ♕a8+ ♔e7 38 ♕a3+ ♔e8 39 ♕a8+ ♔e7 40 ♕a3+ 1-0 Webb**

121 Bagirov-Tukmakov
USSR Final 77

1 d4 ♘f6 2 c4 g6 3 ♘c3 d5 4 ♘f3 ♗g7 5 e3 0-0 6 b4 b6! 7 ♕b3 7 ♗b2 c5 8 dxc5 ♘e4 9 ♕b3 ♗xc3+ 10 ♗xc3 bxc5 11 ♖d1 +=; 8...bxc5! 9 ♘xd5 ♘xd5 10 ♗xg7 ♘xc3!= **c5 8 bxc5 bxc5 9 cxd5 ♘a6 10 ♗e2 ♖b8 11 ♕a4 ♘b4 12 0-0 ♘fxd5 13 ♗d2 ♗d7 14 ♕xa7 ♖a8 15 ♕xc5 ♖c8 16 ♘xd5 ♖xc5 17 ♘xe7+! ♔h8 18 ♗xb4≈ ♖c2 19 ♗d3 ♖b2 20 ♗a3 ♖b8 21 ♘d5 ♖e8 22 ♘f4 ♗b5 23 ♗c5 ♕a5 24 ♖fc1 ♗xd3 25 ♘xd3 ♕a4 26 ♗d6 ♖b6 27 ♗c5 ♖bb8 28 ♗d6 ½-½ Petrosian**

122 Petrosian-Grigorian
USSR Final 77

1 d4 ♘f6 2 c4 g6 3 ♘c3 d5 4 ♗f4 ♗g7 5 e3 0-0 5...c5 6 dxc5 ♕a5 7 ♕a4+ ♕xa4 8 ♘xa4 ♘a6 9 cxd5 ♘xd5 10 ♗b5+ ♗d7 11 ♗xd7+ ♔xd7= **6 ♕b3 c5** 6...dxc4 7 ♗xc4 ♘c6!= **7 cxd5 cxd4 8 exd4 += ♘bd7 9 ♗e2 ♘b6 10 ♗f3 e6!?** 10...♗f5 (Δ ♗d3 c4) 11 ♖d1 ♕d7 12 h3 h5 13 ♘ge2 ♖ad8 14 d6 exd6 += **11 d6!** 11 dxe6 ♗xe6 12 ♕d1 ♘fd5= **♘fd5!?** 11...♘e8 12 ♘ge2 ♘xd6 13 0-0 += **12 ♗xd5** 12 ♗e5 ♗xe5 13 dxe5 ♕g5∞ **exd5** 12...♘xd5 13 ♗e5 ♗xe5 14 dxe5 ♕g5 15 ♘xd5 exd5 16 ♕g3 ♕xg3 17 hxg3 ♖e8 18 f4 f6 19 ♘f3± **13 ♘ge2 ♖e8 14 0-0 ♗f5** 14...♗f8 15 a4 a5 16 ♖fe1± **15 a4 ♗d3 16 ♖fe1 ♗c4 17 ♕b4 ♗f8 18 b3 ♗a6?** 18...a5 19 ♕c5 ♗xb3 20 ♖eb1 ♘d7 21 ♕c7 ♕xc7 22 dxc7 ♗c4∞ **19 ♘b5 ♗xb5 20 ♕xb5 a6** 20...♗xd6 21 a5± **21 ♕b4 a5 22 ♕b5 ♗xd6**

23 ♗d2!± ♘d7 24 ♕xd5 ♘f6 25 ♕f3 ♘e4 26 ♗f4 ♗xf4 27 ♕xf4 ♖c8 28 ♖ac1 ♘d6 29 ♘g3 ♖xe1+ 30 ♖xe1 ♖c3 31 h4! +− Δ h5-6 **h5 32 ♖e5!** Δ ♘xh5/♖d5 **f5?? 33 ♖e6 ♘f7 34 ♖xg6+ ♔h7 35 ♕xf5 ♖c1+ 36 ♘f1 1-0 Petrosian**

123 Onat-Gheorghiu Balkaniad 77

1 d4 ♘f6 2 ♘f3 g6 3 c4 ♗g7 4 ♘c3 d5 5 ♗g5 5 ♗f4; 5 e3; 5 ♕b3 **♘e4 6 cxd5** 6 ♗h4 **♘xg5 7 ♘xg5 e6** 7...c6!?∞ **8 ♘f3** 8 ♕d2 **exd5 9 e3 0-0 10 b4! c6 11 ♗e2 ♗e6 12 0-0 ♘d7 13 ♖c1 ♖c8!=** 13...f5!? **14 ♘e1** 14 b5 cxb5! =+ **♕e7 15 ♘d3 ♘f6 16 ♕a4!** Δ ♘e4 **a6 17 ♘c5 ♖b8 18 ♕b3 ♖fd8 19 a4 ♘d7! 20 a5?!** 20 ♘xd7= **♘xc5 21 bxc5 ♖bc8 22 ♗d3 ♖c7 23 ♖b1 ♖dd7 24 ♖be1 ♕e8! 25 f4? ♖e7!∓ 26 ♘b1 ♗c8 27 ♔f2 ♗f6** 27...♖xe3 28 ♖xe3 ♗xd4 29 ♖fe1 ♖e7 30 ♕d2± **28 ♘d2 ♖e6 29 ♘f3 ♗d8 30 ♗c2 ♖ce7 31 ♕c3 ♗c7 32 ♘g5 ♖f6 33 ♘f3 ♖fe6 34 ♘g5 ♖f6 35 ♘f3 ♗g4! 36 ♔g1 ♗xf3 37 ♖xf3 ♖xf4!∓**

38 ♖h3 ♖f6 39 ♖f3 ♖fe6 40 g3 ♕d8 41 ♖a1 f5 42 ♔f2 h5 43 h4 ♖f7 Δ g5∓ **44 ♔g2 ♕e8 45 ♖af1 ♖fe7 46 ♖e1 ♗d8 47 ♔f2 ♖f7 48 ♖h1 ♗f6 49 ♔g2 ♗g7 50 ♔f2 ♗h6! 51 ♖e1 ♕e7 52 ♗b1 ♖f8 53 ♗c2 ♖e8 54 ♗b1 ♔h8 55 ♗c2 f4!! −+ 56 gxf4 ♕xh4+ 57 ♔g2 ♕e7 58 ♖h1 h4! 59 ♖hh3 g5 60 fxg5 ♕xg5+ 61 ♔f2** 61 ♔h2 ♖g8 −+ **♖g8 62 ♔e2 ♕g1 63 ♔d3 ♖g3! −+ 64 ♖hxg3 hxg3 65 ♕d2 g2 66 ♔c3 ♖xe3+ 67 ♔b2 ♖b3+! −+ 0-1 Gheorghiu**

124 Hardicsay-Vegh Hungary 77

1 c4 ♘f6 2 g3 g6 3 ♗g2 ♗g7 4 ♘f3 0-0 5 0-0 d5 6 d4 ♘c6 7 cxd5 ♘xd5 8 ♘c3 ♘b6 9 e3 e5 10 d5 ♘a5 10...♘e7 **11 e4 h6?!** 11...♗g4!; 11...c6 12 ♗g5 f6 13 ♗e3 cxd5 14 ♗xb6 ♕xb6 15 ♘xd5 ♕d8= **12 b3! c6 13 ♗a3 ♖e8 14 ♗b4! ♘d7 15 ♖c1 ♘f8 16 ♖e1 ♗g4 17 h3 ♗xf3 18 ♗xf3 ♕b6 19 a3 ♖ac8 20 ♗g4! ♖b8 21 ♗e2 ♘h7 22 ♔g2 ♗f8? 23 ♗xf8 ♖xf8 24 b4 +− f5 25 bxa5 ♕xa5 26 ♕b3 ♔g7 27 exf5 ♖xf5 28 ♗d3 ♖f7 29 ♖xe5 ♖bf8 30 f4 cxd5 31 ♖ce1 ♘f6 32 ♖1e2 ♖d8 33 ♖e7 ♖dd7 34 ♖xf7+ ♔xf7 35 ♘e4! ♘xe4 36 ♗xe4 ♔g7 37 ♗b1 d4 38 ♗xg6 ♕a6 39 ♗d3 ♕c6+ 40 ♔h2 ♕d6 1-0 Hardiscay**

125 Timman-Olafsson Tilburg 77

1 d4 ♘f6 2 c4 d6 3 ♘c3 ♘bd7 4 e4 e5 5 ♘ge2 c6 6 g3 g6 7 ♗g2 ♗g7 8 0-0 0-0 9 b3 exd4 10 ♘xd4 ♖e8 11 h3 ♘c5 12 ♖e1 a5 13 ♖b1 a4!? 13...♘fd7 14 ♗e3 ♘e5 15 ♕c2 a4 16 ♖ed1 += Tukmakov-Timman, Reykjavik 76; 15...♕e7 16 ♖bd1 f6 17 f4 ♘f7 18 ♗f2 += Panno-Vukic, Biel 77 **14 ♗f4! axb3 15 axb3 ♘h5 16 ♗e3 ♘f6 17 ♕c2 ♕e7 18 ♖bd1 += ♗d7** 18...♘xe4? 19 ♘xe4 ♘xe4 20 ♗xe4 ♕xe4 21 ♗d2 +− **19 ♗f4** 19 f3!? Δ ♗f2, f4 **♘h5 20 ♗e3** 20 ♘xc6?! **♖a3!?·** 20...♘f6 **21 ♗c1 ♖a1 22 b4!**

♘a6!? 22...♘e6 23 ♘b3 ♖aa8 24 ♔h2±; 24 ♖d3!? **23 ♕b2 ♖xc1 24 ♕xc1 ♘xb4 += 25 ♕b1 c5 26 ♘db5 ♗e5 27 ♕c1** Δ f4 **♕f6 28 ♘e2 ♗xb5 29 cxb5 ♕e6 30 ♕d2 ♖a8 31 ♘c1 ♖a3 32 ♖e3 ♖xe3 33 ♕xe3 ♘c2 34 ♕g5 ♘d4 35 b6 ♔g7 36 ♔h2 ♕c4 37 ♘d3! ♕b3 38 ♕d2 c4** 38...♕xb6 39 f4 ♗f6 40 g4 c4 41 gxh5 cxd3 42 ♕xd3± **39 ♘xe5 dxe5 40 ♖c1 ♘f6**

41 f4! 41 ♕c3? ♘e2 42 ♕xb3 cxb3 43 ♖b1 ♘d4 Δ ♘d7xb6-c4= **♘d7** 41...♘f3+ 42 ♗xf3 ♕xf3 43 ♖xc4 ♘xe4 44 ♕g2 +−; 43...exf4 44 gxf4 ♘xe4 45 ♕d4+ +− **42 fxe5 ♕d3 43 ♕f2! ♘xe5 44 ♖f1 +− ♘dc6 45 ♕f6+ ♔f8 46 ♖a1 ♔e8** 46...♕d8 47 ♖a8! **47 ♖a8+ ♔d7 48 ♖a7! ♔c8 49 ♕h8+ ♔d7 50 ♖xb7+ ♔d6 51 ♕f8+ ♔e6 52 ♖c7 ♕e2 53 ♖xc6+ ♘xc6 54 ♕c8+ ♔d6 55 ♕c7+ ♔c5 56 e5 1-0 Webb**

126 Kovacs-Haik
Reggio Emilia 77/78

1 d4 ♘f6 2 c4 g6 3 ♘c3 ♗g7 4 e4 0-0 5 ♘ge2 d6 6 ♘g3 e5 7 d5 ♘e8 7...♘bd7 8 ♗e2 a6 9 h4 h5 10 ♗g5 ♕e8 11 ♕d2 ♘h7 12 ♗h6 ♘df6 13 ♗xg7 ♔xg7 14 0-0-0 ♗d7 15 ♖dg1 b5 =+ Gligoric **8 h4 h5** 8...f5 9 exf5 gxf5 10 ♗g5 ♕d7 11 ♗d3 ♘a6 12 ♗c2 ♘c5 13 ♘h5 a5 14 ♕e2 ♘f6= Dastkalov-Bobekov, Sofia 60 **9 ♗e2 ♗f6 10 ♗h6 ♘g7 11 ♕d2 ♗xh4 12 0-0-0** 12 ♖xh4? ♕xh4 13 ♗g5 ♕h2 14 0-0-0 f6! =+ **♗e7 13 ♔b1 ♘bd7?** 13...h4! 14 ♘f1 f5 15 g3∞ **14 ♗xh5 ♘xh5 15 ♘xh5 gxh5 16 ♖xh5 f5 17 ♗xf8 ♗xf8 18 exf5 ♘f6 19 ♕g5+ ♔f7** 19...♗g7 20 ♖dh1 ♗xf5+ 21 ♕xf5 ♘xh5 22 ♕e6+ +− **20 ♕g6+ ♔e7 21 ♖h7+ ♘xh7 22 ♕xh7+ ♔e8 23 ♕g6+ ♔e7 24 ♖h1 ♗xf5+** 24...♕e8 25 ♕g5+ ♔d7 26 ♖h7+ ♗e7 27 f6 +− **25 ♕xf5 ♗g7 26 ♕e6+ ♔f8 27 ♖h5 1-0** 27...♕e7 28 ♖f5+ ♔e8 29 ♕g6+ ♔d8 30 ♖f7 +− **Kovacs**

127 Timman-Westerinen Geneva 77

1 ♘f3 ♘f6 2 c4 g6 3 ♘c3 ♗g7 4 e4 d6 5 d4 0-0 6 ♗e2 e5 7 d5 a5 8 ♗g5 h6 9 ♗h4 ♘a6 10 ♘d2 ♕e8! 11 a3 ♗d7 12 b3 ♘h7 13 0-0 f5 14 exf5 ♗xf5 15 ♖e1?! 15 g4!? e4 16 gxf5 ♗xc3 17 fxg6; 15 ♘de4 **g5 16 ♗g3 ♘f6 17 ♘f1 ♘c5 18 ♘e3 ♗g6 19 ♘b5 ♕f7 20 ♖f1 ♘h5 21 b4 axb4 22 axb4 ♖xa1 23 ♕xa1 ♘f4!? 24 ♗g4 ♘cd3 25 ♕a7 h5 26 ♗xf4 ♕xf4 27 ♗e2? ♘c1! 28 ♗f3 ♘b3 29 ♘xc7 ♘d2 30 ♘e6 ♘xf3+ 31 gxf3 ♕xf3 32 ♘xg5** 32 ♕xb7 ♗f6! Δ ♗e4 **♕f6 33 h4 ♗d3 34 ♕a1 ♗h6 35 ♘e6 ♗xe3 36 ♘xf8 ♕g7+ 37 ♔h1 ♗e4+ 38 f3 ♕g3 39 fxe4 ♕h3 mate 0-1**

128 Ivkov-Byrne Bugojno 78

1 d4 ♘f6 2 c4 g6 3 ♘c3 ♗g7 4 e4 d6 5 ♘f3 0-0 6 ♗e2 e5 7 ♗e3 ♕e8?! 7...♕e7; 7...♘bd7 **8 dxe5 ♘g4 9 ♗g5 h6 10 ♗d2 ♘xe5** 10...dxe5? 11 ♘d5 ♘a6 12 h3 +−; 11...♕d8 12 ♗b4 ♖e8 13 h3 ♘f6 14 ♗e7! +− **11 ♘d5 ♘xf3+ 12 ♗xf3 ♕d8 13 ♗c3 ♗xc3+ 14 ♘xc3 ♗e6 15 ♗e2 ♘c6 16 ♕d2 ♔h7 17 f4± f5 18 exf5 ♗xf5 19 0-0-0! ♕f6 20 g4 ♗e6 21 ♖hf1 ♖ae8 22 h4 ♕f7** 22...♕xh4? 23 ♖h1 ♕f6 24 ♖xh6+!; 23...

♕e7 24 f5 **23 h5 gxh5 24 ♗d3+ ♔g8 25 f5 ♗xc4 26 ♗xc4 ♕xc4 27 ♕xh6 +− ♕f7 28 ♖h1 ♕g7 29 ♕xh5** Δ g5 **♖e5 30 ♖h2** 30 ♘d5!? Δ ♘f4 **♘e7 31 ♖dh1 ♘d5! 32 ♘xd5 ♖xd5 33 ♕h8+ ♔f7** 33...♕xh8 34 ♖xh8+ ♔f7 35 ♖1h7+ ♔e8 36 ♖xf8+ ♔xf8 37 ♖xc7 +− **34 ♕xg7+?!** 34 ♕h3 Δ ♕b3 +− **♔xg7 35 ♖h7+ ♔f6 36 ♖xc7 ♖g8 37 ♖c4 ♖c5 38 ♖h6+ ♔g5 39 ♖h5+ ♔f6 40 ♖h6+ ♔g5 41 ♖h5+ ♔f6 42 ♖xc5 dxc5 43 ♖h6+ ♔g5 44 ♖h7** 44 ♖g6+ ♖xg6 45 fxg6 ♔xg6 46 ♔d2 ♔g5 47 ♔d3 ♔xg4 48 ♔c4 ♔f3 49 ♔xc5 ♔e3 50 ♔d6 ♔d2 51 ♔c7 ♔c2= **♔xg4 45 ♖xb7 ♔xf5= 46 ♖c7 ♔e5 47 ♖xc5+ ♔d6 48 ♖c4 ♖g2 49 ♔b1 a5 50 a3 ♖h2 51 ♔a2 ♖g2 52 ♔b3 ♖h2 53 ♔c3 ♖h3+ 54 ♔c2 ♖g3 55 ♖c8 ♖h3 56 ♖c3 ♖h2+ 57 ♔b1** 57 ♔b3 a4+ **♔d5 58 ♖c8 a4 59 ♖a8 ♖h4 60 ♖a5+ ♔c6 61 ♔c2 ♔b6 62 ♖d5 ♖h3 63 ♖d3 ♖h2+ 64 ♔c3 ♔c5 65 ♖g3 ♖h5 ½-½ Webb**

129 Fedorowicz-Boudy Mexico 78
1 c4 ♘f6 2 ♘c3 g6 3 e4 d6 4 d4 ♗g7 5 ♘f3 0-0 6 ♗e2 e5 7 0-0 ♘c6 8 d5 ♘e7 9 b4 ♘h5 10 c5 10 g3!? **♘f4!** 10...h6?! 11 ♘d2 ♘f4 12 ♘c4 f5 13 f3± Tisdall-DeFirmian, USA 76 **11 ♗xf4 exf4 12 ♖c1 h6 13 h3 f5!?** TN 13...g5 14 ♘d4 ♘g6 15 ♗g4 ♗xg4 16 hxg4 ♗xd4! 17 ♕xd4 f3!∓ Larsen-Uhlmann, Zagreb 65; 14 a4! ♘g6 15 a5 ♖e8 16 ♘d2 ♘e5 17 cxd6 cxd6 18 ♘b5± Diesen-Day, Lone Pine 77 **14 cxd6 cxd6 15 exf5?** 15 ♗d3 **♘xf5∓ 16 ♕d2 h5!** Δ g5-g4 **17 ♘b5** 17 ♕xf4? ♗h6 **♖f7 18 a4 a6 19 ♘a3 g5 20 ♘h2**

Diagram

20...g4! 21 hxg4 ♘d4 Δ ♘b3 **22 ♖c4** 22 hxg5!? **♘xe2+ 23 ♕xe2 hxg4 24 ♘xg4 ♕g5 25 f3 b5!!** 25...♕xd5? 26 ♕e8+ ♖f8 27 ♕g6 Δ ♖c7 **26 axb5** 26 ♖e4 ♗f5!∓ **axb5 27 ♘xb5 ♗a6** 27...♕xd5? 28 ♖d1! **28 ♘xd6 ♗d4+! 29 ♘f2 ♗xc4** 29...♖g7? 30 ♕e6+! **30 ♘xc4** 30 ♕xc4? ♖g7 −+ **♖e7! 31 ♕d2 ♖g7 −+ 32 g4 fxg4 33 ♕xd4** 33 ♕xg5 gxf2+ **gxf2+ 34 ♔xf2 ♖a2+ 0-1 Shamkovich**

130 J.Fernandez-Villarreal Mexico 78
1 ♘f3 ♘f6 2 c4 g6 3 ♘c3 ♗g7 4 e4 d6 5 d4 0-0 6 ♗e2 e5 7 0-0 ♘c6 8 d5 ♘e7 9 ♘e1 9 ♘d2; 9 ♗d2; 9 b4 **♘d7 10 ♘d3 f5 11 ♗d2 ♘f6 12 f3 f4 13 c5 g5 14 a4!?** 14 ♖c1 ♘g6 15 cxd6 cxd6 16 ♘b5 ♖f7 17 ♕c2 ♘e8 18 a4 h5 19 ♘f2∝ Spassov-Vukic, Varna 75

14...a5? 14...a6 15 cxd6 cxd6 16 a5 Δ ♘a4-b6; 14...♘g6 15 cxd6 cxd6 16 ♘f2 h5 17 a5∞ **15 ♖c1 h5 16 ♘b5±** Δ cxd6, ♘c7 **♘e8 17 cxd6 cxd6 18 ♘f2 ♖f6** 18...♕b6 19 b4! axb4 20 ♗xb4 Δ a5 **19 ♕c2 b6 20 ♘c7 ♖a7 21 ♘xe8 ♕xe8 22 ♕b3 ♕d8 23 ♖c2 ♖g6** Δ g4 **24 h3! ♗h6 25 ♖fc1± ♔h7 26 ♖c3! g4?** 26...♗d7 27 ♕c2 Δ ♖c7 **27 fxg4 hxg4 28 ♗xg4 ♗xg4 29 ♘xg4 +− ♘g8 30 ♖c8 ♕g5 31 ♕xb6 ♖ag7 32 ♖1c7 ♘f6 33 ♕b8 ♖xc7 34 ♖h8+ 1-0 Shamkovich**

131 Neamtu-Gheorghiu
Rumania Final 77

1 ♘f3 g6 2 c4 ♗g7 3 d4 ♘f6 4 ♘c3 0-0 5 e4 d6 6 ♗e2 e5 7 ♗e3 7 0-0; 7 d5; 7 dxc5 **exd4 8 ♘xd4 ♖e8 9 f3 ♘bd7** 9...c6!∞ **10 0-0 a5 11 ♕c2 c6** 11...♘c5? 12 ♖ad1 c6 13 ♘xc6! +− **12 ♖ad1 ♕c7 13 ♖fe1 ♘c5 14 ♗f1 ♘fd7 15 ♕f2 a4 16 h3 ♕a5 17 ♖b1 ♘e5 18 ♖ed1= f5!? 19 exf5 gxf5 20 ♘c2** 20 f4!+= **♖e6!? 21 ♖xd6?!** Zeitnot 21 f4 ♘f7 22 ♗d4 += **♖xd6 22 ♗xc5 ♘d3! 23 ♗xd3 ♖xd3∓ 24 ♗b6 ♕e5 25 ♖e1 ♕f6 26 ♗c7 ♗e6 27 ♗e5 ♕g6 28 ♗xg7 ♔xg7 29 ♘e3 a3! −+ 30 f4 ♕f6 31 ♕e2 ♕d4! 32 ♘cd1 ♖d2 0-1 Gheorghiu**

132 Dorfman-Grigorian
USSR Final 77

1 c4 ♘f6 2 ♘c3 g6 3 e4 ♗g7 4 d4 d6 5 ♗e2 0-0 6 ♘f3 e5 7 0-0 ♘bd7 8 ♕c2 c6 9 ♖d1 ♕e7 10 d5 c5 11 ♖b1 ♘h5?! 11...♘e8! **12 g3 ♘b6? 13 b4!± cxb4 14 ♖xb4 f5?** 14...♘d7 Δ ♘c5 **15 c5! dxc5 16 d6 +− ♕d7 17 ♖xb6 axb6 18 ♗xb5 ♕d8 19 d7 ♖a5 20 ♕b3+ ♔h8 21 ♘g5 ♖xb5 22 ♘xb5 1-0 Petrosian**

133 Polugaevsky-Kochiev
USSR Final 77

1 c4 g6 2 d4 ♗g7 3 e4 d6 4 ♘c3 e5 5 ♘f3 5 dxe5 dxe5 6 ♕xd8+ ♔xd8= **♘d7 6 ♗e2 ♘gf6 7 0-0 0-0 8 ♖e1** 8 d5= **c6 9 ♗f1 a5 10 ♖b1** 10 h3=; 10 ♗e3!? += **exd4** 10...♖e8 += **11 ♘xd4 ♖e8 12 f3** 12 ♗f4 ♘c5 13 ♕c2 += **d5 13 cxd5 cxd5 14 ♘db5?! dxe4 15 ♘d6 exf3! 16 ♘xe8 ♘g4! 17 ♘e4!** 17 gxf3 ♕b6+ 18 ♗e3 ♘xe3 19 ♕d6 ♗d4 =+; 17 ♕xf3 ♗d4+!? =+ **♕h4 18 h3 f2+ 19 ♘xf2 ♕xf2+ 20 ♔h1 ♗d4!?** 20...♗e5!∓ (Δ ♕g3) 21 ♖xe5 ♘dxe5! 22 ♗g5! ♗d7! 23 hxg4 ♖e8∓; 22...♗f5? 23 hxg4 ♗xb1 24 ♘f6+ Δ ♕xb1± **21 ♗e2 ♘c5!** 21...♘de5? 22 ♖f1 ♕g3 23 ♘f6+! +− **22 ♗g5!=** 22 ♘d6?! ♘d3!! −+ 23 ♗d3 ♕g3 24 ♖c8+ ♔g7 25 ♗h6 ♔xh6 −+ **♘e3?** 22...♘e4!? 23 ♗xg4 ♗xg4 24 ♕xg4 f5! Δ ♖xe8= **23 ♗xe3 ♗xe3 24 ♖f1 ♕g3** 24...♘e4 25 ♘f6+ +− **25 ♘f6+ ♔g7 26 ♘d5** 26 ♖f3!? +=; 26 ♕d8 ♗xh3! **♘e4! 27 ♗f3! ♘f2+ 28 ♖xf2 ♗xf2 29 ♕d2 ♗xh3!?** Δ ♗xg2+ −+ **30 ♕c3+ ♔h6 31 ♖f1! ♗a7 32 ♕c1+ g5?** 32...♔g7= **33 ♕c7! += ♕h4 34 gxh3 ♕xh3+ 35 ♕h2 ♕xh2+ 36 ♔xh2 f5! 37 ♘e7 g4** 37...f4 += **38 ♘xf5 ♔g5 39 ♗xb7 ♖d8 40 ♘g3 ♖d2+ 41 ♔h1 ♖xb2= 42 ♗g2 ♖xa2 ½-½ Kochiev**

134 Dorfman-Kochiev
USSR Final 77

1 c4 g6 2 d4 ♘f6 3 ♘c3 ♗g7 4 e4 d6 5 ♗e2 0-0 6 ♘f3 6 ♗g5!? **e5 7 0-0 ♘bd7** 7...♘c6 +=; 7...c6!? **8 ♖e1 c6 9 ♗f1 a5 10 ♗e3!? exd4?!** 10...♘g4!? **11 ♘xd4 ♖e8 12 f3 d5 13 cxd5 cxd5 14 ♘db5?!** 14 exd5 ♘b6 15 ♗f2 ♖xe1 16 ♕xe1 ♘bxd5 17 ♘xd5 ♘xd5 18 ♖d1± **dxe4 15 ♘d6 ♖f8 16 ♘cxe4 ♘xe4 17 ♘xe4 a4!=** 17...♘f6 18 ♗c5

♘xe4 19 fxe4 ♖e8 20 ♗b5 +− **18 ♝d4!? ♞f6!** 18...♘e5? 19 ♗c5 ♖e8 20 ♕xd8 ♖xd8 21 ♗e7 Δ ♘f6+± **19 ♝c5 ♞xe4 20 ♜xe4** 20 ♗xf8?? ♕b6+ −+ **♝xb2 21 ♜b1= a3 22 ♝xf8 ♛xf8 23 ♜e2 ♝f5 24 ♜bxb2 axb2 25 ♜xb2 ♛a3 26 ♜xb7 ♛xa2 27 ♛b3 ♛xb3 28 ♜xb3 ½-½ Kochiev**

135 Miles-Hort Reykjavik 78
1 c4 ♞f6 2 ♞c3 g6 3 ♞f3 ♝g7 4 e4 d6 5 d4 0-0 6 ♝e2 e5 7 0-0 ♞bd7 8 ♝e3 ♛e7!? 9 dxe5 dxe5 10 ♞d5 ♛d8!? 10...♘xd5 11 cxd5 += **11 ♛c2 ♞g4 12 ♝g5 f6 13 ♝d2 c6 14 ♞e3 += f5!? 15 exf5 ♞xe3 16 ♝xe3 gxf5 17 c5 ♚h8?!** 17...e4!? **18 ♜ad1 f4 19 ♝c1 ♛e7 20 ♜fe1! ♞xc5** 20...♕xc5 21 ♗d3! += **21 b4 ♞e6 22 ♝c4!** 22 ♗d3 ♘g5!? 23 ♘xe5? ♗xe5 24 ♖xe5 ♘f3+! 25 gxf3 ♖g8+ 26 ♔h1 ♕g7 **♛xb4 23 ♜xe5! ♝xe5** 23...♘d4?! 24 ♖xd4 ♗xe5 25 ♘xe5 ♕e1+ 26 ♗f1 ♕xe5 27 ♗b2 ♔g8 28 ♖d7 +− **24 ♞xe5 ♞g7 25 ♞f7+ ♜xf7 26 ♝xf7 ♝f5 27 ♛b3!** 27 ♕e2!? ♖f8? 28 ♗b2! ♖xf7 29 ♖d8+ ♖f8 30 ♕e5! +−; 27...f3! 28 ♕e5 ♕f8!∞ **♛xb3 28 ♝xb3** Δ ♗xf4 ±/+− **f3 29 gxf3?** Zeitnot 29 ♗b2! ♖e8 30 ♗f7! ♖f8 31 ♖e1 Δ ♖e7 +− **♜e8** ∞/+= **30 ♝f7 ♜f8 31 ♝b2 h6 32 ♝b3 ♜e8 33 ♜d6 ♚h7 34 ♜f6 ♜e7 35 ♜f8 ♚g6! 36 h4 ♞h5!= 37 ♜g8+ ♚h7 38 ♜h8+ ♚g6 39 ♜g8+ ♚h7 40 ♝d4 b6 41 ♜h8+ ♚g6 42 ♜g8+ ♚h7 43 ♜h8+ ♚g6 ½-½ Miles**

136 Forintos-Arapovic Sarajevo 78
1 d4 ♞f6 2 c4 g6 3 ♞c3 ♝g7 4 e4 d6 5 ♝e2 0-0 6 ♝g5 c5 7 d5 e5 7...h6; 7...b5 8 cxb5 a6 **8 h4 h6 9 ♝e3 a6** Δ b5 **10 a4 ♛a5 11 ♝d2** Δ h5; 11 ♕d2 b5∞ **h5 12 ♞h3! ♛d8** 12...♘bd7? 13 ♘b5 ♕b6 14 a5 ♕d8 15 ♘xd6 **13 g3 ♞bd7** 13...♘e8 Δ ♘c7, ♘d7-f6 ♗d7 **14 ♝g5! ♛e8** 14...♕a5 15 ♔f1 Δ ♔g2 **15 ♝e3 ♞h7 16 ♚f1! ♛e7 17 ♚g2 ♞df6** 17...f5? 18 exf5 ♖xf5 19 ♘e4± **18 f3** Δ g4± **♞e8 19 ♛d2 f5 20 ♞g5 ♞xg5** 20...♘c7 21 a5! ♖b8 22 ♘a4 Δ b4 +− **21 hxg5 a5 22 exf5 ♝xf5** Δ e4 **23 g4! hxg4 24 fxg4 ♝d7 25 ♞e4 +− b6 26 ♛c2!** 26 ♖hf1?! ♖xf1 27 ♖xf1 ♗xa4∞ **♜a7 27 ♜af1 ♜xf1 28 ♜xf1 ♝c8 29 ♞f6+ ♝xf6** 29...♘xf6 30 gxf6 ♗xf6 31 ♕xg6+ ♗g7 32 ♗d3 **30 gxf6** 30 ♕xg6+ ♗g7 31 ♗d3 ♕f7 **♛h7 31 ♜h1 ♛f7 32 ♝g5 e4 33 ♛xe4 ♞xf6** Zeitnot **34 ♝xf6 ♛xf6 35 ♛e8+ ♚g7 36 ♛h8+ ♚f7 37 ♜h7+ 1-0 Forintos**

137 Harding-Delaney Ireland 78
1 c4 g6 2 e4 d6 3 d4 ♞f6 4 ♞c3 ♝g7 5 ♝e2 0-0 6 ♝g5 h6 7 ♝e3 e5 8 d5 ♞bd7 8...c6!? 9 ♕d2 cxd5 10 cxd5 h5 (10...♔h7!? Uhlmann-Gligoric, Vrbas 77) 11 h3 ♘a6 12 ♗f3 ♗d7 13 ♘ge2 b5 14 a3 Alburt-Gufeld, Vilnius 75, 14...b4!? =+ Gufeld; 12 ♘f3 ♘c5 13 ♕c2 (13 ♗xc5? dxc5 14 ♘xe5 ♖e8 =+ Gufeld) 13...♕c7 14 ♖c1 ♗d7 15 0-0 ♖fc8 16 ♘d2 ♗a4= Holovsky-Harding, corres; 9 h4?! cxd5 10 cxd5 ♘bd7 11 h5 ♘c5! (11...g5? Petrosian-Schweber, Stockholm 62) 12 hxg6 (12 ♕c2!? Smit-Hunter, corres) 12...♘cxe4! 13 ♘xe4 (13 ♗h5 fxg6! Landgraf-Richardson, corres) 13...♘xe4 14 ♗f3 ∞/∓ Byrne-Harding, Ireland Final 77 **9 ♛d2** 9 h4!? ♘c5 10 ♕c2 c6 (10...h5 11 f3 += Polugaevsky-Donner, Amsterdam 70) 11 h5 cxd5 12 cxd5 g5!= Farago-Uhlmann, Leipzig 75; 9 g4!? ♘c5 10 f3 (10 ♗f3? Dennehy-Delaney, Dublin 77) 10...a5 (10...c6 11 ♘h3 cxd5 12 cxd5 Keene-Gligoric, Hastings 70/71;

12...Nh5! Olafsson) 11 h4 h5! 12 g5 Nh7 13 Nh3 f6!∞ Gunnarsson-Keene, Reykjavik 76 **Nc5** 9...h5 10 f3 (10 h3 Nc5 11 Bf3 a5= Uhlmann-Gligoric, Leningrad 73) 10...Nc5 11 Bd1! a5 12 Bc2 Nh7 13 0-0-0 += Farago-Vukcevic, Hastings 76-77; 10...Nh7 11 Nh3 Nc5 12 Nf2 a5 13 0-0-0 b6 (13...f5 14 exf5 gxf5 15 f4± Westerinen) 14 g4 (14 h4! +=) Uhlmann-Westerinen, Solingen 74, 14...hxg4 15 fxg4 f5 16 gxf5 gxf5 17 exf5 Qh4!= Westerinen **10 f3 a5** 10...Nh7 11 h4 h5 12 0-0-0 f5 13 exf5 Bxf5 (13...gxf5!? Sokolov) 14 g4! hxg4 15 fxg4 Ne4!? (15...Bd7 16 Nh3±) 16 Nxe4 Bxe4 17 Rh2 Qd7 18 Nh3 Qa4 19 Nf2! ∞/± Portisch-Gligoric, Ljubljana 75 **11 0-0-0** 11 Bxh6? Nfxe4! **h5 12 h4 Nh7** 12...Bd7 13 Nh3 Rc8 14 Kb1 c6 15 dxc6 Rxc6 16 Ng5 Ne6 17 Nxe6 Bxe6 18 c5 Qh8 19 Bh5 d5!? 20 exd5 Rd8 21 dxe5!± Djindjhashvili-Torre, Geneva 77 **13 g3** 13 Nh3! Qxh4?? 14 Ng5 Qg3 15 Nxh7 Kxh7 16 Bf1! Δ Ne2; 13...f5 **f5 14 Nh3 Nf6 15 Nf2 Bd7 16 Rdg1! c6 17 exf5 gxf5** 17...Bxf5!? 18 g4 **18 g4 fxg4?** 18...f4? 19 Bxc5 dxc5 20 gxh5 Nxh5 21 Nfe4±; 18...hxg4 19 fxg4 f4 20 Bxc5 dxc5 21 Bf3 Δ Ne4; 18...e4!?; 18...cxd5!? **19 fxg4 Nxg4 20 Nxg4 hxg4 21 Bxg4 Kh8 22 Bxd7** 22 Bh6 Rg8 **Qxd7** 22...Nxd7? 23 dxc6 Δ Qxd6 **23 Rg5! Rf5** 23...Qf7 24 Rhg1 **24 Qe2 Qf7 25 Rhg1 Rxg5 26 hxg5** 26 Rxg5!? Rf8∞ **Qg6 27 Bxc5 dxc5 28 dxc6 bxc6** 28...Qxc6? 29 Qh5+ Kg8 30 Nd5 Δ Nf6+ **29 Qe4! Qxe4 30 Nxe4± Rd8?!** 30...Bf8 **31 Nxc5 Rd4 32 b3 Rh4 33 Rd1 e4 34 Ne6 e3! 35 Nxg7** 35 g6? Bf6; 35 Rd8+ Kh7 36 Rd7 e2 37 Rxg7+ Kh8 38 Kd2 Re4 39 Ke1 Rxe6 40 Ra7± **Kxg7 36 Re1 Re4** 36...Rh2 37 a4 **37 Kc2 e2 38 Kd3 Re5 39 Rxe2 Rxg5 40 Re6 Rg3+ 41 Re3 Rg6?** Zeitnot 41...Rg5 42 Re7+ Kf6 43 Rc7 Rg2 44 Rxc6+ Ke7 45 a4 Rg3+ 46 Kc2 Rg2+ 47 Kc3 Rg3+ 48 Kb2 Rg2+ 49 Ka3 Rg5 50 Rb6 Kd7 51 Rb5 +– **42 Kd4 Kf7 43 Kc5 a4 44 b4 Rg2 45 Ra3 Rc2 46 Rxa4 Ke6 47 Ra6 1-0 Harding**

138 Foisov-Georgiev
Balkaniad 77

1 d4 Nf6 2 c4 g6 3 Nc3 Bg7 4 e4 d6 5 f3 0-0 6 Be3 a6 7 Qd2 c6 7...b6 8 0-0-0 c5∞ **8 Nge2 b5 9 h4 e5 10 dxe5 dxe5 11 Qxd8 Rxd8 12 Nc1 Be6 13 Nb3 Nbd7** 13...bxc4 14 Na5± **14 Na5 Rdc8 15 c5!± Nh5 16 g4 Ng3 17 Rg1 Nxf1 18 Kxf1 Bf6 19 g5 Bd8 20 Nb7! a5 21 Kf2 a4 22 Rgd1** Δ Nd6± **Be7 23 Rac1 Rc7 24 Nd6 b4 25 Nd5!** ±/∞

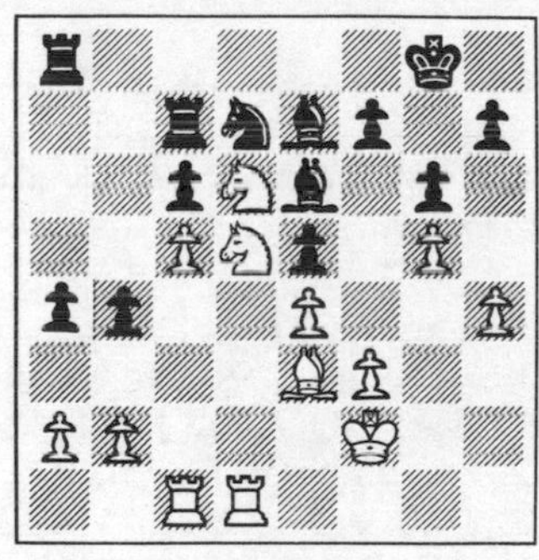

25...cxd5 26 exd5 Bh3 27 Ne4 Bf8 28 c6 Nb8 29 Nf6+ Kh8 30 f4! e4 31 Ne8 Rc8 32 Bd4+ Kg8 33 Nf6+ Kh8 34 Nxe4+ Bg7 35 Nf6 Bf5 36 Re1 b3 37 a3 Bc2 38 Re7 Rf8 39 Rce1 Ra5 40 c7 Na6 41 d6 Bf5 1-0 Gheorghiu

139 Gheorghiu-Tratatovici
Rumania Final 77
1 d4 ♘f6 2 c4 g6 3 ♘c3 ♗g7 4 e4 d6 5 f3 0-0 5...e5; 5...♘c6 **6 ♗e3 b6** 6...♘c6; 6...e5; 6...c6 **7 ♗d3 a6 8 ♘ge2 c5 9 e5! ♘fd7** 9...♘e8 10 exd6 ♘xd6 11 dxc5 +=; 10 ♗e4 ♖a7 11 dxc5± **10 exd6 exd6 11 ♕d2 ♘c6 12 ♗e4 ♗b7 13 0-0 ♘f6∞ 14 ♖ad1!** 14 ♗c2 cxd4 15 ♘xd4 d5= **♘xe4 15 ♘xe4 cxd4** TN 15...♘a5 16 b3 ♗xe4 17 fxe4 ♘c6 18 ♗g5! **16 ♘xd4 ♘e5 17 b3 d5 18 cxd5** 18 ♗g5!± **♕xd5** 18... ♗xd5 19 ♗g5 f6 20 ♗h6± **19 ♗h6! +−**

19...♗xh6 19...♘c6 20 ♗xg7 ♔xg7 21 ♕b2! ♘xd4 22 ♖xd4 ♕e5 23 f4 +− **20 ♕xh6 ♘g4 21 ♕h3! 1-0** 21...f5 22 ♘c3 **Gheorghiu**

140 Portisch-Vukic Bugojno 78
1 d4 ♘f6 2 c4 g6 3 ♘c3 ♗g7 4 e4 d6 5 f3 0-0 6 ♗e3 b6 7 ♗d3 ♗b7 8 ♘h3!? 8 ♘ge2 c5 9 d5 += **e5** 8...c5!? 9 d5 e6 **9 d5 ♗c8 10 ♘g1!± ♘h5 11 ♕d2 f5 12 0-0-0 f4 13 ♗f2 ♗f6 14 ♘ge2 ♗h4 15 ♗g1 a5 16 ♔b1 ♘a6 17 a3 ♗d7 18 ♗c2** Δ ♗a4 **♕e8?!** 18...♘c5!? 19 b4 axb4 20 axb4 ♘a4 21 ♘xa4 ♗xa4 22 ♗xa4 ♖xa4 23 ♕b2 ♕e7 24 ♘c3±; 19 b3!? **19 g3! ♗e7** 19...fxg3 20 hxg3 ♗e7 21 f4 Δ ♗e3 **20 g4 ♘f6 21 h4 ♖b8 22 b3 ♔g7 23 ♔a2 h6 24 ♖b1 ♖a8 25 ♖b2 g5 26 h5 ♔h8 27 ♘c1 b5** 27...♘xg4!? **28 cxb5 ♗xb5 29 ♘xb5 ♕xb5 30 ♗d3 ♕b7 31 ♖c2 ♖fc8 32 ♖h2 ♔g7 33 ♔b2 ♘b8 34 ♗c4 ♔f8 35 ♘a2 c5 36 dxc6 ♖xc6 37 ♕d3 ♘bd7 38 ♘c3 ♘c5 39 ♗xc5 ♖xc5 40 ♗d5 ♘xd5 41 ♘xd5 ♖ac8 42 ♖c3 1-0 Webb**

141 Murei-Liberzon Netanya 77
1 d4 ♘f6 2 c4 g6 3 ♘c3 ♗g7 4 e4 d6 5 f4 5 ♘f3; 5 ♗e2; 5 f3 **c5 6 d5 0-0 7 ♘f3 e6 8 dxe6 fxe6!** 8...♗xe6 9 ♗d3 Δ f5± **9 ♗e2 ♘c6 10 0-0 ♕e7 11 ♔h1 ♗d7 12 ♗e3 ♘g4 13 ♗d2 ♖ac8 14 ♕e1 ♘h6!?** Δ ♘f7∞ **15 ♕g3 ♔h8 16 ♖ae1 ♘b4 17 ♘g5 ♘f7 18 f5!?∞**

18...exf5 19 exf5 ♗xf5 20 ♗g4 ♗e5 21 ♗xf5 gxf5 22 ♘xh7!? ♔xh7 23 ♕h3+ ♔g7 24 ♖xf5 ♕e6! 25 ♘e4 ♕g6 26 ♘g5 ♖c7!! 27 ♖fxe5 ♘xe5 28 ♘e6+ ♔g8! Δ ♘bd3 **29 ♘xf8 ♔xf8 30 ♕h8+ ♔e7 31 h4 ♘bd3 32 ♖f1 ♔d7 33 ♗g5 ♘g4 34 ♕d8+ ♔c6 35 ♔g1 ♕e4 36 ♖f8 ♕d4+ 37 ♔f1 ♕xc4 38 ♕e8+ ♔b6 39 b3 ♕c2 40 g3 ♕d1+ 41 ♔g2 ♘de5 42 ♕d8 ♕e2+ 43 ♔g1 ♘f3+ 0-1 Gheorghiu**

142 Rashkovsky-Geller Sochi 77
1 d4 ♘f6 2 c4 g6 3 ♘c3 ♗g7 4 e4 d6

5 h3 0-0 6 ♗g5 c5! 7 d5 b5 8 cxb5 a6 9 bxa6 ♕a5 10 ♗d2 ♕b4!! 11 ♕c2 ♗xa6 12 ♗xa6 ♘xa6 13 a3?? 13 ♘ge2 ♖fb8 14 ♖b1 ♕c4! 15 a3 ♘b4 16 axb4 cxb4 17 0-0=; 13 ♘ge2 ♕c4!? 14 0-0 ♘b4 Δ ♘d3∞ **♕c4!! 14 ♖b1 ♘b4 15 axb4 cxb4 16 ♘ge2 bxc3 17 ♘xc3 ♖fc8 −+ 18 f3 ♘h5! 19 g4 ♘g3 20 ♖g1 ♘e2 21 ♖g2 ♘d4! 22 ♕d1 ♕d3 23 ♔f2 ♘xf3 24 ♕xf3 ♕xd2+ 25 ♔g1 ♗d4+ 26 ♔h1 ♕e3 27 ♕xe3 ♗xe3 28 ♖c2 ♖ab8 29 ♔g2 ♖b3 30 ♖a1 ♗d4 31 ♖ac1 ♖cb8 32 ♘d1 ♔g7 33 ♖c7 ♗f6 34 ♖1c2 ♖d3 35 ♘f2 ♖e3 36 ♖a7 ♖bb3 37 ♖ac7 h6 38 ♖a7 ♗h4 39 ♖ac7 ♗xf2 40 ♖xf2 ♖xe4 41 ♖d2 ♖be3 42 ♖b7 ♖f4 0-1 Petrosian**

143 Mititelu-Tratatovici
Rumania Final 77
1 d4 ♘f6 2 c4 g6 3 ♘c3 ♗g7 4 e4 d6 5 h3 0-0 6 ♘f3 c5 7 ♗e2 7 d5 b5!?∞ **cxd4 8 ♘xd4 ♘c6 9 ♗e3 ♘xd4 10 ♗xd4 ♗e6 11 0-0 ♖c8 12 b3 ♕a5 13 f4! += ♘h5??** 13...b5! **14 ♗xh5 ♗xd4+ 15 ♕xd4 ♕xh5 16 f5! +−** 16... ♗d7 17 ♘d5! +− **1-0 Gheorghiu**

144 Vukic-Hubner Bugojno 78
1 d4 ♘f6 2 c4 g6 3 ♘f3 ♗g7 4 g3 0-0 5 ♗g2 c5 6 0-0 ♘c6 7 ♘c3 d6 8 d5 ♘a5 9 ♘d2 e5 10 e4 a6 11 b3 ♖b8 12 ♗b2 b5 13 ♕c2 ♘e8 14 ♖ae1 f5 15 exf5 gxf5 16 ♘d1 f4!? N 16...♖b7 17 f4 e4 18 ♗xg7 ♖xg7 19 ♕c3 += Vukic-Tringov Vrsac 75 **17 ♗c3 ♗g4?!** 17...h5!? **18 ♕d3! h5 19 f3 ♗f5 20 ♘e4 h4 21 g4 ♗d7 22 ♕d2!±** 22 ♘df2? bxc4! 23 ♕d2 ♖b5∓; 23 bxc4 ♘xc4 24 ♕xc4 ♗b5 −+ **♘b7 23 ♘df2 a5 24 ♔h1 b4 25 ♗b2 ♘f6 26 ♖g1 ♘xe4 27 ♘xe4 ♕e7 28 ♗h3! ♔f7 29 ♔g2 ♔e8 30 g5 ♔d8 31 ♗xd7 ♕xd7 32 h3!** 32 ♔h1?! h3! **♔c7 33 ♔h2 ♖h8 34 ♖g4 a4 35 ♕c2 ♖a8 36 ♖eg1 ♔b6 37 ♖b1!** Δ a3! **axb3 38 axb3 ♖a2 39 ♖a1 ♖xa1 40 ♗xa1 ♕e8 41 ♗b2 ♕h5 42 ♔g2 ♖a8 43 ♔f1 ♕h8 44 ♔e2 ♖a2 45 ♔d1 ♕h5 46 ♔c1 ♖a8 47 ♕f2 ♖h8 48 ♔c2 ♗f8 49 ♗c1 ♗e7 50 ♗d2 ♔c7 51 ♕e1 ♖a8 52 ♗c1** 52 ♔b2?! ♖a3 Δ ♘a5 **♖h8 53 ♔b2 ♘d8 54 ♗d2 ♘f7 55 ♕a1! +−** 55 ♕g1? ♖g8 56 g6 ♘h6!∓ **♘xg5** 55...♖b8 56 ♕a4 ♖b6 57 ♕e8 ♗d8 58 g6 ♘h6 59 ♕h8 +−; 55...♔b7 56 ♕a4 ♖c8 57 ♕d7+ ♖c7 58 ♕e8 +−; 55...♔b8 56 ♕a6 +− **56 ♕a7+ ♔d8 57 ♖xg5!! ♗xg5 58 ♕b8+ ♔e7 59 ♕xd6+ ♔f7 60 ♕e6+ ♔g7** 60...♔f8 61 ♕f5+ **61 ♕xe5+ ♔g6 62 ♘xg5 ♖f8 63 ♕d6+ ♖f6 64 ♘e6 ♕xf3 65 ♘xf4+ ♔f7 66 ♕xc5 ♕e4 67 ♕a7+ ♔g8 68 ♕e3 ♕h1 69 ♕e8+ ♖f8 70 ♕g6+ ♔h8 71 ♕h5+** 71 ♘e6 ♖f7 72 ♕xf7 ♕b1+ = **♔g8 72 ♕g5+ ♔h7 73 ♕xh4+ ♔g8 74 ♕g5+ ♔h7 75 ♘e6 ♖f7 76 ♕h4+ ♔g8 77 ♕d8+ ♔h7 78 ♘g5+ 1-0 Vukic**

145 Webb-Botterill Hastings 77/8
1 ♘f3 g6 2 d4 ♗g7 3 c4 ♘f6 4 g3 0-0 5 ♗g2 d6 6 ♘c3 ♘c6 7 d5 ♘a5 8 b3 c5 9 ♗b2 ♖b8 10 0-0 a6 11 ♘d2 b5 12 ♕c2 e5 13 ♖ab1 13 ♘d1!? Boleslavsky **♘g4** 13...♗d7 14 e3 ♘g4 15 ♘d1 f5 16 f3 ♘f6 17 f4 e4 18 ♘f2 h5= Hartoch-R.Byrne, Amsterdam 69 **14 ♗a1 b4** 14...f5? 15 cxb5 axb5 16 b4!± **15 ♘d1 f5 16 f3 ♘f6 17 f4 exf4!?** 17...e4= **18 gxf4 ♖b7 19 ♘f2** Δ e4 **♖bf7 20 ♘f3 ♖e7 21 ♘g5 h6 22 ♘e6!** 22 ♘f3 ♖fe8∓ **♗xe6 23 dxe6 ♖xe6 24 e4 ♕e8!!** 24...fxe4 25 ♘xe4± **25 e5 dxe5 26 fxe5 ♘d7** 26...♖xe5 27 ♗xe5 ♕xe5 28 ♖fe1 ♕c7 29 ♖e6!± **27 ♗d5 ♔h7 28 ♘d3**

28 ♗xe6 ♕xe6 Δ ♘c6∓ **♖e7 29 e6 ♖xe6 30 ♖be1! ♖e3 31 ♗xg7 ♔xg7 32 ♕f2 ♖e7 33 ♔h1 ♖f6 34 ♘f4 ♔h7?** 34...♘c6! 35 ♖xe7+ ♕xe7 36 ♕g2 ♘d4 37 ♘h5+ ♔h7 38 ♘xf6+ ♘xf6∓ **35 ♖xe7+ ♕xe7 36 ♖e1 ♕d6?** 36... ♕f8!∞

37 ♘xg6!! ♖xg6 37...♔xg6 38 ♕g2+ +−; 37...♘c6! **38 ♕xf5** (Δ ♖e6) **♘f6 39 ♖g1! ♘xd5 40 ♕f7+ 1-0 Botterill**

146 Portisch-Timman Bugojno 78

1 ♘f3 g6 2 c4 ♗g7 3 d4 ♘f6 4 g3 0-0 5 ♗g2 d6 6 ♘c3 ♘c6 7 0-0 a6 8 d5 ♘a5 9 ♘d2 c5 10 ♕c2 ♖b8 11 b3 b5 12 ♗b2 bxc4 12...♗h6 13 cxb5! axb5 14 e4± **13 bxc4 ♗h6 14 f4 e5 15 dxe6!** 15 ♖ae1?! exf4 16 gxf4 ♘h5 17 e3 ♗g7 18 ♘d1 ♗f5 19 ♗e4!= **♗xe6** 15...fxe6!? **16 ♘d5!± ♗xd5 17 cxd5 ♗g7** 17...♘g4 18 ♗c3 ♘e3 19 ♕a4 ♖b5 20 ♖fb1± Csom-Ghitescu, Moscow 77 **18 ♗c3 ♖e8 19 e4 ♘d7 20 ♗xg7 ♔xg7 21 ♕c3+ ♔g8 22 ♖ab1 ♕c7 23 ♗h3** Δ ♗xd7 **♘b7 24 ♖be1** 24 e5!? dxe5 25 ♗xd7 ♕xd7 26 ♘e4 ♕f5 27 ♖be1 ♔f8 28 ♘g5±; 26...♕e7 27 fxe5 ♕xe5 28 ♘f6+ +−; 24...♘b6 25 ♘e4 ♘xd5 26 ♕d2 +− **♘b6 25 f5?! c4! 26 f6 ♘c5 27 ♕e3 ♘xd5 28 ♕h6 ♘xf6 29 ♖xf6 c3≈ 30 ♘b3 ♘xe4 31 ♖ff1 d5 32 ♗g2 a5 33 ♗xe4 dxe4 34 ♕e3 ♖b4! 35 ♖c1 ♖c4 36 ♖c2 ♖d8** Δ ♖d3 **37 ♘c1 h5 38 ♘e2 ♖d3 39 ♕h6 ♕b6+** 39...e3 40 ♘f4 ♖d2? 41 ♘xg6! **40 ♔g2 e3∓ 41 ♖xf7!** 41 ♘f4 ♖d2+ 42 ♖xd2 cxd2 43 ♘xh5? ♕c6+ **♔xf7 42 ♕h7+ ♔f6 43 ♖c1** 43 ♕h8+ ♔e7 44 ♕g7+ ♔d8 −+ **♖d2 44 ♖f1+ ♔e5 45 ♕g7+ ♔e4** Δ ♔d3 **46 ♖f6!? ♖xe2+ 47 ♔h3 ♕xf6** −+ 47...♖c6? 48 ♕xg6+ +− **48 ♕xf6 c2 49 ♕xg6+ ♔d4 50 ♕d6+ ♔c3 51 ♕e5+ ♔d3 52 ♕f5+ ♖e4 53 ♕b5+** 53 ♕d5+? ♖d4 Δ ♔d2 −+ **♖c4 54 ♕f5+ ♔c3 55 ♕e5+** 55 ♕xa5+ ♔d4 56 ♕b6+ ♔d3 57 ♕b3+ ♔d2 −+; 57 ♕d6+ ♖d4 −+ **♖d4 56 ♕xa5+** 56 ♕c5+ ♔d3 −+ **♔d3 57 ♕a3+ ♔d2 58 ♕b2 ♖d3 59 ♕b4+ ♔d1 60 ♕a4 ♖dd2 0-1 Webb**

147 Smejkal-Peev Leipzig 77

1 d4 ♘f6 2 ♘f3 g6 3 c4 ♗g7 4 g3 0-0 5 ♗g2 d6 6 ♘c3 ♘c6 7 0-0 e5 8 d5 ♘e7 9 e4 c5?! 9...♘e8 **10 ♘e1 ♘e8 11 ♘d3 f5 12 f4 exf4 13 ♗xf4** Δ e5 **fxe4 14 ♘xe4 ♘f5 15 g4! ♘h6** 15... ♗d4+ 16 ♔h1 ♘e3 17 ♗xe3 ♖xf1+ 18 ♕xf1 ♗xe3 19 ♖e1±; 15...♘d4 16 ♗g5± **16 ♗g5 ♖xf1+ 17 ♕xf1 ♕c7 18 h3 ♘f7 19 ♗h4 ♘e5 20 ♘xe5 ♗xe5 21 ♘f6+ ♘xf6 22 ♗xf6 ♗d7** 22... ♗xf6 23 ♕xf6 ♗d7 24 ♖f1 ♖e8 25 ♕f7+ ♔h8 26 ♖f6! Δ ♖e6/♗e4 **23 ♗xe5 dxe5 24 ♕f6! ♖f8 25 d6 ♖xf6 26 dxc7 ♗c8 27 ♖d1 ♖f8 28 g5! ♖e8** 28...♔f7 29 ♖f1+ ♔e7 30 ♖xf8 ♔xf8 31 ♗d5 +− **29 ♖d8 +− ♔f8 30 h4 ♔e7 31 ♖xe8+ ♔xe8 32 ♗d5 a6 33 ♔f2 b5 34 ♔e3 ♔d7 35 ♗g8 ♔xc7 36 ♗xh7 1-0 Webb**

148 Petran-F.Portisch Zalaegerszeg 77

1 d4 ♘f6 2 c4 g6 3 ♘c3 ♗g7 4 ♘f3 0-0

5 g3 d6 6 ♝g2 ♞bd7 7 0-0 e5 8 e4 c6 8...exd4!? 9 ♘xd4 ♘c5 **9 h3 ♜e8 10 ♝e3** 10 d5 **exd4 11 ♞xd4 ♞c5 12 ♛c2** 12 f3!? d5?! 13 ♘xc6± **a5 13 ♜fe1 a4 14 ♜ab1?!** 14 ♖ad1 ♘fd7! 15 ♘de2 ♕a5! 16 ♖xd6 ♘e5! 17 ♖dd1 ♘xc4 18 ♗d4 ♕b4 19 ♗xg7 ♔xg7 20 ♖b1 a3 21 b3 ♘b2 =+ Smyslov-Ciocaltea, Bucharest 53 **♛e7! 15 b4?** 15 f3 **axb3 16 axb3 ♞fxe4!∓ 17 ♞xe4 ♞xe4 18 ♜bd1 ♝d7 19 ♝f4** 19 ♗c1 f5 20 f3 ♗xd4 21 ♖xd4 ♕f6 Δ ♘xg3∓ **f5 20 f3 g5! 21 ♝e3 ♞xg3 22 ♝f2**

22...♛xe1+!! −+ 23 ♝xe1 ♝xd4+ 24 ♚h2 24 ♖xd4 ♘e2+ −+ **♜e2 25 ♝d2 ♝e5 26 ♚g1 f4 27 b4 ♜a3 28 c5 d5** Δ ♗f5 −+ **0-1 Maric**

149 Padevsky-Arnaudov
Bulgaria Final 77

1 d4 g6 2 c4 ♝g7 3 ♞c3 d6 4 ♞f3 ♞d7 5 g3 ♞gf6 6 ♝g2 0-0 7 0-0 c6 8 e4 e5 9 h3 a6 10 d5 c5 11 a3 h6 12 ♞e1 b5 13 b3 ♞e8 14 ♞d3 ♜b8 15 ♝d2 bxc4 16 bxc4 ♞b6 17 ♛b3 ♝d7 18 ♜fb1 f5 19 a4 ♞f6 20 a5 ♞a8 21 ♛xb8 ♛xb8 22 ♜xb8 ♜xb8 23 f3 ♞c7 24 ♜a2 fxe4 25 fxe4 ♝f8 26 ♜b2 ♜xb2 27 ♞xb2 ♚f7 28 ♝f1 ♚g7 29 ♚g2 ♝e7 30 ♝d3 ♞h7 31 ♝c2 ♝g5 32 ♝xg5 ♞xg5 33 h4 ♞f7 34 ♝a4 ♝xa4 35 ♞cxa4 ♚f6 36 ♞d3 ♚e7 37 ♚f3 ♚f6 38 ♞axc5 dxc5 39 ♞xc5 ♚e7 40 ♞d3 ♚f6 41 ♞c5 ♚e7 42 ♞d3 ½-½

150 Smejkal-Vogt Leningrad 77

1 d4 ♞f6 2 c4 g6 3 ♞f3 ♝g7 4 g3 0-0 5 ♝g2 d6 6 0-0 ♞bd7 6...♘c6∝ **7 ♛c2** 7 ♘c3 e5 8 h3 **e5 8 ♜d1 ♜e8 9 ♞c3 e4 10 ♞d2** 10 ♘g5 e3 11 ♗xe3 ♖xe3 12 fxe3 ♘g4 **e3 11 fxe3 ♞b6** 11...♘g4 12 ♘f1 **12 e4! ♞g4 13 ♞f1 ♞xc4 14 h3 ♞f6 15 ♝g5** Δ e5 +− **♝d7! 16 ♜ac1 c6 17 b3 ♞b6 18 ♛d2 ♛e7 19 g4 ♛f8 20 ♛f4**

20...♞xg4∓ 21 hxg4 f6 22 ♝h4 g5 23 ♝xg5 fxg5 24 ♛xg5 ♚h8 25 ♛h4 ♛f4 26 e3 ♛xg4 27 ♛xg4 ♝xg4 28 ♜d2 ♜e7 29 ♜f2 ♜g8 30 ♚h2 ♞d7 31 ♞g3 ♝h6! 32 ♜e1 ♜eg7 33 ♞f5 ♝xf5 34 exf5 ♞f6 Δ ♘g4+ −+ **35 ♝h3 ♜g3** Δ ♗xe3 −+ **36 ♜g2 ♜xg2+ 37 ♝xg2 ♞g4+ 38 ♚h3 ♞xe3 39 ♝e4 d5 40 ♝d3 ♞g2! −+ 41 ♜d1 ♞f4+ 42 ♚h4 ♜g2!** Δ ♗g5 mate **0-1 Gheorghiu**

151 Karner-Petrosian Sochi 77

1 c4 g6 2 ♞c3 ♝g7 3 d4 d6 4 e4 e5 5 dxe5 dxe5 6 ♛xd8+ ♚xd8 7 f4 ♝e6!? 8 ♞f3 ♞d7 9 g3 9 ♘g5 exf4 Δ ♘e5= **h6 10 ♝e3 c6 11 ♝d3** Δ f5± **♝h3! 12 ♝f1 ♝g4 13 ♝e2 exf4 14 gxf4 ♝xc3+! 15 bxc3 ♞gf6∝ 16 ♞d2 ♜e8**

17 e5 g5 18 ♘e4! ♗xe2 19 ♘xf6 ♘xf6 20 ♔xe2 ♘g4 21 ♖hg1 ♘xe3 22 ♔xe3 gxf4+ 23 ♔xf4 ♔e7= 24 ♖ad1?! 24 ♖ab1 b6 25 c5= **♖g8 25 ♖g3 ♖xg3 26 hxg3 h5!** Δ ♖g8-g4∓ **27 ♖b1** 27 ♖h1 ♖d8 (Δ ♖d2/♖d3) 28 ♔e3 ♖g8 =+ **♔e6 28 ♖xb7 ♖g8 29 ♖b4** 29 ♖xa7 ♖g4+ =+ **♖g4+ 30 ♔f3 c5 31 ♖a4 a5 32 ♖xa5 ♖xc4 33 ♖a3?** 33 ♖a7! **♔xe5 34 ♖b3 ♖a4?** 34...f6; 34...f5∓ **35 ♖b7!= ♖xa2 36 ♖xf7 ♖c2 37 ♖h7 ♖xc3+ 38 ♔g2 ♖c2+ 39 ♔h3 c4 40 ♖xh5+ ♔d4 41 ♖h8 ♖e2 42 ♖d8+ ♔e3 43 ♖e8+ ♔d2 44 ♖d8+ ♔c2 45 g4 c3 46 ♔h4 ♖e4 47 ♔h5 ♔b3 48 ♖d1 c2 49 ♖c1 ♔b2 50 ♖xc2+ ♔xc2 51 g5 ♖e1 52 g6 ♖g1 53 ♔h6 ♔d3 54 g7 ♔e4 55 ♔h7 ♔f5 56 g8♕ ♖xg8 57 ♔xg8 ½-½ Petrosian**

152 Stefanov-Ciocaltea
Rumania Final 77

1 c4 g6 2 ♘c3 ♗g7 3 d4 d6 4 ♘f3 ♘d7 5 e4 e5 6 ♗e2 c6 7 0-0 7 d5 ♘h6 8 h4!± **♘h6 8 d5 c5 9 ♗g5 f6 10 ♗d2 0-0 11 a3 ♘f7 12 ♘e1 f5 13 ♘d3 ♘f6 14 f3 b6 15 b4 ♘h5= 16 ♕c1 ♗d7 17 ♖b1 cxb4??** 17...♔h8!= **18 axb4 ♖c8 19 c5!± bxc5 20 bxc5 dxc5 21 ♕a3 c4 22 ♘c5 ♕e7 23 ♗e3 ♗h6! 24 ♗f2! ♗d2 25 ♖b7 ♖fd8 26 d6!**

26...♕xd6 27 ♗xc4 ♖xc5!? 28 ♕xc5! 28 ♗xc5? ♗e3+! **♕xc5 29 ♗xc5 ♗xc3 30 ♗e7 ♗c6 31 ♖c7! +− ♗d4+ 32 ♔h1 ♖b8 33 ♖xc6 ♗b6 34 g4! 1-0 Gheorghiu**

1...b6

153 Filipowicz-N.J.Fries Nielsen
Esbjerg 77

1 ♘f3 b6?! 2 e4 ♗b7 3 ♘c3 e6 4 d4 ♗b4 5 ♗d3 ♘f6 6 ♕e2 d5 7 exd5 7 e5 ♘e4 8 0-0!? ♗xc3 9 bxc3 ♘xc3 10 ♕e3∞ **♘xd5 8 ♗d2 ♘xc3 9 bxc3 ♗e7 10 0-0 ♘d7 11 c4 0-0 12 ♖fe1 ♖e8 13 c3 ♗f6 14 ♗f4 ♗xf3?** 14...c5 15 ♖ad1 Δ ♗c2, ♕d3±/♗a4 **15 ♕xf3 e5 16 ♗f5!!± g6** 16...exf4 17 ♖xe8+ ♕xe8 18 ♗xd7 ♕f8 19 ♕xf4±; 18... ♕d8 19 ♖e1 +− **17 ♗xd7 ♕xd7 18 dxe5 ♕e6 19 ♕d5 ♗g7 20 ♖ad1 ♗f8 21 ♗g5 h6 22 ♗f6 ♗c5** 22...♗e7 **23 ♕xe6 ♖xe6 24 ♖d7 ♗d6! 25 ♖d1!** 25 f4 ♔f8 26 ♖d1 ♔e8!=+ **♖ae8 26 f4 ♗c5+ 27 ♔f1 ♗e7 28 ♗xe7 ♖6xe7 29 ♖xe7 ♖xe7 30 ♔f2 +− ♖e6 31 ♔e3 ♖c6 31 ♖d8+ ♔g7 33 ♔d4 ♖c5 34 ♖d5 ♖c6 35 g4 ♔f8 36 f5 gxf5 37 gxf5 ♔e7 38 h4 h5 39 f6+ ♔e6 40 ♖d8 ♖c5 41 ♖d5 ♖c6 42 a3! ♔f5 43 ♖d7 ♖e6?** 43...♔g6 44 ♖d8 ♖c5 45 ♖g8+ ♔f5 46 ♖g5+ ♔e6 47 ♖xh5 ♖a5 48 ♖h8 ♖xa3 49 ♔e4+−; 43...♖c5 44 ♖xf7 ♖xe5 45 ♖xc7 ♖e4+ (45...♔xf6? 46 ♖f7+! +−) 46 ♔d3 ♖f4 47 f7 ♔g4 48 ♔e3 ♖f6 49 ♖xa7 ♔xh4 50 ♔d4 +− **44 ♖e7!** 44 ♖xf7? c5+ 45 ♔d3 ♖xe5 46 ♖xa7 ♔f6 += **c6 45 ♖xe6 ♔xe6 46 ♔e4 a6 47 ♔f4 a5 48 ♔e4** 48 a4?? b5! 49 cxb5 cxb5 50 axb5 a4 −+ **a4 49 ♔f4 b5 50 cxb5 cxb5 51 ♔e4 ♔d7 52 ♔d5 1-0 Filipowicz**

154 Murei-Keene Netanya 77
1 e4 b6!? 2 d4 ♗b7 3 ♗d3 ♘f6 4 ♘c3 e6 5 ♕f3 5 ♘ge2 Δ 0-0 **d6 6 ♘ge2 ♘bd7 7 ♕h3 g6 8 ♗g5 ♗g7 9 0-0-0 h6** 9...0-0 10 ♗h6 += **10 ♗e3** 10 ♗d2!± **♕e7 11 ♘b5 0-0-0 12 ♘xa7+ ♔b8 13 ♘b5 ♘xe4 14 ♖he1 ♘ef6 15 ♗d2 g5 16 c4 ♗a6 17 ♘ec3 c6 18 ♘a3 ♖c8 19 ♔b1 ♘e8 20 ♕e3 ♕f6 21 ♘c2 d5 22 b3 ♘c7 23 ♗c1 c5 24 cxd5!± cxd4 25 ♘xd4 ♕xd4 26 ♕xd4 ♗xd4 27 ♗xa6!**

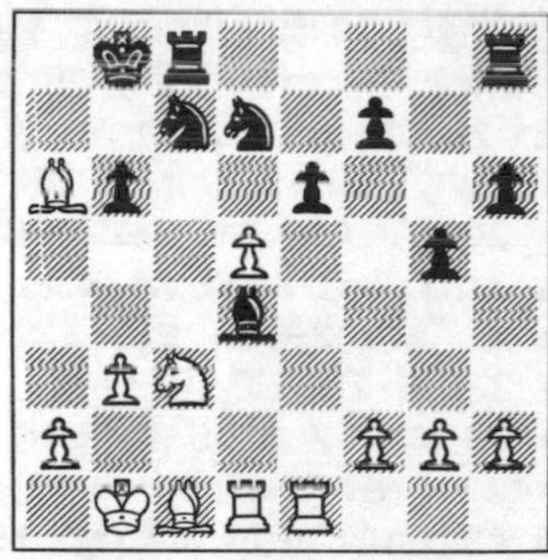

27...♗xc3 28 ♗xc8 ♔xc8 29 ♖e3! ♗g7 30 dxe6 ♘xe6 31 ♖f3 ♘e5 32 ♖f5 ♖e8 33 ♗b2 ♘d8 34 ♖d6 ♔c7 35 ♗xe5 ♗xe5 36 ♖xh6! f6 37 h4 ♘e6 38 hxg5 ♘d4 38...♘xg5 39 f4 **39 ♖fxf6 ♗xf6 40 ♖xf6 ♘e6 41 g6 ♔d6 42 f4! ♔d5 43 g4 b5 44 f5 ♘g5 45 a4! bxa4 46 bxa4 ♔e5 47 ♖b6 ♘e4 48 a5 ♘f6 49 a6 ♘d5 50 ♖b7 ♔f6 51 a7 ♖a8 52 g7 1-0 Gheorghiu**

155 Liberzon-Bohm Netanya 77
1 e4 e6 2 d4 b6!? 2...d5; 2...c5 **3 ♗d3 c5 4 c3 ♗a6 5 ♗xa6 ♘xa6 6 ♘f3 ♘c7 7 ♗g5 ♘f6** 7...♗e7 8 ♗xe7 += **8 ♘bd2 h6 9 ♗xf6 ♕xf6 10 0-0 ♕d8 11 ♕a4 ♗e7 12 dxc5 ♗xc5 13 c4 0-0 14 ♖ad1 a6 15 ♘b3 b5 16 ♕a5 ♗e7 17 c5!± ♕c8 18 ♖d2 ♖d8 19 ♕c3 ♘e8 20 ♘fd4 ♘f6 21 f3 ♕c7 22 ♖c1 ♖ac8 23 ♖dc2 ♘e8 24 ♕a5 ♗g5 25 ♖e1 ♕b7 26 g3 e5 27 ♘f5 d6 28 h4 ♗f6 29 ♖ce1 d5 30 ♕b6! ♕a8** 30...♕xb6 31 cxb6± **31 c6! dxe4 32 fxe4 ♖d3 33 ♕b7! ♘d6 34 ♕xa8 ♖xa8 35 ♘c5! +− ♘xf5 36 ♘xd3 ♘xg3 37 c7 ♖c8 38 ♘b4 ♘xe4 39 ♘d5 ♗xh4 +− 1-0** time/Zeit **Gheorghiu**

1 e4 c5 2 c3

156 M.Tseitlin-A.Lukin USSR 77
1 e4 c5 2 c3 d5 3 exd5 ♕xd5 4 d4 e6 4...♘c6?! 5 dxc5!+= **5 ♘f3 ♘f6 6 ♗d3** 6 ♘a3 **♗e7 7 0-0 0-0 8 c4 ♕d8 9 dxc5! ♘a6 10 ♕e2 += ♘b4** 10 ...♘xc5!? 11 ♗c2 b6 **11 ♖d1 ♕c7 12 ♘c3 ♘xd3 13 ♖xd3 ♕xc5 14 ♘e5 ♖d8** 14...b6!? **15 ♖g3± ♗d7 16 ♗g5 ♔f8?** 16...♗c6!? **17 b4!! ♕xb4 18 ♖b1 ♕d6 19 ♖xb7 ♗e8 20 h3 h6**

21 ♕e3! hxg5 21...♘g8 22 ♖xe7 ♘xe7 23 ♗xh6! ♘f5 24 ♗xg7+! +− **22 ♕xg5 g6 23 ♖f3! ♖d7** 23...♔g7?! 24 ♖xf6 ♗xf6 25 ♕xg6+ **24 ♖xf6! ♗xf6** 24...♖xb7 25 ♘xg6+ +− **25 ♕xf6 ♕xe5!? 26 ♕xe5 ♖xb7 27 ♘e4 ♖b1+ 28 ♔h2 ♔g8 29 h4 ♖ab8 30 h5 +− gxh5 31 ♘f6+ ♔f8 32 ♕c5+ ♔g7 33 ♕g5+ ♔f8 34 ♘h7 mate 1-0 Gufeld**

157 Sveshnikov-Petrosian
USSR Final 77
1 e4 c5 2 c3 ♞f6 3 e5 ♞d5 4 d4 cxd4 5 ♞f3 ♞c6 6 cxd4 d6 7 ♝c4 ♞b6!= 7...e6 += **8 ♝b5 dxe5 9 ♞xe5 ♝d7 10 ♞c3!?** TN 10 ♗xc6 ♗xc6 11 ♘xc6 bxc6 12 0-0 e6= **e6!** 10...♘xe5 11 dxe5 ♗xb5 12 ♘xb5 += **11 ♛g4 h5! 12 ♛e4 ♞xe5 13 dxe5 ♝xb5 14 ♞xb5 ♞d5!= 15 0-0 ♝e7 16 ♝d2 0-0 17 ♞c3 ♞xc3 18 ♝xc3 ♛b6 19 ♜ad1 ½-½ Petrosian**

158 Zuravlev-Podgaets
USSR 77
1 e4 c5 2 c3 ♞f6 3 e5 ♞d5 4 d4 cxd4 5 ♞f3 ♞c6 6 cxd4 d6 7 ♝c4 ♞b6 8 ♝b5 dxe5 9 ♞xe5 ♝d7 10 ♝xc6 ♝xc6 11 0-0 ♜c8?! 11...g6 **12 ♞c3 e6 13 ♛g4?!** 13 ♕h5! g6 14 ♕g4 **h5 14 ♛f4 ♛f6 15 ♛xf6 gxf6 16 ♞xc6 bxc6** 16...♖xc6? 17 d5± **17 ♝f4 f5! 18 ♜ac1 ♜g8 19 ♜fd1 ♚d7 20 ♜d3 ♝e7 21 f3?! ♜gd8 22 ♝g3 ♚e8 23 ♞e2 c5 =+ 24 ♜dc3 cxd4 25 ♜xc8 ♞xc8 26 ♞xd4 ♝f6∓ 27 ♞c6** 27 ♗f2 ♖xd4 28 ♖xc8+ ♔d7 29 ♖c1 ♖a4!∓ **♝xb2 28 ♜c2?** 28 ♘xd8! ♗xc1 29 ♘c6∓ **♜d1+ 29 ♚f2 ♝f6 30 ♝f4 ♜b1! 31 ♝e3 a6 32 a4 ♞e7 −+ 32 ♞d4? f4 0-1 Gufeld**

159 Cuarlas-Sigurjonsson
Bogota 78
1 e4 c5 2 c3 ♞f6 3 e5 ♞d5 4 d4 cxd4 5 cxd4 d6 6 ♞f3 ♞c6 7 ♝c4 dxe5!? 7...e6; 7...♘b6 **8 ♝xd5 ♛xd5 9 ♞c3 ♛d6!** 9...♕a5? 10 d5± **10 d5 ♞d4 11 ♞xd4 exd4 12 ♛xd4 e5 13 ♛d3 ♝d7 14 0-0 ♛g6! 15 ♛e2** 15 ♕xg6 hxg6 16 ♖e1 0-0-0 17 ♖xe5 ♗d6= **♝d6 16 f4 0-0 17 fxe5 ♜fe8 18 ♝f4 ♝xe5! 19 ♝xe5 f6 20 ♛f2 ♜xe5 21 ♜ae1 ♜f5 ½-½ Sigurjonsson**

160 Sznapik-Kuligowski (3) 78
1 e4 c5 2 c3 ♞f6 3 e5 ♞d5 4 d4 cxd4 5 cxd4 d6 6 ♞f3 ♞c6 7 exd6?! ♛xd6 8 ♞c3 g6! 9 ♝c4 ♞b6 10 ♝b3 ♝g7 11 0-0 0-0 12 d5 ♞a5 13 ♝g5 ♞xb3 13...♗g4 **14 ♛xb3 ♝g4 15 ♞d2 ♜ac8 16 h3 ♝f5 17 ♞de4 ♛d7 18 ♜ad1 ♞c4** 18...♗xe4 19 ♘xe4 ♘c4 **19 d6 f6??** 19...♘xd6! 20 ♗xe7 ♗xe4! 21 ♗xf8? ♖xc3∓; 21 ♘xe4 ♕xe7 22 ♘xd6 ♖c6 =+; 21 ♗xd6 ♖e8 22 ♘xe4 ♖xe4 =/=+ **20 dxe7??** 20 ♗e3 +− **♛xe7 21 ♞d6? fxg5∓ 22 ♜fe1** 22 ♘xc4 ♗e6 23 ♘d5 ♕f7 24 ♘ce3 ♖fd8∓ **♝e6 23 ♞d5 ♛xd6 24 ♞f6+ ♜xf6 25 ♜xd6 ♞xd6 26 ♜xe6 ♞f7** 26...♔f8! **27 ♜xf6 ♝xf6 28 ♛xb7 ♜c1+ 29 ♚h2 ♝e5+ 30 g3 ♝d4 31 ♛e4 ♝xf2 32 b4 ♜c3 33 ♚g2 ♝xg3 34 ♛a8+ ♚g7 35 ♛xa7 ♝e5 36 b5 ♜g3+ 37 ♚f1 ♜xh3 38 b6 ♜h2** 38...♖h1+! 39 ♔g2 ♖h2+ **39 a4 ♜b2 40 a5 ♝d4?** 40...h5! **41 ♛d7** 41 ♕c7! **♝xb6 −+ 42 axb6 ♜xb6 43 ♛d4+ ♜f6+ 44 ♚g2 h5 45 ♚h3 ♞h6 46 ♛e5 ♞f5 47 ♚h2 g4 48 ♚g2 ♞h6! 49 ♛d4 ♞f7 50 ♛c3 g5 51 ♚g1 h4! 52 ♛d4 ♞h6 53 ♛e5 ♚g6 54 ♛e8+ ♞f7 55 ♛e4+ ♚h5 56 ♛h7+ ♞h6 57 ♛e7 ♜f4 58 ♛e8+ ♞f7 59 ♚g2 h3+ 60 ♚g1 g3 61 ♛e6 ♚h4 62 ♛a6 ♞d6 63 ♛a1 ♞f5 64 ♛e1 ♞d4 65 ♚h1 ♜f1+ 0-1 Kuligowski**

2 ♞c3/2 d3

161 Sznapik-Kuligowski (1) 78
1 e4 c5 2 ♞c3 d6 3 f4 ♞c6 4 ♞f3 g6 5 ♝c4 ♝g7 6 0-0 e6! 7 f5 exf5 8 d3 ♞e7 9 ♛e1 h6! 10 ♝d2 10 ♕g3≈ **♝e6 11 exf5 ♝xf5 =+ 12 g4 ♝xg4 13 ♝xf7+ ♚xf7 14 ♞e5+ ♚g8 15 ♞xg4 ♛d7 16 ♛g3 ♞e5! 17 h3 ♞xg4!** 17...♔h7?? 18 ♗xh6! +− **18 hxg4 h5! 19 gxh5 ♜xh5∓ 20 ♞e4 ♝d4+ 21**

Kg2 Kg7 22 Bg5 22 Nxd6? Be5 23 Rf7+ Kg8 −+ **Nf5! −+ 23 Rxf5 gxf5!!** 23...Qxf5 24 Rf1 Rxg5 =+ **24 Bf6+ Kf8** 24...Kh7!? 25 Rh1! Rxh1 26 Kxh1 Rg8! −+ **25 Bxd4 fxe4??** 25...cxd4 26 Nf6 Qc6+ 27 Kf2 Qxc2+ 28 Kg1 Kf7 −+ **26 Rf1+ Rf5 27 Qg4! +− Rxf1 28 Qxd7 Rc1 1-0 Kuligowski**

162 Gumrukcioglou-Ermenkov
Balkaniad 77

1 e4 c5 2 Nc3 Nc6 3 f4 g6 4 Nf3 Bg7 5 Bc4 e6 6 d3 Nge7 7 0-0 d5 8 Bb3 Nd4! =+ 9 Nxd4 cxd4 10 Ne2 dxe4 11 dxe4 0-0 12 Qd3 Qb6 13 Bd2 Bd7 14 a4 Δ Bb5!∓ **Bc6 15 Be1 Rad8 16 Bh4 Rd7 17 Bxe7 Rxe7 18 Ng3 Rd8 19 a5 Qb4! 20 Qc4 Qxc4 21 Bxc4 d3!∓**

22 cxd3 Bxb2 23 Ra2 Bd4+ 24 Kh1 Kg7 25 Rb1 Rc7 26 Re2 b5 27 axb6 Bxb6 28 e5 Rd4 29 Rf1 Bd5 30 Ba6 Ra4 31 Bb5 Rb4 32 Ba6 h5 33 Ne4 Ra4 34 Bb5 Ra5 35 Rb2 Bd4 36 Rb4 Ra1 37 Rxa1 Bxa1 38 h3 h4 39 Ra4 Bb2∓ Zeitnot **0-1 Gheorghiu**

163 Villareal-Shamkovich Mexico 78

1 e4 c5 2 Nc3 Nc6 3 g3 g6 4 Bg2 Bg7 5 d3 d6 6 f4 e6 7 Nf3 Nge7 8 0-0 0-0 9 Be3 9 Bd2 Rb8 10 Rb1 b5 11 a3 a5∞ **Nd4 10 Rb1 Rb8 11 Ne2 Nxe2+** 11...Nxf3+ 12 Bxf3 b5 13 c3 a5 14 d4+= Geller **12 Qxe2 b6 13 c3** 13 d4 f5! =+ **Ba6 14 Rfd1 Qd7 15 Qc2 d5 16 c4** 16 e5!?= **Rbc8 17 Bh3?! f5!?** 15...d4= **18 exd5 exd5 19 Bf2 Bb7 20 Bg2 Nc6 21 Qa4** 21 cxd5 Nb4 **Rfd8! 22 Ng5** Δ Bxd5+; 22 cxd5 Nd4 23 Qxd7 Nxf3+ 24 Bxf3 Rxd7 25 d4 c4! Δ Bxd5 =+ **Nd4**

23 Qxa7 23 Qxd7 Rxd7 **Qc6!!** Δ Ra8; 23...Qc7? 24 Bxd4 Bxd4+ 25 Kh1 Ra8 26 Ne6!∞ **24 cxd5** 24 Qa3 Ra8 25 Qc3 Ne2+ −+ **Rxd5 25 Kf1?** 25 b4! Ra8 26 b5 Nxb5 27 Qxb7 Qxb7 28 Rxb5 Qd7! 29 Rxb8 Re8∓ **Ra8 26 Bxd5+ Qxd5 27 Qxb6 Qh1+ 0-1 Shamkovich**

164 Romanishin-Gulko
USSR Final 77

1 e4 c5 2 Nc3 Nc6 3 Nf3 d6 4 g3 g6 5 Bg2 Bg7 6 0-0 Bg4 7 h3 Bxf3 8 Qxf3 e6 9 Ne2 Nge7= 10 Qb3?! 0-0 11 c3 Qd7 12 d3 d5 13 Be3 b6 14 Rad1 d4 =+ 15 Bc1 Rab8 16 f4 b5 17 g4 dxc3 18 bxc3 b4! 19 e5 Rfd8 20 Qc4 Nd5 21 cxb4 21 Qxc5 Bf8 22 Qc4 Na5∓; 22...Rdc8∓ **cxb4 22 d4 Rbc8∓ 23 Qb3 a5 24 f5 a4** 24...Nc3! 25 Nxc3 Nxd4 −+ **25 Qg3** 25 Qxa4 Nxd4 26 Qxd7 Nxe2+ 27 Kf2 Rxd7

28 ♗xd5 ♘c3 ∓+; 25 ♕d3!?∓ **♞c3! 26 ♞xc3 ♞xd4 27 ♝g5 ♜xc3 28 ♛f2 ♜c2! −+ 29 ♛xc2 ♞xc2 30 ♜xd7** 30 ♗d8 ♕a7+ −+ **♜xd7 31 ♝c6 ♜a7 32 ♝e4 b3 33 fxe6 fxe6 34 ♝f6 ♞e3 35 ♜c1 bxa2 36 ♜a1 a3 37 ♜xa2 ♞d1 38 ♝d3 ♞c3 39 ♜a1 ♝xf6 40 exf6 a2 41 ♝c4 ♚f7 42 g5 ♜a5 43 ♚h1 ♜xg5 44 ♝xa2 ♞xa2 0-1 Gufeld**

165 Ciocaltea-Cojocaru
Rumania 78
1 e4 c5 2 ♞f3 e6 3 d3 g6 4 g3 ♝g7 5 ♝g2 ♞e7 6 0-0 ♞bc6 7 ♜e1 0-0 7... d5!? 14/479 **8 c3 d6 9 d4 e5** 9...cxd4! 10 cxd4 e5= **10 dxc5! dxc5 11 ♞a3! +=** **♝g4 12 h3 ♛xd1 13 ♜xd1 ♝xf3 14 ♝xf3 ♜fd8 15 ♝e3 b6 16 ♞b5!± ♝f8 17 g4 h6 18 h4 ♚g7 19 g5 h5 20 ♝e2 ♞c8 21 ♞c7 ♜b8 22 ♝b5 ♜xd1?!** 22...♘ce7!? **23 ♜xd1 ♞8e7 24 ♜d7! ♚g8** 24...♖d8 25 ♗xc6 ♘xc6 26 ♘e6+ **25 ♞d5 ♞xd5 26 ♜xd5 ♞e7 27 ♜d7** 27 ♖xe5? ♖b7 Δ ♗g7 **♞c8 28 ♝c4?** 28 ♖d8! **♝e7** 28...♘d6 29 ♗d5 Δ f4 **29 f4 ♚f8** 29...exf4 30 ♗xf4 ♖a8 31 ♗d5 **30 fxe5 b5 31 ♝d5 b4 32 c4 1-0** time/Zeit **Ciocaltea**

3 ♝b5

166 Ciocaltea-Padevsky Albena 77
1 e4 c5 2 ♞f3 ♞c6 3 ♝b5 e6 4 0-0 ♞ge7 5 c3 5 ♘c3 14/483 **a6 6 ♝a4** 6 ♗xc6 14/482 **b5** 6...d5 7 exd5 ♕xd5 8 d4 ♗d7 9 ♖e1 ♖d8 10 c4!± Spassky-Timman, Amsterdam 77 **7 ♝c2 ♝b7 8 d3 ♞g6 9 ♞g5!? f6** 9...h6!?; 9...♗e7 10 ♕h5 h6 11 ♘xf7! ♔xf7 12 f4± **10 ♞h3 ♝d6 11 f4 0-0 12 ♝e3 ♞ce7 13 ♞d2 ♜c8 14 a4 ♝b8 15 axb5 axb5 16 ♞b3 +=** **♝d6** 16...d6 17 ♘a5 ♗a8 18 f5; 16...c4 17 ♘a5± **17 ♛e2 ♛c7 18 ♛f2! ♝a8 19 ♜a5 c4 20 ♜a7 ♛d8 21 ♞d2** 21 ♘d4!? **♞c6 22 ♜aa1 cxd3 23 ♝xd3 ♜b8 24 b4! ♞ce7 25 ♞b3 f5 26 e5 ♝c7 27 ♞c5** 27 ♗a7! ♗b6 28 ♗xb6 ♕xb6 29 ♕xb6; 27...♖b7 28 ♗c5± **♞d5 28 ♝d4 ♝c6 29 ♞a6 ♜a8 30 ♞xc7 ♛xc7 31 ♝c5 ♜fe8 32 ♛d4 ♛b7** 32...♘h4!? **33 ♜a5! ♞c7 34 ♜f2 ♜a6 35 g3 ♞e7 36 ♝xe7! ♜xe7 37 ♜xa6 ♛xa6?** 37...♘xa6! 38 ♖a2 ♖e8 39 ♘f2 += **38 ♛d6 ♞d5 39 ♛b8+ ♚f7 40 ♞g5+ ♚g6 41 ♛g8 ♞xf4?** 41...♕a1+ 42 ♗f1 h6 43 ♕h7+ ♔h5 44 ♘e4! +−; 44 g4? gxf4 45 ♘e4 ♕a7! **1-0 Ciocaltea**

167 Ciocaltea-Tratatovici
Rumania Final 77
1 e4 c5 2 ♞f3 ♞c6 3 ♝b5 g6 4 0-0 ♞f6 5 ♜e1 ♝g7 6 h3 0-0 7 c3 ♞e8 7...d5 8 e5 ♘e4 **8 d4 cxd4 9 cxd4 ♞c7 10 ♝a4 d5 11 ♝xc6 bxc6 12 e5 ♞e6 13 ♞c3 ♝b7?** 13...f6!∝ **14 ♞a4!± ♜c8 15 ♞g5! ♞xg5 16 ♝xg5 f6 17 ♝f4 c5?? 18 ♞xc5 ♜xc5 19 dxc5 1-0 Gheorghiu**

168 Sarkistan-Veremeichik Kiev 77
1 e4 c5 2 ♞f3 ♞c6 3 ♝b5 g6 4 0-0 ♝g7 5 c3 e5 6 ♞a3 6 d3!? ♘ge7 7 ♗e3 ♕b6? 8 ♘a3 0-0 9 b4 d6 10 ♘c4! ♕xb5 11 a4 ♕a6 12 b5±; 6...♕c7 7 ♗e3 a6 8 ♕a4 d6 9 d4 b5 10 ♕c2 exd4 11 cxd4 ♗g4 12 dxc5! ♗xf3 13 ♕xf3 dxc5 14 ♘c3 ♘ge7 15 ♘d5! += **♞ge7 7 ♜e1 0-0 8 d4?! cxd4 9 cxd4 exd4** 9...♘xd4 10 ♘xd4 exd4 11 ♗g5 += **10 e5 a6 11 ♝xc6 ♞xc6 12 ♞c4 d5! 13 exd6 b5 14 ♝g5?! f6 15 ♛b3** 15 ♘ce5 ♘xe5 16 ♘xe5 ♕b6∓ **♚h8?** 15...bxc4! 16 ♕xc4+ ♔h8 17 ♕xc6 ♗d7! 18 ♕b7 ♖b8 19 ♕a7 fxg5 20 ♖e7 g4 21 ♘g5 ♖xb2?! 22 ♖xd7? ♕xg5 23 ♖xg7 ♕f6! 24 ♖xh7+ ♔g8 25 ♖f1 ♕xf2+! 26 ♖xf2 ♖b1+∓; 22

♕xd7∝; 19...♖a8 20 ♕b7 ♖b8= **16 ♘ce5! ♘xe5 17 ♘xe5 fxg5 18 ♘f7+ ♖xf7 19 ♕xf7 ♗f5 20 d7! ♕xd7** 20...♗xd7 21 ♖e7± **21 ♖e7 ♕xe7 22 ♕xe7 ♗c2 23 ♖e1 ♖f8 24 ♕d7 d3 25 ♖e7 ♗xb2 26 ♖xh7+ ♔g8 27 ♖h3 ♖f6 28 ♕e8+ ♔g7 29 ♖h8! ♖f7 30 ♖g8+ ♔f6 31 ♕c6+ ♔e5 32 ♖e8+ 1-0 Gufeld**

169 Ciocaltea-Antonov
Albena 77
1 e4 c5 2 ♘f3 ♘c6 3 ♗b5 g6 4 0-0 ♗g7 5 c3 e5 5...♘f6!? **6 d4!** 6 d3?! ♘ge7 7 ♗e3 d6 8 d4?! cxd4 9 cxd4 0-0 10 d5 ♘b8 11 ♘fd2 f5 12 f3 f4= Padevsky-Radulov 77 **cxd4 7 cxd4 ♘xd4** 7...exd4 8 ♗f4 ♘ge7 9 ♗d6 0-0 10 a4 += Westerinen-Savon, Dortmund 75; 8...a6 9 ♗c4!? **8 ♘xd4 exd4 9 e5!** 9 f4!?

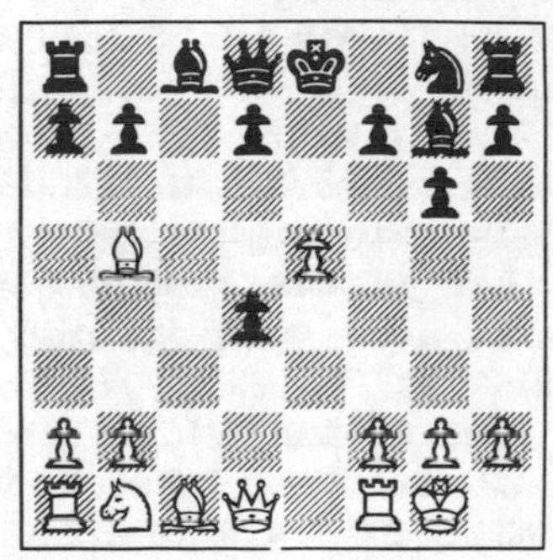

9...♕b6? 9...♘e7?! 10 ♕xd4 ♘c6 11 ♕d6 a6 12 ♘c3! ♗f8? 13 ♖e1! +– Zigura-Tskitishvili, USSR 77 **10 ♘a3! ♘e7 11 ♘c4 ♕c5** 11...♕c7 12 ♘d6+ ♔f8 13 ♕b3 +– **12 b4! ♕d5** 12...♕xb4 13 ♗a3 ♕c3 14 ♖c1 +– **13 ♘d6+ ♔f8 14 f4 d3 15 ♗xd3! ♕d4+ 16 ♔h1 ♕xa1 17 ♕b3 ♘d5 18 ♕xd5 1-0 Ciocaltea**

2...♘c6

170 Honfi-Revesz
Hungary 77
1 e4 c5 2 ♘f3 ♘c6 3 d4 cxd4 4 ♘xd4 e5 5 ♘b5 a6 6 ♘d6+ ♗xd6 7 ♕xd6 ♕f6 8 ♕a3 ♘ge7 9 ♘c3 ♖b8 10 ♗e3 b5 11 ♘d5 ♘xd5 12 exd5 b4 13 ♕a4 N 13 ♕d3 ♘e7 14 d6 ♘f5 15 0-0-0 ♗b7≈ Fichtl-Smejkal, CSSR 63 **♘e7 14 0-0-0 0-0 15 ♔b1?!** 15 d6!? ♘c6 16 ♔b1 ♗b7 17 ♗d3 ♖fc8 18 ♗b6 += Honfi-Baumbach, corr 64/5 **d6 16 ♗e2 ♘f5 17 ♗a7 ♖a8** 17...♖b7 18 ♕xa6 +– **18 ♗b6 ♖b8** 18...a5!? 19 ♗xa5 ♘d4 20 ♗d3 ♕xf2 21 ♕xb4± **19 ♕xb4** 19 ♕a5!? **♕e7!** 19...♘d4 20 ♖xd4 exd4 21 ♕xd4≈ **20 a4 a5 21 ♕b5!** 21 ♕xa5? ♕b7 –+ **♘d4?** 21...♕b7! 22 ♗e3! ♘xe3 23 fxe3 ♗d7!=; 22 ♗xa5?? ♕a7 –+ **22 ♖xd4! exd4 23 ♗d3 ♗d7** 23...♕b7 24 ♗xd4± **24 ♕xa5 ♖a8 25 ♕e1! ♕xe1+ 26 ♖xe1 ♖xa4 27 b3 ♖a3 28 ♖e7 ♖fa8 29 ♗xd4 ♗e8 30 ♖b7 f6 31 ♖b6 ♖d8 32 ♗c3 ♗f7 33 ♗b4 ♖a7 34 c4 ♖da8 35 ♗xd6 ♖a1+ 36 ♔b2 ♖1a2+ 37 ♔c3 ♖xf2 38 ♗e4 f5 39 ♗g3 1-0 Honfi**

171 Tratatovici-Biriescu
Rumania Final 77
1 e4 c5 2 ♘f3 ♘c6 3 d4 cxd4 4 ♘xd4 ♘f6 5 ♘c3 e5 6 ♘db5 d6 7 ♘d5!? 7 ♗g5 **♘xd5 8 exd5 ♘b8 9 c4 a6 10 ♘c3 ♗e7 11 ♗e2 0-0 12 0-0 f5 13 ♔h1** 13 f4!? **♘d7 14 f3** 14 f4∝ **g5 15 ♗e3 ♗f6 16 g4! e4!∝ 17 fxe4?** 17 f4!± **f4 18 ♗d4 ♗xd4 19 ♕xd4 ♘e5 20 ♘d1** 20 c5∓ **h5 21 c5 hxg4** 22 ♘e3?? **fxe3 23 ♖xf8+ ♔xf8 24 ♕xe3 ♔g7 25 cxd6 ♔g6 26 ♕c5 ♗d7 27 ♕c3 ♕h8! 28 ♖f1 ♖c8 29 ♕g3 ♖c2∓ 0-1 Gheorghiu**

172 Mestel-Federowicz
Hastings 77/8
1 e4 c5 2 Nf3 Nc6 3 d4 cxd4 4 Nxd4 Nf6 5 Nc3 e5 5 Ndb5 d6 7 Nd5 Nxd5 8 exd5 Ne7 9 c4 Nf5 10 Bd3

10...a6? 10...Be7 **11 Qa4! Ke7** 11...Bd7 12 Bxf5 axb5 13 Bxd7+ Kxd7 14 Qxb5+; 12...Bxf5? 13 Nxd6+; 11...Qd7? 12 Nc7+ **12 Nc3 f6 13 0-0 g6 14 Ne4 Kf7 15 f4! exf4** 15...Be7 16 fxe5 dxe5 17 c5!; 16...fxe5? 17 g4 **16 Bxf4 Be7 17 c5! dxc5 18 d6 Bf8** 18...Bxd6 19 Bc4+ **19 g4 b5 20 Bxb5 Rb8 21 Bc4+ Kg7 22 gxf5 Bxf5 23 Rae1 Rxb2 24 Qxa6 1-0**

173 Karaklaic-Joksic Borovo 77
1 e4 c5 2 Nf3 Nc6 3 d4 cxd4 4 Nxd4 Nf6 5 Nc3 e5 6 Ndb5 d6 7 Be3 a6 8 Na3 b5 8...Rb8 **9 Nd5 Rb8** 9...Nxd5 10 Qxd5 Qc7 11 c4 Be6 12 Qd2∞ Zaitsev-Titorenko, USSR 74; 10 exd5 Ne7 11 c4 Nf5 12 cxb5 Nxe3 13 fxe3 Qh4+ 14 g3 Qe4 15 Qc2 Qxe3+ 16 Be2 Bd7 17 Qd2± Karaklaic-Denker, Wijk aan Zee 72 **10 Nxf6+ gxf6 11 g3 Bb7 12 Bg2 Ne7 13 c4** 13 0-0 d5! **f5 14 0-0** 14 cxb5 fxe4 15 bxa6 Qa5+ 16 Qd2 Qxd2 17 Bxd2 Ba6! =+ **Bxe4! 15 Bxe4 fxe4 16 Bg5 Rg8 17 Bxe7 Bxe7 18 Qd5 Qd7 19 cxb5 axb5 20 Nc2?!** 20 Qxe4 h5 += **Qb7!= 21 Ne3 Qxd5 22 Nxd5 Kd7 23 f3 exf3 24 Rxf3 Bd8! 25 Nf6+** 25 Rxf7+? Ke6 −+ **Bxf6 26 Rxf6 Ke7 27 Rh6 Rg7 28 Rc1 Rb7 29 Kf2 f6 30 Rc3 Ke6 31 Rh4 Rgc7 32 Rb3 Rc2+ 33 Ke3 d5 34 a4 d4+ 35 Ke4** 35 Kd3 Rf2 36 Rxb5 Rxb5 37 axb5 Kd5 −+ **b4** Zeitnot 35...f5+ 36 Kd3 Rf2 −+; 36 Kf3 Rg7 37 g4 e4+ −+ **36 a5 f5+ 37 Kd3** 37 Kf3 Rg7! −+ **Rf2 38 a6 Rc7 39 Rxb4 Rcc2** 39...Kd5? 40 Rb5+! Rc5 41 Rxd4+!! exd4 42 Rxc5+ Kxc5 43 a7 +− **40 Rb6+ Kf7 41 Rb7+ Kg6** 41...Kf6 **42 Rg4+!? Kh6** 42...fxg4? 43 a7 **43 Rxd4 Rfd2+ 44 Ke3 exd4+ 45 Kf4 Rxb2 46 a7 Rf2+ 47 Ke5 Ra2 48 Kxd4 Ra5 0-1**
Joksic

174 A.Rodriguez-Joksic Pristina 77
1 e4 c5 2 Nf3 Nc6 3 d4 cxd4 4 Nxd4 Nf6 5 Nc3 e5 6 Ndb5 d6 7 Bg5 a6 8 Na3 b5 9 Nab1?! Be7 10 Bxf6 Bxf6 11 a4 b4 12 Nd5 Bg5 13 Bc4 0-0 14 0-0 Be6!? 14...Bb7 15 Nd2 Rc8 16 Nb3 Ne7 17 Nxe7+ Qxe7 18 Qe2?! Qc7 19 Bd3 a5 20 Rfd1 Rfd8 =+ Mnazakanian-Georgadze, USSR 77 **15 Nd2 Ne7 16 Nf3 Bxd5! 17 Bxd5** 17 exd5 Bh6∓ **Nxd5 18 Qxd5 Be7 19 Rfd1 Qc7** 19...Rc8 20 Qb7∞ **20 Rd2 Rac8 21 Rad1** 21 Rc1 Qb6 =+ **Qb6 22 Qb3 Rc6 23 Rd5 Rfc8 24 Ne1 g6 25 R1d2 Rc4 26 Qf3 b3! 27 cxb3 Rb4 28 Nd3** 28 R5d3 Rc1 29 Qe2 d5 30 exd5 Bc5 −+; 28 R2d3 f5! 29 Qh3 Rc1 −+ **Rxb3 29 g3 Rc4 30 a5 Qc6 31 Kg2 Qa4 32 Qd1!? Rxe4 33 f3 Rd4!** 33...Rc4 34 Nc1! Δ b3 +−; 33...Re3 34 Nc1 Rb4 35 Kf2! +− **34 Rxd4 exd4 35 Nc1 Rb4 36 Qxa4 Rxa4 37 Nb3 Bf6 38 Kf2 Rb4 39 Rd3 Kf8∓ 40 Ke2 Ke7 41 Kd1 Ke6 42 Kc2 Kd5 43 Rd1 Bg5 44 f4 Bd8**

45 ♖d3 h5 46 ♖d1 h4 47 ♖d3 ♔e4 48 ♘d2+ ♔f5 49 ♘f3 hxg3 50 hxg3 ♗xa5?! 50...♗f6 −+ **51 ♖a3 ♗b6 52 ♖xa6 ♔g4 53 ♖a3 ♔xg3?!** 53...f5 54 ♘h4 ♔h5 55 ♘f3 ♗d8 56 ♖d3 ♗f6 Δ ♔g4 −+ **54 ♘e5+** 54 ♘g5+? ♔xf4 **♔h4 55 ♘xf7 ♔g4 56 ♘h8 ♔xf4 57 ♘xg6+ ♔e4 58 ♘h4 ♖c4+ −+ 59 ♔d1** 59 ♔b3 ♖c1 Δ d3 −+; 59 ♔d2 ♗d8 60 ♘g2 ♗g5+ −+; 59 ♔b1 d3 −+ **d3 60 ♘g2** 60 ♘f3? ♔xf3 61 ♖xd3+ ♗e3! −+ **♗c5 61 ♖a8 ♖c2 62 ♖a4+ ♗d4 63 ♘f4 ♖xb2 0-1 Joksic**

175 Chiburdanidze-Alexandria (1) 77

1 e4 c5 2 ♘f3 ♘c6 3 d4 cxd4 4 ♘xd4 ♘f6 5 ♘c3 e5 6 ♘db5 d6 7 ♗g5 a6 8 ♘a3 b5 9 ♘d5 ♗e7 10 ♘xe7 10 ♗xf6 ♗xf6 11 c3 **♘xe7!** 10...♕xe7 11 ♗d3 += **11 ♗xf6 gxf6 12 ♕d2** 12 c4?! **♗b7 13 0-0-0 ♗xe4!** N 13...d5 14 exd5 ♕xd5 15 ♕xd5 ♗xd5 16 c4 +=; 15 ♕b4?! ♘c6! =+ **14 ♕xd6 ♕xd6 15 ♖xd6 ♘c6! 16 f3?!** 16 ♖xf6≈ **♔e7 17 ♖d2 ♗f5 18 ♗d3 ♗e6** =+ **19 b3 ♘b4 20 c3 ♖ac8 21 ♔b2 ♘xd3+ 22 ♖xd3 ♖hg8 23 g3** 23 ♖d2 ♖cd8! 24 ♖hd1? ♖xg2 −+ **h5 24 ♖hd1 h4 25 f4!?** 25 g4 f5∓ **♖g4 26 ♘c2 hxg3 27 hxg3 ♖cg8?!** 27...exf4 28 gxf4 ♖xf4 ∝/=+ **28 ♘b4 ♖xg3?** 28...exf4

29 ♘c6+ ♔f8 30 ♖d8+ ♔g7 31 ♖xg8+ ♔xg8 32 f5!± **♖g2+ 33 ♔a3 e4 34 fxe6 fxe6 35 ♖e1** 35 ♘d8!? **f5 36 ♘d8 ♖g6 37 ♔b4 ♔f8 38 ♔c5 ♔e7 39 ♘c6+ ♔f6 40 a4?** c4 +− **bxa4 41 bxa4 ♖g3 42 c4 e3!** 42...♖d3? 43 ♘b4 ♖a3 44 ♘xa6 ♖xa4 45 ♔b5 +−; 42...♔g5 43 ♘e5! +− **43 ♔d4 ♖g4+ 44 ♔d3 f4 45 ♘d4** 45 c5 ♖g5! 46 ♘b8 ♖d5+ 47 ♔e2 ♖d8 48 ♘xa6 e5 49 c6 e4 50 c7 ♖d2+ 51 ♔f1 ♖f2+ 52 ♔g1 ♖c2∝; 47 ♔e4 ♖d8 48 ♘xa6 e5∝; 45 ♖h1 += **e5 46 ♘c6** 46 ♘c2 ♔f5?? 47 ♖xe3 +− **♖g7 47 ♔e4 ♖c7 48 ♘xe5 ♖e7 49 ♔xf4 ♖xe5 50 ♖xe3 ♖a5 51 ♔e4 ♔e6 52 ♔d4+ ♔d6 53 ♖g3 ♖xa4 54 ♖g6+ ♔c7 55 ♔d5 ♖a1 56 ♖g7+ ♔b8 57 ♔c6 ♖h1 58 ♖g6 a5 59 ♖g8+ ♔a7 60 ♖g7+ ♔b8 61 ♔b6 ♖h6+ 62 ♔xa5 ♔c8 63 ♔b5 ♖f6 64 c5 ♖h6 65 c6 ♖h1 ½-½ Gufeld**

176 Gipslis-Jasnikowski
Hradec Kralove 77/8

1 e4 c5 2 ♘f3 ♘c6 3 d4 cxd4 4 ♘xd4 ♘f6 5 ♘c3 e6 6 ♘db5 d6 7 ♗f4 e5 8 ♗g5 a6 9 ♘a3 b5 10 ♘d5 ♗e7 11 ♘xe7 ♘xe7 11...♕xe7 12 ♗d3±; 12 c4!? **12 ♗xf6 gxf6 13 ♕f3 f5** 13...♘g6 14 0-0-0 ♗e6 15 ♔b1 ♔e7 16 c4 ♕a5 17 ♖c1 ♖hc8 18 g3 ♖c5 19 ♗d3 ♖ac8 20 cxb5 axb5 21 ♖xc5 ♖xc5 22 ♕e2± Gaprindashvili-Szabo, Leipzig 77 **14 exf5 ♗xf5 15 ♗d3 ♗xd3** N 15...♗e6 16 0-0± Tringov-Georgadze, Varna 77 **16 ♕xd3 d5 17 c3 ♕b6 18 0-0 f5 19 ♖ae1! e4 20 ♕e3 ♕f6** 20...♕xe3 21 fxe3!± **21 f3 0-0 22 ♘c2 ♖ae8** 22...f4 23 ♕d4±; 22...♘c6!?∝ **23 fxe4 dxe4 24 ♘d4 ♕g6** 24...♕e5 25 ♕g3+ ♘g6!; 25 ♕g5+! ♔h8 26 ♕h5 Δ ♖e3-h3 **25 ♕g3 ♖f6?** 25...♕xg3 26 hxg3±; 25...♖f7 26 ♕e5!± **26 ♖xe4! +− fxe4** 26...♕xg3 27 hxg3 +− **27 ♖xf6 ♕xg3 28 hxg3**

♘d5 29 ♖e6 29 ♖xa6 +− **♖xe6 30 ♘xe6 +− a5** 30...♘e3 31 ♘c7 ♘d1 32 ♘xa6 ♘xb2 33 ♘c7 +− **31 ♔f2 a4 32 a3 ♔f7 33 ♘d4** 33 ♘g5 Δ ♘e4 +− **♘b6 34 ♔e3! +− ♘c4+ 35 ♔xe4 ♘xb2 36 ♘xb5 ♔e6 37 ♔d4 h5 38 c4 ♔f5 39 c5 ♔e6 40 ♘c3** 40 c6 +− **♔d7 41 ♘d5 1-0** 41...♔c6 42 ♘e3 Δ ♔c3 +− **Gipslis**

177 Murei-Radashkovich Netanya 77

1 e4 c5 2 ♘f3 ♘c6 3 d4 cxd4 4 ♘xd4 ♘f6 5 ♘c3 e5 6 ♘db5 d6 7 ♗g5 a6 8 ♘a3 b5 9 ♗xf6 9 ♘d5 ♕a5+ 10 ♗d2 ♕d8 11 ♗g5= **gxf6 10 ♘d5 f5 11 ♘xb5!?** TN 11 exf5; 11 ♗d3 **axb5 12 ♗xb5 ♗d7 13 exf5 ♖b8! 14 a4 ♗g7 15 ♕g4 ♔f8 16 ♕h5??** 16 0-0∞ **♕a5+! −+ 17 c3 ♖xb5 18 b4 ♖xb4 19 ♘xb4 ♘xb4 20 0-0 ♘c6 −+ 21 ♖fd1 ♕c5 22 ♖ab1 ♔e7 23 ♖b7 ♖d8 24 g4 ♘a5 25 ♖b4 ♕xc3 26 ♕h4+ f6 27 ♕xh7 ♔f8 28 ♖e4 ♕f3 29 ♖de1 ♗c6 30 ♖1e3 ♕d1+ 31 ♖e1 ♕f3 32 ♖1e3 ♕d1+ 33 ♖e1 ♕d2! 34 ♖4e3 ♘c4 35 ♖3e2 ♕f4 36 ♕h3 ♕f3! 37 ♕xf3 ♗xf3 38 ♖c2 d5 39 h3 ♖b8 40 ♖c3 e4 0-1 Gheorghiu**

178 Fedorov-Saharov USSR 77

1 e4 c5 2 ♘f3 ♘c6 3 d4 cxd4 4 ♘xd4 ♘f6 5 ♘c3 e5 6 ♘db5 d6 7 ♗g5 a6 8 ♘a3 b5 9 ♗xf6 gxf6 10 ♘d5 f5 11 ♗xb5!? axb5 12 ♘xb5 ♖a7?! 12...♖a4!?; 12...♖b8!? **13 ♘xa7 ♘xa7 14 exf5! ♘b5** 14...♗xf5 15 ♕f3 ♕g5 16 h4 ♕g6 17 g4 ♗e6 18 ♘f6+ ♔d8 19 ♕a8+ ♘c8 20 ♕a5+ ♔e7 21 g5±; 15...♗xc2 16 ♖c1 ♕a5+ 17 b4 ♕xa2 18 0-0 ♕b3 19 ♘e3 +−; 15...♗e6 16 ♘f6+ ♔e7 17 0-0 (17 ♘d5+!? +=) h5 18 a4 ♗g7 (18...d5 19 ♖fd1±) 19 ♘d5+! ♔f8 20 b4 e4 21 ♕xe4 ♗xa1 22 ♖xa1 +=; 14...♗g7 15 ♕f3 ♕g5 16 f6 ♗h6 17 0-0 ♘c6 18 ♕a3 0-0 19 ♕xd6± **15 f6?** 15 c3!± **♗b7 16 c3 ♖g8 17 ♕b3 ♗c6 18 a4 ♘c7 19 ♘xc7 ♕xc7 20 a5 ♗xg2?!** 20...♖xg2 21 ♕b6 ♔d7 =+ **21 ♖g1 ♖g4!** 21...♗d5 22 ♕a4+ ♗c6 23 ♖xg8± **22 f3 ♕c6?!** 22...♕c5!= **23 c4! ♗xf3 24 ♖xg4 ♗xg4 25 ♕b5 += ♗d7 26 ♕xc6 ♗xc6 27 a6 d5 28 a7 ♗a8 29 cxd5 ♔d7 30 ♔e2 ♗c5 31 ♖a5 ♔d6 32 ♔d3 e4+ 33 ♔xe4 ♗b6?±** 33...♗xd5+ += **34 ♖a6 ♔c7 35 ♔e5 ♔b7 36 ♖a3 ♗xa7 37 ♖h3?** 37 ♔d6!± **♗b8+ 38 ♔d4 ♗a7+ 39 ♔c4 ♔c7 40 ♖xh7 ♔d6 41 ♖h5 ♗b7 42 b4 ♗b6 43 h4 ♗d8 44 ♖f5 ♗c8 45 ♖f1 ♗b7 46 h5 ♗xd5+ 47 ♔d4 ♗b6+ 48 ♔d3 ♔e5 49 h6 ♗e4+ 50 ♔c4 ♗e3??** 50...♗h7 += **51 ♖h1!! 1-0**

179 Shamkovich-Wachtel USA 77

1 e4 c5 2 ♘f3 ♘c6 3 d4 cxd4 4 ♘xd4 ♘f6 5 ♘c3 e6 6 ♘db5 d6 7 ♗f4 e5 8 ♗g5 a6 9 ♘a3 b5 9...♗e6!? **10 ♗xf6 gxf6 11 ♘d5 f5 12 c3!? fxe4?** 12...♗g7! **13 ♗xb5! axb5 14 ♘xb5** Δ ♘bc7+, ♕g4+

14...♕g5!? N 14...♖a7? 15 ♘xa7 ♘xa7 16 ♕a4+; 14...♕a5 15 ♘f6+! ♔d8 16 ♘xd6 ♔c7 17 ♘fe8+ ♔b8 18 ♕b3+ ♔a7 19 ♘b5+ ♔b8 20 ♘d4+! +−; 14...♗e6!? 15 ♘bc7+ ♔d7 16 ♘xa8

Bxd5 17 Qxd5 Qxa8 18 Qxe4± Hartoch-Goldenberg, St. Jeans 76 **15 Ndc7+!** 15 Nbc7+ Kd8 16 Nxa8 Qxg2 17 Rf1 Ba6! 18 Ne3 Qf3!∞ **Kd8 16 Qd5!** 16 Nxa8? Qxg2 17 Rf1 Bh3 18 Kd2 e3+! **Bb7** 16...Qxg2 17 0-0-0 **17 Qxf7** Δ Qe8 mate/Ne6+ **Ke7 18 Qf5 Qd7?** 18...Qxc7! 19 Nxc7 Kxc7 20 b4 Δ a4-a5± **19 Qf6+ 1-0 Shamkovich**

180 Ilijin-Urzica
Rumania Final 77

1 e4 c5 2 Nf3 Nc6 3 d4 cxd4 4 Nxd4 Nf6 5 Nc3 e5 6 Ndb5 d6 7 Bg5 7 a4 **a6 8 Na3 b5 9 Bxf6 gxf6** 9...Qxf6? 10 Nd5 Qd8 11 c4 b4 12 Qa4 Bd7 13 Nb5 +− **10 Nd5 f5 11 Bd3 Be6 12 c3 Bg7 13 Qh5 0-0!?** 13...f4 14 0-0 0-0 15 Rfd1 Rb8! 16 Nc2 **14 Rd1?!** N 14 exf5 Bxd5 15 f6 e4 16 fxg7 Re8 17 Be2 Re5 18 Qh6 Rg5 19 Rd1? Qe7 20 c4?! bxc4 21 Nxc4 Bxc4! 22 Bxc4 Ne5! Bena-Pavlov 77 **fxe4! 15 Bxe4 f5! =+ 16 Bc2** 16 Nf4 exf4! 17 Bxc6 Rc8 18 Bd5 Bxd5 19 Rxd5 Re8+ Δ b4 −+ **Rc8 17 0-0 Ne7 18 Bb3 Rc5! 19 Nb4 Bxb3 20 axb3 e4! 21 Nxa6 Re5 22 Qe2 f4! 23 Nxb5 f3! 24 Qc4+ d5 25 Qa4 Rg5 26 Nac7 Rxg2+ 27 Kh1 Nf5! 0-1 Pavlov**

181 Chiburdanidze-Alexandria (3) 77

1 e4 c5 2 Nf3 Nc6 3 d4 cxd4 4 Nxd4 Nf6 5 Nc3 e5 6 Ndb5 d6 7 Bg5 a6 8 Na3 b5 9 Bxf6 gxf6 10 Nd5 f5 11 exf5 Bxf5 12 c3 Bg7 13 Nc2 0-0 14 Nce3 Be4! N 14...Bg6; 14...Be6; 14...Bd7 **15 a4?!** 15 Bd3; 15 Be2 **Ne7! 16 f3??** 16 Nxe7+ Qxe7 17 Be2= **Bxd5 17 Nxd5 Nxd5 18 Qxd5 b4!**

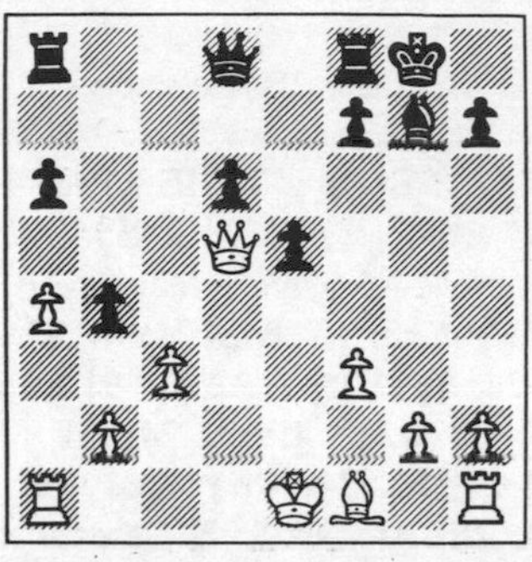

19 Bd3 bxc3 20 bxc3 Qb6∓ 21 Rb1 Qe3+ 22 Kf1 Rac8 23 c4 Rb8 24 Qe4 Qxe4? 24...Rxb1+ 25 Bxb1 Qh6∓ **25 fxe4 Rxb1+ 26 Bxb1 Rb8 27 Ke2 =+ Rb2+ 28 Kf3 Rb4 29 Rd1?!** 29 a5! Rxc4 30 Bd3 Ra4 31 Rc1 **Kf8 30 Bc2?!** 30 a5! **Rxc4 31 Rd2 Ke7 32 Bd1 f5! 33 exf5 e4+!∓ 34 Ke2 Rb4 35 Rd5 Bd4 36 Bc2 Bc5 37 Rd1 Kf6 38 g4 Ke5** 38...Rb2!? **39 Rf1 Rb2 40 Kd1 e3 41 f6!? −+ d5** 41...e2+? 42 Kxe2 Rxc2+ 43 Kd3 Rxh2 44 f7 d5 45 Rf5+! Ke6 46 f8Q =+ **42 f7 Bf8 43 Re1** 43 Kc1 Rb4!? 44 Rf5+ Kd4 45 Rf3 Rc4!! 46 g5 e2 47 Rd3+ Ke4! −+ **d4 44 Re2 Ra2 45 Bxh7 Ra1+ 46 Kc2 Ra2+ 47 Kd1 Ra1+ 48 Kc2 Rxa4 49 g5 Ra3 50 Kb2 Kf4 51 g6 Kf3 52 Re1 Kf2 53 Rd1 e2 54 Rd2 Re3 0-1 Gufeld**

182 Vegh-Perenyi Budapest 77

1 e4 c5 2 Nf3 Nc6 3 d4 cxd4 4 Nxd4 Nf6 5 Nc3 e5 6 Ndb5 d6 7 Bg5 a6 8 Na3 b5 9 Bxf6 gxf6 10 Nd5 f5 11 exf5 Bxf5 12 c3 Bg7 12...Be6 13 Nc2 Bxd5 14 Qxd5 Ne7 15 Qb3 Bg7 16 a4 += Mecking-Ljubojevic, Manila 76 **13 Nc2 0-0 14 Nce3 Bg6** 14...Be6 15 g4! Ra7 16 Bg2 h5 17 h3± Byrne-G.Garcia, Torremolinos 76; 14...Be4

15 ♗d3!? ♗xd5 16 ♘xd5 f5 17 ♕h5 e4 18 ♗c2 b4 19 ♗b3 ♔h8 20 0-0 bxc3 21 bxc3 ♗e5 22 f3± Vegh-Varasdy, Hungary 77 **15 h4 h6 16 g4 e4 17 ♕d2** 17 ♗e2 ♖c8 18 ♘f5∞ Quinteros-Ljubojevic, Manila 76 **♘e5 18 ♗e2 ♖c8 19 ♘f5! ♗xf5 20 gxf5 ♖c5 21 ♖g1! ♔h7 22 0-0-0! b4** 22... ♘d3+ 23 ♗xd3 ♖xd5 24 f6! +− **23 ♘xb4± ♗f6 24 ♔b1 ♖e8 25 ♘d5 ♗xh4 26 ♕f4 ♘d3 27 ♖xd3! exd3 28 f6 +− ♖g8 29 ♗xd3+ ♖g6 30 ♗x g6+ fxg6 31 f7 ♕f8 32 ♘f6+ ♗xf6 33 ♕xf6 ♖g5 34 ♖xg5 hxg5 35 c4 a5 36 b3 g4 37 ♔b2 ♔h6 38 a3 ♔h5 39 ♔b1 ♔h6 40 ♔a2 ♔h7 41 ♔b2 1-0 Tompa**

183 Lanka-Minasjan USSR 78
1 e4 c5 2 ♘f3 ♘c6 3 d4 cxd4 4 ♘xd4 ♘f6 5 ♘c3 e5 6 ♘db5 d6 7 ♗g5 a6 8 ♘a3 b5 9 ♗xf6 gxf6 10 ♘d5 f5 11 g3 fxe4 12 ♗g2 ♗e6 13 ♗xe4 ♗g7 14 ♕h5 ♖c8 15 0-0 ♘e7 16 ♖ad1 ♖c5 17 ♘e3 d5 18 b4 ♖c3 N **19 ♘b1 ♖x e3!? 20 fxe3 ♕b6 21 ♕g5** 21 ♗g2 ♕xe3+ 22 ♔h1 0-0≈ **♔f8?** 21...0-0!? 22 ♗g2 f6∓ **22 ♗g2± h6 23 ♕h5 ♕x e3+ 24 ♔h1 e4 25 ♗h3! ♕b6 26 ♖f4 f5 27 ♖df1 ♗e5 28 ♖xf5+ +− ♗xf5 29 ♗xf5 ♗f6 30 ♘c3 ♕e3 31 ♗e6 1-0 Gipslis**

184 Lanka-Efimov USSR 77
1 e4 c5 2 ♘f3 ♘c6 3 d4 cxd4 4 ♘xd4 ♘f6 5 ♘c3 e5 6 ♘db5 d6 7 ♗g5 a6 8 ♘a3 b5 9 ♗xf6 gxf6 10 ♘d5 f5 11 g3!? fxe4 12 ♗g2 ♗e6 12...♗f5? 13 f3!± ♗g7 14 fxe4 ♗e6 15 0-0 0-0 16 c3 b4 17 ♘c4 bxc3 18 bxc3 ♔h8 19 ♘ce3 Kengis-Lputjan, USSR 77 **13 ♗xe4 ♗g7 14 ♕h5 ♖c8 15 0-0 ♘e7 16 ♖ad1 ♖c5! 17 ♘b4** N 17 ♘e3 d5 18 b4∞ Gaprindashvili-Peters, Lone Pine 77 **♕b6 18 ♕g5 ♔f8!? 19 ♕e3 f5 20 ♗g2 e4 21 c3** 21 ♘d3 ♘d5!? 22 ♕e2 ♖c8∞ **♔f7 22 ♖fe1** Δ ♘d3-f4 **♘g6 23 ♘d3 ♖c6 24 ♕e2 a5?** 24... ♖e8!=

25 g4± d5 26 gxf5 ♗xf5 27 ♕h5 ♔f6 28 ♖e3 28 ♘c2!? **b4 29 ♘c2 bxc3 30 bxc3 ♖xc3 31 ♘de1 ♔e6? 32 ♖xd5!? ♖f8** 32...♔xd5 33 ♕xf5+ ♔d6!? 34 ♖xe4 ♖f8! 35 ♖e6+ ♔c7 36 ♖xb6 ♖xf5 37 ♖b7+± **33 ♗xe4 ♖xe3 34 ♗xf5+ ♔xd5 35 ♘xe3+ ♔c6 36 ♕f3+! ♔b5 37 ♕e2+ ♔c6 38 ♕f3+ ♔b5 39 ♗d3+ ♔c5 40 ♕d5+ ♔b4 41 a3+! ♔c3 42 ♕c4+ ♔b2 43 ♕c2+ ♔a1 44 ♕c1+ 1-0** 44...♔a2 45 ♗c4 mate **Gufeld**

185 Chiburdanidze-Alexandria (5) 77
1 e4 c5 2 ♘f3 ♘c6 3 d4 cxd4 4 ♘xd4 ♘f6 5 ♘c3 e5 6 ♘db5 d6 7 ♗g5 7 a4 **a6 8 ♘a3** 8 ♗xf6 gxf6 9 ♘a3 d5!? **b5 9 ♗xf6** 9 ♘ab1!? **gxf6** 9...♕xf6?! 10 ♘d5± **10 ♘d5 f5 11 g3 fxe4 12 ♗g2 ♗e6** 12...♗f5?! 13 f3!± **13 ♗xe4 ♗g7 14 ♘f6+?** 14 ♕h5!?+= **♗xf6 15 ♗xc6+ ♔e7 =+ 16 c3** 16 ♗xa8 ♕xa8 17 ♖g1 b4 18 ♘b1 ♖c8∓ **♖c8 17 ♗g2** 17 ♗b7 ♖c5 18 ♗xa6 Δ ♕a8 −+; 17 ♗d5 b4∓ **d5 18 ♘c2?** 18 0-0! **d4!∓ 19 cxd4 ♕a5+! 20 ♔f1** 20 ♕d2 ♕xd2+ 21 ♔xd2 ♗g5+ −+ **exd4 21 ♗e4 d3**

22 ♘e3 ♗xb2 −+ 23 ♖b1 d2 23... ♕xa2 −+ **24 ♔g2 ♗d4 25 ♘f5+ ♗xf5 26 ♗xf5 ♖c5 27 ♗c2?!** 27 ♕g4! ♖hd8! 28 ♖b3 ♖c3!! −+ **♖d8 28 ♗b3 ♖f5 29 ♖f1 ♕c3 30 ♕e2+ ♖e5 31 ♕g4 ♕c6+ 32 ♔g1 ♕f6 33 ♖bd1 ♗c3 34 ♕h3 h6 35 ♕g2 ♔f8 36 ♕b7 ♖e7 37 ♕g2 ♔g7 38 ♕h3 ♖d4 39 ♕c8 b4 40 ♕h3 ♕f3 41 ♗c2 ♖e1 42 ♕f5 ♕xf5** 42...♕e2? 43 ♕h7+ ♔f8 44 ♕xh6+ ♔e7 45 ♕h3 **43 ♗xf5 ♖d5 44 ♗c2 ♖a5 45 ♗b3 ♖a3 46 f4 a5 47 g4 a4 48 ♗c4 b3 49 axb3 ♖xd1 50 ♖xd1 ♖a1 51 ♗e2 ♖xd1+ 52 ♗xd1 a3 0-1 Gufeld**

186 Kupreichik-Mochalov Minsk 78
1 e4 c5 2 ♘f3 ♘c6 3 d4 cxd4 4 ♘xd4 ♘f6 5 ♘c3 e5 6 ♘db5 d6 7 ♗g5 a6 8 ♘a3 ♗e6 9 ♘c4 ♖c8 9...♘d4 10 ♗xf6 ♕xf6 11 ♘b6 ♖b8 12 ♘cd5 ♕d8 13 c3 ♗xd5 14 ♘xd5± Tal-Wade, Reykjavik 64 **10 ♗xf6** 10 ♘e3 ♗e7 11 ♗xf6 ♗xf6 12 ♘cd5 ♗g5 13 c3 0-0 14 g3 g6 15 h4 ♗xe3 16 ♘xe3± Georgescu-Vaisman, Rumania Final 73; 10 ♘d5 ♗xd5 11 ♗xf6 ♕xf6!? 12 ♕xd5 ♗e7= Tal **♕xf6!?** N 10...gxf6 11 ♘e3 ♘e7 12 ♗d3 ♕b6 13 0-0 ♕xb2 14 ♘cd5 ♗xd5 15 ♘xd5 Liberzon-Gerusel, Solingen 74 **11 ♘b6 ♖b8 12 ♗e2 ♕d8 13 ♘cd5 ♗e7 14 c3 0-0 15 0-0** 15 a4! ♗g5 16 a5 ♘e7 17 ♗c4± **♗g5 16 ♗c4 ♘e7 17 ♕b3 ♘g6 18 ♖ad1 ♔h8 19 ♕b4 ♗h6 20 f3 f5 21 exf5 ♖xf5 22 ♗d3! +=** 22 ♖fe1 ♘h4 **♖h5 23 ♗xg6 hxg6 24 g3 ♖f5 25 ♘c4?!** 25 ♔g2 **♖f7! 26 ♘db6** 26 ♘xd6? ♖d7 −+ **d5! 27 ♔g2 e4! 28 f4 ♗xf4! 29 gxf4 ♖xf4!∓ 30 ♕d6 ♕g5+ 31 ♔h1 ♖xf1+ 32 ♖xf1 ♖e8 32 ♘e5** Δ ♕xe6 **♔h7 33 ♘bd7 e3 35 ♘f8+ ♖xf8 36 ♖xf8 e2 37 ♘f3 ♕c1+ 38 ♔g2**

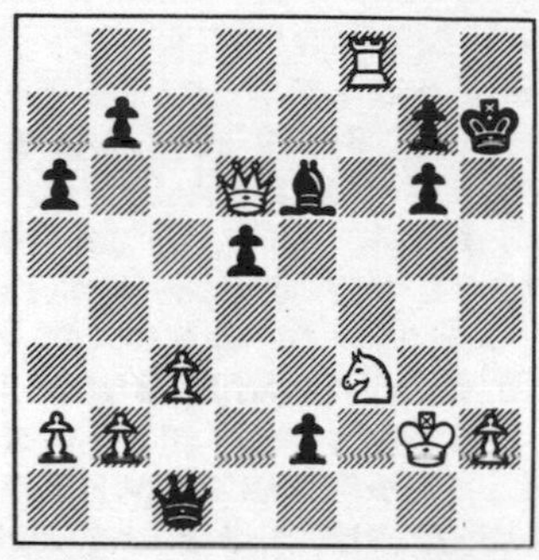

38...♕f1+? 38...♗g4! 39 ♕d8 (39 ♘h4 ♕c2 −+) ♗xf3+ 40 ♔xf3? ♕f1+ 41 ♔g4 ♕g2+ 42 ♔f4 ♕xh2+ 43 ♔g4 ♕g2! 44 ♔f4 g5! 45 ♔f5 g6+ 46 ♔f6 ♕f3! 47 ♔xg5 ♕g3! 48 ♔f6 ♕h4+ −+; 40 ♖xf3! e1♕ 41 ♖h3+ ♕h6 42 ♖xh6+ gxh6=; 40...e1♘+! =+ **39 ♔g3 e1♕+ 40 ♘xe1 ♕xe1+ 41 ♔g2 ♕e4+ 42 ♔f2 ♗f5 43 ♕b4= ♕c2+ 44 ♔g3 ♕d3+ 45 ♔f4 ♕e2 46 ♕d4 ♕xh2+ 47 ♔f3 ♕h3+ 48 ♔e2 ♕h5+ ½-½ Kapengut**

2...♘c6, 4...g6

187 Sigurjonsson-L.Garcia Bogota 78
1 e4 c5 2 ♘f3 ♘c6 3 d4 cxd4 4 ♘xd4 g6 5 ♘c3 ♗g7 6 ♗e3 ♘f6 7 ♗c4 0-0 8 ♗b3 d6 9 h3 ♗d7 10 0-0 ♕a5 11 ♖e1 11 f4 **♖ac8 12 ♕e2 ♘xe4?? 15 ♘xc6! ♗xc6** 13...♘xc3 14 ♘xe7+ ♔h8 15 bxc3 +− **14 ♘xe4 ♗xb2** 14...♗xe4 15 ♗d2! +− **15 ♖ab1 ♗g7 16 ♗d2 +− ♕c7 17 c4 ♖fd8 18 ♖bc1 ♖d7 19 h4! b6 20 h5 ♕b7 21 hxg6 hxg6 22 ♘g5 ♗f6** 22...♗xg2? 23 f3 **23 ♕g4 ♔g7 24 ♗c2** Δ ♘xf7 **♖g8 25 ♗f5! ♖dd8** 25...gxf5 26 ♘e6+ ♔h7 27 ♕h5 mate **26 ♘e6+! fxe6 27 ♕xg6+ ♔f8 28 ♗h6+ ♖g7 29 ♗xe6 ♗e8 30 ♗xg7+** 30 ♕h7?? ♕xg2! mate **1-0 Sigurjonsson**

188 Haag-B.Balogh Hungary 78
1 e4 c5 2 ♞f3 ♞c6 3 d4 cxd4 4 ♞xd4 g6 5 c4 ♞f6 6 ♞c3 d6 7 ♝e2 ♞xd4 8 ♛xd4 ♝g7 9 ♝d2 9 ♗g5; 9 ♗e3 **0-0 10 ♛e3 ♝e6** 10...♘d7; 10...♗d7; 10... e6!? **11 0-0 ♞d7 12 ♜ac1 ♛b6 13 b3 ♛xe3** 13...♗d4 14 ♕g3± **14 ♝xe3 ♞c5 15 f3 a5 16 ♜fd1 ♜fc8?!** 16... f5!?+= **17 ♞b5! ♝d7 18 ♞d4 ♜ab8** 18...♗e8 **19 ♚f2 ♝e8 20 g4! ♜c7 21 g5 ♜bc8 22 ♜b1 ♜b8 23 h4 ♝xd4?! 24 ♝xd4 b5 25 e5! b4 26 exd6 exd6 27 ♝f6±** 27 ♗xc5+= **♜c6 28 ♜d2 a4 29 ♝d1 ♝d7 30 ♝c2 ♝e6 31 ♜bd1 ♜bb6 32 ♝e7 ♝f5 33 ♝xf5 gxf5 34 ♝xd6 ♚g7 35 ♝xc5 ♜xc5 36 ♜d5 ♜xd5 37 ♜xd5 axb3 38 axb3 ♜a6 39 ♜b5 f4 40 ♜xb4 ♜a2+ 41 ♚e1 ♜c2 42 c5 ♜xc5 43 ♜xf4 h6 44 gxh6+ ♚xh6 45 ♚d2 ♚g7 46 b4 ♜h5 47 ♚c3 1-0 Haag**

3 ♝b5+

189 A.Pollard-Browne USA 77
1 e4 c5 2 ♞f3 d6 3 ♝b5+ ♞c6 4 c3 ♞f6 5 ♛e2 ♝d7 6 0-0 a6 7 ♝a4 b5 8 ♝c2 8 ♗b3 **♝g4!** 8...g6 9 d4 += **9 h3 ♝xf3 10 ♛xf3 g6 11 d3 ♝g7 12 ♝e3 ♞d7 13 ♞d2 0-0 14 ♛e2** 14 a4? b4 **♛b6** 14...b4?! 15 ♗a4 **15 ♜ad1 ♜ac8 16 ♞f3 b4!=+ 17 d4 bxc3 18 bxc3 ♛a5** 18...♕b2!? 19 ♗d3! **19 ♝b3 ♛xc3 20 dxc5 ♞xc5 21 ♝xc5 dxc5! 22 ♛xa6 ♞a5??** 22...e6! **23 ♝xf7+!± ♚xf7 24 ♞g5+ ♚g8 25 ♛e6+ ♚h8 26 ♞f7+ ♜xf7 27 ♛xc8+ ♝f8 28 ♜c1 ♛f6 29 ♜xc5?!** 29 ♕xc5± **♛b6 30 ♜c2 e5 31 ♛c3 ♝d6 32 ♜b2 ♛a7 33 ♛c8+?!** 33 ♖d1! **♚g7 34 ♛e6 ♜f6 35 ♛d5 ♝c5! 36 ♜c2 ♝d4 37 ♚h1! ♛b6** 37...♕a6!? **38 ♜fc1 ♜f7 39 ♜c8 ♜xf2!= 40 ♜8c7+ ♚h6 41 ♛d7** 41 ♕g8 **♛f6 42 ♛xh7+ ♚g5 43 h4+** 43 ♕e7? ♕xe7 44 ♖xe7 ♖xa2∓ **♚g4 44 ♛d7+ ♚h5!** 44...♖f5? 45 ♖7c3 ♗xc3 46 ♖xc3 ♕xh4+ 47 ♖h3 ♕e1+ 48 ♔h2 ♕xe4 49 ♖g3+ ♔h4 50 ♕e7+! +−; 44...♔xh4 45 ♕h3+ ♔g5 46 ♕g3+ ♔h6=; 44...♔f4? 45 ♕h3! **45 ♛h7+ ♚g4 46 ♛d7+ ♚h5 ½-½ Browne**

190 Lein-Browne USA Final 77
1 e4 c5 2 ♞f3 d6 3 ♝b5+ ♞c6 4 0-0 ♝d7 5 ♜e1 ♞f6 6 c3 a6 7 ♝f1 7 ♗a4!? **♝g4 8 h3 ♝xf3 9 ♛xf3 g6 10 ♛d1 ♝h6! 11 ♞a3 0-0** 11...e5 12 ♘c2 ♕b6 13 ♘e3! **12 ♞c4!?** 12 ♘c2 e5 13 d4 ♗xc1 14 ♖xc1 cxd4 15 cxd4 ♕b6 16 d5 ♘b4= **d5!?** 12...b5!? 13 ♘e3 ♘xe4 14 ♘g4 ♗g7 15 ♖xe4 f5 +=; 12...♖b8 **13 exd5 ♞xd5 14 ♞e3 ♞xe3 15 dxe3=** 15 fxe3 e5 **♛xd1** 15...♕c7!? △ ♖ad8, ♖d7, ♖fd8 **16 ♜xd1 ♜ad8 17 ♜xd8 ♜xd8 18 f4!** 18 ♗e2 ♘e5 =+ **g5!!**

19 g3 19 f5? ♘e5 20 g4 ♘d3!=+ **gxf4 20 gxf4 e5 21 ♚f2 ♜d6! 22 ♝e2 ♜f6 23 ♚f3 ♞e7!** 23...exf4 24 exf4 ♘e5+ 25 ♔e4 ♘g6 26 f5!± **24 ♝d3 exf4 25 exf4 ♞g6** 25...♘d5? 26 f5 **26 ♝xg6 hxg6 27 h4** 27 ♗e3 ♗xf4! −+ **♜f5** 27...♖b6 28 ♗e3! ♖xb2 29 ♗xc5 ♖c2 30 ♗d4=; 27...♖d6 28 ♗e3 b6 29 b4! **28 ♝e3 ♚f8 29 b4 cxb4 30 cxb4 ♚e8 31 a4 ♝f8!∓ 32 ♜b1 b5 33 axb5**

axb5 34 ♔e4 ♗e7?! 34...♗d6! **35 ♗d4!=+ ♗xh4 36 ♖a1 ♔d7 37 ♖a7+ ♔c6 38 ♖a6+ ♔b7 39 ♖a7+ ♔c6 40 ♖a6+ ♔b7 41 ♖a7+ ♔b8 42 ♖d7 ♔c8 43 ♖a7 ♗e1 44 ♗c5 ♖f6 45 ♗d4! ♖f5 46 ♗c5 ♗h4 47 ♗d6 ♗d8 48 ♗e5 ♗b6 49 ♖e7 ♗d8 50 ♖a7 ♗b6 ½-½ Browne**

191 Alexandria-Ioselani USSR 77

1 e4 c5 2 ♘f3 d6 3 ♗b5+ ♗d7 4 a4 ♘f6 5 e5 dxe5 6 ♘xe5 ♗xb5 7 axb5 ♕d5 8 ♘f3 ♕e4+ 9 ♕e2 ♕xc2! 9...♕xe2+ 10 ♔xe2 += **10 ♘c3 ♘bd7!** 10...e6 11 ♘e5! ♘bd7 12 ♘xd7 ♘xd7 13 ♕f3! += **11 ♘e5 e6?!** 11...♘xe5 12 ♕xe5 ♕d3! 13 ♕xc5 e6 14 ♕c7 ♕d7=+ **12 ♘xd7 ♘xd7 13 0-0?!** 13 ♕f3!? ♘e5 14 ♕xb7 ♘d3+ 15 ♔e2 ♖d8 16 g3! ♘xc1+ 17 ♖hxc1 ♕xd2+ 18 ♔f1 +−; 13...♖b8 14 0-0 ♕f5 15 ♕xf5 exf5 16 ♖e1+ ♔d8 17 ♖xa7 ♗d6 += **♕f5 14 ♖d1** 14 b6 a6 15 ♘b5 ♖c8 16 ♘c7+ ♔d8 −+ **♗d6** 14...♗e7 15 d4 0-0 16 d5 ♘b6 17 d6 ♘f6∓ **15 d4 cxd4 16 ♘e4** 16 ♖xd4 ♕e5∓ **♗b8** 16...♗c7!? **17 ♖a4 ♘f6** 17...0-0! 18 ♖axd4 ♘b6 19 g4?! ♕g6 20 ♘c5 ♘d5 21 ♘xb7 ♗c7∓ **18 ♘xf6+ ♕xf6 19 ♕e4 ♕e5** 19...0-0 20 ♕xb7 ♗d6 21 ♖xa7 ♖ac8∝ **20 ♕xb7 ♕xh2+ 21 ♔f1 ♕h1+ 22 ♔e2 ♕h5+ 23 ♔e1** 23 f3 0-0! 21 ♕xa8 ♕xb5+ **♕e5+?** 23...0-0 24 ♕xa8 ♕h1+ 25 ♔d2 ♗f4+ 26 ♔c2 d3+ −+ **24 ♔f1 ♕d5?** 24...0-0 25 ♖axd4 ♗c7 26 ♗f4 ♕xf4 27 ♖xf4 ♗xf4± **25 ♕xd5 exd5 26 b6 +− ♗d6 27 ♖dxd4 ♔d7 28 bxa7 ♖hc8 29 ♗e3 ♔e7 30 ♖xd5 1-0 Gufeld**

Najdorf

192 Tal-Byrne Bugojno 78

1 e4 c5 2 ♘f3 d6 3 d4 cxd4 4 ♘xd4 ♘f6 5 ♘c3 a6 6 a4!? g6 6...♘c6 **7 ♗e2 ♗g7 8 ♗e3** 8 0-0 ♘c6 9 ♘b3 0-0 10 ♗g5! **0-0 9 0-0 ♘c6 10 f4 ♗d7** 10...♗e6 **11 ♘b3! ♖c8** 11...♘a5 12 e5! **12 ♗f3 ♗e6 13 ♘d5!± ♘d7 14 c3 f5?! 15 exf5 ♗xf5 16 ♘d4!**

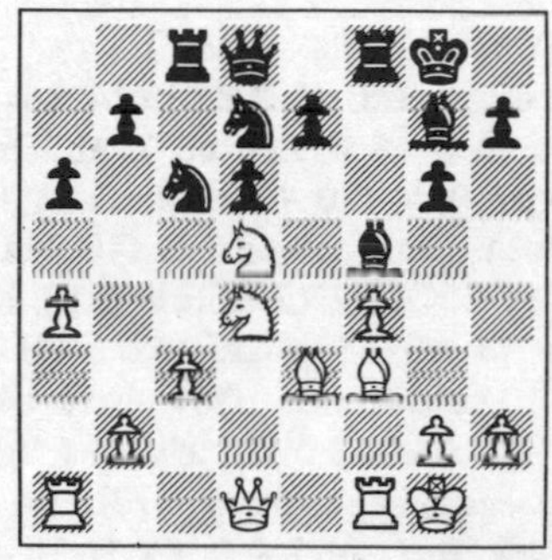

16...e6!? 17 ♘xc6 bxc6 18 ♘b4! c5 19 ♘c6 ♖xc6 20 ♗xc6 ♘f6 21 ♗f3 h5 22 ♕e2 ♕a5 23 ♗f2 d5 24 h3! ♖e8 25 ♖fe1 ♔f7 26 g4! hxg4 27 hxg4 ♗e4 28 ♗h4 c4 29 ♕e3 ♗xf3 30 ♕xf3 ♘e4 31 f5! ♕b6+ 32 ♗f2 ♕xb2 32...♕xf2+ 33 ♕xf2 ♘xf2 34 ♔xf2 gxf5 35 gxf5 exf5 36 ♖xe8 ♔xe8 37 ♖d1 **33 fxe6+ ♔g8** 33...♔xe6 34 ♖xe4+ dxe4 35 ♕xe4+ ♔f7 36 ♕d5+ ♖e6 37 ♖e1 **34 ♕f7+ ♔h7 35 ♗d4 ♖g8 36 e7 ♕b8 37 ♖e3 1-0 Pytel**

193 V.Ivanov-Zhidkov USSR 77

1 e4 c5 2 ♘f3 d6 3 d4 cxd4 4 ♘xd4 ♘f6 5 ♘c3 a6 6 ♗c4 e6 7 ♗b3 b5 7...♘bd7!?; 7...♗e7 **8 0-0** 8 f4 **♗e7** 8...b4?! 9 ♘a4 ♘xe4 10 ♖e1 ♘f6 11 ♗g5±; 8...♗b7 9 ♖e1 ♘c6!?∝ **9 ♕f3?!** 9 f4 0-0 10 e5 dxe5 11 fxe5 ♘fd7 12 ♕h5≈ **♕c7!** 9...♕b6 10 ♗e3 ♕b7 11 ♕g3 g6 12 ♗h6! +−; 9...♗b7?! 10 ♗xe6!± **10 ♕g3** 10 e5? ♗b7!∓; 10 a3

♘c6 11 ♘xc6 ♕xc6 12 ♖e1 0-0 13 ♕g3∝ Velimirovic-Tukmakov, Amsterdam 74 **♞c6!** 10...b4 11 ♘ce2 g6 12 ♗h6! += **11 ♝e3 0-0 12 ♞xc6 ♛xc6 13 ♝d4 ♝b7= 14 ♜ad1?** 14 a3 **b4 15 ♝xf6 ♝xf6 16 ♜xd6 ♛c7 17 ♜fd1?** 17 ♘a4 ♗xe4 =+ **bxc3 18 e5 ♝e7 19 ♜d7 ♜fd8! 0-1 Gufeld**

194 Adorjan-Hulak IBM 77

1 e4 c5 2 ♞f3 d6 3 d4 cxd4 4 ♞xd4 ♞f6 5 ♞c3 a6 6 ♝c4 e6 7 ♝b3 b5 8 0-0 ♝e7 9 f4 0-0 10 e5 dxe5 11 fxe5 ♞fd7 11...♗c5 12 ♗e3 ♗xd4 13 ♗xd4 ♘c6 14 ♖f4 ♘d7 **12 ♛h5 ♞c6 13 ♞xc6 ♛b6+ 14 ♚h1!?** 14 ♗e3 ♕xc6 15 ♔h1 ♗b7 16 ♖f3 ♗c5 17 ♖e1 a5 18 a4 b4 19 ♘b5 ♗xe3 20 ♖exe3 Gheorghiu-Polugaevsky, Petropolis 73; 14...♕xe3+ 15 ♔h1 Δ ♖ae1 **♛xc6 15 ♜f3 ♝b7 16 ♝f4?! ♞c5! 17 ♜g3** 17 ♖g1 ♘e4 **b4! 18 ♝h6** 18 ♕h6? ♕xg2+ 19 ♖xg2 ♗xg2+ 20 ♔xg2 gxh6 −+; 18 ♘e2 **g6 19 ♝xf8 ♝xf8 20 ♞d1 ♞e4 21 ♜g4 ♝g7 22 ♛h4 ♝xe5 23 ♞e3 h5** 23...♗f6 24 ♕e1 ♗xb2 25 ♖d1 ♗c3 26 ♕e2 h5! 27 ♖f4 ♗e5 Δ ♘c3 **24 ♛xh5 ♞f2+ 25 ♚g1 ♞xg4 26 ♛xg4 ♝xb2 27 ♜d1 ♛e4 28 ♛xe4 ♝xe4 29 ♜d7 ♜c8 30 ♞c4 ♝c6 31 ♜xf7 ♝d4+ 0-1** 32 ♔h1 ♔xf7 33 ♘d6+ ♔e7 34 ♘xc8+ ♔d7 +−

195 Eremin-Bangiev corr. 77

1 e4 c5 2 ♞f3 d6 3 d4 cxd4 4 ♞xd4 ♞f6 5 ♞c3 a6 6 ♝e2 e5 7 ♞b3 ♝e6 7...♗e7! **8 0-0** 8 f4 ♕c7 9 g4!? += **♞bd7 9 f4 ♛c7 10 a4 ♝e7 11 ♝e3** 11 ♔h1!? 0-0 12 f5 ♗c4 13 ♗g5!? **0-0 12 ♚h1** 12 a5!? **exf4 13 ♜xf4 ♞e5 14 a5!** 14 ♘d4 ♖ad8! 15 a5 ♕c8! = **♜ae8!?** TN 14...♖fe8 15 ♘d4 ♖ac8 16 ♘f5 ♗f8 17 ♕d2 += **15 ♞d4 ♛c8! 16 ♛d2** 16 ♘xe6 ♕xe6 Δ ♗d8, ♘d6 =+; 16 ♘f5?! ♗xf5 17 ♖xf5? ♘xe4!; 17 exf5 ♘c6! Δ ♗d8 **♞fg4! 17 ♞f5** 17 ♘xe6 ♕xe6= **♞xe3 18 ♛xe3 ♝xf5!** 18...♗g5 19 ♕g3 ♗xf5 20 ♖xf5 ♗d8!; 20 ♕xg5 ♗e6= **19 ♜xf5 ♝d8 20 ♛d2** Δ ♘d5 **♜e6?!** 20...♕e6!? 21 ♘d5 ♘c6 22 ♗d3 g6 23 ♖ff1 ♕e5 =+ **21 b3** 21 ♘d5 ♘c4! **g6 22 ♜ff1 ♝g5 23 ♛d4!** 23 ♕xg5 ♕xc3 =+; 23 ♕e1 ♗h6! Δ ♗g7 **♝h6?** 23...♘c6! 24 ♕c4 ♖e5 25 ♘d5 ♕e6=

24 ♜a2! ♝g7 25 ♞d5 ♚h8?! 25...♕d8 26 ♕b6! +=; 25...♘c6!? 26 ♕c4 ♖e5 **26 ♛d1 ♛d8 27 ♜a4! ♞d7 28 ♞f4 ♜f6 29 g3= ♜e8** 29...♘c5 30 ♖c4! += **30 ♝f3 ♞e5! 31 ♝g2 ♞c6 32 b4 ♞e5 33 ♞d5?! ♜xf1+ 34 ♛xf1 ♛c8 35 c3 ♛c4= 1-0** time/Zeit **Gufeld**

196 Osterman-Bangiev corr. 77

1 e4 c5 2 ♞f3 d6 3 d4 cxd4 4 ♞xd4 ♞f6 5 ♞c3 a6 6 ♝e2 e5 7 ♞b3 ♝e6 8 0-0 ♞bd7 9 f4 ♛c7 10 a4 ♝e7 11 ♝e3 0-0 12 ♚h1 exf4 13 ♜xf4 ♞e5 14 a5! ♜ac8!? 15 ♞d4 ♜fe8 16 ♞f5 16 ♘xe6?! **♝f8 17 ♝d4?!** 17 ♗b6?! ♕c6 18 ♘e3 ♗e7!= **d5! 18 exd5 ♞xd5 19 ♞xd5 ♝xd5 20 ♞e3! ♜cd8?!** 20...♗c4? 21 ♗xc4 +=; 20...♗e6! Δ ♗c5 =+ **21 ♛f1!** Δ ♗b6; Δ ♘xd5 **♞g6 22 ♜g4 ♝c5** 22...h5 23 ♗b6! ♕c6 24 ♖g5 +=; 23 ♖xg6 ♖xe3!∝ **23 ♞xd5 ♜xd5 24**

♗c3 += ♕d7 25 ♗f3! 25 ♗c4? ♖f5! 26 ♕d1 ♕c6! **♖d6 26 ♖e1! ♖xe1 27 ♕xe1 ♖e6 28 ♖e4 ♘f8!** 28...♖xe4 29 ♕xe4 ♕b5 30 ♕d3!± **29 ♖xe6 ♘xe6 30 ♕e4 ♕b5! 31 ♗e2** 31 ♕d3 ♕xd3 32 cxd3 ♘d8! Δ ♘c6 += **♕d7 32 ♗d3?! g6 33 b4** 33 ♕e5 ♗d4! **♗d4 34 ♗xd4** 34 ♗d2 ♕a4!; 34 ♗e1 ♕a4! 35 ♗c4 ♕a1 36 ♗xe6 fxe6= **♘xd4 35 ♔g1 ♘c6= ½-½ Gufeld**

197 Karpov-Bukic Bugojno 78
1 e4 c5 2 ♘f3 d6 3 d4 cxd4 4 ♘xd4 ♘f6 5 ♘c3 a6 6 ♗e2 e5 7 ♘b3 ♗e7 8 0-0 0-0 9 a4 ♘c6 N 9...♗e6 10 f4 ♕c7 **10 ♔h1 ♗e6 11 f4 ♘b4 12 f5 ♗d7 13 ♗g5 ♗c6 14 ♗f3 += ♖c8 15 ♕e2 h6 16 ♗h4 b6 17 ♖fd1 ♕c7** Δ d5 **18 ♗g3! ♗b7 19 ♖d2 ♖fd8 20 ♖ad1 ♘e8** 20...♘d7!? **21 h4** 21 ♘c1? ♗g5 **♘f6 22 ♗f2 ♘d7 23 g3 ♔f8!? 24 ♘c1 ♕c4 25 ♕e1 ♕c7 26 ♕g1 ♘c5 27 ♘1e2 ♗c6 28 b3 ♕b7 29 ♕g2 ♕c7 30 ♗e3 ♗f6 31 ♔h2 ♕e7 32 ♕f2 += ♗b7 33 ♗g2 ♔g8 34 ♕f3 ♔h7? 35 ♕h5± ♕f8 36 ♖f1 ♘d7 37 ♖c1 ♖c6? 38 ♘d5!± ♘xd5** 38...a5!? **39 exd5 ♖cc8 40 ♗e4 +− ♘c5 41 ♗xc5 ♖xc5 42 g4 1-0** 42...♔g8 43 g5 ♗e7 44 f6 gxf6 45 gxf6 ♗xf6 46 ♖g1+ ♗g7 47 ♕f5 **Pytel**

198 Smyslov-Tukmakov
USSR Final 77
1 e4 c5 2 ♘f3 d6 3 d4 cxd4 4 ♘xd4 ♘f6 5 ♘c3 a6 6 ♗e2 e5 7 ♘f3 h6 8 0-0 ♗e6 9 a4 ♘c6 10 b3 ♖c8 11 ♗b2 ♗e7 12 ♖e1 0-0 13 ♗f1 ♕c7≈ 14 ♕d2 ♘b4 14...♗g4!? **15 ♖ac1 ♖fd8 16 ♕e2 ♕b6?!** 16...♗g4 17 h3 ♗h5; 16...♘d7!= **17 ♘b1 ♖c7 18 ♗a3 ♘a2 19 ♖cd1 ♖dc8 20 ♖d2 ♘d7?** 20...♗g4! 21 c4 ♘b4 +=; 21 ♖ed1 ♖c6 +=

21 ♕d1 ♘c3? 21...♖c6 22 c4 ♘b4 23 ♘c3 Δ ♘d5± **22 ♘xc3 ♖xc3 23 ♗xd6 ♗f6 24 ♗a3 ♕c7 25 ♗c4! +− ♖xc4 26 bxc4 ♘c5 27 ♕b1!** 27 ♗xc5 ♕xc5 ∞/+− **b6** 27...♘xa4 28 ♗d6 Δ ♗xc5, ♕xb7 +− **28 h3! ♕c6** 28...♘xa4 29 ♗d6 +− **29 ♗b2 ♘xa4** 29...♕c7 30 ♕a1 ♘d7 31 ♖ed1 +− **30 ♗xe5 ♗e7 31 ♕a1! ♗b4 32 ♗xg7 ♗xd2 33 ♘xd2 ♔h7 34 ♖e3 ♖g8 35 ♖g3 ♗xc4 36 ♕d4 b5 37 ♘f3 ♕c5 38 ♕f6 ♕b6 39 ♕f5+ ♕g6 40 ♖xg6 fxg6 41 ♕f6 1-0 Petrosian**

199 Karpov-Ljubojevic Bugojno 78
1 e4 c5 2 ♘f3 d6 3 d4 cxd4 4 ♘xd4 ♘f6 5 ♘c3 a6 6 ♗e2 e6 7 f4! ♘bd7 8 ♗f3 8 0-0 b5 9 ♗f3 ♗b7∞ **♕c7 9 g4! ♘b6 10 g5 ♘fd7 11 a4 g6!? 12 ♕d3 += ♗g7 13 ♘de2 ♘c5 14 ♕e3 ♘c4 15 ♕f2 ♕a5 16 0-0 0-0 17 ♖a2 ♕b4 18 ♕e1 ♗d7 19 ♔h1 ♕b6 20 b3 ♘a5 21 ♘d1! ♗c6?!** 21...♘c6!? 22 a5! ♕b5 (22...♕c7? 23 b4!) 23 ♘dc3 ♕b4 24 ♗d2!±; 24 ♗a3 ♕a5! **22 b4 ♘xe4 23 ♗e3!± ♘c5 24 bxa5 ♕b1 25 ♖a3 ♕xc2 26 ♕d2 ♗xf3+ 27 ♖xf3 ♕e4 28 ♔g2 ♘xa4 29 ♗d4! e5** 29...♗xd4 30 ♖xa4 **30 ♖xa4 exd4 31 ♘xd4 ♖ac8 32 ♘c3 ♕e8 33 ♖b4 ♕d7 34 ♔g3 ♖c5 35 ♘b3 ♖f5 36 ♘d5 h5 37 h3 ♖e8 38 ♕d3 ♕c6 39**

♘e3 ♖b5 40 ♖xb5 axb5 41 f5 ♖e5 42 h4 ♔h7 43 ♘d4 ♕c1 44 ♘g2 b4 45 ♘e2 ♕c6 46 fxg6+ fxg6 47 ♘ef4 ♖f5 48 ♘e3 +− ♖xf4 49 ♖xf4 ♗e5 50 ♕c4! ♕d7 51 ♘d5 ♕f7 52 ♘f6+ ♔g7 53 ♘xh5+ 1-0 Pytel

200 Zapala-Sigurjonsson
Bogota 78

1 e4 c5 2 ♘f3 d6 3 d4 cxd4 4 ♘xd4 ♘f6 5 ♘c3 e6 6 ♗e2 ♗e7 7 0-0 0-0 8 ♗e3 a6 9 f4 ♕c7 10 ♕e1 b5 11 e5?! 11 ♗f3 **dxe5 12 fxe5 ♕xe5 13 ♗f3 ♗c5! 14 ♕f2!?** 14 ♗xa8 ♘g4!∓ **♖a7 15 ♖fe1** △ ♘dxb5 **♖c7 16 ♖ad1 ♘bd7 17 ♕h4** △ ♗f2 **♗xd4 18 ♗xd4 ♕f5 19 ♕g3 ♖c4 20 ♗e2 ♖c6 21 ♗f3= ♖c4 22 ♗e2 ♖c6 23 ♖f1? ♕g6 24 ♕h4 ♗b7 25 ♗f3 e5! 26 ♗e3** 26 ♗xc6 ♗xc6∓ **♖c4∓ 27 ♕h3 ♗xf3 28 ♖xf3 ♕g4 29 ♕xg4 ♖xg4 30 ♘d5 ♖a4 31 a3 ♖e8 31 ♗g5 ♘xd5 33 ♖xd5 ♘b6 34 ♖d6 ♘c8 35 ♖d7 f6 36 ♗xf6?** Zeitnot **gxf6 37 ♖g3+ ♔f8 38 ♖c3 ♖c4 0-1 Sigurjonsson**

201 Chiricuta-Pavlov
Rumania Final 77

1 e4 c5 2 ♘f3 d6 3 d4 ♘f6 4 ♘c3 cxd4 5 ♘xd4 a6 6 ♗e3 b5?! TN **7 f3?** 7 a4 bxa4?! 8 ♖xa4 ♘bd7! **♗b7 8 ♗d3 ♘bd7 9 a4 b4! 10 ♘a2 e5! 11 ♘b3 d5!=+ 12 0-0 ♗e7** 12...dxe4 13 fxe4 ♗xe4 14 ♗xe4 ♘xe4 15 ♕f3 ♘ef6 16 ♖ad1∝ **13 ♕e2 0-0 14 ♖ad1 ♕c7 15 ♗d2 a5 16 ♗g5 h6! 17 ♗h4 ♘b6 18 ♗xf6 ♗xf6 19 c3 ♘xa4 20 exd5 ♗xd5 21 ♗h7+ ♔xh7 22 ♖xd5 ♔g8 =+ 23 c4 ♖fe8?! 24 ♘ac1 ♘b6 25 ♖c5 ♕e7 26 ♖b5!** 26 ♖xa5?? ♖xa5 27 ♘xa5 ♕c5+ −+ **♘c8 27 ♘xa5 ♘d6 28 ♖d5 ♖ec8 29 ♘cb3 ♕c7! 30 c5?! ♖xa5!**

31 ♘xa5 ♕xa5 32 ♕d3 32 ♖xd6 ♕xc5+ **♘b7 33 ♖fc1 ♖xc5!! 34 ♖dxc5 ♘xc5 35 ♕d5 ♗g5!! −+ 36 ♖e1** 36 ♕xc5? ♕xc5+ 37 ♖xc5 ♗e3+ **♕a7 37 ♔f1 ♕a6+ 38 ♔g1 ♘d3! 39 ♖f1 ♕a7+ 40 ♔h1 ♘f2+ 0-1 Pavlov**

202 Suetin-Platonov USSR 77

1 e4 c5 2 ♘f3 d6 3 d4 cxd4 4 ♘xd4 ♘f6 5 ♘c3 a6 6 ♗e3!? e6 6...e5 7 ♘f3 h6 8 ♗c4 ♗e7 9 ♕e2! += Tseshkovsky-Portisch, Las Palmas 76; 7...♕c7 8 ♗g5 ♘bd7 9 a4 h6 10 ♗h4 ♗e7 11 ♘d2 += Tseshkovsky-Mecking, Manila 76; 6...♘bd7 7 f4 b5!∝ **7 ♗e2 ♕c7** 7... b5!? **8 f4 b5 9 ♗f3** 9 e5?! dxe5 10 fxe5 ♕xe5 11 ♕d2∝ **♗b7 10 a3** 10 e5 dxe5 11 ♗xb7 ♕xb7 12 fxe5 ♕xg2 13 ♖g1 ♕h3 14 ♖g3 ♕xh2∓ **♘bd7 11 ♕e2 e5!?** 11...♗e7 12 g4! += **12 ♘f5 h6** 12...g6 13 fxe5 dxe5 14 ♘h6 += **13 0-0!?** 13 ♘d5! ♘xd5 14 exd5 g6 15 ♘g3 ♗g7 16 f5!±; 13...♗xd5 14 exd5 e4 15 ♗d4± **g6 14 ♘g3 exf4 15 ♗xf4 ♘e5= 16 ♖ad1 ♗g7 17 ♔h1 0-0 18 ♖f2** 18 ♕d2 ♘c4 19 ♕c1 ♔h7 =+ **♖fe8 19 ♕f1 ♖ad8 20 ♗xe5 ♖xe5! =+**

Diagram

21 ♖fd2 h5 22 ♕d3 ♖c5 23 ♘f1 ♘e8

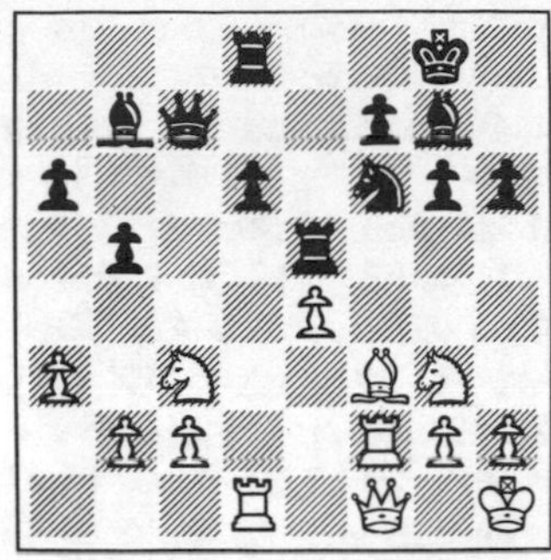

△ ♗xc3 **24 e5!? ♖xe5 25 ♗xb7 ♕xb7 26 ♘d5 ♘f6 27 ♘xf6+ ♗xf6∓ 28 ♖f2 ♕e7 29 c4 ♗g7 30 cxb5 axb5 31 ♘d2 ♖e1+ 32 ♖xe1** 32 ♖f1 ♖xd1 33 ♖xd1 ♗xb2∓ **♕xe1+ 33 ♖f1 ♕e8 34 ♘f3 ♕c6 35 ♘g5 ♖f8 36 b3 d5 37 ♕f3 ♕d7 38 a4 bxa4 39 bxa4 ♗h6 40 ♕f6 d4 41 ♘f3 d3 42 ♕a1 d2 −+ 43 a5 ♖c8 44 ♘xd2 ♕xd2 45 a6 ♖c2 46 ♖g1 ♖a2 0-1 Gufeld**

203 Tisdall-Petrosian Hastings 77/8
1 e4 c5 2 ♘f3 e6 3 d4 cxd4 4 ♘xd4 ♘f6 5 ♘c3 d6 6 ♗e3 a6 7 f4 b5 8 ♕f3 ♗b7 9 ♗d3 ♘bd7 9...b4!? **10 0-0 ♖c8 11 a3 ♗e7** 11...♖xc3 12 bxc3 ♘c5 13 ♘b3 ♘cxe4 14 ♗d4 ∝/+= **12 ♖ae1 0-0?!** 12...♖xc3 13 bxc3 ♕a8 **13 ♕h3! ♔h8** 13...♖xc3 14 bxc3 ♘xe4 15 ♘xe6! +− **14 ♘f3 e5 15 ♘h4 g6 16 fxe5?=+** 16 ♘f3!± **♘xe5 17 ♗d4 ♘fd7 18 ♘f3 ♗f6 =+ 19 ♗e3?** 19 ♘xe5=+ **♔g8 20 ♘d4 ♗g7 21 ♖d1 ♘b6! 22 ♘f3 ♘bc4 23 ♗xc4 ♖xc4!∓ 24 ♘d4?** −+ 24 ♘d2∓ **h5** △ ♘g4 **25 ♔h1 ♘g4 26 ♗g1 ♖e8 27 ♕f3 f5 0-1 Petrosian**

204 Honfi-Cserna Hungary 77
1 e4 c5 2 ♘f3 d6 3 d4 cxd4 4 ♘xd4 ♘f6 5 ♘c3 a6 6 f4 ♕c7 7 ♗d3 g6 8 0-0 ♘bd7 9 ♘f3 ♗g7 10 ♕e1 e5 11 a4 11 ♔h1 **b6 12 ♕h4 ♗b7 13 fxe5 dxe5 14 ♗h6 0-0 15 ♘g5 ♕d6!?** N 15...♘h5?? 16 ♗xg7 ♔xg7 17 ♖xf7+ +− **16 g4 ♖fc8 17 ♗xg7** 17 ♖f3 ♗xh6 18 ♕xh6 ♕f8 19 ♘xf7 ♕xf7 20 g5 ♕g7= **♔xg7 18 ♘xf7!? ♔xf7 19 ♕xh7+!?** 19 g5 ♔g7 20 gxf6+ ♘xf6= **♔e6!** 19...♔e8 20 ♕xg6+ ♔d8 21 g5 ♘e8 22 ♕h7≈

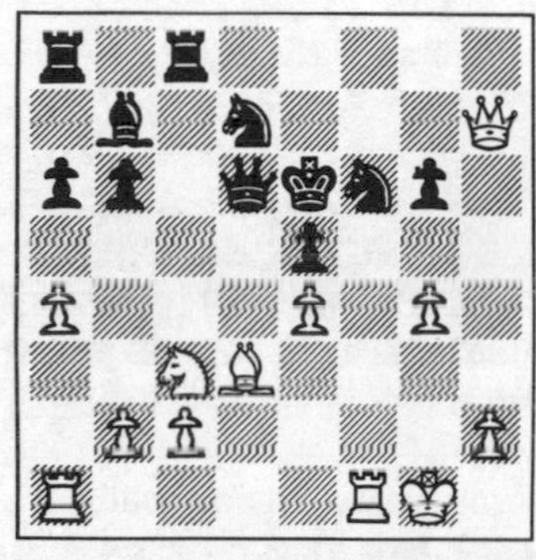

20 ♖xf6+! ♘xf6! 20...♔xf6? 21 ♖f1+ ♔g5 22 ♗e2 +− **21 ♕xb7 ♕c5+** 21...♕c7 22 ♕xc7 ♖xc7 23 h3 ♖h7 24 ♗f1≈ **22 ♔h1 ♖cb8 23 ♕g7 ♖g8 24 ♕h6!** 24 ♕b7? ♘xg4 25 ♘d5 ♖h8−+ **♖h8 25 ♗c4+!!** 25 ♕xg6? ♖xh2+ 26 ♔xh2 ♕f2+ −+; 25 ♕d2? ♘xg4 −+ **♕xc4** 25...♔d6? 26 ♖d1+ ♔c6 27 ♗d5+ ♘xd5 28 exd5+ ♔b7 29 ♕g7+ ♔c7 30 ♕xg6 +− **26 ♕xg6 ♖ag8 27 ♕f5+ ♔e7 28 g5 ♘d7??** 28...♘h5! 29 ♕xe5+ ♕e6 30 ♕c7+ ♕d7 31 ♕e5+ ♕e6= **29 ♘d5+ ♔e8 30 ♕xd7+ ♔xd7 31 ♘xb6+ ♔e6?!** 31...♔c6 32 ♘xc4 ♖xg5 33 b4 ♖h4 34 ♖e1≈ **32 ♘xc4 ♖xg5 33 ♖d1 ♖hg8?** 33...♖h4! 34 ♘d2 ♖gh5 35 ♘f1± **34 ♘e3 ♖f8 35 ♘f5 ♔f7 36 ♖d7+ ♔g6 37 h3 ♖h8 38 ♔h2 ♖gh5 39 ♖d3 ♖b8 40 b3 ♔g5 41 ♔g3 ♖hh8 1-0 Honfi**

205 Durao-Petrosian Sochi 77
1 e4 c5 2 ♘f3 d6 3 d4 cxd4 4 ♘xd4 ♘f6 5 ♘c3 a6 6 f4 ♕c7 7 ♗d3 g6 8

0-0 ♝g7 9 ♞f3 ♝g4?! 10 ♛e1 ♝xf3 11 ♜xf3 ♞bd7 12 ♚h1 e6!? 12...0-0 13 ♕h4 Δ ♖h3± **13 ♝d2 ♞b6** Δ ♘c4 **14 ♜d1 ♞fd7** 14...♘c4 15 ♗c1 **15 ♝f1 ♜d8 16 ♛h4 h6 17 e5??** 17 ♗e3 Δ ♗d4± **dxe5 18 ♞e4** Δ ♗b4 **0-0! 19 ♜c3** 19 ♗b4 ♕xc2 **♛b8 20 f5 exf5 21 ♝xh6 fxe4 22 ♜h3 ♞f6?** 22...f5 −+ **23 ♝xg7 ♞h5** 23...♔xg7 24 ♕h6+ +− **24 ♜xd8 ♜xd8 25 ♝f6??** −+ 25 g4! ♖d1 26 gxh5 ♖xf1+ 27 ♔g2 ♖f4 28 ♗xe5!!∞ ♕xe5 29 ♕d8+ ♔g7 30 hxg6 ♖g4+ 31 ♔h1; 28 ♗xe5!! ♖xh4 29 ♗xb8 += **♜d1 26 ♛f2 ♞d5 27 ♝g5 ♞hf4 28 ♝xf4 exf4 29 ♚g1 ♞e3 30 ♜xe3 fxe3 31 ♛xe3 ♛e5 32 ♚f2 ♛f5+ 0-1 Petrosian**

206 Durao-Ochoa Spain Final 77

1 e4 c5 2 ♞f3 d6 3 d4 cxd4 4 ♞xd4 ♞f6 5 ♞c3 a6 6 f4 ♛c7 7 ♝d3 g6 8 0-0 ♝g7 9 ♞f3 0-0 10 ♛e1 ♞bd7 11 ♚h1 e5 12 ♛h4 b5 13 fxe5 dxe5 14 ♝h6 b4 15 ♞d5 ♞xd5 16 exd5 ♝xh6 17 ♛xh6 f5? 17...f6! **18 ♜ae1! e4 19 d6 ♛xd6 20 ♝c4+ ♚h8 21 ♞g5 ♛e7 22 ♜xe4 ♛g7 23 ♛xg7+ ♚xg7 24 ♞e6+ ♚h8 25 ♞xf8 fxe4 26 ♝d5 ♜b8 27 ♜f7 ♞xf8 28 ♜xf8+ ♚g7 29 ♜g8+ ♚f6 30 ♝xe4 b3 31 axb3 ♜b4 32 ♜f8+ ♚g5?! 33 ♜xc8 ♜xe4 34 ♜c5+ ♚f6 35 ♚g1 ♜e2 36 ♚f1 ♜d2 37 b4 ♜d1+ 38 ♚e2 ♜g1 39 ♚f2 ♜b1 40 b3 ♜c1 41 ♜c6+ ♚e5 42 h3 ♚d5 43 ♜c5+ 1-0 Ochoa**

207 Kapengut-Platonov Vilnius 77

1 e4 c5 2 ♞f3 d6 3 d4 cxd4 4 ♞xd4 ♞f6 5 ♞c3 a6 6 f4 e6 6...♘bd7!? 7 ♗d3 b5 8 ♕e2 e5 9 ♘b3 ♗e7 10 ♗d2 0-0; 6...♕c7!? **7 ♝d3!?** 7 ♗e2 ♕c7 8 0-0 += **b5 8 0-0 ♝b7 9 ♛e2 e5 10 ♞b3 ♞bd7 11 ♝d2 ♝e7 12 ♞d1!+= ♞c5** 12...♖c8 13 ♘a5 ♗a8 14 a4! += **13 ♞f2?!** 13 ♘xc5! dxc5 14 fxe5 ♕d4+ 15 ♗e3 ♕xe5 16 ♗xb5! +=; 14...c4 15 exf6 cxd3 16 cxd3! ♗xf6 17 ♗c3 +=; 14...♘d7!? **♞xd3 14 cxd3 ♜c8 15 a4 ♝c6 16 ♞a5 ♝d7 17 axb5 axb5** 17...♗xb5!? **18 ♝b4 ♛b6** 18...0-0? 19 fxe5 dxe5 20 ♘b7 ♕e8 21 ♘xd6 ♗xd6 22 ♗xd6± **19 ♚h1 += exf4 20 e5!** 20 ♕f3 0-0 21 ♕xf4 +=; 20...♕e3! =+ **dxe5 21 ♝xe7 ♚xe7 22 ♛xe5+ ♝e6 23 ♞e4** 23 ♕xf4 ♖hd8 =+ **♜hd8!** 23...♘xe4 24 dxe4 f6 25 ♕xf4 += **24 ♞xf6 gxf6 25 ♛xf4 ♛d4! =+ 26 ♛f3 ♝d5 27 ♛e2+ ♚d7** 27...♕e5 28 ♕f2!+=; 27...♔f8?! 28 ♕h5! **28 ♜ad1 ♜g8?!** 28...♖e8! 29 ♕d2 ♖g8 30 ♖f2 ♖g5∓ **29 ♜f2 ♜ce8 30 ♛f1 ♜e5 31 ♞c4! ♜eg5 32 ♜dd2 ♚c7∓ 33 ♞a3** Zeitnot **♝c6 34 ♞c2** 34 ♘b1 b4! **♛xb2! 35 ♞e1 ♛a1 −+ 36 ♜xf6 ♜c5!** Δ ♖c1 **37 ♞c2 ♛xf1+ 38 ♜xf1 ♜xg2 39 ♜xf7+ ♚d8 40 ♜xg2 ♜xc2 41 ♜fg7 ♜xg2 0-1** 42 ♖xg2 b4 −+ **Gufeld**

208 Kagan-Shamkovich
Hastings 77/8

1 e4 c5 2 ♞f3 d6 3 d4 cxd4 4 ♞xd4 ♞f6 5 ♞c3 a6 6 g3 e6 7 ♝g2 ♛c7 8 0-0 ♝e7 9 ♞ce2 9 ♘de2!? Δ h3, g4, ♘g3 **0-0 10 b3 e5! 11 ♞f5 ♝xf5 12 exf5 d5 13 ♝b2?** 13 ♗xd5 ♖d8 14 c4 ♘c6 15 ♘c3 ♗b4= **♜d8∓ 14 c4?! d4!** 14...dxc4? 15 ♕c2 **15 h3** Δ g4 **h5! 16 ♚h1? ♞c6 17 a3 ♛c8 18 ♛d3**

Diagram

18...e4! 19 ♝xe4 ♞e5 20 ♛b1 d3! 21 ♝xe5 21 ♘c3 ♘xe4 22 ♘xe4 ♕xf5 −+ **♞xe4 22 ♞f4 ♛xf5 23 ♛b2** Δ ♗xg7 **f6 24 ♝d4 ♝d6 25 ♚g2 ♝xf4 26 gxf4 ♛xf4 −+ 27 ♝e3 ♛f5 28 ♜ad1 ♞g5! 29 ♝xg5 ♛xg5+ 30 ♚h2 ♛f4+ 31**

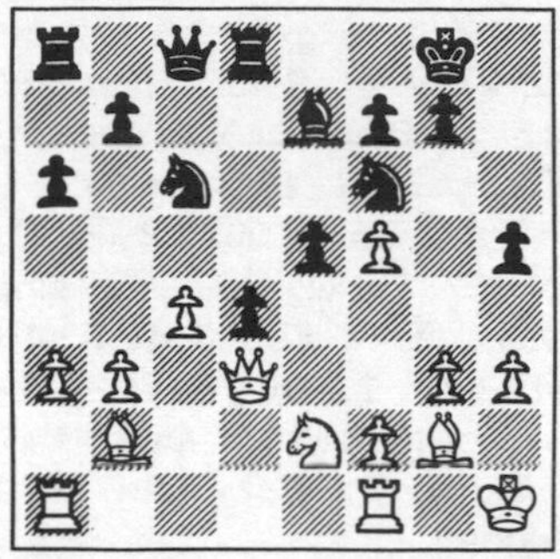

♔g2 d2 32 ♕c2 ♖ac8 33 ♖g1 ♖c5 34 ♔f1 ♖f5 35 ♖g2 h4! 36 b4 ♖d4 37 c5 ♕f3! 38 ♔g1 38 ♖xd2 ♖xd2 39 ♕xd2 ♖d5 –+ **♖e5** Δ ♖e1+ **39 ♔h2 ♕f4+ 40 ♔h1 ♖e1+ 41 ♖g1 ♕f3+ 0-1 Shamkovich**

209 Katalymov-Gofshtein USSR 77

1 e4 c5 2 ♘f3 d6 3 d4 cxd4 4 ♘xd4 ♘f6 5 ♘c3 a6 6 ♗g5 e6 7 ♕d3 b5 7... ♗e7 8 0-0-0 h6 9 ♗h4 ♘bd7 **8 f4 ♘bd7 9 0-0-0 ♗b7 10 e5** 10 a3 ♖c8 =+ **dxe5 11 fxe5 ♘xe5 12 ♕g3 ♘ed7 13 ♘cxb5?!** 13 ♗xf6 gxf6 14 ♗e2∞; 13 ♘dxb5 axb5 14 ♗xb5 ♗c8 15 ♖d2 ♗e7 16 ♖hd1 h6∞ **axb5 14 ♗xb5 ♖xa2! 15 ♔b1** 15 ♘b3 ♕a8! 16 ♖xd7 ♘xd7 17 ♖d1 ♖a1+! 18 ♘xa1 ♕xa1+ 19 ♔d2 ♕a5+ 20 ♔c1! ♕xb5 21 ♕b8+! ♘xb8 22 ♖d8 mate; 20... ♕a1+!=; 16 ♗xf6 ♖a1+ 17 ♔d2 ♖xd1+ 18 ♖xd1 gxf6 19 ♕c7 ♕c8!∓ **♕a8! 16 ♘b3 ♗d5 17 ♗xf6 ♖a1+! 18 ♘xa1 ♕a2+ 19 ♔c1 ♕xa1+ 20 ♔d2 ♕a5+ 21 ♗c3 ♕xb5 =+ 22 ♖hf1 ♘f6 23 ♔c1 ♗e7 24 ♔b1** 24 ♕xg7 ♖g8 25 ♕h6 ♖g6∓ **♘e4 25 ♕xg7 ♘xc3+ 26 ♕xc3 0-0 27 ♕g3+ ♔h8 28 ♖f4 f5 29 b3 ♗f6!∓ 30 c4 ♕a5 31 cxd5 ♕a1+ 32 ♔c2 ♕b2+ 33 ♔d3 ♖c8! 34 ♖d2 ♖c3+ 35 ♔e2 ♖xg3 36 hxg3** 36 ♖xb2 ♖xg2+ 37 ♔f3 (37 ♔f1!?) ♖xb2 38 dxe6 ♖xb3+ 39 ♔g2 ♖b5∓ **♕xb3 37 dxe6 ♕xg3 38 ♖f2 ♕e5+ 39 ♔f1 ♕a1+ 40 ♔e2 ♕a6+ 41 ♔e1 ♕xe6+! 42 ♖de2** 42 ♔f1 ♕c4+ 43 ♔e1 ♕c1+ 44 ♖d1 ♗c3+ 45 ♔e2 ♕c2+ –+ **♕d5** Δ ♗c3+, ♕d1+ **43 ♔f1** 43 ♖e8+ ♔g7 44 ♖fe2 ♗h4 –+ **♗h4 44 ♖d2 ♕c4+ 0-1 Gufeld**

210 Lanka-Feldman corr. 77

1 e4 c5 2 ♘f3 d6 3 d4 cxd4 4 ♘xd4 ♘f6 5 ♘c3 a6 6 ♗g5 e6 7 f4 b5 8 e5 dxe5 9 fxe5 ♕c7 10 ♕e2 ♘fd7 11 0-0-0 ♗b7 12 ♕g4 12 ♕h5 g6 13 ♕h4 ♗g7 14 ♗e7 ♕xe5 15 ♗xb5 ♕h5! 16 ♗xd7+ ♘xd7 17 ♕xh5 gxh5 18 ♗g5? ♖g8 19 ♗h4 ♗e5∓ Quinteros-Polugaevsky, Manila 75; **♕xe5** 12... ♕b6 13 ♗e2 ♘xe5 14 ♕h3 (14 ♕h5!?) ♘bd7 15 ♖he1 h6 16 ♗h4 g5 17 ♗xg5 ♖g8 Kavalek-Polugaevsky, Manila 75; 18 ♗h4 ♗xg2 19 ♕e3 ♗c5 20 ♗h5∞ **13 ♗d3** 13 ♗xb5 axb5 14 ♘cxb5 h5? 15 ♘c7+!! +– Vereznik-Iznjin, USSR 76; 14 ♖he1 h5 15 ♕h4 ♕c5 16 ♘cxb5 ♗d5 17 ♖d3 ♘a6 18 a3!± Torre-Mariotti, Manila 76 **h6 14 ♗h4 g5 15 ♗g3** 15 ♖he1 h5! 16 ♕xg5 ♗h6 17 ♘xe6 Ljubojevic-Mariotti, Manila 76 ∞ Minic **♕e3+ 16 ♔b1 h5 17 ♖he1 ♕xe1 18 ♕xg5 ♗h6 19 ♕xh5 ♕e3 20 ♘xe6 ♕xe6 21 ♖e1 ♕xe1+ 22 ♗xe1 ♗g7 23 ♕g4 ♔f8!** 23...0-0 24 ♕h4!± Litvinov-Zarenko, USSR 73 **24 ♘e4 ♖h6 25 ♗b4+ ♔g8 26 ♗c3 ♖g6 27 ♘g5 ♘f6 28 ♕f4 ♖xg5 29 ♕xg5 ♘bd7 30 ♗f5 b4! 31 ♗xb4 ♖e8 32 ♗c3 ♘e5 33 h4 ♘e4?** 33...♘d5 34 ♗xe5 ♖xe5 35 ♕d8+ ♗f8 36 ♕g5+ ♗g7 37 ♕d8+ = **34 ♗xe4! ♗xe4 35 h5 ♔h7 36 ♕g5 ♗g7 37 ♕f4 ♗d5 38 g5 ♔g8 39 ♕d4 ♗f3 40 h6 ♗h8 41 ♕f4 ♗h5 42 a4 +– ♗g6 43 b4! f6 44 b5 axb5 45 axb5 fxg5 46 ♕b4! g4?**

47 b6 g3 48 b7 g2 49 b8♛+ 1-0 Gipslis

211 Matulovic-Bohmfeld
Dortmund 77

1 e4 c5 2 ♞f3 d6 3 d4 cxd4 4 ♞xd4 ♞f6 5 ♞c3 a6 6 ♝g5 e6 7 f4 b5!? 8 e5 dxe5 9 fxe5 ♛c7 10 exf6 ♛e5+ 11 ♝e2 ♛xg5 12 ♛d3 ♛xf6 13 ♜f1 ♛g6!? 13...♕e5 14 0-0-0 ♖a7 15 ♘f3 ♕f4+ 16 ♘d2 ♕c7 17 ♗h5 Gheorghiu-Ljubojevic, IBM 75; 17 ♘de4!? **14 ♛e3 ♝c5 15 ♝f3 ♜a7 16 ♞e4 ♝b4+ 17 c3 ♝e7 18 ♞xe6! ♛xe6 19 ♛xa7 ♞c6 20 ♛c7 f5 21 0-0-0 fxe4**

22 ♜fe1!± N 22 ♗h5+ g6 23 ♗g4 ♕xg4 24 ♕xc6+ ♗d7 25 ♖xd7! ♕xd7 26 ♕a8+ ♕d8 27 ♕c6+ = Matulovic-Polugaevsky, Belgrade-Moscow 74 **0-0?** 22...♕h6+!? 23 ♔b1 ♗f5 24 ♗xe4 ♗xe4+ 25 ♖xe4 0-0 26 ♖xe7 ♘xe7 27 ♕xe7 ♕xh2 28 ♕e6+ ♔h8 29 ♕xa6± **23 ♝xe4 ♛h6+** 23...♗g5+ Δ ♘e7 **24 ♚b1 ♝g4? 25 ♝xc6 ♝xd1 26 ♝d5+ 1-0 Maric**

212 Tratatovici-Urzica
Rumania Final 77

1 e4 c5 2 ♞f3 d6 3 d4 cxd4 4 ♞xd4 ♞f6 5 ♞c3 a6 6 ♝g5 e6 7 f4 ♛b6 8 ♛d2 ♛xb2 9 ♜b1 9 ♘b3 ♕a3; 9 ♘b3 ♘bd7! 10 ♗xf6 gxf6 11 ♗e2 b5 12 0-0 ♗b7 Δ ♖ac8 Timman **♛a3 10 f5 ♞c6 11 fxe6 fxe6 12 ♞xc6 bxc6 13 e5 dxe5 14 ♝xf6 gxf6 15 ♞e4 ♝e7 16 ♝e2 h5 17 0-0?!** 17 ♖b3 ♕a4 18 c4 f5 19 ♘g3 h4 20 ♘h5!?∞ Bronstein **f5 18 ♜b3 ♛a4 19 c4 fxe4 20 ♛d1 ♝c5+ 21 ♚h1 ♝d4! 22 ♝xh5+ ♚d8 23 ♛g4 ♜a7 24 ♛g5+ ♜e7 25 ♜d1 ♛xc4! 26 ♜c1 ♜f8!** Δ ♖f1+ **0-1 Pavlov**

213 A.Rodriguez-Marjanovic
Vrnjacka Banja 77

1 e4 c5 2 ♞f3 d6 3 d4 ♞f6 4 ♞c3 cxd4 5 ♞xd4 a6 6 ♝g5 e6 7 f4 ♛b6 8 ♛d2 ♛xb2 9 ♞b3 ♞c6 9...♕a3 Fischer **10 ♝xf6 gxf6 11 ♞a4!? ♛a3 12 ♞b6 ♜b8 13 ♞c4 ♛a4 14 ♝e2! d5** 14... b5 15 ♘xd6+ ♗xd6 16 ♕xd6 ♕b4+ 17 ♕xb4 ♘xb4 18 ♔f2+= **15 exd5 exd5 16 ♞b6 ♛b4 17 ♞xd5 ♛xd2+ 18 ♚xd2 ♝g7 19 ♚e3!± 0-0 20 c4 a5 21 a4 ♜e8+ 22 ♚f2 ♝f5 23 ♜ac1 ♝e4 24 ♝f3 f5 25 ♝xe4 ♜xe4 26 ♜he1 ♜be8 27 ♜xe4 fxe4 28 ♚e3! f5 29 h3 h5 30 g4! hxg4 31 hxg4 fxg4 32 ♜g1 ♚f7 33 ♜xg4 ♝h6 34 ♜h4 ♝g7 35 ♞c7 ♜d8 36 ♞d5 ♜e8 37 ♜h5 ♝b2 38 ♞c7 ♜g8 39 ♚xe4 ♜g3 40 ♜b5 ♜c3 41 c5!+− ♜c4+ 42 ♚f3 ♜xa4 43 ♜xb7 ♞d8 44 ♜a7 ♞c6 45 ♜a6 ♜a3 46 ♜xc6 a4 47 ♚e4 axb3 48 ♞d5 ♝h8 49 ♜b6 b2 50 c6 ♜a6 51 ♜b7+ ♚f8 52 c7 ♜c6 53 f5 ♝c3 54 ♞f4! ♚e8 55 ♞e6 ♝a5** 55...♗f6? 56 ♔d5 Δ ♘c5 +− **56 ♜b8+ ♚d7 57 ♜xb2 ♚d6 58 ♜b7 ♜c4+ 59 ♚f3 ♜c1 60 ♜a7 1-0 Maric**

214 Efimov-Kengis USSR 77

1 e4 c5 2 ♞f3 d6 3 d4 cxd4 4 ♞xd4 ♞f6 5 ♞c3 a6 6 ♝g5 e6 7 f4 ♛c7 7... ♘bd7; 7...b5 **8 ♝xf6 gxf6 9 ♝e2 b5**

10 ♗h5 b4 11 ♘ce2 ♗g7 12 f5 += 0-0 13 fxe6 fxe6 14 ♘f4 ♕e7 14...e5 15 ♘d5 **15 0-0 a5!?** N 15...e5 16 ♘d5 ♕d8 17 ♘f5 **16 ♔h1 ♘a6 17 ♕g4!± ♘c7 18 ♖ae1 ♔h8?** 18...a4 (Δ ♖a5-g5) 19 ♖e3 ♗d7 20 ♕h4 ♖a5? 21 ♘g6! ♕f7 22 ♘e5 +−; 21...hxg6 22 ♗xg6 ♗h8 23 ♘f5 +− **19 ♕h4** Δ ♘g6+ **♔g8 20 ♖e3 e5 21 ♘c6 ♕d7 22 ♘d5 +− ♘xd5 23 exd5 f5 24 ♘e7+ ♔h8 25 ♗g6 1-0 Gufeld**

215 Timman-Mecking
Wijk aan Zee 78

1 e4 c5 2 ♘f3 d6 3 d4 cxd4 4 ♘xd4 ♘f6 5 ♘c3 a6 6 ♗g5 e6 7 f4 ♘bd7 8 ♕f3 ♕c7 9 0-0-0 b5 10 ♗d3 10 e5 ♗b7 11 ♕h3 dxe5 12 ♘xe6 fxe6 13 ♕xe6+ ♗e7∞; 10 ♗xb5!? **♗b7 11 ♖he1 ♕b6** 11...b4? 12 ♘d5! exd5 13 exd5+ ♔d8 14 ♗f5! ♗e7 15 ♗e6!± Kavalek-Gheorghiu, Skopje 72; 11... 0-0-0 12 ♔b1 +=; 11...h6 12 ♕h3! **12 ♘b3 b4 13 ♘a4 ♕c7 14 ♘d4 ♗e7 15 ♕h3 0-0-0** N 15...♘c5 16 ♘xc5 dxc5 17 ♘xe6 fxe6 18 ♗c4!± Spassky-Tukmakov 73 **16 f5 ♘c5?!** 16...e5!?

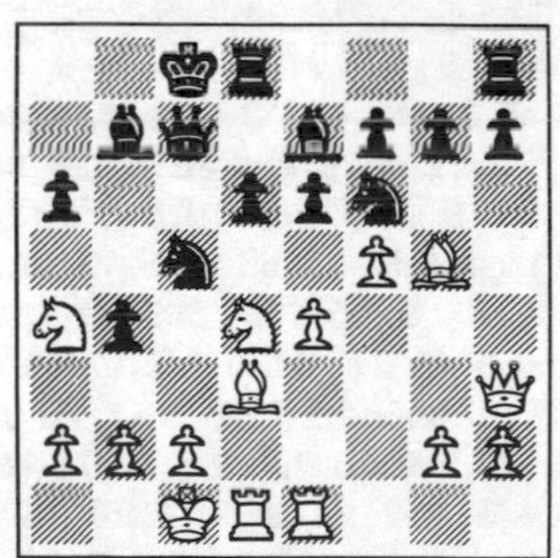

17 fxe6! 17 ♘xc5 dxc5∓ **♘xa4 18 exf7+ ♔b8 19 ♘e6 ♕a5! 20 e5 ♖c8 21 exf6 gxf6 22 ♗f4 ♘xb2?** 22... ♘c3!!∞ **23 ♔xb2 ♖c3 42 ♔c1 ♖hc8 25 ♘d4! ♗f8 26 ♖e8 ♕xa2 27 ♖xf8 ♖xf8 28 ♗xd6+ ♔a8 29 ♗xf8 ♕xf7 30 ♗xb4 +− ♖c7 31 ♕e6 ♕g7 32 ♗e4 ♕g5+ 33 ♔b2 ♗xe4 34 ♕xa6+! ♔b8 35 ♗d6 1-0 Pytel**

216 Saharov-V.Zuravlev corr. 76/77

1 e4 c5 2 ♘f3 d6 3 d4 cxd4 4 ♘xd4 ♘f6 5 ♘c3 a6 6 ♗g5 e6 7 f4 ♗e7 8 ♕f3 ♕c7 9 0-0-0 ♘bd7 10 ♗d3 b5 10...b6? 11 ♖he1 ♗b7 12 ♕g3 0-0-0 13 ♗xf6 ♗xf6 14 ♗xa6±; 12...h6 13 ♗h4 g5 14 fxg5 ♖g8 15 g6! ♖xg6 16 ♘xe6 ♕c6 17 ♕h3 fxe6 18 e5±; 12...h6 13 ♗h4 e5 14 ♘f5! exf4 15 ♕xg7! ♖h7 16 ♕xh7 ♘xh7 17 ♗xe7± Sakharov-Buben, corr. 75 **11 ♖he1 ♗b7 12 ♕g3 b4!** 12...0-0-0 13 ♗xb5!± **13 ♘d5 exd5 14 e5** 14 exd5 ♔d8 15 ♕e3 ♖e8 16 ♘f5 +=; 15...♘b6! =+ **dxe5 15 fxe5 ♘h5** 15...♘e4? **16 ♕h4** 16 e6= **♗xg5+ 17 ♕xg5 g6 18 e6 ♕f4+?** 18...♘df6 19 exf7+ ♔xf7 20 ♘e6 ♕d6 21 ♕h6∞; 18...♘c5 19 exf7+ ♔xf7 20 ♖f1+ ♔g8 21 ♘f5 ♘e6=; 19...♔f8!? 20 ♔b1!? Δ g4 **19 ♕xf4 ♘xf4 20 exd7+ ♔xd7 21 ♖f1 += ♘xd3+ 22 ♖xd3 ♖hf8** 22...f5 23 g4± **23 ♖df3 ♔e7 24 ♖e3+ ♔d7 25 ♖f6 a5 26 ♖ef3 ♔e7 27 ♖b6 ♗c8 28 ♖e3+ ♔d7?** 28...♗e6 29 ♘xe6 fxe6 30 ♖exe6+ ♔f7 31 ♖ed6 ♖ad8 32 ♖xd8 ♖xd8 33 ♖a6±; 31...♔g8!; 31 ♔d2 += **29 ♖e5 +− ♖e8 30 ♖xd5+ ♔e7 31 ♘c6+ 1-0 Gufeld**

217 Biriescu-Georgescu
Rumania Final 77

1 e4 c5 2 ♘f3 d6 3 d4 ♘f6 4 ♘c3 cxd4 5 ♘xd4 5 ♕xd4 a6! 6 ♗g5 ♘c6 7 ♕d2 e6 8 0-0-0 h6 9 ♗h4 b5 10 ♗d3 Ciocaltea-Ungureanu, Rumania Final 77 **a6 6 ♗g5 e6 7 f4 ♗e7 8 ♕f3 ♕c7 9 0-0-0 ♘bd7 10 ♗d3** 10 ♗e2?!; 10 ♕g3!? **h6 11 ♗h4?!** 11 h4!? ♘c5! 12

f5!; 11...♕b6? 12 ♘de2 ♘f8 13 ♗xf6 ♗xf6 14 e5 += Velimirovic-Garcia 75; 11 ♕h3! ♘b6 12 f5 e5 13 ♘de2 ♗d7 14 ♔b1 ♗c6! **g5! 12 e5?!** 12 fxg5 ♘e5 13 ♕e2 ♘fg4 14 ♘f3 hxg5 15 ♗g3 ♗d7 16 h3 ♘xf3 17 hxg4! ♘h4 18 ♖h3 0-0-0 19 ♗xa6 bxa6 20 ♗xh4 gxh4! 21 ♘d5 exd5 22 ♖c3 ♕xc3 23 ♕xa6+ = Estrin-Alexeev 76 **gxh4! 13 exf6 ♞xf6 14 f5 e5 15 ♞de2 ♝d7 16 ♞e4 d5!!** TN **17 ♞xf6+ ♝xf6 18 ♛xd5 =+** 18 ♘c3?! ♗g5+! 19 ♔b1 d4 20 ♘d5 ♕d6 21 f6 ♗c6 22 ♗e4 ♖d8 23 ♘c3 ♕xf6! 24 ♗xc6+ bxc6 =+ 25 ♕xf6 ♗xf6 26 ♘e4 ♗e7 27 ♖f1 0-0 28 ♖f5 f6; 20 ♘e4 f6 21 ♗c4 0-0-0; 21 g3!? **♝c6 19 ♛c5 0-0-0** Δ ♗xg2, h3 **20 ♜hg1 ♚b8 21 g3 h3! 22 ♜ge1 ♝g5+ 23 ♚b1 ♝f3! 24 ♛xc7+ ♚xc7 −+ 25 a4 ♜d7 26 ♝c4 ♝d2! 27 ♞g1** 27 ♖g1 ♖hd8 **♝xd1! 28 ♜xd1 ♜hd8 29 ♞xh3 ♝e3 30 ♜d3 ♜xd3 31 cxd3 f6 32 ♚c2 ♚c6 33 b4 b5 34 axb5 axb5 0-1** 35 ♗e6 ♖a8 Δ ♖a1-h1 **Pavlov**

218 Lanka-Bangiev corr. 76/77

1 e4 c5 2 ♞f3 d6 3 d4 cxd4 4 ♞xd4 ♞f6 5 ♞c3 a6 6 ♝g5 e6 7 f4 ♝e7 8 ♛f3 ♛c7 9 0-0-0 ♞bd7 10 ♛g3!? 10 g4; 10 ♗d3 **h6!** 10...b5? 11 ♗xf6 ♗xf6 12 ♗xb5 axb5 13 ♘dxb5±; 11...gxf6 += **11 ♝h4** 11 ♗xf6 ♗xf6! **g5!? 12 fxg5 ♞h5** 12...♖g8?! 13 ♗e2± **13 ♛e3** 13 ♕g4?! hxg5 14 ♗xg5 ♘e5 15 ♕h4 ♘g6= **♛c5 14 ♚b1 hxg5 15 ♝f2 ♞e5 16 ♛d2 ♛c7 17 ♞f3 ♜g8?!** 17...♘xf3! 18 gxf3 ♗d7= **18 ♞xe5 dxe5 19 ♝e2** 19 ♘a4?! b5 20 ♘b6 ♖b8 =+ **♞f6?!** 19...♘f4! **20 ♝e3 ♞d7 21 ♜hf1! ♜g7** 21...b5 22 ♘d5! exd5 23 ♕xd5± **22 ♝h5 b5?!** 22...♘f6 23 g4 ♘xh5 24 gxh5 f6 25 ♕e2 Δ h6, ♕h5±

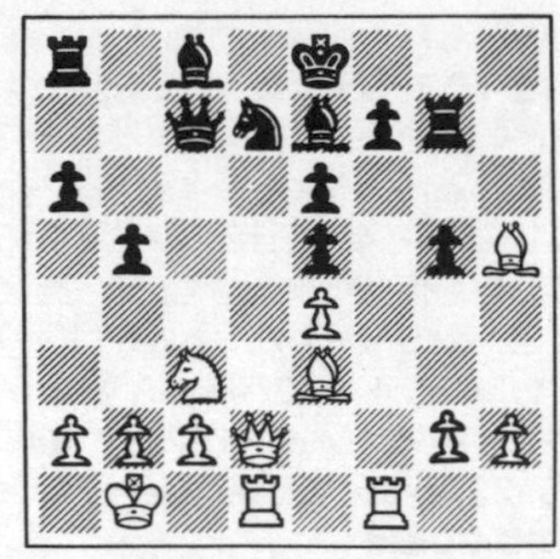

27 ♜xf7! ♜xf7 24 ♛f2 ♞f6 25 ♜f1 Δ ♗xg5 **♝d7** 25...♗b7!? **26 ♝xf7+** 26 ♗xg5 0-0-0! 27 ♗xf7 ♖f8! =+ **♚xf7 27 ♝xg5 ♛d8 28 g4! ♚g6 29 ♝xf6 ♝xf6 30 g5! ♝xg5 31 ♛f7+± ♚h6 32 h4! ♝xh4** 32...♗f4 33 ♖g1 +− **33 ♜g1! ♝g5?** 33...♕f6± **34 ♜d1! ♝e7** 34...♖a7 35 ♖h1+ ♗h4 36 ♕f2 +− **35 ♞e2 ♜c8 36 ♞g3 ♛e8 37 ♜h1+ ♚g5 38 ♛g7+ 1-0** 38...♔f4 39 ♘e2+ ♔e3 40 ♕g3+ ♔xe4 41 ♕g2+! ♔e3 42 ♖h3+ +− **Gufeld**

Sozin

219 Georgescu-Tratatovici
Rumania Final 77

1 e4 c5 2 ♞f3 ♞c6 3 d4 cxd4 4 ♞xd4 ♞f6 5 ♞c3 d6 6 ♝c4 e6 7 ♝e3 ♝e7 8 ♛e2 0-0 9 ♝b3 ♛c7 10 ♜g1 10 0-0-0 **a6 11 g4 ♞d7 12 g5 ♞c5 13 ♛h5 g6 14 ♛h6 ♞xb3** 14...♖e8 Δ ♗f8∞ **15 axb3 f6 16 0-0-0 b5 17 f4 fxg5 18 f5!± ♞e5 19 fxe6 ♝b7 20 ♝xg5 ♝xg5 21 ♛xg5 b4 22 ♞d5± ♝xd5 23 exd5 ♜f2 24 ♜g2! ♜ff8 25 ♚b1 a5 26 ♜e2 a4 27 e7 ♜fe8 28 ♞f5** 28 ♖xe5 dxe5 29 ♘f5; 29 ♘c6∞ **axb3 29 ♛f6 gxf5 30 ♜g1+ ♞g4 31 ♜xg4+ fxg4 32 ♛e6+ ♚h8 33 cxb3??** 33 ♕f6+ = **♜a1+!! −+ 0-1** 34 ♔xa1 ♕c1+ 35 ♔a2 ♖a8 mate **Gheorghiu**

220 Tratatovici-Stefanov
Rumania Final 77
1 e4 c5 2 ♘f3 d6 3 d4 cxd4 4 ♘xd4 ♘f6 5 ♘c3 ♘c6 6 ♗c4 e6 7 ♗e3 ♗e7 8 ♕e2 a6 9 0-0-0 9 ♗b3 ♕c7 10 ♖g1!? **♕c7 10 ♗b3 0-0 11 ♖hg1 ♘d7 12 ♔b1** Velimirovic **♘c5 13 ♕h5** TN **♗d7 14 g4 ♘xd4?** 14...♖fc8 **15 ♗xd4! f6? 16 ♗xc5!! dxc5** 16...♕xc5 17 ♕xc5 dxc5 18 ♖xd7

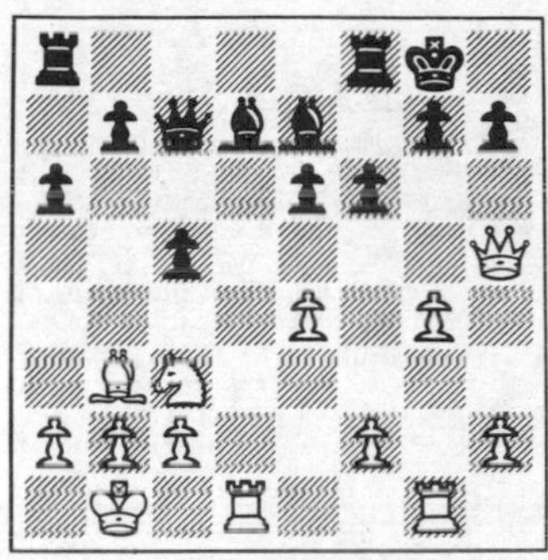

17 ♘d5! +− **exd5** 17...♕d8 18 ♘f4 ♕c8 19 ♖xd7 +− **18 ♕xd5+ ♔h8 19 ♕xd7 ♖ac8 20 ♗e6 ♖fd8 21 ♕xc7 ♖xd1+ 22 ♖xd1 ♖xc7 23 c3 ♖c6 24 ♗d7 ♖c7 25 ♖d5** +− **♔g8 26 ♗e6+ ♔f8 27 h4 ♖c6 28 ♗d7 ♖c7 29 ♔c2 ♔f7 30 ♗f5 g6 31 ♗d7 ♗f8 32 g5 h6 33 gxf6 ♔xf6 34 h5 g5 35 e5+ ♔e7 36 ♗g4 ♔e8 37 e6 b6 38 ♔d3 ♗e7 39 ♔e4 c4 40 ♖d7 ♖xd7 41 exd7+ ♔d8 42 ♔d5 b5 43 ♔c6 1-0 Pavlov**

221 E.Kuzmin-Vdovin corr. 76/77
1 e4 c5 2 ♘f3 ♘c6 3 d4 cxd4 4 ♘xd4 ♘f6 5 ♘c3 d6 6 ♗c4 e6 7 ♗e3 ♗e7 8 ♕e2 a6 9 0-0-0 ♕c7 10 ♗b3 0-0 11 g4 11 ♖hg1 b5 12 g4 b4 13 ♘xc6 ♕xc6 14 ♘d5 exd5 15 g5 ♘xe4 16 ♗xd5 ♕a4 17 ♗xa8! ♘xc3 18 bxc3 ♗e6 19 ♗d4 ♖xa8? 20 g6 +−; 19...bxc3 20 ♗xc3 ♖xa8 += **♘xd4 12 ♖xd4 b5 13 g5 ♘d7 14 ♕h5** 14 ♖g1 g6 15 f4?! ♘c5 16 f5 exf5 17 ♘d5 ♕d8 18 e5 dxe5 19 ♘f6+ ♗xf6 20 ♖xd8 ♘xb3+ 21 axb3 ♗xd8 =+; 15 h4! +=; 14...♘c5!∞ **♖d8 15 ♘d5?! exd5 16 ♗xd5 ♘e5 17 f4** 17 ♗xa8? ♗g4 18 ♕h4 ♗f3 −+ **♗g4** 17...g6? 18 ♕h4 ♘f3 19 ♗xf7+ ♔xf7 20 ♕xh7+ = **18 ♕h4 ♖ac8 19 c3 ♗e6!** 19...♗f3? 20 ♖e1! += **20 ♗xe6** 20 fxe5 dxe5 21 ♗xe6? exd4 −+; 21 ♖dd1 ♗xd5 22 exd5 b4∓; 21 ♖d3 b4∓ **♘g6!∓**

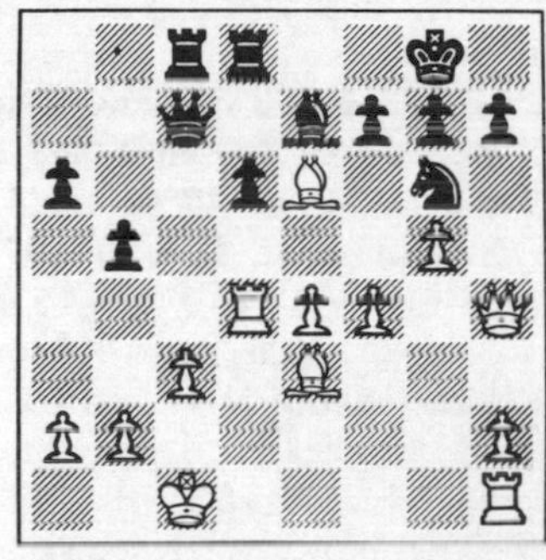

21 ♕g4 fxe6 22 ♕xe6+ ♔h8 23 h4 ♕d7 24 ♕xd7 ♖xd7 25 h5 ♘f8 26 f5 h6?! 27 gxh6 gxh6 28 ♗xh6 ♗f6 29 ♖b4 ♘h7 30 a4 ♖c4 31 ♖xc4 bxc4 32 ♔c2 ♘g5 33 ♗xg5 ♗xg5 34 ♖d1 ♗f4 35 ♖d4 ♖c7 36 b3 cxb3+ 37 ♔xb3 ♔g7 38 ♖c4 ♖b7+ 39 ♔c2 ♗e5 40 ♖c6 a5 41 ♖a6 ♖c7 42 ♖xa5 ♖xc3+ −+ **43 ♔d2 ♖a3 44 ♖a8 ♔h6 45 a5 ♔xh5 46 a6 ♗d4 0-1 Gufeld**

222 Irtaev-Ubilava USSR 77
1 e4 c5 2 ♘f3 d6 3 d4 cxd4 4 ♘xd4 ♘f6 5 ♘c3 ♘c6 6 ♗c4 e6 7 ♗e3 ♗e7 8 ♕e2 a6 9 0-0-0 ♕c7 10 ♗b3 10 ♖g1 0-0 11 g4 ♘xe4 12 ♘xe4 d5 13 ♗d3 dxe4 14 ♗xe4 e5 15 ♘f5 ♗e6∞ **0-0 11 ♖hg1 ♘d7 12 g4** 12 ♔b1 ♘c5 13 ♕h5 Δ g4, ♖g3-h3 **♘c5 13 g5 b5?!** 13...♗d7 14 ♕h5 ♖fc8 15 ♖g3 g6 16 ♕h6 ♗f8 17 ♕h4 ♗e7= **14 ♕h5?!**

14 ♗d5! ♗d7 15 ♘xc6 ♗xc6 16 ♗xc5 dxc5 17 ♗xc6 ♕xc6 18 e5 Δ ♘e4-f6+± **b4 15 ♖g3?!** 15 ♘a4 ♗d7 16 ♘xc5 ♘xd4 17 ♘xd7 ♘xb3+ 18 axb3 ♖fc8 19 ♖d2 ♕d7= **bxc3 16 ♖h3 ♘xb3+ 17 axb3 cxb2+ 18 ♔b1 h6 19 ♘xc6** 19 ♖g1 ♘xd4 20 ♗xd4 e5 21 gxh6 g6 22 ♖xg6+ ♔h8 −+ **♕xc6 20 ♖g1 ♕xe4 −+ 21 g6** 21 gxh6 g6 −+ **e5 22 ♖hg3 ♗f5 0-1 Gufeld**

223 H.Olafsson-Mednis
New York 77
1 e4 c5 2 ♘f3 ♘c6 3 d4 cxd4 4 ♘xd4 ♘f6 5 ♘c3 d6 6 ♗c4 e6 7 ♗e3 ♗e7 8 ♗b3 0-0 9 0-0 a6 10 f4 ♘xd4 11 ♗xd4 b5 12 e5 dxe5 13 fxe5 ♘d7 14 ♘e4 14 ♕h5?! – 13/410 **♗b7 15 ♘d6** 15 ♖f4?! – 13/409 **♗xd6 16 exd6 ♕g5 17 ♖f2! ♖ad8!** N 17...e5 18 ♗c3 += e4? 19 ♕f1± Bangiev-Starin, Volgograd 71; 17...♗d5 18 ♖d2 += Bangiev-Chernikov, Chelyabinsk 75; 17...a5?! 18 a4 ♖a6 19 axb5 ♖xd6 20 ♕d2 ♕g4 21 ♖a4!± Ciric-Suradiradja, Belgrade 77 **18 ♕d2!** 18 ♕e2?! ♗d5! 19 ♖d1 ♗xb3 20 axb3 e5 21 ♗e3 ♕g6 22 c4 f5 =+ **♕xd2 19 ♖xd2 ♘f6! = 20 ♗xf6 gxf6 21 c4!** 21 d7?! ♗d5! **bxc4 22 ♗xc4 ♖d7 23 b4** 23 ♖ad1! ♖c8 24 ♗b3 ♖c5 25 ♖d4! +=; 23...♖fd8! 24 b4 f5! 25 b5 ♖c8= **♖c8 24 ♗b3= ½-½** 24...♖cd8! 25 ♖ad1 ♗d5 26 ♗xd5 ♖xd6 27 ♔f2! exd5= **Mednis**

Richter-Rauzer

224 Dorfman-Gulko (6) 78
1 e4 c5 2 ♘f3 ♘c6 3 d4 cxd4 4 ♘xd4 ♘f6 5 ♘c3 d6 6 ♗g5 ♕b6 7 ♘b3 e6 8 ♗d3 8 ♗e3 ♕c7 9 ♗e2 ♗e7 10 0-0 a6 11 a4 b6 12 f4 0-0 13 ♗f3 ♖b8 14 ♕e2 ♘a5 15 ♘xa5 bxa5 16 ♖ab1 ♖b4 =+ Chekhov-Gulko, USSR 75; 8 g4 a6 9 ♗e3 ♕c7 10 g5 ♘d7 11 f4 b5 12 a3 Vasyukov-Gulko, USSR Final 74; 8 h4; 8 ♗xf6 **a6 9 a4 ♘a5 10 ♗e3 ♕c7 11 ♘xa5 ♕xa5 12 0-0 ♗e7 13 ♕e1 ♗d7** 13...0-0 14 ♘d5 **14 h3 ♖c8 15 f4 ♗c6 16 ♖b1 ♕c7 17 b4 0-0 18 b5**

18...♗xb5! 18...♗d7 19 bxa6! ♕xc3? 20 ♕xc3 ♖xc3 21 axb7; 19...bxa6 20 ♖b3 **19 ♘xb5 axb5 20 ♖xb5 d5 21 e5 ♘e4 22 ♗d4 ♗c5 23 c3 ♕c6 24 ♔h2 b6 25 ♗xe4 dxe4 26 ♗xc5 bxc5 27 ♕e3 ♕d5 28 ♖e1 ♕c4 ½-½**

225 Holmov-Ubilava USSR 77
1 e4 c5 2 ♘f3 ♘c6 3 d4 cxd4 4 ♘xd4 ♘f6 5 ♘c3 d6 6 ♗g5 ♗d7 7 ♕d2 ♖c8 8 ♘b3 8 0-0-0 **h6** 8...a6 **9 ♗xf6** 9 ♗h4 g5! 10 ♗g3 ♗g7 11 0-0-0 h5 12 h4 g4≈ **gxf6 10 f4** 10 ♗d3!? **f5 11 exf5** 11 ♗d3 fxe4 12 ♗xe4 ♗g7∝ **♗xf5 12 ♗d3 ♕d7 13 0-0 ♗g7 14 ♖ae1 0-0 15 ♗xf5** 15 ♘d5!? ♖fe8 16 c4!+= ♗xd3 17 ♕xd3 ♗xb2 18 f5! ∝/+= **♕xf5 16 ♘d5 ♖fe8 17 c3 a5! 18 ♔h1 b5 19 ♘c1 b4 20 c4 ♕b1! 21 b3 ♕b2 22 ♕e3 e6 23 ♘b6 ♖cd8** 23...♖b8 24 f5 ♕d4 25 ♕g3 Δ ♘d7, f6 **24 ♖d1 ♘d4! =+ 25 ♘a4 ♘f5 26 ♕f3 ♕f6 27 ♘e2 d5 28 c5 d4?!** 28... ♖e7 Δ ♖c7, ♗f8∓ **29 ♖d2 ♖e7 30**

♖fd1 ♖c7 31 ♖c1 ♕e7 31...♕g6!? Δ h5, ♕g4 **32 ♕e4 h5 33 ♖d3 ♖d5 34 g3 ♕e8** Zeitnot **35 h3** Zeitnot **♕c6 35 ♔g1 ♘e3 37 ♔f2 h4 38 g4 f5 39 gxf5 ♘xf5 40 ♖g1 ♖f7** 40...♔f8!? Δ ♗f6, ♖g7 =+ **41 ♖g6 ♖f6 42 ♖g5 ♕c7 43 ♔e1 ♔f7 44 ♘b6!? ♖xc5 45 ♘c4 ♖h6 46 ♘g1! ♕c6** 46...♗f6!? 47 ♘f3 ♗xg5 48 fxg5 ♖h5 ∞/=+ **47 ♕xc6 ♖xc6 48 ♘f3 ♖c5? 49 ♘xd4 ♖xc4 50 ♘xf5 ♖e4+ 51 ♘e3 ♗d4 =+ 52 ♔d2 ♖xf4 53 ♘g4 ♖h8 54 ♖xa5 ♖c8 55 ♖b5 ♖e4??** 55...♖a8∓ 56 ♖xb4 ♖xa2+ −+ **56 ♖f3+ ♔g6 57 ♔d3 ♖xg4 58 hxg4 ♖c3+?** 58...e5! 59 ♖xb4 ♔g5 **59 ♔e4 e5 60 ♖xb4 ♖c2 61 ♖b8 1-0 Gufeld**

226 Klovan-Ubilava USSR 77

1 e4 c5 2 ♘f3 d6 3 d4 cxd4 4 ♘xd4 ♘f6 5 ♘c3 ♘c6 6 ♗g5 ♗d7 7 ♕d2 ♖c8 8 0-0-0 ♘xd4 9 ♕xd4 ♕a5 10 ♗d2 10 f4 ♖xc3!? 11 bxc3 e5 12 ♕b4 ♕xb4 13 cxb4 ♘xe4 14 ♗h4 g5! 15 fxg5 ♗e7 ∞/+=; 10 ♗e3 a6 11 ♗c4 b5 12 ♗b3 e6= **e5** 10...a6 11 f3 e5 12 ♕e3 ♗e6 13 a3 ♕c7 14 g4 0-0 15 ♗d3 += **11 ♕d3**

11...♖xc3!? TN **12 ♗xc3** 12 ♕xc3? ♕xa2∓ **♕xa2 13 f3!? g6 14 ♔d2! ♕e6 15 ♔e1!** 15 ♗e2 d5! **♗c6 16 ♗b4 d5 17 ♗xf8 ♔xf8 18 exd5 ♘xd5 19 c4** 19 ♕a3+ ♔g7 20 ♕xa7 ♖c8 ∞/+= **♘f4 20 ♕d6+ ♕xd6 21 ♖xd6 ♔e7 22 ♖d2 a5 23 ♔f2** 23 ♗d3? ♘xg2+ 24 ♖xg2 ♗xf3 25 ♖hg1 ♗xg2 26 ♖xg2 f5∓ **♖c8! 24 g3 ♘e6 25 ♗g2 ♘c5 26 ♖e1 f6 27 ♖e3** 27 f4 e4 28 g4! ∞+= **a4 28 ♗f1 ♗d7 29 ♗e2 h5! 30 ♗d1 ♗e6 31 ♗c2 g5 32 ♖a3 ♗d7 33 b4 axb3 34 ♗xb3 ♗e6 35 ♗a2 ½-½ Gufeld**

227 Radev-Zaichik USSR 77

1 e4 c5 2 ♘f3 d6 3 d4 cxd4 4 ♘xd4 ♘f6 5 ♘c3 ♘c6 6 ♗g5 ♗d7 7 ♕d2 ♖c8 8 0-0-0 ♘xd4 9 ♕xd4 ♕a5 10 f4 10 ♗d2 **♖xc3!? 11 bxc3 e5 12 ♕b4 ♕xb4 13 cxb4 ♘xe4 14 ♗h4 g5 15 fxg5 ♗e7 16 ♗c4 h6 17 ♖hf1 0-0** 17...♗e6!? **18 ♖de1 hxg5 19 ♖xe4 gxh4 20 ♗d5 ♔g7 += 21 ♔b2?! b5! 22 ♖e3 ♗d8 23 ♖a3 ♗b6 24 ♖af3 f5= 25 ♔b1?** 25 ♗e4! ♔g6? 26 g4! +=; 25...f4= **♔g6∓ 26 a3** 26 ♗e4 ♗e6 27 g4 hxg3 28 hxg3 d5∓ **♖c8 27 ♔c1 ♗d4 28 h3 e4∓ 29 ♖b3 ♖e8 30 ♗b7 ♗e6 31 ♖bb1 ♗c4 32 ♖fe1 e3 0-1 Gufeld**

228 Santos-Robatsch Guarda 77

1 e4 c5 2 ♘f3 d6 3 d4 cxd4 4 ♘xd4 ♘f6 5 ♘c3 ♘c6 6 ♗g5 ♗d7 7 ♗e2 ♕a5 8 ♗xf6 gxf6 9 ♘b3 ♕g5 10 ♘d5! ♖c8? 10...0-0-0 Boleslavsky **11 f4? ♕xg2 12 ♗f3 ♕h3! 13 ♕e2 ♕h4+ 14 ♕f2 ♕xf2 15 ♔xf2 ♗h6 16 c3 f5 17 ♖hg1 fxe4 18 ♗xe4 f5?! 19 ♗f3 ♗e6 20 ♖ad1 ♗xd5! 21 ♖xd5** 21...♗xd5!? **♗xf4 22 ♗h5+?! ♔d8 23 ♖xf5?! ♗xh2 24 ♖h1 ♗e5 25 ♗f3 e6 26 ♖fh5 ♖c7 27 ♖h6 ♖e7 28 ♗e4 ♖f8+ 29 ♔e2 ♖f4 30 ♗xh7 ♖g4 31 ♖f1 ♖g2+ 32 ♖f2 ♖xf2+ 33 ♔xf2 ♖f7+ 34 ♔e2 ♔e7 35 ♗d3?!** 35 ♗c2!? **♗g7 36 ♖h3? d5 37 ♖h7! ♘e5 38 ♗c2 ♔d6 39 ♘d4 a6 40 ♗f5? exf5! 41 ♖xg7 f4! 42 ♖g5 f3+ 43 ♔f1 ♘c4 44 ♖g6+ ♔d7 45**

♔f2 ♘xb2 46 ♘xf3 ♘d3+ 0-1 Ochoa

229 Shamkovich-Peters
USA Final 77
1 e4 c5 2 ♘f3 ♘c6 3 d4 cxd4 4 ♘xd4 ♘f6 5 ♘c3 d6 6 ♗g5 e6 7 ♕d2 a6 8 0-0-0 ♗d7 9 f3!? ♗e7 9...h6 10 ♗e3 b5 11 ♘xc6 ♗xc6 12 ♘e2!? e5?! 13 ♘c3± Radulov-Gheorghiu, Athens 76; 12...♗e7 **10 ♗e3 b5** 10...0-0 11 g4 ♘xd4 12 ♗xd4 ♗c6 **11 g4 0-0** 11...♘xd4 12 ♗xd4 b4 13 ♘e2 e5 14 ♗e3 a5∞; 12 ♕xd4!? **12 g5 ♘e8 13 h4 ♘c7 14 ♖g1?** 14 ♘xc6 ♗xc6 15 ♖g1 b4 16 ♘e2± **b4?** 14...♘xd4! 15 ♗xd4 b4 16 ♘e2 ♘b5!= **15 ♘xc6! ♗xc6 16 ♘e2 d5?** 16...e5!? **17 ♘d4 ♗b7 18 e5±** Δ f4-f5; Δ h5, g6 **g6 19 h5 ♖e8 20 ♖h1 +− ♗f8 21 ♕h2 ♗g7 22 hxg6 hxg6 23 ♘b3! a5 24 ♕h7+ ♔f8 25 ♗c5+ ♖e7 26 f4** 26 ♕h8+! ♗xh8 27 ♖xh8+ ♔g7 28 ♖xd8 +− **a4 27 ♘d4 b3 28 a3! 1-0 Shamkovich**

230 Taborov-Zhidkov Kiev 77
1 e4 c5 2 ♘f3 d6 3 d4 cxd4 4 ♘xd4 ♘f6 5 ♘c3 ♘c6 6 ♗g5 e6 7 ♕d2 a6 8 0-0-0 ♗d7 9 f4 9 f3 ♘xd4 10 ♕xd4 ♗e7 11 g4 ♗c6 12 ♗e3 0-0 13 g5 ♘d7 14 h4 b5 15 ♕d2 += **b5 10 ♘xc6** 10 ♗xf6 gxf6 11 f5 ♘xd4 12 ♕xd4 ♗h6+ 13 ♔b1 ♗f4 14 ♕d3 ♗e5 15 ♘e2 ♕b6 16 ♘g1 0-0-0 17 ♘f3= Matanovic-Tal, Kiev 76 **♗xc6 11 ♗d3 ♗e7!** 11...♕a5 += **12 e5?!** 12 ♖he1 0-0 13 e5 dxe5 14 ♕f2!? h6! 15 ♗xf6 ♗xf6 16 fxe5 ♗h4 17 g3 ♗g5+ 18 ♔b1 ♕c7 19 h4= Karpov-Tal, Moscow 76 **dxe5 13 fxe5 ♘d7** 13...♘d5 14 ♘e4 0-0 15 ♗xe7 ♕xe7 16 ♖hf1 += **14 ♗xe7 ♕xe7 15 ♗e4** 15 ♕f4 ♘c5 16 ♘e4 ♗xe4 17 ♗xe4 ♖c8! 18 ♖d6 0-0 19 ♔b1 ♘xe4 20 ♕xe4 ♖c4= Mecking-Polugaevsky (8) 77 **♕c5!** 15...♘xe5? 16 ♕d4! f6 17 ♕xe5!± Boleslavsky; 15...♗xe4 16 ♘xe4 ♘xe5 17 ♘d6+ ♔f8 18 ♖hf1± **16 ♖he1** 16 ♗xc6 ♕xc6 17 ♘e4 0-0! 18 ♕xd7 ♕xe4 =+ **♖c8 17 ♔b1** 17 ♗xc6 ♕xc6 18 ♘e4 0-0 =+ **♖c7 18 ♕d3 h6 19 ♕d6?** 19 ♕g3! 0-0 20 ♗xc6 ♕xc6 21 ♖d4 ♕c5 22 ♖g4! b4 23 ♖xg7+ ♔h8 24 ♖g4 bxc3 25 ♖h4 ♔h7 26 ♕f4±; 21...♘c5! 22 ♖g4 f5!= **♕xd6 =+ 20 exd6** 20 ♖xd6? ♘e5∓ **♖c8 21 ♗xc6 ♖xc6 22 a4** 22 ♘d5? ♖xd6 23 ♘f6+ ♔e7 24 ♖xd6 ♔xd6 25 ♖d1+ ♔e7 26 ♘xd7 ♖d8∓; 23 ♘c7+ ♔e7 24 ♖xd6 ♔xd6 25 ♘xa6 ♖c8 =+ **bxa4 23 ♘xa4 ♘c5** 23...0-0? 24 ♖e3 Δ ♖c3 += **24 ♘xc5 ♖xc5 25 ♖e3 ♔d7 26 ♖a3 ♖a8 27 ♖ad3?** 27 ♖b3! ♖b5! 28 ♖c3 ♖c8 29 ♖xc8 ♔xc8 30 d7+ ♔d8 31 ♖d6 a5 Δ ♖d5 =+ **♖b8 28 ♔c1 ♖b6 29 b3 ♖cc6?** 29...♖h5! 30 h3 ♖c5 Δ ♖cc6 =+ **30 ♖f3 f5 31 ♖g3 g5 32 ♖h3 ♖xd6 33 ♖xh6 ♖xd1+ 34 ♔xd1 ♖d6+ 35 ♔e2 ♖c6 36 ♔d2 ♖d6+ ½-½ Gufeld**

231 Radulov-Ermenkov
Bulgaria 77
1 e4 c5 2 ♘f3 ♘c6 3 d4 cxd4 4 ♘xd4 ♘f6 5 ♘c3 d6 6 ♗g5 e6 7 ♕d2 a6 8 0-0-0 ♗d7 9 f4 b5 10 ♘xc6 ♗xc6 11 ♕e3 ♗e7 12 ♗xf6

12...gxf6 12...♗xf6! 13 e5 ♗e7 14

exd6 ♗xd6 15 ♕d4 ♗f8! 16 ♕e3 ♗d6=; 14 ♕d4 dxe5 15 ♕xe5 ♕b8!= Gufeld **13 f5 ♕a5 14 fxe6 fxe6 15 ♔b1 b4 16 ♘e2 e5 17 ♘g3 d5 18 ♗e2 0-0-0 19 exd5 ♗xd5 20 ♖xd5 ♕xd5 21 ♕a7 ♖d6 22 ♘f5 ♖e8 1-0**

232 Westerinen-Mednis
New York 77

1 e4 c5 2 ♘f3 ♘c6 3 d4 cxd4 4 ♘xd4 ♘f6 5 ♘c3 d6 6 ♗g5 e6 7 ♕d2 a6 8 0-0-0 ♗d7 9 f4 b5 10 ♗xf6 gxf6 11 ♔b1 ♕b6 12 ♘xc6 ♗xc6 13 ♗d3 0-0-0 13...♕c5 14 ♖hf1 0-0-0 15 f5 += Vogt-Bielczyk, DDR-Poland 77 **14 a3?!** 14 ♖hf1 **♔b8?!** 14...d5!=; 14...a5! Δ b4 **15 ♖hf1 h5?!** 15...d5; 15...a5 **16 ♕e2 d5 17 exd5 exd5?!** 17...♗xd5 18 ♘xd5 ♖xd5 19 ♗e4 ♖d6 20 ♗f3 h4 21 ♕e4 ♔c7= **18 ♘a2 += ♗c5?!** 18...a5! 19 b4 ♔c7! **19 ♕f3 ♗b7 20 ♖fe1 ♗c8 21 h3 h4 22 ♖e2 ♗b7 23 ♗f5 ♕c7 24 ♘b4 ♕d6 25 ♘d3 ♗b6 26 ♕f1 ♖de8** 26...a5!? **27 ♖de1 ♕d8 28 ♗g4 ♖e4 29 ♗f3 f5!?** 29...♖c4 30 ♖e7 ♖c7 += **30 ♗xe4 fxe4 31 ♘e5 ♕e7?!** 31...♕c7! += **32 ♖d1** 32 c3!± **♕e6?!** 32...d4! += **33 c3± ♖g8?!** 33...a5! Δ b4 **34 ♘f3! ♕f6 35 ♘d4 ♗c7 36 ♕f2! ♖g7 37 ♖f1 ♗b6 38 ♔a2 ♖g8 39 ♖d1 ♗c7 40 ♖f1 ♗b6 41 ♖d2! ♖g7 42 ♕e2 ♕g6 43 f5 ♕f6 44 ♕h5** +− **♖g8 45 ♖f4 ♖h8 46 ♕e2 ♔a8 47 ♕e3 ♗c7 48 ♖g4 ♗e5 49 ♖d1 ♔b8 50 ♘b3! ♖d8 51 ♕g5 ♕xg5 52 ♖xg5 ♗f6 53 ♖h5 e3 54 ♘d4 ♖e8 55 ♖e1 ♔c7 56 ♔b3 ♗c8 57 ♖e2 ♖g8 58 ♔c2 ♖g3 59 ♖h7 ♔d6 60 ♖xf7 ♗e5 61 ♘f3 ♗f4 62 ♘xh4 1-0 Mednis**

233 Klovan-Tukmakov USSR 77

1 e4 c5 2 ♘f3 d6 3 d4 cxd4 4 ♘xd4 ♘f6 5 ♘c3 ♘c6 6 ♗g5 e6 7 ♕d2 a6 8 0-0-0 ♗d7 9 f4 b5 10 ♗xf6 10 ♘xc6 ♗xc6 11 ♕e1 **gxf6** 10...♕xf6?! e5! **11 ♘xc6** 11 ♔b1 ♕b6 12 ♘ce2!? += **♗xc6 12 ♗d3 ♕b6 13 ♔b1 0-0-0 14 f5 d5! 15 exd5** 15 fxe6 dxe4 16 ♘xe4 ♗xe4 17 ♕c3+ ♗c6 18 ♗e4 ♗c5 19 ♗xc6+ ♕xc6 20 b4 fxe6≈; 17...♕c6 18 ♗xe4 ♖xd1+ 19 ♖xd1 ♕xc3 20 bxc3 fxe6= **exd5 16 ♘e2 d4!** 16...♗d6 17 c3 ♗e5 18 ♘d4! ♗xd4 19 cxd4 ♕xd4 20 ♗xb5!± **17 ♘g3 h5 18 ♖he1** 18 ♗e4?! h4 19 ♗xc6 ♕xc6 20 ♘e2 ♕xg2∓ **♗h6 19 ♕b4 ♗xg2** 19...♗f8!? **20 ♗e4 ♗xe4 21 ♖xe4 ♗e3 22 ♖e7 ♔b8 23 ♖xf7 ♖c8 24 ♘e4** 24 ♕e7 ♖c7 25 ♕xf6 ♕xf6 26 ♖xf6 ♖hc8 ∞/=+ **♕c6 25 ♕d6+ ♕xd6 26 ♘xd6 ♖cf8! 27 ♖b7+ ♔a8 28 ♖b6 ♔a7 29 ♖b7+ ½-½ Gufeld**

234 Tal-Spassov Sochi 77

1 e4 c5 2 ♘f3 d6 3 d4 cxd4 4 ♘xd4 ♘f6 5 ♘c6 ♘c6 6 ♗g5 e6 7 ♕d2 a6 8 0-0-0 ♗d7 9 f4 ♗e7 10 ♗e2!? 0-0 11 ♘f3! N 11 ♗f3? h6 12 ♗h4 ♘xe4 13 ♗xe7 ♘xd2 14 ♗xd8 ♘xf3 15 ♘xf3 ♖fxd8 16 ♖xd6 ♔f8 =+ Fischer-Spassky 72 **♕e8 12 ♗xe7 ♘xe7 13 e5! d5 14 ♗d3± ♕c7 15 g4** Δ ♗xh7+ **f6 16 ♖he1 fxe5 17 ♘xe5 ♖d8 18 ♕f2! ♗c8 19 ♕h4! g6 20 ♕g3** Δ f5, h4-h5 **♘c6 21 f5!** +− **d4 22 ♘xc6 ♕xc6 23 ♘e2! exf5 24 gxf5 ♕d6** 24...♗xf5 25 ♗xf5 ♖xf5 26 ♘xd4 **25 fxg6 hxg6 26 ♕xg6+ ♕xg6 27 ♗xg6 ♖f2 28 ♘xd4 ♘f6 29 ♖e2 ♖f4 30 ♘e6 ♖xd1+ 31 ♔xd1 ♖b4 32 ♔c1 ♘d5 33 ♗f5 ♘f4 34 ♘xf4 ♗xf5 35 ♘d5 1-0 Petrosian**

235 Beljavsky-Tal Leningrad 77

1 e4 c5 2 ♘f3 d6 3 d4 cxd4 4 ♘xd4 ♘f6 5 ♘c3 ♘c6 6 ♗g5 e6 7 ♕d2 7 ♕d3!?∞ **a6 8 0-0-0 ♗d7** 8...h6!?

9 ♗f4; 9 ♗e3!± **9 f4 ♗e7** 9...b5 **10 ♘f3 b5 11 ♗xf6** 11 e5 b4!=+ **gxf6 12 f5 ♕b6 13 ♔b1 0-0-0! 14 g3 ♔b8 15 fxe6 fxe6 16 ♗h3 ♗c8 17 ♕h6 ♕c5! 18 ♖hf1 a5 19 ♘e2** Δ ♘ed4/♘f4 **d5 20 exd5 ♘b4!∓** Tal; ∞ Beljavsky

21 ♘ed4? 21 ♘fd4∞ **♕xd5 22 b3 e5! 23 ♘e6 ♕c6!!** Δ ♕xc2+ −+ **24 c3 0-1** 24...♕e4+! **Gheorghiu**

Scheveningen

236 Sigurjonsson-Olafsson
Reykjavik 78

1 e4 c5 2 ♘f3 ♘c6 3 d4 cxd4 4 ♘xd4 e6 5 ♘c3 d6 6 ♗e3 ♘ge7 6...♘f6 **7 ♘b3 a6 8 a4 b6 9 ♗e2 ♘a5!?** 9...♗b7 Δ ♘c8, ♗e7 **10 0-0 ♘ec6 11 ♘xa5 bxa5!** 11...♘xa5 12 b4± **12 ♗c4 ♗e7 13 f4 0-0 14 ♗b3 ♖b8 15 ♕e2 ♗f6 16 ♖ad1 ♕c7 17 f5! ♖b4! 18 ♕h5! ♕e7** 18...♗xc3?! 19 bxc3 ♖xe4 20 f6± **19 ♖f3** Δ ♖h3 **g6 20 ♕h6 ♗g7 21 ♕h3 exf5! 22 exf5** 22 ♘d5 ♕xe4∓ **♘d4 23 ♘d5 ♕e4 24 ♘xb4 axb4!** 24...♘xf3+ 25 ♕xf3 ♕xf3 26 gxf3 axb4 27 fxg6 hxg6 28 ♖xd6± **25 ♗xd4 ♗xd4+ 26 ♔h1 ♗xf5 27 ♖xf5** 27 ♕g3∞ **gxf5 28 ♕g3+ ♔h8 29 ♕xd6 ♖e8 30 ♕xb4 ♗xb2 31 ♕xe4 fxe4 32 ♗xf7 ♖c8 33 ♖e1 ♖xc2 34 g3 ♖c1 ½-½ Sigurjonsson**

237 Gipslis-Tukmakov Parnu 77

1 e4 c5 2 ♘f3 ♘c6 3 d4 cxd4 4 ♘xd4 ♘f6 5 ♘c3 d6 6 ♗e3 ♘g4 6...e5 7 ♘f3 ♗e7 8 ♗c4 h6 9 0-0 0-0 10 ♕e2 ♗g4 11 ♖ad1± Kapengut-Ubilava, USSR 74 **7 ♗b5 ♘xe3 8 fxe3 ♗d7 9 ♗xc6** 9 0-0!? **bxc6 10 0-0 e6** 10...e5!? **11 e5 ♗e7** 11...d5 12 ♕f3 ♕e7 13 b4! Δ b5± **12 ♕h5 0-0 13 exd6 ♗xd6 14 ♘e4 ♗e7 15 ♖ad1 ♕b6** 15...♕c7 16 ♘g5 ♗xg5 17 ♕xg5 e5 18 ♘b3 f6 19 ♕g3 ♗e6 20 ♘c5 ♕e7 21 b4!± Gipslis-Spassov, Budapest 77 **16 ♖f3 ♗e8!** N 16...♕xb2? 17 ♖h3 h6 18 ♖g3 ♔h8 19 ♖f1!± Kordali-Dordevic, corr. 70

17 ♖h3 h6 18 ♖g3 ♔h7 19 ♖f1 ♕d8!∓ 19...♖d8 20 ♖f6! ♖d5 21 ♖xg7+ ♔xg7 22 ♕xh6+ ♔g8 23 ♘g5! +− **20 c4 a5 21 ♕e5** 21 h3!? g6∞ **♖g8 22 ♘xc6?! ♗xc6 23 ♖xf7 ♕d1+ 24 ♔f2** 24 ♖f1 ♕d3 25 ♖f7 ♕b1+!∓ **♕c2+ 25 ♔g1 ♕b1+ 26 ♔f2 ♕c2+ 27 ♔g1 ♕b1+ 28 ♔f2 ♗f8! −+ 29 ♘f6+** 29 ♘g5+ ♔h8 30 ♖c7 ♗e8! −+ **♔h8 30 ♘xg8 ♖d8! −+ 31 ♕c3** 31 ♖gxg7 ♖d2+ 32 ♔g3 ♖xg2+ 33 ♔h4 ♗xg7 34 ♘f6 ♕xb2! −+ **♕d1 32 e4 ♖d2+ 33 ♔e3 ♕e1+ 0-1 Gipslis**

238 Zhidkov-Fojgel USSR 77
1 e4 c5 2 ♘f3 e6 3 d4 cxd4 4 ♘xd4 ♘f6 5 ♘c3 d6 6 f4 ♘c6 6...a6 **7 ♗e3** 7 ♘b3 ♗e7 8 ♗d3∞ **♗d7!?** 7...♗e7 8 ♕f3 e5 9 ♘xc6 bxc6 10 fxe5 dxe5 11 ♗c4 ♗e6= **8 ♕f3 ♘xd4** 8...♗e7 9 ♗c4 ♘a5 10 ♗b3 0-0-0 11 0-0-0 ♘xb3+ 12 axb3 ♕a5 13 ♔b1 ♖fc8 14 g4 += **9 ♗xd4 ♗c6 10 0-0-0 ♕a5 11 ♔b1!?** 11 ♗c4! += **♗e7 12 ♗c4 ♖d8** 12...♘xe4? 13 ♘xe4 d5 14 ♕h5± **13 ♖he1 0-0 14 ♗b3 e5** 14...b5? 15 ♘d5± **15 ♗e3 b5 16 fxe5 dxe5 17 ♗g5 b4?** 17...♖xd1+ 18 ♖xd1 ♖d8 += **18 ♗xf6 ♗xf6 19 ♘d5 ♗xd5 20 ♗xd5± ♕c5 21 ♖f1! a5 22 ♕b3** Δ ♗xf7+! **♖b8 23 ♖f5 ♕a7 24 g4 a4 25 ♕g3 ♖be8 26 g5 ♗d8 27 g6! 1-0 Gufeld**

239 Kuzmin-Kochiev
USSR Final 77
1 e4 c5 2 ♘f3 e6 3 d4 cxd4 4 ♘xd4 ♘c6 5 ♘c3 d6 6 g3 ♘f6 7 ♗g2 ♗d7 8 0-0 ♗e7 9 ♘xc6 9 ♗e3 0-0 10 ♕e2 a6 11 ♘xc6 ♗xc6 12 a4 ♕a5 13 ♖fd1 ♖fd8 14 ♗d4 e5 15 ♗e3 h6 16 ♕c4! ♖dc8 17 ♕b3 ♕d8 18 a5± Kuzmin-Kochiev, Baku 76 **♗xc6 10 ♕e2 0-0 11 a4 ♕c7 12 ♘b5! ♕c8 13 c4 b6± 14 ♗f4 ♖d8 15 ♖fe1 ♘e8 16 h4 a6 17 ♘d4 ♗b7 18 a5 bxa5 19 ♘b3!**

19...♖b8 20 ♘xa5 ♗a8 21 ♖ab1! ♖d7 22 b4 ♗d8 23 ♕a2 h6 24 ♕a4 ♗xa5 25 bxa5 ♖xb1 26 ♖xb1 ♗c6 26...♖c7 27 ♖b4; 26...♖b7 27 ♖b6 **27 ♕a3 e5 28 ♗e3 ♘f6 29 f3 +− ♕c7 30 ♖b6 ♖d8 31 ♖xa6 ♘d7 32 ♗h3 ♕b7 33 ♖a7 ♕b1+ 34 ♕c1 ♕a2 35 ♕d2 ♕a3 36 ♖c7 ♖b8 37 ♖xc6 ♖b2 38 ♕e1 ♕b3 1-0 Petrosian**

240 Shalnev-Podgaets USSR 76
1 e4 c5 2 ♘f3 ♘c6 3 d4 cxd4 4 ♘xd4 ♘f6 5 ♘c3 d6 6 g3 ♗g4 6...e5 7 ♘de2 ♗e7 8 ♗g2 0-0 9 0-0 +=; 6...♘xd4!? Δ g6 **7 f3 ♗d7** 7...♘xd4?! 8 ♕xd4 ♗xf3? 9 ♗b5+ ♘d7 10 0-0± **8 ♗e3** 8 ♗g2 a6 9 ♘b3 **g6** 8...e6 9 ♗g2 a6 **9 ♕d2 ♗g7 10 ♗c4?** 10 g4! += **♖c8 11 ♗b3 ♘e5 12 g4 b5! 13 g5 b4 =+ 14 ♘ce2 ♘h5 15 ♘g3** 15 ♕xb4 a5 16 ♕a3 0-0 Δ a4!∓ **♘xg3 16 hxg3 a5 17 a4 bxa3 18 ♖xa3 a4! 19 ♖xa4** 19 ♗a2 ♕b6 20 c3 ♕xb2! 21 ♕xb2 ♘d3+ 22 ♔e2 ♘xb2 23 ♖b1 ♘c4 24 ♗xc4 ♖xc4 25 ♖b8+ ♗c8 26 ♔d3 0-0!∓; 20 b3 ♕xd4! 21 ♗xd4 ♘xf3+ 22 ♔d1 ♘xd2 23 ♗xg7 ♘xe4 =+; 20 b4 ♕a6∓ **♗xa4 20 ♗xa4+ ♔f8 21 ♗b3 ♘c4 22 ♗xc4 ♖xc4∓ 23 ♔f2 ♕a8 24 c3 ♖a4 25 ♘c2 ♖a2 26 ♘b4 ♖a1 27 ♖xa1 ♕xa1 28 ♔g2 ♗e5! 29 ♘d5** 29 f4 ♗g7 Δ h6∓ **♕b1 30 ♗b6 ♔g7! 31 ♘xe7 ♖a8 32 f4 ♖a2 33 ♗f2 ♕xe4+ 34 ♔h2 ♖a1 −+ 35 ♗g1 ♖e1 36 ♕g2 ♖e2 37 ♗f2 ♗xc3 38 bxc3 ♕xe7 39 g4 ♕e4 40 ♕xe4 ♖xe4 0-1 Gufeld**

Dragon

241 Honfi-Fabian Hungary 77
1 e4 c5 2 ♘f3 ♘c6 3 d4 cxd4 4 ♘xd4 ♘f6 5 ♘c3 g6 6 ♘xc6 bxc6 7 e5 ♘g8 8 ♗c4 ♕a5 9 ♗f4 ♗g7 10 0-0 ♗xe5 11 ♗xe5 11 b4 ♕c7 12 ♘d5 cxd5 13 ♕xd5 ♘f6 14 ♕xf7+ ♔d8∞ Kurajica-

Ostojic, Skopje 69 **♕xe5 12 ♖e1 ♕f4** 12...♕c7? 13 ♕d4 f6 14 ♗xg8 ♖xg8 Fischer-Ostojic 70 15 ♘d5! +−; 12... ♕g7 13 ♕d6 +− **13 ♖e4 ♕f6** 13... ♕c7 14 ♕d4 f6 15 ♗xg8 ♖xg8 16 ♘d5 +− **14 ♖e3! d5 15 ♗xd5! cxd5 16 ♕xd5 ♖b8 17 ♘e4 ♕g7** 17...♕xb2? 18 ♘d6+ ♔d8 19 ♘c4+ +−; 17...♕e6 18 ♘d6+ exd6 19 ♖xe6+ fxe6 20 ♕d4 e5 21 ♕xd6 ♖b5 22 c4 +−; 19... ♗xe6 20 ♕d4 f6 21 ♖e1 ♔f7 22 ♕xa7+ ♘e7 23 ♕e3 +− **18 ♖b3! ♗b7** 18... ♖xb3 19 ♕c6+ +− **19 ♖xb7 ♖d8 20 ♕b5+ ♔f8 21 ♖b8 ♕d4 22 c3 1-0 Honfi**

242 Timman-Miles
Wijk aan Zee 78

1 e4 c5 2 ♘f3 ♘c6 3 d4 cxd4 4 ♘xd4 g6 5 c4 ♘f6 6 ♘c3 d6 7 ♘c2 ♗g7 8 ♗e2 0-0 9 0-0 ♘d7 10 ♗d2 ♘c5 11 b3 ♗d7 11...a5; 11...♗xc3!? 12 ♗xc3 ♘xe4≈ **12 f3 a5 13 ♔h1 b6?!** 13...♘b4 **14 ♗e1 ♕b8 15 ♖c1 ♕b7 16 ♘d5 f5 17 exf5 ♗xf5 18 ♗f2** 18 ♘ce3!? ♗b2 19 ♘xf5 ♗xc1 20 ♘xd6 ≈ **♖ad8 19 ♘d4 ♘xd4 20 ♗xd4 ♗xd4 21 ♕xd4 e5! += 22 ♕e3 ♗e6 23 ♘c3** 23 ♖cd1 **♗d7 24 ♖cd1 ♗c6 25 ♗d3** 25 ♘d5 **♖f4 26 ♗c2** Δ a3, b4 **b5 27 cxb5 ♗xb5 28 ♖f2 ♗c6 29 ♔g1** 29 ♖fd2? ♗xf3 **♖f6 30 ♖fd2 ♔g7 31 ♘d5 ♗xd5 32 ♖xd5 ♕b6 33 h4 ♖c8 34 ♖1d2 a4?** 34...h5!? += **35 h5 ♘d7 36 h6+ ♔f7 37 ♕xb6 ♘xb6 38 ♖b5 ♘d7 39 ♖b7 ♔e7 40 bxa4?!±** 40 b4! ♖a8 41 ♗e4 ♖b8 42 ♖a7 +− **♖ff8 41 ♗d3 ♖c1+ 42 ♔h2 ♖fc8 43 a5 ♖1c7 44 a6 ♘c5 45 ♖xc7+ ♖xc7 46 ♖b2!** 46 ♗xg6!? hxg6 47 h7 ♖c8 48 a7 ♘a4 49 ♖c2 ♖h8 50 ♖c7+ ♔f6 51 ♔g3 ♘c5 52 a4 Δ a5, a6, ♖b7 ≈ **♘xd3** 46...d5 47 ♗xg6 hxg6 48 h7 ♖c8 49 a7 Δ ♖b8 +−; 47 ♖b6 +− **47 ♖b7 ♔d7 48 a7 ♖xb7 49 a8♕ +− ♖c7** 49...♘c5 50 a4 +− **50 a4 ♘f4 51 a5 ♔e7 52 a6 ♖c2 53 ♕b7+ ♔f6 54 a7 ♔g5 55 ♕e7+ ♔h5 56 a8♕ g5 57 ♕f7+ ♔h4 58 ♕xf4+ exf4 59 ♕b7 ♖e2 60 ♕d7 1-0 Miles**

243 Bukic-Romanishin Moscow 77

1 d4 g6 2 c4 c5 3 ♘f3 cxd4 4 ♘xd4 ♘c6 5 e4 ♘f6 6 ♘c3 d6 7 ♗e2 ♘xd4 8 ♕xd4 ♗g7 9 ♗g5!? ♗e6 10 0-0 10 ♖d1 **0-0 11 ♕d2 ♖c8 12 b3 b5? 13 e5 b4** 13...dxe5?! 14 ♕xd8 ♖fxd8 15 ♘xb5±; 13...♘e8 14 ♘xb5 ♗xe5 15 ♘xa7± **14 exf6 exf6 15 ♗e3± bxc3 16 ♕xc3 f5** 16...d5 17 c5! Δ ♗d4, b4± **17 ♗d4 ♗xd4 18 ♕xd4 ♕a5 19 ♖fd1 ♖fd8** Δ d5 **20 ♗f3 ♖c5?! 21 ♕f6 ♖d7** Δ ♕d8

22 b4!+− ♕xb4 23 ♖db1 ♕xc4 24 ♗e2! 1-0 24...♕c2 25 ♗d3 ♕c3 26 ♖b8+ ♖c8 27 ♕xc3 +− **Maric**

244 Kuligowski-Sznapik (2) 78

1 c4 ♘f6 2 ♘c3 c5 3 ♘f3 g6 4 d4 ♗g7 5 e4 cxd4 6 ♘xd4 ♘c6 7 ♗e3 d6 8 ♗e2 0-0 9 0-0 ♘d7?! 10 ♕d2 ♘c5 11 ♖ad1 ♗d7 12 f4! ♘xd4 13 ♗xd4 ♗xd4+ 14 ♕xd4 ♗c6 15 e5! 15 f5 ♕b6 16 f6? e5! **♕b6 16 exd6 ♖fd8 17 ♘d5! ♗xd5 18 dxe7 ♖e8 19 cxd5 ♖xe7 20 ♗f3 ♕d6!± 21 ♖fe1 ♖ae8 22**

♖xe7 ♖xe7 23 ♖c1 ♘d7?? 23...♖c7! 24 ♕e5?? ♘d3 −+; 24 ♖e1± **24 ♖c8+ 1-0** 24...♘f8 25 ♖xf8+ ♔xf8 26 ♕h8 mate **Kuligowski**

245 Spassky-Miles Bugojno 78
1 e4 c5 2 ♘f3 d6 3 d4 cxd4 4 ♘xd4 ♘f6 5 ♘c3 g6 6 ♗e2 ♗g7 7 ♗e3 0-0 8 0-0 ♘c6 9 ♘b3 ♗e6 10 f4 b5!? N 10... ♘a5; 10...♕c8 **11 f5** 11 ♘xb5 ♘xe4; 11 ♗xb5 ♘g4! **b4** 11...♗d7 12 ♗xb5 **12 fxe6 bxc3 13 exf7+ ♔h8** 13...♖xf7 14 ♗c4 **14 bxc3 += ♘e5 15 ♗d4 ♘xe4 16 ♗f3! ♘xf3+ 17 ♕xf3 ♘f6 18 ♖ad1 ♕c8 19 ♗xf6 ♗xf6 20 ♖xd6! ♖xf7 21 ♖c6 ♕e8 22 ♕e4 ♖d8 23 g3 ♗g7 24 ♕e6 ♖xf1+ 25 ♔xf1 ♗f6 26 ♘c5 ♗xc3 27 ♘e4 ♗d4 28 c3 ♗b6 29 ♔e2! ♕d7 30 ♕xd7 ♖xd7 31 c4 ♖d4? 32 ♘g5 h6? 38 ♖c8+ 1-0** 38...♔g7 39 ♘e6+ **Pytel**

246 Savon-Sosonko Portoroz 77
1 e4 c5 2 ♘f3 d6 3 d4 cxd4 4 ♘xd4 ♘f6 5 ♘c3 g6 6 ♗e2 ♗g7 7 0-0 ♘c6 8 ♘b3 0-0 9 ♗e3 ♗e6 10 f4 ♕c8 11 ♔h1 ♗g4 12 ♗g1 b6 12...♖e8!? **13 ♘d5! ♗xe2 14 ♕xe2 ♕b7 15 ♖ad1 ♖fe8 16 c3± ♖ac8 17 ♗f2 ♘b8 18 ♕f3** 18 ♗h4 ♘bd7 **♕a6 19 ♘xf6+ ♗xf6**

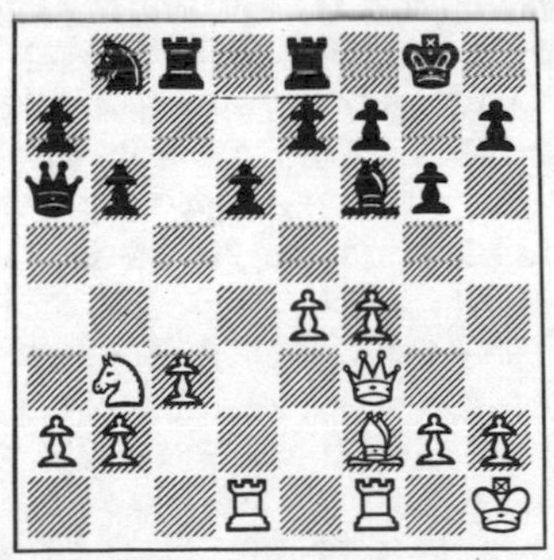

20 e5! ♗g7 20...dxe5? 21 fxe5 ♗xe5 22 ♗d4 +− **21 exd6 ♕xa2 22 ♘c1 ♕c4 23 b3 ♕b5?!** 23...♕a6!? **24 d7 ♘xd7 25 c4 ♕f5 26 g4 ♘e5 27 gxf5 +− ♘xf3 28 ♔g2 ♘xh2 29 ♔xh2 gxf5 30 ♘e2 ♖ed8 31 ♘g3 e6 32 ♘h5 ♗b2 33 ♗h4 ♖xd1 34 ♖xd1 h6 35 ♘f6+ ♔f8 36 ♘d7+ ♔e8 37 ♘e5 a5 38 ♗f6 ♗a3 39 ♖g1 1-0** 39...♔f8 40 ♘d7+ ♔e8 41 ♘xb6 +− **Maric**

247 Dolmatov-Ristic
USSR-Jugoslavia 77
1 e4 c5 2 ♘f3 d6 3 d4 cxd4 4 ♘xd4 ♘f6 5 ♘c3 g6 6 ♗e2 ♗g7 7 0-0 ♘c6 8 ♘b3 0-0 9 ♗g5 ♗e6 10 f4 10 ♔h1 ♘a5 11 f4 ♘a5 10...b5!∞ **11 f5 ♗c4 12 ♔h1 ♖c8 13 ♗d3** 13 e5?! ♗xe2 14 ♘xe2 (14 ♕xe2 dxe5 15 ♖ad1 ♕c7 16 ♗xf6 ♗xf6! 17 ♘d5 ♕c4 =+) ♘e4 (14...♘xb3!?) 15 ♘xa5 ♘xg5 16 f6 (16 ♘xb7!?) ♕xa5 (16...exf6 17 ♘xb7!; 17 exf6∞) 17 fxe7 ♖fe8 18 exd6 ♖b8 19 ♕d3 ♗e5 20 ♖ad1 ♘e6 21 ♕f3 ♘g5 22 ♕e3 f6 23 b4 ♕xb4 24 d7 ♖xe7 25 d8♕+ ♖xd8 26 ♕b3+ ♕xb3 27 ♖xd8+ ♔f7 28 axb3 ♗c7!∞ Dolmatov-Ristic, USSR-Jugoslavia 77 **b5 14 ♕d2 b4 15 ♘e2 d5! 16 ♘xa5 ♕xa5 17 exd5?!** 17 e5 ♘e4 18 ♗xe4 dxe4 19 f6 exf6 20 ♗xf6∞ **♗xd3! 18 ♕xd3 ♕xd5 =+ 19 ♖ac1?! ♕xa2∓ 20 c3 ♖fd8 21 ♕f3 bxc3 22 bxc3 ♕d5! 23 c4 ♕xf3 24 ♖xf3 ♖d7! 25 h3 ♘e4 −+ 26 ♗e3 ♘d2! 27 ♗xd2 ♖xd2 28 ♘f4 ♖d4 29 fxg6 hxg6 30 c5 ♗h6** △ e5 **0-1 Rajkovic**

248 Georgiev-Sequeira Innsbruck 77
1 e4 c5 2 ♘f3 d6 3 d4 cxd4 4 ♘xd4 ♘f6 5 ♘c3 g6 6 ♗e3 ♗g7 7 f3 0-0 8 ♗c4 ♘c6 9 ♕d2 ♗d7 10 h4 ♘e5 11 ♗b3 ♖c8 12 0-0-0 ♘c4 13 ♗xc4 ♖xc4 14 h5 ♘xh5 15 g4 ♘f6 16 ♘de2 ♖e8 17 ♗h6 ♗h8 18 e5 ♘xg4 19 fxg4 ♗xe5 20 ♗f4 ♕a5 21 ♗xe5 ♕xe5 22

♘d5 ♖xg4 23 ♘ec3 ♕g5 24 ♖de1 ♗c6 25 ♕xg5 ♖xg5 26 ♖xe7 26 ♘xe7+?? ♖xe7 **♖xe7 27 ♘xe7+ ♔g7 28 ♖d1 h5 29 ♘xc6 bxc6 30 ♖xd6 h4 31 ♖d3 f5!? 32 ♘e2 ♖g2 33 ♔d1 g5 34 ♔e1 g4 35 b4 h3 36 ♔f1 ♔h6 37 a4 ♔g5 38 b5 cxb5 39 axb5 ♔h4 40 ♖d7 g3 41 ♖xa7 f4! 42 b6 ♖h2 43 ♖h7+ ♔g4 44 ♖g7+ ♔f3 45 ♘g1+ ♔e4 46 ♖e7+ ♔d5 47 ♘xh3 ♖xh3 48 ♖f7 ♔e4 49 b7 f3 50 ♖e7+ ♔d4 51 ♖d7+ ♔e3 52 ♖e7+ ♔d2 53 ♖d7+ ♔c1?** 53...♔xc2! **54 ♔g1 g2 55 ♔f2 ♖h8 56 ♔xf3?? ♔xc2?? = 1-0** time/Zeit **Ochoa**

249 Nunn-Mestel
Hastings 77/78

1 e4 c5 2 ♘f3 d6 3 d4 cxd4 4 ♘xd4 ♘f6 5 ♘c3 g6 6 ♗e3 ♗g7 7 f3 ♘c6 8 ♕d2 ♗d7 9 0-0-0 ♖c8 10 ♔b1 ♘e5 11 ♗h6 ♗xh6 12 ♕xh6 ♖xc3 13 bxc3 ♕b6+ 14 ♔a1 ♕c5 15 ♕d2 15 ♔b2 ♕b6+ = **0-0 16 ♖b1 b6 17 ♗b5?** 17 h3 Δ f4; 17 ♗d3

17...♖c8 18 ♗xd7 ♘fxd7 19 f4 ♘c4 20 ♕c1 a6 20...e5 21 ♖b5 **21 h4 e5 22 fxe5 dxe5 23 ♘e2 ♕f2! 24 ♕d1 ♘c5 25 h5** 25 ♖f1 ♕xg2 26 ♕d5 ♘e6 27 ♖xf7 ♔xf7 28 ♕d7+ ♔f6 Δ ♕xe2 **♘e3 26 ♕d2 ♘xe4 27 ♕d3 ♘xc3! 28 hxg6** 28 ♘xc3 ♘xc2+ 29 ♔b2 ♘b4+ 30 ♕e2 ♘d3+ 31 ♔a1+ ♕d4! −+ **hxg6 29 ♖xb6 e4! 30 ♕xa6 ♘xc2+ 31 ♔b2 ♕xb6+ 0-1**

250 Nicevski-Ubilava USSR 77

1 e4 c5 2 ♘f3 d6 3 d4 cxd4 4 ♘xd4 ♘f6 5 ♘c3 ♘c6 6 f4 g6 7 ♘xc6 bxc6 8 e5 ♘d7 9 ♕f3 9 exd6 exd6 10 ♗e3 **d5!?** N 9...♗g7 10 ♕xc6 ♖b8 11 exd6 0-0∞ **10 h4 h5! 11 ♗e3** 11 e6!? ♘f6 12 exf7+ ♔xf7 13 ♗d3 ♗g4 14 ♕f2 ♕b6= **e6** 11...♘b6 Δ ♗f5 **12 g4?! ♖b8 13 gxh5** 13 0-0-0 ♕a5 14 ♗d2 ♕a3!! −+ **♖xh5** 13...♖xb2? 14 hxg6 fxg6 15 ♗d3± **14 b3 ♗a3! 15 ♘a4 c5 16 ♕g3 ♗a6! 17 ♗g2** 17 ♗xa6 ♕a5+∓ **d4 18 ♗d2 ♗b7 19 ♗xb7 ♖xb7 20 ♕f3 ♕c8 =+ 21 c3 ♘b6 22 cxd4 cxd4 23 0-0?** 23 ♘xb6 axb6 24 0-0 =+ **♘d5∓ 24 ♕d3 ♖xh4 25 ♔g2 ♘e3+ 26 ♗xe3 ♕c6+ 27 ♖f3** 27 ♔g3 ♖g4+ 28 ♔xg4 ♕g2+ 29 ♔h4 ♗e7 mate **♖g4+ 28 ♔f2 dxe3+ 29 ♔xe3** 29 ♕xe3 ♕c2+ −+ **♗c1+ 30 ♔f2 ♖d7 31 ♕c3 ♖d2+ −+ 32 ♔f1 ♖d1+ 33 ♔e2 ♕e4+ 34 ♖e3** 34 ♔xd1 ♖g1+ −+ **♖d2+ 0-1 Gufeld**

251 Zuravlev-Krogius Sochi 77

1 e4 c5 2 ♘f3 d6 3 d4 cxd4 4 ♘xd4 ♘f6 5 ♘c3 g6 6 g3 ♘c6 7 ♗g2 ♘xd4 8 ♕xd4 ♗g7 9 ♗g5 0-0?! 9...h6!? **10 ♕d2 += ♖e8 11 0-0 ♗e6 12 ♘d5 ♗xd5? 13 exd5 ♕c7 14 c3 a5 15 ♖fe1 ♖ab8 16 ♖ac1 b5 17 ♖e2 a4?** 17...♖b7 Δ b4 **18 a3!± ♘g4 19 ♖ce1 ♘e5 20 ♖e4 ♖b7 21 ♕e2 h6 22 ♗c1 ♖bb8 23 ♖h4!** 23 f4 ♘c4 24 ♖xe7!±; 23...f5! 24 ♖e3 ♘g4 Δ ♕c5+ **e6** 23...g5 24 ♖e4 +−; 23...h5± **24 ♗xh6! exd5 25 ♗xg7!! ♔xg7 +−** 25...♘f3+ 26 ♗xf3 ♖xe2 27 ♗f6 ♖xe1+ 28 ♔g2 **26 ♕d2 ♖h8 27 ♖f4 ♖be8 28 ♗xd5 ♖e7 29 ♔g2 ♕d7 30 h4 f6** 30...g5 31 ♖fe4 gxh4 32 ♕g5+ +− **31 ♖d1**

g5 32 ♖xf6 ♖h5 33 hxg5 ♖e8 34 ♔g1 ♖eh8 35 ♕f4 ♕e8 36 ♖xd6 ♖f8 37 ♖f6 1-0 Petrosian

4 ♕xd4

252 Radulov-Inkiov Primorsko 77
1 e4 c5 2 ♘f3 d6 3 d4 cxd4 4 ♕xd4 a6 5 c4 ♘c6 6 ♕d2 g6 7 b3 ♗g7 8 ♗b2 ♘f6 9 ♘c3 ♗g4 10 ♗e2 0-0 11 0-0 ♕a5 12 ♖fd1 ♘d7 13 h3 ♗xf3 14 ♗xf3 ♘c5 15 g3 ♘d4 16 ♗g2 e5 17 ♘d5 ♕xd2 18 ♖xd2 a5 19 ♖ad1 ♘a6 20 ♗c3 ♘c5 21 ♘c7 ♖ac8 22 ♗xa5 ♗h6 23 ♖b2 ♘ce6 24 ♘d5 ♖a8 25 ♗b6 ♖a3 26 ♘c7 ♖c8 27 ♗xd4 ♘xd4 28 ♘b5 ♘xb5 29 cxb5 ♖ca8 30 ♖xd6 ♖xa2 31 ♖xa2 ♖xa2 32 ♖d7 b6 33 ♗f1 ♗f8 34 ♗c4 ♗c5 35 ♖xf7 ♔h8 36 h4 h5 37 ♔f1 ♖d2 38 f4 exf4 39 gxf4 ♖d8 40 f5 gxf5 41 e5 ♖f8 42 ♖b7 ♖e8 43 e6 ♖e7 44 ♖b8+ ♔g7 45 ♔e2 ♔g6 46 b4 ♗d4 47 ♖d8 ♗e5 48 ♖g8+ ♔f6 49 ♖f8+ ♔g6 50 ♖g8+ ♔f6 51 ♖g5 ♖h7 52 ♗d3 ♖h8 53 ♔e3 ♔xe6 54 ♗xf5+ ♔e7 55 ♗g6 ♗f6 56 ♖f5 ♗xh4 57 ♗xh5 ♗e1 58 ♔e4 ♗xh4 59 ♔d5 ♖h6 60 ♖f7+ ♔d8 61 ♗g4 ♖d6+ 62 ♔e5 ♖d2 63 ♗f5 ♗c5 64 ♗e4 ♖d7 ½-½

253 Ciocaltea-Giurumia
Rumania 78
1 e4 c5 2 ♘f3 d6 3 d4 ♘f6 4 ♘c3 cxd4 5 ♕xd4 N **a6 6 ♗g5 ♘c6 7 ♕d2 h6** 7...♗d7 8 0-0-0 b5 9 ♔b1 e6 10 ♗d3 ♗e7 11 ♖he1 b4 12 ♘e2 h6 13 ♗h4 ♕b6 14 ♘c1 g5 15 ♗g3 e5 16 h4= Ciocaltea-Minic, Bar 77 **8 ♗f4** 8 ♗e3!? **e5 9 ♗e3 ♗e6! 10 ♗e2 ♖c8** 10...d5!= **11 0-0 g5?! 12 ♖fd1! ♗e7 13 ♘e1 b5 14 f3 ♘a5 15 b3 ♕c7!** 15...0-0 16 a4! **16 ♘d5 ♘xd5 17 exd5 ♗d7 18 ♖ac1 0-0 19 ♘d3 ♗d8** 19...f5 20 ♘xe5 dxe5 21 d6± **20 h4 f5 21 hxg5 f4 22 ♗f2 hxg5 23 ♘b4 ♕b7 24 ♘c6!**

24...♘xc6 25 dxc6 ♖xc6 26 c4! ♗b6 27 c5 ♗a7 28 b4 ♔g7 29 a4! ♔f6 30 axb5 axb5 31 ♗d3 ♗e6 31...d5 32 ♗b1 ♗e6 33 ♕d3 ♖g8 34 ♔f1 ♗b7 35 ♔e2 ♖a6 36 ♖h1 +− **32 ♗e4 d5 33 ♗xd5 ♗b8!? 34 ♕d3 ♖h8 35 ♕e4 ♗f5 36 ♕e2** 36 ♗xc6? ♕h7 −+ **♕h7 37 ♔f1 ♕h1+ 38 ♗g1 ♖h2** 38...♖cc8 39 ♕xb5± **39 ♗xc6 ♖xg2 40 ♕xg2 ♗h3 +− 41 ♖c2! g4 42 fxg4 ♗xg2+ 43 ♖xg2 ♔g5** 43...♕h3 44 g5+ **44 ♗e4! ♕h8 45 ♖h2 ♕g8 46 ♖d5 f3 47 ♗xf3 ♔f4 48 ♔g2! ♕g6 49 ♖h5 1-0 Ciocaltea**

254 Remlinger-Browne USA 77
1 e4 c5 2 ♘f3 d6 3 d4 cxd4 4 ♕xd4 ♘c6 4...a6 5 c4 ♘c6 6 ♕d2 g6 7 ♘c3 ♗h6!? **5 ♗b5 ♗d7** 5...♘f6? 6 e5! **6 ♗xc6 ♗xc6 7 ♘c3 ♘f6 8 ♗g5 e6** 8...g6?! **9 0-0-0 ♗e7 10 ♖he1 0-0 11 ♕d2** 11 e5?! dxe5 12 ♕h4 ♕c7 13 ♘xe5 ♖fd8! 14 ♘g4 ♘xg4 15 ♗xe7 ♖xd1+ 16 ♖xd1 ♕f4+ = **♕c7** 11...♕a5!? 12 ♔b1 **12 ♘d4 ♖fd8! 13 ♖e3?! b5** TN **14 ♘cxb5** 14 a3 a5! 14 ♘xc6? ♕xc6; 14 ♔b1? b4 **♗xb5 f5 ♘xb5 ♕c5! 16 ♗xf6 ♗xf6 17 ♖b3** 17 ♘xd6? ♗g5 18 ♘b7 ♖xd2 19 ♘xc5 ♖xf2 −+; 17 ♘c3? ♗g5 −+ **d5!** 17...a5!? **18 e5?!**

♗xe5 19 f4 ♗f6 20 ♘d4 ♖ab8! 21 ♔b1 21 ♖c3 ♖xb3 22 ♘xb3 ♕c4 23 g3 h6 24 ♕d3 ♕c7 24...♖b8!? 25 c3! 25 c3 ♕b6 26 ♘d4 ♖c8! Δ ♖c4 27 ♔a1 27 ♕b5?? ♗xd4 −+ a5! 28 ♖d2 a4! 29 a3 ♖c4 30 ♕e3 30 f5 e5 31 ♘c2 e4 32 ♕xd5 ♖xc3! 33 ♕xe4 ♖c4 34 ♕e8+ ♔h7 35 ♘b4 ♖c1+ 36 ♔a2 ♕g1 −+ e5! −+ 31 fxe5 31 ♘f5 d4! 32 cxd4 exd4 33 ♕d3 ♖c1+ 34 ♔a2 ♕e6+ −+ ♗g5 32 ♕d3 ♗xd2 33 ♕xd2 ♕g6! 34 ♕e3?! ♕e4! 35 ♕f2 35 ♕xe4 dxe4 36 ♔b1 ♖c5! 37 e6 fxe6 38 ♘xe6 ♖f5 39 ♘f4 g5 −+ ♕xe5 36 ♔a2 h5 37 ♕d2 g6 38 ♕f2 ♔g7 39 ♕d2 ♖c8 40 ♕d1 ♖c4 41 ♕d2 ♖c8 42 ♕d1 ♖a8 43 ♘c6 ♕e4 44 ♘d4 44 ♘b4 ♕c4+ 45 ♔b1 ♖e8 −+ ♖a6 45 ♕d2 ♖f6 46 ♕d1 ♕e8! 47 ♕c2 ♖f1 48 h4 ♕e1 49 ♕xa4 ♕b1+ 50 ♔b3 ♖f2 51 ♘e6+ fxe6 0-1 Browne

2...e6, 4...a6

255 Suradiradja-Joksic
Jugoslavia 77
1 e4 c5 2 ♘f3 e6 3 d4 cxd4 4 ♘xd4 a6 5 c4 ♘f6 6 ♘c3 ♕c7 7 a3 ♘c6 8 ♗e3 b6 9 ♗e2 ♗b7 10 f4 ♗c5 11 e5 ♘xd4 12 ♗xd4 12 exf6 ♘f5∓ ♘e4 13 ♘xe4 ♗xe4 14 0-0 ♕c6 15 ♖f2 15 ♗f3 ♗xf3 16 ♖xf3 d6=+ a5! 16 ♕d2 0-0 17 ♖d1 d5 18 exd6 ♕xd6 19 ♕e3 ♕c6 20 ♗xc5 bxc5 21 ♗f1 ♖fd8 22 ♖fd2 ♖xd2 23 ♖xd2 23 ♕xd2 g6 Δ ♖b8 h6 24 ♕c3 ♕c7 25 ♕e3 ♗f5 26 ♗e2 ♖d8! 27 h3 Zeitnot 27 ♖xd8+ ♕xd8 28 ♕xc5 ♕d2 29 ♗f1 ♕xb2 30 ♕xa5 ♕d4+ 31 ♔h1 ♕xf4 32 ♕d8+ ♔h7 33 ♕d1 e5 =+ ♖xd2 28 ♕xd2 ♗e4 29 ♗f1 ♕b6 30 ♔h2 ♕b3 31 ♕xa5 ♕d1 32 ♔g1 ♕d4+ 32...♗d3? 33 ♕d8+ +− 33 ♔h1 ♕f2 34 ♕d8+ ♔h7 35 ♕d1 ♕xb2 36 ♕e2 36 ♗d3 f5!∓ ♕b1 37 ♔h2 f5 38 g3 ♕b3 39 ♗g2 ♗d3 40 ♕xe6 ♕c2 Δ ♗e4 41 ♔g1?! ♗xc4∓ 42 ♕e3 ♗d3 43 g4 c4 44 g5 hxg5 45 fxg5 c3 46 h4 ♕e2 47 g6+ ♔xg6 48 ♕g5+ ♔h7 0-1 Joksic

256 Radulov-Velikov
Bulgaria Final 77
1 e4 c5 2 ♘f3 e6 3 d4 cxd4 4 ♘xd4 a6 5 ♘d2 ♘c6 6 ♘xc6 bxc6 7 e5 ♕a5 8 f4 ♘e7 9 c3 ♘d5 10 ♘e4 f5 11 exf6 ♘xf6 12 ♘d6+ ♗xd6 13 ♕xd6 ♕d5 14 ♕xd5 cxd5 15 ♗e3 a5 16 a4 ♘e4 17 ♗d3 0-0 18 0-0-0 ♖f7 19 ♗xe4 dxe4 20 ♖d6 ♗b7 21 ♖hd1 ♗c6 22 b3 ♖ff8 23 ♔c2 ♖fb8 24 ♖xd7 ♗xd7 25 ♖xd7 ♖d8 26 ♖e7 ♖e8 27 ♖xe8+ ♖xe8 28 b4 axb4 29 cxb4 ♔f7 30 b5 ♔e7 31 a5 ♔d6 32 a6 ♖a8 33 ♔c3 ♔c7 34 ♗d4 ♖d8 35 b6+ ♔c6 36 b7 1-0

257 Arnason-Miles Reykjavik 78
1 e4 c5 2 ♘f3 e6 3 d4 cxd4 4 ♘xd4 a6 5 ♗d3 ♘c6 6 ♘xc6 dxc6!? 7 f4 7 0-0 +=/= e5 8 f5 ♘f6 N 8...h5?! Quinteros-Camara, Fortaleza 75; 8...b5 9 ♕f3 ♗e7 10 ♗e3 b5 11 0-0 11 a4 c5! Δ c4 12 ♖d1 ♕c7 13 c4 b4 =+/= 14 ♘d2 ♗b7 15 ♗c2 0-0?! 15...♗c6 16 g4 ♘d7 17 ♘f1 17 g5 h6 18 ♕g3 ♗g5 19 ♗xg5 19 h4 ♗f4 hxg5 20 h4 ♘f6! 21 hxg5 ♘h7! 22 f6 22 ♕e3!? ♕e7 23 f6∞ ♘xg5 23 fxg7 ♔xg7 24 ♕e3 f6 24...♕e7 25 ♖d7?! ♕xd7? 26 ♕xg5+; 25...♘h3+! −+; 25 ♘g3! 25 ♘g3 ♖ad8 26 ♘h5+ ♔g6 27 ♖xd8 ♖xd8 28 ♖f1 ♖f8 29 ♖f5 ♘h7 29...♗c8? 30 ♘xf6! ♗xf5 31 ♘d5 Δ exf5+± 30 ♖f2 ♗c8∓ 31 ♗a4! ♕e7 31...♘g5?? 32 ♗e8+! +− 32 ♗c6 ♘g5 33 ♖g2 ♗xg4 34 ♖xg4 ♔xh5 35 ♕e2! ♕e6 35...♔g6 36 ♖h4 Δ ♕h5+∞; 35...♖h8!?

36 Rxg5+ Kxg5 37 Qg2+ Kh6 38 Qh3+ Kg7 39 Qg4+ Kf7 40 Bd5+ Kf8 41 Qc8+ Qe8 42 Qxc5+ ∞/=+; 35... Qg7 36 Rg2+ Kg6 37 Qg4!

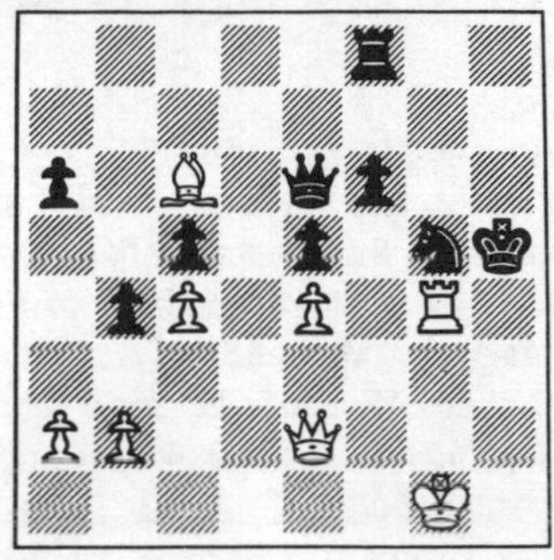

36 Rg3+? 36 Rxg5+! Kxg5 37 Qd2+! Kg6 38 Qg2+ Kf7 39 Bd5 Qxd5 40 exd5! Rg8 41 Qxg8+ Kxg8 42 Kf2 f5 43 Ke3 Kf7 44 Kf3 e4+ 45 Ke3 Ke7 46 Kf4 Kf6 47 Ke3 Ke5 48 Ke2 f4 49 Kf2 f3 50 Ke3 Kf5 51 Kf2 a5 52 b3 Kf4 (52...a4!? 53 bxa4 Kf4) 53 d6 e3+ 54 Kf1 f2 55 Ke2 Kg3 56 d7 Kg2 57 d8Q f1Q+ 58 Kxe3 Qe1+ ∞/∓ **Kg6 37 Bd5 Qc8 −+ 38 Qg2 Rh8 39 Rf3 Rh4 40 Rf5 Rf4 41 Bf7+ Kxf7 42 Qxg5 Rxf5 43 Qxf5 Qxf5 44 exf5 Kg7 45 Kf2 Kh6 46 Kf3 Kg5 47 Ke4 a5 48 b3 Kg4 49 Kd5 Kf4 50 Kxc5 e4 0-1 Miles**

2...e6, 4...Nc6

258 Kovacs-Piasetski Stip 77

1 e4 c5 2 Nf3 Nc6 3 Nc3 e6 4 d4 cxd4 5 Nxd4 Nf6 6 Be2 Bb4 7 0-0 Qa5?! 7...0-0?! 8 Nxc6 bxc6 9 e5 Nd5 10 Ne4 += Kovacs-Rajkovic 14/630; 7...Bxc3! 8 bxc3 Nxe4 9 Bd3 d5 10 Ba3 Nxd4 11 cxd4 Qa5 12 Qc1 Bd7 13 Rb1 Bc6 14 Bb4 Qc7= Geller-Hasin, USSR Final 58 **8 Ndb5 a6 9 Nd6+ Ke7 10 Bf4 Ne5 11 Nd5+! Nxd5** 11...exd5 12 Nf5+ Ke6 13 Nxg7+ Kd6 14 Qd4! +− **12 Bxe5 Bxd6 13 Bxd6+ Kxd6 14 c4 += Ke7 15 exd5 Re8 16 Qd3** 16 d6+! Kf8 17 Bf3 Δ a3, b4, c5 += **Qb6 17 Rab1 exd5 18 Qxh7 Qh6 19 Qd3 dxc4 20 Qxc4 Kf8 21 Bf3 d6 22 Rbd1 Be6 23 Qb4 += Kg8 24 Rxd6 a5 25 Qd4 Rac8 26 Bxb7 Rc4 27 Qd2 Qxd2 28 Rxd2 Rb4** 28...Rb8 29 b3! Rb4 30 Bc6 +− **29 Bc6 Reb8 30 b3 Rc8 31 Ba4 Kf8 32 Rfd1 Rc5 33 f3 g5 34 h3 Kg7 35 Kf2 Kf6 36 Kg3 Rc3 37 Rd3 Rc5 38 R1d2 Rb8 39 Rd6 Ke5 40 Ra6 Rbc8 41 Bd7! Bxd7** 41...Rd8 42 Re2+ Kd4 43 Bxe6 fxe6 44 Raxe6 +− **42 Rxd7 f6** 42...f5 43 Rg7 +− **43 Rda7 Rc2 44 Rxa5+ Kd4 45 R7a6 Rb2 46 Rxf6 Rcc2 47 Rd6+ 1-0** 47...Kc3 48 Rc6+ Δ Rxc2 +− **L.Kovacs**

259 Martin-Taimanov Montilla 77

1 e4 c5 2 Nf3 Nc6 3 d4 cxd4 4 Nxd4 e6 5 Nc3 a6 6 Be2 Nge7 7 Be3 Nxd4 8 Qxd4 b5 9 f4 Nc6 10 Qd2 Be7 11 0-0-0 11 Bf3; 11 0-0 **Qa5! 12 e5** 12 Kb1 b4 13 Nd5 exd5 14 exd5 Nd8 15 Bf3 **b4 13 Ne4 Qxa2 14 Nd6+ Bxd6 15 Qxd6** Δ Bf3 **Qa1+ 16 Kd2 Qxb2 17 Bc5** 17 Bf3 **Qc3+ 18 Kc1 b3!**

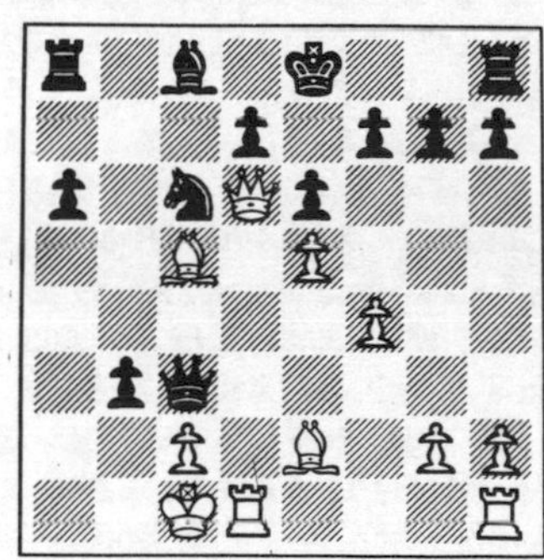

19 ♝d3 ♜b8 20 ♜he1 ♜b5! 21 ♝a3 ♞b4! 22 ♜e2 22 ♗xb4 ♖xb4 Δ ♖a4 −+ **b2+! 0-1** 23 ♗xb2 ♘a2+ 24 ♔b1 ♕xb2 mate; 23 ♔b1 ♕xa3 −+

260 Aleksic-Cabrilo Jugoslavia 77
1 e4 c5 2 ♞f3 e6 3 d4 cxd4 4 ♞xd4 ♞c6 5 ♞c3 a6 6 g3 d6 7 ♝g2 ♝d7 8 ♞de2 ♞f6 9 0-0 ♝e7 10 h3 b5 11 a3 0-0 12 f4 ♜b8 13 g4 a5 14 ♞g3 b4 15 axb4 axb4 16 ♞ce2 ♛b6+ 17 ♚h1 ♜fd8 18 g5 ♞e8 19 f5 ♞e5 20 ♞d4 ♝f8 21 b3 ♞c7 22 ♝b2 ♞a6 23 ♜f4 ♞c5 24 ♜h4 g6 25 ♞h5 gxh5 26 ♛xh5 h6 27 gxh6 ♝e8 28 h7+ ♚h8 29 ♛g5 1-0

261 Radulov-Kirov
Bulgaria Final 77
1 e4 c5 2 ♞f3 e6 3 d4 cxd4 4 ♞xd4 ♞c6 5 ♞c3 a6 6 g3 d6 7 ♝g2 ♝d7 8 0-0 ♞f6 9 ♞de2 ♝e7 10 h3 0-0 11 g4 b5 12 a3 ♜b8 13 ♞g3 b4 14 axb4 ♞xb4 15 g5 ♞e8 16 f4 ♞c7 17 h4 ♜e8 18 f5 ♝f8 19 f6 ♞b5 20 ♞ce2 ♛b6+ 21 ♚h2 g6 22 h5 ♞c6 23 hxg6 hxg6 24 ♞f4 ♞e5 25 ♞d3 ♞xd3 26 ♛xd3 ♞c7 27 ♜f4 ♛b5 28 ♛f3 e5 29 ♜h4 d5 30 ♞f5 gxf5 31 ♛h5 1-0

262 Janosevic-Damjanovic
Jugoslavia 77
1 e4 c5 2 ♞f3 ♞c6 3 d4 cxd4 4 ♞xd4 ♛c7 5 ♞c3 e6 6 ♝e2 a6 7 0-0 ♞f6 8 ♝e3 d6 9 f4 ♝d7 10 ♛e1 ♝e7 11 ♛g3 0-0 12 ♜ad1 ♞xd4 13 ♝xd4 ♝c6 14 e5 dxe5 15 ♝xe5 ♛b6+ 16 ♚h1 ♜ad8 17 ♝d3 ♞h5 18 ♛h3 g6 19 ♞e4 f5 20 ♞g5 ♝xg5 21 fxg5 ♛c5 22 ♜de1 b5 23 a3 ♝d5 24 ♝c3 ♜f7 25 ♛e3 ♛xe3 26 ♜xe3 ♜c8 27 ♝e2 ♜d7 28 ♚g1 ♞g7 29 ♜d1 ♜dc7 30 ♝f3 f4 31 ♜ed3 ♝xf3 32 ♜d8+ ♜xd8 33 ♜xd8+ ♚f7 34 gxf3 ♞h5 35 ♜h8 ♜c5 36 ♜xh7+ ♚e8 37 h4 a5 Δ b4 **38 ♜b7 e5 39 ♚f2 ♞g3 40 ♜b6 ♚d7 41 ♚e1 ♞f5 42 h5 gxh5 43 g6 ♚e7 44 ♝xa5 ♜xc2 45 ♝b4+ ♚d7 46 ♝c3 h4 47 g7 ♞xg7 48 ♜b7+ ♚e6 49 ♜xg7 1-0**

263 Larsen-Hort Bugojno 78
1 e4 c5 2 ♞f3 e6 3 d4 cxd4 4 ♞xd4 ♞c6 5 ♞c3 ♛c7 6 ♝e2 ♞f6 7 0-0 a6 8 ♚h1 ♝e7 8...♗b4 9 ♗g5! **9 f4 d6 10 ♝e3 0-0 11 ♛e1 ♝d7** 11...♘xd4 12 ♗xd4 ♗c6 13 ♕g3 **12 ♛g3 ♚h8 13 ♜ad1 b5 14 e5!? dxe5** 14...♘e8!? **15 fxe5 ♞e8** 15...♘xe5? 16 ♗f4 ♗d6 17 ♘b3 Δ ♖xd6; 15...♕xe5!? 16 ♗f4 ♕c5∞ **16 ♞f3±**

16...♝c8 17 ♞e4 ♚g8 17...f5 18 exf6 ♕xg3? 19 fxe7!+− **18 ♝f4 ♞b4 19 ♞f6+ ♚h8 20 ♞g5! +− ♛xc2 21 ♞fxh7 ♝xg5 22 ♞xg5 ♛g6 23 ♝d2 1-0 Pytel**

264 Planinc-Matulovic Jugoslavia 77
1 e4 c5 2 ♞f3 ♞c6 3 d4 cxd4 4 ♞xd4 ♛c7 5 ♞c3 e6 6 g3 a6 7 ♝g2 ♞f6 8 0-0 ♝e7 9 ♜e1 ♞xd4 10 ♛xd4 ♝c5 11 ♛d1 d6 12 ♝e3 12 ♘a4 ♗a7 13 c4 ♗d7 14 ♗e3 Novoselski-Matulovic, Jugoslavia 77 **e5 13 ♛d2 ♝e6 14 ♜ad1 ♚e7 15 ♝g5 h6 16 ♝xf6+ ♚xf6 17 ♞d5+ ♝xd5 18 ♛xd5 g6 19 ♚h1 ♜ad8**

20 f4 ♚g7 21 ♜f1 f6 22 ♜d3 ♜hf8 23 c3 ♛f7 24 fxe5 ♛xd5 25 exf6+ ♜xf6 26 ♜xd5 ♜xf1+ 27 ♝xf1 ♚f6 28 e5+ ♚e7 29 ♝d3 g5 30 ♚g2 ♝e3 31 b3 ♝c1 32 ♚f3 ♝b2 33 exd6+ ♜xd6 34 ♜xd6 ♚xd6 35 ♚g4 ♝xc3 36 ♚h5 ♝g7 37 ♚g6 ♝f8 38 ♚f7 ♝e7 39 ♝e2 a5 40 a4 b6 41 ♝f3 ♚d7 42 ♚g7 ♚e6 43 ♚xh6 ♚f5 44 ♚h5 ♚f6 46 h4 ½-½

265 Ochoa-Santos Guarda 77
1 e4 e6 2 d4 c5 3 ♞f3 cxd4 4 ♞xd4 ♞c6 5 ♞xc6 bxc6 6 ♝d3 ♞f6 7 c4 ♛c7 8 0-0 ♝e7 9 f4 d6 10 ♛f3 0-0 11 ♞c3 e5 12 ♝e3 ♞g4 13 ♝c1 exf4 14 ♝xf4 ♝f6 15 ♛g3 ♝e5 16 c5 ♝xf4 17 ♜xf4 ♞e5 18 cxd6 ♛xd6 19 ♝c2 ♛b4 20 ♝b3 a5 21 ♜f2 ♞c4 22 e5! ♝e6 23 ♚h1 ♜ad8 24 ♞e4 ♜d4 25 ♜f4! ♞xe5? 26 ♞f6+ ♚h8 27 ♛h4 1-0 Ochoa

2...e6, 4...♞f6

266 Kuzmin-Tal
USSR Final 77
1 e4 c5 2 ♞f3 e6 3 d4 cxd4 4 ♞xd4 ♞f6 5 ♞c3 d6 6 g3 ♝e7 7 ♝g2 a6 8 0-0 ♛c7 9 a4 ♞c6 10 ♝e3 0-0 11 h3 ♝d7 12 ♛e2 ♜ab8 13 ♜fd1 ♜fc8 14 ♞xc6 14 ♘b3 (Δ a5) ♘a5≈ **bxc6!** 14...♗xc6 15 a5 += **15 ♛xa6 ♜xb2∝ 16 ♜db1 ♜cb8** 16...♖xc2 17 ♕d3 **17 ♜xb2 ♜xb2 18 a5 c5!** 18...♖xc2 19 ♕d3!? ♖b2 20 a5±; 19 ♕b6!?± **19 ♛d3 ♛a7 20 a6** 20 e5!? **♞e8 21 ♜a5?=+** 21 ♗f1!∝ **♝c6 22 ♛c4 ♛b6! 23 ♜a3??** 23 ♖a1 =+ **♛b4! −+ 24 ♛xb4 cxb4 25 ♜a4 ♝xa4 0-1 Petrosian**

267 Wedberg-Vogt
Sweden-DDR 77
1 e4 c5 2 ♞f3 e6 3 d4 cxd4 4 ♞xd4 ♞f6 5 ♞c3 d6 6 g3 ♝e7 7 ♝g2 0-0 8 0-0 a6 9 ♜e1 ♛c7 10 a4 ♞c6 11 ♞b3 b6 12 f4 ♝b7 13 ♛e2 ♜fe8 14 ♝e3 ♞d7 15 ♛f2 ♞c5 15...♗f6 **16 g4 ♝f6** 16...♘b4 17 ♘d4 **17 g5** 17 ♘d4 ♘xd4 18 ♗xd4 ♗xd4 19 ♕xd4 e5=+ **♝xc3 18 bxc3 ♞e7** 18...♖ac8 **19 a5! bxa5** 19...♘xe4? 20 ♗xb6 ♘xf2 21 ♗xc7 ♗xg2 22 ♔xg2 ♘g4 23 h3 ♘d5 24 ♗b6 ♘xf4+ 25 ♔g3±; 20...♕c4 21 ♗xc4 ♗xc4 22 ♘d2± **20 ♝xc5! dxc5 21 ♜xa5?!** 21 ♘xa5 ♗c8 22 f5 ♖b8∝ **♞g6! 22 ♜f1** 22 f5 exf5 23 ♖xc5 ♕e7 24 ♖xf5 ♘e5 =+ **c4! 23 ♜c5** 23 ♕c5 ♕b8!∓ **♛xf4 =+ 24 ♞a5 ♛xf2+ 25 ♚xf2** 25 ♖xf2 ♖e7 26 ♘xb7 ♖xb7 27 e5 ♖b1+∓ **♜ab8 26 ♜d1 ♝a8 27 ♞xc4 ♜b5! 28 ♜xb5 axb5 29 ♞d6** 29 ♘a3 ♗c6; 29...♘f4=+ **♜d8 30 ♝f1 ♝xe4 31 ♝xb5 ♝xc2 32 ♜d2 ♞e5 33 ♜xc2 ♜xd6 34 c4 ♞d3+ 35 ♚e3 ♞c5∓ 36 ♜a2 ♜d3+ 37 ♚f4 ♜d8 38 ♜a7 h6 39 gxh6 gxh6 40 ♜c7 ♞d3+ 41 ♚e3 ♞b4! 42 ♚e4 ♚g7 43 c5? ♞d5 44 ♜b7 ♞c3+ 45 ♚f3 ♞xb5 46 ♜xb5 ♜d5 47 ♜a5 ♚f6 48 ♚f4 ♜h5 49 ♚g3 ♜f5 50 ♜b5 ♜d5 0-1** 51 ♔f4 ♖d2 52 ♔g3 ♖c2 53 ♖a5 ♔g5 54 c6+ f5 −+; 52 c6 ♖c2 53 ♖b6 ♖c4+ 54 ♔f3 ♔e5 −+ **Vogt**

268 Formanek-Wagman
Reggio Emilia 77/78
1 e4 c5 2 ♞f3 d6 3 d4 cxd4 4 ♞xd4 ♞f6 5 ♞c3 e6 6 g4 h6 6...a6; 6...♘c6 **7 ♜g1** 7 g5 hxg5 8 ♗xg5 ♘c6 9 ♕d2 ♕b6 **♞c6 8 h4 d5 9 ♝b5 ♝d7 10 exd5? ♞xd5 11 ♞xd5 exd5 12 ♛e2+?** 12 ♗e3 ♕xh4 13 ♕f3 **♝e7 13 ♞f3** 13 ♗e3 ♘xd4 14 ♗xd7+ ♕xd7 15 ♗xd4 0-0 =+; 13 ♘f5!? **0-0 14 g5 ♜e8 15 ♚d1 ♝f8** 15...♗xg5! 16 ♗xg5 hxg5 17 ♕d3 ♘b4 18 ♕d2 ♕f6 −+; 16 ♕d3 ♘b4 −+ **16 ♛d2 ♜e4 17 ♝d3 ♜g4 18 ♜e1 ♛b6 19 a3 ♜g2 20 gxh6 ♝g4**

21 ♗e2 21 ♕f4 ♕xf2 22 ♖f1 ♖g1

21...♖e8? 21...♕xf2! 22 ♕e3 ♕xe3 23 ♗xe3 ♖e8 24 ♖g1 ♖xe3 25 ♖xg2 ♗xf3 −+; 22 ♘g5 ♖e8 **22 h7+ ♔h8 23 ♕f4 ♕xf2?** 23...♗xf3 24 ♕xf3 ♖xf2 25 ♕g4 ♘d4 26 ♗d3 ♖xe1+ 27 ♔xe1 ♘xc2+ 28 ♗xc2 ♖xc2 −+ **24 ♕xf7 ♕xe1+ 25 ♔xe1** 25 ♘xe1? ♗xe2+ 26 ♔d2 ♗h5+ −+ **♖exe2+?** 25... ♖gxe2+! 26 ♔d1 ♔xh7 (Δ ♘d4) 27 c3 ♖8e7! 28 ♕xf8 ♖f2 −+; 28 ♕f4 ♖7e4 29 ♕g3 ♗d6! −+; 26 ♔f1 ♗h3+ 27 ♔g1 ♗c5+ 28 ♔h1 ♗g2+ −+ **26 ♔d1 ♔xh7 27 ♘g5+ ♔h6 28 ♘f3+ ♔h7 29 ♘g5+ ½-½ Paoli**

269 Suradiradja-Adamski
Primorsko 77

1 e4 c5 2 ♘f3 d6 3 d4 ♘f6 4 ♘c3 cxd4 5 ♘xd4 e6 6 g4 h6 7 g5 hxg5 8 ♗xg5 a6 9 ♕d2 ♘c6 10 0-0-0 ♕b6 11 ♘b3 ♕c7 12 h4 ♗e7 13 f4 b5 14 ♗g2 ♗b7 15 ♖h3 0-0-0 16 ♘d5 exd5 17 exd5 ♘xd5 18 ♗xd5 ♔b8 19 ♖c3 ♗xg5 20 hxg5 ♕d7 21 ♗xc6 ♗xc6 22 ♕d4 ♗b7 23 ♕b6 ♖he8 24 ♘c5 dxc5 25 ♖cd3 ♕xd3 26 ♖xd3 ♖e1+ 27 ♔d2 ♖de8 28 ♖d8+ 1-0

270 Furman-Beljavsky USSR 77

1 e4 c5 2 ♘f3 e6 3 d4 cxd4 4 ♘xd4 ♘f6 5 ♘c3 d6 6 g4 h6 7 g5 hxg5 8 ♗xg5 ♘c6 9 ♕d2 ♕b6 10 ♘b3 a6 11 0-0-0 ♕c7 12 f4 b5 13 ♕e3 ♗b7 14 ♗h3?! 14 h4 += **b4 15 ♗xf6** 15 ♘e2 ♖xh3!? 16 ♕xh3 ♘xe4 ∞/=+ **gxf6 16 ♘e2 ♘e5!∓ 17 ♔b1 ♘c4 18 ♕d3 0-0-0 19 ♘ed4?! ♖e8** 19...♘xb2 20 ♔xb2 ♕c3+ −+ **20 ♖he1?! ♔b8?** 20...♘xb2! **21 ♖e2?** 21 ♗f1 += **♗h6 22 ♖f2 ♖c8∓ 23 ♗g2 ♕b6 24 ♕e2 a5 25 ♖f3 a4 26 ♘c1 ♖hg8 27 ♗h3**

27...♖g1! 28 ♗f1 f5! 29 exf5 e5! 30 fxe5 dxe5 31 ♕f2 ♗xf3 32 ♕xf3 ♗xc1 0-1 Gufeld

271 Tseshkovsky-Kurajica
Ljubljana 77

1 e4 c5 2 ♘f3 e6 3 d4 cxd4 4 ♘xd4 ♘f6 5 ♘c3 d6 6 g4 h6 7 g5 7 h4; 7 h3 Δ ♗e3, f4 **hxg5 8 ♗xg5 ♘c6 9 h4 ♗d7!? 10 ♘b3?!** 10 ♕d2 ♕b6 11 ♘b3 ♘e5 12 ♕e2 += **♕c7?!** 10...a6; 10...♖c8! Δ ♘e5, ♘a5 **11 h5?!** 11 ♕e2! Δ 0-0-0 += **a6 12 f4 b5 13 ♗g2 ♖c8 14 ♕e2 b4 15 ♘d1 a5 16 a4 bxa3 17 ♖xa3 ♕b8 18 ♘e3 ♗e7 19 ♖h3 ♖c7! 20 f5 ♖a7 21 fxe6 fxe6 22 c3 ♖b7??** 22...a4 23 ♘c1 ♘e5∓

Diagram

23 h6! gxh6 23...♖xb3? 24 hxg7

Rxh3 25 Rxb3 Qxb3 26 Bxf6 Kf7 27 g8Q+! Kxg8 28 Qg4+ +–; 24...Rg8 25 Rxb3 Qxb3 26 Rh8 Kf7 27 Bxf6 +– **24 e5 Nxe5 25 Bxb7 Qxb7 26 Nxa5 Qe4**∞ **27 Nac4** 27 Bxf6? Bxf6 28 Nac4 Nxc4 29 Nxc4 Bh4 –+ **Nxc4 28 Nxc4 Qb1+ 29 Qd1 Qe4+ 30 Qe2= ½-½ Kurajica**

272 Radulov-Balaskas Balkaniad 77
1 e4 c5 2 Nf3 e6 3 d4 cxd4 4 Nxd4 Nf6 5 Nc3 d6 6 g4 6 f4; 6 Be3; 6 Be2 **h6 7 h4 Be7 8 Rg1 d5! 9 f3** 9 Bb5+ Kf8∞ **a6??** 9...dxe4 10 g5 hxg5 11 hxg5 Nd5 12 Nxe4∞ **10 g5 hxg5 11 hxg5 Nh7 12 exd5 exd5 13 Qe2!± Nc6 14 Be3 Kf8 15 f4 Qd6 16 0-0-0 Be6 17 Bg2 Rc8 18 Kb1 Na5 19 Nb3 Rxc3 20 bxc3 Nc4 21 Bc5 Qc7 22 Bxe7+ Qxe7 23 Bxd5 1-0 Gheorghiu**

2...Nf6

273 Arapovic-Minic Jugoslavia 77
1 e4 c5 2 Nf3 Nf6 3 e5 Nd5 4 Nc3 e6 5 Bc4 5 Nxd5; Ne4!? **Nb6 6 Bd3** 6 Qe2 Nc6 7 0-0 a6 8 d3 d5 Zhilin-Mats, Novosibirsk 62 **Nc6 7 0-0 d6 8 exd6 Bxd6 9 Ne4 Be7 10 b3 f5 11 Ng3 0-0 12 Bb2 Bf6 13 Bxf6 Qxf6 14 Bb5 Nd4 15 Nxd4 Qxd4 16 c3 Qd6 17 Re1 e5 18 Qe2 e4 19 f3 exf3 20 gxf3 a6 21 Bc4+ Nxc4 22 Qxc4+ Kh8 23 d4 cxd4 24 Rad1 f4 25 Rxd4 Qb6 26 Ne4 Qg6+ 27 Kh1 Qh5 28 Nd2 Bh3 29 Rxf4 Rfc8 30 Qd4 Rd8 31 Qf2 Rac8 32 Rg1 Rxc3 32 Qd4 1-0**

274 Tal-Zaitsev Sochi 77
1 e4 c5 2 Nf3 Nf6 3 e5 Nd5 4 d4 cxd4 5 Qxd4 e6 6 Bc4 Nc6 7 Qe4 f5?!± 7...d6 8 exd6 Nf6 9 Qh4; 9 Qe2 += **8 Qe2** 8 exf6 Nxf6 9 Qe2≈ **Nde7** TN **9 Nc3 a6 10 h4 b5 11 Bb3 Qc7 12 Bd2 Bb7?** 12...Ng6!? **13 0-0-0 Na5 14 Kb1 Nxb3?** 14...Nec6 △ Be7, 0-0 **15 cxb3 b4 16 Na4 +– Be4+ 17 Ka1 Nc6 18 Bg5! h6** 18... Bxf3 19 Qxf3 Qxe5 20 Rxd7! +– **19 Bf4 g6 20 Qe3 Rb8 21 Nd2 Bxg2?? 22 Qg3 1-0 Petrosian**

2...g6

275 Baretic-Novoselski Jugoslavia 77
1 e4 c5 2 Nf3 g6 3 d4 cxd4 4 Nxd4 Nc6 5 Nc3 Bg7 6 Be3 Nf6 7 Bc4 Qa5 8 0-0 0-0 9 Nb3 Qc7 10 f4 d6 11 f5 a5 12 a4 Nb4 13 Be2 Bd7 14 Qd2 Nxe4 15 Nxe4 Qxc2

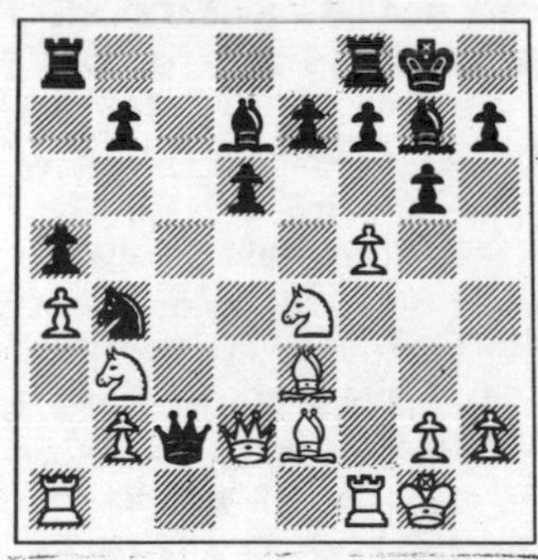

16 f6 exf6 17 Nxf6+ Bxf6 18 Rxf6 Qxb3 19 Bh6 Nc2 20 Raf1 Bxa4 21

♛xd6 ♛xb2 22 ♝c4 ♝b3 23 ♜xf7 ♜xf7 24 ♜xf7 ♛d4+ 25 ♛xd4 ♞xd4 26 ♜f8 mate 1-0

276 Hulak-Barlov Jugoslavia 77
1 e4 c5 2 ♞f3 g6 3 d4 cxd4 4 ♛xd4 ♞f6 5 ♛a4 ♛b6 6 e5 ♞d5 7 a3 ♞c6 8 ♛e4 ♞c7 9 ♞c3 ♝g7 10 ♝c4 ♞a5 11 ♝a2 ♛c6 12 ♛b4 b6 13 ♝g5 ♛c5 14 ♛h4 ♝b7 15 ♝e3 ♛c6 16 0-0-0 b5 17 ♞g5 ♞c4 18 ♞xb5 ♞xe3 19 ♞xc7+ ♛xc7 20 ♝xf7+ ♚f8 21 fxe3 ♛xe5 22 c3 ♜c8 23 ♜hf1 ♜xc3+ 0-1

1 e4 c6

277 Sax-Vadasz Tungsram 77
1 e4 c6 2 d3 d5 3 ♞d2 ♞f6!? 4 ♞gf3 ♝g4 5 h3 ♝h5 6 ♛e2! 6 e5 ♘cd7 7 e6 fxe6 8 g4 ♗g6!= **♛c7!** 6...e6? 7 g4 ♗g6 8 h4 h5 9 ♘e5 ♘xg4 10 ♘xg6 fxg6 11 exd5± **7 g4 ♝g6 8 ♝g2 e6 9 0-0 ♝e7 10 ♞h4 dxe4** 10...♘xe4? 11 ♘xg6 ♘xd2 12 ♘xe7 ♘xf1 13 ♘f5 +− **11 dxe4 ♞bd7 12 ♞f5?** 12 f4! ♘xe4? 13 ♘xg6 ♘xd2 14 ♘xe7 ♘xf1 15 ♘f5 0-0 16 ♘h4 ♘g3 17 ♕f3±; 12...♗xe4! 13 ♘xe4 ♘xe4 14 ♕xe4 ♗xh4 15 g5! h6 16 f5! hxg5! 17 fxe6 ♘f6 18 exf7+ ♔xf7 19 ♕c4+ +− **exf5 13 exf5 ♝xf5 14 gxf5 ♞b6 15 ♜e1 ♞bd5??** 15... ♖d8! 16 ♘b3 ♘c8 17 ♗g5 0-0 =+; 15...♘c8!? **16 ♞b3 b5 17 a4 b4 18 c4! bxc3 19 bxc3 0-0** 19...♘xc3 20 ♗xc6+ +− **20 c4 ♝b4 21 cxd5 ♝xe1 22 ♛c4?!** 22 ♕xe1 cxd5 23 ♘d4± **♛e5?** Zeitnot 22...♘xd5! 23 ♗xd5 ♕b6 24 ♗g2 ♕xf2+ 25 ♔h1 ♖b8∞ **23 dxc6 ♛c3 24 ♛xc3 ♝xc3 25 ♜b1 ♝e5 26 ♞c5 ♝d4 27 ♞a6 ♜ac8 28 c7 ♝b6 29 ♝f4 ♜fe8 30 ♝b7 g5 31 fxg6 hxg6 32 ♝xc8 ♜xc8 33 ♜b5 ♚f8 34 a5 1-0 Vadasz**

278 Pribyl-Kozma CSSR 77
1 e4 c6 2 d3 d5 3 ♞d2 g6 4 ♞gf3 ♝g7 5 g3 e5 6 ♝g2 ♞e7 7 0-0 0-0 8 b4!? 8 ♖e1 d4!; 8 ♕e2 ♕c7 9 exd5 cxd5 10 c4 dxc4 11 ♘xc4 ♘bc6= **a5!** 8... dxe4 9 dxe4 ♕c7 10 ♗b2 ♗g4 11 h3 ♗xf3 12 ♕xf3 ♘d7 13 ♖fd1 +=; 8...♘d7 9 ♗b2 b6 10 d4!? += **9 bxa5 ♛xa5** 9...♖xa5 10 ♗b2 ♘d7 11 ♕e2 dxe4 12 dxe4 ♖a4 13 ♘c4 += Pribyl-Spiridonov, Brno 75; 10...♕c7 11 ♖e1!? d4 12 ♘c4 ♖a6 13 c3+= **10 ♝b2 ♛c7** 10...d4 11 ♘c4 ♕c7 12 a4 c5 13 ♘fd2 ♗h6 14 c3 ♘ec6 Hartoch-Vukic, Banja Luka 74; 10...♘bd7 11 ♖e1 d4 (11...f6 12 d4!+=) 12 a4 ♕d8 13 ♘c4 c5 14 c3 b6 15 cxd4 cxd4 16 ♗a3 ♗a6 17 ♕b3 += Zinn-Kolarov, Kapfenberg 69 **11 a4 b6?!** TN 11...d4 12 c3 c5 13 cxd4 cxd4 14 ♘c4 ♘ec6 15 ♗a3 += Pribyl-Filip, CSSR 74; 11...♘bd7!? 12 ♕e2 d4 13 c3 dxc3?! 14 ♗xc3 c5 15 ♘c4 ♘c6 16 ♕b2 ♘d4 17 a5± Pribyl-Meduna, Praha 74 **12 exd5!? cxd5 13 ♜e1 ♞ec6 14 c4 d4 15 ♝a3 += ♜d8 16 ♛c2 ♞a6? 17 ♞xe5!! ♝xe5 18 ♝xc6 ♛xc6 19 ♜xe5 ♝b7 20 f3 ♜e8≈ 21 ♜ae1! ♜xe5 22 ♜xe5 ♞c5?** 22...♘c7 23 ♖e7 ♘e6≈ **23 ♝xc5 bxc5 24 ♞e4!± ♜xa4 25 ♜xc5 ♜a1+ 26 ♚g2 ♛a6 27 ♜b5!± ♝c6 28 ♜b1 f5 29 ♜xa1 ♛xa1 30 ♞f6+ ♚g7 31 ♞d5 ♛e1 32 ♛a2 ♛e5?!** 32...♗xd5!? 33 cxd5± **33 ♞b4! +− ♝b7** 33...♗d7 34 f4 ♕e3 35 ♕f2! **34 ♛f2 g5 35 ♞c2! ♚g6** 35...g4 36 ♕xd4 ♗xf3+ 37 ♔f2 ♔f6 38 ♕xe5+ ♔xe5 39 ♔e3 +− **36 ♚f1 ♛c7 37 ♞xd4 ♛a5 38 ♛e3 ♛a1+ 39 ♚f2 ♛b2+ 40 ♞e2 g4 41 ♛e6+ 1-0 Pribyl**

279 Kochiev-Smyslov USSR Final 77
1 e4 c6 2 d3 d5 3 ♞d2 g6 4 g3 ♝g7 5 ♝g2 e5 6 ♞gf3 ♞e7 7 0-0 0-0 8 ♛e2

♕c7 9 b3 d4 10 a4! Δ ♗a3, ♘c4 ♘a6 11 ♗a3 c5 12 ♘c4 ♘c6 13 ♘e1! += 13 ♘h4 ♕e7!= ♘ab4 14 f4 exf4 15 gxf4 f5 16 e5 ♗e6 17 h4! 17 ♘f3 ♗h6! ♕e7 18 ♘f3 h6 19 ♕f2± ♖ad8 20 ♔h2 ♘d5 21 ♕g3 ♘cb4 22 ♖f2 ♗f7 23 h5?! 23 ♗h3!?± ♘xf4!

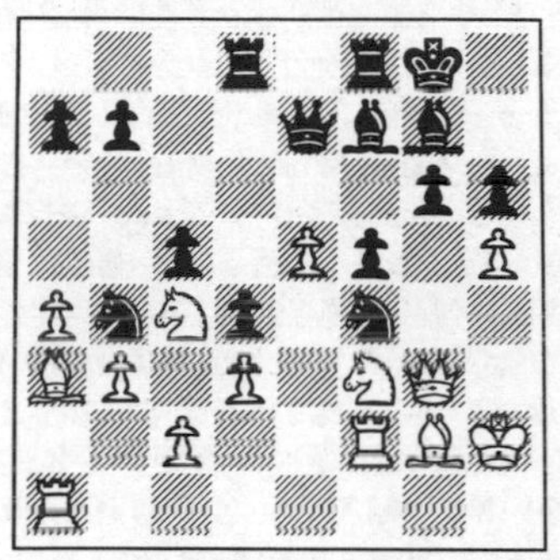

24 hxg6!? 24 ♕xf4 g5∞ ♘xg6 25 ♖e1! Δ e6 f4? 26 ♕g4+= Δ e6 ♕e6 27 ♗h3! ♕xg4 28 ♗xg4 Δ e6 ♗xc4 29 bxc4± ♖fe8 30 e6 ♖e7 31 ♗f5 ♘f8 32 ♗c1! ♖d6 33 ♗xf4 ♖a6 34 ♖fe2 ♘a2 35 ♖g2! ♘xe6 36 ♗xh6 +− ♔f8 37 ♗xe6 ♖axe6 38 ♗xg7+ ♔e8 39 ♖xe6 ♖xe6 40 ♗e5 ♘b4 1-0 Kochiev

280 Perenyi-Gereben
Budapest 1 77

1 e4 c6 2 d4 d5 3 ♘d2 dxe4 4 ♘xe4 ♘d7 5 ♗c4 ♘gf6 6 ♘g5 6 ♘xf6+ ♘xf6 7 c3 b5 8 ♗d3 ♗g4 9 ♘e2 e6 10 ♕c2 ♗e7 11 h3 ♗h5 12 ♘f4 += e6 7 ♕e2 ♘d5 7...♘b6 8 ♗d3 h6 9 ♘5f3 c5 10 dxc5 ♗xc5 11 ♘e5 ♘bd7 12 ♘gf3 ♘xe5 13 ♘xe5 0-0 14 0-0 b6 15 ♗f4 ♗b7 16 ♖ad1 8 ♗d2 ♗e7 9 ♘1h3 h6 10 ♘e4 b5 11 ♗d3 ♘b4 12 ♗xb4 ♗xb4+ 13 c3 ♗e7 14 ♘f4 += ♘f6 14...0-0 15 ♘h5 ♘f6 16 ♘exf6+ ♗xf6 17 ♕e4± 15 ♕f3 ♗d7 16 ♘xf6+ gxf6 17 0-0± f5 18 ♖fe1 ♕c7 19 d5! cxd5 20 ♗xf5 ♕c5 21 ♖ad1!! 0-0-0 22 ♘xd5 ♗g5 23 ♘b4 ♕b6 23...exf5 24 ♘a6 24 ♗e4 a5 25 ♗c6 ♗xc6 26 ♘xc6 ♖xd1 27 ♖xd1 f5 28 ♘xa5! ♕xa5 29 ♕c6+ ♕c7 30 ♕a8+ ♕b8 31 ♕a6+ ♔c7 31...♕b7 32 ♕xe6+ ♔c7 33 ♕e5+ 32 ♖d6 ♕a8 33 ♕b6+ ♔c8 34 ♖c6+ ♔d7 35 ♖c7+ 1-0 B.Balogh

281 Karpov-Hort Bugojno 78

1 e4 c6 2 d4 d5 3 ♘d2 dxe4 4 ♘xe4 ♘d7 5 ♘f3 ♘gf6 6 ♘xf6+ ♘xf6 7 ♘e5! 7 c3 ♗g4!=; 7 ♗c4!? ♗f5 7...♗c6!? 8 c4 g6!; 7...♘d7 8 ♘d3! 8 c3 e6 8...♘d7 9 ♘xf7! ♔xf7 10 ♕f3 e6 11 g4 ♕f6 12 gxf5 ♕xf5 13 ♕e3 += Spassky-Donner, San Juan 69 9 g4 ♗g6 10 h4 h5?! 10...♗d6 11 ♕e2! c5 12 ♗g2! cxd4 13 h5 dxc3 14 ♕b5+ ♔f8 15 hxg6± Ciric; 12 h5? ♗e4 13 f3 cxd4∞ Karpov-A.Zaitsev, USSR 70 11 g5 ♘d5 12 ♘xg6± fxg6 13 ♕c2 ♔f7 14 ♖h3! ♘e7 15 ♗c4 ♘f5 16 ♖f3 ♕d7 16...♔e7!? 17 ♖xf5+! gxf5 18 ♕xf5+ ♔e7 19 ♕e4 ♖e8 20 ♗f4 ♔d8 21 ♕e5 ♖g8 22 0-0-0 g6 23 ♖e1 ♗g7 24 ♕b8+ ♔e7 24...♕c8 25 ♖xe6+! 1-0 25...♕xe6 26 ♕c7+ ♕d7 27 ♗d6 mate

282 Spassky-Larsen Bugojno 78

1 e4 c6 2 d4 d5 3 ♘c3 dxe4 4 ♘xe4 ♗f5 5 ♘g3 ♗g6 6 ♘f3 ♘d7 7 ♗d3 7 h4! ♕a5+?! N 7...♗xd3 8 ♕xd3 e6 9 0-0 ♘gf6 10 ♗f4 ♗e7 11 ♖fe1 0-0 12 c4 += Matulovic-Milic, Jugoslavia 55; 7...e6! 8 0-0 ♘gf6 9 ♖e1 ♗e7 10 c4 0-0 11 ♗xg6 hxg6 12 ♗f4 ♖e8 13 ♕c2 c5 14 ♖ad1 cxd4 15 ♘xd4 += Najdorf-Kotov, Zurich 53 8 ♗d2 ♕c7 9 ♗xg6 hxg6 10 ♕e2 e6 11 ♘e4± 0-0-0? 11...♘gf6 12 g3! c5 13 ♗f4 ♕c6 14 0-0-0 c4

15 ♘c3 +− Δ d5 **♘h6 16 d5 exd5 17 ♖xd5 ♗c5 18 ♖hd1 f6 19 ♖d6! ♗xd6 20 ♖xd6 ♕c5 21 ♖d5 1-0** 21...♕c6 22 ♘d4 ♕a6 23 ♘db5 **Pytel**

283 Karpov-Larsen Bugojno 78
1 e4 c6 2 d4 d5 3 ♘d2 3 ♘c3 g6 4 ♘f3 ♗g4 **dxe4 4 ♘xe4 ♗f5 5 ♘g3 ♗g6 6 ♘f3 ♘d7 7 h4 h5?!** 7...h6 **8 ♗d3 ♗xd3 9 ♕xd3 e6 10 ♘e4 ♕a5+ 11 ♗d2 ♕f5!? 12 0-0-0 0-0-0 13 ♗e3 ♘h6** 13...♘gf6 14 ♘xf6 ♕xd3 15 ♖xd3 ♘xf6 16 ♘g5 ♖d7 17 ♗f4± **14 ♘eg5! ♕xd3 15 ♖xd3 ♗e7 16 ♖e1 += ♖hf8 17 ♘h3 ♘g4 18 ♗g5! ♖fe8 19 ♗xe7 ♖xe7 20 ♘fg5 ♘df6 21 ♖d2 ♖ed7**

22 ♖ee2! g6 23 c3 b6?! 24 ♘f3 c5? 24...♔c7+= **25 dxc5 bxc5 26 ♘hg5 ♔c7 27 ♖xd7+ ♖xd7 28 ♘d2± ♘d5 29 g3 ♖e7 30 ♘ge4 ♔c6 31 ♘b3! c4 32 ♘d4+ ♔b6 33 ♘c2 +−** Δ ♘a3 **f5 34 ♘d2 ♔c5 35 ♘a3 ♘b6 36 f3 ♘f6 37 ♖e5+ ♘fd5 38 ♔c2 ♘d7 39 ♖e1 ♘5b6 40 ♘dxc4 e5** 40...♘xc4 41 b4+ ♔d5 42 ♖d1+ **41 ♖d1 ♘xc4 42 b4+ ♔c6 43 ♘xc4 ♖g7 44 ♖d6+ ♔c7 45 ♖a6 g5 46 hxg5 ♖xg5 47 ♖xa7+ ♔d8 48 f4! exf4 49 gxf4 ♖g2+ 50 ♔b3 ♖f2 51 ♘e3 ♘f6** 51...♖xf4? 52 ♘d5 **52 ♘xf5 ♖xf4 53 ♘d4 ♖f1 54 ♖a8+ ♔e7 55 a4 ♔f7 56 a5 ♔g7 57 a6 ♘d5 58 ♖d8 1-0 Pytel**

284 Ulman-Jone corr. 74/77
1 e4 c6 2 d4 d5 3 ♘c3 dxe4 4 ♘xe4 ♗f5 5 ♘g3 ♗g6 6 h4 h6 7 ♘f3 ♘d7 8 h5 ♗h7 9 ♗d3 ♗xd3 10 ♕xd3 ♕c7 11 ♗d2 e6 12 ♕e2 ♘gf6 13 0-0-0 0-0-0 14 ♘e5 ♘b6 15 ♗a5 ♖d5 16 b4 ♖xa5 17 bxa5 ♗a3+ 18 ♔b1 ♘a4 19 ♕f3! ♗b4 20 ♖d3 ♕xa5 21 ♘e2 ♘d5! 22 ♖h3 22 ♕xf7 ♘ac3+ 23 ♘xc3 ♗xc3 ∓/∝ **f6 23 ♘g6 ♖d8 24 ♘gf4** 24 a3!? **♘dc3+! 25 ♘xc3** 25 ♖xc3 ♗xc3 26 ♘xc3 ♕b4+ **♗xc3 26 ♖xc3 ♕b4+ 27 ♔c1 ♖xd4 28 ♖d3 ♖xf4 29 ♖b3** N 29 ♕e3 ♕b2+ 30 ♔d2 e5 31 ♕xa7 ♘b5∓ Scheper-Tarnai, corr 72 **♕e1+ 30 ♕d1 ♕e5 31 ♖he3** 31 ♖hd1 ♕c7 **♖e4 32 ♕e2 ♕a1+ 33 ♖b1 ♕xa2! 34 ♕d3** 34 ♖xe4 ♘c3 **♖xe3 35 ♕xe3 ♕c4 36 ♖b3 b6 37 ♕d3 ♕f4+ 38 ♕e3 ♕g5 39 ♖a3 b5 40 ♔b1 ♕g4 41 ♖d3 ♕b4+ 42 ♔c1 ♕e7** 42...♕b2+ 43 ♔d2 ♕b4+ 44 ♔e2 ♕g4+ 45 ♕f3 **43 ♕e4 ♔c7 44 ♕h7 ♔b6 45 ♕g8 e5 46 ♕b8+ ♔c5 47 ♕d8 ♕xd8** 47...♕f7 48 g4 f5 49 ♖d7 **48 ♖xd8± ♘c3 49 ♖d7 ♘e2+ 50 ♔d2 ♘f4 51 ♖xa7 ♘e6** 51...♘xh5!? 52 g4 ♘f4 53 ♖xg7 ♔d4 54 ♖h7 c5∝ **52 ♖d7! f5 53 g3 b4 54 ♔d3 f4 55 g4 f3 56 ♔e4 ♘g5+ 57 ♔xe5 ♔c4 58 ♖xg7 1-0 Gipslis**

285 Ubilava-Fedorov USSR 77
1 e4 c6 2 d4 d5 3 ♘d2 dxe4 4 ♘xe4 ♗f5 4...♘bd7 5 c3 ♘gf6 6 ♘xf6+ ♘xf6 7 ♗c4 ♘d5 8 ♘e2 ♗g4 9 0-0 += Ubilava-Holmov, USSR 76 **5 ♘g3 ♗g6 6 ♘f3 ♘d7 7 h4 h6 8 h5 ♗h7 9 ♗d3 ♗xd3 10 ♕xd3 e6 11 ♗d2 ♘gf6 12 ♕e2 ♕c7 13 0-0-0 0-0-0 14 ♘e5 += ♘b6 15 ♖h4!?** 15 ♗a5 ♖d5 16 b4∝ **c5 16 ♗a5! cxd4** 16...♗d6 17 dxc5 ♗xe5 18 ♖xd8+ ♖xd8 19 cxb6 ♗f4+ 20 ♔b1 axb6 21 ♗xb6 +−

Ubilava-Shereshevsky, USSR 74; 19... axb6 20 ♖c4 +− **17 ♖dxd4! ♗c5 18 ♖c4 ♖d5 19 ♘d3 ♔d7!** 19...♔b8 20 b4 ♗e3+ 21 ♕xe3 ♘xc4 22 ♗xc7+ +− **20 ♖c3 ♖c8 21 ♘e4** 21 b4? ♗e3+ **♘xe4 22 ♕xe4** 22 ♖xe4 ♕h2! **♕b8** 22...♕d6 23 ♕f3± **23 ♘xc5+ ♖dxc5 24 ♖xc5 ♖xc5 25 ♗c3 +− ♖g5 26 ♗xg7 ♘d5 27 ♗xh6 ♖e5 28 ♕a4+ b5 29 ♕d4 ♖e1+ 30 ♔d2 ♖g1 31 ♗e3 ♔e8? 32 ♕h8+ 1-0 Gufeld**

286 Gilezetdinov-Saharov
corr. 76/77

1 e4 c6 2 d4 d5 3 ♘c3 dxe4 4 ♘xe4 ♗f5 5 ♘g3 ♗g6 6 h4 h6 7 ♘f3 ♘d7 8 h5 ♗h7 9 ♗d3 ♗xd3 10 ♕xd3 ♕c7 11 ♖h4 e6 12 ♗f4 ♕a5+! N 12...♗d6 13 ♗xd6 ♕xd6 14 ♘e4 ♕e7 15 ♕a3 += **13 ♗d2 ♕b6** 13...♕c7!? 14 0-0-0 ♗e7 15 ♖hh1 ♘gf6= **14 0-0-0 ♗e7 15 ♖hh1 ♘gf6 16 c4 ♕a6 17 ♔b1 ♗d6 18 ♘e2 ♘g4 19 ♗e1 0-0-0= 20 ♕c2** 20 ♘d2 **c5 21 ♖d3?! cxd4 22 c5 ♗e7 =+** 22...♘xc5? 23 ♖xd4± **23 ♘exd4 ♘de5 24 ♖c3?! ♘xf3 25 ♘xf3 ♗f6 26 ♖b3** 26 ♖a3 ♕b5 27 ♖xa7? ♖d1+ −+; 27 ♖b3 ♕c6 =+ **♖d5 27 ♖b4? ♖hd8 28 a3** 28 ♗c3 ♘xf2! 29 ♕xf2 ♖d1+ 30 ♖xd1 ♖xd1+ 31 ♔c2 ♕d3+ 32 ♔b3 ♗xc3 −+ **♖d1+ 29 ♔a2**

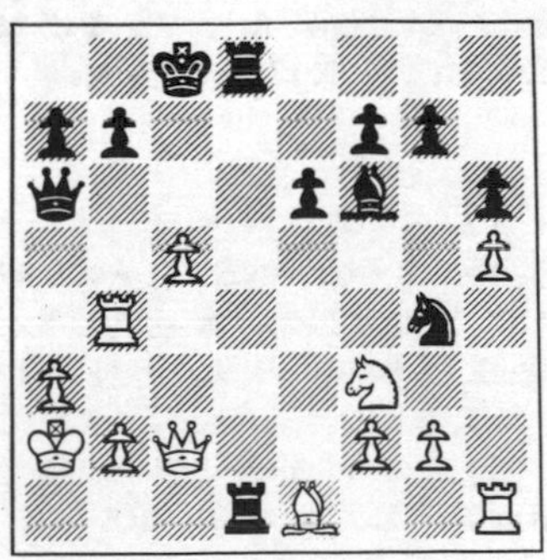

29...♘xf2! 30 ♕xf2 ♖a1+! 31 ♔b3 31 ♔xa1 ♕xa3+ 32 ♔b1 ♖d1+ 33 ♔c3 ♕d3 mate **♕d3+ 32 ♔a4 a5 33 ♖bh4** 33 ♖b6 ♕c4+ 34 ♔xa5 ♖d5 −+; 33 ♖f4 ♕d7+ 34 ♔xa5 ♕c7+ −+ **♖d5 34 ♖1h3** 34 ♗xa5 b5+! 35 ♔b4 ♗c3+! 36 bxc3 ♖b1+ −+; 34 ♗c3 ♗xc3 35 ♖xa1 b5+! −+; 34 ♗d2 b5+ 35 ♔xa5 ♗d8+ 36 ♔b4 ♖xh1 −+; 34 ♕d2! b5+ 35 ♔xa5 ♖xa3+! 36 bxa3 ♕xa3+ 37 ♔xb5 ♕xc5+ 38 ♔a4 ♕b5+ 39 ♔a3 ♖d3+ 40 ♕xd3 ♕xd3+ 41 ♔a4 ♗xh4∓ **♖xa3+! −+ 35 bxa3 b5+ 36 ♔xa5 ♗d8+ 0-1 Gufeld**

287 Sveshnikov-Djindjihashvili
Hastings 77/78

1 e4 c6 2 d4 d5 3 exd5 cxd5 4 c4 ♘f6 5 ♘c3 e6 5...♘c6; 5...g6 **6 ♘f3 ♗e7 7 cxd5 exd5** 7...♘xd5 8 ♗d3 += **8 ♗b5+ ♗d7 9 ♗xd7+** 9 ♕b3 0-0= **♘bxd7 10 0-0 0-0 11 ♗g5** 11 ♕b3 ♘b6 12 a4 +=; 11...♕a5!∝ **♕a5 12 ♘e5 ♖fe8** 12...♗b4! 13 ♘xd7 ♘xd7 14 ♕g4 f5!∝ **13 ♕b3 ♘xe5 14 dxe5 ♘e4 15 ♗e3 ♗f8 16 ♘xe4** 16 e6!? ♖xe6 17 ♕xb7 ♖d8 18 ♘xe4 ♖e7! 19 ♘f6+ gxf6∝ **dxe4 17 ♗d4 ♗c5 18 ♗c3 ♕b6 19 ♕d5 ♗b4?!** 19...e3! 20 fxe3 ♗xe3+ 21 ♔h1 ♖e6!+= **20 ♕xe4 ♗xc3 21 bxc3 ♕c5 22 ♖ae1 ♖e7 23 ♖e3± f6 24 e6** 24 f4± **♖ae8 25 ♖fe1?** 25 ♕g4! f5 26 ♕e2 f4 27 ♖e4± **♖xe6 26 ♕xe6+ ♖xe6 27 ♖xe6 += ♕xc3 28 h3** 28 ♖e8+ ♔f7 29 ♖8e7+ ♔g6 30 h4!+=; 29...♔f8 △ ♕b4∝ **h5! 29 ♖e7 b5 30 h4 a5 31 g3 b4 32 ♖d1 a4 33 ♖b7 ♕b2 34 ♖d8+ ♔h7 35 ♖db8 ♕b1+ 36 ♔g2 ♕e4+ 37 ♔g1 ♕e1+ 38 ♔g2 ½-½ Sveshnikov**

288 Vadasz-Sapi
Hungary Final 77

1 c4 c6 2 e4 d5 3 exd5 cxd5 4 cxd5 ♕xd5? 4...♘f6! 5 ♗b5+ ♘bd7 6 ♘c3 g6? 7 d4 ♗g7 8 d6 e6 9 d5 e5 10 ♘f3 0-0 11 0-0 ♘e8 12 ♖e1 ♘xd6? 13 ♗xd7 ♗xd7 14 ♘xe5± Sax-Orso, Hungary Final 77 **5 ♘c3 ♕d8 6 d4 ♘f6 7 ♘f3 e6 8 ♗d3 ♗e7 9 ♗g5!** 9 0-0 0-0 10 ♗g5 ♘c6 11 a3 b6 12 ♖e1 ♗b7 13 ♗c2 ♖c8 14 ♕d3 g6 15 ♖ad1 ♘d5 16 ♗h6 ♖e8 17 ♗a4 ♗f6 += Sax-Haag, Tungsram 76 **0-0** 9...♘bd7 10 ♘e5! ♘xe5 11 dxe5 ♘d5 12 ♗xe7 ♕xe7 13 ♘xd5 exd5 14 ♗b5+ += **10 ♗c2 ♘c6 11 a3 b6 12 ♕d3 g6 13 h4!**

13...a5?! 13...♘d5!? 14 ♘e4 ♗b7 15 h5 ♖c8 16 ♕d2 ♘a5 17 hxg6 fxg6 18 ♘e5± **14 h5 ♗a6 15 ♕d2 ♕c7** 15...♘xh5? 16 ♗h6 ♖e8 17 ♖xh5 gxh5 18 ♕f4 +− **16 hxg6 fxg6** 16...hxg6 17 ♗f4 ♕d7 18 ♗e5± Δ ♕h6 **17 ♗b3! ♘d8 18 ♕e3 ♗c4 19 ♗xc4 ♕xc4 20 ♘e5 ♕a6** 20...♕c7 21 ♕g3! ♕b7 22 ♗h6± **21 ♗h6 ♖e8 22 ♕g3 ♗d6 23 ♗f4** 23 ♕g5! ♗xe5 24 ♕xe5 ♔f7 25 ♘e4 +− **♗xe5 24 ♗xe5 ♘d7 25 ♕h4 ♘f8?** 25...h5 26 ♕g3 ♘xe5 27 dxe5 ♔h7 28 ♘e4 +− **26 ♕f6 1-0 Vadasz**

289 Kuzmin-Bagirov
USSR Final 77

1 c4 c6 2 e4 d5 3 cxd5 cxd5 4 exd5 ♘f6 5 ♘c3 ♘xd5 6 ♘f3 ♘c6 7 d4 ♗g4 8 ♗c4 8 ♕b3 ♗xf3 9 gxf3 ♘b6 10 d5 ♘d4 11 ♕d1 e5∞; 8 ♗b5 ♕a5 9 ♕b3 ♘xc3 10 bxc3 ♗xf3 11 gxf3 e6 12 d5 a6!= Keene-Roth, Aarhus 76 **e6 9 0-0 ♗e7 10 h3 ♗h5 11 ♖e1 0-0 12 ♗xd5 exd5 13 g4 ♗g6 14 ♘e5 ♗b4 15 ♗f4 ♘xe5 16 ♖xe5 ♗xc3 17 bxc3 ♖e8 18 ♕e2 f6 19 ♖xe8+ ♕xe8 20 ♖e1 ♕xe2 21 ♖xe2 ♖c8 22 ♖e7 ♖xc3 23 ♖xb7 ♖xh3 24 ♖b3** 24 ♖xa7 ♗e4 25 ♔f1 ♗f3 **♖xb3 25 axb3 ♗c2 26 b4 g5 27 ♗b8 ♗d1 28 ♗xa7 ♗xg4 29 b5 ♔f7 30 b6 ♗c8 31 ♗b8 ♔g6 32 ♗c7 f5 33 f4 g4 34 ♔f2 ♔f7 35 ♗d8 ♔e6 36 ♗h4 ♔d7 37 ♔e3 ♔c6 38 ♔d3 ♗a6+ 39 ♔c3= ½-½**

1 e4 e5 2 ♘c3

290 Inkiov-Radulov (2) 78

1 e4 e5 2 ♘c3 ♗c5 3 ♘f3 d6 4 d4 exd4 5 ♘xd4 ♘c6 6 ♗e3 ♘xd4 7 ♗xd4 ♗xd4 8 ♕xd4 ♘f6 9 0-0-0 0-0 10 e5 ♘e8 11 f4 ♕h4 12 ♗c4 dxe5 13 fxe5 ♕xd4 14 ♖xd4 c6 15 ♖d8 b5 16 ♗b3 ♗b7 17 ♖d7 ♗c8 18 ♖xf7 ♖xf7 19 ♖f1 ♘f6 20 exf6 ♗d7 21 ♘e4 ♗e8 22 ♘d6 c5 23 ♗xf7+ 23 ♘xe8? c4 **♗xf7 24 fxg7 ♗d5 25 ♖f5 ♗xg2 26 ♖g5 ♗h3 27 ♖g3 ♗e6 28 ♘e4**

291 Mamatov-Podgaets
USSR 77

1 e4 e5 2 ♘c3 ♘c6 3 ♗c4 ♘f6 4 d3 ♗b4 5 ♘ge2 d5= 6 exd5 ♘xd5 7 0-0 ♗e6 8 ♘e4?! 8 ♗b5 **♗e7 9 f4?! exf4 10 ♗xd5** 10 ♘xf4? ♘xf4 11 ♗xf4 ♕d4+ −+ **♗xd5 11 ♗xf4 ♗xe4 12 dxe4 0-0 13 ♕e1 ♗f6 14 ♕g3 ♕e7∓**

15 ♝xc7 ♝xb2 16 ♜ab1 ♞d4! 17 ♜f2 ♛c5! 18 ♚h1 ♛xc2! 19 ♜xb2 ♛xb2 20 ♝e5 ♛a1+! 21 ♞g1 f6 22 ♜xf6 ♛xg1+! 0-1 Gufeld

1 e4 e5 2 ♞f3 ♞c6 3 ♝b5

292 Mednis-Lein New York 77

1 e4 e5 2 ♞f3 ♞c6 3 ♝b5 a6 4 ♝a4 d6 5 c3 ♝d7 6 d4 ♞f6 7 0-0 ♝e7 8 ♜e1 0-0 9 ♞bd2 ♜e8 10 ♞f1 ♝f8!? 10...h6 **11 ♞g3** 11 ♗g5! h6? 12 ♗xf6 ♕xf6 13 dxe5! ♘xe5 14 ♘xe5 ♗xa4 15 ♘g4!± Matulovic-Sokolov, Jugoslavia 61; 11...b5! N 12 ♗b3 (12 ♗c2!? h6 13 ♗h4) 12...h6 13 ♗xf6 ♕xf6 14 ♘e3 ♕d8 (14...g6!? Δ ♗g7) 15 a4! ♘a5?! 16 ♗c2± Sigurjonsson-Lein, New York 77; 15...exd4? 16 cxd4 ♖xe4?! 17 ♗d5 ♖e7 18 ♖c1 ♕e8 19 ♘h4! ♔h8 20 ♘hf5! +−; 15...g6! += **g6 12 h3 ♝g7 13 a3** 13 ♗b3!?; 13 ♗c2!? **a5!= 14 dxe5** 14 ♗c2 a4 **♞xe5 15 ♞xe5 dxe5 16 ♝e3** 16 ♗xd7?! =+ **b5 17 ♝c2 a4 18 ♝d3! ♛e7 19 c4 b4 20 axb4 ♛xb4 21 ♛c2= ♝c6 22 ♞e2 ♞h5 23 ♞c3 ♞f4 24 ♝f1 ♞e6 25 ♞d5 ♛b7 26 ♜eb1 ♜ab8 27 ♝d3 ♜ed8 28 ♛e2 ♞f4 29 ♛c2** 29 ♘xf4? exf4 30 ♗xf4 ♖xd3! 31 ♕xd3 ♗xe4∓ **♝e8 30 ♝f1 ♞e6 31 ♞c3!= ♞d4!? 32 ♝xd4 exd4 33 ♞xa4 ♛b4 34 ♝d3 ♜a8 35 b3 ♜db8 36 ♛e2 ♝c6 37 ♛c2 ♝f8 38 ♛e2 ♛b7 39 ♛c2 ♝b4 40 ♜d1 ♜a5 41 ♜ab1 ♜e8 42 f3 ♛a7 43 ♜a1 ♝d7?!** 43...♗d6≈ **44 ♚h1 c5 45 f4! ♜a8 46 e5 ♝xa4 47 ♜xa4 ♜xa4 48 bxa4 ♛xa4 49 ♛e2 += ♜e8! ½-½ Mednis**

293 Mihailov-Vitolin,E. corr. 77

1 e4 e5 2 ♞f3 ♞c6 3 ♝b5 a6 4 ♝a4 d6 5 c3 f5 6 exf5 ♝xf5 7 d4 e4 8 ♞g5 d5 9 f3 e3 10 f4 ♞f6 11 0-0 ♝d6 12 ♝xe3 0-0 13 ♞f3 ♞g4 14 ♝c1 14 ♕d2!? ♘a5 15 ♗b3 ♘xb3 16 axb3 ♘xe3 17 ♕xe3 ♗xf4= **♞a5 15 h3 ♞f6 16 ♝c2 N** 16 ♘e5 ♘e4 17 ♘d2 c5 =I Germans-Ciocaltea, Lugano 68 **♝xc2 17 ♛xc2 c5 18 ♞e5 cxd4 19 cxd4 ♛b6!** 19...♖c8 20 ♘c3± **20 ♝e3** 20 ♕d3!? **♝xe5 21 fxe5 ♞c4! 22 ♛d3 ♞d7 23 ♜e1** 23 ♘c3 ♘dxe5! **♜ac8 24 b3** 24 ♘c3 ♘xb2 25 ♕c2 ♕b4; 25...♘c4 **♞dxe5 25 dxe5 ♞xe3 26 ♜xe3** 26 ♕xe3?! ♕xe3+ 27 ♖xe3 ♖c1+ 28 ♔h2 ♖ff1 29 e6 ♔f8 30 ♖f3+ ♖xf3 31 gxf3 d4∓; 29 ♖d3 ♖cd1! 30 ♖xd1 ♖xd1∓ **♜c1+ 27 ♚h2 ♛e6 28 a4 ♜ff1 29 ♜a2 ♜xb1+ 30 ♜f2! ♜xf2 31 ♛xb1 ♛f7 32 e6 ♛f4+ 33 ♜g3 ♛e5 34 ♛c1 ♛xe6 35 ♛c7 g6 36 ♜g5!** 36 ♕xb7 ♕d6!∓ **♛f7 37 ♛xf7+ ♚xf7 38 ♜xd5 ½-½ Gipslis**

294 Tseitlin-Klovan USSR 77

1 e4 e5 2 ♞f3 ♞c6 3 ♝b5 a6 4 ♝a4 d6 5 0-0 ♝g4 6 c3 6 h3 **♞f6 7 d3 g6 8 ♞bd2 ♝g7 9 ♜e1 0-0 10 ♞f1 ♝d7 11 a3** 11 ♘e3!? b5 12 ♗c2 Δ b4, a4 += **b5 12 ♝b3** 12 ♗c2 d5 **♞a5 13 ♝a2 c5= 14 ♝g5 h6 15 ♝h4 ♞c6 16 ♞e3 ♛b6 17 h3** 17 ♘d2 Δ ♕f3 **♜ae8 18 a4** 18 ♘h2 ♔h8 19 ♕f3 ♘g8 Δ f5 **♞e7 19 ♞h2 ♚h8 20 axb5**

axb5 21 Bb3 Qb7 22 Qf3?! g5 23 Bg3 c4!=+

24 Bc2 24 dxc4 Nxe4 25 cxb5 f5∓; 25 Nd5 Nc5 26 Nxe7 Qxf3 27 Nxf3 Nxb3∓ **cxd3 25 Bxd3 d5∓ 26 exd5** 26 Nxd5 Nexd5 27 exd5 e4 28 Bxe4 Nxe4 29 Rxe4 Rxe4 30 Qxe4 f5 Δ f4 −+ **e4 27 Qd1** 27 Bxe4 Nxe4 28 Qxe4 f5 Δ f4 −+ **exd3 −+ 28 Bd6 Rg8 29 Bxe7 Rxe7 30 Qxd3 Rge8 31 Nf3 Nh5 32 Rad1 Nf4 33 Qd2 Re4 34 Kh2 Qb6 35 d6 Qb7 36 h4 gxh4 37 Nxh4 Nd3 38 Qxd3 Rxh4+ 39 Kg1 Rhe4 40 Ra1 f5 41 Red1 R8e5 42 Nf1 Rg4 43 g3 f4 44 Nh2 Rgg5 0-1 Gufeld**

295 Kapengut-Vorotnikov Vilnius 77

1 e4 e5 2 Nf3 Nc6 3 Bb5 a6 4 Ba4 d6 5 0-0 Bg4 6 h3 h5 6...Bh5 7 c3 Nf6 8 Re1 +=; 7...Qf6 8 g4 Bg6 9 d4! Bxe4 10 Nbd2 += **7 d4** 7 Bxc6 bxc6 8 d4 Qf6 9 Nbd2 Be6!?; 7 d3 c4= **b5** 7...Qf6?! 8 dxe5 Δ hxg4 **8 Bb3 Nxd4 9 hxg4 hxg4 10 Ng5** 10 Bxf7+!? **Nh6 11 g3!** N 11 c3 Nxb3 12 axb3 Be7 13 Qd5 Rc8 14 Rxa6 Bxg5 15 Qc6+ Kf8∝; 11 f4 d5! 12 Bxd5 Bc5 13 Be3 Qd6 14 b4 Bb6 15 c4∝ **c6!** 11...Qd7 12 Bd5! c6 13 c3! += **12 f4 Be7! 13 Be3 Nxb3 14 cxb3!** 14 axb3 d5!=+ **d5 15 Qc2** 15 Nd2 d4!; 15 exd5 Nf5! **Rc8 16 Bc5! d4** 16...Bxg5 17 fxg5 Qxg5 18 Nd2 d4 19 Rf2! Δ Nf1± **17 b4!? Bxg5** 17...Qd7?! **18 fxg5 Qxg5∝ 19 Qd2!** 19 Rf2 Qe3! 20 Kg2 Ng8 21 Nd2 Rh2+!?; 21 Qe2 Qh6!∓; 21 Qd2 Qxe4+ **Qh5** Δ Nf5 **20 Rf2! Nf5?!** 20...Qh3 21 Rg2 f6 22 Qf2 Nf7 23 Rh2 Ng5! 24 Nd2!+=; 20...f6!? **21 Rh2! Qxh2+ 22 Qxh2 Rxh2 23 Kxh2 Ne3 24 Nd2 Kd7 25 Nf1! Rh8+ 26 Kg1 Nxf1 27 Rxf1 += f6 28 a4! Ke6 29 axb5 cxb5 30 Ra1 Ra8 31 Kf2 g6** 31...f5 32 exf5+ Kxf5 33 Ke2 Ke4 34 Rh1± **32 Ke2 f5 33 Kd3!± Kf6 34 Bb6! Kf7 35 Rc1! Re8!** 35...Rh8 36 Rc7+ Ke6 37 Rc6+ Kf7 38 Bc7± **36 Bc7 Re6 37 Rc5 Kf6 38 Bd8+ Kf7 39 Rc7+ Ke8 40 Bg5! Kf8 41 Bh6+ Kg8 42 Bg7! Re8 43 Bf6 Re6 44 Rc8+ Kf7 45 Bh8! Ke7 46 Rc5 f4 47 Rxe5 +− 1-0 Gufeld**

296 Egenberger-Klovan corr. 75/77

1 e4 e5 2 Nf3 Nc6 3 Bb5 a6 4 Ba4 Nf6 5 d4 exd4 6 0-0 Be7 7 e5 Ne4 8 b4 0-0 9 a3 9 Re1 Ng5 10 Nxd4 Nxd4 11 Qxd4 Ne6 12 Qe4 d5 13 exd6 Qxd6 14 c3 Bf6∓ **b5** 9...d5?! 10 Bxc6 bxc6 11 Nxd4± **10 Bb3 d5 11 c3** 11 Nxd4 Nxe5 12 Bf4 Ng6 13 Nc6 Qe8! 14 Nxe7+ (14 Bxd5 Bf6∓) Qxe7 15 Bxd5 (15 Qxd5 Nxf4 16 Qxa8 Bd3∓) Rd8 16 Bxa8 Rxd1 17 Rxd1 Nxf2 18 Kxf2 Nxf4∓ **Nxc3 12 Nxc3 dxc3 13 Qxd5** 13 Bxd5 c2 14 Qd2 Bb7 15 Ne1 (15 Be4 Qxd2 16 Bxd2 d5∓; 15 Bb2 Nxe5∓) 15... a5 16 Nxc2 axb4 17 Bxc6 Bxc6∓ **Bb7 14 Rd1 Qxd5 15 Rxd5 Rfd8 16 Bg5 Rxd5 17 Bxd5 Rd8! −+ 18 Bb3 Bxg5 19 Nxg5 Nxe5! 20 Re1** 20 Rc1 h6! 21 Nh3 Nd3! 22 Rxc3

♖e8 –+ **♗d5 21 ♖d1 c6 22 f4 ♘g4 0-1 Gipslis**

297 Kuzmin-Beljavsky
USSR ½-Final 77
1 e4 e5 2 ♘f3 ♘c6 3 ♗b5 a6 4 ♗a4 ♘f6 5 0-0 ♘xe4 6 d4 b5 7 ♗b3 d5 8 dxe5 ♗e6 9 ♘bd2 ♘c5 10 c3 ♘xb3? 10...d4! 11 ♗xe6 ♘xe6≈ **11 ♘xb3 ♗e7 12 ♘fd4!± ♘xe5** 12...♘xd4 13 cxd4±; 12...♕d7 13 f4± **13 ♖e1 ♘g6 14 ♘xe6 fxe6 15 ♘d4! +–**

15...♘f8 15...e5 16 ♘e6 ♕d7 17 ♕xd5 +– **16 ♕g4 h5 17 ♕xg7 ♗f6 18 ♕g3 ♕d7 19 ♗f4 0-0-0 20 a4 c5 21 ♗e5 h4** 21...♖h6 **22 ♕f4 ♗xe5 23 ♕xe5 ♖h6 24 axb5 1-0 Gufeld**

298 Pereira-Weiner corr. 76/77
1 e4 e5 2 ♘f3 ♘c6 3 ♗b5 a6 4 ♗a4 ♘f6 5 0-0 ♘xe4 6 d4 b5 7 ♗b3 d5 8 dxe5 ♗e6 9 c3 ♗c5!? 9...♗e7+= Gheorghiu **10 ♘bd2 0-0 11 ♗c2 ♗f5 12 ♘b3 ♗g4!** 12...♗b6? 13 ♘fd4!± Gheorghiu **13 ♘xc5 ♘xc5 14 ♖e1 ♖e8 15 ♗f4 d4 16 h3 d3** 16...♗h5 17 cxd4 ♗xf3 18 ♕xf3 ♘xd4 19 ♕c3 ♘xc2 20 ♕xc2 ♘e6 21 ♖ad1 ♕e7 22 ♗e3 ♖ed8 23 f4!± Karpov-Beljavsky, Leningrad 77; 17 g4? d3!∓ Gheorghiu **17 hxg4 dxc2 18 ♕xc2 ♕d3 19 ♕e2 ♖ad8 20 ♕e3 ♕xe3 21 ♖xe3 ♖d5 22 ♗g3 ♖ed8 23 ♔f1 h6 24 g5 hxg5 25 ♘xg5 ♘d3 26 e6 ♖xg5 27 ♗h4 ♖h5 28 ♗xd8 ♖h1+ 29 ♔e2 ½-½**

299 Haag-Karsa Hungary 78
1 e4 e5 2 ♘f3 ♘c6 3 ♗b5 a6 4 ♗a4 ♘f6 5 0-0 ♘xe4 6 d4 b5 7 ♗b3 d5 8 dxe5 ♗e6 9 c3 ♗c5 10 ♘bd2 0-0 11 ♗c2 ♗f5 12 ♘b3 ♗g4 13 ♘xc5 ♘xc5 14 ♖e1 ♖e8 15 ♗f4 ♕d7!? 15...♘e6 16 ♕d3 += **16 ♕d2 ♗h5! 17 ♘d4 ♗g6 18 ♖ad1 ♘e7 19 ♗e3?! ♗xc2 20 ♕xc2 ♘g6 21 b4 ♘a4! 22 f4 ♘b6 23 ♕f2 ♘c4 24 ♘b3 ♕f5 25 ♘d4 ♕d7 26 ♘b3 ♕f5 27 ♘d4 ♕d7 28 ♘b3 ½-½ Haag**

300 Shamkovich-Tarjan
Hastings 77/78
1 e4 e5 2 ♘f3 ♘c6 3 ♗b5 a6 4 ♗a4 ♘f6 5 0-0 ♘xe4 6 d4 b5 7 ♗b3 d5 8 dxe5 ♗e6 9 c3 ♗e7 10 ♗c2 0-0 10...♗g4!? **11 ♕e2 ♕d7** 11...♘c5 12 ♘d4 ♕d7 13 ♘d2 f6∞ **12 ♘d4 f5 13 f3! N** 13 exf6 ♘xd4 14 cxd4 ♗xf6∞ **♘c5** 13...♘g5 14 ♗xg5 ♗xg5 15 ♘xe6 ♕xe6 16 f4 ♗e7 17 ♘d2 += **14 ♗e3 f4!?** 14...♘xe5? 15 b4 ♘b7 16 ♗f4 +– **15 ♗f2 ♗f7 16 ♖e1 ♘e6 17 ♘d2 ♘cxd4?!** 17...♘cd8 **18 cxd4 += ♗g6 19 ♖ec1 ♗xc2 20 ♖xc2 a5 21 ♖ac1** 21 ♘b3!? Δ ♘c1-d3 **♖a6 22 ♕d3 a4! 23 ♘b1** Δ ♘c3-e2 **♖b6 24 b3** 24 ♘c3 b4 25 ♘e2 b3!∞ **g6?** 24...b4!

Diagram

25 ♘c3 axb3 26 axb3 ♖a8 27 ♘e2± ♖ba6 28 ♕d2 Δ ♘xf4, ♗e3 **g5 29 ♕d3 ♖a1 30 h4! ♖xc1+ 31 ♖xc1 gxh4 32 ♕f5 ♗g5 33 ♕g4 ♔h8 34 ♗xh4 ♖g8 35 ♗xg5 ♖xg5 36 ♕h3** Δ ♘xf4 **♕e8 37 ♖a1 ♕c6 38 ♕h4**

♖f5 39 ♕e7 Δ ♔f2, ♖h1 **♖f8 40 ♔f2 ♔g8 41 ♕b4** 41 ♖h1 ♖f7 42 ♕h4 ♕c2! **♕b6 42 ♖c1 ♖a8 43 ♕d2 ♖f8 44 ♕d3 ♖f7 45 b4!+− ♖f8 46 ♖h1 ♖f7 47 ♖a1** Δ ♖a5 **c6 48 ♖a8+ ♔g7 49 ♖e8 ♘c7 50 ♖d8! ♘a6** 50...♘e6 57 ♖d6 ♖e7 52 ♕f5+− **51 ♖d6 ♕b8** 51...♘xb4 52 ♕d2 ♕a5 53 ♘xf4 +− **52 ♕d2 ♕f8 53 ♔e1! ♘b8 54 g3! ♖a7** 54...fxg3 55 ♕g5+ **55 ♘xf4 ♕f5 56 ♔f2 ♘d7 57 g4 ♕b1 58 ♘e2** 58 ♘h5+ ♔h8 59 ♖xc6 Δ ♖c8+ **♘f8 59 ♕h6+ ♔g8 60 ♖d8 ♕xb4 61 ♕xc6 ♖a1 62 ♕xd5+ ♔g7 63 ♕d6! 1-0 Shamkovich**

301 Loktev-Grebenshikov corr. 77
1 e4 e5 2 ♘f3 ♘c6 3 ♗b5 a6 4 ♗a4 ♘f6 5 0-0 ♘xe4 6 d4 b5 7 ♗b3 d5 8 dxe5 ♗e6 9 ♕e2 ♗e7 10 ♖d1 ♘c5 11 c4 d4 12 cxb5 ♘xb3 13 axb3 axb5 14 ♖xa8 ♕xa8 15 ♗g5 ♗xb3 16 ♘c1 ♗xg5 17 ♘xg5 h6 18 e6! N 18 ♘f3 0-0 19 ♕xb5 ♗a4 20 ♕c5 ♖b8!= Mecking-Korchnoi, (4) 74 **hxg5 19 exf7+ ♔f8** 19...♔xf7 20 ♕f3+ Δ ♕xb3 **20 ♕xb5!** 20 ♕f3 **♗a4 21 ♕d5! ♖h6?** 21...♕a5 22 ♕xa5 ♘xa5 23 ♖xc7± **22 ♖e1!+− ♖d6 23 ♖e8+ ♕xe8 24 fxe8♕+ ♔xe8 25 ♕g8+ ♔d7 26 b3 ♗b5 27 ♕xg7+ ♔c8 28 ♕xg5 ♗e2 29 h4 d3 30 ♘d2 ♘d4 31 h5 1-0 Gipslis**

302 Tal-Smyslov
USSR Final 77
1 e4 e5 2 ♘f3 ♘c6 3 ♗b5 a6 4 ♗a4 ♘f6 5 0-0 ♘xe4 6 d4 b5 7 ♗b3 ♗e7?! 8 ♘xe5 8 dxe5+= **♘xe5 9 dxe5 ♗b7** 9...♘c5?! 10 ♗xf7+ ♔xf7 11 ♕f3+ ♔e8 12 ♕xa8 g6 13 ♕a7± **10 ♕g4 0-0 11 f3** 11 ♘c3 ♘xc3 12 ♗h6 ♗f6! 13 exf6 ♕xf6 14 ♗g5 ♕d4≈ **♘g5** 11...♗c5+? 12 ♔h1 ♘f2+ 13 ♖xf2 ♗xf2 14 ♗g5 h5 15 ♕f4 +− **12 f4??** 12 ♘c3 ♔h8 13 f4 ♘e4 12...♗c5+!? **13 f5 ♔h8** 13...♗c5+!? 14 ♔h1 ♔h8 15 ♘c3 ♘f2+ 16 ♖xf2 ♗xf2 17 ♗g5 f6 18 exf6 gxf6 19 ♗h6 ♖g8 −+ **14 ♖f3?** 14 ♗e3!=+ **♗c5+!∓**

15 ♔f1 15 ♗e3 ♕e7! **d6 16 f6 g6** 16...gxf6? 17 ♖h3 Δ ♖xh7+ = **17 ♕h4 dxe5 18 ♔e2** 18 c3 g5! 19 ♗xg5 ♘xg5 20 ♕xg5 ♖g8−+ **♕d4** Δ ♘c3+ **19 ♖h3 ♕f2+ 20 ♕xf2 ♘xf2 21 ♖h4 ♘e4 22 ♗h6 ♘xf6 23 ♗xf8 ♖xf8 −+ 24 ♔f1 ♖d8 25 c4 g5 26 ♖h3 g4 27 ♖c3 b4 28 ♖c1 ♖d4 29 g3 ♗f3 30 a3 a5 31 axb4 axb4 32 ♖a5 ♘d7 33 ♗c2 e4 34 ♖e1 ♗b6 35 ♖a8+ ♔g7 36 ♖d8 f5 37 ♗a4 ♘e5 38 ♖xd4 ♗xd4 39 ♘d2 ♗xb2 40 ♘b3 ♗c3 0-1 Gufeld**

303 Panchenko-Zaitsev Sochi 77
1 e4 e5 2 ♘f3 ♘c6 3 ♗b5 a6 4 ♗a4 ♘f6 5 0-0 ♗e7 6 ♖e1 b5 7 ♗b3 d6 8

c3 0-0 9 d4 ♝g4 10 ♝e3 ♝h5!? N 11 h3 ♝g6?! 11...♕d7!? Δ d5/exd4, d5 **12 ♞bd2! exd4** 12...♘xe4 13 ♗d5 ♘xd2 14 ♗xd2! ♕d7 15 dxe5 dxe5 16 ♗xc6 ♕xc6 17 ♘xe5±; 14 ♘xd2? exd4 15 cxd4 ♘b4 16 ♗xa8 ♕xa8∞ **13 ♞xd4** 13 cxd4 ♘b4 **♞a5 14 ♝c2 c5 15 ♞4f3 d5?** 15...♘c6 Δ d5 **16 e5 ♝xc2 17 ♛xc2 ♞e8 18 ♜ad1! ♞c7?** 18...♕c8 19 ♗g5!± **19 ♞e4!± ♞b7 20 ♝g5! h6** 20...♔h8!? **21 ♞f6+ ±/+− gxf6** 21...♗xf6 22 exf6 hxg5 23 ♘xg5 g6 24 ♖e7 Δ ♘xf7 Panchenko **22 ♝xh6 fxe5 23 ♜xe5 f5** 23...♕d6 24 ♗f4 ♕d7 25 ♗g5! ♖fe8 26 ♗xe7 ♖xe7 27 ♖g5+ ♔f8 28 ♕h7 +− Panchenko **24 ♜de1 ♜f7 25 ♜xf5 ♝f6 26 ♞g5 ♞d6 27 ♞xf7 ♞xf7 28 ♜h5 ♞xh6 29 ♜xh6 ♝g7 30 ♛h7+ ♚f8 31 ♜g6 1-0 Petrosian**

304 Gulko-Ivkov Polanica 77

1 e4 e5 2 ♞f3 ♞c6 3 ♝b5 a6 4 ♝a4 ♞f6 5 0-0 ♝e7 6 ♜e1 b5 7 ♝b3 d6 8 c3 0-0 9 d4 ♝g4 10 ♝e3 exd4 11 cxd4 ♞a5 12 ♝c2 ♞c4 13 ♝c1 c5 14 b3 ♞a5 14...♘b6! Tal-Portisch, Biel 76 **15 d5 ♞d7 16 ♞bd2 ♝f6 17 ♜ab1 ♝c3 18 h3 ♝xf3** 18...♗h5 19 g4± Gulko-Unzicker, Tallinn 77 **19 ♛xf3 b4 20 ♜f1** 20 ♖d1 += Bronstein-Smyslov, Petropolis 73 **♜fe8 21 ♛d3 ♞e5 22 ♛e2!** 22 ♕g3 c4! 23 f4 cxb3 24 axb3 ♖c8! **♛b6 23 f4 ♞d3** 23... c4+!

Diagram

24 ♞f3! 24 ♗xd3? c4+ =+ **♞xc1 25 ♜bxc1 c4+ 26 ♚h1 cxb3 27 axb3 g6** 27...f6 28 e5! dxe5 29 ♕e4 g6 30 f5! g5 31 ♘g5!± **28 e5! dxe5 29 fxe5 ♛f6 30 ♛e3! ♝xe5 31 ♞g5 ♝b2 32 ♛g3 ♛e5 33 ♛h4 ♛g7** 33...h5 34 ♘xf7! **34 ♜xf7 ♛xf7 35 ♞xf7 ♝xc1 36 d6 ♞b7 37 ♝e4 ♜ab8 38 ♝d5 ♛g7 39 ♛d4+ 1-0 Pytel**

305 Gufeld-Beljavsky USSR 77

1 e4 e5 2 ♞f3 ♞c6 3 ♝b5 a6 4 ♝a4 ♞f6 5 0-0 ♝e7 6 ♜e1 b5 7 ♝b3 0-0 8 c3 d6 9 h3 ♞a5 10 ♝c2 c5 11 d4 ♛c7 12 ♞bd2 cxd4 13 cxd4 ♞c6 14 ♞b3 a5 15 ♝e3 a4 16 ♞bd2 ♞b4 16... ♗e6 **17 ♝b1 ♝d7** 17...a3?! 18 bxa3 ♕c3 19 ♘b3± **18 a3 ♞c6 19 ♝d3 += ♞a5 20 ♛e2 ♛b8 21 ♜ac1 ♜e8 22 ♜c2 ♝d8 23 ♜ec1 b4 24 axb4 ♛xb4 25 dxe5 dxe5 26 ♝c5** 26 ♘c4!?+= **♛b8 27 ♝a3?! ♞h5= 28 ♛e3** 28 g3 ♗xh3 29 ♗b5 ♖e6 30 ♗d7 ♘f4! −+ **♞f4 29 ♝f1 h6 30 ♞c4 ♞xc4 31 ♝xc4 ♝b6 32 ♝c5** 32 ♕d2!? += ♕a7? 33 ♗xf7+ ♔xf7 34 ♖c7! +− **♝xc5 33 ♛xc5 ♝e6 34 ♝xe6** 34 ♗f1= **♜xe6 35 ♛c8+?!** 35 ♕c4=; 35 ♕e3= **♚h7 36 ♛d7?!** 36 ♕c4= **♜a7 37 ♜c7?? ♛xb2 −+ 38 ♛d8** 38 ♕xf7 ♕xc1+ −+ **♜xc7 39 ♜xc7 ♛b1+ 40 ♚h2 ♛f1 41 ♞h4 ♜g6 0-1 Gufeld**

306 Beljavsky-Klovan USSR 77

1 e4 e5 2 ♞f3 ♞c6 3 ♝b5 a6 4 ♝a4 ♞f6 5 0-0 ♝e7 6 ♜e1 b5 7 ♝b3 d6 8 c3 0-0 9 h3 ♝b7 10 d4 ♞a5 10...♖e8 **11 ♝c2 ♞c4 12 b3 ♞b6 13 ♞bd2**

♜e8 14 ♞f1 14 dxe5 dxe5 15 ♘xe5 ♗c5 16 ♘d3 ♘xe4 17 ♘xe4 ♗xe4 18 ♘xc5 ♗xc2 19 ♕xd8 ♖exd8 20 ♗e3 += **c5 15 ♞g3 ♝f8 16 a4 c4 17 a5 exd4 18 cxd4** 18 axb6 d3 19 ♗b1 ♘xe4 20 ♘xe4 ♖xe4 21 ♖xe4 ♗xe4 22 ♘d2 ♗d5 23 bxc4 bxc4 24 ♗a2±; 19...♕xb6 20 bxc4 bxc4 21 ♗a2∞ **cxb3 19 ♝xb3 ♞c4 20 ♝xc4 bxc4 21 d5 += ♜c8 22 ♝e3 ♞d7** 22...♘xe4? 23 ♗b6+− **23 ♛b1 ♝a8 24 ♜c1 g6 25 ♜a4 ♞c5 26 ♝xc5 ♜xc5 27 ♜cxc4 ♜xc4 28 ♜xc4 ♛xa5 29 ♛c1 ♝b7 30 ♚h2** 30 ♘d4?? ♗xd5 **♛b6 31 ♛f4 ♛d8?!** 31...♖e7 32 ♘d4 ♖c7; 31...♖c8? 32 ♘g5 ♖c7 33 ♕f6 h6 34 ♕d8 +− **32 ♞d4± ♛b6 33 ♞c6 a5?** Zeitnot 33...♖c8!? 34 ♖b4 ♕c7 35 ♕c1 a5 36 ♖c4 ♕b6 37 ♕c2 += **34 ♜c3 a4??** 34...♗xc6 35 dxc6 ♖c8 36 ♘h5! ♖xc6 37 ♘f6+ ♔g7 38 ♘d7 ♕c7 39 ♕f6+ ♔g8 40 ♖xc6 ♕xc6 41 ♕d8 +−; 36...♕d4 37 ♘f6+ ♔g7 38 ♘d5± **35 ♞h5 +− ♜c8 36 ♞f6+ ♚g7 37 ♞d7 ♛b2** 37...♕c7 38 ♕f6+ ♔g8 39 ♘xf8 ♗xc6 40 ♖xc6 ♕d8 41 ♘e6! +− **38 ♛f6+ ♚g8 39 ♞e7+ ♝xe7 40 ♜xc8 ♝xc8 41 ♛xb2 ♝xd7 42 ♛b7 1-0 Gufeld**

307 Dorfman-Romanishin
USSR Final 77

1 e4 e5 2 ♞f3 ♞c6 3 ♝b5 a6 4 ♝a4 ♞f6 5 0-0 ♝e7 6 ♜e1 b5 7 ♝b3 d6 8 c3 0-0 9 h3 ♞b8 10 d4 ♞bd7 11 ♞bd2 ♝b7 12 ♝c2 12 ♘f1 ♖e8 13 ♘g3 ♗f8 14 d5 c5 15 ♗c2 c4 16 ♗e3 ♘c5 17 ♕d2 += Timoshenko-A.Petrosian, USSR ½-Final 77 **♜e8 13 b3** 13 ♘f1 ♗f8 14 ♗g5 h6 15 ♗h4 g5 16 dxe5∞ Romanishin-Kraidman, Hastings 76/77; 13 b4 **♝f8 14 a4** 14 ♗b2 g6 15 a4 ♘h5 16 c4 c6 17 ♘f1 bxc4 18 bxc4 exd4 19 ♗xd4 ♕c7 20 ♖b1 ♗g7 21 ♗xg7 ♘xg7 22 ♘e3 h5 23 ♕d4 ♘e6 24 ♕d2 ♘e5 25 ♘h4 ♗c8 26 ♘ef5 Romanishin-A.Petrosian, Moscow 72; 17...exd4 **g6 15 d5 c6 16 c4 ♛c7** 16...bxc4 17 bxc4 a5; 17 dxc6 cxb3!; 17...♗xc6 18 ♘xc4 **17 ♝a3 ♜ec8 18 ♝d3 cxd5 19 cxd5 ♛b6 20 g3** 20 axb5 axb5 21 ♕e2 ♘h5 22 ♗xb5 ♘g3 23 ♕d3 ♖xa3 24 ♖xa3 ♘c5 25 ♕b1 ♕xb5 26 b4!; 21...b4 22 ♗b2 ♘c5 23 ♘c4 ♕d8 24 ♗c2 **♞h5 21 ♚g2 ♞c5 22 ♝c2 ♝g7** 22...♗h6 **23 a5 ♛d8 24 b4 ♞d7 25 ♝d3** 25 ♘f1 **♛f8! 26 ♚g1 ♝h6** 26...f5 27 exf5 gxf5 28 ♘h4 e4 **27 ♛e2 ♞g7 28 h4 f5 29 ♞g5 ♞f6 30 ♜ad1 fxe4 31 ♞dxe4**

31...♞xe4? 31...♗xd5? 32 ♘xf6+ ♕xf6 33 ♗xb5 ♗b3 34 ♗xa6 ♗xd1 35 ♖xd1 ♖f8 36 ♗c4+ ♔h8 37 ♘e4 ♕f3 38 ♕xf3 ♖xf3 39 ♘xd6; 31...♘xd5! 32 ♕a2 ♔h8 33 ♘xd6 ♗xg5 34 ♘xb7 ♘c3!; 32 ♗b1 ♗xg5 33 ♗a2 ♗e7 **32 ♞xe4 ♞f5 33 ♝b2 ♜c7** 33...♗xd5 **34 f4 ♝g7** 34...♖f7 35 fxe5 dxe5 36 ♗xe5 ♖e8; 35 h5 ♗xd5 36 hxg6 hxg6 37 ♕g4 **35 fxe5 ♝xe5 36 ♝xe5 dxe5 37 d6! ♞d4 38 ♛a2+ ♛f7 39 ♛xf7+ ♜xf7 40 ♜f1 ♜xf1+ 41 ♜xf1 ♝xe4** 41...♖d8 42 ♘c5? ♗c6 43 ♘xa6 e4 44 ♗b1 ♖xd6 45 ♗a2+ ♔g7 46 ♖f7+ ♔h6 47 ♔f2 ♘f5!; 42 ♘f6+! ♔g7 43

Be4 **42 Bxe4 Ra7?** 42...Rd8 43 Bd5+ Kh8 44 Rf6? Nf5 45 Bb7 Kg7!; 44 Bb7! Rxd6 45 Rf8+ Kg7 46 Ra8 Rd7 47 Bxa6 e4 48 Rb8 Kh6 49 Re8! **43 g4! Kg7 44 g5 Rf7 45 Rf2** 45 Rxf7+ Kxf7 46 Bd5+ Ke8 47 Bb7 Kd7 48 Bxa6 Kxd6 49 Bb7 Kc7 50 Be4! Ne2+ 51 Kf2 Nc3 52 Kf3 **Nf5 46 Bxf5 gxf5 47 Rc2 Kg6 48 Rc6 Rd7 49 Rxa6 Kh5 50 Rb6 Kxh4 51 Kf2 Kxg5 52 a6 Ra7 53 d7! Rxd7 54 Rxb5 Kf4 55 Ra5 1-0**

308 Korsunsky-Klovan USSR 77

1 e4 e5 2 Nf3 Nc6 3 Bb5 a6 4 Bxc6 dxc6 5 0-0 f6 6 d4 Bg4 7 dxe5 Qxd1 8 Rxd1 fxe5 9 Rd3 Bd6 10 Nbd2 b5 10...Nf6 11 Nc4 Nxe4 += **11 c4** 11 b3!? **Nf6 12 c5 Bxc5 13 Nxe5 Be2** 13...0-0? 14 Nb3 Bd6 15 Nxc6± Vaulin-Klovan, USSR 77 **14 Rc3 Bb6** 14...Bd4 15 Rxc6 Bxe5 16 Rxe6+ ± **15 Rxc6 0-0-0! 16 Nf7 Nxe4 17 Nxh8 Bxf2+ 18 Kh1 Bb6 19 h3** 19 Rxb6 cxb6 20 Nf7 Rd5=+; 19 Nf7 Nf2+ 20 Kg1 Nh3+ += **Nxd2 20 Nf7** 20 Bxd2 Rxd2 21 Rac1 Kb7 22 R6c2 Rxc2 23 Rxc2 Bc4 24 b3 Bd5∓ **Ne4!** 20...Rd5 21 Re6!± **21 Nxd8** 21 Bf4 Rf8 22 Nd6! Kd7∓ ½-½ 21...Ng3+ 22 Kh2 Nf1+ = **Gipslis**

309 Radulov-Inkiov (1) 78

1 e4 e5 2 Nf3 Nc6 3 Bb5 a6 4 Bxc6 dxc6 5 0-0 Bg4 6 d3 6 h3 Bh5 7 g4! Bg6 8 Ne5 Qh4 9 Qf3 **Bd6 7 Nbd2 Ne7 8 h3 Bh5 9 b3 f6 10 Bb2 Qd7 11 Nc4 Bf7 12 Ne3 c5 13 c3 0-0 14 d4 cxd4 15 cxd4 exd4 16 Nxd4 Rad8 17 Ndf5 Nxf5 18 Nxf5 Be6 19 Nxd6 Qxd6 20 Qxd6 cxd6** 20...Rxd6? 21 Ba3 +− **21 Ba3 Rf7 22 Rfe1 Rc7 23 Re2 d5 24 Rd1 Rcd7 25 e5** 25 Red1? dxe4= **fxe5 26 Rxe5 Bf7 27 Bc5 h6 28 Bd4 Re8 29 Rxe8+ Bxe8 30 Re1 Bg6 31 Rc1 Kf7 32 f3 Bd3 33 Kf2 Bb5 34 Rc8 Bc6 35 g4 Re7 36 Kg3 g5 37 Rh8 Kg6 38 Rg8+ Kh7 39 Rf8 Re2 40 Rf7+ Kg8 41 Rg7+ Kf8 42 Rh7 Rd2 43 Bc5+ Ke8 44 Re7+ Kd8 45 Re1 Rxa2 46 Bf8 Ra5 47 Re5 Rb5 48 Bxh6 Rxb3 49 Bxg5+ Kd7 50 Re3 Rxe3 51 Bxe3 b5 52 h4 Ke6 53 h5 b4 54 Bd4 Kf7 55 g5 Be8 56 f4 Ke6 57 Kg4 1-0**

310 Timoshenko-Klovan USSR 77

1 e4 e5 2 Nf3 Nc6 3 Bb5 Bc5 4 0-0 4 c3 **Nd4 5 Nxd4 Bxd4 6 c3 Bb6 7 d4 c6 8 Ba4 exd4** 8...d6 **9 cxd4 d5 10 exd5 Qxd5 11 Bb3!?** N 11 Re1+ Be6 12 Nc3 Qxd4 13 Qf3∞ **Qxd4 12 Qh5 Qf6 13 Bg5** 13 Nc3!? Bf5 14 Re1+ Kf8 ∞/+= **Qg6≈ 14 Re1+ Kf8 15 Qh4 Nf6 16 Nd2** 16 Qb4+ c5 17 Qf4 h6 18 Qd6+ Kg8 19 Re8+ Kh7 20 Rxh8+ Kxh8 21 Qf8+ Kh7 22 Bxf6 gxf6∞; 16...Kg8? 17 Bxf6 gxf6 18 Re7 +− **h6 17 Bf4** 17 Nf3 Bg4 18 Bxf7 Qxf7 19 Ne5 hxg5! 20 Qxh8+ Qg8 21 Ng6+ Kf7 22 Ne5+ =; 18 Bxf6? Bxf3 **Qg4!=+** 17...Nd5?! 18 Nc4 ∞/+= **18 Bd6+ Kg8 19 Nf3** 19 Qxg4?! Bxg4 20 Re7 Rd8 21 Bxf7+ Kh7 22 Nc4 Rxd6! 23 Nxd6 Bc5∓ **Qxh4 20 Nxh4 Nd5! 21 Rad1 Bg4 22 Rd3 g5?!** 22...Rd8! 23 Be5 Re8 24 Rg3 Bc7!∓

Diagram

23 Ng6! 23 Nf3 Bf5 24 Rdd1 Kh7∓ **Bf5** 23...fxg6 24 Rxd5 +− **24 Ne7+** 24 Rxd5? Bxg6∓ **Nxe7 25 Rxe7** 25 Rf3 Be6 26 Bxe6 fxe6 27 Bxe7 Re8= **Bxd3 26 Bxf7+ Kg7 27 Bc4+ Kf6 28 Re6+ Kg7 29 Re7+ ½-½ Gufeld**

Opposite B's accentuate advantage

311 Lafite-Mechkarov France 77
1 e4 e5 2 ♘f3 ♘c6 3 ♗b5 ♗c5 4 0-0 ♘f6 5 d3 d6 6 c3 0-0 7 h3 7 ♘bd2 ♕e7 8 b4 ♗b6 9 ♘c4 ♘d8 10 ♘xb6 axb6= Panov-Tolush, USSR 40 **♘e7 8 ♖e1 c6 9 ♗a4 ♘g6 10 ♘bd2 ♘h5 11 d4 ♗b6 12 ♘f1 ♘hf4 13 ♕c2 ♕f6 14 ♕d1 h6 15 ♘g3 ♗e6 16 ♗b3 ♖ad8 17 d5 ♗xh3 18 gxh3 ♘xh3+ 19 ♔g2 ♘xf2 20 ♘h5 ♘f4+ 21 ♔h2 ♘xh5 22 ♕e2 ♘f4 23 ♕f1 ♘4d3 0-1**

312 Bangiev-Fokin USSR 77
1 e4 e5 2 ♘f3 ♘c6 3 ♗b5 ♘d4?! 4 ♘xd4 exd4 5 0-0 c6 6 ♗a4!? 6 ♗c4 += **♗c5** 6...♘f6 7 d3 d5 8 ♗g5 dxe4 9 dxe4 ♗e7 10 e5+=; 6...d5?! 7 exd5 ♕xd5 8 ♗b3 ♕f5 9 ♖e1+ ♗e7 10 d3 ♗d7 11 ♘bd2 += **7 d3 ♘e7 8 ♘bd2** 8 ♗g5! 0-0 9 ♗b3 h6 10 ♗h4 d6 11 f4 += **0-0?!** 8...d5! 9 exd5 ♘xd5 10 ♖e1+ ♗e6 11 ♘e4 ♗e7 12 ♗b3 0-0 13 ♗d2 += **9 ♕h5! d6** 9...d5 10 ♗b3 ♗e6 11 ♘f3 h6 12 ♗d2 += **10 ♘f3 h6** 10...♗e6? 11 ♘g5 **11 ♗b3!** 11 ♗xh6? gxh6 12 ♕xh6 f6! **♗e6?!** 11...d5! += **12 ♗xh6! ♗xb3 13 ♗d2! f6** 13...♗e6 14 ♘g5 ♖e8 15 ♕h7+ ♔f8 16 ♕h8+ ♘g8 17 ♘h7+± **14 axb3 ♕d7 15 ♖ae1** 15 ♘h4! **♕e6?** 15...g6 **16 ♘h4 ♕f7 17 ♕g4 ♖fe8 18 ♖e2!? a5 19 ♖a1! ♗b4 20 ♗xb4 axb4 21 ♖ee1** Δ ♕d7 **d5 22 ♘f3! dxe4 23 ♖xa8 ♖xa8 24 ♕xe4 ♘d5 25 ♕xd4 ♖e8 26 ♖e4!± ♖e6 27 ♕a7! ♕e7 28 ♕b8+ ♔f7** 28...♔h7 29 ♕c8 ♖xe4 30 ♕f5+± **29 ♖xe6 ♔xe6 30 ♕g8+! ♔d7! 31 h4! +– ♔c7 32 h5 ♘f4 33 ♕h7** Δ h6 **♘d5 34 c4! bxc3 35 bxc3 ♔b6** 35...♘xc3 36 h6 +– **36 c4 ♘f4 37 h6 ♘e6 38 ♕e4 1-0 Gufeld**

313 Shamkovich-Stopa USA 77
1 e4 e5 2 ♘f3 ♘c6 3 ♗b5 ♘d4 4 ♘xd4 exd4 5 0-0 c6 6 ♗a4 ♗c5 6...♘f6!? **7 d3 ♘e7 8 ♕h5!** N 8 ♗g5 0-0 9 ♗b3 h6 10 ♗h4 d6 11 f4± Honfi-Thielement, Monte Carlo 67; 9...d5! 10 exd5 cxd5 11 ♕h5 ♗e6 12 f4 f6 =+ **d6** 11...d5?! 12 ♗b3 0-0 13 ♘d2 0-0 14 ♘f3± **9 ♘d2 ♗e6** 9...0-0 10 ♘f3 Δ ♘g5 **10 ♘f3 += ♕a5?!** 10...0-0 11 ♘g5 h6 12 ♘xe6 fxe6 13 ♗b3 += **11 ♗b3 ♗xb3 12 cxb3±** Δ ♘xd4 **♕c7** 12...♕b5 13 ♘g5 ♘g6 14 ♕h3! h6 15 ♘xf7! **13 ♘g5 ♘g6 14 f4!±**

14...0-0-0 15 ♗d2 ♕e7? 15...h6 **16 b4 ♗b6 17 a4 ♕f6** 17...h6 18 ♘f3 a6 19 b5!± **18 ♕h3 ♔b8 19 e5! ♕e7** 19...dxe5 20 fxe5 ♕xe5 21 ♘xf7 +– **20 exd6 ♖xd6 21 ♖ae1 ♕d7 22 f5! +– f6 23 ♘e4 ♘e5 24 ♘xd6 ♕xd6**

25 ♗f4 ♗c7 26 ♗xe5 fxe5 27 b5 cxb5 28 axb5 ♕b4 29 ♕g4 ♕e7 30 ♖f3 Δ ♖g3 **h5 31 ♕g6 ♖h6 32 f6! ♕b4 33 ♕e8+ 1-0 Shamkovich**

314 Radulov-Inkiov (3) 78

1 e4 e5 2 ♘f3 ♘c6 3 ♗b5 f5 4 ♘c3 fxe4 4...♘d4; 4...♘f6 **5 ♘xe4 ♘f6** 5...d5 **6 ♕e2!?** 6 ♘xf6+ ♕xf6 7 ♕e2 ♗e7 8 ♗xc6 bxc6 9 ♕xe5 ♕f7 10 0-0 d6 11 ♕g3 0-0≈ Penrose-Boey, Lugano 68; 10 d3 d6 11 ♕f4 += **♕e7** 6...d5 7 ♘xf6+ gxf6 8 d4 e4 9 ♘e5=; 9 ♘h4± **7 0-0 d5 8 ♘c3 e4 9 ♘d4 ♗d7 10 ♗xc6 bxc6 11 d3 c5 12 ♘db5 ♗c6 13 ♗g5 d4 14 ♗xf6 gxf6 15 ♘xe4 ♗xb5 16 ♕h5+ ♔d8 17 ♕d5+ ♕d7 18 ♕xa8+ ♔e7 19 ♘xc5 ♗c6 20 ♕xa7 ♕d8 21 ♖fe1+ ♔f7 22 ♘e6 ♕d5 23 ♕xc7+ ♗e7 24 ♘d8+ ♖xd8** 24...♕xd8 25 ♕xc6 +− **25 ♖xe7+ ♔f8 26 ♖f7+ ♕xf7 27 ♕xd8+ ♔g7 28 ♖e1 ♕g6 29 ♕c7+ 1-0**

315 Vitolins-Lanka USSR 77

1 e4 e5 2 ♘f3 ♘c6 3 ♗b5 f5 4 ♕e2 fxe4 5 ♕xe4 ♘f6 6 ♕e2 ♗d6! 7 d4 e4 8 ♘g5 ♕e7 9 c3 h6 10 ♘h3 0-0 10... g5!? 11 ♘d2 b6 12 ♘c4 ♗b7 13 ♘xd6 ♕xd6 14 f4 g4 15 ♘f2 0-0-0 =+ Konstantinov-Zak, USSR 59 **11 ♘d2 a6 12 ♗a4 b5 13 ♗c2 ♗b7 14 ♘f1 ♘a5 15 ♘g3 ♕e6 16 0-0 ♘c4 17 a4 ♗d5 18 a5 e3?!**

Diagram

19 b3?! 19 ♗xe3± **♘g4?** 19...exf2+ 20 ♖xf2 ♗xg3 21 hxg3 ♕xe2 22 ♖xe2 ♘d6= **20 f3 ♘xh2 21 ♔xh2 ♗xg3+ 22 ♔xg3 ♕d6+ 23 f4! +− g5 24 bxc4 ♗xc4 25 ♗d3 ♖ae8 26 ♗xc4+ bxc4 27 ♗xe3 ♕e6 28 ♖ae1 ♔h8 29 fxg5 ♕d6+ 30 ♘f4 ♖f5 31 gxh6 ♖g5+ 32 ♔h2 1-0 Gipslis**

316 Gipslis-Gonsior
Hradec Kralove 77/78

1 e4 e5 2 ♘f3 ♘c6 3 ♗b5 ♘f6 4 0-0 ♗c5 5 ♘xe5! ♘xe4 5...♘xe5 6 d4 c6 7 dxe5 ♘xe4 8 ♗d3± **6 ♕e2 ♘xe5 7 d4! ♕e7** 7...♗e7 8 dxe5 ♘c5 9 ♖d1! 0-0 10 ♗c4 c6 11 a4± O'Kelly-Duckstein, 60 **8 dxc5 ♘xc5 9 b4!±** 9 ♖e1?! ♘g6 10 ♕f1 ♘e6∓ **a6** 9...♘a6 10 ♖e1 +− **10 bxc5 axb5 11 ♖e1 f6** 11...d6; 11 cxd6 cxd6 12 f4± **12 f4 ♕xc5+ 13 ♗e3 ♕c4! 14 fxe5 ♕xe2** 14...fxe5 15 ♕h5+ +− **15 ♖xe2 fxe5 16 ♘c3 d6** 16...c6 17 ♗c5! +−; 16...b4 17 ♘d5 +− **17 ♘xb5 ♔d7 18 a4** 18 ♖f1 ♔c6 Δ ♗e6≈ **♖f8! 19 ♖d2 ♖f6 20 ♘c3?** 20 c4 Δ a5± **♖f7 21 ♖dd1 ♔c6 22 ♘b5 ♗e6 23 ♖a3 b6!** 23... ♗c4 24 ♘a7+ ♔d7 25 ♖c3±; 24... ♖xa7 25 ♗xa7 b6 26 a5! +− **24 ♖c3+ ♔b7 25 ♘xd6+ cxd6 26 ♖xd6 ♖xa4** Δ ♖a1+ **27 ♖xb6+ ♔a8 28 h3 ♗c4 29 ♖c6 ♗a6 30 ♖e6 ♗c4 31 ♖xe5± ♔b7 32 ♖e8 ♗a6 33 ♖e6 ♗c4 34 ♖d6** 34 ♖b6+ Δ ♖c6± **♖a1+ 35 ♔h2 ♖a4 36 ♖d8** 36 ♖b6+!? Δ ♖c6 **g6 37 ♔g3 ♗e6 38 ♖d6 ♗c4 39 ♗f4 g5? 40 ♗xg5 ♖g7 41 h4 +− ♖a6 42 ♖d4 ♗e6** 42...h6 43 ♖cxc4 +− **43 ♔f2 ♖c6 44 ♖b4+ ♖b6 45 ♖e4 ♗d5 46**

♜d4 ♜b5 46...♖c6 47 ♖xc6 ♔xc6 48 g4!+− **47 g3 h5 48 ♝f4 ♝c6 49 ♜d8 ♝e4 51 ♜b8+ 1-0** 51...♔a6 52 ♖c6+ ♔a5 53 ♗d2+ +− **Gipslis**

317 Shulman-Zvigelsky USSR 77
1 e4 e5 2 ♞f3 ♞c6 3 ♝b5 ♞f6 4 0-0 ♝c5 5 ♞xe5 ♞xe4 6 ♛e2 ♞xe5 7 ♛xe4 ♛e7 8 d4 ♞c6 9 ♛g4 9 ♗xc6 dxc6 10 ♖e1 ♕xe4 11 ♖xe4+ ♗e7= **h5!** 9...f5 10 ♕h5+ g6 11 ♕d1± **10 ♛xg7** N **♝xd4 11 ♛g3 a6** 11...d6!? Δ ♗d7 **12 ♝c4 h4 13 ♛d3 d6 14 ♝d5 ♝f6 15 ♝xc6+ bxc6 16 ♛f3 d5** 16...♗d7 **17 ♞d2 ♜g8 18 h3 ♝e6 19 ♞b3 ♚d7 20 ♝e3!? ♝xb2 21 ♜ad1 ♝a3?!** 21...♕f6!? **22 c4! ♝d6 23 ♞d4± ♜g6 24 ♞xc6! ♛f6 25 ♛xf6 ♜xf6 26 cxd5 ♝xd5 27 ♜xd5 ♚xc6 28 ♜d4± ♜g8** 28...♖h8 29 ♖c1+ Δ ♗g5± **29 ♜xh4 ♜fg6 30 g4 +− f5 31 f3 fxg4 32 hxg4 ♚d7 33 ♚f2 ♜f8 34 g5 ♝e7?! 35 ♜h7 ♚e8 36 ♜xe7+ ♚xe7 37 ♝c5+ ♚f7 38 ♝xf8 ♚xf8 39 f4 ♚f7 40 ♜c1 1-0 Gipslis**

318 Perenyi-Tsinka
Budapest I 77
1 e4 e5 2 ♞f3 ♞c6 3 ♝b5 g6 4 c3 d6 5 d4 ♝d7 6 ♛b3 N 6 dxe5 dxe5 7 ♕e2 ♗g7 8 ♗e3 ♘ge7 9 ♘bd2 a6 10 ♗c4 ♕c8 11 0-0 0-0 12 b4 ♘d8=; 7 ♗c4 ♕f6 8 0-0 h6 9 ♗e3 ♘ge7 10 b4 ♗g7= **♝h6! 7 0-0 ♝xc1 8 ♜xc1 ♞ge7 9 ♞a3 0-0 10 dxe5 dxe5 11 ♞c4 ♝e6 12 ♝xc6 ♝xc4 13 ♛xc4 ♞xc6 14 ♜d1 ♛e7 15 ♜d5 += ♜ad8 16 ♜e1 a6** 16...♔g7 17 b4 f6 18 ♕b4 += **17 b4 ♜fe8 18 a4 ♚g7 19 b5 ♞a5 20 ♛b4!±**

Diagram

20...♜xd5 21 exd5 ♛xb4 22 cxb4 ♞c4 23 bxa6 bxa6 24 ♜c1 ♞b6 25 ♜xc7 ♞xd5 26 ♜b7 ♚f6 27 h4 h6 27...♖c8! **28 ♞d2 ♞c3 29 a5 ♜d8 30 ♞c4 ♜d4 31 ♜b6+ ♚g7** 31...♔f5 32 ♘d6+ **32 ♞xe5 ♜xh4 33 f3! ♞d5 34 g4! h5 35 ♜b7 ♚f6 36 b5 +− ♚xe5 37 bxa6 hxg4 38 a7 gxf3 39 a8♛ ♜g4+ 40 ♚f2 ♚e4 41 ♜b4+ 1-0 B.Balogh**

319 Zaitsev-Zuravlev Sochi 77
1 e4 e5 2 ♞f3 ♞c6 3 ♝b5 g6 4 d4 ♞xd4 5 ♞xd4 exd4 6 ♛xd4 ♛f6 7 e5 ♛b6 8 ♛a4! N **c6 9 ♝d3 ♛b4+ 10 ♛xb4 ♝xb4+ 11 ♝d2± ♝e7 12 ♞c3 f6** 12...d5 13 exd6 ♗xd6 14 0-0-0± **13 f4 f5 14 0-0-0 ♞h6 15 h3 b5 16 ♞e2** 16 g4! **♝b7 17 ♝e3 a6 18 c4 b4 19 c5 a5 20 ♞g1?!** 20 ♘d4 (Δ e6) ♗xc5 21 ♘xf5 +− **♝a6 21 ♞f3 ♞f7 22 ♝xa6 ♜xa6 23 ♜d2?** 23 ♗d4! Δ e6 **♞d8! 24 ♜hd1 ♜a7 25 ♜c2 ♞e6 26 ♜d3 ♜b7 27 a4 bxa3 =+ ½-½ Petrosian**

1 e4 e5 2 ♞f3 ♞c6 3 ♞c3

320 Mititelu-Ene Rumania 77
1 e4 e5 2 ♞f3 ♞c6 3 ♞c3 g6 4 d4 exd4 5 ♞d5 5 ♘xd4 ♗g7 6 ♗e3 ♘f6 7 ♗e2 0-0 8 0-0 ♖e8 9 ♘xc6 bxc6 10 ♗f3 ♗b7 11 ♕d2 d6= Spassky-Larsen (5) 68 **♝g7 6 ♝g5 ♞ce7** 6...

Nge7? 7 Nxd4!; 6...f6 7 Bf4 += **7 Nxd4** 7 e5 h6! 8 Bxe7 Nxe7 9 Qxd4=; 8 Bh4 g5 9 Nxe7 Qxe7 =+ Winawer-Steinitz, London 1883 **c6 8 Nxe7** 8 Nc3 h6 9 Be3 Nf6 10 Bc4 0-0 11 Qf3 d5!± Gufeld-Petrosian, USSR 69 **Nxe7 9 Qd2 h6 10 Bf4** 10 Bh4 d5 11 exd5 Qxd5= Cesnauskas-Nei, USSR 64 **d5! 11 exd5** 11 0-0-0 g5= **Qxd5 12 Be3?!** 12 c3 **0-0 13 c4 Qe5 14 0-0-0 Rd8 15 f4** 15 Qc3 Nf5 16 Nxf5 Rxd1+ 17 Kxd1 Qxf5∓ **Qf6 16 Qf2 Nf5! 17 Nxf5 Rxd1+ 18 Kxd1 Bxf5 19 h3 Rd8+ 20 Kc1** 20 Ke1 Qe7! **Qd6 21 Qe1** 21 Qe2? Bxb2+ 22 Kxb2 Qb4+; 21 Qd2? Qe7 22 Qf2 Qe4 **c5! 22 g4**

22...Bxb2+! 23 Kxb2 Qb6+ 24 Ka3 24 Ka1 Qf6+ **Rd1! 25 Bd2 Rxe1 26 Bxe1 Qc6 27 Rg1 Qf3+ 28 Kb2 Qe3 29 Rh1 Be4 0-1 Ciocaltea**

1 e4 e5 2 Nf3 d6

321 Zaitsev-Durao Sochi 77
1 e4 e5 2 Nf3 d6 3 d4 Nf6 3...exd4 4 Nxd4 g6 Larsen 5 Nc3 Bg7 6 Be2?! Nc6 7 Be3 Nf6 8 0-0 0-0 9 Re1 Re8 10 Nxc6 bxc6 11 Bf3 Nd7= Karpov-Keene, Bad Lauterberg 77; 6 f3!? Nc6 7 Be3 Nf6 8 Qd2 0-0 9 0-0-0 Re8 += Tseshkovsky-Lehmann, Albena 77 **4 Nc3 Nbd7 5 Bc4 Be7 6 0-0 0-0 7 Qe2 c6 8 a4 Qc7 9 Ba2** 9 h3 Δ Be3 **b6 10 Be3 Bb7** 10...Ng4 **11 Nh4!? exd4** 11...g6 12 dxe5 dxe5? 13 Bh6 Rfe8 14 Bxf7+ +−; 12...Nxe5 13 Bh6 Rfe8 14 f4 Neg4 15 Bg5 d5! 16 e5 Bc5+ 17 Kh1 h6!; 13 h3 Nfd7!; 13 f4 Ned7 **12 Bxd4 c5 13 Be3** 13 Nf5 cxd4 14 Nxe7+ Kh8 15 Ncd5 Bxd5 16 Nxd5 Bxd5 17 Bxd5 Rac8 18 Rac1 Nf6 **Nxe4 14 Nf5 Bf6?** 14...Ndf6 15 Bh6! gxh6 16 Nd5 Nxd5 17 Qxe4 **15 Nd5 Bxd5** 15...Qd8 16 Qg4 Re8 17 Bh6+ Kf8 18 Nxf7! **16 Bxd5 Ng5** 16...Rae8 17 Qg4 **17 Bxa8 Rxa8 18 Bxg5 Bxg5 19 Rad1 Rd8 20 Nxd6 1-0**

322 Haag-Titkos Hungary 78
1 e4 c6 2 d4 d6 3 Nf3 Nf6 4 Nc3 Bg4 5 Be2 Nbd7 6 0-0 e5 7 Be3 Be7 8 Nh4! Bxe2 9 Qxe2 g6 10 Rad1 0-0 11 g3 Ne8 12 dxe5! dxe5 12...Bxh4 13 gxh4± **13 Bh6 Ng7 14 Bxg7 Kxg7 15 Qg4 Nf6 16 Nf5+ Kh8 17 Rxd8 Nxg4 18 Rxa8 Rxa8 19 Nxe7 Re8 20 Nxc6 bxc6 21 Rd1 Rb8 22 b3 Rb7 23 h3 Nh6 24 Rd8+ Kg7 25 Kf1 1-0 Haag**

1 e4 e5 2 Nf3 Nf6

323 Tal-Suetin Sochi 77
1 e4 e5 2 Nf3 Nf6 3 Nxe5 d6 4 Nf3 Nxe4 5 d4 d5 6 Bd3 Be7 7 0-0 Nc6 8 c4 Nf6. 8...Bg4 9 Nc3 Nxc3 10 bxc3 0-0 11 Rb1 dxc4 12 Bxc4 Na5 13 Bd3 c5=; 8...Nb4; 8...Be6 **9 Nc3** 9 cxd5 Nxd5 10 Nc3 += **0-0 10 Re1 dxc4 11 Bxc4 Bg4 12 Be3 Na5** 12...Bxf3 13 Qxf3 Nxd4 14 Qxb7 Nc2 15 Rad1 Qb8! **13 Bd3 Re8 14 h3 Bh5 15 a3 a6 16 d5?!** 16 b4! Nc6 17 g4 Bg6 18 Bc4 **c5!**

17 ♗g5 b5 18 ♖e5 18 d6 ♕xd6 19 ♗xf6 ♗xf6 20 ♗xh7+; 19...♕xf6 20 ♗d5; 19...gxf6 **♗g6 19 ♗xg6 hxg6 20 d6? ♕xd6 21 ♕e2 ♘c4 22 ♘e4 ♕d8 23 ♖d1**

23...♘xe5! **24 ♖xd8 ♘xf3+ 25 ♕xf3 ♖axd8 26 ♗xf6 ♗xf6 27 ♘xf6+ gxf6 28 ♕xf6 ♖d2 29 ♕xa6 ♖xb2 30 ♕c6 ♖e1+ 31 ♔h2 ♖ee2 32 g4 c4 33 ♔g3 ♖b3+ 34 ♔h4 ♖xf2 35 ♔g5 ♖xh3 36 a4 c3 37 axb5 c2 0-1** 38 b6 ♔g7 (Δ f6+) 39 ♕c7 ♖h1 −+

1 e4 e6

324 Kavalek-Korchnoi
Wijk aan Zee 78

1 e4 e6 2 d3 b6!? 3 g3 ♗b7 4 ♗g2 c5 5 ♘f3 ♘f6 6 0-0 ♗e7 7 e5?! ♘d5 8 d4 c4!=+ 9 c3 0-0 10 ♘bd2 b5 11 ♖e1 d6 12 ♕c2 dxe5 13 ♘xe5 ♘d7 14 ♘df3 ♖c8 15 a3 ♘xe5 16 dxe5? 16 ♘xe5 **♖c7! 17 ♘d4 a6 18 ♗e4 h6 19 ♕e2 ♗c5 20 ♖d1 ♖d7∓ 21 ♗c2** Δ ♕e4 **♘e7! 22 ♗xh6?!** 22 ♗e3 ♕c7∓ **gxh6 23 ♕g4+ ♔h8 −+ 24 ♘e2** 24 ♕h5 ♘g8 **♘g6! 25 h4 ♖d2 26 ♘f4 ♘xe5 27 ♕h5 ♖xd1+ 28 ♖xd1 ♕f6 0-1 Pytel**

325 Sigurjonsson-Mednis New York 77

1 e4 e6 2 d4 d5 3 ♘c3 ♗b4 4 e5 b6 5 ♗d2 ♘e7?! 5...♕d7 6 ♘f3 ♗f8!? 7 ♗e2 ♗a6 8 0-0 ♘e7 += Timman-Seirawan, Lone Pine 78 **6 ♘f3!** 6 ♕g4?! ♘f5 7 ♘f3 ♗a6 8 ♗xa6 ♘xa6 9 ♕f4 c5= Tseshkovsky-Petrosian, USSR Final 76 **♗a6** 6...♕d7!? 7 ♗e2 ♗a6 **7 ♗xa6 ♘xa6 8 ♘e2! ♗xd2+** 8...♘f5 += **9 ♕xd2 h5?!** 9...c5 += **10 a4! ♘b8 11 a5 b5** 11...♘bc6 12 axb6 axb6 13 ♖xa8 ♕xa8 14 0-0± **12 b4! ♘d7 13 0-0-0± ♘f8 14 ♘f4 ♘eg6 15 ♘d3 ♘d7 16 ♘g5 ♘df8 17 ♖de1 ♘h7 18 ♘xh7 ♖xh7 19 ♘c5 ♖h6 20 f4 ♘e7 21 g3 ♘f5 22 ♕d3 c6 23 h3 h4 24 g4 ♘g3 25 ♘b7 ♕e7 26 ♘d6+ ♔f8 27 ♕c3!** 27 ♖h2 ♖d8 28 ♕c3 ♖xd6! 29 exd6 ♕xd6 += **♘xh1 28 ♕xc6 ♖b8 29 ♖xh1 ♔g8 30 ♔b2 f6 31 ♖e1 fxe5 32 ♖xe5??** 32 fxe5! g6!± Δ ♖h7 **♖d8! 33 ♘xb5 ♕xb4+ 34 ♔c1 ♖b8** 34...♕xa5! −+ **35 g5 ♖g6** 35...♖xb5? 36 gxh6 ♕b2+ 37 ♔d1 ♕xd4+ 38 ♔e2±; 35...♕xb5?! = **36 c4** 36 ♖xe6 ♖xe6 37 ♕xe6+ ♔h8 (37...♔h7? 38 g6+ ♔h6?? (38...♔h8=) 39 ♕e5! +−) 38 ♘d6 ♕b2+ 39 ♔d1 ♕xd4+ 40 ♔e2 ♕xf4! −+ 41 ♘f7+ ♔g8! 42 ♘e5+ ♔h7 43 g6+ ♔h6; 41 g6 ♕f6! **dxc4 37 a6 c3! −+ 38 ♘xc3 ♕xd4 39 ♘e2 ♕a1+ 40 ♔d2 ♖b2+ 41 ♔e3 ♕f1! 42 ♕c4 ♕xh3+ 43 ♔d4 ♖d2+ 44 ♔e4 ♖d5! 0-1** 45 ♖xd5 exd5+ 46 ♕xd5+ ♕e6+; 45 ♘d4 ♕g2+ 46 ♘f3 ♖xe5+ 47 fxe5 h3 **Mednis**

326 Mecking-Andersson
Wijk aan Zee 78

1 e4 e6 2 d4 d5 3 ♘c3 ♗b4 4 e5 b6 5 ♘f3 ♕d7 6 ♗d2 ♗a6 6...♗f8 7 a4! **7 ♗xa6 ♘xa6 8 ♘e2** 8 0-0 ♘b8 9 ♘e2 ♗e7 10 ♖c1± Δ c4 Geller-Karpov, USSR Final 76; 9...♗xd2 10 ♕xd2 += **♗f8** 8...♗xd2+ 9 ♕xd2 ♘e7 += **9 0-0?!**

9 ♘f4! c5 10 ♕e2 ♘b4 11 ♗e3 ♘h6 12 dxc5 bxc5 13 c3 ♘c6 14 c4 += Liberzon-Hubner, Bad Lauterberg 77 **c5 10 c3 ♘e7 11 ♘f4 ♘b8 12 ♖c1** 12 c4!? cxd4 13 cxd5 ♘xd5 14 ♘xd4 += **c4 13 b3 ♘bc6** 13...b5 14 a4 a6 15 ♖a1 += **14 ♘h5** 14 bxc4!? dxc4 15 ♘g5 += Δ ♘e4 **h6 15 ♗e3 ♘a5 16 ♘d2 0-0-0 17 g4 g6 18 ♘g3 ♔b8 19 ♕e2 ♖c8 20 f4 h5!**

21 b4?! 21 h3; 21 f5!? **♘ac6 22 gxh5?** 22 h3; 22 f5!? **gxh5 23 ♘xh5 ♘f5 =+ 24 ♘g3 ♘ce7 25 ♘f3 ♗h6 26 ♔f2 ♖h7 27 ♖g1 ♖ch8** Δ ♘g6 **28 ♘h5 ♗g7 29 ♘xg7 ♘xg7 30 ♖g4 ♘gf5 31 ♖cg1 ♕a4! 32 ♗c1 ♖h3 33 ♔g2** 33 ♖1g2!? Δ ♔g1 **♘g6 34 ♕f2 ♔b7** Δ ♕e8 **35 ♕e2 ♖8h6 36 ♖f1 ♕e8 37 ♖g1 ♕h8 38 ♔f2?** 38 ♖h1∓ **♘gh4 −+ 39 ♘xh4 ♖6xh4 40 ♗d2 ♖xh2+ 41 ♖1g2 ♖4h3 42 ♕f1 ♖xg2+ 43 ♖xg2 ♕h4+ 44 ♔e2 ♘g3+ 0-1 Webb**

327 Tal-Petrosian
USSR Final 77

1 e4 e6 2 d4 d5 3 ♘c3 ♗b4 4 e5 b6?! 5 ♕g4 ♗f8 6 ♘f3 ♕d7 6...♗a6!? **7 a4 ♘c6** 7...♗a6 8 ♘b5 c6 9 ♘d6+± **8 ♗d2 ♘ge7** 8...♘b4 9 ♖c1± **9 ♗e2?!** 9 ♘d1; 9 ♘e2 **♘f5!** Δ h5, g5, ♘xd4/ h5, g6, ♗h6, ♘xd4 **10 0-0 h5 11 ♕f4 g6** 11...g5 12 ♕xg5 ♗h6 13 ♕xh5 **12 ♗b5 ♗h6** 12...a6!? 13 ♗xc6 ♕xc6 Δ ♗h6, ♕c4∓ **13 ♘g5 ♘fxd4 14 ♖ad1! ♔f8?? +−** 14...0-0 15 ♕xd4 ♘xd4 16 ♗xd7 ♗xd7 17 ♘xe6 fxe6 18 ♗xh6 ♘xc2∞; 14...a6 15 ♗xc6 ♘xc6 16 ♕f6 0-0 17 ♘f3 ∞/=+ **15 ♗xc6 ♘xc6 16 ♘ce4** Δ ♘f6, ♘gh7+ **♗xg5 17 ♘xg5 ♗a6 18 ♖fe1 ♔g8 19 b4 ♗c4 20 b5 ♘d8 21 ♗b4 ♕e8 22 ♖e4?! ♗xb5 23 axb5 dxe4 24 c4!** 24 ♘xe4 ♕xb5∞ **c5 25 ♘xe4 ♕f8 26 ♘f6+** 26 ♗c3! **♔g7 27 ♗c3** 27 ♗e1! ♘b7 28 ♘d7! +− **♘b7 28 ♕f3** 28 ♖d7 ♖d8! 29 ♖xb7?? ♖d1+ −+ **♘a5 29 ♖d7 ♖d8 30 ♖xa7 ♘xc4 31 h4 ♖a8 32 ♘xh5+?!** 32 ♖b7! +− **gxh5 33 ♕f6+ ♔g8 34 ♕g5+ ♔h7 35 ♕xh5+ ♔g8 36 ♕g5+ ♔h7 37 ♕xh5+ ♔g8 38 ♕g4+ ♔h7 39 ♕e4+ ♔g7 40 ♕g4+ ♔h7 ½-½ Petrosian**

328 Ivanovic-Planinc
Jugoslavia Final 78

1 e4 e6 2 d4 d5 3 ♘c3 ♗b4 4 e5 b6 5 ♘h3 5 ♗d2; 5 a3 **♕d7 6 ♘f4 ♘c6 7 ♗e2 ♗b7 8 0-0 0-0-0 9 ♘a4** 9 ♗g4!? **♗f8 10 c3 f6 11 b4 ♘h6** 11...fxe5? 12 ♘xe6 **12 ♘d3 ♘f7 13 f4 f5 14 ♖ab1 += ♗e7 15 ♕b3 ♖dg8 16 ♔h1 h5 17 ♖b2 h4 18 ♗e3 g5 19 ♖fb1!** Δ ♘ac5 **gxf4 20 ♗xf4 ♗g5 21 ♕d1** 21 ♘ac5 ♕e7 22 ♘xb7 ♗xf4≈ **♕e7 22 ♗f3 ♗xf4 23 ♘xf4 ♘g5 24 ♕d3 h3 25 ♖e1** 25 c4? dxc4 26 ♕xc4 ♘xf3 27 gxf3 ♘xe5; 25 ♘c5 ♗a8 **♘e4 26 ♗xe4 dxe4 27 ♕e3 hxg2+ 28 ♖xg2 ♖xg2 29 ♔xg2 ♖g8+ 30 ♔h1 ♕h4!** Δ ♘xe5, ♕xf4 **31 ♖f1** 31 ♘xe6? ♘xe5 32 dxe5 ♕xe1+ **♗a6 32 ♕f2** 32 ♖f2 ♕g4! 33 ♖g2 ♕d1+ 34 ♕g1 ♕f3 −+; 32 ♖g1 ♖xg1+ 33 ♔xg1 ♕g4+ 34 ♔f2 ♕d1 −+ **♕xf2 33 ♖xf2 ♘xe5!? 34 ♖g2** 34 dxe5!? e3 35 ♖g2 ♗b7 36 ♘b2 ♖g4 37 ♘bd3≈; 34...♖g4 35 ♘g2!≈; 34...♗b7 35 ♘b2 ♖g4! −+; 35 ♖g2! e3 36 ♘b2≈

Rxg2 35 Kxg2 Nd3! −+ **36 Nxd3 exd3 37 Nb2 d2 38 Kf2 f4 39 a4 Bc4 40 h4 Kd7 41 Kf3 Ke7 42 h5 Kf6 43 Kxf4 Be2 44 h6 d1Q 45 Nxd1 Bxd1 46 a5 Bc2 47 c4 Bd3 48 c5 bxa5 49 bxa5 a6 50 Ke3 Bh7 51 Kf4 c6 0-1 Webb**

329 Van der Sterren-Korchnoi
Wijk aan Zee 78

1 e4 e6 2 d4 d5 3 Nc3 Bb4 4 e5 c5 5 a3 Bxc3+ 6 bxc3 Ne7 7 Nf3 Nbc6 7...Bd7! 8 Bd3 Ba4; 8 a4 Qa5 **8 Bd3 Qa5 9 0-0 c4 10 Be2 Bd7?!** 10...Qxc3 11 Bd2 Qb2= **11 a4 Nc8** 11...f6 12 Qd2 Δ Ba3± **12 Qd2 Nb6 13 Qg5?!** 13 Ba3! Nxa4 14 Bd6± **Rg8** 13...Qxc3 14 Qxg7 0-0-0≈; 14 Ra2! Nxd4 15 Bd2! Nxf3+ 16 Bxf3 Qd4 17 Be3 Qc3= **14 Ra3 h6 15 Qh5± Nxa4 16 g3** 16 Nh4!? Δ f4, f5 **b5 17 Bd2 Qd8 18 Rb1 Qe7 19 Raa1 a6** += **20 Nh4 0-0-0 21 Ng2!** 21 f4 f5! **Kc7 22 Ne3 Ra8 23 f4 Nb6** 23...f5!? 24 exf6 Qxf6 Δ Nb6/Be8 25 g4!± **24 f5 b4?!** 24...exf5 += **25 Rf1** Δ f6 **g6 26 fxg6 Rxg6 27 Qf3 Be8 28 Qf4** Δ Bh5/cxb4 **bxc3 29 Bxc3 Qg5 30 Qf3 a5 31 Ng2 Nb4 32 Nf4 Rg8 33 Rfb1 Qd8** 33...Qe7? 34 Rxa5

34 Qf1! Δ Qc1 **Nc6 35 Rb5 a4** 35...Nxd4 36 Rc5+ Nc6 37 Bxa5 +− **36 Qb1 Ra6 37 Qb2 Bd7** 37...Qe7 38 Rc5 Δ Qa3 **38 Qa3 Nxd4 39 Qc5+! Kb7** 39...Nc6 40 Ba5 Kb7 41 Bxb6 Rxb6 42 Rab1 +− **40 Bxd4 Bxb5 41 Qxb5** +− **a3 42 Bh5 Qc7 43 Ne2 Qe7 44 Nc3 Qd7 45 Qb4 Rg5 46 Rxa3! Rxa3 47 Qxb6+ Ka8 48 Nb5 Qb7 49 Qd8+ Qb8 50 Qd7 Qb7** 50...Rxh5 51 Nc7+ Kb7 52 Nxd5+ Ka6 53 Qc6+ Ka5 54 Bb6+ **51 Qe8+ Qb8 52 Qc6+ Qb7 53 Qe8+ Qb8 54 Qc6+ Qb7 55 Qd6 Raxg3+ 56 hxg3 Qxb5 57 Qf8+ Kb7 58 Qxf7+ Kb8 59 Kg2 Qa4 60 Qf8+ 1-0 Webb**

330 Mecking-Korchnoi
Wijk aan Zee 78

1 e4 e6 2 d4 d5 3 Nc3 Bb4 4 e5 c5 5 a3 Bxc3+ 6 bxc3 Ne7 7 Qg4 0-0!? 8 Nf3 8 Bg5 Qa5! 9 Bxe7? Qxc3+ 10 Ke2 Nc6! −+ **Nbc6 9 Bd3 f5 10 exf6 Rxf6 11 Qh5?!** 11 Bg5! Rf7 12 Bxe7 Rxe7 13 Qh4 g6 14 0-0 c4 15 Be2 Bd7 16 Rb1 b6 17 Rfe1 Qf8 18 Bf1 Ree8 19 Re2 Kg7 20 Ra1 Qf5 21 Qg3 g5 22 Rae1 h6= Tunak-Pytel, Poland 77 **h6 12 0-0** 12 Ne5?! Nxe5 13 dxe5 Rf8 14 g4? c4 15 Bg6? Nxg6 16 Qxg6 Qh4 17 Be3 Bd7 18 0-0-0 Qe7! 19 Qh5 Be8 20 Qh3 Bg6 −+ Shaposhnikov-Boleslavsky, USSR 51 **c4 13 Be2 Qa5 14 Bd2 Bd7 15 Rfb1 Qc7=+ 16 Nh4 Raf8 17 f4 Be8 18 Qg4 Ng6! 19 Nxg6** 19 g3 **Bxg6 20 Ra2 Ne7 21 Rab2 b6 22 Qh3 Nf5 23 Re1 Qe7 24 Ra2 Nd6 25 Bf3 Ne4 26 Bxe4 Bxe4∓ 27 g3 Qf7 28 Qg4 g5! 27 Raa1 Rf5! 30 Rf1** 30 fxg5 h5 31 g6 Qf6 32 Qh3 Rf2 33 Bf4 Rg2+ 34 Kf1 Qxf4+! 35 gxf4 Rxf4+ 36 Qf3 Bxf3 **Bxc2 31 Rf2 Qg6 32 Re1 Be4! 33 Rxe4 dxe4 34 Kf1 Rb5 35 Qe2 Rb1+ 36 Kg2 Rb2 37 Qxc4 e3!** −+ **38 Bxe3 Qe4+ 39 Kh3 Rxf2**

40 ♗xf2 gxf4 41 gxf4 ♖xf4 42 ♗g3 ♖f5 43 ♕c8+ ♖f8 44 ♕c4 h5 45 ♕b5 ♕g4+ 46 ♔g2 h4 0-1 Pytel

331 Velimirovic-Kovacevic
Jugoslavia Final 78

1 e4 e6 2 d4 d5 3 ♘c3 ♗b4 4 e5 f6 4...c5; 4...b6 **5 a3** 5 ♕g4 ♕e7 6 ♗d3 ♕f7 7 ♘e2 c5 8 dxc5 ♘c6 9 f4 ♗xc5 10 ♕g3 Alekhine-Pavlov, Moscow 09; 6 ♘f3! +=; 5 ♘f3 c5 6 a3 (6 ♗b5+ ♘c6+=) ♗a5 7 b4 cxb4 8 ♘b5 ♘c6 9 axb4 ♗c7 10 c3 ♘ge7 11 exf6 gxf6 12 ♗d3 0-0 13 0-0 ♗d7 14 ♗h6± Botvinnik-Ragozin, Moscow 27 **♗f8 6 ♗d3 ♕d7 7 ♘f3 ♘c6 8 0-0 fxe5 9 ♗b5 ♗d6** 9...exd4?? 10 ♘e5 **10 ♗xc6 bxc6 11 ♘xe5 ♗xe5 12 ♕h5+ ♕f7 13 ♕xe5 ♘f6 14 ♗f4 0-0 15 ♕xc7 ♘e4 16 ♕xf7+** 16 ♕xc6?? ♗d7 17 ♕c7 ♖ac8 −+ **♖xf7 17 ♗e5 ♘xc3 18 bxc3 ♗a6 19 ♖fb1 ♖b7 20 ♖xb7 ♗xb7 21 ♖b1 ♗a6 22 a4 ♔f7 23 f3 g5 24 ♖b8 ♖xb8 25 ♗xb8 ♗e2 26 ♗xa7 ♗d1 27 a5 ♗xc2 28 ♗b6 ♗d3 29 ♗d8 h6 30 ♔f2 ♗a6 31 g4 c5 32 ♔e3 cxd4+ 33 cxd4 ♔g6 34 f4 ♗c4 35 fxg5 hxg5 36 h4 gxh4 37 ♗xh4 1-0**

332 Kuzmin-Petrosian
USSR Final 77

1 e4 e6 2 d4 d5 3 ♘c3 dxe4 4 ♘xe4 ♘d7 5 ♘f3 ♘gf6 6 ♘xf6+ ♘xf6 7 ♗d3 c5 8 0-0 cxd4 9 ♘xd4 += ♗e7 10 ♗f4! 0-0 11 c3 ♘d5 12 ♗g3 ♗f6 13 ♘f3 ♗d7 14 ♕e2 ♕a5 15 a4 ♗c6 16 ♘d2!? Δ ♘c4-d6; 16 ♘e5!± **♕d8 17 ♘c4 g6 18 ♖fd1 ♗h4 19 ♘e5 ♗xg3 20 hxg3 ♕c7 21 ♗c2 ♖ad8 22 ♖d4 ♘f6 23 ♖ad1 ♖d5 24 ♖xd5 ♗xd5 25 ♕e3 ♗e4!= 26 ♘d7** 26 ♗xe4 ♕xe5 27 ♗xb7 ♕xe3 28 fxe3 ♖b8!= **♘xd7 27 ♗xe4 ♘f6 28 ♗f3 b6 29 ♕d4 ♔g7 30 c4 ♖c8 31 b3 ♕e7 32 ♕c3 a5!= 33 ♕e5 ♕b4 34 ♖d4 ♖c5 35 ♕e3 ♖c8?!** 35...h6!?= **36 ♖h4 ♕c5** 36...h5!? 37 g4 ♕c5!= **37 ♕h6+ ♔g8 38 g4 g5! 39 ♖h3 ♕e5 40 ♗e2**

40...♖d8?? +− 40...♔h8 Δ ♖g8-g6-g7 **41 ♖e3 ♕f4 42 g3! +− ♘xg4 43 ♗xg4 ♕xg4 44 ♖e5! ♕d4 45 ♖xg5+ ♔h8 46 ♖h5 ♕g7 47 ♕e3 ♕d4** 47...♖d4 48 c5+−; 48 ♖b5 Δ c5+−; 48 ♔g2 Δ c5 +− **48 ♕xd4 ♖xd4 49 ♖b5 ♖d6 50 ♔f1 ♔g7 51 ♔e2 ♖c6 52 c5 ♖xc5** 52...bxc5 53 ♖xa5 c4 54 b4 c3 55 ♔d1 +− **53 ♖xc5 bxc5 54 ♔d3 e5 55 ♔c4 f5 56 ♔xc5 h5 57 b4 axb4 58 ♔xb4 f4 59 a5 e4 60 ♔c3 e3 61 ♔d3 1-0 Petrosian**

333 Pytel-Sioris Kallithea 77

1 e4 e6 2 d4 d5 3 ♘c3 dxe4 4 ♘xe4 ♘d7 5 ♘f3 ♘gf6 6 ♘xf6+ ♘xf6 7 ♗g5 7 ♘e5 ♕d5 8 ♗e2! +=; 7 ♗d3 b6 8 ♕e2±; 7...♗e7!+= **♗e7 8 ♗d3 0-0 9 ♕e2 c5** 9...b6? 10 ♗xf6 ♗xf6 11 ♕e4+− **10 dxc5! ♕a5+ 11 c3 ♕xc5 12 ♖d1!?** N 12 0-0 ♖d8 13 ♖ad1 ♗d7 14 ♘e5 ♗e8 15 ♖fe1 ♖ac8!=; 12 0-0-0 ♖d8 13 ♘e5 += Keres; 13... h6 14 h4!± **♘d5?!** 12...♗d7? 13 ♗xf6 ♗xf6 14 ♗xh7+ +−; 12...♖d8!? **13 ♗xe7 ♘xe7** 13...♕xe7? 14 ♗xh7+ ♔xh7 15 ♖xd5 +− **14 0-0± ♘c6 15 ♖fe1 g6 16 ♗e4 ♖b8 17 ♖d2 a6 18**

♖ed1 e5?! 18...b5? 19 b4 ♕xc3 20 ♖c2 +− **19 ♗xc6 ♕xc6 20 ♘xe5 ♕c7 21 ♘d7 +− ♗xd7 22 ♖xd7 ♕a5 23 a3 ♕a4 24 g3 ♖be8 25 ♕f3 ♖e1+ 26 ♔g2 ♕b5 27 ♕d3 ♕xd3 28 ♖1xd3 b5 29 ♖3d6 ♖e2 30 ♖d2 ♖fe8 31 ♔f3 ♖xd2 32 ♖xd2 ♖e6 33 ♖e2 ♖d6 34 ♔e3 ♔f8 35 ♖d2 ♖e6+ 36 ♔d3 ♖f6 37 ♖e2 g5 38 c4 bxc4+ 39 ♔xc4 g4 40 b4 ♖f3** 40...♖h6 41 a4 ♖xh2 42 b5 **41 a4 ♖a3 42 a5 h5 43 ♔c5 ♖f3 44 ♔b6 ♖f6+ 45 ♔b7 1-0 Pytel**

334 Klovan-Gusev USSR 77
1 e4 e6 2 d4 d5 3 ♘c3 ♘f6 4 ♗g5 ♗b4 5 e5 h6 6 ♗d2 ♗xc3 7 bxc3 7 ♗xc3 ♘e4= **♘e4 8 ♕g4 g6 9 ♗c1 c5! 10 ♗d3 ♘xc3 11 dxc5 ♕a5 12 ♗d2 ♕a4! 13 h3 ♘e4 14 ♗xe4 ♕d4!** 14...dxe4 += **15 ♖b1 ♕xe5 16 ♖b4!?** N 16 ♘e2=+ **dxe4!** 16...♘c6 17 ♘f3! ♕a1+ 18 ♔e2 ♕xh1 19 ♗xg6! ♘xb4 20 ♘e5! +− **17 ♘e2 ♘c6 18 ♖xe4 ♕xc5 19 ♕f4 f5 20 ♗c3 ♖h7 21 ♖e3 ♗d7 22 0-0 0-0-0 23 ♖b1**

23...e5! 24 ♗xe5 g5 25 ♕f3 f4 26 ♗d4! ♕xc2 27 ♖eb3 ♗f5! =+ 28 ♖c1 ♕xc1+? 28...♕e4! 29 ♕xe4 ♗xe4 30 ♗xa7 ♖d2=+ **29 ♘xc1 ♘xd4 30 ♖c3+ ♔b8 31 ♕d1± f3** 31...♖hd7 **32 ♕e1! ♔a8 33 ♕e5 ♖hh8 34 ♖c4 ♘e2+ 35 ♔h2 ♖hf8** 35...♘xc1 36 ♕xf5 +− **36 gxf3 ♘f4 37 ♘b3 ♘g6** 37...♘xh3+?! **38 ♕a5 ♘h4 39 f4 ♗d7 40 ♘d4 +− a6 41 ♕b6** Δ ♖c7 **♗c8** 41...gxf4 42 ♖c7 ♗c8 43 ♘c6! +− **42 ♘c6! 1-0 Gufeld**

335 Klovan-Shereshevsky USSR 77
1 e4 e6 2 d4 d5 3 ♘c3 ♘f6 4 ♗g5 ♗b4 5 e5 h6 6 ♗e3 6 ♗d2 **♘e4 7 ♕g4 ♔f8** 7...g6 8 a3 ♗xc3+ 9 bxc3 ♘xc3 10 ♗d3 ♕e7 11 h4 α/+= Zuravlev-Shereshevsky, USSR 77 **8 a3 ♗xc3+ 9 bxc3 ♘xc3 10 ♗d3 c5 11 dxc5 ♘c6 12 ♘f3 f5 13 exf6 ♕xf6 14 ♕h5 e5 15 ♗g6** 15 ♘h4?! e4 16 ♘g6+ ♔g8 17 ♘xh8 exd3≈; 15 ♗g5?! hxg5 16 ♕xh8+ ♔e7≈ **♗d7 16 0-0 ♔g8 17 ♖fe1?!** 17 ♖ae1 ♖f8 18 ♗d2 ♘e4 19 ♗xe4 dxe4 20 ♖xe4 g6 21 ♕h4 ♕xh4 22 ♘xh4 g5 23 ♘f3 ♗f5=; 17 ♗d2! ♘e4 18 c4 ♘xd2 19 ♘xd2 d4 20 ♘e4 += **♖f8 18 ♗d2 ♘e4 19 ♖ad1 ♗f5 20 ♗xf5 ♕xf5 21 ♕xf5 ♖xf5= 22 c4** 22 ♗c1 ♘c3 23 ♖d3 d4 =+ **♘xd2 23 ♘xd2** 23 ♖xd2?! dxc4 =+ **d4 24 ♖b1 ♖f7 25 ♘e4 ♔h7?** 25...♖d7 26 ♘d6 b6 27 ♘e4 bxc5 28 ♖b5 ♔f7 29 ♖xc5 ♖c8= **26 ♘d6 += ♖c7 27 ♘xb7 ♖b8 28 ♘d6 ♖xb1 29 ♖xb1 ♘d8 30 ♖b8 ♘e6 31 ♖e8 ♘xc5 32 ♖xe5 ♘b7 33 ♘xb7 ♖xb7 34 ♔f1 ♖b3?!** 34...♖b2 35 ♔e1± **35 ♖a5± d3** 35...♖c3 **36 ♔e1 ♖b2 37 ♖xa7 +− ♖e2+ 38 ♔d1 ♖xf2 39 ♖d7 ♖xg2 40 ♖xd3 ♖xh2 41 c5 ♖h5 1-0 Gufeld**

336 Planinc-Raicevic
Jugoslavia Final 78
1 e4 e6 2 d4 d5 3 ♘c3 ♘f6 4 ♗g5 ♗e7 5 e5 ♘fd7 6 h4 c5 7 ♗xe7 ♕xe7!? 7...♔xe7 8 ♕g4 ♔f8≈ **8 ♘b5 0-0 9 ♘c7 cxd4 10 ♘xa8 f6!** 10...♕b4+ 11 ♕d2 ♕xb2 12 ♖d1 f6 13 ♕xd4; 12...♘c6 13 ♘f3 **11 ♕xd4!?** 11 ♕d2

fxe5 Δ ♘c6≈; 11 exf6 ♕b4+ 12 ♕d2 ♕xb2 13 ♖d1 ♘c6≈ **fxe5 12 ♕xa7 ♕b4+ 13 ♔d1 ♕xb2 14 ♖c1 ♘c6 15 ♕e3** 15 ♕a4?! ♖xf2 16 ♘f3 e4; 16 ♕b5 ♘b4! **♘f6 16 f3 ♘g4 17 ♕b6 ♕a3** 17...♕xb6 18 ♘xb6 ♘f2+ 19 ♔e1 ♘xh1 20 ♘e2±; 20 g4!? **18 ♗d3 ♘b4!? 19 ♘e2 e4!?**

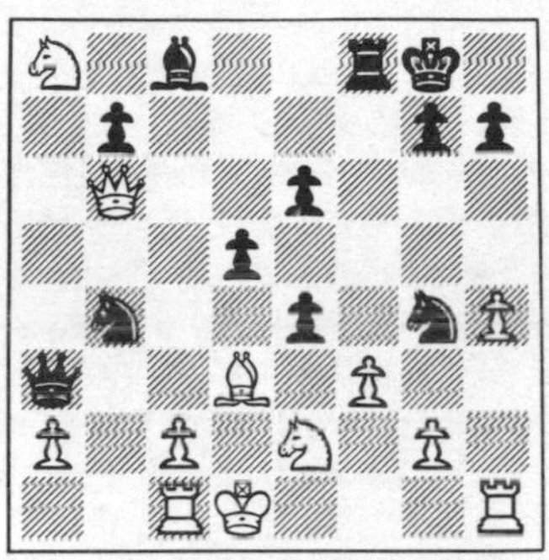

20 fxg4 20 ♗xc4 dxe4 21 fxg4 ♘d5≈; 21...e5!?; 20 ♗b5 exf3 21 gxf3 ♕xf3∓ **exd3 21 cxd3 ♗d7!** 21...e5? 22 ♖xc8! **22 ♖c3 ♕b2 23 a3 ♗a4+ 24 ♔e1 ♕a1+** 24...♘xd3+?! 25 ♖xd3 ♕a1+ 26 ♔d2 ♕a2+ 27 ♔e3 +− **25 ♖c1 ♘xd3+ 26 ♔d2 ♘xc1 27 ♕xe6+ ♔h8 28 ♖xc1 ♕xa3 29 ♖c8 h6?** 29...♕b2+! 30 ♔c1 ♕b1+ 31 ♘c1? ♕b4+; 30 ♔e3 ♕b3+? 31 ♘c3 d4+ 32 ♔xd4!; 30...d4+! 31 ♘xd4 ♕f2+ 32 ♔e4 ♕xg2+ 33 ♔e5 ♕g3+ 34 ♔d5? ♗b3+; 32 ♔d3 ♕f1+ 33 ♘e2 ♗b5+ 34 ♔d2 ♗xe2!= **30 ♖xf8+ ♕xf8 31 ♘b6 +− ♕b4+ 32 ♔e3 ♗c6 33 ♕c8+ ♔h7 34 ♕f5+ ♔h8 35 ♘c8 ♕c5+ 36 ♔d2 ♗b5 37 ♘c3 ♕d4+ 38 ♔c2 ♗c4 39 ♘e7 1-0 Webb**

337 Krogius-Karner Sochi 77

1 d4 e6 2 e4 d5 3 ♘d2 a6 4 e5 ♗d7! Δ ♗b5 **5 ♘df3** 5 a4 c5! Δ ♘c6 **♗b5 6 ♗xb5+ axb5 7 ♕d3 ♕d7 8 ♘e2 b6 9 0-0 c5 10 c3 c4?!** 10...♘e7!? **11 ♕c2 ♘e7?!** 11...♘c6! 12 ♘g3 g6∞ **12 ♘g3 h5 13 ♗g5! += ♘g6 14 ♘h4 ♘xh4 15 ♗xh4 ♗e7?** 15...♘c6 16 ♕e2 ♗e7 17 ♗xe7 ♕xe7 18 ♘xh5 ♕h4 19 g4 g6 20 ♘f6+ +−; 16...g6+= **16 ♗xe7 ♕xe7 17 a4! h4 18 ♘e2 ♕a7 19 f4 g6 20 b3 cxb3 21 ♕xb3 bxa4 22 ♕b5+ ♘d7?** 22...♕d7 23 ♕xb6 ♘c6 Δ 0-0, ♘e7 **23 c4! dxc4 24 ♘c3!!** Δ ♘e4/♖xa4 **0-0 25 ♖xa4 ♕b7 26 ♖xc4 ♖fc8 27 d5 ♖xc4?** 27...♖a5 28 ♖xc8+ ♕xc8 29 ♕c6 ♖c5 += **28 ♕xc4 ♖c8 29 ♕d4 h3?+−** 29...b5!? **30 gxh3 exd5 31 ♘xd5 ♖c2 32 f5! ♘f8 38 e6 fxe6 34 ♘f6+ ♔f7 35 fxg6+ ♔e7 36 ♘e4 ♕d5 37 ♕xd5 1-0 Petrosian**

338 Nunn-Botterill Hastings 77/8

1 e4 e6 2 d4 d5 3 ♘d2 c5 4 ♘gf3 ♘c6 5 exd5 exd5 6 ♗b5 ♗d6 7 dxc5 ♗xc5 8 0-0 ♘ge7 9 ♘b3 ♗d6 10 ♗d2!? 10 ♘bd4; 10 ♗g5 0-0 11 ♗h4 ♕b6! 12 ♗d3 a5! Gulko; 11 ♖e1 f6! 12 ♗h4 ♕b6 13 ♗e2 ♗e6 14 ♗g3 ♘e5 15 ♘fd4 ♗d7= Gipslis-Korchnoi, IBM 76 **0-0 11 ♖e1 ♕c7 12 ♗c3 a6** 12...♗f5 Δ ♗g6≈ **13 ♗d3?!** 13 ♗f1! += **f6 14 h3 ♗d7 15 ♘bd4 ♘e5 16 a3 ♕b6!= 17 ♕d2 ♘7c6 18 ♖ad1** 18 ♘xe5 fxe5 19 ♘xc6 ♗xc6 20 ♗xe5 ♖xf2! 21 ♗d4! ♖xd2 22 ♗xb6 d4 23 ♖e2= **♖ae8 19 b4 ♘xd3 20 ♖xe8 ♖xe8 21 ♕xd3 ♘e5 22 ♘xe5 fxe5 23 ♘f3 ♗c6 24 ♗a1** 24 ♕f5 ♕c7=+ **♕c7 25 ♘d2 ♕f7 26 c4 e4 27 ♕e2 ♗f4! 28 cxd5 ♗b5!?** 28...♗xd5 =+ **29 ♘c4** 29 ♕e1? e3 −+; 29 ♕g4? h5−+ **♖c8 30 ♖d4**

Diagram

30...♕g6!? 30...♗e5? 31 ♘xe5 ♖c1+ 32 ♕d1! ♖xd1+ 33 ♖xd1 +−; 30... ♕f6? 31 ♕d1! ♗xc4 32 ♖xc4 ♖xc4 33 ♗xf6 gxf6 34 d6! ♖c1 35 ♕xc1

♗xc1 36 d7 +−; 30...e3!! 31 fxe3 ♗g3!∓ Δ ♗xc4, ♖xc4, ♕f2+ Mestel **31 ♕a2 h6 32 d6 ♔h7 33 d7** Zeitnot **♖d8 34 g3 ♖xd7 35 ♖xd7 ♗xd7 36 ♔h2 ♗b8 37 ♗e5** 37 ♘e5 ♗xe5 38 ♗xe5 ♕f5 −+ **♗a7∓ 38 ♕e2 ♕f5 39 g4 ♕xf2+ 40 ♕xf2 ♗xf2 41 ♘d6 ♗c6 42 ♗f4 e3 43 ♗g3 ♔g6 44 ♘c4 ♔f6 45 ♘b2 ♗xg3+ 46 ♔xg3 ♔e5 0-1 Botterill**

339 Dorfman-Gulko (4) 78

1 e4 e6 2 d4 d5 3 ♘d2 c5 4 exd5 exd5 5 ♘gf3 ♘c6 6 ♗b5 ♗d6 7 dxc5 ♗xc5 8 0-0 ♘e7 9 ♘b3 ♗d6 10 ♗g5 0-0 11 ♖e1 ♗g4 12 ♗e2 12 h3 ♗h5 13 ♗e2 h6 14 ♗d2 ♗c7 15 ♗c3 ♕d6 16 ♘bd4 a6 17 g3 ♗g6 18 ♗d3 ♗h5 19 ♗e2 ♗g6 20 ♗d3 ½-½ Geller-Gulko, USSR Final 77 **h6 13 ♗xe7 ♗xe7 14 ♘fd4 ♗xe2 15 ♖xe2 ♗f6 16 c3 += ♖e8 17 ♘f3 ♖xe2 18 ♕xe2 ♕b6 19 ♖d1 ♖d8?** 19...♘e7 20 ♘e5 += **20 ♖xd5± ♖xd5 21 ♕e8+ ♔h7 22 ♕e4+ g6 23 ♕xd5 ♔g7 24 g3 ♕a6 25 ♘bd2 ♕e2 26 ♔g2 ♗d8 27 ♕c4 ♕e7 28 ♕e4 ♕c5 29 ♘b3 ♕b5 30 ♘fd4 ♕a6 31 ♘xc6 bxc6 32 ♘c1 ♗f6 33 a3 ♕b5 34 ♘d3 a5 35 a4 ♕b6 36 ♕c4 h5 37 h4 ♕d8 38 ♔f1 ♕e8 39 b4 ♕d8 40 ♔e2 ♕a8 41 ♘c5 ♕e8+ 42 ♕e4 ♕c8 43 ♔d2 ♕d8+ 44 ♔c2 axb4 45 cxb4 ♗d4 46 ♕xc6 ♗xf2 47 ♘e4 ♗e1 48 b5 ♗a5 49 ♕d6 ♕c8+ 50 ♔b3 ♕c1 51 ♕e5+ +− ♔g8 52 ♕e8+ ♔g7 53 ♕e5+ ♔g8 54 ♘f6+ ♔g7** 54...♔f8 55 ♘d7+ +− **55 ♘xh5+ ♔f8 56 ♕b8+ ♔e7 57 ♕b7+ ♔d6 58 ♕a6+ ♔e5 59 ♕f6+ ♔e4 60 ♕f4+ ♕xf4 61 ♘xf4 ♔d4 62 g4 ♗d2 63 ♘e2 ♔e3 64 b6 1-0 Gufeld**

340 Ostojic-Vaganian Rome 77

1 e4 e6 2 d4 d5 3 ♘d2 ♘c6 4 ♘gf3 ♘f6 5 e5 ♘d7 6 ♘b3 ♗e7 6...f6 7 ♗b5 ♘cb8 8 0-0 c6 9 ♗d3 f5 10 g4 g6 11 ♘g5 Padevsky-Kolarov, Bulgaria 77; 6...a5 7 a4 b6 8 h4! **7 ♗b5 a5!?** N **8 a4 ♘cb8 9 0-0** 9 h4! Δ ♗g5 **b6 10 c3** 10 ♗d2 **0-0 11 ♗e3 c6 12 ♗d3 ♗a6= 13 ♘e1 c5 14 ♗xa6 ♘xa6 15 f4** 15 ♘c2! Δ ♘a3-b5= **f5! 16 exf6 ♘xf6 17 ♕e2 ♗d6 18 ♘d2 ♕e8=+ 19 ♘d3 c4! 20 ♘e5 ♘c7 21 ♕d1 b5 22 axb5 ♕xb5 23 ♕c2** 23 b3!? **♖fb8 24 ♖a2 ♖a6 25 f5?! ♖f8 26 h3 ♗xe5!∓ 27 dxe5 ♘d7 28 ♗d4 exf5 29 ♖xf5 ♖xf5 30 ♕xf5 ♘e6 31 ♘f3 ♘df8 32 ♕c2 a4 33 ♖a3 ♘f4 34 ♕f5?! ♕xb2 35 ♕xf4 ♕xa3 36 ♕f5 ♘e6 37 ♗e3 ♕f8 38 ♕b1 a3 39 ♕b5 ♕c8 0-1 Pytel**

341 Matulovic-Arapovic Jugoslavia 77

1 e4 e6 2 d4 d5 3 ♘d2 ♘c6 4 ♘gf3 g6 4...♘f6 **5 e5** 5 c3 ♗g7 6 ♗d3 ♘h6 7 0-0 0-0 8 ♖e1 f6 9 b4 a6 10 a4 ♘f7 11 ♗a3 ♖e8 12 ♕b3 ♘e7 13 b5 axb5 14 axb5 ♕d7 15 c4 += Keres-Troianescu, Moscow 56; 10...♖e8 11 ♕b3 ♘e7 12 ♗b2 b6 13 c4 ♘f7 14 ♖e2 ♕d7 15 ♖ae1+= Sokolsky-Korchnoi, USSR Final 54; 6 ♗b5!? **♘h6 6 ♘b3 f6 7 exf6 ♕xf6 8 ♗g5 ♕g7 9 ♗b5 ♘f7 10 ♗f4 ♗d6 11 ♗xc6+ bxc6 12 ♗g3 0-0 13 0-0 e5 14 ♘xe5 ♘xe5 15 dxe5**

Bxe5 16 Bxe5 Qxe5 17 c3 a5 18 a4 Qg5 Δ Bh3 **19 f3 Rb8 20 Rf2 Qe3 21 Nxa5 Rxb2 22 Qd4 Qxd4 23 cxd4 Rb6** 23...Rb4? 24 Nxc6 Rc4 25 Ne7+ **24 Rc2 Bd7 25 Rac1 Ra8 26 Nxc6 Bxc6 27 Rxc6 Rxc6 28 Rxc6 Rxa4 29 Rxc7 Rxd4 30 Kf2 Rd2+ 31 Kg3 h6 32 f4 d4 33 Kf3 d3 34 Rd7 Rd1 35 g3 Kf8 36 Rd4 Kf7 37 Ke3 Rh1 38 h4 Rg1 39 Kf2 ½-½**

342 Zhidkov-Gofstein USSR 77
1 e4 e6 2 d4 d5 3 Nd2 Nf6 4 e5 Nfd7 5 Bd3 c5 6 c3 b6!? 6...Nc6 7 Ne2 += **7 Ne2** 7 Qg4!? **Ba6 8 Bxa6** 8 Bb1!? **Nxa6 9 0-0** 9 Nf4!? **Nc7** 9...Be7 10 f4 f5 11 exf6 Bxf6 12 f5 **10 f4** 10 Ng3!? Δ Qg4; 10 Nf4! += **f5! 11 Nf3** 11 exf6 Nxf6 12 Ng3∝ **Nb8?!** N 11...Be7! Δ 0-0= **12 Be3 Nc6 13 dxc5! += bxc5** 13...Bxc5 14 Ned4 += **14 b4!**

14...d4!? 14...cxb4 15 cxb4 Bxb4 16 Qa4 Qd7 17 Rac1±; 15...Nxb4 16 Ned4 += **15 cxd4?** 15 Qa4! dxe3 16 Rfd1±; 15...Qd7 16 b5!± **Nd5!∓ 16 Qa4 Rc8 17 Bd2 cxb4 18 Rfc1 Nb6! 19 Qb3 Qd5 20 Ng5 Kd7! 21 Qd3 Be7 22 Nf3 Rc7 23 Ne1 Rhc8 24 Nc2 Nc4 25 Be1 a5 26 Qb3 Na7 27 Rd1 Nb5?!** 27...Nb2! **28 Qa4 Nb6 29 Qxa5 Rxc2 30 Rd2 Rxd2 0-1 Gufeld**

343 Jurczynska-B.Pytel
Poland 77
1 e4 e6 2 d4 d5 3 Nd2 Nf6 4 e5 Nfd7 5 Bd3 c5 6 c3 Nc6 7 Ne2 cxd4 8 cxd4 f6 9 exf6 Nxf6 10 0-0 10 Nf3 Bd6 11 Bf4 Qa5+ 12 Bd2 Qc7 Matulovic-Pytel, Le Havre 77; 10...0-0!? **Bd6 11 Nf3** 11 f4!? **0-0 12 a3 e5 13 dxe5 Nxe5 14 Nxe5 Bxe5 15 Qb3 Qc7 16 h3 Be6 17 Be3 Qf7 18 Bd4 Bd6 19 Rac1 Ne4! 20 Bxe4 dxe4 21 Qe3 Qg6 22 Rfd1 Rf3! 23 Qd2 Bxh3 24 g3 Rd3! 25 Qe1 Bg4 26 Rc3 Bf3 27 Rdxd3 exd3 0-1 Pytel**

344 Ostojic-Arapovic
Jugoslavia 77
1 e4 e6 2 d4 d5 3 Nd2 Nf6 4 e5 Nfd7 5 f4 c5 6 c3 Nc6 7 Ndf3 Qa5 8 Ne2 8 Kf2; 8 dxc5 **b5 9 Be3** 9 Bd2 b4 10 g4 bxc3 11 bxc3 Nb6= S.Garcia-Korchnoi, Skopje 72; 10 cxb4 Nxb4 11 Nc3 c4 12 a3 Nc6 13 b3 Matanovic-Portisch, Ljubljana 73 **b4 10 Kf2 Ba6 11 cxb4 Nxb4 12 Nc3 Rb8 13 a3 Nc6 14 b4 cxb4 15 axb4 Qxb4 16 Rxa6 Qxc3 17 Bd2 Rb2 18 Be2 Qc2 19 Qa1 Nxd4 20 Rc1 Bc5 21 Kf1 Qe4 22 Nxd4 Qxd4 23 Rxc5 Nxc5 24 Bb5+ Kf8 25 Rxa7 g6 26 Qa5 Kg7 27 Rxf7+ Kh6** 27...Kxf7? 28 Qc7+ = **28 Qa3 Rb3 29 Qc1** Δ f5+ **Ne4 30 Be1 Rxb5 31 Qa3 Qc4+ 32 Kg1 Qc5+ 0-1**

345 Tatai-Korchnoi
Beersheva 78
1 e4 e6 2 d4 d5 3 exd5 exd5 4 Bd3 c5!? N **5 Nf3 Nc6** 5...c4!? **6 Qe2+ Be7! 7 dxc5 Nf6 8 h3** 8 0-0 **0-0 9 0-0 Bxc5 10 c3 Re8=+ 11 Qc2 Qd6 12 Nbd2?** 12 Kh1

12...Qg3!! −+ 13 Bf5 13 Nb3 Bxh3; 13 Kh1 Bxf2 **Re2 14 Nd4 Nxd4 0-1** 15 cxd4 Bxd4 16 Bxc8 Rxf2 **Pytel**

346 Bielczyk-Joksic Zabrze 77
1 e4 e6 2 d4 d5 3 e5 c5 4 c3 a6 5 Nf3 Nc6 6 Bd3 f5 7 exf6 Nxf6 8 0-0 Bd6 9 Re1 cxd4 10 cxd4 Qc7 11 Nc3 0-0 12 Qe2?! 12 h3 e5 **Ng4!=+ 13 Bxh7+ Kh8 14 Ne5** 14 Ng5? Bxh2+ −+; 14 g3 e5! 15 dxe5 Bc5−+ **Bxe5** 14...Ncxe5 15 dxe5 Bc5 16 Qxg4! Bxf2+ 17 Kh1 Bxe1 18 Bd3!∞ **15 dxe5 Ncxe5∓ 16 f4 Qc5+ 17 Kh1** 17 Be3 Nxe3 18 Qxe3 Qxe3+ 19 Rxe3 Ng4 20 Rh3 Nh6 21 Bd3 Rxf4 −+ **Nf2+ 18 Kg1 Neg4! 19 Be3 Qxe3 20 Qxe3 Nxe3 21 Kxf2** 21 Rxe3 Ng4 22 Rh3 Nh6 23 Bd3 Rxf4 −+ **d4 22 Bd3 e5 23 Kg1 Rxf4 24 Nd1 Nxd1 25 Raxd1 Bg4 26 Rc1 Re8 27 Rc5** Zeitnot **e4 28 Rd5? exd3 29 Rxe8+ Kh7 30 Red8 d2 31 Rxd4 Rxd4 32 Rxd4 0-1** time **Joksic**

347 Bjelajac-Despotovic
Jugoslavia 77
1 e4 e6 2 d4 d5 3 e5 c5 4 c3 Nc6 5 Nf3 f6 5...Nge7 **6 Bb5 Qb6** 6...Bd7 7 0-0 Qb6 8 Bxc6 bxc6 9 exf6 Nxf6 10 Ne5 Bd6 11 dxc5 Bxc5 12 Bg5!± Nimzovich-Levenfish, Karlovy Vary 11 **7 Bxc6+ bxc6 8 0-0 f5 9 dxc5 Bxc5 10 b4 Bf8 11 Be3 Qc7 12 Nbd2 h6 13 Nb3 Ne7 14 Bc5 Ng6 15 Re1 Bxc5 16 Nxc5 0-0 17 Nd4 Re8 18 Qh5 Qf7 19 Qh3** 19 Nxc6 Nxe5 **Bd7 20 a4 Nf8 21 a5 Rec8 22 f4 Rc7 23 a6 Re8 24 Nb7 Rb8 25 Qe3 Bc8 26 Nc5 Nh7 27 Qh3 Nf8 28 Kh1 Qg6 29 Qh4 Qf7 30 Qd8 Kh7 31 Ndxe6 Nxe6 32 Nxe6 Re7 33 Nf8+ Kg8 34 Nd7+! Re8 35 e6 Qg6 36 Qc7 Bxd7 37 exd7 Red8 38 Qxa7 Qf7 39 Qxb8! Rxb8 40 a7 Ra8 41 Re8+ 1-0**

1 e4 Nf6

348 Planinc-Kovacevic
Jugoslavia Final 78
1 e4 Nf6 2 Nc3 d5 3 e5 Nfd7 4 Nxd5 Nxe5 5 Ne3 c5 6 b3!? 6 f4; 6 b4?! Nec6 7 bxc5 e5 8 Bb2 Bxc5∞ **Nbc6 7 Bb2 a6?!** 7...e6 8 f4 Ng6 9 g3 Be7!? 10 Bg2 Rg8 11 Bc3? Nxf4! 12 Bb5 Nd5=+ **8 f4 Nd7 9 Nf3 Nf6 10 Bc4 e6**

10...b5 11 Ne5! Nxe5 12 fxe5 bxc4 13 exf6 gxf6 14 Nxc4 **11 f5! b5** 11...exf5 12 Ng5 **12 fxe6!! bxc4 13 exf7+ Kxf7 14 Ng5+ Kg6** 14...Ke7 15 Qe2; 14...Ke8 15 0-0 Δ Bxf6 **15 Qf3! Kxg5?!** 15...Nd4 16 Qxa8 Kxg5∞ **16 Qxc6 Bd7 17 Qf3 h5 18**

0-0 cxb3?! 18...♗e7 19 ♘xc4 Δ ♘e5 +− **19 ♖ae1! ♔g6 20 ♘d5 ♖h6** 20... ♘xd5 21 ♕xd5 Δ ♕f7+ +− **21 ♘xf6 gxf6 22 ♗xf6 +− ♕c8 23 ♗b2 ♗f5 24 ♖e8! 1-0 Maric**

349 Smyslov-Alburt
USSR Final 77

1 e4 ♘f6 2 ♘c3 d5 3 e5 ♘e4 4 ♘ce2 4 d4? ♘xc3 5 bxc3 e6= Heidenfeld-Hecht, Nice 74 **f6** 4...d5 5 c3! +− Sahovic-Gliksman, Jugoslavia 73 **5 ♘f3 fxe5** 5...♗g4 6 d3 ♘c5 7 d4 ♘e4 8 h3! ♗d7 9 ♘h4 Knezevic-Alburt, Decin 76 **6 d3 ♘d6 7 ♘xe5 ♘d7 8 ♘xd7 ♗xd7 9 ♘f4 c6 10 ♕e2 ♘f7 11 d4 g6 12 ♘e6 ♗xe6 13 ♕xe6 ♗g7 14 c3 ♕d6 15 ♕xd6 ♘xd6 16 f4 ♔d7 17 ♗d3 b5 18 a3 a5 19 ♔e2 b4 20 ♗d2 bxc3 21 bxc3 a4 22 ♖hb1 ♖hb8 23 ♖b4 ♖xb4 24 axb4 e6 25 ♗c2 ♘c4 26 ♖xa4 ♖xa4 27 ♗xa4 ♘xd2 28 ♔xd2 ♗h6 29 ♔e3 g5 30 g3 gxf4+ 31 gxf4 ♗f8 32 ♔f3 h6 33 ♔g4 ♗d6 34 h3 ♗c7 35 h4 ♗d6 36 h5 ♗e7 ½-½**

350 Sveshnikov-Shamkovich
Hastings 77/78

1 e4 ♘f6 2 e5 ♘d5 3 c4 ♘b6 4 c5 ♘d5 5 d4 5 ♗c4 e6 6 ♘c3≈ **d6** 5...b6 **6 exd6 exd6** 6...cxd6 7 ♘f3 **7 ♘f3 ♗e7** 7...♘c6 8 ♗b5 a6 9 ♗xc6+ bxc6 10 ♗g5 ♗e7 11 ♗xe7 ♘xe7 12 0-0 += Sveshnikov-L.Popov, Plovdiv 73 **8 ♘c3 c6** 8...dxe5 9 ♘xe5 ♗e6 10 ♗d3 ♘d7 **9 ♗e2 0-0 10 0-0** 10 ♘xd5 cxd5 11 0-0 += **♘xc3?!** 10...dxe5 11 ♘xd5 ♕xd5 12 ♘xe5 ♗e6 13 ♗c4 ♕d6 14 ♖fe1 +=; 10...♗e6 11 ♘e4 += **11 bxc3 ♗f5 12 ♕b3 ♕b6** 12...♕c7 13 ♗f4 d5 14 ♘e1 += **13 ♗a3 c5** 13... ♖d8 14 ♖fe1 Δ ♗c4 **14 ♕d5!?** 14 exd6 ♗xd6 15 dxc5 ♗xc5 16 ♗xc5 ♕xc5 17 ♕xb7 ♘c6 18 ♕b5 += **♗e6** 14...♕c6 15 ♕xc6 ♘xc6 16 exd6 ♗xd6 17 dxc5 ♗e7 18 ♘d4 ♗e4 19 ♘b5 Δ ♘d6± **15 ♕e4 d5 16 ♕e3 ♘d7 17 ♖ab1 ♕c7 18 dxc5! ♗f5** 18...♗xc5 19 ♗xc5 ♘xc5 20 ♘d4 Δ f4± **19 ♖bd1 ♗xc5** 19...♗e4 20 c4 ♗xf3 21 ♗xf3 dxc4 22 e6! ♘f6! 23 exf7+ ♖xf7 24 ♖c1±; 22 c6 ♘xe5 23 cxb7 ♘xf3+ 24 ♕xf3 ♖b8= **20 ♗xc5 ♘xc5 21 ♖xd5± b6 22 ♘d4 ♗e4 23 ♘b5 ♕c6 24 ♖d6 ♕b7**

25 ♖d4!? 25 f3± **♗xg2** 25...♗c6 26 ♘d6± **26 ♘d6 ♕c6 27 ♖fe1** 27 ♖fd1! **a6 28 ♘f5 ♖ae8 29 ♕g5 ♕g6** 29...g6 30 ♘h6+ ♔g7 31 ♘g4 Δ ♕h6+, ♘f6 +− **30 ♕xg6 hxg6 31 ♘d6 ♗h3 32 ♘xe8 ♖xe8 33 ♗f1 +− ♗e6 34 c4 g5 35 ♖ed1 g6 36 ♖d6 ♘a4 37 a3 ♔f8 38 ♖b1 ♖b8 39 ♖b4 ♘c5 40 ♖bxb6 ♖xb6 41 ♖xb6 ♔e7 42 ♔g2 ♗c8 43 ♔f3 ♔d7 44 ♔e3 1-0 Sveshnikov**

351 Hulak-Vukic
Jugoslavia Final 78

1 e4 ♘f6 2 e5 ♘d5 3 d4 d6 4 ♘f3 ♗g4 5 ♗e2 e6 6 0-0 ♗e7 7 h3 ♗h5 8 c4 ♘b6 9 exd6 cxd6 10 ♘bd2 0-0 11 b3 ♘c6 12 ♗b2 ♗g6! 13 a3 a5 14 ♗c3?! 14 ♖e1! d5 15 c5 ♘d7 16 ♗b5! += Kagan-Vukic, Biel 77 **♗f6 15 ♖e1 e5!= 16 dxe5** 16 d5 ♘d4 17 ♖c1 ♘d7 18 b4 axb4 19 axb4 ♕b6= **dxe5 17 ♗f1?**

17 Qc1!? Δ Qb2; 17 b4? Na4! **Nd7 18 b4?** 18 Qc1!? **e4! 19 Bxf6 Nxf6 20 b5** 20 Ng5? axb4∓ **exf3 21 bxc6 fxg2 22 Bxg2 bxc6 23 Bxc6 Ra6 24 Bg2 Rd6 25 Ra2 Nh5! 26 c5 Rd3 27 Re3 Rxe3 28 fxe3 Qe7 29 Nc4 Qxc5 30 Qd5 Qc7 31 Rd2** 31 Nxa5? Rd8 32 Qb5 Rd1+ 33 Kf2 Qg3+ 34 Ke2 Bd3+ −+ **Nf6 32 Qb5 Be4 −+ 33 Rd6 Bxg2 34 Kxg2 Ne4 35 Qc6 Qe7 36 Rd4 f5 37 Qd5+ Kh8 38 Qe5 Qg5+ 39 Kh2 Qh5** 39...Qh4? 40 Qf4= **40 Qf4 Ng5 41 Ne5 Qxh3+ 42 Kg1 Ne6 0-1 Vukic**

352 Tal-Bagirov
USSR Final 77
1 e4 Nf6 2 e5 Nd5 3 d4 d6 4 Nf3 Bg4 5 Be2 e6 6 0-0 Be7 7 h3 Bh5 8 c4 Nb6 9 exd6 cxd6 10 Nbd2 Nc6 11 b3 0-0 12 Bb2 Bg6 12...d5 13 c5 Nd7 14 a3 f6 15 b4 a6 16 Re1 += Medina-Hecht, Malaga 72 **13 a3** 13 Ne1?! d5 14 c5 Nd7 15 Ndf3 b6= Blumenfeld-Vukic, New York 76 **a5 14 Bc3 Bf6 15 Re1 e5 16 Nf1 e4 17 N3h2 d5 18 Ng4 Bg5 19 Ne5 Nxe5 20 dxe5 dxc4 21 bxc4 Qxd1 22 Rexd1 Rfc8 23 Ne3 Bxe3 24 fxe3 Nxc4 25 Bd4 Bf5 26 Rdb1 b6 27 Bxc4 Rxc4 28 Rxb6 ½-½**

353 Ortel-Honfi Hungary 77
1 e4 Nf6 2 e5 Nd5 3 d4 d6 4 Nf3 g6 5 c4 Nb6 6 exd6 cxd6 7 Be2 Bg7 8 0-0 0-0 9 Nc3 Nc6 10 Be3 Bg4 11 b3 e6 11...d5!? **12 Qd2** 12 h3 Bxf3 13 Bxf3 Qf6 14 Ne2 d5≈ **d5 13 c5 Nc8** 13...Nd7!? 14 Rac1 Bxf3 15 Bxf3 f5∞ Ozsvath-Honfi, Budapest 53 **14 Rab1 N8e7 15 b4 Bxf3 16 Bxf3 Nf5 17 Ne2 a6 18 g3?!** 18 a4 **h6 19 Bg4?! Nxe3 20 Qxe3** 20 fxe3 Qg5 21 Bf3 e5!=+ **Qf6 21 Rfd1 e5 22 dxe5 Nxe5 23 Bh3 Nf3+ 24 Kg2 Ng5∓ 25 Nf4** 25 Rxd5?? Rfe8 26 Qd2 Nxh3 27 Kxh3 Qe6+ −+ **d4 26 Qd3 Qc6+ 27 f3 a5 28 b5** 28 a3? axb4 29 axb4 Ra2+ −+ **Qxc5 29 Rbc1 Qd6 30 Re1 Rfe8 31 Qb3 Rad8 32 Bg4 Re3! 33 Rxe3 dxe3 34 Qxe3 Qd2+ 35 Qxd2 Rxd2+ 36 Kf1 Rxh2 37 Rc8+ Kh7 38 Rc7 f5 39 Bxf5 gxf5 40 Rxb7 Kg8 41 Ng6 Bd4 42 Ne7+ Kf8 43 Nxf5 Rf2+ 44 Ke1 Nxf3+ 45 Kd1 Rd2+ 46 Kc1 Bb2+ 47 Kb1 Ba3 0-1 Honfi**

1 e4 g6

354 Knezevic-Planinc
Jugoslavia Final 78
1 Nf3 g6 2 e4 Bg7 3 d4 d6 4 c3 Nf6 5 Bd3 0-0 6 0-0 Nbd7?! 6...Nc6 Δ e5 **7 Nbd2 e5 8 Re1 exd4?** 8...Re8 **9 cxd4 c5 10 e5! dxe5 11 dxe5 Ng4 12 Nc4± b5 13 Bg5 Qc7 14 Be4 Bb7?** 14...Rb8 15 Qd6 Qxd6 16 Nxd6 Ngxe5 17 Be7 Nxf3+ 18 Bxf3 Ne5! **15 Bxb7 Qxb7 16 Nd6 Qc6**

17 Nxf7! Rxf7 18 e6 Rxf3 18...Rf5 19 exd7 Rd5 20 Re8+! Kf7 21 Rxa8 +−; 20...Rxe8 21 Qxd5+ **19 exd7 Rf7 20 Re7!** 20 d8Q+ Rxd8 21 Qxd8+ Rf8 Δ Rxf2 **Bf6 21 Rxf7 +−**

Kxf7 22 Bxf6 Qxf6 23 Qd5+ Kg7 24 Qxa8 Qxf2+ 25 Kh1 Qf4 26 g3 Qd2 27 Qg2 Qxd7 28 Re1 Ne5 29 Rf1 29 Rxe5? Qd1+ = **Qc6 30 Qxc6 Nxc6 31 Rd1 c4** 31...Nd4 32 b4+− **32 Rd7+ Kh6 33 Rc7 Nb4 34 a4 bxa4 35 Rxc4 a5 36 Rc3 Kg5 37 Ra3 Kg4 38 Rxa4 Kf3 39 Rxa5 Nd3 40 Ra3 1-0 Maric**

355 Tal-Vadasz Tallinn 77

1 e4 g6 2 d4 Bg7 3 c3 d6 4 f4 Nf6 5 e5 dxe5 6 fxe5 Nd5 7 Nf3 0-0 8 Bc4 c5! 9 0-0 cxd4 10 cxd4 10 Qxd4 e6 11 Bg5 Nc6 12 Bxd8 Nxd4 13 cxd4 Rxd8= **Nc6 11 Nc3 Be6 12 Bb3** 12 Ng5? Nxc3 13 Nxe6 Nxd1 14 Nxd8 Raxd8 15 Rxd1 Nxd4 −+ **Na5! 13 Ng5 Nxc3!** 13...Nxb3? 14 Nxe6 Nxc3 15 bxc3 fxe6 16 Rxf8+ Bxf8 17 axb3± Nei-Saidy, Tallinn 73 **14 bxc3** 14 Nxe6? Nxd1 15 Nxd8 Nxb3 16 axb3 Rfxd8 17 Rxd1 Bxe5 −+ **Bd5 15 e6!?** 15 Rb1 h6 16 Nf3 Rc8 17 Qd3 Nc4 =+ **Nxb3 16 exf7+ Rxf7! 17 Nxf7 Qa5! 18 Nh6+ Kh8!** 18...Bxh6? 19 Bxh6 Nxa1 20 Qe1! Qc7 21 Qf2 Qd8 22 Rxa1 +− **19 Rb1??** 19 axb3? Qxa1 20 Qe1 Qa2 21 Rf2 Qxb3 −+; 19 c4! Bxd4 20 Kh1 Bxa1? 21 axb3! Bc6 22 Bd2 Bc3 23 b4!! Qxb4 24 Qe1 +−; 20...Bc6! 21 axb3 Qxa1 22 Qe2 Bf6 =+; 19... Nxc1 20 Qxc1 Bxd4+ 21 Kh1 Rc8!? 22 Qf4 Bxa1 23 Rxa1 Qc3=+; 22 Nf7+ Kg8 23 Nh6+ Kg7 24 Qg5 Bf6!; 22 Rd1 Rc4 23 Qg5 Rc2 **Nxc1 20 Nf7+** 20 Qxc1 Qxa2 21 Rb2 Bxh6 22 Qxh6 Qxb2 23 Rf8+ Rxf8 24 Qxf8+ Bg8 −+ **Bxf7 21 Qxc1 Bc4 22 Rf2 Qc7 23 Qe3 b5 24 h4 Qd6 25 Rd1 Bf6 26 g3 Rd8 27 Rdd2 a5 28 Kg2 Bd5+ 29 Kg1 Qe6 30 Qf4 Qe4 31 Qxe4 Bxe4 32 Kf1 Rc8 33 Rfe2 Bd5 34 Re3 g5 35 h5 g4 36 Rf2 b4 37 Rc2 Bxd4 38 Rxe7 Rf8+ 0-1 Vadasz**

356 Gulko-Petrosian
USSR Final 77

1 d4 g6 2 e4 Bg7 3 Nc3 d6 4 Nge2 c6 5 a4 e5 6 Be3 Nf6 7 dxe5 dxe5 8 Qxd8+ Kxd8 9 h3 Be6 10 Ng1!? Δ Nf3-d2-c4/Bc4 **Nbd7 11 Nf3 h6 12 Nd2 Kc7 13 Bc4! Rhe8 14 0-0-0 Bf8! 15 f4 Bc5 16 Bxc5** 16 Bxe6 fxe6 17 Bxc5 Nxc5 18 fxe5±; 16...Rxe6 17 Bxc5 Nxc5 18 f5 +=; 16...Bxe3! 17 Bxf7 Re7 18 Bxg6 exf4!=+ **Nxc5 17 fxe5 Nfd7 18 Bxe6 =+** 18 b4 Nxe5! ∓ **Rxe6 19 Nf3 Nxe5 20 Rhf1 Raf8 21 Nd4 Re7 22 b3 Ned7 23 Rf4 a5 24 Rdf1 h5?** 24...b6 Δ Nb7-d6, Nc5∓

25 Rd1 Nb6? 25...b6! **26 Rdf1 Ncd7 27 Nf3 f6 28 g4 hxg4 29 Rxg4 g5 30 h4 gxh4 31 Rxh4 ½-½ Petrosian**

357 Benjamin-Mednis
New York 77

1 e4 d6 2 d4 Nf6 3 Nc3 g6 4 Be3 c6 5 a4 Bg7 6 Qd2 Nbd7 6...Ng4!? 7 Bg5 h6 (7...Qb6!?) 8 Bh4 a5?! 9 f4 Nf6 10 0-0-0 Na6 11 Nf3 Bg4 12 Be2 d5 13 h3± Westerinen-Brasket, New York 77; 8...Qb6! 9 h3 Nf6 10 a5 Qc7 =+ Timman **7 Be2 e5 8 Rd1 Qa5 9 f3 0-0 10 Nh3 d5?!** 10...Re8! **11 exd5! Nxd5 12 Nxd5 Qxd2+** 12...Qxd5?! 13 c4! Qd6 14 d5!± **13 Rxd2 cxd5 14 Nf2?!** 14 dxe5! Nxe5 15 Rxd5! += **Re8= 15 c3 exd4 16 Bxd4 Bh6 17 Rc2 Nb8! 18 Ng4! Bxg4 19 fxg4 Nc6 20 Bf2?** 20 Bf6!= **Rac8!∓** Δ Nb4 **21 Kd1 Nb4! 22 Bf3** 22 Bb5?! Nxc2 23 Bxe8? Rxe8 24 Kxc2 Re2+ Zeitnot **Nxc2 23 Kxc2 Be3! 24 Bxe3 Rxe3 25 Rd1 Re5** Zeitnot **26 Bxd5 Rc7 27 Bf3 b6 28 h3 Kg7 29 Rd6 Ree7 30 b3 Red7 31 Rxd7 Rxd7 32 c4 Kf6 33 Kc3 Ke5 34 b4 Rc7 35 Kd3 f6 36 Bd5 a5! 37 b5?** 37 Kc3 Rc8! −+ **Kd6 −+ 38 Kd4 Re7 39 Be4 Re5 40 Bd5 Re1 41 Bg8 h6 42 Bf7 g5 43 Bd5** 43 Kc3 Re3+ 44 Kd4 Ra3 **Ra1 44 Ke4 Rxa4 45 Kf5 Rb4 46 Kxf6 a4 0-1 Mednis**

358 Balashov-Donchenko
USSR 77

1 e4 d6 2 d4 Nf6 3 Nc3 g6 4 Be3 c6 4...Ng4 5 Bg5∝ **5 Qd2 Nbd7 6 Nf3?!** 6 f3 **e5 7 0-0-0** 7 h3!? **Ng4 8 Bg5 Be7 9 Bc4?!** 9 h3 Bxg5 10 Nxg5 Nxf2 11 Bc4 Nxd1 12 Nxf7 Qe7 13 Nxh8 Nxc3= **0-0** 9...exd4! 10 Bxe7 dxc3 11 Qd4 Kxe7!∓; 10 Qf4 Nde5∓ **10 h3 Bxg5 11 Nxg5 Ngf6 12 f4 += Qe7 13 fxe5?!** 13 Rhf1!+= **dxe5 14 d5 Kg7= 15 dxc6** 15 d6!? Qd8? 16 Bxf7!; 15...Qe8 **bxc6 16 Qd6 Qxd6 17 Rxd6 Ne8 18 Rd2** 18 Rxc6 Bb7 =+ **h6 19 Nf3 Nef6 20 Rf1 Nb6?** 20...Bb7 21 Rdf2 Rae8= **21 Nxe5 Nxc4** 21...Re8 22 Rdf2 Rxe5 23 Rxf6 Nxc4 24 Rxf7+ +− **22 Nxc4 Ba6 23 Rd6!± Nxe4 24 Rxc6 Ng3** 24...Bxc4 25 Rxc4 Nxc3 26 Rxc3± **25 Rf2 Bc8 26 Rc7 Be6 27 Nd6 a6 28 b3 +− h5 29 Nce4 Nxe4 30 Nxe4 Rac8 31 Ra7 Ra8 32 Rxa8 Rxa8 33 Nc5 1-0 Gufeld**

359 Sveshnikov-Botterill
Hastings 77/78

1 e4 d6 2 d4 g6 3 Nc3 Bg7 4 Be3 c6 5 g3 Nf6 6 h3 0-0 7 Bg2 e5 8 Nge2 Qe7 N 8...Nbd7; 8...b5!? 9 dxe5 dxe5 10 Bc5 += **9 a4!** 9 0-0 b5!∝ **a5 10 0-0 Na6!?** 10...Bd7 **11 Qd2** 11 g4 Nb4 12 Ng3 d5!= **exd4 12 Bxd4** 12 Nxd4 Nc5 13 Bg5 h6!=; 13 f3!+= **Nc5 13 f3** 13 Bxc5 dxc5= **Be6 14 b3 Rad8 15 Rae1** 15 Qe3 += **b6 16 f4** 16 Qe3 d5= **d5 17 Bxf6!** 17 f5? Nfxe4 18 Nxe4 Nxe4 19 Bxe4 dxe4 20 f6? Bxf6 21 Bxf6 Qxf6! −+; 17 e5 Nfe4 18 Qe3 f5! 19 exf6 Nxf6 =+ **Qxf6 18 e5 Qe7 19 Nd4 Qd7 20 g4 f5** 20...Ne4 21 Nxe4 dxe4 22 Rd1 f5∝ **21 gxf5 gxf5** 21...Bxf5 22 Qe3= **22 Qe3 Rf7** 22...Bh6! Δ Kh8, Rg8, Ne4∝ **23 Nce2 Bf8 24 Kh2 Qc7 25 Bf3 Be7 26 Rg1+ Kh8 27 Rg2 Rff8 28 Reg1 Rg8 29 Ng3 Qd7** 29...Rdf8 30 Nh5±

30 Ngxf5! Rxg2+ 31 Rxg2 Bxf5 32 e6 Qc7 33 Nxf5 Bf6 33...d4 34 Nh6 Bf6 37 e7! +− **34 e7** 34 Nh6? Nxe6∝ **Re8 35 Bh5** 35 Nh6 Bg7 **Rxe7 36 Bf7! +− h6 37 Qg3 Qxf4 38 Qxf4 1-0** 38...Be5 39 Nxe7 +− **Sveshnikov**

360 Mednis-Soltis New York 77

1 e4 g6 2 d4 Bg7 3 Nc3 d6 4 Nf3 a6!? 4...Nf6 **5 a4** 5 Be2!? b5 6 0-0 Bb7 7 Re1 Nd7 8 Bf1 += Honfi-Vadasz, Kecskemet 75; 5 Bc4!? b5?! (5...Nf6 6 0-0 += Δ e5) 6 Bb3 Nf6 7 0-0 0-0 8 e5 dxe5 9 dxe5 Qxd1 10 Rxd1 Ng4 11 Bf4± Shamkovich-Goodman, Lone Pine 77 **Bg4 6 Be2 Nc6 7 d5** 7 Be3 e5 **Bxf3 8 Bxf3 Ne5** 8...Nd4!= **9 Be2 c6** 9...a5!? **10 0-0** 10 a5! += **a5! 11 Be3 Nf6 12 Ra3?!** 12 f4 Ned7 13 Kh1 += **Ned7! 13 f4 0-0 14 Kh1 Qc7 15 Qe1 Rfe8!= 16 Qf2 e6 17 dxe6 Rxe6 18 Bf3 Rae8 19 Bd4 b6! 20 Raa1! Nc5 21 e5 dxe5 22 Bxe5 Qe7 23 Rad1 Ncd7! 24 Bd4 Qb4 25 b3 c5 26 f5!= Rd6** 26...gxf5 27 Bxf6 Nxf6 28 Nd5 Nxd5 29 Bxd5= **27 Bxf6 Rxd1 28 Rxd1 Nxf6 29 Nd5** 29 fxg6! Qxc3?! 30 gxf7+ Kxf7 31 Bh5+ Kf8 32 Bxe8±; 29...hxg6?! 30 Nd5±; 29...fxg6!= **Nxd5 30 Bxd5 Qg4! 31 Qf3 Qxf3 32 Bxf3 gxf5 33 Kg1 Bd4+ 34 Kf1 Re3 35 Rd3!= Rxd3** 35...Kg7 36 Rxe3!= **36 cxd3 Kg7 ½-½ Mednis**

361 Botterill-Kagan Hastings 77/78

1 d4 g6 2 e4 Bg7 3 Nc3 d6 4 Nf3 c6!? 5 Be2 b5 5...Nd7, Δ Nh6!?, f5 Suttles **6 0-0** 6 a3 a6 7 0-0 Qc7 8 Be3 Nd7 9 Qd2 Nb6? 10 e5 d5 11 b3 Bg4 12 Ng5 += Uusi-Gurgenidze, Irkutsk 65; 9...e5!= **Nd7 7 a3 Bb7 8 Re1 a6** Δ e5, c5 **9 Bf1 e5 10 d5 c5 11 a4! b4 12 Nb1 Ngf6 13 a5 0-0 14 c3 bxc3 15 Nxc3 Ne8 16 Nd2 f5= 17 Nc4 Rb8 18 Ra3** 18 g3 f4 19 Bh3 Bc8∞ **fxe4 19 Nxe4 Ndf6 20 Bg5 Qc7 21 Nxf6+?!** 21 Bxf6! Bxf6 22 Rb3 += **Bxf6! 22 Bxf6 Nxf6** 22...Rxf6 Δ Ng7-f5-d4 =+ **23 Nb6 Nd7! 24 Rb3 Nxb6 25 Rxb6 c4?** 25...Ba8!∓ **26 Qd2 Qc5 27 Rc1!± Rf4** 27...Bxd5? 28 b4! Qd4 29 Qxd4 exd4 30 Bxc4± **28 g3 Rd4 29 Qb4! +- Qxb4 30 Rxb4 c3 31 Rb6** Δ Bxa6 **Rc8 32 Rxb7 c2 33 Be2 Rxd5 34 Bg4 Rd4 35 Bxc8 Rd1+ 36 Kg2 Rxc1 37 Rc7 d5 38 Bxa6 e4 39 Bb7 Kh8 40 a6 d4 1-0 Botterill**

362 Pribyl-Selfert
Hradec Kralove 77/78

1 e4 g6 2 d4 Bg7 3 Nc3 d6 4 Nf3 Nc6 4...Nd7? 5 Bc4!; 4...Bg4?! 5 Be3 Nc6 6 Bb5 += **5 Bb5 Bd7?** 5...Bg4 6 Be3 a6 7 Bxc6+ bxc6 8 h3 Bd7? 9 Qd2 Qb8 10 Rb1 Nf6 11 Bh6 0-0 12 0-0 Qb7 13 Rfe1 Rae8 14 e5!± Stean-Kotov, London 77; 8...Bxf3! 9 Qxf3 e6 10 e5! Ne7 11 Ne4 Nd5 12 Bg5 += Smyslov-Timman, Waz 72 **6 0-0 e6 7 Bg5! Nge7 8 d5!± Ncb8 9 dxe6 fxe6 10 Nd4 Nbc6** 10...c6 11 Bc4 d5 12 exd5 cxd5 13 Bxd5! +-

11 Nxe6!! Bxe6 12 Nd5 0-0? 12...Bxd5 13 exd5 a6 14 dxc6 axb5 15 cxb7 Rb8 16 Re1 Bf8 17 Qd4 Rg8 18 Rxe7+ Bxe7 19 Re1 c5!∞; 15 Re1! Bf8 16 Qd4 Rg8 17 Rxe7+! Bxe7 18 Re1 +- Rxa2? 19 Qd5!; 18...bxc6 19 Qf6 Kd7 20 Qe6+; 18...Kf7 19 Qd5+ Kf8 20 Bxe7+ Qxe7 21 Rxe7 Kxe7 22 cxb7 +- **13 Bxc6 Bxd5 14**

Bxd5+ Kh8 15 c3 +− Qd7 16 Bb3 Rae8 17 Qd2 Ng8?! 18 f3 h6?! 19 Be3 Kh7 20 Rad1 Nf6 21 Rfe1 Nh5 22 Bc2 Qe7 23 g4!? 23 c4 +− **Nf6 24 Qg2 Kh8 25 g5?!** 25 Qh3! h5 26 e5 +− **Nh5 26 gxh6?** 26 e5! Nf4 27 Bxf4 Rxf4 28 Bxg6 Ref8 29 exd6 +− **Be5 27 Bb3?** 27 Qg4! +− **Qh4 28 Rf1** 28 Bg5? Bxh2+! **Nf4 29 Qd2 Qxh6≈ 30 Kh1 Qh5 31 Bd4 Re7 32 Qe3 Rh7 33 Rd2 Qh3 34 Rff2 b6 35 Bc4 g5 36 Rd1 Qh5 37 Rfd2?** 37 Bxe5+ dxe5 38 Rfd2 g4 39 fxg4 Qxg4 40 Rg1! Qh5 41 Qg3± **Ng6! 38 Rg1??** 38 Rg2! Rxf3 39 Be2! Rxe3 40 Bxh5 Nf4 (40...Bxd4 41 Bxg6 +=) 41 Bxe3 Nxg2 =; 38 R1f1∞ **Qxh2+!! 39 Rxh2 Rxh2 mate 0-1 Pribyl**

363 Pribyl-Sapi
Hradec Kralove 77/78

1 e4 d6 2 d4 Nf6 3 Nc3 g6 4 Nf3 Bg7 5 Be2 0-0 6 0-0 c6 7 a4 Nbd7?! 7...a5; 7...Qc7 **8 e5! dxe5** 8...Nd5? 9 Nxd5 cxd5 10 exd6 exd6 11 c3± **9 dxe5 Nd5** 9...Ne8 10 Bf4 Nc7 11 Qc1 += **10 Nxd5 cxd5 11 Bf4** 11 Qxd5 Nxe5= **Nc5?!** TN 11...Qc7 12 Kh1! e6 13 Ra3 Nxe5 14 Rc3 Qb8 15 Re3 f6 16 b3 Δ Qa1± Keene **12 h3 b6 13 Re1 += Ne6** 13...Ba6!? **14 Bg3 Bb7 15 c3 Qc8 16 a5! Bc6 17 Bf1± Qd7 18 Nd4 Nxd4 19 Qxd4 Qb7 20 b4 b5 21 a6! Qd7 22 f4 f5 23 Bf2 e6 24 Qd2 Rf7 25 Bd4 Bf8 26 Bd3 Be7 27 Kh2** 27 g4! **h5 28 g4 hxg4 29 hxg4 Rh7+ 30 Kg2 Rf8 31 Rh1 Rff7 32 Qf2 Bd8 33 Qg3 Kf8 34 Kf2 Rxh1 35 Rxh1 Rh7 36 Rh3! +− Bb6?! 37 Bxb6 axb6 38 Qh2! Rxh3 39 Qxh3 Qg7 40 Qh4 Be8 41 Qf6+ Qxf6 42 exf6 fxg4** 42...Kf7 43 g5 +− **43 a7 Bc6 44 Bxg6 d4 45 cxd4 Bb7 46 Kg3 Bf3 47 Bh5 1-0 Pribyl**

364 Holek-Ftacnik CSSR 78

1 e4 g6 2 d4 Bg7 3 Nf3 d6 4 Nc3 Nf6 5 Be2 0-0 6 0-0 a6? 7 Bg5!? N 7 Bf4 b5 8 e5 Nfd7 9 a4 += Najdorf-Stahlberg, 50; 7 Re1 b5 8 e5 Nfd7 9 e6 fxe6 10 Ng5± Holmov-Gipslis 63; 7 a4?! b6 8 Re1 Bb7 9 Bc4 e6= Kavalek-Suttles 74 **b5 8 e5 Ne8?** 8...Nfd7 **9 a4 f6 10 exf6 exf6 11 Bh4 b4 12 Nd5 a5 13 Re1± Kh8 14 Bd3 c6 15 Nf4 Nc7**

16 Bxg6!! Bh6 16...hxg6 17 Nxg6+ Kg8 18 Ne7+ Kf7 19 Ng5+! fxg5 20 Qh5+ Δ Qg6 mate **17 Bxh7! Bxf4 18 Ne5!! dxe5** 18...Kxh7 19 Qh5+ Kg7 20 Qg6+ Kh8 21 Nf7+ Rxf7 22 Qxf7 Bg5 23 Bxg5 fxg5 24 Re7 +− **19 Qh5 Bg4!** 19...Qe7 20 Bg6+ Kg8 21 dxe5 +− **20 Qxg4 Kxh7 21 dxe5!± Bg5** 21...Nd5!? 22 exf6 (Δ Qg7 mate) Ra7 23 Re7+! Rxe7 24 fxe7 Nxe7 25 Re1 Bd6 26 Re6 Rf7 27 Bf6! Rxf6 28 Rxf6 Be5 29 Qh4+ +−; 27 Qh5+? Kg8 28 Rh6 Be5!! −+; 25...Rf7 26 Bxe7 Rxe7? 27 Qh4+ **22 exf6 Bxf6 23 Re5!! +− Qd5** 23...Bxe5 24 Bxd8 Rxd8 25 Qh4+ +− **24 Bxf6! Rxf6 25 Rae1! Nba6** 25...Qf7 26 Re7 Nd5 27 Rxf7+ Rxf7 28 Re8 Nf6 29 Qh4+ Kg7 30 Qg3+ Kh7 31 Rxb8 **26 Rh5+ Qxh5 27 Qxh5+ +− Kg8 28 Re7 Ne6 29 Qg4+?** 29

♕h7+! ♔f8 30 ♖d7! ♔e8 31 ♕e7 mate **♔f8 30 ♖xe6 ♖xe6 31 ♕xe6 ♖e8 32 ♕f6+ ♔g8 33 ♕g5+ ♔f8 34 ♕f4+ ♔g7 35 ♕d4+ ♔f8 36 h4 ♖e1+ 1-0 Pribyl**

365 Zhidkov-Chikovani
USSR 77

1 e4 d6 2 d4 ♘f6 3 ♘c3 g6 4 ♘f3 ♗g7 5 ♗e2 0-0 6 0-0 c6 7 a4 7 h3 b5!? 8 e5 ♘e8 9 ♗f4!+=; 7 ♖e1!? **♕c7 8 ♗f4!?** 8 a5!+= **♘bd7!?** 8...♘h5 9 ♗e3 e5 10 ♕d2+= **9 e5! += dxe5** 9...♘d5? 10 ♘xd5 cxd5 11 exd6 exd6 12 c3±; 9...♘h5 10 exd6 exd6 11 ♗e3+= **10 ♘xe5 ♘xe5 11 ♗xe5** 11 dxe5 ♘d5! = **♕d8 12 a5! ♗e6 13 ♗f3 ♖c8 14 ♖e1 ♗d5** 14...♘d5 15 ♗xd5 ♗xd5 16 ♗xg7 ♔xg7 17 ♕e2 += **15 ♘xd5 cxd5 16 c3 e6 17 ♕b3 ♕d7 18 ♖a4! ♖fe8** 18...♘e8 19 ♗f4± **19 g3 ♖e7 20 c4 ♖d8** 20...dxc4 21 ♖xc4 ♖xc4 22 ♕xc4 ♘d5 23 ♗xg7 ♔xg7 24 ♗xd5 exd5 25 ♖xe7 ♕xe7 26 ♕d5± **21 c5 ♘e8 22 ♗f4 f6 23 a6!± g5**

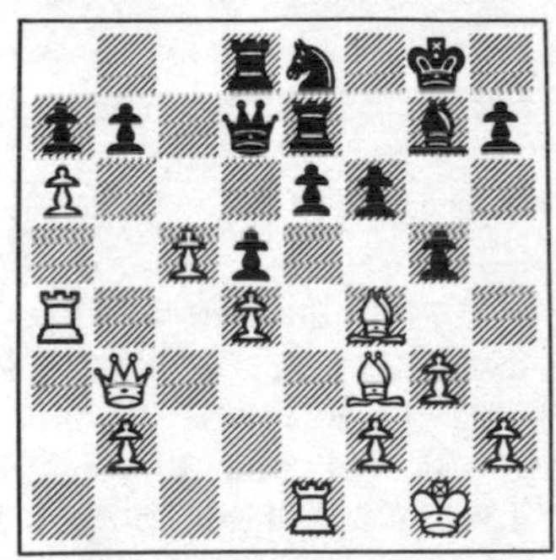

24 axb7! gxf4 24...♕xb7 25 ♕xb7 ♖xb7 26 ♖xe6 gxf4 27 ♖xe8+!± **25 ♖xa7 ♖b8 26 ♖xe6!! ♖xe6 27 ♗xd5 ♔f7!** 27...♔h8 28 ♗xe6 ♕xd4 29 ♖a8 ♕d8 30 ♕d5± **28 c6 ♕d6 29 ♗xe6+ ♔e7** 29...♕xe6 30 ♕xe6+ ♔xe6 31 ♖a8 **30 ♖a8+− ♔d8 31 ♕b6+ ♔e7 32 ♕c5 ♕xc5 33 dxc5 f5 34 ♖xb8 ♗e5 35 ♖c8 1-0 Gufeld**

366 Gipslis-Vadasz Budapest 77

1 e4 g6 2 d4 ♗g7 3 ♘c3 d6 4 ♘f3 ♘f6 5 ♗e2 0-0 6 0-0 ♘c6 7 d5 ♘b4 7...♘b8 8 h3 c6 9 ♗g5 ♗d7 10 a4 a5 11 ♖e1 += **8 h3** 8 ♗g5 h6 9 ♗e3 e6 10 a3 ♘a6 11 dxe6 ♗xe6 12 ♕d2 ♘c5! Vogts-Vadasz, Budapest 76; 8 a3 ♘a6 9 ♖e1 ♘c5 10 ♗f1 e6 11 dxe6 ♘xe6 12 h3 b6 13 ♗c4 ♗b7 14 ♗d5 ♕c8 15 ♕d2± Gaprindashvili-Vadasz, Budapest 77 **e6** 8...c6!? **9 ♗g5 h6 10 ♗e3 exd5 11 exd5 ♔h7 12 a3 ♘a6 13 b4 ♘b8 14 ♖b1 ♘bd7 15 ♖e1 a5** 15...♘b6 16 a4 a5 17 bxa5 ♖xa5 18 ♗xb6 cxb6 19 ♗b5 += **16 ♘b5! axb4 17 axb4 ♘b6 18 c4 ♗d7 19 ♘fd4 ♖e8 20 ♗d3± ♗xb5 21 ♘xb5 ♘fd7 22 ♕b3 ♘c8 23 ♗c2 ♘f6 24 ♖ed1 ♕d7 25 ♗d4 ♘e7** 25...♘xd5± **26 ♕f3 ♘eg8 27 ♘c3 ♖a3 28 c5! ♔h8** 28...♘h5 29 ♕xh5?! ♗xd4 Δ ♖xc3; 29 c6! bxc6 30 ♗a4! ♖xa4 31 ♘xa4 ♗xd4 32 ♖xd4 c5 33 bxc5±; 32...cxd5 33 ♘c3 c6 34 b5!± **29 c6 bxc6 30 dxc6 ♕e6 31 b5 ♕c4 32 ♕d3! ♕xd3 33 ♗xd3 ♘e7 34 ♖e1! ♘xc6?!** Zeitnot 34...♖aa8± **35 bxc6 +− ♖xe1+ 36 ♖xe1 ♘h5 37 ♗xg7+ ♔xg7 38 ♖c1 ♘f4 39 ♗f1 1-0 Gipslis**

367 Bangiev-Hait USSR 77

1 e4 d6 2 d4 ♘f6 3 ♘c3 g6 4 ♘f3 ♗g7 5 ♗e2 0-0 6 0-0 ♘c6 6...c6!? 7 a4 a5 **7 ♗e3** 7 d5 **♗g4 8 ♕d2 e5 9 d5 ♘e7 10 ♖ad1** 10 a4 ♗c8!? 11 ♘e1 ♘d7 12 a5 a6 13 ♘d3 f5∞ **♗d7! 11 ♘e1** 11 h3 b5! **b5!** N **12 f3** 12 ♘d3 c6!?; 12...a5! **♕b8!** 12...b4 13 ♘b1 a5 14 c4 += **13 ♘d3 a5** 13...c6?! 14 dxc6 ♘xc6 15 ♘f2 +=; 14...♗xc6 15 ♘b4 += **14 ♘f2!** Δ f4 **♘h5** 14...♖d8 15 f4 b4

16 ♘b1 exf4 17 ♗xf4 += **15 b3?! ♘f4! 16 g3! b4?** 16...♘xe2+ 17 ♘xe2 f5 18 c4= **17 gxf4 exf4?** 17...bxc3 18 ♕xc3 exf4 19 ♗d4 ♗xd4 20 ♕xd4 g5!; 18 ♕c1! exf4 19 ♗xf4 += **18 ♗d4! bxc3 19 ♕xf4 ♗xd4 20 ♖xd4 f5 21 ♕e3 f4 22 ♕xc3+= g5** Δ ♘g6 **23 e5!? dxe5 24 ♖e4** 24 ♗c4? exd4 25 d6+ ♖f7! 26 ♕xd4 cxd6∓ **♘g6 25 ♗c4?!** 25 ♔h1! += **♕b4! 26 ♕a1 ♕d6! 27 ♖e2** Δ ♘e4 **♗f5 28 ♔h1 ♖ae8?! 29 ♖g1 h6 30 ♘e4 ♗xe4 31 ♖xe4 += ♘h4?! 32 ♕c3! ♕b4** 32...♘f5 33 ♕xa5+=; 32...a4 33 ♖ge1 **33 ♕d3 ♕d6 34 ♗b5! ♖e7 35 ♖c4! c5?!** 35...♘f5 36 ♖c6 ♕d8 37 ♗c4 ♔h8 **36 dxc6 ♕xd3 37 cxd3 ♖c7** 37...♘xf3? 38 c7 ♖c8 39 ♖gc1 +− **31 ♖f1 ♔g7 39 ♔g1 +− ♘f5 40 ♖c5 ♔f6 41 ♔f2 ♘d4 42 ♗a4 ♖fc8 43 ♖e1 1-0 Gufeld**

368 Tringov-Arnaudov
Bulgaria Final 77

1 e4 g6 2 d4 ♗g7 3 ♘f3 d6 4 ♘c3 ♘f6 5 ♗e2 0-0 6 0-0 ♗g4 7 ♗e3 ♘c6 8 ♕d2 e5 9 d5 ♘e7 10 ♖ad1 a6 10...♗d7 11 ♗h6 ♗xh6 12 ♕xh6 ♔h8 13 ♘e1 ♘eg8 14 ♕d2 ♕e7 15 f4 += Planinc-Ree, Wijk aan Zee 74; 10...♘d7 11 ♘g5± Spassky-Parma, Havana 66; 10...♗xf3 11 ♗xf3 ♘d7 12 ♗e2 f5 13 g3 ♘f6 14 f3 ♕d7 15 ♗b5 Δ ♖f2± Spassky-Parma, San Juan 69 **11 ♘e1 ♗xe2 12 ♕xe2 ♘h5 13 ♘d3 f5 14 exf5 ♘xf5 15 ♘e4 ♘xe3 16 ♕xe3 ♘f4 17 c4 ♕h4 18 f3 ♗h6 19 ♕e1 ♕e7 20 ♘xf4 ♖xf4 21 b4 ♖af8 22 c5 g5 23 h3 ♗g7 24 ♕e2 h5 25 g3 ♖4f7 26 ♔g2 ♗h6 27 ♕d3 h4 28 g4 ♖f4 29 ♖c1 ♖8f7 30 a4 ♕f8 31 ♖c3 ♔g7 32 a5 ♕b8 33 ♕e2 ♖f8 34 ♖fc1 ♖4f7 35 cxd6 cxd6 36 b5 axb5 37 ♕xb5 ♖d8 38 ♕b6 ♖fd7 39 ♖c7 ♔f8 40 ♖xd7 ♖xd7 41 a6 ♔e7 42 a7 1-0**

369 Ubilava-Kaiszauri USSR 77

1 e4 d6 2 d4 ♘f6 3 ♘c3 g6 4 ♘f3 ♗g7 5 ♗e2 0-0 6 0-0 ♗g4 7 ♗e3 ♘c6 8 d5 8 ♕d2 **♗xf3 9 ♗xf3 ♘e5 10 ♗e2 c6 11 f4 ♘ed7 12 dxc6 bxc6 13 ♕d2= ♖b8 14 b3 ♕a5** 14...♖b4 15 ♗f3 ♘c5 16 e5+= **15 ♖ad1 ♖fe8 16 ♗f3 ♖bd8 17 ♘d5!?+= ♕a3** 17...♕xd2 18 ♘xf6+ ♗xf6 19 ♖xd2 += **18 ♘xf6+ ♗xf6 19 c4 a5 20 ♕f2 ♖f8** 20...a4? 21 e5 dxe5 22 ♗xc6 ♘b8 **21 ♖d2** 21 e5?! dxe5 22 ♗xc6 ♘b8 **a4 22 e5 ♗g7** 22...dxe5 23 ♗xc6 ♘b8 24 ♗xa4± **23 ♗xc6 axb3 24 axb3 ♕xb3 25 ♗b5** 25 exd6 exd6 26 ♖xd6? ♘f6 **♕b4?!** 25...♘c5! 26 ♗xc5 dxc5 27 ♖xd8 ♖xd8 28 ♕xc5 e6≈ **26 ♖fd1±**

26...♕a5 27 exd6 exd6 28 ♖xd6 +− ♘f6 29 ♕d2 ♖xd6 30 ♕xd6 ♘e4 31 ♕b6 ♕a2 32 ♖c1 ♘c3 33 ♔h1 ♕e2 Zeitnot **34 ♗g1 ♘a2 35 c5 ♕b2 36 ♖f1 ♗d4 37 ♗c4 ♕xb6 38 cxb6 ♗xg1 1-0 Gufeld**

370 Inkiov-Arnaudov
Bulgaria Final 77

1 e4 g6 2 d4 ♗g7 3 ♘c3 d6 4 f4 a6 4...♘a6 5 ♘f3 ♗g4 6 ♗e3 c6 7 h3 ♗xf3 8 ♕xf3 ♘c7 9 0-0-0 d5 10 e5 ♕d7 11 g4± Gligoric-Ljubojevic,

Teesside 72 **5 ♘f3 b5** 5...♘d7 6 ♗c4 e6 7 a4 ♘e7 8 0-0 0-0 9 ♗e3 d5 10 ♗d3± Honfi-Sandor, Wijk aan Zee 69 **6 ♗d3** 6 a3 ♗b7 7 ♗e3 ♘d7 8 ♗d3 c5 9 e5!? cxd4 10 ♗xd4 ♗xf3 11 ♕xf3 dxe5 12 fxe5 ♗xe5 13 0-0-0!≈ Levy-Friedgood, Johannesburg 72 **b4** 6...♗b7 7 a4 b4 8 ♘e2 ♘d7 9 c3 bxc3 10 bxc3 c5 11 ♖b1 ♖b8 12 0-0 e6 13 f5± Ljubojevic-Day, Canada 74 **7 ♘e2 d5 8 e5 ♗g4 9 0-0 e6 10 a3 ♘c6 11 ♗d2 ♗f5 12 ♗xb4 ♗f8 13 ♗xf8 ♔xf8 14 ♗xf5 gxf5 15 ♕d3 ♘ge7 16 b4 ♕b8 17 c3 ♕b5 18 ♕d1 ♘b8 19 a4 ♕b7 20 ♘c1 ♘d7 21 ♘d3 ♖d8 22 ♘g5 h5 23 ♖b1 ♕c6 24 ♕c2 ♘c8 25 b5 axb5 26 axb5 ♕b6 27 ♕a4 ♔g7 28 ♕b4 c6 29 ♘c5 cxb5 30 ♕xb5 ♘xc5 31 ♕xb6 ♘xb6 32 dxc5 ♘a4 33 ♖b7 ♘xc5 34 ♖xf7+ ♔g8 35 ♖c7 ♘a6 36 ♖c6 1-0**

371 Hort-Torre Polanica 77

1 e4 d6 2 d4 ♘f6 3 ♘c3 g6 4 f4 ♗g7 5 ♘f3 c5 6 ♗b5+ ♗d7 7 ♗xd7+!? 7 e5 **♘fxd7** 7...♘bxd7? 8 e5 ♘g4 9 e6 fxe6 10 ♘g5! **8 d5 ♘a6 9 ♕e2 0-0 10 0-0 ♘c7 11 a4 a6 12 ♖fd1 ♖ab8 13 a5 b5 14 axb6 ♘xb6 15 ♗d2! ♕c8 16 ♗e1 ♕d7** 16...♘b5 17 e5!± **17 ♕d3 ♘c8?! 18 ♖a2 ♘a7 19 e5 ♘ab5 20 ♘e2! ♘a7 21 c4! ♘c8 22 ♘g3± e6 23 exd6 ♕xd6 24 ♘e4 ♕b6** 24...♕xf4? 25 ♗g3 **25 ♗a5 ♕a7 26 d6! +− ♘d5 27 d7!** 27 cxd5?? c4+ **♘ce7** 27...♕xd7 28 cxd5 **28 d8♕ ♖fxd8 29 ♗xd8 ♘c6** 29...♖xd8 30 ♕f1! **30 ♗h4 ♘db4 31 ♕b1 ♘xa2 32 ♕xa2 ♖xb2 33 ♕a4 ♕b6 34 ♘f6+ ♗xf6 35 ♗xf6 ♖b1 36 ♖xb1 1-0** 36...♕xb1+ 37 ♔f2 ♕b6 38 ♘e5 **Pytel**

372 Klovan-Gofshtein USSR 77

1 e4 d6 2 d4 ♘f6 3 ♘c3 g6 4 f4 ♗g7 5 ♘f3 c5! 6 ♗b5+ 6 e5! ♘fd7 7 exd6 0-0 8 ♗e3 ♕b6?! 9 dxe7 ♖e8 10 ♕d2± Matanovic-Rukavina, Jugoslavia 75; 8...exd6 9 ♕d2 ♘c6 10 ♗b5! ♕b6 11 0-0-0+= Matulovic-Sigurjonsson, Vrsac 77; 6 dxc5∝ **♗d7 7 e5 ♘g4 8 h3** 8 ♗xd7+ ♕xd7 9 d5 dxe5 10 h3 e4 11 ♘xe4 +=; 8...e6∝ **cxd4** 8...♗xb5 9 ♘xb5 dxe5 10 hxg4 ♕a5+ 11 c3 ♕xb5 12 dxe5 += **9 ♕xd4 dxe5** 9...♘h6!? 10 g4 ♗xb5!? 11 ♘xb5 ♕a5+ 12 ♘c3 ♘c6 13 ♕e4 0-0-0∝ Hermlin-Chipashvili, USSR 76 **10 ♕c4?!** N 10 ♕d5! e4 11 ♘g5 ♘h6 12 ♕xb7 ♗xc3+ 13 bxc3 ♗xb5 14 ♕xa8 ♗c6 15 ♕xa7 0-0 16 g4 +=; 11...♗xc3+!? **e4! 11 hxg4!?** 11 ♘g5 ♘h6 12 ♗e3+= **exf3 12 gxf3 ♘c6 13 ♗d2 a6 14 ♗xc6 ♗xc6 15 ♕e2 ♕c7 16 0-0-0 0-0-0=+ 17 ♘e4 ♕b6 18 ♗c3 ♗xc3 19 ♘xc3 ♕b4 20 ♕e3 ♖xd1+ 21 ♖xd1 ♖d8 22 ♖xd8+ ♔xd8 23 g5 f6?** 23...♕c4∓ **24 b3!= ♕d6 25 ♘e4 ♕e6 26 ♕d4+ ♔e8 27 gxf6 ♗xe4 28 fxe7! ♗d5 29 c4 ♕e1+ 30 ♔b2 ♕e2+ 31 ♔b1 ½-½ Gufeld**

373 Klovan-Rimov USSR 77

1 e4 d6 2 d4 ♘f6 3 ♘c3 g6 4 f4 ♗g7 5 ♘f3 c5 6 dxc5 ♕a5 7 ♗d3 ♕xc5 8 ♕e2 ♘c6 9 ♗e3 ♕a5 10 0-0 0-0?! 10...♗g4! 11 h3 ♗xf3 12 ♕xf3 0-0 += **11 h3 ♘b4?! 12 ♕f2 ♗e6 13 ♘g5 ♘xd3 14 cxd3 ♗d7 15 ♖ae1± ♗c6 16 ♕h4 h6 17 ♘f3 ♕h5 18 ♕f2 ♕a5 19 ♘d4 ♕a6 20 ♕d2 b5 21 f5 +− g5 22 h4 b4 23 ♘xc6 ♕xc6 24 ♘d5** 24 ♘e2!? ♘g4 25 hxg5 hxg5 26 ♗xg5 ♕b6+ 27 d4 +− **♘xd5 25 exd5 ♕xd5 26 hxg5 hxg5 27 ♗xg5 ♕d4+ 28 ♔h1 ♕xb2 29 ♕f4 f6?!** 29...e5!? **30 ♕c4+ ♖f7** 32...♔h7 33 ♖f3 +− **31 ♖xe7 ♖f8 32 ♗f4 ♕c3 33 ♕d5 ♕c5 34 ♕e6 ♕d4 35 ♖f3 d5**

36 ♗d6 ♗h6 37 ♖xf7 ♖xf7 38 ♕e8+ ♔g7 39 ♖g3+ ♗g5 40 ♖xg5+ 1-0 Gufeld

374 Zuravlev-Adorjan
Sochi 77

1 e4 g6 2 d4 ♗g7 3 ♘c3 d6 4 f4 ♘f6 5 ♘f3 0-0 6 e5 dxe5 7 dxe5 ♕xd1+ 8 ♔xd1 ♘h5!? Δ ♘c6, f6 **9 ♗c4** 9 ♗e3 ♘c6 10 ♗c4 ♗g4 11 ♖f1 ♘a5 12 ♗d3 f6! 13 exf6 ♗xf6 14 h3 ♗e6 15 ♘d2 ♘g3=+ Panchenko-Adorjan, Sochi 77 **♘c6 10 ♖f1 ♗h6?!** 10...♗g4 11 ♔e1 ♘a5 12 ♗d3 f6∞ **11 ♘e2 ♖d8+ 12 ♔e1 ♘b4 13 ♗b3 ♗e6** 13...♘g7 Δ ♗e6 **14 a3 ♗xb3** 14...♘d3+ 15 cxd3 ♗xb3 16 g4 ♘g7 17 g5 +− **15 axb4 ♗c4 16 g3 ♘g7?!** 16...♗f8 Δ ♘g7, f6= **17 b3 ♗d5?** 17...♗xe2 18 ♔xe2 a6 += **18 ♘c3?** 18 ♗b2! **♗xf3 19 ♖xf3 f6 20 exf6 exf6 21 ♗b2 ♘e6?** 21...♘e8= **22 ♘e4 f5 23 ♘f6+ ♔f7!** 23...♔h8 24 ♖d1 ♗g7 25 ♖e3 ♖xd1+ 26 ♔xd1 ♖d8+ 27 ♔c1 +− **24 ♘xh7± ♗g7?+−** 24...♘d4 25 ♖f2 ♖d6 26 ♖d1 ♖ad8 27 ♔f1 a6± **25 ♗xg7 ♔xg7 26 ♘g5 ♘xg5 27 fxg5 a6 28 ♖d1 ♖xd1+ 29 ♔xd1 ♔f7 30 ♔d2 ♔e6 31 ♖e3+ ♔d6 32 ♖d3+ ♔e6 33 ♖d4! c6 34 ♖h4 ♖d8+ 35 ♔e3 b5 36 ♖h7 ♖d6 37 ♖a7 ♖d1 38 ♖xa6 ♖e1+ 39 ♔f2 1-0 Petrosian**

375 Cuartas-A.Zapata
Bogota 78

1 d4 ♘f6 2 ♘f3 g6 3 ♗f4 ♗g7 4 ♘c3 c5 4...d5 **5 dxc5 ♕a5 6 ♕d2 ♕xc5 7 e4 0-0 8 e5?! ♘g4 9 ♘d5 e6!** 9...♘xf2? 10 ♗e3 **10 ♘f6+ ♘xf6 11 exf6 ♗xf6 12 ♗d6 ♕c6?** 12...♕b6! 13 ♗xf8 ♕xb2 **13 0-0-0 ♕b6 14 c3 ♘c6 15 ♗xf8 ♔xf8 16 h4 d5 17 h5 e5! 18 ♘g5! ♔g8 19 hxg6 hxg6**

20 ♘xf7!? ♔xf7 21 ♕xd5+ ♔g7? 21...♗e6! 22 ♖h7+ ♗g7 23 ♖xg7+ ♔xg7 24 ♕xe6 ♕xf2∞ **22 ♖h7+! ♔xh7 23 ♕f7+ ♔h6** 23...♗g7 24 ♗d3 Δ ♖h1+ **24 ♕xf6 ♗g4 25 ♗e2!! 1-0** 25...♗xe2 26 ♖h1+ ♗h5 27 g4 (Δ ♖xh5 mate) ♔h7 28 gxh5 g5 29 ♕f7+ ♔h8 30 h6 ♖g8 31 h7 +− **Sigurjonsson**

376 Honfi-Nagy Hungary 77

1 e4 d6 2 d4 ♘f6 3 ♘c3 g6 4 g3 ♗g7 5 ♗g2 0-0 6 ♘ge2 c6 6...e5 7 0-0 ♘c6 **7 a4 b6?!** N **8 0-0 ♗b7 9 f4 ♕c8 10 h3 c5 11 d5 ♘a6 12 g4 ♘c7 13 f5 ♘d7 14 ♕e1 a6 15 ♕h4 b5 16 ♗h6!±** 16 fxg6 fxg6 17 ♕xe7 ♖xf1+ 18 ♔xf1 ♗f6 19 ♕xd6 ♗e5= **b4 17 ♘d1 ♕e8 18 g5 f6 19 ♗xg7 ♔xg7 20 ♕h6+ ♔g8 21 ♘f4 ♘e5** Δ ♘f7 **22 fxg6 hxg6 23 ♘e3 ♖f7 24 ♕h4** 24 gxf6 exf6 25 ♘xg6? ♖h7 −+ **♗c8 25 ♘d3 ♘xd3 26 cxd3 ♕f8 27 gxf6 exf6 28 ♖f2 ♘e8 29 ♖af1 ♖h7 30 ♕g3 ♕h6?** 30...♖aa7 31 ♘c4 ♖ag7 32 e5 dxe5 33 d6 ♗e6 34 ♕xe5± **31 ♖xf6! ♘xf6 32 ♖xf6 ♖g7 33 ♘c4 ♕c1+?!** 33...♗d7 34 ♖xd6 ♗e8 35 ♖f6± **34 ♔h2 ♗d7 35 ♖xg6 ♖xg6 36 ♕xg6+ ♔h8 37 ♕f6+ ♔g8 38 ♘xd6 ♗e8 39 e5!? ♕xb2 40 ♕e6+ ♔f8 41 ♕f6+ ♔g8 42 ♘xe8 ♖xe8 43 d6! ♕d4** 43...♕xe5+?

44 Qxe5 Rxe5 45 d7 +− **44 Qg6+ Kf8 45 Qf5+ Kg8 46 d7 Rf8 47 Qg5+ Kf7 50 Qf6+ Kg8 51 Qg6+ Kh8 50 e6 Qe5+ 51 Qg3 Qf6** 51... Qxe6 52 Qh4+ Kg7 53 Qg5+ Kh8 54 d8Q+− **52 Qe3 Qe7 53 Qh6+ Kg8 54 Be4 b3 55 Qg6+ Kh8 56 Qh5+ Kg7 57 Qg6+ Kh8 58 Qh6+ Kg8 59 Qh7+ Qxh7 60 Bxh7+ Kxh7 61 e7 Rf2+ 62 Kg3 b2 63 e8Q b1Q 64 Qe7+ Kg6** 64...Kh6 65 Qd6+ Kh5 66 Kxf2+− **65 Kxf2 Qb2+** 65...Qc2+ 66 Qe2+− **66 Kf3 1-0 Honfi**

377 Babdman-Nikolaevsky USSR 77

1 e4 d6 2 d4 g6 3 Nc3 Bg7 4 Bg5 c6 5 Qd2 b5 6 0-0-0 Qa5 7 f4 Nd7 7...b4 8 Nb1 Qxa2 9 Qxb4 ∞/+= **8 Nf3 Ngf6 9 Bd3 0-0** 9...b4 10 Ne2+= **10 Kb1 b4 11 Ne2 Rb8 12 f5?! c5! 13 Bh6 c4! 14 Bxc4 Nxe4 15 Qe3 Ndf6 16 fxg6 hxg6 17 Bxg7 Kxg7 18 Ng3 d5 19 Nxe4 dxc4! 20 Nxf6 exf6 21 Nh4 Rb6 22 Qe2 Be6 23 d5 Bxd5 24 Qf2** Δ Nf5+ **Be4 25 Qe2**

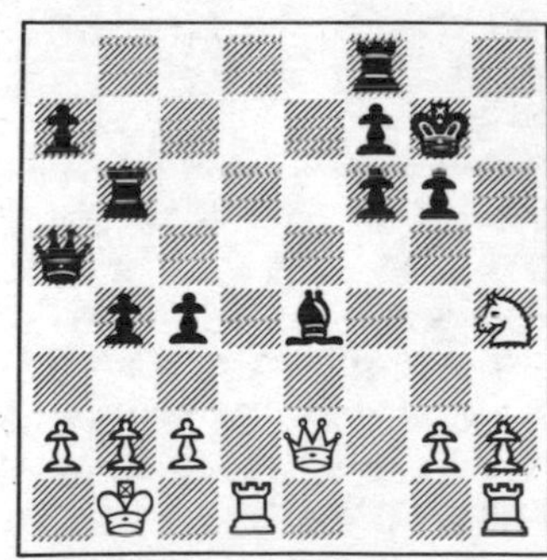

25...b3! 26 Qxe4 bxa2+ 27 Ka1 c3! 0-1 Gufeld

378 Shamkovich-Botterill Hastings 77/78

1 d4 g6 2 e4 d6 3 Nf3 Bg7 4 Bc4 Nf6 5 Qe2 c6 6 Bb3 0-0 7 0-0 7 e5!? **Bg4 8 Nbd2 e5 9 dxe5 dxe5 10 Nc4** 10 h3 Bxf3 11 Qxf3 Δ Nc4 Qe7! **11 h3** 11 Bd2!? Nbd7 12 h3 Bxf3 13 Qxf3 Nc5? 14 Bb4!± **Bxf3 12 Qxf3 b5! 13 Ne3** 13 Na5 Qb4! **Nbd7= 14 a4!? Nc5 15 axb5 Nxb3** 15... cxb5? 16 Nd5± **16 cxb3 cxb5 17 Ra6! Rfd8 18 Rd1 Rd4?** 18...Rxd1+ 19 Nxd1 Ne8! 20 Nc3 Nc7=

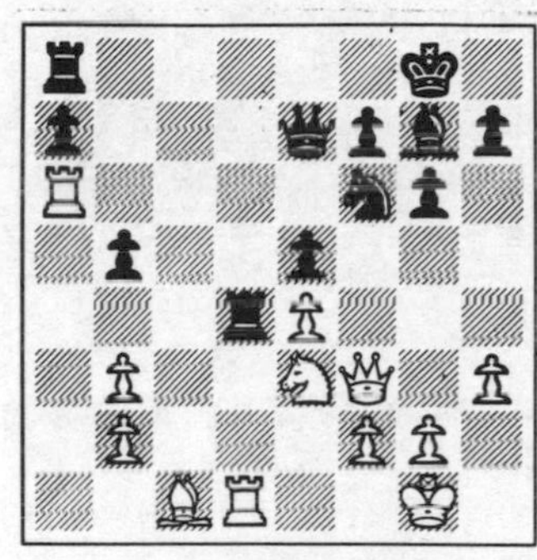

19 Rxd4 exd4 20 e5 Rc8 21 exf6 Rxc1+ 22 Nf1 Qe1 23 Rxa7! 23 Qd3? Rd1 24 Qxb5 d3 −+; 23 fxg7 Qxf1+ 24 Kh2 Qg1+ 25 Kg3 Rc5!∓ **Bf8** 23...Qxf1+ 24 Kh2 Qe1 (24... Bf8?? 25 Qd5!) 25 Ra8+ Bf8 26 Qf4! Ra1 27 Rd8! Ra6 28 Qh6! +−; 24...Qg1+ 25 Kg3 Qe1 26 Re7!! Qb4 27 Qd5!+− **24 Qd5 Qe6** 24... Qxf1+? 25 Kh2 Δ Qxf7+ **25 Qxd4 Qe2** Δ Rxf1+; 25...Rc6 26 Rb7! Qxf6 27 Qxf6 Rxf6 28 Rxb5 +− **26 Ra8! Rxf1+** 26...Qxf1+ 27 Kh2 Qg1+ 28 Kg3 Qd1 29 Qb4!+− **27 Kh2 Rxf2** 27...Qe6 28 Qc5! **28 Rxf8+! Kxf8 29 Qc5+! 1-0 Shamkovich**

379 Polugaevsky-Gulko USSR Final 77

1 Nf3 g6 2 d4 d6 3 e4 Nf6 4 Nbd2 Bg7 5 Bc4 0-0 6 Bb3 Nc6 7 c3 Bg4

8 h3 ♗xf3 9 ♕xf3 e5 10 d5 ♘e7 11 ♘c4 ♘d7 12 g4 ♘c5 13 ♗e3 b5 14 ♘a3 ♘xb3 15 axb3 c6! 16 dxc6 ♘xc6 17 ♘xb5 ♕b8 18 ♕e2 a6 19 ♘a3 ♕xb3 20 ♘c4 d5! 21 exd5 ♘d4!

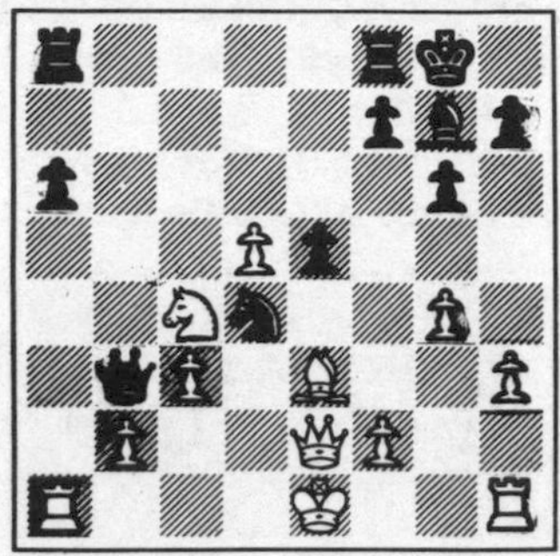

22 cxd4 exd4 23 ♖a3 ♕b5 23...♕b7 24 0-0 **24 ♖a5** 24 0-0 ♖fc8 **♕b8 25 ♖a3 ½-½**

1 ♘f3

380 Suetin-Kupreichik USSR 78

1 ♘f3 d5 2 c4 d4 3 g3 ♘c6 4 ♗g2 e5 5 d3 ♗b4+ 6 ♗d2 a5 7 0-0 ♘f6 8 e3!? N 8 ♘a3 **0-0 9 exd4 exd4 10 ♘a3 ♗f5 11 ♗f4 h6 12 ♘b5!? ♖c8 13 ♘e5?** 13 a3 ♗c5 14 ♖e1 ♖e8 15 ♕d2 += **g5! 14 ♗xc6 bxc6 15 ♘xc6 ♕d7 16 ♗e5 ♕xc6!** 16...♘g4 17 h3!; 16...♗g4 17 f3 ♗h3 18 ♘xb4 axb4 19 ♗xf6± **17 ♘xd4 ♕d7 18 ♗xf6 ♗g4!∓ 19 f3 ♗h3 20 ♘c2 ♕f5 21 ♗d4 ♗xf1 22 ♕xf1 ♖fd8 23 ♔g2 c5 24 ♗f2 ♗d2! 25 ♖d1 ♖xd3 26 ♕e2 ♖cd8 27 ♕e4 ♕xe4 28 fxe4 ♗b4 29 ♖xd3 ♖xd3 30 a3?! ♗d2 31 ♗xc5 ♗c1! −+ 32 ♔f1 ♖d2 33 ♘d4 ♖xb2 34 ♘b5 ♖c2 35 ♘d6 ♖xh2 36 ♔e1 ♖a2 37 ♘b5 ♖c2 38 ♘d6 ♖c3 39 g4 ♗xa3 40 ♗xa3 ♖xa3 41 ♔d2 ♔f8 42 c5 ♔e7 43 ♘f5+ ♔d7 44 ♘xh6 ♖f3 45 ♘f5 ♖f4 0-1 Suetin**

381 Larsen-Ivkov Bugojno 78

1 c4 e6 2 ♘f3 d5 3 b3 ♘f6 4 ♗b2 ♗e7 5 g3 0-0 6 ♗g2 c5 7 cxd5 ♘xd5 8 0-0 ♗f6= 9 ♕c1 ♘c6 10 ♗xf6 ♕xf6 11 ♘c3 ♘xc3 12 ♕xc3 ♕xc3 13 dxc3 ♖d8 14 ♖fd1 ♗d7 15 ♘g5 ♗e8 16 ♘e4 ♖xd1+ 17 ♖xd1 b6 18 ♘d6 ♖d8 19 ♔f1 ♘e7 20 ♔e1 ♗c6 21 ♗xc6 ♘xc6 22 ♘c4 ♖xd1+ 23 ♔xd1 ♔f8 24 a4 ♔e7 25 ♔d2 g5 25...e5!?= **26 e4 f5 27 ♔e3 ♘a5?** 27...♔f6 += **28 ♘xa5 bxa5**

20 h3 h6 29...♔f6? 30 ♔d3 +−; 29...♔d6 30 f4 g4 31 hxg4 fxg4 32 e5+ ♔e7 33 ♔e4 +− **30 f3! a6** 30...♔d6 31 f4 g4 32 hxg4 fxg4 33 e5+ +− **31 f4 gxf4+** 31...g4 32 hxg4 fxg4 33 e5 ♔f7 34 ♔e4 ♔g6 35 f5+! exf5 36 ♔f4 h5 37 c4 +− **32 ♔xf4 ♔f6 33 exf5 exf5 34 h4 +− ♔e6 35 g4 fxg4 36 ♔xg4 ♔d5** 36...♔f6 37 c4 ♔g6 38 h5+ ♔f6 39 ♔f4 +− **37 ♔h5 c4 38 bxc4+ ♔xc4 39 ♔xh6 ♔b3 40 h5 ♔xa4 41 ♔g5 ♔b3 42 h6 a4 43 h7 a3 44 h8♕ 1-0 Webb**

382 Korchnoi-Sosonko
Wijk aan Zee 78

1 c4 ♘f6 2 ♘f3 e6 3 g3 d5 4 ♗g2 dxc4 5 ♘e5 ♘bd7 6 ♘xc4 e5!= 7 ♘c3 ♗c5 8 0-0 0-0 9 b3 ♖e8 10 ♗b2 c6 11 ♕c2 ♘b6 12 e3 Δ f4/♘xe5 **♘xc4**

13 bxc4 ♗e6 14 ♘e4!? ♗f5 15 ♖ad1 ♘xe4 15...♔h8 16 f4! **16 ♗xe4 ♗xe4 17 ♕xe4 ♕a5 18 f4?!** 18 ♗c3 ♗b4 19 ♗xb4 ♕xb4 20 d3= **♖ad8 19 ♗c3 ♗b4 20 ♗xb4 ♕xb4 21 fxe5 f6!** 21...♖xd2 22 ♕f4 ♖f8 23 ♖xd2 ♕xd2 24 e6± **22 ♕g4 fxe5 23 ♖f2 e4 =+ 24 ♖df1 ♕xc4** 24...♖xd2? 25 ♖f7 ♕b2 26 ♖f8+! **25 d4 ♕d5** 25...c5!? **26 h4 h5 27 ♕g6 ♖f8 28 ♖f5 ♕d7 29 ♖xh5 ♖xf1+ 30 ♔xf1 ♕f7+ 31 ♕xf7+ ♔xf7= 32 ♖f5+ ♔g6 33 ♖e5 ♖d5 34 ♖xe4** 34 ♖xd5 cxd5 35 g4 b5 36 ♔e2 a5= **♖a5 35 ♖e7 b5 36 ♖e6+** 36 c4?! ♖xa2 37 ♖e6+ ♔f7 38 ♖xc6 b4∓ **♔f5 37 ♖xc6 ♖xa2 38 ♖c5+ ♔e4 39 ♖xb5 ♔f3 40 ♖f5+ ♔xe3 41 d5 ♖d2 42 ♔e1 ♖d4 43 ♖g5 a5 44 ♖xg7 a4 45 ♖a7 ♔f3 46 ♖a5 ♔xg3 47 ♔e2 ♔f4 48 h5 ♔e5 49 ♔f3 a3 50 ♖xa3 ♔xd5 51 ♖a6 ♔e5 52 h6 ♔f5 ½-½ Webb**

383 Vadasz-Ribli
Hungary Final 77

1 ♘f3 ♘f6 2 g3 d5 3 ♗g2 c6 4 c4! dxc4 5 ♕c2! b5 6 a4 ♗b7 7 b3 cxb3 8 ♕xb3 a6 9 ♗a3 ♘bd7 10 0-0 e6 11 ♗xf8 ♔xf8 11...♘xf8? 12 ♘e5! ♕d6 13 ♘c4 ♕c5 14 axb5 axb5 15 ♖xa8 ♗xa8 16 ♕a2 ♗b7 17 ♘a5 ♕a7 18 ♘c3 +−; 12...♕d4 13 ♘xc6 ♕xa1 14 ♘c3 +− **12 ♖c1 ♖c8 13 d3! g6** 13...h6 14 ♘bd2 ♔g8 15 ♘d4 ♕b6 16 ♘xe6 fxe6 17 ♕xe6+ ♔f8 18 axb5 axb5 19 ♘e4 ♖e8 20 ♕d6+ ♔f7 21 ♘xf6 ♘xf6 22 ♗xc6± **14 ♘bd2 ♔g7 15 ♕b2 ♕b6** 15...♕e7 16 ♘e5 ♘xe5 17 ♕xe5 ♖hd8 18 axb5 axb5 19 ♘e4± **16 ♘e5 ♘xe5 17 ♕xe5 ♕c7 18 ♕b2! e5 19 axb5 axb5 20 ♖a7 ♕b6?** 20...♕b8! 21 ♕a1 ♖he8 22 ♘b3 ♗a8 23 d4 ♖c7 24 ♖xc7 ♕xc7 25 d5+=; 22...♘d7 23 ♗h3 f5 24 e4 +−; 22...♖c7 23 ♕a5! **21 ♕xe5! ♕xa7** 21...♖he8 22 ♕a1 ♖xe2 23 ♘e4± **22 ♘e4 ♖he8 23 ♕xf6+ ♔g8 24 ♘d6 ♗a8 25 ♗d5 cxd5** 25...♖f8 26 ♘xc8 ♖xc8 27 h4 ♕d7 28 h5!± **26 ♘xc8 ♕b8?** 26...♕d7 27 ♘d6 ♖f8! 28 h4 b4 29 h5 ♕d8 30 ♕e5± **27 ♘d6?** 27 ♘e7+! ♔f8 28 ♖c8! ♖xc8 29 ♘xc8+= **♖f8 28 ♖c8 ♕xc8** 28...♖xc8 29 ♕xf7+ ♔h8 30 ♕f6+ ♔g8 31 ♕e6+ ♔g7 32 ♘xc8 ♕c7 33 ♘d6 ♗c6 34 h4 b4 35 h5 b3 36 h6+± **29 ♘xc8 ♖xc8 30 d4 ♗c6 31 ♕d6 ♗e8 32 f3 ♖c2 33 ♔f2 ♗c6 34 h4 h5 35 g4 hxg4 36 fxg4 b4 37 ♕xb4 ♗d7 38 ♕b8+ ♖c8 39 ♕f4 ♖e8 40 h5 ♗e6 41 h6 ♔h7 42 g5 ♗f5 43 ♕d6 ♗e4 44 ♕f6 ♖g8 45 ♕e5 f5 46 ♕c7+ ♔h8 47 ♔e3 f4+ 48 ♔xf4 1-0 Vadasz**

384 Larsen-Ljubojevic Bugojno 78

1 ♘f3 c5 2 g3 d5 3 ♗g2 ♘c6 4 0-0 e5 5 d3 ♗e7 6 e4 d4 7 a4 g5!? 8 ♘bd2 ♗e6 9 ♘c4 f6 10 h4!? 10 ♘e1≈ △ f4/♗h3 **h6 11 ♘h2 gxh4 12 ♕h5+**

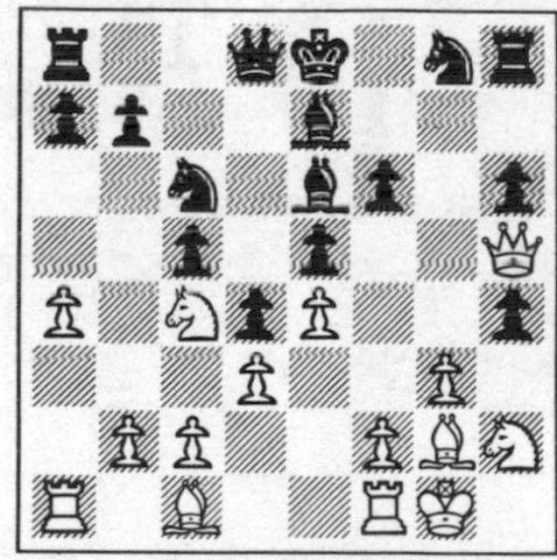

12...♔d7! 13 ♕xh4?! 13 gxh4= **f5 14 ♕h5 ♘f6 15 ♕e2 fxe4 16 dxe4 ♕g8 17 b3 h5∓ 18 f4 ♗xc4** 18...♕xg3?! 19 fxe5 ♘g4 20 ♗f4 ♕h4? 21 ♘f3 +− **19 ♕xc4 ♕xc4** 19...♕xg3? 20 fxe5 △ ♗f4 **20 bxc4 ♖ag8 21 fxe5 ♘xe5 22 ♗f4 ♗d6** 22...♘xc4? 23 e5 ♘g4 24

Nxg4 hxg4 25 Bd5 **23 Rab1 Kc7 24 Nf3** 24 Bxe5 Bxe5 25 Rf5 Nd7∓ **Nxf3+ 25 Rxf3 Nxe4 26 Rfb3** 26 Rff1!? Bxf4 27 Bxe4=+ **b6! 27 Bxd6+** 27 Bxe4 Bxf4 28 Kh2 Rxg3! −+; 28 Kf2 Be3+ **Nxd6 28 Bd5 Rg5 29 Re1 Rh7 30 Kg2 Rhg7 31 Kh2 Nf5 −+ 32 a5 Ne3! 33 axb6+ axb6 34 Ra1 Nxd5 35 cxd5 Kd6 36 Rxb6+ Kxd5 37 Ra3 h4 38 gxh4 Rg2+ 39 Kh3 Rg1** 40 Kh2 R7g2+ 41 Kh3 Rxc2 −+ **0-1 Webb**

385 Gurevich-Kuperman USSR 78

1 Nf3 d5 2 g3 Nf6 3 Bg2 c6 4 d3 Bf5 5 Nbd2 h6 6 b3 e6 7 Bb2 Nbd7 8 c4 Bd6 9 Qc2 0-0 10 a3 e5?! 11 0-0 a5 12 e4! Be6 12...Bh7 13 Nh4 Δ Nf5 +=; 12...dxe4 13 dxe4 Bh7 14 Nh4 Δ Nf5 += **13 d4! Qb8** 13...dxe4 14 dxe5 exf3 15 Nxf3 += **14 c5 Bc7 15 dxe5 Nxe5 16 Nd4± Bd7** 16...dxe4 17 Nxe6± **17 f4 Neg4**

18 Qc3! dxe4 19 Bxe4! Re8 19... Nxe4? 20 Nxe4 f6 21 h3! +− **20 Rae1** Δ h3 **h5 21 N4f3** Δ Ng5 **b6 22 Ng5 h4 23 h3 Nh6 24 Bh7+! Kf8** 24...Kh8 25 Qxf6!! +− **25 Nde4 Bd8 26 Bg6!! fxg6 27 Nh7+ Kf7 28 Nhxf6 gxf6 29 Nxf6 Rxe1 30 Rxe1 Be6 31 Nd7! 1-0 Gufeld**

386 Vadasz-Nei Tallinn 77

1 Nf3 d5 2 g3 g6 3 Bg2 Bg7 4 d4 e6!? 5 0-0 Ne7 6 Nbd2 0-0 7 e4! 7 c4 Nf5 8 e3 a5 9 b3 b6 10 Ba3 Re8 11 Rc1 c6 12 Qc2 b5 13 Rfd1 b4 14 Bb2 Ne7 15 e4 Nd7 16 a3 Bb7 17 Ra1 Qb6 18 Ne5 Nxe5 19 dxe5 bxa3 =+ Pribyl-Nei, Tallinn 77 **b6 8 Re1 Ba6?! 9 h4! Nbc6 10 c3 Na5 11 h5 gxh5** 11...c5 12 hxg6 hxg6 13 dxc5 bxc5 14 Ng5! Δ Qg4-h4 +− **12 Nh4 c5 13 dxc5 dxe4** 13...bxc5 14 Qxh5 d4 15 e5± **14 Bxe4 Bb7 15 Qxh5 Ng6 16 Ndf3 Bxe4 17 Rxe4 Qd5! 18 Qxd5** 18 Ng5!? h6 19 Nxg6 fxg6 20 Qxg6 hxg5 21 Bxg5 Qf5 22 Qxe6+ Qxe6 23 Rxe6 bxc5 24 Rd1∝ **exd5 19 Ra4! Nc4 20 cxb6 Nxb6 21 Rb4 Rfb8 22 Nf5 a5** 22...Bf8 23 Rb3 Na4 24 Rxb8 Rxb8 25 b3 Nxc3 26 Bb2 Ne4 27 Rd1 += **23 Rb5 Na4 24 Rxb8+ Rxb8 25 Nxg7 Kxg7 26 b3 Nc5 27 Be3 Ne6 28 Rd1 Ne7 29 Nd4 Kf6 30 Kg2 a4 31 Rh1! axb3 32 axb3 Kg7 33 b4 Nxd4** Zeitnot **34 Bxd4+ f6 35 Bc5 Nc6 36 Rd1 Rd8 37 f4 Kf7 38 Kf3 Rd7 39 c4 d4 40 b5 Na5 41 Rxd4 Rxd4 42 Bxd4 Nxc4 43 b6 Nd6 44 f5 1-0 Vadasz**

387 Timman-Larsen Bugojno 78

1 Nf3 Nf6 2 c4 b6 3 g3 Bb7 4 Bg2 c5 5 0-0 g6 6 b3 Bg7 7 Bb2 0-0 8 Nc3 d5 9 d4 Nbd7 10 cxd5 Nxd5 11 e3 Nxc3 12 Bxc3 Rc8 13 Qe2 cxd4 14 Bxd4 Bxd4 15 Nxd4 Bxg2 16 Kxg2 Nc5 17 Rfd1 Qd5+ 18 Kg1 Ne4 19 Qf3 Rfd8 20 Rac1 Nc3 21 Qxd5 Rxd5 Δ Rxd4 **22 Rd3 Rdc5**

Diagram

23 Rc2 a5 24 Kf1 e5 25 Ne2 Ne4

25...♘xe2 26 ♖xe2 ♖c2 27 ♖dd2 **26 ♜xc5 ♜xc5 27 f3 ♞g5 28 e4 ♜c2 29 h4 ♞e6 30 ♜d6 ♜xa2 31 ♜xb6 ♚g7 32 ♜b7 ♜b2 33 f4** 33 ♖b5?? ♖xe2 **exf4 34 gxf4 a4 35 f5 ♞c5 36 ♜c7 a3! 37 ♜xc5 a2 38 ♜a5 ♜b1+ 39 ♚f2 a1♛ 40 ♜xa1 ♜xa1 41 fxg6 fxg6 42 ♞d4 ♚h6 43 b4 ♚h5 44 ♚e3 ♚xh4 45 b5 g5 46 ♞f5+ ♚h3 47 e5 ♜e1+ 48 ♚d4 g4 0-1** 49 b6 g3 50 ♘xg3 ♔xg3 51 ♔d5 ♔f4! 52 e6 ♔f5 53 b7 ♖d1+ 54 ♔c6 ♔xe6 −+

388 Portisch-Larsen Bugojno 78

1 ♞f3 ♞f6 2 c4 b6 3 g3 ♝b7 4 ♝g2 c5 5 0-0 g6 6 ♞c3 ♝g7 7 d4 ♞e4 8 ♞d5!? ♞c6 8...0-0 9 ♘g5! ♘a6 10 ♗f4± **9 dxc5 bxc5** 9...♘xc5 10 ♖b1 += **10 ♞e1 f5 11 ♞d3 d6 12 ♞3f4 ♝c8≈** 12...♕d7? 13 ♘e6 **13 f3?!** 13 ♕a4 ♗d7 14 ♘e6 ♗xe6 15 ♕xc6+ ♔f7 16 ♘c7 ♖c8 17 ♘xe6 ♖xc6 =+; 13 ♘c3 ♗xc3 14 bxc3 ♘e5= **♞f6 14 e4 fxe4 15 fxe4 ♜b8! 16 ♛a4 ♝d7 17 ♞e6** 17 ♗h3!? **♝xe6 18 ♛xc6+** 18 e5?! ♘xd5 19 cxd5 ♕a5!∓ **♛d7 19 ♞c7+ ♚f7 20 ♛xd7 ♝xd7∓ 21 ♞d5** 21 e5!? **♚e8! 22 ♚h1** 22 ♘c3 ♘g4! −+ **♞xd5 23 cxd5 c4!** △ c3 **24 a4 ♜f8** 24...♗xb2?! 25 ♖b1 c3 26 ♗xb2∓ **25 ♜d1** 25 ♖xf8+ ♔xf8 26 ♖a2 c3 27 bxc3 ♖b1 −+ **♝g4 −+ 26 ♜e1 c3 27 bxc3 ♝xc3 28 ♝f4 ♝xa1 29 ♜xa1 ♜b3 30 ♜c1 ♜d3 31 ♚g1 ♜d1+ 32 ♜xd1 ♝xd1 33 a5 ♝e2 34 h4 ♚d7 35 ♝e3 a6 36 ♝h3+ ♚c7 37 ♝g5 ♝f3 38 e5 ♜e8 39 exd6+ ♚xd6 40 ♝f1 ♜a8 41 ♝d3 ♝xd5 42 h5 gxh5 43 ♝e3 ♚e5 44 ♝b6 ♝b7 45 ♝e2 ♜f8 46 ♝c7+ ♚d4 47 ♝b6+ ♚c3 48 ♝c5 ♜f5 49 ♝f2 ♚d2 0-1 Webb**

389 Vukic-Karpov Bugojno 78

1 ♞f3 ♞f6 2 g3 b5 3 ♝g2 ♝b7 4 0-0 e6 5 d3 5 b3 ♗e7 6 c4 bxc4 7 bxc4 c5= Kochiev-G.Garcia, Leningrad 77 **d6 6 e4 c5 7 a4 a6 8 axb5 axb5 9 ♜xa8 ♝xa8 10 ♞a3 ♝c6 11 e5! += ♞fd7 12 exd6 ♝xd6 13 ♞g5 b4 14 ♞c4 ♞f6** 14...♗e7? 15 ♘xf7 **15 ♛e2 ♝xg2 16 ♚xg2 ♝e7** 16...0-0? 17 ♘xe6 **17 ♝e3 0-0 18 ♜a1 ♞d5 19 ♞e4 ♛c7 20 f3 ♞d7 21 ♝f2 ♜e8 22 ♛e1 f5 23 ♞ed2 ♝f8 24 ♜a6 e5 25 ♛a1 ♞5f6 26 ♛a2 ♚h8 27 ♛a4** 27 ♘e3!? g6 28 ♘d5 += **♜c8 28 ♜e6 ♛b8 29 ♛a6 ♜e8 30 ♞e3 ♜xe6 31 ♛xe6 g6**

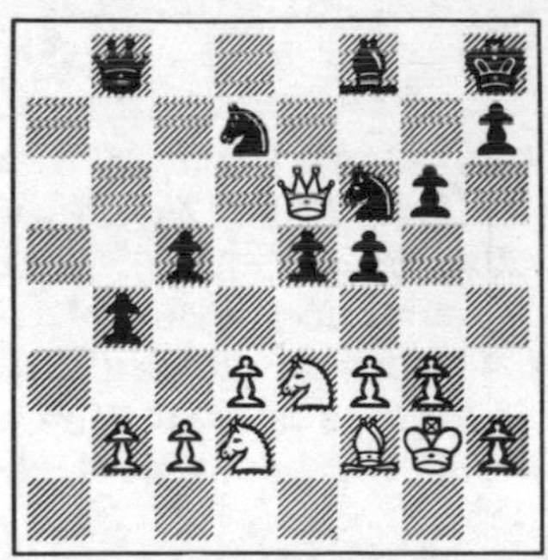

32 ♞d5 32 g4?! fxg4 33 fxg4 ♕a8+≈; 32 h3!? △ g4 **♛e8 33 ♛c6 ♞xd5 34 ♛xd5 ♞b6 35 ♛b7 ♛e6 36 ♛a6 ♛d6 37 ♞b3 ♞d7 38 ♛b7 ♝e7 39 ♞a5 ♛e6 40 ♞c4 ♚g7= 41 ♚f1** 41 h3 h5! **g5 42 ♚g2 h5 43 h3 ♚h6 44 ♞e3 f4 45 ♛d5 ♛xd5 46 ♞xd5 fxg3**

47 ♗xg3 ♗f8 48 ♔f2 ♔g6 49 ♔e2 ♔f5 50 c3 bxc3 51 bxc3 ♔e6 52 ♘e3 ♗g7 53 ♗e1 ♘f8 54 ♗d2 ♘g6 55 ♘f1 ♘f4+ 56 ♗xf4 exf4 57 ♘d2 ½-½ Webb

390 Grigorian-Bagirov Baku 77

1 ♘f3 d5 2 g3 ♗g4 3 ♗g2 c6 4 0-0 e6 5 d3 ♗d6 6 ♘bd2 ♘e7 7 h3 ♗h5 8 b3 0-0 9 ♗b2 ♘d7 10 ♕e1 a5 11 a3 11 a4 **♕b6 12 g4 ♗g6 13 a4 ♖fe8 14 e3** 14 e4!? c5!? 15 e5 ♗c7 16 ♘h4 ♘c6 17 f4 c4+ 18 ♔h1 cxd3 19 f5 exf5 20 gxf5 ♗h5∓ **f6 15 ♔h1 ♗f7 16 ♘d4 e5 17 ♘f5 ♘xf5 18 gxf5 g6** 18...g5 **19 ♖g1 ♔f8 20 ♕e2 ♔e7 21 c4 gxf5 22 d4∞**

22...♖g8! 23 ♖ac1 ♖g6 24 c5 ♘xc5 25 dxc5 ♗xc5 26 ♘f3 ♗e6 27 ♘d4 27 ♘h4 ♖h6 28 ♕c2 ♗xe3! 29 ♘xf5+ ♗xf5 30 ♕xf5 ♗xc1∓ **♗d6** 27...exd4? 28 exd4 Δ ♖ce1 +− **28 ♘xe6 ♔xe6 =+ 29 ♕c2 ♖ag8 30 ♗c3 ♕c7 31 f4 e4 32 ♕f2 b6 33 ♔h2 ♗a3 34 ♖cd1 ♗b4 35 ♗b2 ♗c5 36 ♗h1 ♕g7 37 ♖xg6 hxg6 38 ♖c1 g5 39 ♗d4 ♗xd4** 39...gxf4!? 40 ♗xc5 f3 Δ ♕c7+∞ **40 exd4 ♕c7 41 ♕g3** 41 ♖f1 ♕xf4+ 42 ♕xf4 gxf4∓ **♖g7 42 fxg5 fxg5 43 ♗g2 c5 44 dxc5 bxc5 45 ♗f1 d4 46 ♗c4 ♔f6∓ 47 ♔g2 ♕xg3+ 48 ♔xg3 d3** 48...f4+∓ 49 ♔g4? ♖h7 Δ ♖h4 mate **49 ♗b5 ♖c7 50 ♔f2 ♔e5 51 ♔e3 f4+ 52 ♔d2 ♔d4?!** 52...c4!−+ **53 ♖c4+ ♔d5 54 ♗a6 ♖h7??** 54...♖a7 −+ **55 ♖xe4! ♖xh3 56 ♗xd3 ♖g3 57 ♖e8 g4! 58 ♖d8+ ♔e5 59 ♖e8+ ♔d5 60 ♖d8+ ♔e5 61 ♖f8 ♖f3 62 ♖e8+ ♔f6 63 ♔e2 ♔g5 64 ♖e5+ ♔h4 65 ♖xc5 ♖e3+ 66 ♔d2 g3 67 ♖c4 ½-½** 67...g2 68 ♖xf4+ ♔g5 69 ♖f5+ ♔g4 70 ♔xe3 g1♕+ 71 ♔d2= **Horton**

1 f4

391 Vaiser-Klovan USSR 77

1 f4 d5 2 ♘f3 ♘f6 3 g3 c5 3...♘c6 4 ♗g2 ♗g4 5 0-0 ♗xf3 6 ♖xf3 e5 7 fxe5 ♘xe5 8 ♖f5 ♘eg4 9 c4?! ♕d7 10 ♕f1 dxc4 11 ♗xb7 ♖b8∓ Quinteros-Pomar, Olot 61; 3...♗g4 4 ♗g2 ♘bd7 5 d3 c6 6 ♘bd2 ♕b6! 7 a4 a5 8 h3 ♗xf3 9 ♘xf3 e6 10 e3 ♗d6 11 0-0 0-0= Jakobsen-Hennings, Kapfenberg 70 **4 ♗g2 ♘c6 5 0-0 g6 6 d3 ♗g7 7 c3 0-0 8 ♘a3** 8 ♕c2 d4 9 ♘a3 ♘d5 10 ♗d2 ♗g4 11 ♖ae1 ♖c8 12 ♘c4 ♗xf3 13 ♗xf3 b5 14 e4? dxc3 15 bxc3 ♘db4! =+ S.Garcia-Uhlmann, Havana 69 **b6** 8...d4 9 e4 e5 10 f5? gxf5 11 exf5 dxc3 12 bxc3 e4!=+ Radulov-Spiridonov, Bulgaria 69 **9 ♕a4!?** 9 e4 dxe4 10 dxe4 ♗a6 11 ♕xd8 ♖axd8 12 ♖e1 e5 =+ Rossetto-Bilek, Amsterdam 64 **♗d7 10 e4** N 10 ♕c2 d4 11 ♘c4 ♖c8 12 e4 dxe3 13 ♘xe3 ♘g4 14 ♘xg4 ♗xg4 =+ Defotis-Podgaets, Mayaguez 71 **dxe4 11 dxe4 e5 12 ♕c2 ♖e8 13 ♘c4 exf4 14 e5 ♘h5 15 gxf4± ♗f8 16 ♘g5** Δ ♗d5 **b5**

Diagram

17 f5! ♘xe5 17...♗xf5? 18 ♖xf5 gxf5 19 ♕xf5 +−; 17...bxc4? 18 fxg6 +−; 17...gxf5?! 18 ♗xc6 ♗xc6 19 ♕xf5 +− **18 fxg6 ♘xg6 19 ♕f2 +− ♗e6** 19...♕e7

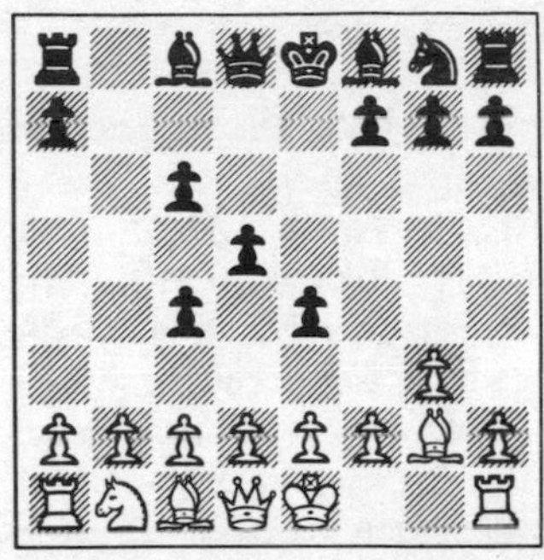

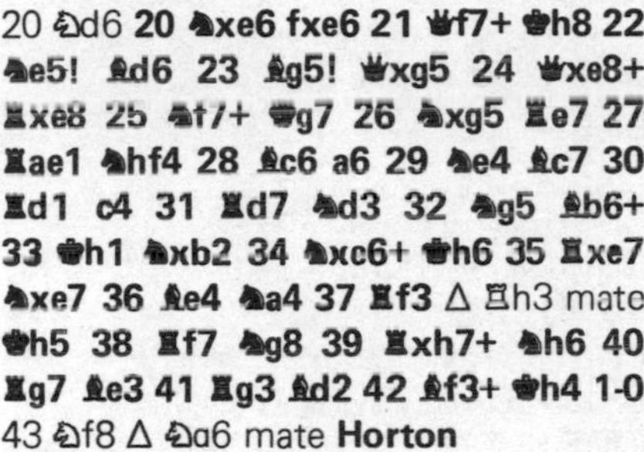

20 ♘d6 **20 ♞xe6 fxe6 21 ♛f7+ ♚h8 22 ♞e5! ♝d6 23 ♝g5! ♛xg5 24 ♛xe8+ ♜xe8 25 ♞f7+ ♚g7 26 ♞xg5 ♜e7 27 ♜ae1 ♞hf4 28 ♝c6 a6 29 ♞e4 ♝c7 30 ♜d1 c4 31 ♜d7 ♞d3 32 ♞g5 ♝b6+ 33 ♚h1 ♞xb2 34 ♞xc6+ ♚h6 35 ♜xe7 ♞xe7 36 ♝e4 ♞a4 37 ♜f3** Δ ♖h3 mate **♚h5 38 ♜f7 ♞g8 39 ♜xh7+ ♞h6 40 ♜g7 ♝e3 41 ♜g3 ♝d2 42 ♝f3+ ♚h4 1-0** 43 ♘f8 Δ ♘g6 mate **Horton**

1 g3

392 Grigorian-Alburt
USSR Final 77

1 g3 d5 2 ♝g2 e5 3 ♞f3 e4 4 ♞d4 c5 5 ♞b3 c4!? 6 ♞d4 ♞c6 7 ♞xc6 bxc6 8 d3 cxd3 9 cxd3 f5 10 0-0 ♞f6 11 ♛c2 ♝d7 12 ♞d2 h5 13 ♞b3 h4 14 ♝f4 hxg3 15 hxg3 ♛e7 16 ♜fd1 ♛f7 17 ♞c5 ♝xc5 18 ♛xc5 ♛h5 19 f3 ♚f7 20 ♚f2 g5 21 ♝e5 f4 22 ♜h1 e3+ 23 ♚g1 ♛g6 24 ♜xh8 ♜xh8 25 ♛xa7 ♛f5 26 ♝xf6 ♚xf6 27 ♜c1 fxg3 28 ♛c7 ♜c8 29 ♛d6+ ♛e6 30 ♛xg3 ♛e5 31 f4 gxf4 32 ♜f1 ♚e7 33 ♜xf4 Δ ♖f7+ +− **♛xb2 34 ♛xe3+ ♚d6 35 ♛g3 ♚c5 36 ♛f2+ d4 37 ♜e4 ♛c1+ 38 ♚h2 ♜h8+ 39 ♜h4 ♛e3 40 ♛g3 ♜xh4+ 41 ♛xh4 ♛e5+ 42 ♚g1 ♛xe2 43 ♛d8 ♛d1+ 44 ♚h2 ♛h5+ ½-½**

Games Index